*E*THICS FOR MODERN LIFE

FIFTH EDITION

*E*THICS FOR MODERN LIFE

FIFTH EDITION

RAZIEL ABELSON
New York University

MARIE-LOUISE FRIQUEGNON
William Patterson College

ST. MARTIN'S PRESS

New York

Editor: Sabra Scribner
Managing editor: Patricia Mansfield Phelan
Project editor: Alda D. Trabucchi
Production supervisor: Joe Ford
Art director: Sheree Goodman
Text design: Lee Goldstein
Cover design: Paul Shaw/Letter Design

Library of Congress Catalog Card Number: 94-65221

Manufactured in the United States of America.

9 8 7 6 5
f e d c b a

For information, write:
St. Martin's Press, Inc.
175 Fifth Avenue
New York, NY 10010

ISBN: 0-312-09967-3

PREFACE

The main purpose of this fifth edition of *Ethics for Modern Life,* in addition to the usual purposes of deleting out-of-date topics and adding more timely and lively essays, lies in the decision to streamline Part Four, "The Good Life." The previous edition offered formulations of great religious and ethical world views—namely, Buddhism, Christianity, Epicureanism, Nietzschean existentialism, and Aristotelian eudaemonism, subjects that are too rich to be done adequate justice in one section of an anthology. Consequently, we have lowered our sights to what we hope is a manageable level. Our new Part Four comprises essays on particular ingredients of a happy life: skillful activity, pleasure, self-assertion, sexual fulfillment, and religious enlightenment, and we leave it to the reader to incorporate them into his or her own view of the world.

We have also deepened and enriched the theoretical part of this book by adding formulations of contractarianism (Rawls), virtue ethics (Foot), and feminist ethics (Baier) to chapter 1, which, together with chapter 2 (the exploration of the grounds of moral responsibility), constitutes the purely theoretical part of the book.

Each of the four main parts of this volume begins with an introductory commentary on the issues under discussion and briefly sketches the main arguments for each position, as well as objections that might be raised against them. We believe that these commentaries will prove helpful to readers in finding their way through the thickets of philosophical controversy. At the end of each chapter, discussion questions and suggestions for further reading are provided for the convenience of both teachers and students.

The order in which the various topics are considered is of course not sacrosanct. Many will prefer to begin with the more practical concerns and turn later to theoretical issues, and will therefore begin with Parts Two and Three and proceed later to Parts One and Four, while others may choose to save Part One for last. Should theory precede practice or should practice precede theory? However one decides, the important thing is to do justice to both.

We would like to thank those who carefully reviewed the fifth edition: Lynne Boughton, DePaul University; James W. Gustafson, Northern Essex Community College; Steven Fleishman, University of Maryland; David J. Detmer, Purdue University-Calumet; Antony Khoury, Tuskegee University; Douglas Lackey, Bernard Baruch College, City University of New York; John

Olson and Dale Lugenbehl, Palomar College; and Robert Tucker, Florida Southern College.

At St. Martin's Press, we would like to give special thanks to Sabra Scribner, who guided us and the manuscript to completion; Don Reisman, who initiated the fifth edition; Kerry Abrams, who cleared permissions; Elizabeth Bast, who prepared the manuscript; and Alda Trabucchi, who coordinated the project from manuscript through typesetting.

RAZIEL ABELSON
MARIE-LOUISE FRIQUEGNON

CONTENTS

ETHICS FOR MODERN LIFE

FIFTH EDITION

General Introduction

WHY STUDY ETHICAL PHILOSOPHY?

Some years ago, a city official was convicted for embezzlement and extortion. While his case was being appealed, the official enrolled in a course in ethical philosophy in order, he told reporters, to learn what had somehow until then escaped his notice: the difference between right and wrong. This belated attempt at self-improvement seemed insincere as well as futile, since a man of bad character, as Aristotle observed, is not likely to be reformed by lectures. In the hope of escaping punishment, the official was pretending that his fault was intellectual rather than moral.

But if studying ethical philosophy is not a means of moral reformation, then what's the point of it? What can a student learn from books like this and from the courses in which they are used? The answer is that although philosophy alone will not make us virtuous, it can help us think more clearly about our principles of action and unravel the logical knots in our reasoning about ethical problems.

Many people besides our convicted embezzler might be shocked to hear that ethical philosophy provides nothing more grandiose than clarification of what we already know in a more obscure and implicit way. Underestimating the value of intellectual clarity is a widespread phenomenon, since we do not feel the need for clarity until we have reached a fairly high level of reflective consciousness. We get along fairly well in daily life without help from philosophy. Only when we address ourselves to dilemmas in which we have either no traditional guides or too many conflicting guides do we become concerned about clarity and consistency. That stealing is wrong and that an employee who loafs on the job deserves to be fired are matters as thoroughly understood and as firmly dealt with by the butcher and the baker as by the philosopher. But when we denounce an act of murder in the name of the sanctity of human life and then, as members of a jury, are asked to ordain the execution of the culprit, we feel uneasy. For if life is sacred, then what right have we to take the life of the murderer? The principle that human life is sacred instructs us to spare the defendant, but the principle

1

that the punishment should fit the crime calls for the ultimate penalty. We must then decide that one principle has priority, or qualify both so that they no longer collide.

Social problems provoke more philosophical reflection and debate than personal problems because of their far-reaching consequences and the conflicts of interest they involve. When people are affected by a practice, many points of view toward that practice are elicited. The resulting disputes should then be settled by rational discussion. When we look beyond the narrow horizon of our personal affairs and take an active interest in social and political questions, we find ourselves having to choose between social upheaval and infringement of minority rights, between national loyalty and moral conscience, between abundance at home and the alleviation of misery abroad. Automatic responses to familiar situations are now crude and inappropriate. Yet few of us have been trained to handle large-scale decisions in a routine way. The rules of conduct we have been following in our daily lives without conscious deliberation must now be modified—or perhaps be replaced by new rules—and this process of revision requires philosophical reflection.

Ethical philosophy is the effort to resolve conflicts rationally, when our automatic responses and implicit rules of action collide with contrary responses and rules. When opposition from others or from our own conscience makes us aware of arguments against our actions and policies, it becomes necessary for us to provide reasons for them, and thus to engage in philosophical discussion. The purpose of such discussion is not to improve our moral character but to refine our conceptual equipment for supporting or rejecting disputed courses of action, so that the course we choose will be rationally justified.

But weighing reasons for and against alternative decisions is only the practical side of ethical philosophy. People skilled in distinguishing the better from the worse and in giving cogent reasons for their judgments are, in this practical sense, ethical philosophers, even if they have never taught a course in ethics or written an article on the subject. But reflection on practice leads eventually to theory, and on the theoretical level, special training is essential for philosophical work. When plausible reasons are cited on both sides of a practical controversy, we begin to wonder, not just which course of action is best, but which of the competing reasons is most compelling, and why. We ascend from practical reasoning about actions and policies to theoretical reasoning about standards and principles, and we find ourselves on the lofty terrain of ethical theory.

ETHICAL THEORY AND SCIENTIFIC THEORY

The term "ethical theory" should not mislead anyone into thinking that there can be a science of ethics in any way analogous to the sciences of physics and chemistry. Theories in science are generalizations from observed patterns of events together with explanatory hypotheses that make possible the prediction of new events. The experimental scientist discovers new facts, and the theoretical scientist constructs a theory that explains them and predicts further discoveries. In contrast, an ethical theory reasons from common-sense facts known to everyone, and it formulates principles and standards whose function is not to predict new events but to guide our choices and actions. This difference is often summed up by saying that science is "descriptive" while ethics is "normative," meaning that science tells us what was, is, or will be the case, whether we like it or not, while ethics tells us what ought to be and what we ought to do. Science gives us information about the world, while ethics gives us rules and standards for changing the world to fit our requirements. A scientific theory provides a hypothesis for predicting what will happen, while an ethical theory provides a rule or a standard for making things happen.

Of course, standards are employed in science as well as in ethics—for example, the meter bar as a standard of length or the amount of foreign particles as a standard of chemical purity. But these are standards of measurement and classification, not standards of choice and action. Scientific standards are adopted because of their uniformity and the ease with which they can be identified. The meter bar is, for practical purposes, unchanging—it does not expand or contract or bend—and everyone who uses it can agree on how many times its length an object extends. Such considerations are independent of the needs, desires, and aspirations of those who employ the standard. But standards of evaluation have their reason for being in just such needs, desires, and aspirations. Ripeness and sweetness of taste are standards for evaluating apples because we want ripe, sweet apples; honesty and intelligence are standards of political statesmanship because they are the qualities needed for social stability and improvement.

Finally, ethical standards differ from scientific standards, and ethical principles differ from scientific laws, in their logical relations to the judgments they support. Once a scientific standard has been agreed upon, any object that satisfies it must be judged to have passed the test; for example, if a boat measures ten feet in length, we must judge that it is ten feet long whether we approve of it or not. But an ethical standard is importantly different in that, when an object or action is found to conform to it, we may decide to modify the standard rather than approve of the object in question. For example, a teacher grading examination papers will look for features like accuracy of information, clarity of expression, and unity of structure as the standards a good paper should meet. But suppose the teacher reads a paper that meets these standards yet seems a dull and mechanical repetition of the class lectures. The teacher may then decide that some other standard should take precedence in determining the grade. The paper lacks originality, and this fact outweighs the others. Thus ethical standards are subject to modification when they support judgments that contradict our moral intuitions or frustrate our deepest desires.

These differences between science and ethics may account for the difference in the kind of knowledge we have of them. While theories, laws, and standards of measurement are well known to all qualified scientists, ethical principles and standards remain for the most part obscurely at work in our actions and choices, and require philosophical analysis to be brought to conscious attention. We often know what we approve of without knowing why—that is, without being able to state just what features merit our approval. And in ordinary circumstances this lack of awareness of our reasons for our judgments does not occasion any difficulty. But when we are uncertain of our choices and decisions, when we vacillate between alternative courses of action, we find it necessary to engage in philosophical reflection in order to make clear to ourselves where the source of the conflict lies and to assess the merit of the reasons on either side. Thus while scientific knowledge advances through new discoveries, ethical understanding advances through clarification of what we already know.

THE ROLE OF ETHICAL PHILOSOPHY TODAY

In our world of rapid change and continual conflict, many established principles of action and standards of judgment have proved inadequate or inapplicable. "Defend free elections" seems irrelevant to a starving and illiterate peasantry in a feudal society in Asia or South America. "Grade everyone alike" strikes the teacher, sensitive to the enormous differences in background and training of pupils from different socioeconomic backgrounds, as masking the perpetuation of social injustice behind the façade of pedagogical impartiality. "All violations of the law must be punished" sounds unrealistic to the police officer faced with a possible riot if a teenager is arrested for opening a fire hydrant on a hot summer night.

Where can philosophers find new or revised principles to replace those that have failed us, and what authority have they to say what they should be? Philosophers have no legal authority to legislate for others. But it is their task to clarify the rules and standards implicit in our common judgments and preferences and, where these are found to be in conflict, to suggest whatever revisions might resolve the conflict with a minimum of shock to our common system of values. This task of clarification and revision involves two levels: the practical level, on which the philosopher articulates existing rules and standards, shows where they come into conflict, and suggests modifications; and the theoretical level, on which the underlying concept— such as morality, responsibility, happiness, or justice—is defined in terms of the practical proposals it can justify.

THE STRUCTURE OF THIS BOOK

Each of the four parts of this book marks out an area of ethical concern. Part One presents the efforts of philosophers to formulate the standards of moral right and wrong in accordance with which actions and policies can be justified. Fundamental moral principles that have evolved through millennia of human experience are articulated in chapter 1, and the theoretical grounds for ascribing moral responsibility are studied in chapter 2.

Part Two is concerned with the moral evaluation of taking human life: one's own in chapter 3; that of a suffering invalid in chapter 4; that of a fetus in chapter 5; and that of a convicted murderer in chapter 6.

Part Three deals with disputed issues of social policies aimed at realizing social justice. Environmental obligations involving famine relief and population control, affirmative action in behalf of underprivileged minorities, paternalism and the right of privacy, and humane treatment of animals are both criticized and defended, as applications of the moral standards articulated in chapter 1.

The format changes somewhat in Part Four, wherein the topics are less matters of debate than of personal choice. They are also self-regarding, rather than other-regarding, aspects of conduct, as more or less essential ingredients of happiness. In chapter 12, skillful activity, cultivated pleasures, sexual fulfillment, self-assertion, mystical enlightenment, and spiritual love are explored as paths to the good life.

*E*THICAL THEORIES

What is morality? Is an action right or wrong only in relation to certain conditions, or is it right or wrong independent of any conditions? Are the grounds for judging human conduct always the same, or should they vary with social and individual needs, customs, and historical evolution? Theories of morality may be classified as relativist or absolutist depending on the answers they offer to these questions. But either relativism or absolutism may involve different general assumptions and may support different moral principles. An absolutist may argue for the invariant character of particular rules of conduct on the ground that they are divine commands, or that they are laws of nature, or that they are deducible from the concept of reason, or that they are intuitively self-evident. A relativist may hold that the rules of right conduct vary with human conventions, or with social traditions, or with political, psychological, economic, or biological needs. The history of ethical philosophy is a continuous dialogue between progressively more refined forms of absolutism and relativism. Although the basic issue between the rival theoretical standpoints represented in chapter 1 is still unsettled, each view contributes important discoveries about the meaning of our ethical statements. As the dialogue continues, we progress in untangling the complex logic of ethical judgment.

Space does not permit a complete survey of the myriad philosophical theories of morality that history offers us. We shall limit our study to examples of seven major schools of thought—religious absolutism, cultural relativism, rational absolutism, utilitarianism, prescriptivism, contractarianism, virtue ethics, and feminism, since the many other positions that philosophers have formulated are variations on these fundamental themes.

RELIGIOUS ABSOLUTISM

In our first selection, Robert C. Mortimer, Anglican bishop of Exeter, defends what is probably the oldest conception of moral right and wrong, the religious view that the meaning of "right" is obedience to divine commands. Assuming that natural processes reflect the will of their Creator and that conscience is the voice of God in the human soul, Mortimer maintains that natural law, personal conscience, and church pronouncements are the agencies for interpreting scriptural revelations and discovering what God requires us to do. An act is right, he maintains, "because God commands it." To be moral is to have those qualities of character, such as humility and charity, that motivate us to obey the dictates of our conscience as it represents the will of God.

The definition of right action as obedience to a superior being is strongly suggested by the way children develop moral awareness. A child first learns the difference between right and wrong from what his parents permit or forbid him to do. Later, the child adopts rules independently and evaluates his or her parents' conduct in turn. The Judaeo-Christian-Islamic concept of God compares the relation between God and man to that of father and child. But unlike the child who develops personal standards of conduct, man does not "grow up" to become independent of his heavenly Father, and God's commands, unlike those of human parents, are never subject to His children's criticism. Parental authority, the original standard of ethical judgment for the child, is thus infinitely extended in the religious concept of divine authority, and this extension provides an absolute basis for rules of conduct, since the commands of God are to be followed under any and all conditions.

While he claims that divine authority is the ultimate basis of moral right, there are, according to Mortimer, several subsidiary standards for deciding whether an action conforms to the will of God. The authority of the church, the rational recognition of natural law, and the promptings of one's conscience are subsidiary standards against which actions may be judged. This plurality of standards suggests the question: what if two or more of these standards justify incompatible actions? Mortimer recognizes the possibility of such conflicts and concludes that none of his three subsidiary standards is infallible when applied by fallible humans. Whichever method we use to interpret the will of God may be misapplied and lead to error, but this does not alter the fact that the will of God is always, by definition, right.

But can any authority, divine or human, be immune from ethical criticism? When we describe God as good, merciful, benevolent, and just, we express ethical judgments about God, and such judgments seem to be grounded on standards independent of divine authority. Does it make sense to say that what God does is right or good, if it makes no sense to say that what He does *could* be wrong or bad? In other words, if "right" *means* "in accordance with the will of God," then the statement "God is always right" seems to amount to "the will of God is in accordance with the will of God," which is empty truism. The problem of whether divine commandments are the foundation of right and therefore right by definition, or whether their rightness can be supported by more fundamental ethical standards, lies at the center of the controversy between religious and secular ethics.

CULTURAL RELATIVISM

The religious conception of right as obedience to the commands of a superior being develops naturally out of an authoritarian social structure where strict rules of conduct are decreed and enforced by those in power. When authoritarian society gives way to democratic society, in which individuals compete on equal terms, a different view of morality is apt to develop, a view in which the arbiter of rules of conduct is not a superior person, but a consensus of opinion among equals. When commercial and industrial democracies supplanted the agrarian monarchies of ancient Greece, the conventionalist ethics of the Sophists became dominant. In the seventeenth and eighteenth centuries, as Western Europe evolved from feudal to industrial societies, philosophers renewed their interest in the conventional origins of ethical standards.

Cultural relativism regards the validity of rules of conduct as dependent on the laws, customs, and agreements—the "conventions"—of the social group in which the conduct is judged. But it has one important feature in common with religious absolutism. Both positions identify moral rules with commands issued by an authority (social in the one case and divine in the other). Neither view allows for rational criticism of the basic rules. In both, ethical judgment arrives at a point beyond which one can no longer reason about what is right or wrong, but can only insist: it is the law or custom of our society, or it is what God has commanded, and therefore, it is right by definition. Just as religious absolutism requires an uncritical acceptance of divine authority, so cultural relativism requires an uncritical conformity to social authority. Both positions imply that ethical reasoning must terminate with an appeal to an authority whose might makes his or her decisions right.

Ruth Benedict's classic anthropological study, *Patterns of Culture,* does not explicitly identify morality with custom, indeed, the words "morality" and "ethics" never appear in the book, but this very fact might well be taken to imply an identification of morality with custom. This interpretation seems borne out by passages in which she seems to approve of tolerating actions that are socially accepted in the culture she describes, although in most other cultures they are the epitome of immorality, as in the following passage:

> Among the Eskimo, when one man has killed another, the family of the man who has been murdered may take the murderer to replace the loss within its own group. The murderer then becomes the husband of the woman who has been widowed by his act. This is an emphasis on restitution that ignores all other aspects of the situation—those which seem to us the only important ones; but when tradition selects some such objective it is quite in character that it should disregard all else. (p. 256)

"It is quite in character" sounds very much like approval.

Benedict describes three strikingly different primitive cultures: the gentle Zuñi of the American Southwest, the murderous and paranoidal Dobu of New Guinea, and the fanatically competitive Kwakiutal of Vancouver Island. What is accepted and admired in one of these societies is, she knows, precisely what is abhorred in another and vice versa. As a reputable anthropologist she makes no value judgments as to who is right and who is wrong, but therein lies the weakness of cultural relativism. If what is right and wrong depends solely on the customs and institutions of a society, then what grounds can we have for evaluating those customs and institutions? How could reformers be justified in criticizing prejudice, discrimination, slavery, cruelty, or tyranny when such practices are enshrined in their own institutions and ways of life? What right would we then have to condemn our slave-trading and Indian-massacring ancestors, or the Nazi and Stalinist regimes of our own time? The cultural relativist would seem to renounce any claim to justifiable social criticism and demand for social reforms from outsiders.

RATIONAL ABSOLUTISM

Many philosophers who agree that rules of conduct must have an unquestionable authority behind them insist that it cannot be identified with any person, not even a divine person. They argue that moral principles ought to be followed out of respect for the principles themselves and not out of fear of the person who promulgates them. The important difference between the rudimentary consciousness of children or savages and the mature consciousness of civilized adults is, the rational absolutist claims, the ability of the latter to judge matters for themselves and to follow their own rules of conduct. Not that one's own rules would differ from those of others—this admission would lead to relativism. Since reason is the same faculty in all, the rules discovered by one person's reason must be identical with those discovered by any other person, so that, as Kant put it, when I legislate for myself I legislate for everyone else as well, and, conversely, everyone legislates for me.

Immanuel Kant (1724–1804) was a devout Pietist who regarded Christianity as the highest moral ideal, but he made ethics more fundamental than theology. Instead of deriving his ethical principles from his beliefs about God, he derived his beliefs about God from what he regarded as purely rational ethical beliefs. Moral principles are, in Kant's view, commands of reason rather than commands of a divine parent. He conceived of God not as willful, issuing decrees, but as a perfect lawgiver and judge who recognizes the same rational principles that human reason discovers. The "categorical imperatives" of morality, unlike arbitrary commands of an individual, are universal and unconditional, applying to all persons and in all situations. Like the laws of logic, moral laws can be deduced from the concept of reason, without reference to any special facts of experience. In contrast to relativistic views of morality, Kant maintains that we can expect people to follow the same moral rules whatever their cultural backgrounds and personal needs. The single condition that qualifies a rule of conduct as a *moral law* is that it be logically possible to want every rational being to follow it under any conditions. In this way, Kant makes logical consistency the single standard of what is morally right.

While Kant's view pays remarkable homage to our intuitive sense of morality—that morality is impersonal, universal, rational, and yet a product of the individual's personal judgment—it is not free from logical difficulties. It seems impossible to formulate any rule of conduct that we would want everyone to follow under all circumstances. Kant's examples of such rules, which he calls "moral duties" ("Do not make false promises," "Do not take your own life"), seem to demand exceptions. Would it be wrong, for example, to break a promise made to a vicious criminal who threatens you with death? Kant claimed that such a promise must be kept, but this seems contrary to the common-sense attitudes he says his theory must explain and justify.

A second difficulty is that Kant frequently appeals to practical social consequences to justify rules that he insists should be deducible from the mere concept of a rational being. For instance, he argues that we cannot will it as a universal law that people make false promises when it is to their interest to do so, on the ground that if such a rule were followed, people would stop trusting each other. But it may be argued that this consideration is practical or utilitarian, rather than purely logical, and that there is nothing logically self-contradictory in proposing such a rule. Some writers, noticing this implicit utilitarianism in Kant, propose a compromise between utilitarian relativism and rational absolutism based on the distinction between rule and act. They suggest that an action is right if it conforms to a right rule, and that a rule is right if following it without exception produces socially beneficial results.

UTILITARIANISM

The Kantian account of moral right as conformity to universal and unconditional rules prompts the question: just which rules are universal and unconditional? The difficulty of answering to everyone's satisfaction leads the relativist to conclude that the question itself is a mistake and that the criterion of moral right must be something other than formal universality. Utilitarians offer a relativistic criterion, one which yields different results under different conditions. They classify moral right as that species of good which affects society as a whole, rather than one or a few individuals, and they propose that an act may be judged morally right if it produces pleasure or alleviates pain for most people. John Stuart Mill (1806–1873), the nineteenth-century British leader of liberalism and philosophical empiricism, formulated the slogan "the greatest happiness for the greatest number."

J. J. C. Smart, professor of philosophy emeritus at the University of Adelaide, Australia, is one of the most influential proponents today of utilitarian ethical theory. Smart argues for act-utilitarianism, which applies the greatest happiness principle of J. S. Mill to individual actions, as against rule-utilitarianism, which enjoins us to obey strict rules that, in turn, have been adopted because following them tends to maximize social benefit. Rule-utilitarianism is a compromise between rational absolutism (or deontology, as it is often called) and act-utilitarianism. Smart rejects this compromise as "law-worship" because it requires us to follow a moral rule such as "Do not lie" even when doing so does more harm than good. A moral rule, he asserts, is only a "rule of thumb," or rough guide, not a law.

Smart acknowledges that it is good for people to develop the habits of conduct that are called moral virtues, such as honesty, kindness, fairness, and temperance, because these "habits" usually maximize social benefit, but they should prevail only when action is uncontroversial enough to be automatic. When the situation is complex enough to require deliberation, a utilitarian estimate of benefits should take the place of virtuous habits and even override them.

Perhaps the most vulnerable aspect of act-utilitarianism lies in its approach to problems of justice. Justice to most people seems a far stricter requirement than, say, kindness, to the point of appearing an absolute rule. Replying, in the essay included here, to McCloskey's argument that a sheriff must not frame an innocent man even to avoid a terrible race riot, Smart grasps the nettle and boldly maintains that this "common sense" moral attitude is simply mistaken, and that in this case injustice is morally required, thus demonstrating that even rules of justice are fallible guides, rather than strict laws.

PRESCRIPTIVISM

The difficulties we have already encountered in justifying any particular standard of moral right and wrong, and the plethora of theories on this subject that vie for our allegiance, have persuaded many thinkers, (from the Sophists and Sceptics of Ancient Greece, to the present-day noncognitivists, that no standards are provably correct, for the reason that the primary role of value judgments, of which moral judgments are the central subspecies, is to guide action rather than to convey information. Consequently, whatever standards of value and morality we choose to employ cannot be justified on the ground that they are closer to truth than their rivals.

An early and extreme form of noncognitivism was proposed by the logical positivists, a philosophical movement that began in Vienna in the 1920s and became dominant in Great Britain and America in the 1930s and 1940s. The British philosopher A. J. Ayer, in his classic manifesto, *Language, Truth and Logic,* asserts that statements about what is good or bad, right or wrong have no "cognitive" (that is, informative) meaning, but merely express positive or negative feelings, like "groovy" and "yech."

The British philosopher R. M. Hare developed a more moderate view, which he called "prescriptivism," that preserves the noncognitive emphasis on the action-guiding role of value judgments, while also accounting for a secondary informative function that explains why we feel there is a point in reasoning about such judgments and in trying to decide which are true and which are false. According to Hare, the primary role of declarations like "X is good" or "A is wrong" is to commend the choice of X or to urge the avoidance of A, but such declarations are normally grounded on the satisfaction by X of certain criteria of evaluation, or on the failure of A to satisfy certain criteria of right action. Thus both declarations convey the information that those criteria have or have not been met (provided there is prior agreement on what they are). Disputes about value and morality acquire their hopelessly interminable "reach for your gun" character when the parties involved do not agree on the criteria of goodness or moral right. There are occasional uses of "good" and "right" when one does not have any definite criteria in mind, as in "Is that a good thing, whatever it is?", but they are quite rare.

There are, Hare grants, some uses of value terms that are primarily informative, where "good" and "right" indicate that the thing so described performs its characteristic function, as in "good motor car" or "the right wrench." But these uses are dependent on conventional agreement as to the function to be performed, and are therefore derivative from prior commendations of such objects. There is also the special use Hare calls the "inverted comma use" of value terms to signify that others would commend or prescribe, or condemn or forbid, the object or action in question, as when we speak of a "good burglar" or the "right weapon for an assassination." His general point concerning the rule, further confirmed by these very exceptions, is that evaluative language is primarily action guiding, while descriptive language is primarily informative, and that this difference accounts for the impossibility of reaching universal agreement on judgments of the former kind.

CONTRACTARIANISM

An influential synthesis of rational absolutism and utilitarianism, incorporating the 18th century doctrine of a social contract, was developed in recent years by the eminent American philosopher, John Rawls. Kant tried to deduce moral principles from his formal rule of universalizability, but the question then arose, why universalize one rule rather than another? Rawls' theory of rational choice of moral principles "under a veil of ignorance" seems to many to provide a satisfactory answer to that question.

In his early essay, "Justice as Fairness," excerpted in this chapter, Rawls offers a justification of two moral principles that, he maintains, define justice: the principle of Equality of Liberty and the principle of Difference. The Principle of Equality grants everyone an equal right to the maximum degree of liberty consistent with the liberty of others. The Principle of Difference specifies that inequalities of wealth and privilege are justified only if they are open to all in fair competition and if they are to the benefit of everyone alike. (In his later book, *A Theory of Justice,* he transformed this into what has come to be called the "maximin" principle, that inequalities are justified only if they benefit those who are worst off, even if they don't benefit everyone.)

Rawls offers two main arguments for his principles of justice (and, by implication, for other moral principles as well), one empirical, the other *a priori.* The first is that, in deciding on rules for adjudicating conflicting claims, rationally self-interested persons will always choose these two principles for their own protection, because, having no assurance that inequalities will be to their personal advantage, they will tend to play it safe. This argument assumes that it is more rational to be cautious than to gamble on success, that is, to prefer minimal risk to the chance for maximum gain. Critics have argued that it is no less rational to gamble for "winner take all."

Rawls' second argument deduces his two principles from the concept of a community of persons. To be a person among other persons, he maintains, is to have rights and liberties that are mutually acknowledged. The sense of fairness that involves acknowledgement of equal rights is "simply the possession of one of the forms of conduct in which the recognition of others as persons is manifested. To be a member of a community of persons is to recognize the equal rights and liberties of all." This argument is subject to the criticism that not all rights or liberties can be assigned equally or we would have social chaos, and it is not clear just which rights and liberties apply to persons as such, independently of their social roles.

VIRTUE ETHICS

Many contemporary philosophers, led by Philippa Foot, consider the theorists we have already considered to be too preoccupied with justifying rules of action, rather than with clarifying the traits of character that dispose agents to act well and serve as goals of moral education. Issues as to how we should act are less important, they think, than issues as to what we should be like, since a person of good character will usually do the right thing whether guided by a rule of action or not, while one of bad character will often act wrongly no matter what rules of action he professes. Thus the main task of ethical theory should be to distinguish the various virtues that make up a good moral character and to resolve apparent conflicts among them.

Clearly, this position is not in competition with the others with respect to offering an alternative standard of morally right action to that of social utility, divine command, social custom, or Kantian universalizability. Philippa Foot's own implicit standard seems to be the Aristotelian one of personal well-being (*eudaimonia*), but other virtue ethicists favor somewhat different standards. Bernard Williams inclines toward universalizability, while A. C. MacIntyre seems closer to social custom. What they have in common is their focus on the way we ought to *be*, rather than what we ought to *do*.

For models of moral theory Philippa Foot refers us to Aristotle and St. Thomas Aquinas to define the central virtues, such as courage, temperance, prudence, and justice; explain how they contribute to well-being; and resolve apparent conflicts among them. Foot distinguishes genuinely moral virtues from what are sometimes called "social" virtues (for example, being witty or having a pleasing personality) and also from desirable skills (athletic or musical virtuosity, for example). The reason Foot prefers to focus on virtues rather than on rules of action is that she believes that moral conduct is best encouraged and justified by showing that it is to the advantage of the moral agent, as well as socially beneficial, to behave morally. She holds that the classical emphasis on rules, whether Kantian, utilitarian, or culturally relative, fails to perform that critical task. A Kantian might well reply to that argument by maintaining (as Henry Prichard did in a well-known essay entitled "Does Moral Philosophy Rest on a Mistake?") that to be concerned with how one can profit from morality is expressive of a preference for self-interest over moral duty and is therefore just the wrong kind of question to ask. One might also object that moral virtues are tendencies to act in morally right ways, so that we need standards for judging what those right ways of acting are in order to define the virtues and that, for this reason, rules of conduct must take precedence over virtuous dispositions.

FEMINIST ETHICS

The distinguished American philosopher Annette Baier, like Philippa Foot, disdains offering a rival principle or set of principles of right action in what she considers the too-narrow sense of moral theory as "a systematic account of a large area of moral philosophy with a keystone [that is, a general rule] supporting all the rest" and proposes, instead, a new focus on the concept of trust, in contrast with the concept of obligation preferred by male philosophers and that of love preferred by some female philosophers. Baier thinks trust combines the merits of both approaches, so that a moral theory in the more general sense will inform us whom to trust and why for the coercive enforcement of moral rules, as well as whom to trust and why to care for and assist us and thus do the work of love. She does not try to delineate such a general theory of trust, but merely to explain the need for it.

Baier claims that an ethics of obligation, à la Mortimer or Kant, for example, emphasizes coercive restraint on liberty (what one must not do, under threat of blame or punishment), and therefore does weakly and inadequately what the criminal law does better, since a would-be miscreant would be more effectively deterred by threat of criminal sanctions than by that of moral disapproval. This is a controversial claim, worth exploring in depth. On the other hand, she maintains, a pure ethics of love, like that of many Christian sects, supports a more comprehensive and helpful way of life, but fails to provide us with guidelines as to whom to trust and to what degree. Moreover, it fails to explain the specific kind of trust involved in authorizing certain persons to coerce others to behave decently. Here again, Baier seems to be assuming that obligatory rules of action require special social authorities such as police, prosecutors, and judges, and cannot be effectively supported by public and private criticism and exhortation. It might be argued that Baier here displays excessive trust in social authority. Is it true that the rules of obligatory conduct, the central moral rules, can be entrusted to the police and the courts to articulate and uphold, rather than to the consciences of the man and woman in the street? And as for love, does it really need an ethics? Can anyone tell us whom to love and how much? More to the point: *should* anyone tell us? Can there be an ethics of trust *prior* to an ethics of obligation? Should we trust anyone who fails to meet his or her moral obligations? These are issues worth exploring further, as Baier suggests we do. But where that exploration leads us, whether to a more masculine, a more feminine, or a gender-neutral ethics, remains to be seen.

THE GROUNDS FOR MORAL RESPONSIBILITY

Assuming that we now understand how to judge acts to be right and people to be moral, can we do anything with our newly acquired wisdom? Suppose that whatever we do is determined by causes we cannot control. Deliberating about what is right is pointless if we are powerless to change our behavior in accordance with our moral judgments, so that it makes no practical difference *what* we believe. In short, if there is no free will, ethical discussion seems useless.

Again, using ethical standards to judge the conduct and character of others assumes that our judgments affect those we judge. We say that X behaved badly and Y has an evil character because we hope to reform X and Y, by either shaming or punishing them. But to do this is to hold X and Y responsible for their conduct. The applicability of ethical theory therefore depends on our knowledge of the conditions under which people are responsible for their actions. To say that a man has done the right thing is to praise his conduct and sometimes to suggest that he be rewarded. To say that a man is vicious is to punish him verbally and often to propose more tangible modes of punishment. But when, if ever, are we *justified* in meting out praise and blame or reward and punishment?

The conditions for assigning moral responsibility are most needed in deciding when to punish people for their actions. Everyday rules of procedure—products of centuries of human experience—often serve well enough, but at times ascribing responsibility becomes slippery. Were the German people responsible for the atrocities of the Third Reich? Were some more responsible than others? If so, to what degree? Is an insane person responsible for a brutal crime? Does neurosis excuse antisocial conduct? Is a juvenile delinquent from a broken home in a slum less responsible for his actions than one who rebels against wealthy and indulgent parents? In determining more exactly the conditions under which a person can or cannot help doing what he does, the sharp line between free and compulsive, voluntary and involuntary behavior melts away, and we turn to philosophy for clearer definitions of "free will," "voluntary," and "responsible."

Classical thought identified the problem of moral responsibility with whether or not the will is free, assuming that only freely willed action is responsible action. In turn, the will was described as a faculty of the mind, and philosophers sought to determine whether it does or does not have a certain quality called "freedom." Plato ascribed all good powers to the intellect and all evil ones to the faculty of desire. He concluded that wrong action is always due to intellectual error, so that "no man does evil voluntarily." Aristotle noted that punishment is justified only if we distinguish voluntary from involuntary infractions of law or moral principle, and he suggested distinctions among involuntary, nonvoluntary, impulsive, and deliberate action that have guided legal and moral judgment ever since.

The Greek Stoics held the fatalistic view that no one can help acting as he does, and yet made rigorous self-control the cornerstone of their system of ethics, unaware of the paradox until it was pointed out by Cicero. Epicurus and his followers rejected Stoic fatalism and accounted for freedom of the will by the unpredictable and spontaneous motions of the atoms that are the human soul. Christians, conceiving of the soul as intangible and indestructable, thought of the will as part of the soul substance having its own personality. Christian philosophers argued over whether this personalized will was free to direct the body until St. Augustine proposed a compromise that became authoritative doctrine but was vague enough to permit diverse interpretations by later Christian philosophers. Augustine transformed the Stoic notion of a blind naturalistic fatalism into the doctrine of divine predestination, according to which God has so arranged the world that He knows in advance how everyone will choose to act, despite the fact that He created man with the ability to choose freely.

The rise of modern science in the seventeenth century inspired a new, more secular form of determinism, proclaimed by Hobbes and Spinoza, and accepted by many scientists and philosophers to the present day. In this view, every event can, in principle, be explained as a predictable outcome of antecedent causes in accordance with rigorous scientific laws. Some philosophers and scientists have concluded that free will is an illusion and that praise and blame or reward and punishment are inappropriate responses to human actions, due to our ignorance of their causes. If we knew the causes of an action we would know that the agent has no alternative to performing it, and since the ability to do otherwise is a necessary condition for moral responsibility, it would be unfair to hold a person morally responsible for what he cannot help doing. This conclusion from the principle of determinism, which holds it to be incompatible with freedom of the will, was baptized "hard" determinism by William James, and distinguished from "soft" determinism, which holds determinism to be compatible with freedom and responsibility. Libertarians agree with hard determinists that determinism is incompatible with free will and moral responsibility but, contending that freedom and responsibility are facts of life that it is absurd to deny, they conclude that where human actions are concerned, determinism must be false. The libertarian reasons that we know we are free, and we merely conjecture that our actions are causally determined. If these two beliefs are incompatible, then it is the conjecture that must go, not the known fact.

Soft determinists differ from both hard determinists and libertarians in denying that freely willed action and causal determinism are incompatible. Beginning with Aristotle, who distinguished voluntary from involuntary action in terms of whether the causes or motives of action are internal to the agent (e.g., his own desires, purposes, and decisions) or external (e.g., threats, physical force, or hypnotic influence), soft determinists propose that freely willed or voluntary action be defined in terms of the *kind* of causes that produce it, rather than as action having no causes at all. They argue that uncaused action would be so unpredictable and capricious that, if it occurred, we would not blame it on the agent. Thus libertarian freedom, in the sense of uncaused action, provides no reasonable basis for holding people morally responsible for their actions, while freedom understood as caused by the agent's rational motives explains why coercion, ignorance, and psychic compulsion excuse agents from responsibility for their actions, since under these conditions the agent cannot be deterred from acting by threat of punishment or by rational argument.

Neither hard nor soft determinists deny the phenomenon we call "choice" or "decision." But both reject the interpretation that libertarians like Roderick Chisholm make of this phenomenon. Considered merely as a mental event, the reality of choice or decision is beyond dispute; however, the appearance that there are genuine alternatives, say A and B, such that it is just as likely that the agent will choose to do A as to do B, may be illusory. For when a person does A by choice, no doubt he could instead have chosen to do B in the sense that *if* he had chosen to do B he would have done B, but it may not have been possible, the determinist claims, for the agent to have so chosen. As Paul Edwards maintains, our tendency to assume that alternative courses of action are open to us may simply result from our limited knowledge of the internal and external forces acting on us. As the eighteenth-century philosopher Baron d'Holbach put it, it may just be because "the mechanism of... sensations... perceptions, and the manner they engrave ideas on the brain of man, are not known to him; because he is unable to unravel all these motions; because he cannot perceive the chain of operations in his soul or the motive principle that acts within him, that he supposes himself a free agent." Thus the mere mental occurrence of the appearance of choosing may be indisputable, but the belief that one has real alternatives is illusory, due to the ignorance of what goes on inside us.

The arguments for determinism are of two kinds: first, there is the great success of physics, chemistry, and biology in finding causal explanations of phenomena. Although the laws of physics on a subatomic level are now thought to be statistical rather than deterministic, the achievements of the last few centuries in these natural sciences have convinced almost everyone that, on a macroscopic level, the laws of nature reign supreme. Second, there is the somewhat less overwhelming, but nevertheless impressive, success in the last century of experimental psychology, economics, and other behavioral sciences.

Paul Edwards supports hard determinism against both soft determinism and libertarianism by accepting a distinction proposed by the libertarian theologian C. A. Campbell between a popular conception and a more reflective conception of moral responsibility. The former, unreflective conception is that one is morally responsible for one's action only if one is not being coerced, but is doing what one wants to do. (This is the soft determinist conception.) The reflective conception, according to Campbell, requires that the agent could have chosen otherwise. Edwards revises this as follows: "The reflective person, I should prefer to express it, requires not only that the agent was not coerced; he also requires that the agent *originally chose his own character*—the character that now displays itself in his choices and desires and efforts." Edwards agrees with Campbell that this reflective conception of the conditions for moral responsibility is the correct one, but unlike Campbell, he doesn't believe that it is ever realized. He holds, like the famous defense attorney of the early twentieth century, Clarence Darrow, that we are all products of our heredity and formed character, so that it is never really the case that we could have acted otherwise, and therefore no one is really morally responsible for what he or she does, in the "reflective sense" of the term.

Roderick Chisholm defends the libertarian view that to act of one's own free will and thus to be morally responsible for one's action entails being able to do otherwise, that is, to choose between alternative courses of action, and that this condition is incompatible with determinism: "If the act which he *did* perform was an act that was also in his power *not* to perform, then *it* could not have been caused or determined by any event that was not within his power either to bring about or not bring about."

Chisholm considers, and then rejects, a possible solution to this conflict between determinism and free will suggested by the early American philosopher Jonathan Edwards, and revived in this century by the British philosopher G. E. Moore, consisting in what has come to be called the "hypothetical" as contrasted with the "categorical" interpretation of "could have done otherwise." On this hypothetical interpretation, (1) "She could have done otherwise" means the same as (2) "If she had chosen to do otherwise, she would have done so." This stratagem, he claims, simply does not work, for the second statement might be true while the first was false. Chisholm's positive account of free will is that the agent, rather than any external or internal event, causes her own action, so that her action is not uncaused, but is an instance of what he calls "immanent" rather than "transeunt" causation. This concept of two radically different kinds of causation lies at the heart of libertarianism and provokes unending controversy.

Patrick Nowell-Smith, a contemporary British philosopher, defends a soft determinist view that avoids the problems raised by the obscure libertarian concept of agent ("immanent") causation of one's own actions, by defining free action as not only compatible with but actually entailing determinism. We are acting freely and responsibly, he suggests, when we could do otherwise in the "hypothetical sense" that, *if* we were given adequate reasons for doing otherwise, we *would* make that alternative choice. We have already seen that theorists of the other two persuasions reject the hypothetical interpretation. But if we accept that interpretation, Nowell-Smith argues, we can then define a freely willed action as one that the agent would not have performed if she had recognized good reasons not to do so. In brief, a free act is one that is caused (motivated) by reasons and would have been caused not to be performed had the agent been in possession of better reasons (such as certainty of punishment) to refrain.

Nowell-Smith's formulation of the soft determinist position is quite persuasive. It conforms to and explains our common-sense criteria of responsibility, while avoiding obscure notions of immanent or agent causation and a self distinct from one's formed character, as well as that of a completely uncaused action. It makes no advance commitments as to which of our actions are free and responsible, leaving these matters to psychologists and social scientists to decide after adequate empirical investigation. But it is not invulnerable to philosophical criticism, for it makes freely willed action compatible with determinism only by broadening the meaning of "cause" to what may be an unwarranted extent, to include reasons for acting that are not at all compelling.

Susan Wolf, a contemporary American philosopher, offers a controversially broad interpretation of the term *determination* in holding that actions are usually determined by motives, and motives by heredity and environment. She calls this kind of determination "psychological determination." This concept enables Wolf to offer a compromise between the soft determinist compatibilism of Nowell-Smith and the incompatibilism of both hard determinism as propounded by Edwards and libertarianism as championed by Chisholm.

Wolf proposes an "asymmetrical" account of free will, according to which it is compatible with psychological determinism when the action is determined by good reasons, but not when it is determined by bad reasons. It follows that "an agent can be morally praiseworthy even though he is determined.... But ... an agent cannot be morally blameworthy if he is determined." Wolf thus reaches the rather paradoxical conclusion that responsibility is asymmetrical with respect to freedom. We are free to perform good actions, and always worthy of praise or reward when we do, but we are seldom free when we do bad things, and therefore we should seldom be blamed or punished.

Wolf's analysis has the merit of bringing out the partial truth in each of the three classical views and in explaining why none is entirely true. But it would not be easy to apply her criteria of moral responsibility to actual cases. When is a miscreant capable of refraining from wrongdoing, and when not? Are all reasons for acting equally compelling? If not, when is a person determined by reasons, and when is he or she only influenced but not determined? Is good action always determined, unlike bad action, which, Wolf suggests, is only sometimes determined? This is an asymmetry Wolf does not consider and explain.

1

*T*HE STANDARDS OF MORAL RIGHT AND WRONG

*R*ELIGIOUS ABSOLUTISM

Robert C. Mortimer

THE BIBLE AND ETHICS

The Christian religion is essentially a revelation of the nature of God. It tells men that God has done certain things. And from the nature of these actions we can infer what God is like. In the second place the Christian religion tells men what is the will of God for them, how they must live if they would please God. This second message is clearly dependent on the first. The kind of conduct which will please God depends on the kind of person God is. This is what is meant by saying that belief influences conduct. The once popular view that it does not matter what a man believes so long as he acts decently is nonsense. Because what he considers decent depends on what he believes. If you are a Nazi you will behave as a Nazi, if you are a Communist you will behave as a Communist, and if you are a Christian you will behave as a Christian. At least, in general; for a man does not always do what he knows he ought to do, and he does not always recognize clearly the implications for conduct of his belief. But in general, our conduct, or at least our notions of what constitutes right conduct, are shaped by our beliefs. The man who knows about God—has a right faith—knows or may learn what conduct is pleasing to God and therefore right.

The Christian religion has a clear revelation of the nature of God, and by means of it instructs and enlightens the consciences of men. The first foundation is the doctrine of God the Creator. God made us and all the world.

Because of that he has an absolute claim on our obedience. We do not exist in our own right, but only as His creatures, who ought therefore to do and be what He desires. We do not possess anything in the world, absolutely, not even our own bodies; we hold things in trust for God, who created them, and are bound, therefore, to use them only as He intends that they should be used. This is the doctrine contained in the first chapters of Genesis. God created man and placed him in the Garden of Eden with all the animals and the fruits of the earth at his disposal, subject to God's own law. "Of the fruit of the tree of the knowledge of good and evil thou shalt not eat." Man's ownership and use of the material world is not absolute, but subject to the law of God.

From the doctrine of God as the Creator and source of all that is, it follows that a thing is not right simply because we think it is, still less because it seems to be expedient. It is right because God commands it. This means that there is a real distinction between right and wrong which is independent of what we happen to think. It is rooted in the nature and will of God. When a man's conscience tells him that a thing is right, which is in fact what God wills, his conscience is true and its judgment correct; when a man's conscience tells him a thing is right which is, in fact, contrary to God's will, his conscience is false and telling him a lie. It is a lamentably common experience for a man's conscience to play him false, so that in all good faith he does what is wrong, thinking it to be right. "Yea the time cometh that whosoever killeth you will think that he doeth God service." But this does not mean that whatever you think is right is right. It means that even conscience can be wrong: that the light which is in you can be darkness.

There is such a thing as human nature, which is the same in all men. It exists, like everything else, in order to become fully itself, to achieve its end. What that end is can be perceived, at any rate to a great extent, by the use of reason alone, unaided by any special divine revelation. For example, everybody has some idea of what is meant by a good man or a noble man. Everybody has some idea of what makes a society "advanced" or developed and what makes it primitive or decadent. Or again, that mind should control matter, the reason order the emotions, is clearly demanded by the very structure of our nature, in which there is a hierarchy of spirit, mind, and body. To make the body obey the reason is in harmony with nature, to allow the body to dominate the mind is to violate nature. Temperance, self-control, has always been recognized as a virtue. Indeed there has always been a general recognition of what the virtues are: justice, courage, temperance, consideration for others. The man who has these is well on the way to realizing his true nature, to becoming a man. The coward, the thief, the libertine, the ruthless oppressor is stunting and maiming himself. He becomes less and less a man, as he becomes more and more the slave of some dominant impulse and obsession. He is unbalanced and only partially developed.

All this means that there is a pattern of general behavior, a code of things to do and not to do, which derives necessarily from nature itself, from the simple fact that man is man. It is what is called natural law. The knowledge of it is not peculiar to Christians: it is common to man. It may make things plainer to give an illustration or two.

It is clear that man's power of memory, by means of which he can use the experience of the past as a guide for the present and can in some measure forecast the future and so provide for coming needs out of present superfluity—it is clear that this power of memory indicates the duty of thrift and prudence and condemns prodigality as unnatural. Man is meant to acquire control of his environment by such use of reason and to live free of the bondage of chance and desperate need. Wilful neglect to make provision for the future is to violate the law of nature and to incur the risk of the penalties which such violations incur.

Again, nature makes it abundantly clear that the survival and education of human offspring require a long and close union of the two parents. Kittens and puppies may survive birth from promiscuous unions, being adequately cared for by the mother alone, and quickly reaching an age of self-sufficiency. Not so human babies, whose slow development to maturity involves them in a long helpless dependence on their parents, and creates for the parents a long period of shared responsibility for the lives they have brought into the world. Hence the institution of marriage, found at all levels of human culture, and the general recognition of the virtue of chastity and of fidelity to the marriage bond.

Again, it is clear that the isolated individual man, the fictional solitary inhabitant of a desert island, cannot, or does not, easily attain to the full development of his personality and power. It is by sharing the fruits of their diverse labour, by each contributing that for which he has a special aptitude, that men accumulate wealth, and by wealth get leisure. It is by mutual intercourse and the exchange of thought that men acquire and distribute wisdom, and are able to practise and appreciate the arts. It is by living together that men develop their spiritual and mental powers and become persons. In other words, as Aristotle said, Man is by nature a political animal. He is not meant to live alone but in society. From this follows the universal recognition of the virtue of justice. Without justice there can be no stable society. Justice demands that all respect each other's rights, so that all may live together in peaceful enjoyment of that which is their own. The particular determinations of justice, the decision as to what are each man's rights has always been difficult, and subject to constant variation; but the general principle that rights are to be respected has been universally admitted and finds expression in such universal prohibitions as "thou shalt not kill," and "thou shalt not steal." . . .

It is certain that human perception of the content and implications of natural law has developed with the emergence of man from his primitive condition—the history of the institution of marriage is but one, if the clearest, illustration of this. It is equally certain that it has also regressed; that from time to time different human societies have lost, or failed to reach, a grasp of certain of the most elementary of its contents. Anthropologists have little difficulty in showing that there is scarcely one of the generally accepted moral axioms which has not somewhere at some time been denied. Cannibalism, thievery, even prostitution have in some societies not merely been practiced, but extolled as moral duties. And in our own day we have been amazed at the Nazi moral code, which inculcated cruelty and lies as patriotic virtues.

Some have used these facts as an argument in favor of relativism and against the very existence of the natural law of divinely constituted human behavior. But the facts will not bear this argument, any more than ignorance of the solar system proves that the earth does not go round the sun. Existence of law and knowledge of that law are not the same thing. The law may well exist, and yet men be in ignorance of it. Knowledge of the law of nature in its more delicate implications and determinations demands refinement of moral sensitiveness and a quality of prophetic insight. Even in its elementary content, in such precepts as the ten commandments, passion, self-interest, long-standing custom can blind men to truths which to others seem self-evident. The elementary right to individual freedom has often been denied to slaves in the name of the law of nature itself. There is no limit to the perversity of the human reason when clouded and weakened by unredeemed sin. It is the fact of universal human selfishness, or as theologians call it, the Fall, which prevents men from attaining a clear and persistent understanding of what constitutes right behavior. And it is this which establishes the permanent need of Revelation, and places Christians in a privileged and especially responsible position.

The pattern of conduct which God has laid down for man is the same for all men. It is universally valid. When we speak of Christian ethics we do not mean that there is one law for Christians and another for non-Christians. We mean the Christian understanding and statement of the one common law for all men. Unbelievers also know or can be persuaded of that law or of part of it: Christians have a fuller and better knowledge. The reason for this is that Christians have by revelation a fuller and truer knowledge both of the nature of God Himself and of the nature of man. As has been well said, "Christian men, in order to learn what is the place of the Natural Law and its products in the economy of salvation, must look to the Bible as the witness of God's operations and as the record of God's supernatural destiny for man, to which the Natural Law is itself oriented and subordinated. Only with such a perspective, and with the will to purification of perception and purpose thereby created, will they be able to perceive or affirm the Natural Law in its completeness as an expression of the Lordship of Jesus Christ."

The Revelation in the Bible plays a three-fold part. In the first place it recalls and restates in simple and even violent language fundamental moral judgments which men are always in danger of forgetting or explaining away. It thus provides a norm and standard of human behavior in the broadest and simplest outline. Man's duty to worship God and love the truth, to respect lawful authority, to refrain from violence and robbery, to live in chastity, to be fair and even merciful in his dealings with his neighbor—and all this as the declared will of God, the way man *must* live if he would achieve his end—this is the constant theme of the Bible. The effect of it is not to reveal something new which men could not have found out for themselves, but to recall them to what they have forgotten or with culpable blindness have failed to perceive.

It is not easy to exaggerate the power of human self-deception nor man's ingenuity in persuading himself that black is white; manifest injustice can be depicted as justice, and unchastity acclaimed as "a venture of bold living." For example in times of shortages to exploit the needs and miseries of the poor by a strictly legal use of the markets may easily be represented as a perfectly proper use of one's opportunities, a quite legitimate advancement of oneself and one's family. The complacency born of such long and widespread practice is shattered by the violence of Revelation. "Thus saith the Lord: For three transgressions of Israel, and for four, I will not turn away the punishment thereof; because they sold the righteous for silver and the poor for a pair of shoes . . ." (Amos ii, 6). This, then, is the first work of Revelation; it continuously sets forth the broad paths of right conduct. Lies are lies by whatever name you call them, and injustice however fairly screened and decked. They who read the Scriptures constantly and with attention cannot fail to ask themselves not only how far they have knowingly and willfully transgressed the law of God, but also how far even that conduct which has seemed above question and reproach comes under divine condemnation.

And this leads to the second work of Revelation. The conduct which God demands of men, He demands out of His own Holiness and Righteousness. "Be ye perfect, as your Father in Heaven is perfect." Not the service of the lips but of the heart, not obedience in the letter but in the Spirit is commanded. The standard is too high: the Judge too all-seeing and just. The grandeur and majesty of the moral law proclaims the weakness and impotence of man. It shatters human pride and self-sufficiency: it overthrows that complacency with which the righteous regard the tattered robes of their partial virtues, and that satisfaction with which rogues rejoice to discover other men more evil than themselves. The revelation of the holiness of God and His Law, once struck home, drives men to confess their need of grace and brings them to Christ their Savior.

Lastly, Revelation, by the light which it throws on the nature of God and man, suggests new emphases and new precepts, a new scale of values which could not at all, or could not easily, have been perceived as part of the Natural Law for man without it. Thus it comes about that Christian ethics is at once old and new. It covers the same ground of human conduct as the law of the Old Testament and the "law of the Gentiles written in their hearts." Many of its precepts are the same precepts. Yet all is seen in a different light and in a new perspective—the perspective of God's love manifested in Christ. It will be worthwhile to give one or two illustrations of this.

Revelation throws into sharp relief the supreme value of each individual human being. Every man is an immortal soul created by God and designed for an eternal inheritance. The love of God effected by the Incarnation the restoration and renewal of fallen human nature in order that all men alike might benefit thereby. The Son of God showed particular care and concern for the fallen, the outcast, the weak and the despised. He came, not to call the righteous, but sinners to repentance. Like a good shepherd, He sought especially for the sheep which was lost. Moreover, the divine drama of Calvary which was the cost of man's redemption, the price necessary to give him again a clear picture of what human nature was designed to be and to provide him with the inspiration to strive towards it and the assurance that he is not irrevocably tied and bound to his sinful, selfish, past, makes it equally clear that in the eyes of the Creator His creature man is of infinite worth and value.

The lesson is plain and clear: all men equally are the children of God, all men equally are the object of His love. In consequence of this, Christian ethics has always asserted that every man is a person possessed of certain inalienable rights, that he is an end in himself, never to be used merely as a means to something else. And he is this in virtue of his being a man, no matter what his race or color, no matter how well or poorly endowed with talents, no matter how primitive or developed. And further, since man is an end in himself, and that end transcends this world of time and space, being fully attained only in heaven, it follows that the individual takes precedence over society, in the sense that society exists for the good of its individual members, not those members for society. However much the good of the whole is greater than the good of any one of its parts, and whatever the duties each man owes to society, individual persons constitute the supreme value, and society itself exists only to promote the good of those persons.

This principle of the infinite worth of the individual is explicit in Scripture, and in the light of it all totalitarian doctrines of the State stand condemned. However, the implications of this principle for human living and for the organization of society are not explicit, but need to be perceived and worked out by the human conscience. How obtuse that conscience can be, even when illumined by revelation, is startlingly illustrated by the long centuries in which Christianity tolerated the institution of slavery. In view of the constant tendency of man to exploit his fellow men and use them as the instruments of his greed and selfishness, two things are certain. First, that the Scriptural revelation of the innate inalienable dignity and value of the individual is an indispensable bulwark of human freedom and growth. And second, that our knowledge of the implication of this revelation is far indeed from being perfect; there is constant need of further refinement of our moral perceptions, a refinement which can only emerge as the fruit of a deeper penetration of the Gospel of God's love into human life and thought.

Another illustration of the effect of Scripture upon ethics is given by the surrender of the principle of exact retribution in favor of the principle of mercy. Natural justice would seem to require exact retributive punishment, an eye for an eye, a tooth for a tooth. The codes of primitive peoples, and the long history of blood feuds show how the human conscience has approved of this concept. The revelation of the divine love and the explicit teaching of the Son of God have demonstrated the superiority of mercy, and have pointed the proper role of punishment as correction and not vengeance. Because of the revelation that in God justice is never unaccompanied by mercy, in Christian ethics there has always been an emphasis on the patient endurance of wrongs in imitation of Calvary, and on the suppression of all emotions of vindictive anger. As a means to soften human relations, as a restraint of human anger and cruelty, so easily disguised under the cloak of justice, the history of the world has nothing to show comparable to this Christian emphasis on patience and mercy, this insistence that even the just satisfaction of our wrongs yields to the divine example of forebearance. We are to be content with the reform or at least the restraint of the evildoer, never to seek or demand vengeance.

It is well known how great a store Aristotle set by the "magnanimous" man, the man who holds himself to be intellectually and morally superior to his fellows, and is so. The concept of humility as a virtue is, I think, peculiar to the Christian code of ethics. It is inspired wholly by the example of the Son of God who came down from Heaven and lived as a man, and suffered the shameful death of the Cross. "The Son of Man came not to be ministered unto but to minister." "He that is greatest among you, let him be as one that serveth."

The duty of the great and highly placed not to seek their own advantage, but to devote themselves to the service of those over whom they bear rule; the conviction that all are equal in the sight of God, though different men have different functions; the recognition that all authority, power and wealth are from above, held in trust for God to whom account must one day be given; the understanding that respect, deference, prestige, rank are not things to be eagerly grasped at, but that, in imitation of Him who counted not His equality with God, a prize to be snatched at, their surrender is nobler than their acquisition, their responsibility weightier than their privileges: these are insights not easily gained by the natural man but plain in the Revelation and always emphasized in the Christian tradition. Humility in high and low alike is that virtue by which men are conscious of their own frailty and unworthiness, and grateful for the divine mercy and help upon which they constantly depend; by it they see in their own virtues only the triumph of God's grace and a divine commission to the service of others. This lovely quality is perhaps the noblest of all the gifts of Christianity to the human race. . . .

These are only a few of the matters on which the human conscience is enlightened by the Revelation contained in the Christian tradition. Nor are all the implications of the Revelation anything like fully realized even now after nearly two thousand years. No doubt, so long as humanity exists, among those who humbly and patiently seek to live under the Gospel there will develop an ever clearer and more delicate perception of what the divine pattern for human conduct is. It is certain that where the Revelation is ignored, the darkness of degeneracy and barbarism sets in. Sin-ridden man needs the Scriptures to rebuke his errors, to correct the distortion with which he perceives the natural law, to hold him firmly to its elementary principles and to lighten his eyes to its hidden depths. Christian ethics is the exposition of the moral truths implicit in the Revelation, and the application of them to human living. It interprets to man the natural law on the basis of that superior knowledge of the nature of God, of man, and of the end for which man is created, which Revelation contains.

AUTHORITY AND CONSCIENCE

Because the content of Christian ethics is thus determined by the nature of the divine revelation in Scripture, the Church has always held a high position of authority in the matter of morals. Just as it is her duty and function to define what is the Christian faith, and to guard it from false teaching, so it is her duty to define what is the Christian conduct which follows from that faith, and to denounce practices which are opposed to it. The most important part of her duty in this respect is to proclaim the broad principles and general duties of Christian behavior. It is her duty constantly to remind men of those obvious moral truths which they are always in danger of forgetting under the influence of passion and self-interest. The "duty towards God" and "the duty towards my neighbor" in the English Church Catechism are illustrations of the Church performing this kind of work. The two "duties" set out the ordinary Christian duties. They are stated without argument and on authority—the authority of Scripture and of the Church interpreting Scripture. The clergy, armed with the same authority, preach these duties and expound them.

In addition to this duty of constantly emphasizing general principles, the Church has also the duty of applying these principles to changing circumstances. This is a task of very considerable difficulty—a difficulty not clearly realized by those who glibly call "for a lead from the Church" whenever any fresh moral problem arises. The difficulty is created by the tension between the "magisterium" or "teaching authority" of the Church in faith and morals on the one hand, and the autonomy of every individual conscience on the other.

Once the Church has "pronounced" on any question of morals, there is a prima facie obligation on Christians to obey: for the Church has authority in such matters. Yet if the pronouncement is contrary to a man's own conscientious judgment there is a higher obligation, as we shall see in a moment, to obey one's own conscience. It is for this reason, in order to avoid a conflict of this kind, that the Protestant Churches, at least, are reluctant to issue detailed and authoritative statements on new moral problems. After all, the guidance of the Holy Spirit is promised to the Church as a whole; the Spirit dwells in every member of the Church from the highest and most instructed to the lowest and least gifted. Authoritative pronouncements are only properly made when they express and articulate the common mind of the whole Church. To determine what this mind is is a slow and difficult matter. It is not necessarily what those in authority in the Church hold to be true at the moment of the first impact of the new problem; neither is it necessarily the half-instinctive reaction of the general mass of Christians. The common Spirit-guided judgment more often emerges or crystallizes slowly after debate and reflection.

Nevertheless, life has to be lived. And men naturally and rightly demand of the Church help and advice in solving their moral problems and in applying the principles of Christian ethics to the situation in which they daily find themselves. It is much easier to perceive and admit, for example, the claims of justice in general, than to decide what is in fact just within the framework of a given social order. The Church has an undeniable duty to ease this difficulty, sometimes by re-proclaiming the general principles and outline of justice, sometimes by going further and asserting positively that this or that practice is demanded or is condemned by those principles. This duty brings the Church not only into the area of personal ethics but also into the spheres of politics and economics. Her voice is to be heard both declaring and expounding, for example, the duties of marriage and also teaching the laws of war, the requirements of honesty in business or the mutual duties of employer and employed.

In many cases, perhaps in most, the Church does not try so much to lay down the solutions of moral problems or to dictate in detail the moral conduct appropriate to particular circumstances, as to set forth the principles which must be borne in mind by those faced with such problems, and with which conduct must conform in this or that set of circumstances. Thus, in time of war, the Church will not necessarily condemn out of hand any particular method of warfare—for she may have altogether inadequate material for passing a judgment—but she will remind belligerents of the duties of mercy and humanity and of the general claims of justice. And in this way she will call on those in authority to see to it that their conduct of the war does not infringe these principles. Or again, in matters of the marketplace, the Church will not herself lay down what is the just price, or at what point profits turn into profiteering: she will not herself determine what is a fair wage, or what is the proper number of hours to be worked in a day or a week. But she will insist that merchants aim at a just price, that manufacturers be content with a moderate profit, that masters and men have a common Master in Heaven, that the laborer is worthy of his hire, that power and advantage are not rightly used as opportunities to exploit or coerce. And she will call on those engaged in the marketplace to see to it that in their conduct they do not wilfully and flagrantly violate those principles.

When new inventions suddenly create new situations, it becomes the duty of the Church to assist Christians to form their moral judgments by stating clearly the moral issues which are involved. She assists them by showing what is genuinely new in the new situation and what is old, by disentangling the various elements which go to form the situation, and so presenting a clearer picture of the problem which has to be solved.

These are some of the ways in which the Protestant Churches, at least, try to discharge their duty of guiding and teaching Christian people in matters of morals. Occasionally, and in the case of the Roman Church more often, the Church will authoritatively forbid particular practices as certainly contrary to the laws of God. For example, divorce and remarriage is condemned as a violation of the marriage bond. The compulsory sterilization of the mentally defective is forbidden as constituting a denial of an essential human right, and their extermination as an unjustifiable subordination of the individual to the community. The institution of slavery is condemned as unjust in its affront to human dignity and its denial of human rights.

Whether the Church commands or reminds or advises, precisely because she is the divinely constituted guardian and interpreter of the Christian faith in which Christian ethics is rooted, her voice is not to be disregarded. She is not to be carelessly and lightly dismissed as though she had no right to speak, and were guilty of an unwarrantable intrusion into matters outside of the sphere of religion. All Christians are morally bound to pay her the greatest attention; they are to take account in their conduct of those principles which she lays down as governing particular matters, and where she issues a definite command or prohibition, they are under a moral obligation to obey. Yet, because the application of moral principles to particular situations and the conquest determination of where duty lies is the primary task of the individual conscience, the Church, however authoritative her teaching, is not the final arbiter. The last word lies with conscience.

The statement that Christians are under a moral obligation to obey the Church in matters of morals presupposes that their own consciences are not at variance with the teaching of the Church. No man lightly sets up his own judgment against that of the Church, nor acquiesces in conscientious disagreement without the most serious and painful effort to understand and make his own the Church's judgment; but in the last resort his own conscience must be allowed to be supreme. Deeply embedded in the heart of Christian ethics is the dictum "Conscience is always to be obeyed."

It must be so. Conscience is a man's reason making moral judgments. It is by the use of this reason that man apprehends truth, if he apprehends it at all. What, therefore, a man perceives to be true he must hold to be true or else deny that he can ever perceive truth at all.

A judgment of conscience is a perception or apprehension of moral truth. It takes the form "this is right" or "this is wrong." The foundation of all morality is the innate instinctive universal recognition that right is to be done, wrong is not to be done. When, therefore, a man judges, by his reason, that "this is right," at the same moment he recognizes that "this ought to be done." To hold that "this is right, yet it ought not to be done" is the same as to say "this is right, though I know it to be wrong" or "I accept as true what I know to be untrue." In other words, a man can never be acting rightly when he goes against his conscience.

This does not mean . . . that he is necessarily acting rightly whenever he obeys his conscience. It is nonsense to suppose that whatever a man thinks is right must be right. But it does mean that whenever a man disobeys his conscience, whether his conscience is right or wrong, he is acting wrongly.

For every time he does so, he says in effect "I am doing what I judge to be wrong." Hence, in the last resort, no matter how much others may denounce my judgment as false, no matter with what authority of tradition and learning the contrary opinion be invested, if my own conscience is clear and certain, it must be followed. For not to follow it would be to refuse to do what I know to be right, what I know to be the will of God.

From this fundamental principle of the supremacy of the individual conscience, as constituting for each individual the norm and standard of moral conduct from which there is no appeal, there flow two important corollaries. The first is that it becomes at times a duty to disobey lawful authority. The second is that it is at all times a duty to take moral problems seriously.

Although . . . it is the teaching of Christian ethics that subjects are under a moral obligation to obey their lawful superiors—that such obedience is the will of God, to be rendered "for conscience sake" and not merely from compulsion—yet the obedience so enjoined is not blind and undiscriminating. It is due to superiors because and in so far as they are the agents of God. It follows, therefore, that no obedience is due where the superiors command anything which is against the will of God. On the contrary, such commands not only may but must be disobeyed. For we are to obey God rather than men. In consequence it is the duty of subjects in every state to scrutinize the laws passed upon them, to make sure that they will not, by obeying them, transgress the laws of God. In a democratic state they have the further duty of taking the appropriate constitutional steps to have such laws repealed and to ensure that no more such laws be enacted.

Cultural Relativism

Ruth Benedict

The vast proportion of all individuals who are born into any society always and whatever the idiosyncrasies of its institutions, assume, as we have seen, the behaviour dictated by the society. This fact is always interpreted by the carriers of the culture as being due to the fact that their particular institutions reflect an ultimate and universal sanity. The actual reason is quite different. Most people are shaped to the form of their culture because of the enormous malleability of their original endowment. They are plastic to the moulding force of the society into which they are born. It does not matter whether, with the Northwest Coast, it requires delusions of self-reference, or with our own civilization the amassing of possessions. In any case the great mass of individuals take quite readily the form that is presented to them.

They do not all, however, find it equally congenial, and those are favoured and fortunate whose potentialities most nearly coincide with the type of behaviour selected by their society. Those who, in a situation in which they are frustrated, naturally seek ways of putting the occasion out of sight as expeditiously as possible are well served in Pueblo culture. Southwest institutions. . . minimize the situations in which serious frustrations can arise, and when it cannot be avoided, as in death, they provide means to put it behind them with all speed.

On the other hand, those who react to frustration as to an insult and whose first thought is to get even are amply provided for on the Northwest Coast. They may extend their native reaction to situations in which their paddle breaks or their canoe overturns or to the loss of relatives by death. They rise from their first reaction of sulking to thrust back in return, to "fight" with property or with weapons. Those who can assuage despair by the act of bringing shame to others can register freely and without conflict in this society, because their proclivities are deeply channelled in their culture. In Dobu those whose first impulse is to select a victim and project their misery upon him in procedures of punishment are equally fortunate.

It happens that none of the three cultures we have described meets frustration in a realistic manner by stressing the resumption of the original and interrupted experience. It might even seem that in the case of death this is impossible. But the institutions of many cultures nevertheless attempt nothing less. Some of the forms the restitution takes are repugnant to us, but that only makes it clearer that in cultures where frustration is handled by giving rein to this potential behaviour, the institutions of that society carry this course to extraordinary lengths. Among the Eskimo, when one man has killed another, the family of the man who has been murdered may take the murderer to replace the loss within its own group. The murderer then becomes the husband of the woman who has been widowed by his act. This is an emphasis upon restitution that ignores all other aspects of the situation—those which seem to us the only important ones; but when tradition selects some such objective it is quite in character that it should disregard all else.

Restitution may be carried out in mourning situations in ways that are less uncongenial to the standards of Western civilization. Among certain of the Central Algonkian Indians south of the Great Lakes the usual procedure was adoption. Upon the death of a child a similar child was put into his place. This similarity was determined in all sorts of ways: often a captive brought in from a raid was taken into the family in the full sense and given all the privileges and the tenderness that had originally been given to the dead child. Or quite as often it was the child's closest playmate, or a child from another related settlement who resembled the dead child in height and features. In such cases the family from which the child was chosen was supposed to be pleased, and indeed in most cases it was by no means the great step that it would be under our institutions. The child had always recognized many "mothers" and many homes where he was on familiar footing. The new allegiance made him thoroughly at home in still another household. From the point of view of the bereaved parents, the situation had been met by a restitution of the *status quo* that existed before the death of their child.

Persons who primarily mourn the situation rather than the lost individual are provided for in these cultures to a degree which is unimaginable under our institutions. We recognize the possibility of such solace, but we are careful to minimize its connection with the original loss. We do not use it as a mourning technique, and individuals who would be well satisfied with such a solution are left unsupported until the difficult crisis is past.

There is another possible attitude toward frustration. It is the precise opposite of the Pueblo attitude, and we have described it among the other Dionysian reactions of the Plains Indians. Instead of trying to get past the experience with the least possible discomfiture, it finds relief in the most extravagant expression of grief. The Indians of the plains capitalized the utmost indulgences and exacted violent demonstrations of emotion as a matter of course.

In any group of individuals we can recognize those to whom these different reactions to frustration and grief are congenial: ignoring it, indulging it by uninhibited expression, getting even, punishing a victim, and seeking restitution of the original situation. In the psychiatric records of our own society, some of these impulses are recognized as bad ways of dealing with the situation, some as good. The bad ones are said to lead to maladjustments and insanities, the good ones to adequate social functioning. It is clear, however, that the correlation does not lie between any one "bad" tendency and abnormality in any absolute sense. The desire to run away from grief, to leave it behind at all costs, does not foster psychotic behaviour where, as among the Pueblos, it is mapped out by institutions and supported by every attitude of the group. The Pueblos are not a neurotic people. Their culture gives the impression of fostering mental health. Similarly, the paranoid attitudes so violently expressed among the Kwakiutl are known in psychiatric theory derived from our own civilization as thoroughly "bad"; that is, they lead in various ways to the breakdown of personality. But it is just those individuals among the Kwakiutl who find it congenial to give the freest expression of these attitudes who nevertheless are the leaders of Kwakiutl society and find greatest personal fulfilment in its culture.

Obviously, adequate personal adjustment does not depend upon following certain motivations and eschewing others. The correlation is in a different direction. Just as those are favoured whose congenial responses are closest to that behaviour which characterizes their society, so those are disoriented whose congenial responses fall in that arc of behaviour which is not capitalized by their culture. These abnormals are those who are not supported by the institutions of their civilization. They are the exceptions who have not easily taken the traditional forms of their culture.

For a valid comparative psychiatry, these disoriented persons who have failed to adapt themselves adequately to their cultures are of first importance. The issue in psychiatry has been too often confused by starting from a fixed list of symptoms instead of from the study of those whose characteristic reactions are denied validity in their society.

The tribes we have described have all of them their nonparticipating "abnormal" individuals. The individual in Dobu who was thoroughly disoriented was the man who was naturally friendly and found activity an end in itself. He was a pleasant fellow who did not seek to overthrow his fellows or to punish them. He worked for anyone who asked him, and he was tireless in carrying out their commands. He was not filled by a terror of the dark like his fellows, and he did not, as they did, utterly inhibit simple public responses of friendliness toward women closely related, like a wife or sister. He often patted them playfully in public. In any other Dobuan this was scandalous behaviour, but in him it was regarded as merely silly. The village treated him in a kindly enough fashion, not taking advantage of him or making a sport of ridiculing him, but he was definitely regarded as one who was outside the game.

The behaviour congenial to the Dobuan simpleton has been made the ideal in certain periods of our own civilization, and there are still vocations in which his responses are accepted in most Western communities. Especially if a woman is in question, she is well provided for even today in our *mores,* and functions honourably in her family and community. The fact that the Dobuan could not function in his culture was not a consequence of the particular responses that were congenial to him, but of the chasm between them and the cultural pattern.

Most ethnologists have had similar experiences in recognizing that the persons who are put outside the pale of society with contempt are not those who would be placed there by another culture. Lowie found among the Crow Indians of the plains a man of exceptional knowledge of his cultural forms. He was interested in considering these objectively and in correlating different facets. He had an interest in genealogical facts and was invaluable on points of history. Altogether he was an ideal interpreter of Crow life. These traits, however, were not those which were the password to honour among the Crow. He had a definite shrinking from physical danger, and bravado was the tribal virtue. To make matters worse he had attempted to gain recognition by claiming a war honour which was fraudulent. He was proved not to have brought in, as he claimed, a picketed horse from the enemy's camp. To lay false claim to war honours was a paramount sin among the Crow, and by the general opinion, constantly reiterated, he was regarded as irresponsible and incompetent.

Such situations can be paralleled with the attitude in our civilization toward a man who does not succeed in regarding personal possessions as supremely important. Our hobo population is constantly fed by those to whom the accumulation of property is not a sufficient motivation. In case these individuals ally themselves with the hoboes, public opinion regards them as potentially vicious, as indeed because of the asocial situation into which they are thrust they readily become. In case, however, these men compensate by emphasizing their artistic temperament and become members of expatriated groups of petty artists, opinion regards them not as vicious but as silly. In any case they are unsupported by the forms of their society, and the effort to express themselves satisfactorily is ordinarily a greater task than they can achieve.

The dilemma of such an individual is often most successfully solved by doing violence to his strongest natural impulses and accepting the rôle the culture honours. In case he is a person to whom social recognition is necessary, it is ordinarily his only possible course. One of the most striking individuals in Zuñi had accepted this necessity. In a society that thoroughly distrusts authority of any sort, he had a native personal magnetism that singled him out in any group. In a society that exalts moderation and the easiest way, he was turbulent and could act violently upon occasion. In a society that praises a pliant personality that "talks lots"—that is, that chatters in a friendly fashion—he was scornful and aloof. Zuñi's only reaction to such personalities is to brand them as witches. He was said to have been seen peering through a window from outside, and this is a sure mark of a witch. At any rate, he got drunk one day and boasted that they could not kill him. He was taken before the war priests who hung him by his thumbs from the rafters till he should confess to his witchcraft. However, he dispatched a messenger to the government troops. When they came, his shoulders were already crippled for life, and the officer of the law was left with no recourse but to imprison the war priests who had been responsible for the enormity. One of these war priests was probably the most respected and important person in recent Zuñi history, and when he returned after imprisonment in the state penitentiary he never resumed his priestly offices. He regarded his power as broken. It was a revenge that is probably unique in Zuñi history. It involved, of course, a challenge to the priesthoods, against whom the witch by his act openly aligned himself.

The course of his life in the forty years that followed this defiance was not, however, what we might easily predict. A witch is not barred from his membership in cult groups because he has been condemned, and the way to recognition lay through such activity. He possessed a remarkable verbal memory and a sweet singing voice. He learned unbelievable stores of mythology, of esoteric ritual, of cult songs. Many hundreds of pages of stories and ritual poetry were taken down from his dictation before he died, and he regarded his songs as much more extensive. He became indispensable in ceremonial life and before he died was the governor of Zuñi. The congenial bent of his personality threw him into irreconcilable conflict with his society, and he solved his dilemma by turning an incidental talent to account. As we might well expect, he was not a happy man. As governor of Zuñi, and high in his cult groups, a marked man in his community, he was obsessed by death. He was a cheated man in the midst of a mildly happy populace.

It is easy to imagine the life he might have lived among the Plains Indians, where every institution favoured the traits that were native to him. The personal authority, the turbulance, the scorn, would all have been honoured in the career he could have made his own. The unhappiness that was inseparable from his temperament as a successful priest and governor of the Zuñi would have had no place as a war chief of the Cheyenne; it was not a function of the traits of his native endowment but of the standards of the culture in which he found no outlet for his native responses.

The individuals we have so far discussed are not in any sense psychopathic. They illustrate the dilemma of the individual whose congenial drives are not provided for in the institutions of his culture. This dilemma becomes of psychiatric importance when the behaviour in question is regarded as categorically abnormal in a society. Western civilization tends to regard even a mild homosexual as an abnormal. The clinical picture of homosexuality stresses the neuroses and psychoses to which it gives rise, and emphasizes almost equally the inadequate functioning of the invert and his behaviour. We have only to turn to other cultures, however, to realize that homosexuals have by no means been uniformly inadequate to the social situation. They have not always failed to function. In some societies they have even been especially acclaimed. Plato's *Republic* is, of course, the most convincing statement of the honourable estate of homosexuality. It is presented as a major means to the good life, and Plato's high ethical evaluation of this response was upheld in the customary behaviour of Greece at that period.

The American Indians do not make Plato's high moral claims for homo-

Ethics for Modern Life
Fifth Edition
by RAZIEL ABELSON and MARIE-LOUISE FRIQUEGNON

When ordering, please use this ISBN: **0-312-09967-3**

This examination copy is sent to you with the compliments of your St. Martin's Press representative. May we have your comments on it, please? They will help us estimate printing requirements, assist us in preparing revisions, and guide us in shaping future books to your needs.

❒ You may quote me in your advertising.
❒ I have adopted this book for _____ semester, 19___.
❒ I am seriously considering this book for use with my classes.

Comments: Date_____

Name _____   Department _____

School _____   Phone Number _____

City _____   State _____   Zip _____

Course Title _____   Enrollment _____

Present Text _____

Do you plan to change texts this year?   Yes ❒   No ❒   When is your decision due? _____

Is your decision   ❒ Individual   ❒ Committee   ❒ Department

If committee or department, please list others involved:

_____

BUSINESS REPLY MAIL

FIRST CLASS   PERMIT NO. 1147   NEW YORK, NY

POSTAGE WILL BE PAID BY

College Department
ST. MARTIN'S PRESS, INC.
175 FIFTH AVENUE
NEW YORK, N.Y. 10010

sexuality, but homosexuals are often regarded as exceptionally able. In most of North America there exists the institution of the *berdache,* as the French called them. These men-women were men who at puberty or thereafter took the dress and the occupations of women. Sometimes they married other men and lived with them. Sometimes they were men with no inversion, persons of weak sexual endowment who chose this rôle to avoid the jeers of the women. The berdaches were never regarded as of first-rate supernatural power, as similar men-women were in Siberia, but rather as leaders in women's occupations, good healers in certain diseases, or, among certain tribes, as the genial organizers of social affairs. They were usually, in spite of the manner in which they were accepted, regarded with a certain embarrassment. It was thought slightly ridiculous to address as "she" a person who was known to be a man and who, as in Zuñi, would be buried on the men's side of the cemetery. But they were socially placed. The emphasis in most tribes was upon the fact that men who took over women's occupations excelled by reason of their strength and initiative and were therefore leaders in women's techniques and in the accumulation of those forms of property made by women. One of the best known of all the Zuñis of a generation ago was the man-woman We-wha, who was, in the words of his friend, Mrs. Stevenson, "certainly the strongest person in Zuñi, both mentally and physically." His remarkable memory for ritual made him a chief personage on ceremonial occasions, and his strength and intelligence made him a leader in all kinds of crafts.

The men-women of Zuñi are not all strong, self-reliant personages. Some of them take this refuge to protect themselves against their inability to take part in men's activities. One is almost a simpleton, and one, hardly more than a little boy, has delicate features like a girl's. There are obviously several reasons why a person becomes a berdache in Zuñi, but whatever the reason, men who have chosen openly to assume women's dress have the same chance as any other persons to establish themselves as functioning members of the society. Their response is socially recognized. If they have native ability, they can give it scope; if they are weak creatures, they fail in terms of their weakness of character, not in terms of their inversion.

The Indian institution of the berdache was most strongly developed on the plains. The Dakota had a saying, "fine possessions like a berdache's," and it was the epitome of praise for any woman's household possessions. A berdache had two strings to his bow, he was supreme in women's techniques, and he could also support his *ménage* by the man's activity of hunting. Therefore no one was richer. When especially fine beadwork or dressed skins were desired for ceremonial occasions, the berdache's work was sought in preference to any other's. It was his social adequacy that was stressed above all else. As in Zuñi, the attitude toward him is ambivalent and touched with malaise in the face of a recognized incongruity. Social scorn, however, was visited not upon the berdache but upon the man who lived with him. The latter was regarded as a weak man who had chosen an easy berth instead of the recognized goals of their culture; he did not contribute to the household, which was already a model for all households through the sole efforts of the berdache. His sexual adjustment was not singled out in the judgment that was passed upon him, but in terms of his economic adjustment he was an outcast.

When the homosexual response is regarded as a perversion, however, the invert is immediately exposed to all the conflicts to which aberrants are always exposed. His guilt, his sense of inadequacy, his failures, are consequences of the disrepute which social tradition visits upon him, and few people can achieve a satisfactory life unsupported by the standards of their society. The adjustments that society demands of them would strain any man's vitality, and the consequences of this conflict we identify with their homosexuality.

Trance is a similar abnormality in our society. Even a very mild mystic is aberrant in Western civilization. In order to study trance or catalepsy within our own social groups, we have to go to the case histories of the abnormal. Therefore the correlation between trance experience and the neurotic and psychotic seems perfect. As in the case of the homosexual, however, it is a local correlation characteristic of our century. Even in our own cultural background other eras give different results. In the Middle Ages when Catholicism made the ecstatic experience the mark of sainthood, the trance experience was greatly valued, and those to whom the response was congenial instead of being overwhelmed by a catastrophe as in our century, were given confidence in the pursuit of their careers. It was a validation of ambitions, not a stigma of insanity. Individuals who were susceptible to trance, therefore, succeeded or failed in terms of their native capacities, but since trance experience was highly valued, a great leader was very likely to be capable of it.

Among primitive peoples, trance and catalepsy have been honoured in the extreme. Some of the Indian tribes of California accorded prestige principally to those who passed through certain trance experiences. Not all of these tribes believed that it was exclusively women who were so blessed, but among the Shasta this was the convention. Their shamans were women, and they were accorded the greatest prestige in the community. They were chosen because of their constitutional liability to trance and allied manifestations. One day the woman who was so destined, while she was about her usual work, fell suddenly to the ground. She had heard a voice speaking to her in tones of the greatest intensity. Turning, she had seen a man with drawn bow and arrow. He commanded her to sing on pain of being shot through the heart by his arrow, but under the stress of the experience she fell senseless. Her family gathered. She was lying rigid, hardly breathing. They knew that for some time she had had dreams of a special character which indicated a shamanistic calling, dreams of escaping grizzly bears, falling off cliffs or trees, or of being surrounded by swarms of yellow-jackets. The community knew therefore what to expect. After a few hours the woman began to moan gently and to roll about upon the ground, trembling violently. She was supposed to be repeating the song which she had been told to sing and which during the trance had been taught her by the spirit. As she revived, her moaning became more and more clearly the spirit's song until at last she called out the name of the spirit itself, and immediately blood oozed from her mouth.

When the woman had come to herself after the first encounter with her spirit, she danced that night her first initiatory shaman's dance. For three nights she danced, holding herself by a rope that was swung from the ceiling. On the third night she had to receive in her body her power from her spirit. She was dancing, and as she felt the approach of the moment she called out, "He will shoot me, he will shoot me." Her friends stood close, for when she reeled in a kind of cataleptic seizure, they had to seize her before she fell or she would die. From this time on she had in her body a visible materialization of her spirit's power, an icicle-like object which in her dances thereafter she would exhibit, producing it from one part of her body and returning it to another part. From this time on she continued to validate her supernatural power by further cataleptic demonstrations, and she was called upon in great emergencies of life and death, for curing and for divination and for counsel. She became, in other words, by this procedure a woman of great power and importance.

It is clear that, far from regarding cataleptic seizures as blots upon the family escutcheon and as evidences of dreaded disease, cultural approval had seized upon them and made of them the pathway to authority over one's fellows. They were the outstanding characteristic of the most respected social type, the type which functioned with most honour and reward in the community. It was precisely the cataleptic individuals who in this culture were singled out for authority and leadership.

The possible usefulness of "abnormal" types in a social structure, provided they are types that are culturally selected by that group, is illustrated from every part of the world. The shamans of Siberia dominate their communities. According to the ideas of these peoples, they are individuals who by submission to the will of the spirits have been cured of a grievous illness—the onset of the seizures—and have acquired by this means great supernatural power and incomparable vigour and health. Some, during the period of the call, are violently insane for several years; others irresponsible to the point where they have to be constantly watched lest they wander off in the snow and freeze to death; others ill and emaciated to the point of death, sometimes with bloody sweat. It is the shamanistic practice which constitutes their cure, and the extreme exertion of a Siberian séance leaves them, they claim, rested and able to enter immediately upon a similar peformance. Cataleptic seizures are regarded as an essential part of any shamanistic performance.

A good description of the neurotic condition of the shaman and the attention given him by his society is an old one by Canon Callaway, recorded in the words of an old Zulu of South Africa:

> The condition of a man who is about to become a diviner is this; at first
> he is apparently robust, but in the process of time he begins to be delicate,

not having any real disease, but being delicate. He habitually avoids certain kinds of food, choosing what he likes, and he does not eat much of that; he is continually complaining of pains in different parts of his body. And he tells them that he has dreamt that he was carried away by a river. He dreams of many things, and his body is muddied [as a river] and he becomes a house of dreams. He dreams constantly of many things, and on awaking tells his friends, "My body is muddied today; I dreamt many men were killing me, and I escaped I know not how. On waking one part of my body felt different from other parts; it was no longer alike all over." At last that man is very ill, and they go to the diviners to enquire.

The diviners do not at once see that he is about to have a soft head [that is, the sensitivity associated with shamanism]. It is difficult for them to see the truth; they continually talk nonsense and make false statements, until all the man's cattle are devoured at their command, they saying that the spirit of his people demands cattle, that it may eat food. At length all the man's property is expended, he still being ill, and they no longer know what to do, for he has no more cattle, and his friends help him in such things as he needs.

At length a diviner comes and says that all the others are wrong. He says, "He is possessed by the spirits. There is nothing else. They move in him, being divided into two parties; some say, 'No, we do not wish our child injured. We do not wish it.' It is for that reason he does not get well. If you bar the way against the spirits, you will be killing him. For he will not be a diviner; neither will he ever be a man again."

So the man may be ill two years without getting better; perhaps even longer than that. He is confined to his house. This continues till his hair falls off. And his body is dry and scurfy; he does not like to anoint himself. He shows that he is about to be a diviner by yawning again and again, and by sneezing continually. It is apparent also from his being very fond of snuff; not allowing any long time to pass without taking some. And people begin to see that he has had what is good given to him.

After that he is ill; he has convulsions, and when water has been poured on him they then cease for a time. He habitually sheds tears, at first slight, then at last he weeps aloud and when the people are asleep he is heard making a noise and wakes the people by his singing; he has composed a song, and the men and women awake and go to sing in concert with him. All the people of the village are troubled by want of sleep; for a man who is becoming a diviner causes great trouble, for he does not sleep, but works constantly with his brain; his sleep is merely by snatches, and he wakes up singing many songs; and people who are near quit their villages by night when they hear him singing aloud and go to sing in concert. Perhaps he sings till morning, no one having slept. And then he leaps about the house like a frog; and the house becomes too small for him, and he goes out leaping and singing, and shaking like a reed in the water, and dripping with perspiration.

In this state of things they daily expect his death; he is now but skin and bones, and they think that tomorrow's sun will not leave him alive. At this time many cattle are eaten, for the people encourage his becoming a diviner. At length [in a dream] an ancient ancestral spirit is pointed out to him. This spirit says to him, "Go to So-and-so and he will churn for you an emetic [the medicine the drinking of which is a part of shamanistic initiation] that you may be a diviner altogether." Then he is quiet a few days, having gone to the diviner to have the medicine churned for him; and he comes back quite another man, being now cleansed and a diviner indeed.

Thereafter for life, when he is possessed by his spirits, he foretells events and finds lost articles.

It is clear that culture may value and make socially available even highly unstable human types. If it chooses to treat their peculiarities as the most valued variants of human behaviour, the individuals in question will rise to the occasion and perform their social rôles without reference to our usual ideas of the types who can make social adjustments and those who cannot. Those who function inadequately in any society are not those with certain fixed "abnormal" traits, but may well be those whose responses have received no support in the institutions of their culture. The weakness of these aberrants is in great measure illusory. It springs, not from the fact that they are lacking in necessary vigour, but that they are individuals whose native responses are not reaffirmed by society. They are, as Sapir phrases it, "alienated from an impossible world."

The person unsupported by the standards of his time and place and left naked to the winds of ridicule has been unforgettably drawn in European literature in the figure of Don Quixote. Cervantes turned upon a tradition still honoured in the abstract the limelight of a changed set of practical standards, and his poor old man, the orthodox upholder of the romantic chivalry of another generation, became a simpleton. The windmills with which he tilted were the serious antagonists of a hardly vanished world, but to tilt with them when the world no longer called them serious was to rave. He loved his Dulcinea in the best traditional manner of chivalry, but another version of love was fashionable for the moment, and his fervour was counted to him for madness.

These contrasting worlds which, in the primitive cultures we have considered, are separated from one another in space, in modern Occidental history more often succeed one another in time. The major issue is the same in either case, but the importance of understanding the phenomenon is far greater in the modern world where we cannot escape if we would from the succession of configurations in time. When each culture is a world in itself, relatively stable like the Eskimo culture, for example, and geographically isolated from all others, the issue is academic. But our civilization must deal with cultural standards that go down under our eyes and new ones that arise from a shadow upon the horizon. We must be willing to take account of changing normalities even when the question is of the morality in which we were bred. Just as we are handicapped in dealing with ethical problems so long as we hold to an absolute definition of morality, so we are handicapped in dealing with human society so long as we identify our local normalities with the inevitable necessities of existence.

No society has yet attempted a self-conscious direction of the process by which its new normalities are created in the next generation. Dewey has pointed out how possible and yet how drastic such social engineering would be. For some traditional arrangements it is obvious that very high prices are paid, reckoned in terms of human suffering and frustration. If these arrangements presented themselves to us merely as arrangements and not as categorical imperatives, our reasonable course would be to adapt them by whatever means to rationally selected goals. What we do instead is to ridicule our Don Quixotes, the ludicrous embodiments of an outmoded tradition, and continue to regard our own as final and prescribed in the nature of things.

In the meantime the therapeutic problem of dealing with our psychopaths of this type is often misunderstood. Their alienation from the actual world can often be more intelligently handled than by insisting that they adopt the modes that are alien to them. Two other courses are always possible. In the first place, the misfit individual may cultivate a greater objective interest in his own preferences and learn how to manage with greater equanimity his deviation from the type. If he learns to recognize the extent to which his suffering has been due to his lack of support in a traditional ethos, he may gradually educate himself to accept his degree of difference with less suffering. Both the exaggerated emotional disturbances of the manic depressive and the seclusion of the schizophrenic add certain values to existence which are not open to those differently constituted. The unsupported individual who valiantly accepts his favourite and native virtues may attain a feasible course of behaviour that makes it unnecessary for him to take refuge in a private world he has fashioned for himself. He may gradually achieve a more independent and less tortured attitude toward his deviations and upon this attitude he may be able to build an adequately functioning existence.

In the second place, an increased tolerance in society toward its less usual types must keep pace with the self-education of the patient. The possibilities in this direction are endless. Tradition is as neurotic as any patient; its overgrown fear of deviation from its fortuitous standards conforms to all the usual definitions of the psychopathic. This fear does not depend upon observation of the limits within which conformity is necessary to the social good. Much more deviation is allowed to the individual in some cultures than in others, and those in which much is allowed cannot be shown to suffer from their peculiarity. It is probable that social orders of the future will carry this tolerance and encouragement of individual difference much further than any cultures of which we have experience.

The American tendency at the present time leans so far to the opposite extreme that it is not easy for us to picture the changes that such an attitude would bring about. Middletown is a typical example of our usual urban fear of seeming in however slight an act different from our neighbours. Eccentricity is more feared than parasitism. Every sacrifice of time and tranquility is made in order that no one in the family may have any taint of nonconformity attached to him. Children in school make their great tragedies out of not wearing a certain kind of stockings, not joining a certain dancing-class, not driving a certain car. The fear of being different is the dominating motivation recorded in Middletown.

The psychopathic toll that such a motivation exacts is evident in every institution for mental diseases in our country. In a society in which it existed only as a minor motive among many others, the psychiatric picture would be a very different one. At all events, there can be no reasonable doubt that one of the most effective ways in which to deal with the staggering burden of psychopathic tragedies in America at the present time is by means of an educational program which fosters tolerance in society and a kind of self-respect and independence that is foreign to Middletown and our urban traditions.

Not all psychopaths, of course, are individuals whose native responses are at variance with those of their civilization. Another large group are those who are merely inadequate and who are strongly enough motivated so that their failure is more than they can bear. In a society in which the will-to-power is most highly rewarded, those who fail may not be those who are differently constituted, but simply those who are insufficiently endowed. The inferiority complex takes a great toll of suffering in our society. It is necessary that sufferers of this type have a history of frustration in the sense that strong native bents have been inhibited; their frustration is often enough only the reflection of their inability to reach a certain goal. There is a cultural implication here, too, in that the traditional goal may be accessible to large numbers or to very few, and in proportion as success is obsessive and is limited to the few, a greater and greater number will be liable to the extreme penalties of maladjustment.

To a certain extent, therefore, civilization in setting higher and possibly more worthwhile goals may increase the number of its abnormals. But the point may very easily be overemphasized, for very small changes in social attitudes may far outweigh this correlation. On the whole, since the social possibilities of tolerance and recognition of individual difference are so little explored in practice, pessimism seems premature. Certainly other quite different social factors which we have just discussed are more directly responsible for the great proportion of our neurotics and psychotics, and with these other factors civilizations could, if they would, deal without intrinsic loss.

We have been considering individuals from the point of view of their ability to function adequately in their society. This adequate functioning is one of the ways in which normality is clinically defined. It is also defined in terms of fixed symptoms, and the tendency is to identify normality with the statistically average. In practice this average is one arrived at in the laboratory, and deviations from it are defined as abnormal.

From the point of view of a single culture this procedure is very useful. It shows the clinical picture of the civilization and gives considerable information about its socially approved behaviour. To generalize this as an absolute normal, however, is a different matter. As we have seen, the range of normality in different cultures does not coincide. Some, like Zuñi and the Kwakiutl, are so far removed from each other that they overlap only slightly. The statistically determined normal on the Northwest Coast would be far outside the extreme boundaries of abnormality in the Pueblos. The normal Kwakiutl rivalry contest would only be understood as madness in Zuñi, and the traditional Zuñi indifference to dominance and the humiliation of others would be the fatuousness of a simpleton in a man of noble family on the Northwest Coast. Aberrant behaviour in either culture could never be determined in relation to any least common denominator of behaviour. Any society, according to its major preoccupations, may increase and intensify even hysterical, epileptic, or paranoid symptoms, at the same time relying socially in a greater and greater degree upon the very individuals who display them.

This fact is important in psychiatry because it makes clear another group of abnormals which probably exists in every culture: the abnormals who represent the extreme development of the local cultural type. This group is socially in the opposite situation from the group we have discussed, those whose responses are at variance with their cultural standards. Society, instead of exposing the former group at every point, supports them in their furthest aberrations. They have a licence which they may almost endlessly exploit. For this reason these persons almost never fall within the scope of any contemporary psychiatry. They are unlikely to be described even in the most careful manuals of the generation that fosters them. Yet from the point of view of another generation or culture they are ordinarily the most bizarre of the psychopathic types of the period.

The Puritan divines of New England in the eighteenth century were the last persons whom contemporary opinion in the colonies regarded as psychopathic. Few prestige groups in any culture have been allowed such complete intellectual and emotional dictatorship as they were. They were the voice of God. Yet to a modern observer it is they, not the confused and tormented women they put to death as witches, who were the psychoneurotics of Puritan New England. A sense of guilt as extreme as they portrayed and demanded both in their own conversion experiences and in those of their converts is found in a slightly saner civilization only in institutions for mental diseases. They admitted no salvation without a conviction of sin that prostrated the victim, sometimes for years, with remorse and terrible anguish. It was the duty of the minister to put the fear of hell into the heart of even the youngest child, and to exact of every convert emotional acceptance of his damnation if God saw fit to damn him. It does not matter where we turn among the records of New England Puritan churches of this period, whether to those dealing with witches or with unsaved children not yet in their teens or with such themes as damnation and predestination, we are faced with the fact that the group of people who carried out to the greatest extreme and in the fullest honour the cultural doctrine of the moment are by the slightly altered standards of our generation the victims of intolerable aberrations. From the point of view of a comparative psychiatry they fall in the category of the abnormal.

In our own generation extreme forms of ego-gratification are culturally supported in a similar fashion. Arrogant and unbridled egoists as family men, as officers of the law and in business, have been again and again portrayed by novelists and dramatists, and they are familiar in every community. Like the behaviour of Puritan divines, their courses of action are often more asocial than those of the inmates of penitentiaries. In terms of the suffering and frustration that they spread about them there is probably no comparison. There is very possibly at least as great a degree of mental warping. Yet they are entrusted with positions of great influence and importance and are as a rule fathers of families. Their impress both upon their own children and upon the structure of our society is indelible. They are not described in our manuals of psychiatry because they are supported by every tenet of our civilization. They are sure of themselves in real life in a way that is possible only to those who are oriented to the points of the compass laid down in their own culture. Nevertheless a future psychiatry may well ransack our novels and letters and public records for illumination upon a type of abnormality to which it would not otherwise give credence. In every society it is among this very group of the culturally encouraged and fortified that some of the most extreme types of human behaviour are fostered.

Social thinking at the present time has no more important task before it than that of taking adequate account of cultural relativity. In the fields of both sociology and psychology the implications are fundamental, and modern thought about contracts of peoples and about our changing standards is greatly in need of sane and scientific direction. The sophisticated modern temper has made of social relativity, even in the small area which it has recognized, a doctrine of despair. It has pointed out its incongruity with the orthodox dreams of permanence and ideality and with the individual's illusions of autonomy. It has argued that if human experience must give up these, the nutshell of existence is empty. But to interpret our dilemma in these terms is to be guilty of an anachronism. It is only the inevitable cultural lag that makes us insist that the old must be discovered again in the new, that there is no solution but to find the old certainty and stability in the new plasticity. The recognition of cultural relativity carries with it its own values, which need not be those of the absolutist philosophies. It challenges customary opinions and causes those who have been bred to them acute discomfort. It rouses pessimism because it throws old formulas into confusion, not because it contains anything intrinsically difficult. As soon as the new opinion is embraced as customary belief, it will be another trusted bulwark of the good life. We shall arrive then at a more realistic social faith, accepting as grounds of hope and as new bases for tolerance the coexisting and equally valid patterns of life which mankind has created for itself from the raw materials of existence.

Rational Absolutism

Immanuel Kant

PART ONE

Nothing in the whole world, or even outside of the world, can possibly be regarded as good without limitation except a *good will.* No doubt it is a good and desirable thing to have intelligence, sagacity, judgment, and other intellectual gifts, by whatever name they may be called; it is also good and desirable in many respects to possess by nature such qualities as courage, resolution, and perseverance; but all these gifts of nature may be in the highest degree pernicious and hurtful, if the will which directs them, or what is called the *character,* is not itself good. The same thing applies to *gifts of fortune.* Power, wealth, honor, even good health, and that general well-being and contentment with one's lot which we call *happiness,* give rise to pride and not infrequently to insolence, if a man's will is not good; nor can a reflective and impartial spectator ever look with satisfaction upon the unbroken prosperity of a man who is destitute of the ornament of a pure and good will. A good will would therefore seem to be the indispensable condition without which no one is even worthy to be happy.

A man's will is good, not because the consequences which flow from it are good, nor because it is capable of attaining the end which it seeks, but it is good in itself, or because it wills the good. By a good will is not meant mere well-wishing; it consists in a resolute employment of all the means within one's reach, and its intrinsic value is in no way increased by success or lessened by failure.

This idea of the absolute value of mere will seems so extraordinary that, although it is endorsed even by the popular judgment, we must subject it to careful scrutiny.

If nature had meant to provide simply for the maintenance, the well-being, in a word the happiness, of beings which have reason and will, it must be confessed that, in making use of their reason, it has hit upon a very poor way of attaining its end. As a matter of fact the very worst way a man of refinement and culture can take to secure enjoyment and happiness is to make use of his reason for that purpose. Hence there is apt to arise in his mind a certain degree of *misology,* or hatred of reason. Finding that the arts which minister to luxury, and even the sciences, instead of bringing him happiness, only lay a heavier yoke on his neck, he at length comes to envy, rather than to despise, men of less refinement, who follow more closely the promptings of their natural impulses, and pay little heed to what reason tells them to do or to leave undone. It must at least be admitted, that one may deny reason to have much or indeed any value in the production of happiness and contentment, without taking a morose or ungrateful view of the goodness with which the world is governed. Such a judgment really means that life has another and a much nobler end than happiness, and that the true vocation of reason is to secure that end.

The true object of reason then, in so far as it is practical, or capable of influencing the will, must be to produce a will which is *good in itself,* and not merely good *as a means* to something else. This will is not the only or the whole good, but it is the highest good, and the condition of all other good, even of the desire for happiness itself. It is therefore not inconsistent with the wisdom of nature that the cultivation of reason which is essential to the furtherance of its first and unconditioned object, the production of a good will, in this life at least, in many ways limit, or even make impossible, the attainment of happiness, which is its second and conditioned object.

To bring to clear consciousness the conception of a will which is good in itself, a conception already familiar to the popular mind, let us examine the conception of *duty,* which involves the idea of a good will as manifested under certain subjective limitations and hindrances.

I pass over actions which are admittedly violations of duty, for these, however useful they may be in the attainment of this or that end, manifestly do not proceed *from* duty. I set aside also those actions which are not actually inconsistent with duty, but which yet are done under the impulse of some natural inclination, although *not a direct inclination* to do these particular actions; for in these it is easy to determine whether the action that is consistent with duty, is done *from duty* or with some selfish object in view. It is more difficult to make a clear distinction of motives when there is a *direct* inclination to do a certain action, which is itself in conformity with duty. The preservation of one's own life, for instance, is a duty; but, as everyone has a natural inclination to preserve his life, the anxious care which most men usually devote to this object, has no intrinsic value, nor the maximum from which they act any moral import. They preserve their life *in accordance with* duty, but not *because of* duty. But, suppose adversity and hopeless sorrow to have taken away all desire for life; suppose that the wretched man would welcome death as a release, and yet takes means to prolong his life simply from a sense of duty; then his maxim has a genuine moral import.

But, secondly, an action that is done from duty gets its moral value, *not from the object* which it is intended to secure, but from the maximum by which it is determined. Accordingly, the action has the same moral value whether the object is attained or not, if only the *principle* by which the will is determined to act is independent of every object of sensuous desire. What was said above makes it clear, that it is not the object aimed at, or, in other words, the consequences which flow from an action when these are made the end and motive of the will, that can give to the action an unconditioned and moral value. In what, then, can the moral value of an action consist, if it does not lie in the will itself, as directed to the attainment of a certain object? It can lie only in the principle of the will, no matter whether the object sought can be attained by the action or not. For the will stands as it were at the parting of the ways, between its *a priori* principle, which is formal, and its *a posteriori* material motive. As so standing it must be determined by something, and, as no action which is done from duty can be determined by a material principle, it can be determined only by the formal principle of all volition.

From the two propositions just set forth a third directly follows, which may be thus stated: *Duty is the obligation to act from reverence for law.* Now, I may have a natural *inclination* for the object that I expect to follow from my action, but I can never have *reverence* for that which is not a spontaneous activity of my will, but merely an effect of it; neither can I have reverence for any natural inclination, whether it is my own or another's. If it is my own, I can at most only approve of it; if it is manifested by another, I may regard it as conducive to my own interest, and hence I may in certain cases even be said to have a love for it. But the only thing which I can reverence or which can lay me under an obligation to act, is the law which is connected with my will, not as a consequence, but as a principle; a principle which is not dependent upon natural inclination, but overmasters it, or at least allows it to have no influence whatever in determining my course of action. Now if an action which is done out of regard for duty sets entirely aside the influence of natural inclination and along with it every object of the will, nothing else is left by which the will can be determined but objectively the *law* itself, and subjectively *pure reverence* for the law as a principle of action. Thus there arises the maxim, to obey the moral law even at the sacrifice of all my natural inclinations.

The supreme good which we call moral can therefore be nothing but the *idea of the law* in itself, in so far as it is this idea which determines the will, and not any consequences that are expected to follow. Only a *rational* being can have such an idea, and hence a man who acts from the idea of the law is already morally good, no matter whether the consequences which he expects from his action follow or not.

Now what must be the nature of a law, the idea of which is to determine the will, even apart from the effects expected to follow, and which is therefore itself entitled to be called good absolutely and without qualification? As the will must not be moved to act from any desire for the results expected to follow from obedience to a certain law, the only principle of the will which remains is that of the conformity of actions to universal law. In all cases I must act in such a way *that I can at the same time will that my maxim should become a universal law.* This is what is meant by conformity to law pure and simple; and this is the principle which serves, and must serve, to determine the will, if the idea of duty is not to be regarded as empty and chimerical. As a matter of fact the judgments which we are wont to pass upon conduct perfectly agree with this principle, and in making them we always have it before our eyes.

May I, for instance, under the pressure of circumstances, make a promise which I have no intention of keeping? The question is not, whether it is prudent to make a false promise, but whether it is morally right. To enable me to answer this question shortly and conclusively, the best way is for me to ask myself whether it would satisfy me that the maximum to extricate myself from embarrassment by giving a false promise should have the force of a universal law, applying to others as well as to myself. And I see at once, that, while I can certainly will the lie, I cannot will that lying should be a universal law. If lying were universal, there would, properly speaking, be no promises whatever. I might say that I intended to do a certain thing at some future time, but nobody would believe me, or if he did at the moment trust to my promise, he would afterwards pay me back in my own coin. My maxim thus proves itself to be self-destructive, so soon as it is taken as a universal law.

Duty, then, consists in the obligation to act from *pure* reverence for the moral law. To this motive all others must give way, for it is the condition of a will which is good *in itself,* and which has a value with which nothing else is comparable.

There is, however, in man a strong feeling of antagonism to the commands of duty, although his reason tells him that those commands are worthy of the highest reverence. For man not only possesses reason, but he has certain natural wants and inclinations, the complete satisfaction of which he calls happiness. These natural inclinations clamorously demand to have their seemingly reasonable claims respected; but reason issues its commands inflexibly, refusing to promise anything to the natural desires, and treating their claims with a sort of neglect and contempt. From this there arises a *natural dialectic,* that is, a disposition to explain away the strict laws of duty, to cast doubt upon their validity, or at least, upon their purity and stringency, and in this way to make them yield to the demands of the natural inclinations.

Thus men are forced to go beyond the narrow circle of ideas within which their reason ordinarily moves, and to take a step into the field of *moral philosophy,* not indeed from any perception of speculative difficulties, but simply on practical grounds. The practical reason of men cannot be long exercised any more than the theoretical, without falling insensibly into a dialectic, which compels it to call in the aid of philosophy; and in the one case as in the other, rest can be found only in a thorough criticism of human reason.

PART TWO

So far, we have drawn our conception of duty from the manner in which men employ it in the ordinary exercise of their practical reason. The conception of duty, however, we must not suppose to be therefore derived from experience. On the contrary, we hear frequent complaints, the justice of which we cannot but admit, that no one can point to a single instance in which an action has undoubtedly been done purely from a regard for duty; that there are certainly many actions which are not *opposed* to duty, but none which are indisputably done *from* duty and therefore have a moral value. Nothing indeed can secure us against the complete loss of our ideas of duty, and maintain in the soul a well-grounded respect for the moral law, but the clear conviction, that reason issues its commands on its own authority, without caring in the least whether the actions of men have, as a matter of fact, been done purely from ideas of duty. For reason commands inflexibly that certain actions should be done, which perhaps never have been done; actions, the very possibility of which may seem doubtful to one who bases everything upon experience. Perfect disinterestedness in friendship, for instance, is demanded of every man, although there may never have been a sincere friend; for pure friendship is bound up with the idea of duty as duty, and belongs to the very idea of a reason which determines the will on *a priori* grounds, prior to all experience.

It is, moreover, beyond dispute, that unless we are to deny to morality all truth and all reference to a possible object, the moral law has so wide an application that it is binding, not merely upon man, but upon all *rational beings,* and not merely under certain contingent conditions, and with certain limitations, but absolutely and necessarily. And it is plain, that no experience could ever lead us to suppose that laws of this apodictic character are even possible.

There is, therefore, no genuine supreme principle of morality, which is not independent of all experience, and based entirely upon pure reason. If, then, we are to have a philosophy of morality at all, as distinguished from a popular moral philosophy, we may take it for granted without further investigation, that moral conceptions, together with the principles which flow from them, are given *a priori* and must be presented in their generality (*in abstracto*).

Such a metaphysic of morality, which must be entirely free from all admixture of empirical psychology, theology, physics and hyperphysics, and above all from all occult or, as we may call them, hypophysical qualities, is not only indispensable as a foundation for a sound theory of duties, but it is also of the highest importance in the practical realization of moral precepts. For the pure idea of duty, unmixed with any foreign ingredient of sensuous desire, in a word, the idea of the moral law, influences the heart of man much more powerfully through his reason, which in this way only becomes conscious that it can of itself be practical, than do all the motives which have their source in experience. Conscious of its own dignity, the moral law treats all sensuous desires with contempt, and is able to master them one by one.

From what has been said it is evident, that all moral conceptions have their seat and origin in reason entirely *a priori,* and are apprehended by the ordinary reason of men as well as by reason in its purely speculative activity.

We have also seen that it is of the greatest importance, not only in the construction by speculative reason of a theory of morality, but also with a view to the practical conduct of life, to derive the conceptions and laws of morality from pure reason, to present them pure and unmixed, and to mark out the sphere of this whole practical or pure knowledge of reason. Nor is it permissible, in seeking to determine the whole faculty of pure practical reason, to make its principles dependent upon the peculiar nature of human reason, as we were allowed to do, and sometimes were even forced to do, in speculative philosophy; for moral laws must apply to every rational being, and must therefore be derived from the very conception of a rational being as such.

To show the need of advancing not only from the common moral judgments of men to the philosophical, but from a popular philosophy, which merely gropes its way by the help of examples, to a metaphysic of morality, we must begin at the point where the practical faculty of reason supplies general rules of action, and exhibit clearly the steps by which it attains to the conception of duty.

Everything in nature acts in conformity with law. Only a rational being has the faculty of acting in conformity with the *idea* of law, or from principles; only a rational being, in other words, has a will. And as without reason actions cannot proceed from laws, will is simply practical reason. If the will is infallibly determined by reason, the actions of a rational being are subjectively as well as objectively necessary; that is, will must be regarded as a faculty of choosing *that only* which reason, independently of natural inclination, declares to be practically necessary or good. On the other hand, if the will is not invariably determined by reason alone, but is subject to certain subjective conditions or motives, which are not always in harmony with the objective conditions; if the will, as actually is the case with *man,* is not in perfect conformity with reason; actions which are recognized to be objectively necessary, are subjectively contingent. The determination of such a will according to objective laws is therefore called *obligation.* That is to say, if the will of a rational being is not absolutely good, we conceive of it as capable of being determined by objective laws of reason, but not as by its very nature necessarily obeying them.

The idea that a certain principle is objective, and binding upon the will, is a command of reason, and the statement of the command in a formula is an *imperative.*

All imperatives are expressed by the word *ought,* to indicate that the will upon which they are binding is not by its subjective constitution necessarily determined in conformity with the objective law of reason. An imperative says, that the doing, or leaving undone of a certain thing would be good, but it addresses a will which does not always do a thing simply because it is good. Now, that is practically *good* which determines the will by ideas of reason, in other words, that which determines it, not by subjective influences, but by principles which are objective, or apply to all rational beings as such. *Good* and *pleasure* are quite distinct. Pleasure results from the influence of purely subjective causes upon the will of the subject, and these vary with the susceptibility of this or that individual, while a principle of reason is valid for all.

A perfectly good will would, like the will of man, stand under objective laws, laws of the good, but it could not be said to be under an *obligation* to act in conformity with those laws. Such a will by its subjective constitution could be determined only by the idea of the good. In reference to the Divine will, or any other holy will, imperatives have no meaning; for here the will is by its very nature necessarily in harmony with the law, and therefore *ought* has no application to it. Imperatives are formulae, which express merely the relation of objective laws of volition in general to the imperfect will of this or that rational being, as for instance, the will of man.

Now, all imperatives command either *hypothetically* or *categorically*. A hypothetical imperative states that a certain thing must be done, if something else which is willed, or at least might be willed, is to be attained. The categorical imperative declares that an act is in itself or objectively necessary, without any reference to another end.

Every practical law represents a possible action as good, and therefore as obligatory for a subject that is capable of being determined to act by reason. Hence all imperatives are formulae for the determination of an action which is obligatory according to the principle of a will that is in some sense good. If the action is good only because it is a means to *something else,* the imperative is *hypothetical;* if the action is conceived to be good *in itself,* the imperative, as the necessary principle of a will that in itself conforms to reason, is *categorical.*

An imperative, then, states what possible action of mine would be good. It supplies the practical rule for a will which does not at once do an act simply because it is good, either because the subject does not know it to be good, or because, knowing it to be good, he is influenced by maxims which are opposed to the objective principles of a practical reason.

The hypothetical imperative says only that an action is good relatively to a certain *possible* end or to a certain *actual* end. In the former case it is *problematic,* in the latter case *assertoric.* The categorical imperative, which affirms that an action is in itself or objectively necessary without regard to an end, that is, without regard to any other end than itself, is an *apodictic* practical principle.

Whatever is within the power of a rational being may be conceived to be capable of being willed by some rational being, and hence the principles which determine what actions are necessary in the attainment of certain possible ends, are infinite in number.

Yet there is one thing which we may assume that all finite rational beings actually make their end, and there is therefore one object which may safely be regarded, not simply as something that they *may* seek, but as something that by a necessity of their nature they actually *do* seek. This object is *happiness.* The hypothetical imperative, which affirms the practical necessity of an action as the means of attaining happiness, is *assertoric.*

We must not think of happiness as simply a possible and problematic end, but as an end that we may with confidence presuppose *a priori* to be sought by everyone, belonging as it does to the very nature of man. Now skill in the choice of means to his own greatest well-being may be called *prudence*, taking the word in its more restricted sense. An imperative, therefore, which relates merely to the choice of means to one's own happiness, that is, a maxim of prudence, must be hypothetical; it commands an action, not absolutely, but only as a means to another end.

Lastly, there is an imperative which directly commands an action, without presupposing as its condition that some other end is to be attained by means of that action. This imperative is *categorical.* It has to do, not with the matter of an action and the result expected to follow from it, but simply with the form and principle from which the action itself proceeds. The action is essentially good if the motive of the agent is good, let the consequences be what they may. This imperative may be called the imperative of *morality.*

How are all these imperatives possible? The question is not, How is an action which an imperative commands actually realized? but, How can we think of the will as placed under obligation by each of those imperatives? Very little need be said to show an imperative of skill is possible. He who wills the end, wills also the means in his power which are indispensable to the attainment of the end. Looking simply at the act of will, we must say that this proposition is analytic. If a certain object is to follow as an effect from my volition, my causality must be conceived as active in the production of the effect, or as employing the means by which the effect will take place. The imperative, therefore, simply states that in the conception of the willing of this end there is directly implied the conception of actions necessary to this end. No doubt certain synthetic propositions are required to determine the particular means by which a given end may be attained, but these have nothing to do with the principle or act of the will, but merely state how the object may actually be realized.

Were it as easy to give a definite conception of happiness as of a particular end, the imperatives of prudence would be of exactly the same nature as the imperatives of skill, and would therefore be analytic. For, we should be able to say, that he who wills the end wills also the only means in his power for the attainment of the end. But, unfortunately, the conception of happiness is so indefinite, that, although every man desires to obtain it, he is unable to give a definite and self-consistent statement of what he actually desires and wills. The truth is, that, strictly speaking, the imperatives of prudence are not commands at all. They do not say that actions are objective or *necessary,* and hence they must be regarded as counsels (*consilia*), not as commands (*praecepta*) of reason. Still, the imperative of prudence would be an analytic proposition, if the means to happiness could only be known with certainty. For the only difference in the two cases is that in the imperative of skill the end is merely possible, in the imperative of prudence it is actually given; and as in both all that is commanded is the means to an end which is assumed to be willed, the imperative which commands that he who wills the end should also will the means, is in both cases analytic. There is therefore no real difficulty in seeing how an imperative of prudence is possible.

The only question which is difficult of solution, is, how the imperative of morality is possible. Here the imperative is not hypothetical, and hence we cannot derive its objective necessity from any presupposition. Nor must it for a moment be forgotten, that an imperative of this sort cannot be established by instances taken from experience. We must therefore find out by careful investigation, whether imperatives which seem to be categorical may not be simply hypothetical imperatives in disguise.

One thing is plain at the very outset, namely, that only a categorical imperative can have the dignity of a practical *law,* and that the other imperatives, while they may no doubt be called *principles* of the will, cannot be called laws. An action which is necessary merely as a means to an arbitrary end, may be regarded as itself contingent, and if the end is abandoned, the maxim which prescribes the action has no longer any force. An unconditioned command, on the other hand, does not permit the will to choose the opposite, and therefore it carries with it the necessity which is essential to a law.

It is, however, very hard to see how there can be a categorical imperative or law of morality at all. Such a law is an *a priori* synthetic proposition, and we cannot expect that there will be less difficulty in showing how a proposition of that sort is possible in the sphere of morality than we have found it to be in the sphere of knowledge.

In attempting to solve this problem, we shall first of all inquire, whether the mere conception of a categorical imperative may not perhaps supply us with a formula, which contains the only proposition that can possibly be a categorical imperative. The more difficult question, how such an absolute command is possible at all, will require a special investigation, which must be postponed to the last section.

If I take the mere conception of a hypothetical imperative, I cannot tell what it may contain until the condition under which it applies is presented to me. But I can tell at once from the very conception of a categorical imperative what it must contain. Viewed apart from the law, the imperative simply affirms that the maxim, or subjective principle of action, must conform to the objective principle or law. Now the law contains no condition to which it is restricted, and hence nothing remains but the statement, that the maxim ought to conform to the universality of the law as such. It is only this conformity to law that the imperative can be said to represent as necessary.

There is therefore but one categorical imperative, which may be thus stated: *Act in comformity with that maxim, and that maxim only, which you can at the same time will to be a universal law.*

Now, if from this single imperative, as from their principle, all imperatives of duty can be derived, we shall at least be able to indicate what we mean by the categorical imperative and what the conception of it implies, although we shall not be able to say whether the conception of duty may not itself be empty.

The universality of the law which governs the succession of events, is what we mean by *nature,* in the most general sense, that is, the existence of things, in so far as their existence is determined in conformity with universal laws. The universal imperative of duty might therefore be put in this way: *Act as if the maxim from which you act were to become through your will a universal law of nature.*

If we attend to what goes on in ourselves in every transgression of a duty, we find, that we do not will that our maxim should become a universal law. We find it in fact impossible to do so, and we really will that the opposite of our maxim should remain a universal law, at the same time that we assume the liberty of making an exception in favor of natural inclination in our own case, or perhaps only for this particular occasion. Hence, if we looked at all cases from the same point of view, that is, from the point of view of reason, we should see that there was here a contradiction in our will. The contradiction is, that a certain principle is admitted to be necessary objectively or as a universal law, and yet is held not to be universal subjectively, but to admit of exceptions. What we do is, to consider our action at one time from the point of view of a will that is in perfect conformity with reason, and at another time from the point of view of a will that is under the influence of natural inclination. There is, therefore, here no real contradiction, but merely an antagonism of inclination to the command of reason. The universality of the principle is changed into a mere generality, in order that the practical principle of reason may meet the maxim half way. Not only is this limitation condemned by our impartial judgment, but it proves that we actually recognize the validity of the categorical imperative, and merely allow ourselves to make a few exceptions in our own favor which we try to consider as of no importance, or as a necessary concession to circumstances.

This much at least we have learned, that if the idea of duty is to have any meaning and to lay down the laws of our actions, it must be expressed in categorical and not in hypothetical imperatives. We have also obtained a clear and distinct conception (a very important thing), of what is implied in a categorical imperative which contains the principle of duty for all cases, granting such an imperative to be possible at all. But we have not yet been able to prove *a priori,* that there actually is such an imperative; that there is a practical law which commands absolutely on its own authority, and is independent of all sensuous impulses; and that duty consists in obedience to this law.

In seeking to reach this point, it is of the greatest importance to observe, that the reality of this principle cannot possibly be derived from the *peculiar constitution of human nature.* For by duty is meant the practically unconditioned necessity of an act, and hence we can show that duty is a law for the will of all human beings, only by showing that it is applicable to all rational beings, or rather to all rational beings to whom an imperative applies to all.

The question, then, is this: Is it a necessary law *for all rational beings* that they must always estimate the value of their actions by asking whether they can will that their maxims should serve as universal laws? If there is such a law, it must be possible to prove entirely *a priori,* that it is bound up with the very idea of the will of a rational being. To show that there is such a connection we must, however reluctantly, take a step into the realm of metaphysic; not, however, into the realm of speculative philosophy, but into the metaphysic of morality. For we have here to deal with objective practical laws, and therefore with the relation of the will to itself, in so far as it is determined purely by reason. All relation of the will to what is empirical is excluded as a matter of course, for if reason determines the relation *entirely by itself,* it must necessarily do so *a priori.*

Will is conceived of as a faculty of determining itself to action *in accordance with the idea of certain laws.* Such a faculty can belong only to a rational being. Now that which serves as an objective principle for the self-determination of the will is an *end,* and if this end is given purely by reason, it must hold for all rational beings. On the other hand, that which is merely the condition of the possibility of an action the effect of which is the end, is called the *means.* The subjective ground of desire is natural inclination, the objective ground of volition is a motive; hence there is a distinction between subjective ends, which depend upon natural inclination, and objective ends, which are connected with motives that hold for every rational being. Practical principles that abstract from all subjective ends are *formal;* those that presuppose subjective ends, and therefore natural inclinations, are *material.* The ends which a rational being arbitrarily sets before himself as material ends to be produced by his actions, are all merely relative; for that which gives to them their value is simply their relation to the peculiar susceptibility of the subject. They can therefore yield no universal and necessary principles, or practical laws, applicable to all rational beings, and binding upon every will. Upon such relative ends, therefore, only hypothetical imperatives can be based.

Suppose, however, that there is something the existence of which has in itself an absolute value, something which, *as an end in itself,* can be a ground of definite laws; then, there would lie in that, and only in that, the ground of a possible categorical imperative or practical law.

Now, I say, that man, and indeed every rational being as such, *exists* as an end in himself, *not merely as a means* to be made use of by this or that will, and therefore man in all his actions, whether these are directed towards himself or towards other rational beings, must always be regarded as an end. No object of natural desire has more than a conditional value; for if the natural desires, and the wants to which they give rise, did not exist, the object to which they are directed would have no value at all. So far are the natural desires and wants from having an absolute value, so far are they from being sought simply for themselves, that every rational being must wish to be entirely free from their influence. The value of every object which human action is the means of obtaining, is, therefore, always conditioned. And even beings whose existence depends upon nature, not upon our will, if they are without reason, have only the relative value of means, and are therefore called *things.* Rational beings, on the other hand, are called *persons,* because their very nature shows them to be ends in themselves, that is, something which cannot be made use of simply as a means. A person being thus an object of respect, a certain limit is placed upon arbitrary will. Persons are not purely subjective ends, whose existence has a value *for us* as the effect of our actions, but they are *objective ends,* or beings whose existence is an end in itself, for which no other end can be substituted. If all value were conditioned, and therefore contingent, it would be impossible to show that there is any supreme practical principle whatever.

If, then, there is a supreme practical principle, a principle which in relation to the human will is a categorical imperative, it must be an *objective* principle of the will, and must be able to serve as a universal practical law. For, such a principle must be derived from the idea of that which is necessarily an end for every one because it is an *end in itself.* Its foundation is this, that *rational nature exists as an end in itself.* Man necessarily conceives of his own existence in this way, and so far this is a *subjective* principle of human action. But in this way also every other rational being conceives of his own existence, and for the very same reason; hence the principle is also *objective,* and from it, as the highest practical ground, all laws of the will must be capable of being derived. The practical imperative will therefore be this: *Act so as to use humanity, whether in your own person or in the person of another, always as an end, never as merely a means.*

The principle, that humanity and every rational nature is an end in itself, is not borrowed from experience. For, in the first place, because of its universality it applies to all rational beings, and no experience can apply so widely. In the second place, it does not regard humanity subjectively, as an end of man, that is, as an object which the subject of himself actually makes his end, but as an objective end, which ought to be regarded as a law that constitutes the supreme limiting condition of all subjective ends, and which must therefore have its source in pure reason. The objective ground of all practical laws consists in the *rule* and the form of universality, which makes them capable of serving as laws, but their *subjective* ground consists in the *end* to which they are directed. Now, by the second principle, every rational being, as an end in himself, is the subject of all ends. From this follows the third practical principle of the will, which is the supreme condition of its harmony with universal practical reason, namely, the idea of *the will of every rational being as a will which lays down universal laws of action.*

This formula implies, that a will which is itself the supreme lawgiver cannot possibly act from interest of any sort in the law, although no doubt a will may under the law, and may yet be attached to it by the bond of interest.

At the point we have now reached, it does not seem surprising that all previous attempts to find out the principle of morality should have ended in failure. It was seen that man is bound under law by duty, but it did not strike anyone, that the *universal* system of laws to which he is subject are laws which he *imposes upon himself,* and that he is only under obligation to act in conformity with his own will, a will which by the purpose of nature prescribes universal laws. Now so long as man is thought to be merely subject to law, no matter what the law may be, he must be regarded as stimulated or constrained to obey the law from interest of some kind; for as the law does not proceed from *his* own will, there must be *something external* to his will which compels him to act in conformity with it. This perfectly necessary conclusion frustrated every attempt to find a supreme principle of duty. Duty was never established, but merely the necessity of acting from some form of interest, private or public. The imperative was therefore necessarily always conditioned, and could not possibly have the force of a moral command. The supreme principle of morality I shall therefore call the principle of the *autonomy* of the will, to distinguish it from all other principles, which I call principles of *heteronomy.*

The conception that every rational being in all the maxims of his will must regard himself as prescribing universal laws, by reference to which himself and all his actions are to be judged, leads to a cognate and very fruitful conception, that of a *kingdom of ends.*

By *kingdom,* I mean the systematic combination of different rational beings through the medium of common laws. Now, laws determine certain ends as universal, and hence, if abstraction is made from the individual differences of rational beings, and from all that is peculiar to their private ends, we get the idea of a complete totality of ends combined in a system; in other words, we are able to conceive of a kingdom of ends, which conforms to the principles formulated above.

All rational beings stand under the law, that each should treat himself and others, *never simply as means,* but always as *at the same time ends in themselves.* Thus there arises a systematic combination of rational beings through the medium of common objective laws. This may well be called a kingdom of ends, because the object of those laws is just to relate all rational beings to one another as ends and means. Of course this kingdom of ends is merely an ideal.

Morality, then, consists in the relation of all action to the system of laws which alone makes possible a kingdom of ends. These laws must belong to the nature of every rational being, and must proceed from his own will. The principle of the will, therefore, is, that no action should be done from any other maxim than one which is consistent with a universal law. This may be expressed in the formula: *Act so that the will may regard itself as in its maxims laying down universal laws.* Now, if the maxims of rational beings are not by their very nature in harmony with this objective principle, the principle of a universal system of laws, the necessity of acting in conformity with that principle is called practical obligation or *duty.* No doubt duty does not apply to the sovereign will in the kingdom of ends, but it applies to every member of it, and to all in equal measure. *Autonomy* is thus the foundation of the moral value of man and of every other rational being.

The three ways in which the principle of morality has been formulated are at bottom simply different statements of the same law, and each implies the other two.

An absolutely good will, then, the principle of which must be a categorical imperative, will be undetermined as regards all objects, and will contain merely the *form of volition* in general, a form which rests upon the *autonomy* of the will. The one law which the will of every rational being imposes upon itself, and imposes without reference to any natural impulse or any interest, is, that the maxims of every good will must be capable of being made a universal law.

*U*TILITARIANISM

J. J. C. Smart

According to the act-utilitarian, . . . the rational way to decide what to do is to decide to perform that one of those alternative actions open to us which is likely to maximize the probable happiness or well-being of humanity as a whole, or more accurately, of all sentient beings. The utilitarian position is here put forward as a criterion of rational choice. It is true that we may choose to habituate ourselves to behave in accordance with certain rules, such as to keep promises, in the belief that behaving in accordance with these rules is generally optimific, and in the knowledge that we most often just do not have time to work out individual pros and cons. When we act in such an habitual fashion we do not of course deliberate or make a choice. The act-utilitarian will, however, regard these rules as mere rules of thumb, and will use them only as rough guides. Normally he will act in accordance with them when he has no time for considering probable consequences or when the advantages of such a consideration of consequences are likely to be outweighed by the disadvantage of the waste of time involved. He acts in accordance with rules, in short, when there is no time to think, and since he does not think the actions which he does habitually are not the outcome of moral thinking. When he has to think what to do, then there is a question of deliberation or choice, and it is precisely for such situations that the utilitarian criterion is intended.

It is, moreover, important to realize that there is no inconsistency whatever in an act-utilitarian's schooling himself to act, in normal circumstances, habitually and in accordance with stereotyped rules. He knows that a man about to save a drowning person has no time to consider various possibilities, such as that the drowning person is a dangerous criminal who will cause death and destruction, or that he is suffering from a painful and incapacitating disease from which death would be a merciful release, or that various timid people, watching from the bank, will suffer a heart attack if they see anyone else in the water. No, he knows that it is almost always right to save a drowning man, and in he goes. Again, he knows that we would go mad if we went in detail into the probable consequences of keeping or not keeping every trivial promise: we will do most good and reserve our mental energies for more important matters if we simply habituate ourselves to keep promises in all normal situations. Moreover he may suspect that on some occasions personal bias may prevent him from reasoning in a correct utilitarian fashion. Suppose he is trying to decide between two jobs, one of which is more highly paid than the other, though he has given an informal promise that he will take the lesser paid one. He may well deceive himself by underestimating the effects of breaking the promise (in causing loss of confidence) and by overestimating the good he can do in the highly paid job. He may well feel that if he trusts to the accepted rules he is more likely to act in the way that an unbiased act-utilitarian would recommend than he would be if he tried to evaluate the consequences of his possible actions himself. Indeed Moore argued on act-utilitarian grounds that one should never in concrete cases think as an act-utilitarian.

This, however, is surely to exaggerate both the usefulness of rules and the human mind's propensity to unconscious bias. Nevertheless, right or wrong, this attitude of Moore's has a rational basis and (though his argument from probability considerations is faulty in detail) is not the law worship of the rule-utilitarian, who would say that we ought to keep to a rule that is the most generally optimific, even though we *knew* that obeying it in this particular instance would have bad consequences.

Nor is this utilitarian doctrine incompatible, as M. A. Kaplan has suggested it is, with a recognition of the importance of warm and spontaneous expressions of emotion. Consider a case in which a man sees that his wife is tired, and simply from a spontaneous feeling of affection for her he offers to wash the dishes. Does utilitarianism imply that he should have stopped to calculate the various consequences of his different possible courses of action? Certainly not. This would make married life a misery and the utilitarian knows very well as a rule of thumb that on occasions of this sort it is best to act spontaneously and without calculation. Moreover I have said that act-utilitarianism is meant to give a method of deciding what to do in those cases in which we do indeed decide what to do. On these occasions when we do not act as a result of deliberation and choice, that is, when we act spontaneously, no method of decision, whether utilitarian or non-utilitarian, comes into the matter. What does arise for the utilitarian is the question of whether or not he should consciously encourage in himself the tendency to certain types of spontaneous feeling. There are in fact very good utilitarian reasons why we should by all means cultivate in ourselves the tendency to certain types of warm and spontaneous feeling.

Though even the act-utilitarian may on occasion act habitually and in accordance with particular rules, his criterion is, as we have said, *applied* in cases in which he does not act habitually but in which he deliberates and chooses what to do. Now the right action for an agent in given circumstances is, we have said, that action which produces better results than any alternative action. If two or more actions produce equally good results, and if these results are better than the results of any other action open to the agent, then there is no such thing as *the* right action: there are two or more actions which are *a* right action. However this is a very exceptional state of affairs, which may well never in fact occur, and so usually I will speak loosely of the action which is *the* right one. We are now able to specify more clearly what is meant by "alternative action" here. The fact that the utilitarian criterion is meant to apply in situations of deliberation and choice enables us to say that the class of alternative actions which we have in mind when we talk about an action having the best possible results is the class of actions which the agent could have performed if he had tried. For example, it would be better to bring a man back to life than to offer financial assistance to his dependants, but because it is technologically impossible to bring a man back to life, bringing the man back to life is not something we could do if we tried. On the other hand it may well be possible for us to give financial assistance to the dependants, and this then may be the right action. The right action is the action among those which we could do, i.e. those which we *would* do if we chose to, which has the best possible results.

It is true that the general concept of action is wider than that of deliberate choice. Many actions are performed habitually and without deliberation. But the actions for whose rightness we as agents want a criterion are, in the nature of the case, those done thinkingly and deliberately. An action is at any rate that sort of human performance which it is appropriate to praise, blame, punish or reward, and since it is often appropriate to praise, blame, punish, or reward habitual performance, the concept of action cannot be identified with that of the outcome of deliberation and choice. With habitual actions the only question that arises for an agent is that of whether or not he should strengthen the habit or break himself of it. And individual acts of habit-strengthening or habit-breaking can themselves be deliberate.

The utilitarian criterion, then, is designed to help a person, who could do various things if he chose to do them, to decide which of these things he should do. His utilitarian deliberation is one of the causal antecedents of his action, and it would be pointless if it were not. The utilitarian view is therefore perfectly compatible with determinism. The only sense of "he could have done otherwise" that we require is the sense "he would have done otherwise if he had chosen." Whether the utilitarian view necessitates complete metaphysical determinism is another matter. All that it requires is that deliberation should determine actions in the way that everyone knows it does anyway. If it is argued that any indeterminism in the universe entails that we can never know the outcome of our actions, we can reply that in normal cases these indeterminacies will be so numerous as approximately to cancel one another out, and anyway all that we require for rational action is that some consequences of our actions should be *more probable* than others, and this is something which no indeterminist is likely to deny.

The utilitarian may now conveniently make a terminological recommendation. Let us use the word "rational" as a term of commendation for that action which is, on the evidence available to the agent, *likely* to produce the best results, and to reverse the word "right" as a term of commendation for the action which does *in fact* produce the best results. That is, let us say that what is rational is to try to perform the right action, to try to produce the best results. Or at least this formulation will do where there is an equal probability of achieving each possible set of results. If there is a very low probability of producing very good results, then it is natural to say that the rational agent would perhaps go for other more probable though not quite so good results. For a more accurate formulation we should have to weight the goodness of the results with their probabilities. However, neglecting this complication, we can say, roughly, that it is rational to perform the action which is on the available evidence the one which will produce the best results. This allows us to say, for example, that the agent did the right thing but irrationally (he was trying to do something else, or was trying to do this very thing but went about it unscientifically) and that he acted rationally but by bad luck did the wrong thing, because the things that seemed probable to him, for the best reasons, just did not happen.

Roughly, then: we shall use "right" and "wrong" to appraise choices on account of their actual success in promoting the general happiness, and we shall use "rational" and "irrational" to appraise them on account of their likely success. As was noted above "likely success" must be interpreted in terms of maximizing the probable benefit, not in terms of probably maximizing the benefit. In effect, it is rational to do what you reasonably think to be right, and what will be right is what will maximize the probable benefit. We need, however, to make one qualification to this. A person may unreasonably believe what it would in fact be reasonable to believe. We shall still call such a person's action irrational. If the agent has been unscientific in his calculation of means-ends relationships he may decide that a certain course of action is probably best for human happiness, and it may indeed be so. When he performs this action we may still call his action irrational, because it was pure luck, not sound reasoning, that brought him to his conclusion.

"Rational" and "irrational" and "right" and "wrong" so far have been introduced as terms of appraisal for chosen or deliberate actions only. There is no reason why we should not use the pair of terms "right" and "wrong" more widely so as to appraise even habitual actions. Nevertheless we shall not have much occasion to appraise actions that are not the outcome of choice. What we do need is a pair of terms of appraisal for *agents* and *motives*. I suggest that we use the terms "good" and "bad" for these purposes. A good agent is one who acts more nearly in a generally optimific way than does the average one. A bad agent is one who acts in a less optimific way than the average. A good motive is one which generally results in beneficent actions, and a bad motive is one which generally ends in maleficent actions. Clearly there is no inconsistency in saying that on a particular occasion a good man did a wrong action, that a bad man did a right action, that a right action was done from a bad motive, or that a wrong action was done from a good motive. Many specious arguments against utilitarianism come from obscuring these distinctions. Thus one may be got to admit that an action is "right," meaning no more than that it is done from a good motive and is praiseworthy, and then it is pointed out that the action is not "right" in the sense of being optimific. I do not wish to legislate as to how other people (particularly non-utilitarians) should use words like "right" and "wrong," but in the interests of clarity it is important for me to state how I propose to use them myself, and to try to keep the various distinctions clear.

It should be noted that in making this terminological recommendation I am not trying to smuggle in valuations under the guise of definitions, as Ardon Lyon, in a review of the first edition of this monograph, has suggested that I have done. It is merely a recommendation to pre-empt the already evaluative words "rational" and "irrational" for one lot of commendatory or discommendatory jobs, the already evaluative words "right" and "wrong" for another lot of commendatory or discommendatory jobs, and the already evaluative words "good" and "bad" for yet another lot of commendatory or discommendatory jobs.

We can also use "good" and "bad" as terms of commendation or discommendation of actions themselves. In this case to commend or discommend an action is to commend or discommend the motive from which it sprang. This allows us to say that a man performed a bad action but that it was the right one, or that he performed a good action but that it was wrong. For example, a man near Berchtesgaden in 1938 might have jumped into a river and rescued a drowning man, only to find that it was Hitler. He would have done the wrong thing, for he would have saved the world a lot of trouble if he had left Hitler below the surface. On the other hand his motive, the desire to save life, would have been one which we approve of people having: in general, though not in this case, the desire to save life leads to acting rightly. It is worth our while to strengthen such a desire. Not only should we praise the action (thus expressing our approval of it) but we should perhaps even give the man a medal, thus encouraging others to emulate it. Indeed praise itself comes to have some of the social functions of medal giving: we come to like praise for its own sake, and are thus influenced by the possibility of being given it. Praising a person is thus an important action in itself—it has significant effects. A utilitarian must therefore learn to control his acts of praise and dispraise, thus perhaps concealing his approval of an action when he thinks that the expression of such approval might have bad effects, and perhaps even praising actions of which he does not really approve. Consider, for example, the case of an act-utilitarian, fighting in a war, who succeeds in capturing the commander of an enemy submarine. Assuming that it is a just war and that the act-utilitarian is fighting on the right side, the very courage and ability of the submarine commander has a tendency which is the reverse of optimific. Everything that the submarine commander has been doing was (in my proposed sense of the word) wrong. (I do not of course mean that he did anything wrong in the technological sense: presumably he knew how to manoeuvre his ship in the right way.) He has kept his boat cunningly concealed, when it would have been better for humanity if it had been a sitting duck, he has kept the morale of his crew high when it would have been better if they had been cowardly and inefficient, and has aimed his torpedoes with deadly effect so as to do the maximum harm. Nevertheless, once the enemy commander is captured, or even perhaps before he is captured, our act-utilitarian sailor does the right thing in praising the enemy commander, behaving chivalrously towards him, giving him honour and so on, for he is powerfully influencing his own men to aspire to similar professional courage and efficiency, to the ultimate benefit of mankind.

What I have said in the last paragraph about the occasional utility of praising harmful actions applies, I think, even when the utilitarian is speaking to other utilitarians. It applies even more when, as is more usually the case, the utilitarian is speaking to a predominantly non-utilitarian audience. To take an extreme case, suppose that the utilitarian is speaking to people who live in a society governed by a form of magical taboo ethics. He may consider that though on occasion keeping to the taboos does harm, on the whole the tendency of the taboo ethics is more beneficial than the sort of moral anarchy into which these people might fall if their reverence for their taboos was weakened. While, therefore, he would recognize that the system of taboos which governed these people's conduct was markedly inferior to a utilitarian ethic, nevertheless he might also recognize that these people's cultural background was such that they could not easily be persuaded to adopt a utilitarian ethic. He will, therefore, on act-utilitarian grounds, dispute his praise and blame in such a way as to strengthen, not to weaken, the system of taboo.

In an ordinary society we do not find such an extreme situation. Many people can be got to adopt a utilitarian, or almost utilitarian, way of thought, but many cannot. We may consider whether it may not be better to throw our weight on the side of the prevailing traditional morality, rather than on the side of trying to improve it with the risk of weakening respect for morality altogether. Sometimes the answer to this question will be "yes," and sometimes "no." As Sidgwick said:

> The doctrine that Universal Happiness is the ultimate *standard* must not be understood to imply that Universal Benevolence is . . . always the best *motive* of action. For . . . it is not necessary that the end which gives the criterion of rightness should always be the end at which we consciously aim: and if experience shows that the general happiness will be more satisfactorily attained if men frequently act from other motives than pure universal philanthropy, it is obvious that these other motives are to be preferred on Utilitarian principles.

In general, we may note, it is always dangerous to influence a person contrary to his conviction of what is right. More harm may be done in weakening his regard for duty than would be saved by preventing the particular action in question. Furthermore, to quote Sidgwick again, "any particular existing moral rule, though not the ideally best even for such beings, as existing men under the existing circumstances, may yet be the best that they can be got to obey." We must also remember that some motives are likely to be present in excess rather than defect: in which case, however necessary they may be, it is not expedient to praise them. It is obviously useful to praise altruism, even though this is not pure generalized benevolence, the treating of oneself as neither more nor less important than anyone else, simply because most people err on the opposite side, from too much self-love and not enough altruism. It is, similarly, inexpedient to praise self-love, important though this is when it is kept in due proportion. In short, to quote Sidgwick once more, "in distributing our praise of human qualities, on utilitarian principles, we have to consider not primarily the usefulness of the quality, but the usefulness of the praise."

Most men, we must never forget, are not act-utilitarians, and do not use the words "good" and "bad," when applied to agents or to motives, quite in the way which has here been recommended. When a man says that another is wicked he may even be saying something of a partly metaphysical or superstitious connotation. He may be saying that there is something like a yellow stain on the other man's soul. Of course he would not think this quite literally. If you asked him whether souls could be coloured, or whether yellow was a particularly abhorrent colour, he would of course laugh at you. His views about sin and wickedness may be left in comfortable obscurity. Nevertheless the things he *does* say may indeed entail something *like* the yellow stain view. "Wicked" has thus come to have much more force than the utilitarian "likely to be very harmful" or "probably a menace." To stigmatize a man as wicked is not, as things are, just to make men wary of him, but to make him the object of a peculiar and very powerful abhorrence, over and above the natural abhorrence one has from a dangerous natural object such as a typhoon or an octopus. And it may well be to the act-utilitarian's advantage, *qua* act-utilitarian, to acquiesce in this way of talking when he is in the company of non-utilitarians. He himself will not believe in yellow stains in souls, or anything like it. *Tout comprendre c'est tout pardonner;* a man is the result of heredity and environment. Nevertheless the utilitarian may influence behaviour in the way he desires by using "wicked" in a quasi-superstitious way. Similarly a man about to be boiled alive by cannibals may usefully say that an imminent eclipse is a sign of the gods' displeasure at the proposed culinary activities. We have seen that in a completely utilitarian society the utility of praise of an agent's motives does not always go along with the utility of the action. Still more may this be so in a non-utilitarian society. . . .

So far, I have done my best to state utilitarianism in a way which is conceptually clear and to rebut many common objections to it. At the time I wrote the earlier edition of this monograph I did so as a pretty single-minded utilitarian myself. It seemed to me then that since the utilitarian principle expressed the attitude of generalized benevolence, anyone who rejected utilitarianism would have to be hard hearted, i.e. to some extent non-benevolent, or else would have to be the prey of conceptual confusion or an unthinking adherent of traditional ways of thought, or perhaps be an adherent of some religious system of ethics, which could be undermined by metaphysical criticism. Admittedly utilitarianism does have consequences which are incompatible with the common moral consciousness, but I tended to take the view "so much the worse for the common moral consciousness." That is, I was inclined to reject the common methodology of testing general ethical principles by seeing how they square with our feelings in particular instances.

After all, one may feel somewhat as follows. What is the purpose of morality? (Answering this question is to make a moral judgement. To think that one could answer the question "What is the purpose of morality?" without making a moral judgement would be to condone the naturalistic fallacy, the fallacy of deducing an "ought" from an "is.") Suppose that we say, as it is surely at least tempting to do, that the purpose of morality is to subserve the general happiness. Then it immediately seems to follow that we ought to reject any putative moral rule, or any particular moral feeling, which conflicts with the utilitarian principle. It is undeniable that we do have anti-utilitarian moral feelings in particular cases, but perhaps they should be discounted as far as possible, as due to our moral conditioning in childhood. (The weakness of this line of thought is that approval of the general principle of utilitarianism may be due to moral conditioning too. And even if benevolence were in some way a "natural," not an "artificial," attitude, this consideration could at best have persuasive force, without any clear rationale. To argue from the naturalness to the correctness of a moral attitude would be to commit the naturalistic fallacy.) Nevertheless in some moods the general principle of utilitarianism may recommend itself to us so much the more than do particular moral precepts, precisely because it *is* so general. We may therefore feel inclined to reject an ethical methodology which implies that we should test our general principles by our reactions in particular cases. Rather, we may come to feel, we should test our reactions in particular cases by reference to the most general principles. The analogy with science is not a good one, since it is not far off the truth to say that observation statements are more firmly based than the theories they test. But why should our more particular moral feelings be more worthy of notice than our more generalized ones? That there should be a disanalogy between ethics and science is quite plausible if we accept a non-cognitivist theory of meta-ethics.

The utilitarian, then, will test his particular feelings by reference to his general principle, and not the general principle by reference to his particular feelings. Now while I have some tendency to take this point of view (and if I had not I would not have been impelled to state and defend utilitarianism as a system of normative ethics) I have also some tendency to feel the opposite, that we should sometimes test our general principles by how we feel about particular applications of them. (I am a bit like G. E. Moore in his reply to C. L. Stevenson, where he feels both that he is right and Stevenson wrong and that he is wrong and Stevenson is right. My own indecisiveness may be harder to resolve, since in my case it is a matter of feeling, rather than intellect, which is involved.)

It is not difficult to show that utilitarianism could, in certain exceptional circumstances, have some very horrible consequences. In a very lucid and concise discussion note, H. J. McCloskey has considered such a case. Suppose that the sheriff of a small town can prevent serious riots (in which hundreds of people will be killed) only by "framing" and executing (as a scapegoat) an innocent man. In actual cases of this sort the utilitarian will usually be able to agree with our normal moral feelings about such matters. He will be able to point out that there would be some possibility of the sheriff's dishonesty being found out, with consequent weakening of confidence and respect for law and order in the community, the consequences of which would be far worse even than the painful deaths of hundreds of citizens. But as McCloskey is ready to point out, the case can be presented in such a way that these objections do not apply. For example, it can be imagined that the sheriff could have first-rate empirical evidence that he will not be found out. So the objection that the sheriff *knows* that the man he "frames" will be killed, whereas he has only probable belief that the riot will occur unless he frames the man, is not a sound one. Someone like McCloskey can always strengthen his story to the point that we would just have to admit that if utilitarianism is correct, then the sheriff must frame the innocent man. (McCloskey also has cogently argued that similar objectionable consequences are also implied by rule-utilitarianism. That is, an unjust *system* of punishment might be more *useful* than a just one. Hence even if rule-utilitarianism can clearly be distinguished from act-utilitarianism, a utilitarian will not be able to avoid offensive consequences of his theory by retreating from the "act" form to the "rule" form.) Now though a utilitarian might argue that it is empirically unlikely that some such situation as McCloskey envisages would ever occur, McCloskey will point out that it is *logically* possible that such a situation will arise. If the utilitarian rejects the unjust act (or system) he is clearly giving up his utilitarianism. McCloskey then remarks: "But as far as I know, only J. J. C. Smart among the contemporary utilitarians, is happy to adopt this 'solution'." Here I must lodge a mild protest. McCloskey's use of the word "happy" surely makes me look a most reprehensible person. Even in my most utilitarian moods I am not *happy* about this consequence of utilitarianism. Nevertheless, however unhappy about it he may be, the utilitarian must admit that he draws the consequence that he might find himself in circumstances where he ought to be unjust. Let us hope that this is a logical possibility and not a factual one. In hoping thus I am not being inconsistent with utilitarianism, since any injustice causes misery and so can be justified only as the lesser of two evils. The fewer the situations in which the utilitarian is forced to choose the lesser of two evils, the better he will be pleased. One must not think of the utilitarian as the sort of person who you would not trust further than you could kick him. As a matter of untutored sociological observation, I should say that in general utilitarians are more than usually trustworthy people, and that the sort of people who might do you down are rarely utilitarians.

It is also true that we should probably dislike and fear a man who could bring himself to do the right utilitarian act in a case of the sort envisaged by McCloskey. Though the man in this case might have done the right utilitarian act, his act would betoken a toughness and lack of squeamishness which would make him a dangerous person. We must remember that people have egoistic tendencies as well as beneficent ones, and should such a person be tempted to act wrongly he could act very wrongly indeed. A utilitarian who remembers the possible moral weakness of men might quite consistently prefer to be the sort of person who would not always be able to bring himself to do the right utilitarian act and to surround himself by people who would be too squeamish to act in a utilitarian manner in such extreme cases.

No, I am not happy to draw the conclusion that McCloskey quite rightly says that the utilitarian must draw. But neither am I happy with the anti-utilitarian conclusion. For if a case really *did* arise in which injustice was the lesser of two evils (in terms of human happiness and misery), then the anti-utilitarian conclusion is a very unpalatable one too, namely that in some circumstances one must choose the greater misery, the *very much* greater misery, such as that of hundreds of people suffering painful deaths.

Still, to be consistent, the utilitarian must accept McCloskey's challenge. Let us hope that the sort of possibility which he envisages will always be no more than a logical possibility and will never become an actuality. At any rate, even though I have suggested that in ethics we should test particular feelings by general attitudes, McCloskey's example makes me somewhat sympathetic to the opposite point of view. Perhaps indeed it is too much to hope that there is *any* possible ethical system which will appeal to all sides of our nature and to all our moods. It is perfectly possible to have conflicting attitudes within oneself. It is quite conceivable that there is *no* possible ethical theory which will be conformable with all our attitudes. If the theory is utilitarian, then the possibility that sometimes it would be right to commit injustice will be felt to be acutely unsatisfactory by someone with a normal civilized upbringing. If on the other hand it is not utilitarian but has deontological elements, then it will have the unsatisfactory implication that sometimes avoidable misery (perhaps very great avoidable misery) ought not to be avoided. It might be thought that some compromise theory, on the lines of Sir David Ross's, in which there is some "balancing up" between considerations of utility and those of deontology, might provide an acceptable compromise. The trouble with this, however, is that such a "balancing" may not be possible: one can easily feel pulled sometimes one way and sometimes the other. How can one "balance" a serious injustice, on the one hand, and hundreds of painful deaths, on the other hand? Even if we disregard our purely self-interested attitudes, for the sake of interpersonal discussions, so as to treat ourselves neither more nor less favourably than other people, it is still possible that there is no ethical system which would be satisfactory to all men, or even to one man at different times. It is possible that something similar is the case with science, that no scientific theory (known or unknown) is correct. If so, the world is more chaotic than we believe and hope that it is. But even though the world is not chaotic, men's moral feelings may be. On anthropological grounds it is only too likely that these feelings are to some extent chaotic. Both as children and as adults, we have probably had many different moral conditionings, which can easily be incompatible with one another.

Meanwhile, among possible options, utilitarianism does have its appeal. With its empirical attitude to questions of means and ends it is congenial to the scientific temper and it has flexibility to deal with a changing world. This last consideration is, however, more self-recommendation than justification. For if flexibility is a recommendation, this is because of the utility of flexibility.

PRESCRIPTIVISM

R. M. Hare

There are two sorts of things that we can say, for example, about strawberries; the first sort is usually called *descriptive,* the second sort *evaluative.* Examples of the first sort of remark are "This strawberry is sweet" and "This strawberry is large, red, and juicy." Examples of the second sort of remark are "This is a good strawberry" and "This strawberry is just as strawberries ought to be." The first sort of remark is often given as a reason for making the second sort of remark; but the first sort does not by itself entail the second sort, nor vice versa. Yet there seems to be some close logical connection between them. Our problem is: "What is this connection?"; for no light is shed by saying that there is a connection, unless we can say what it is.

The problem may also be put in this way: if we knew all the descriptive properties which a particular strawberry had (knew, of every descriptive sentence relating to the strawberry, whether it was true or false), and if we knew also the meaning of the word "good," then what else should we require to know, in order to be able to tell whether a strawberry was a good one? Once the question is put in this way, the answer should be apparent. We should require to know, what are the criteria in virtue of which a strawberry is to be called a good one, or what are the characteristics that make a strawberry a good one, or what is the standard of goodness in strawberries. We should require to be given the major premise. We have already seen that we can know the meaning of "good strawberry" without knowing any of these latter things—though there is also a sense of the sentence "What does it mean to call a strawberry a good one?" in which we should not know the answer to it, unless we also knew the answer to these other questions. It is now time to elucidate and distinguish these two ways in which we can be said to know what it means to call an object a good member of its class. This will help us to see more clearly both the differences and the similarities between "good" and words like "red" and "sweet."

Since we have been dwelling for some time on the differences, it will do no harm now to mention some of the similarities. For this purpose, let us consider the two sentences "M is a red motor-car" and "M is a good motor-car." It will be noticed that "motor-car," unlike "strawberry," is a functional word, as defined in the preceding chapter. Reference to the *Shorter Oxford English Dictionary* shows that a motor-car is a carriage, and a carriage a

"Prescriptivism," by R. M. Hare. Reprinted from *The Language of Morals* (1952) by permission of Oxford University Press.

means of conveyance. Thus, if a motor-car will not convey anything, we know from the definition of motor-car that it is not a good one. But when we know this, we know so little, compared with what is required in order to know the full criteria of a good motor-car, that I propose in what follows to ignore, for the sake of simplicity, this complicating factor. I shall treat "motor-car" as if it did not have to be defined functionally: that is to say, I shall assume that we could learn the meaning of "motor-car" (as in a sense we can) simply by being shown examples of motor-cars. It is, of course, not always easy to say whether or not a word is a functional word; it depends, like all questions of meaning, on how the word is taken by a particular speaker.

The first similarity between "M is a red motor-car" and "M is a good motor-car" is that both can be, and often are, used for conveying information of a purely factual or descriptive character. If I say to someone "M is a good motor-car," and he himself has not seen, and knows nothing of M, but does on the other hand know what sorts of motor-car we are accustomed to call "good" (knows what is the accepted standard of goodness in motor-cars) he undoubtedly receives information from my remark about what sort of motor-car it is. He will complain that I have misled him, if he subsequently discovers that M will not go over 30 m.p.h., or uses as much oil as petrol, or is covered with rust, or has large holes in the roof. His reason for complaining will be the same as it would have been if I had said that the car was red and he subsequently discovered that it was black. I should have led him to expect the motor-car to be of a certain description when in fact it was of a quite different description.

The second similarity between the two sentences is this. Sometimes we use them, not for actually conveying information, but for putting our hearer into a position subsequently to use the word "good" or "red" for giving or getting information. Suppose, for example, that he is utterly unfamiliar with motor-cars, in the same sort of way as most of us are unfamiliar with horses nowadays, and knows no more about motor-cars than is necessary in order to distinguish a motor-car from a hansom cab. In that case, my saying to him "M is a good motor-car" will not give him any information about M, beyond the information that it is a motor-car. But if he is able then or subsequently to examine M, he will have learned something. He will have learned that some of the characteristics which M has, are characteristics which make people—or at any rate me—call it a good motor-car. This may not be to learn very much. But suppose that I make judgments of this sort about a great many motor-cars, calling some good and some not good, and he is able to examine all or most of the motor cars about which I am speaking; he will in the end learn quite a lot, always presuming that I observe a consistent standard in calling them good or not good. He will eventually, if he pays careful attention, get into the position in which he knows, after I have said that a motor-car is a good one, what sort of motor-car he may expect it to be—for example, fast, stable on the road, and so on.

Now, if we are dealing not with "good," but with "red," we should call this process "explaining the meaning of the word"—and we might indeed, in a sense, say that what I have been doing is explaining what one means by a "good motor-car." This is a sense of "mean" about which, as we have seen, we must be on our guard. The processes, however, are very similar. I might explain the meaning of "red" by continually saying of various motor-cars "M is a red motor-car," "N is not a red motor-car," and so on. If he were attentive enough, he would soon get into a position in which he was able to use the word "red" for giving or getting information, at any rate about motor-cars. And so, both with "good" and with "red," there is this process, which in the case of "red" we may call "explaining the meaning," but in the case of "good" may only call it so loosely and in a secondary sense; to be clear, we must call it something like "explaining or conveying or setting forth the standard of goodness in motor-cars."

The standard of "goodness," like the meaning of "red," is normally something which is public and commonly accepted. When I explain to someone the meaning of "red motor-car," he expects, unless I am known to be very eccentric, that he will find other people using it in the same way. And similarly, at any rate with objects like motor-cars where there is a commonly accepted standard, he will expect, having learnt from me what is the standard of goodness in motor-cars, to be able, by using the expression "good motor-car," to give information to other people, and get it from them, without confusion.

A third respect in which "good motor-car" resembles "red motor-car" is the following: both "good" and "red" can vary as regards the exactitude or vagueness of the information which they do or can convey. We normally use the expression "red motor-car" very loosely. Any motor-car that lies somewhere between the unmistakably purple and the unmistakably orange could without abuse of language be called a red motor-car. And similarly, the standard for calling motor-cars good is commonly very loose. There are certain characteristics, such as inability to exceed 30 m.p.h., which to anyone but an eccentric would be sufficient conditions for refusing to call it a good motor-car; but there is no precise set of accepted criteria such that we can say "If a motor-car satisfies these conditions, it is a good one; if not, not." And in both cases we would be precise if we wanted to. We could, for certain purposes, agree not to say that a motor-car was "really red" unless the redness of its paint reached a certain measurable degree of purity and saturation; and similarly, we might adopt a very exact standard of goodness in motor-cars. We might refuse the name "good motor-car" to any car that would not go round a certain race-track without mishap in a certain limited time, that did not conform to certain other rigid specifications as regards accommodation, etc. This sort of thing has not been done for the expression "good motor-car"; but it has been done by the Ministry of Agriculture for the expression "super apple."

It is important to notice that the exactness or looseness of their criteria does absolutely nothing to distinguish words like "good" from words like "red." Words in both classes may be descriptively loose or exact, according to how rigidly the criteria have been laid down by custom or convention. It certainly is not true that value-words are distinguished from descriptive words in that the former are looser, descriptively, than the latter. There are loose and rigid examples of both sorts of word. Words like "red" can be extremely loose without becoming to the least degree evaluative; and expressions like "good sewage effluent" can be the subject of very rigid criteria, without in the least ceasing to be evaluative.

It is important to notice also, how easy it is, in view of these resemblances between "good" and "red," to think that there are no differences—to think that to set forth the standard of goodness in motor-cars is to set forth the meaning, in all senses that there are of that word, of the expression "good motor-car"; to think that "M is a good motor-car" means neither more nor less than "M has certain characteristics of which 'good' is the name."

It is worth noticing here that the functions of the word "good" which are concerned with information could be performed equally well if "good" had no commendatory function at all. This can be made clear by substituting another word, made up for the purpose, which is to be supposed to lack the commendatory force of "good." Let us use "doog" as this new word. "Doog" like "good," can be used for conveying information only if the criteria for its application are known; but this makes it, unlike "good," altogether meaningless until these criteria are made known. I make the criteria known by pointing out various motor-cars, and saying "M is a doog motor-car," "N is not a doog motor-car," and so on. We must imagine that, although "doog" has no commendatory force, the criteria for doogness in motor-cars which I am employing are the same as those, which in the previous example, I employed for goodness in motor-cars. And so, as in the previous example, the learner, if he is sufficiently attentive, becomes able to use the word "doog" for giving or getting information; when I say to him, "Z is a doog motor-car," he knows what characteristics to expect it to have; and if he wants to convey to someone else that a motor-car Y has those same characteristics, he can do so by saying "Y is a doog motor-car."

Thus the word "doog" does (though only in connection with motor-cars) half the jobs that the word "good" does—namely, all those jobs that are concerned with the giving, or learning to give or get, information. It does not do those jobs which are concerned with commendation. Thus we might say that "doog" functions just like a descriptive word. First my learner learns to use it by my giving him examples of its application and then he uses it by applying it to fresh examples. It would be quite natural to say that what I was doing was teaching my learner the *meaning* of "doog"; and this shows us again how natural it is to say that, when we are learning a similar lesson for the expression "good motor-car" (i.e. learning the criteria of its application), we are learning its meaning. But with the word "good" it is misleading to say this; for the meaning of "good motor-car" (in another sense of "meaning") is something that might be known by someone who did not know the criteria of its application; he would know, if someone said that a motor-car was a good one, that he was commending it; and to know that, would be to know the meaning of the expression. Further, as we saw earlier, someone might know about "good" all the things which my learner learned about the word "doog" (namely, how to apply the word to the right objects, and use it for giving and getting information) and yet be said not to know its meaning; for he might not know that to call a motor-car good was to commend it.

It is time now to justify my calling the descriptive meaning of "good" secondary to the evaluative meaning. My reasons for doing so are two. First, the evaluative meaning is constant for every class of object for which the word is used. When we call a motor-car or a chronometer or a cricket-bat or a picture good, we are commending all of them. But because we are commending all of them for different reasons, the descriptive meaning is different in all cases. We have knowledge of the evaluative meaning of "good" from our earliest years; but we are constantly learning to use it in new descriptive meanings, as the classes of objects whose virtues we learn to distinguish grow more numerous. Sometimes we learn to use "good" in a new descriptive meaning through being taught it by an expert in a particular field—for example, a horse man might teach me how to recognize a good hunter. Sometimes, on the other hand, we make up a new descriptive meaning for ourselves. This happens when we start having a standard for a class of objects, certain members of which we have started needing to place in order of merit, but for which there has hitherto been no standard. . . .

The second reason for calling the evaluative meaning primary is, that we can use the evaluative force of the word in order to *change* the descriptive meaning for any class of objects. This is what the moral reformer often does in morals; but the same process occurs outside morals. It may happen that motor-cars will in the near future change considerably in design (e.g., by our seeking economy at the expense of size). It may be that then we shall cease giving the name "a good motor-car" to a car that now would rightly and with the concurrence of all be allowed that name. How, linguistically speaking, would this have happened? At present, we are roughly agreed (though only roughly) on the necessary and sufficient criteria for calling a motor-car a good one. If what I have described takes place, we may begin to say "No cars of the nineteen-fifties were really good; there weren't any good ones till 1960." Now here we cannot be using "good" with the same descriptive meaning as it is now generally used with; for some of the cars of 1950 do indubitably have those characteristics which entitle them to the name "good motor-car" in the 1950 descriptive sense of that word. What is happening is that the evaluative meaning of the word is being used in order to shift the descriptive meaning; we are doing what would be called, if "good" were a purely descriptive word, redefining it. But we cannot call it that, for the evaluative meaning remains constant; we are rather altering the standard. This is similar to the process called by Professor Stevenson "persuasive definition"; the process is not necessarily, however, highly colored with emotion.

Although with "good" the evaluative meaning is primary, there are other words in which the evaluative meaning is secondary to the descriptive. Such words are "tidy" and "industrious." Both are normally used to commend; but we can say, without any hint of irony, "too tidy" or "too industrious." It is the descriptive meaning of these words that is most firmly attached to them; and therefore although we must for certain purposes class them as value-words (for if we treat them as purely descriptive, logical errors result), they are so in a less full sense than "good." If the evaluative meaning of a word, which was primary, comes to be secondary, that is a sign that the standard to which the word appeals has become conventional. It is, of course, impossible to say *exactly* when this has happened; it is a process like the coming of winter.

Although the evaluative meaning of "good" is primary, the secondary descriptive meaning is never wholly absent. Even when we are using the word "good" evaluatively in order to set up a new standard, the word still has a descriptive meaning, not in the sense that it is used to *convey* information, but in the sense that its use in setting up the new standard is an essential preliminary—like definition in the case of a purely descriptive word—to its subsequent use with a new descriptive meaning. It is also to be noticed that the relative prominence of the descriptive and evaluative meanings of "good" varies according to the class of objects within which commendation is being given. We may illustrate this by taking two extreme examples. If I talk of a "good egg," it is at once known to what description of egg I am referring—namely, one that is not decomposed. Here the descriptive meaning predominates, because we have very fixed standards for assessing the goodness of eggs. On the other hand, if I say that a poem is a good one, very little information is given about what description of poem it is—for there is no accepted standard of goodness in poems. But it must not be thought that "good egg" is exclusively descriptive, or "good poem" exclusively evaluative. If, as the Chinese are alleged to do, we chose to eat eggs that are decomposed, we should call that kind of egg good, just as, because we choose to eat game that is slightly decomposed, we call it "well hung" (compare also the expression "good Stilton cheese"). And if I said that a poem was good, and was not a very eccentric person, my hearer would be justified that the poem was not "Happy Birthday to You"!

In general, the more fixed and accepted the standard, the more information is conveyed. But it must not be thought that the evaluative force of the word varies at all exactly in inverse proportion to the descriptive. The two vary independently: where a standard is firmly established and is as firmly believed in, a judgment containing "good" may be highly informative, without being any the less commendatory. Consider the following description of the Oxford Sewage Farm:

> The method employed is primitive but efficient. The farm is unsightly, obnoxious to people dwelling near it, and not very remunerative, but the effluent from it is, in the technical sense, good.

Now here, as may be seen by consulting handbooks on the subject, there are perfectly well recognized tests for determining whether effluent is good or bad. One manual gives a simple field test, and another gives a series of more comprehensive tests which take up seventeen pages. This might tempt us to say that the word is used in a purely descriptive sense and has no evaluative force. But, although admittedly in calling effluent good in this technical sense we are commending it as effluent and not as perfume, we are nevertheless commending it; it is not a neutral chemical or biological fact about it that is good; to say that it was bad would be to give a very good reason for sacking the sewage-farmer or taking other steps to see that it was good in future. The proper comment on such a lapse was made by a former Archbishop of York, speaking to the Congress of the Royal Sanitary Institute, 1912.

> There is now, I hope, no need of the trenchant eloquence of that noble-hearted pioneer of sanitary science, Charles Kingsley, to insist that it is not religion, but something more nearly approaching blasphemy, to say that an outbreak of disease is God's will being done, when patently it is man's duty which is being left undone.

It is true that, if the word "good" in a certain sentence has very little evaluative meaning, it is likely that it has a fair amount of descriptive meaning, and vice versa. That is because, if it had very little of either, it would have very little meaning at all, and would not be worth uttering. To this extent the meanings vary inversely. But this is only a tendency; we may do justice to the logical phenomena by saying that "good" normally has at least some of both sorts of meaning; that it normally has sufficient of both sorts taken together to make it worth uttering; and that, provided that the first two conditions are satisfied, the amounts of the two sorts of meaning vary independently.

There are, however, cases in which we use the word "good" with no commendatory meaning at all. We must distinguish several kinds of such non-commendatory uses. The first has been called the *inverted-commas* use. If I were not accustomed to commend any but the most modern styles of architecture, I might still say "The new chamber of the House of Commons is very good Gothic revival." I might mean this in several senses. The first is that in which it is equivalent to "a good example to choose, if one is seeking to illustrate the typical features of Gothic revival" or "a good specimen of Gothic revival." This is a specialized evaluative sense, with which we are not here concerned. I might mean, on the other hand, "genuinely preferable to most other examples of Gothic revival, and therefore to be commended *within* the class of Gothic revival buildings in general." With this sense, too, we are not now concerned; it is a commendatory use, with a limited class of comparison. The sense with which we are concerned is that in which it means, roughly, "the sort of Gothic revival building about which a certain sort of people—you know who—would say 'that is a good building.' " It is characteristic of this use of "good" that in expanding it we often want to put the word "good" inside inverted commas; hence the name. We are, in this use, not making a value-judgment ourselves, but alluding to the value-judgment of other people. This type of use is extremely important for the logic of moral judgments, in which it has caused some confusion.

It is to be noticed that it is easiest to use "good" in an inverted-commas sense, when a certain class of people, who are sufficiently numerous and prominent for their value-judgments to be well known (e.g. the "best" people in any field), have a rigid standard of commendation for that class of object. In such cases, the inverted-commas use can verge into an *ironic* use, in which not only is no commendation being given, but rather the reverse. If I had a low opinion of Carlo Dolci, I might say "If you want to see a really 'good' Carlo Dolci, go and look at one in. . . . "

There is another use in which the absence of evaluative content is not sufficiently obvious to the speaker for us to call it either an inverted-commas or an ironic use. This is the *conventional* use, in which the speaker is merely paying lip-service to a convention, by commending, or saying commendatory things about, an object just because everyone else does. I might, if I myself had no preference at all about the design of furniture, still say "This piece of furniture is of good design," not because I wished to guide my own or anyone else's choice of furniture, but simply because I had been taught the characteristics which are generally held to be criteria of good design, and wished to show that I had "good taste" in furniture. It would be difficult in such a case to say whether I was evaluating the furniture or not. If I were not a logician, I should not ask myself the questions which would determine whether I was. Such a question would be "If someone (not connected in any way with the furniture trade), consistently and regardless of cost filled his house with furniture not conforming to the canons by which you judge the design of this furniture to be good, would you regard that as evidence that he did not agree with you?" If I replied "No, I would not; for what furniture is of good design is one question, and what furniture one chooses for oneself is another," then we might conclude that I had not been really commending the design by calling it good, but only paying lip-service to a convention. . . .

These are only some of the many ways in which we use the word "good." A logician cannot do justice to the infinite subtlety of language; all he can do is point out some of the main features of our use of a word, and thereby put people on their guard against the main dangers. A full understanding of the logic of value-terms can only be achieved by continual and sensitive attention to the way we use them.

COMMENDING AND CHOOSING

It is now time to inquire into the reasons for the logical features of "good" that we have been describing and to ask why it is that it has this peculiar combination of evaluative and descriptive meaning. The reason will be found in the purposes for which it, like other value-words, is used in our discourse. The examination of these purposes will reveal the relevance of the matters discussed in the first part of this book to the study of evaluative language.

I have said that the primary function of the word "good" is to commend. We have, therefore, to inquire what commending is. When we commend or condemn anything, it is always in order, at least indirectly, to guide choices, our own or other people's, now or in the future. Suppose that I say, "The South Bank Exhibition is very good." In what context should I appropriately say this, and what would be my purpose in so doing? It would be natural for me to say it to someone who was wondering whether to go to London to see the Exhibition, or, if he was in London, whether to pay it a visit. It would, however, be too much to say that the reference to choices is always as direct as this. An American returning from London to New York, and speaking to some people who had no intention of going to London in the near future, might still make the same remark. In order, therefore, to show that critical value-judgments are all ultimately related to choices, and would not be made if they were not so related, we require to ask, for what purpose we have standards.

It has been pointed out by Mr. Urmson that we do not speak generally of "good" wireworms. This is because we never have any occasion for choosing between wireworms, and therefore require no guidance in so doing. We therefore need to have no standards for wireworms. But it is easy to imagine circumstances in which this situation might alter. Suppose that wireworms came into use as a special kind of bait for fishermen. Then we might speak of having dug up a very good wireworm (one, for example, that was exceptionally fat and attractive to fish), just as now, no doubt, sea-fishermen might talk of having dug up a very good lugworm. We only have standards for a class of objects, we only talk of the virtues of one specimen against another, we only use value-words about them, when occasions are known to exist, or are conceivable, in which we, or someone else, would have to choose between specimens. We should not call pictures good or bad if no one ever had the choice of seeing them, or not seeing them (or of studying them or not studying them in the way that art students study pictures, or of buying them or not buying them). Lest, by the way, I should seem to have introduced a certain vagueness by specifying so many alternative kinds of choices, it must be pointed out that the matter can, if desired, be made as precise as we require; for we can specify, when we have called a picture a good one, within what class we have called it good; for example, we can say "I meant a good picture to study, but not to buy."

Some further examples may be given. We should not speak of good sunsets, unless sometimes the decision had to be made, whether to go to the window to look at the sunset; we should not speak of good billiard-cues, unless sometimes we had to choose one billiard-cue in preference to another; we should not speak of good men unless we had the choice, what sort of men to try to become. Leibniz, when he spoke of "the best of all possible worlds," had in mind a creator choosing between the possibilities. The choice that is envisaged need not ever occur, nor even be expected ever to occur; it is enough for it to be envisaged as occurring, in order that we should be able to make a value-judgment with reference to it. It must be admitted, however, that the most useful value-judgments are those which have references to choices that we might very likely have to make.

CONTRACTARIANISM

John Rawls

I

It might seem at first sight that the concepts of justice and fairness are the same, and that there is no reason to distinguish them, or to say that one is more fundamental than the other. I think that this impression is mistaken. In this paper I wish to show that the fundamental idea in the concept of justice is fairness; and I wish to offer an analysis of the concept of justice from this point of view. To bring out the force of this claim, and the analysis based upon it, I shall then argue that it is this aspect of justice for which utilitarianism, in its classical form, is unable to account, but which is expressed, even if misleadingly, by the idea of the social contract.

To start with I shall develop a particular conception of justice by stating and commenting upon two principles which specify it, and by considering the circumstances and conditions under which they may be thought to arise. The principles defining this conception, and the conception itself, are, of course, familiar. It may be possible, however, by using the notion of fairness as a framework, to assemble and to look at them in a new way. Before stating this conception, however, the following preliminary matters should be kept in mind.

Throughout I consider justice only as a virtue of social institutions, or what I shall call practices. The principles of justice are regarded as formulating restrictions as to how practices may define positions and offices, and assign thereto powers and liabilities, rights and duties. Justice as a virtue of particular actions or of persons I do not take up at all. It is important to distinguish these various subjects of justice, since the meaning of the concept varies according to whether it is applied to practices, particular actions, or persons. These meanings are, indeed, connected, but they are not identical. I shall confine my discussion to the sense of justice as applied to practices, since this sense is the basic one. Once it is understood, the other senses should go quite easily.

Justice is to be understood in its customary sense as representing but *one* of the many virtues of social institutions, for these may be antiquated, inefficient, degrading, or any number of other things, without being unjust. Justice is not to be confused with an all-inclusive vision of a good society; it is only one part of any such conception. It is important, for example, to distinguish that sense of equality which is an aspect of the concept of justice from that sense of equality which belongs to a more comprehensive social ideal. There may well be inequalities which one concedes are just, or at least not unjust, but which, nevertheless, one wishes, on other grounds, to do away with. I shall focus attention, then, on the usual sense of justice in which it is essentially the elimination of arbitrary distinctions and the establishment, within the structure of a practice, of a proper balance between competing claims.

Finally, there is no need to consider the principles discussed below as *the* principles of justice. For the moment it is sufficient that they are typical of a family of principles normally associated with the concept of justice. The way in which the principles of this family resemble one another, as shown by the background against which they may be thought to arise, will be made clear by the whole of the subsequent argument.

II

The conception of justice which I want to develop may be stated in the form of two principles as follows: first, each person participating in a practice, or affected by it, has an equal right to the most extensive liberty compatible with a like liberty for all; and second, inequalities are arbitrary unless it is reasonable to expect that they will work out for everyone's advantage, and provided the positions and offices to which they attach, or from which they may be gained, are open to all. These principles express justice as a complex of three ideas: liberty, equality, and reward for services contributing to the common good.

The term "person" is to be construed variously depending on the circumstances. On some occasions it will mean human individuals, but in others it may refer to nations, provinces, business firms, churches, teams, and so on. The principles of justice apply in all these instances, although there is a certain logical priority to the case of human individuals. As I shall use the term "person," it will be ambiguous in the manner indicated.

The first principle holds, of course, only if other things are equal: that is, while there must always be a justification for departing from the initial position of equal liberty (which is defined by the pattern of rights and duties, powers and liabilities, established by a practice), and the burden of proof is placed on him who would depart from it; nevertheless, there can be, and often there is, a justification for doing so. Now, that similar particular cases, as defined by a practice, should be treated similarly as they arise, is part of the very concept of a practice; it is involved in the notion of an activity in accordance with rules. The first principle expresses an analogous conception, but as applied to the structure of practices themselves. It holds, for example, that there is a presumption against the distinctions and classifications made by legal systems and other practices to the extent that they infringe on the original and equal liberty of the persons participating in them. The second principle defines how this presumption may be rebutted.

It might be argued at this point that justice requires only an equal liberty. If, however, a greater liberty were possible for all without loss or conflict, then it would be irrational to settle on a lesser liberty. There is no reason for circumscribing rights unless their exercise would be incompatible, or would render the practice defining them less effective. Therefore no serious distortion of the concept of justice is likely to follow from including within it the concept of the greatest equal liberty.

The second principle defines what sorts of inequalities are permissible; it specifies how the presumption laid down by the first principle may be put aside. Now by inequalities it is best to understand not *any* differences between offices and positions, but differences in the benefits and burdens attached to them either directly or indirectly, such as prestige and wealth, or liability to taxation and compulsory services. Players in a game do not protest against there being different positions, such as batter, pitcher, catcher, and the like, nor to there being various privileges and powers as specified by the rules; nor do the citizens of a country object to there being the different offices of government such as president, senator, governor, judge, and so on, each with their special rights and duties. It is not differences of this kind that are normally thought of as inequalities, but differences in the resulting distribution established by a practice, or made possible by it, of the things men strive to attain or avoid. Thus they may complain about the pattern of honors and rewards set up by a practice (e.g., the privileges and salaries of government officials) or they may object to the distribution of power and wealth which results from the various ways in which men avail themselves of the opportunities allowed by it (e.g., the concentration of wealth which may develop in a free price system allowing large entrepreneurial or speculative gains).

It should be noted that the second principle holds that an inequality is allowed only if there is reason to believe that the practice with the inequality, or resulting in it, will work for the advantage of *every* party engaging in it. Here it is important to stress that *every* party must gain from the inequality. Since the principle applies to practices, it implies that the representative man in every office or position defined by a practice, when he views it as a going concern, must find it reasonable to prefer his conditions and prospects with the inequality to what they would be under the practice without it. The principle excludes, therefore, the justification of inequalities on the grounds that the disadvantages of those in one position are outweighed by the disadvantages of those in another position. This rather simple restriction is the main modification I wish to make in the utilitarian principle as usually understood. When coupled with the notion of a practice, it is a restriction of consequence, and one which some utilitarians, for example, Hume and Mill, have used in their discussions of justice without realizing apparently its significance, or at least without calling attention to it. Why it is a significant modification of principle, changing one's conception of justice entirely, the whole of my argument will show.

Further, it is also necessary that the various offices to which special benefits or burdens attach are open to all. It may be, for example, to the common advantage, as just defined, to attach special benefits to certain offices. Perhaps by doing so the requisite talent can be attracted to them and encouraged to give its best efforts. But any offices having special benefits must be won in a fair competition in which contestants are judged on their merits. If some offices were not open, those excluded would normally be justified in feeling unjustly treated, even if they benefited from the greater efforts of those who were allowed to compete for them. Now if one can assume that offices are open, it is necessary only to consider the design of practices themselves and how they jointly, as a system, work together. It will be a mistake to focus attention on the varying relative positions of particular persons, who may be known to us by their proper names, and to require that each such change, as a once for all transaction viewed in isolation, must be in itself just. It is the system of practices which is to be judged, and judged from a general point of view: unless one is prepared to criticize it from the standpoint of a representative man holding some particular office, one has no complaint against it.

III

Given these principles, one might try to derive them from *a priori* principles of reason, or claim that they were known by intuition. These are familiar enough steps and, at least in the case of the first principle, might be made with some success. Usually, however, such arguments, made at the point, are unconvincing. They are not likely to lead to an understanding of the basis of the principles of justice, not at least as principles of justice. I wish, therefore, to look at the principles in a different way.

Imagine a society of persons amongst whom a certain system of practices is *already* well-established. Now suppose that by and large they are mutually self-interested; their allegiance to their established practices is normally founded on the prospect of self-advantage. One need not assume that, in all senses of the term "person," the persons in this society are mutually self-interested. If the characterization as mutually self-interested applies when the line of division is the family, it may still be true that members of families are bound by ties of sentiment and affection and willingly acknowledge duties in contradiction to self-interest. Mutual self-interestedness in the relations between families, nations, churches, and the like, is commonly associated with intense loyalty and devotion on the part of individual members. Therefore, one can form a more realistic conception of this society if one thinks of mutually self-interested families, or some other association. Further, it is not necessary to suppose that these persons are mutually self-interested under all circumstances, but only in the usual situation in which they participate in their common practices.

Now suppose also that these persons are rational: they know their own interests more or less accurately; they are capable of tracing out the likely consequences of adopting one practice rather than another; they are capable of adhering to a course of action once they have decided upon it; they can resist present temptations and the enticements of immediate gain; and the bare knowledge or perception of the difference between their condition and that of others is not, within certain limits and in itself, a source of great dissatisfaction. Only the last point adds anything to the usual definition of rationality. This definition should allow, I think, for the idea that a rational man would not be greatly downcast from knowing, or seeing, that others are in a better position than himself, unless he thought their being so was the result of injustice, or the consequence of letting chance work itself out for no useful common purpose, and so on. So if these persons strike us as unpleasantly egoistic, they are at least free in some degree from the fault of envy.

Finally, assume that these persons have roughly similar needs and interests, or needs and interests in various ways complementary, so that fruitful cooperation amongst them is possible; and suppose that they are sufficiently equal in power and ability to guarantee that in normal circumstances none is able to dominate the others. This condition (as well as the others) may seem excessively vague; but in view of the conception of justice to which the argument leads, there seems no reason for making it more exact here.

Since these persons are conceived as engaging in their common practices, which are already established, there is no question of our supposing them to come together to deliberate as to how they will set these practices up for the first time. Yet we can imagine that from time to time they discuss with one another whether any of them has a legitimate complaint against their established institutions. Such discussions are perfectly natural in any normal society. Now suppose that they have settled on doing this in the following way. They first try to arrive at the principles by which complaints, and so practices themselves, are to be judged. Their procedure for this is to let each person propose the principles upon which he wishes his complaints to be tried with the understanding that, if acknowledged, the complaints of others will be similarly tried, and that no complaints will be heard at all until everyone is roughly of one mind as to how complaints are to be judged. They each understand further that the principles proposed and acknowledged on this occasion are binding on future occasions. Thus each will be wary of proposing a principle which would give him a peculiar advantage, in his present circumstances, supposing it to be accepted. Each person knows that he will be bound by it in future circumstances the peculiarities of which cannot be known, and which might well be such that the principle is then to his disadvantage. The idea is that everyone should be required to make *in advance* a firm commitment, which others also may reasonably be expected to make, and that no one be given the opportunity to tailor the canons of a legitimate complaint to fit his own special condition, and then to discard them when they no longer suit his purpose. Hence each person will propose principles of a general kind which will, to a large degree, gain their sense from the various applications to be made of them, the particular circumstances of which being as yet unknown. These principles will express the conditions in accordance with which each is the least unwilling to have his interests limited in the design of practices, given the competing interests of the others, on the supposition that the interests of others will be limited likewise. The restrictions which would so arise might be thought of as those a person would keep in mind if he were designing a practice in which his enemy were to assign him his place.

The two main parts of this conjectural account have a definite significance. The character and respective situations of the parties reflect the typical circumstances in which questions of justice arise. The procedure whereby principles are proposed and acknowledged represents constraints, analogous to those of having a morality, whereby rational and mutually self-interested persons are brought to act reasonably. Thus the first part reflects the fact that questions of justice arise when conflicting claims are made upon the design of a practice and where it is taken for granted that each person will insist, as far as possible, on what he considers his rights. It is typical of cases of justice, to involve persons who are pressing on one another their claims, between which a fair balance or equilibrium must be found. On the other hand, as expressed by the second part, having a morality must at least imply the acknowledgment of principles as impartially applying to one's own conduct as well as to another's, and moreover principles which may constitute a constraint, or limitation, upon the pursuit of one's own interests. There are, of course, other aspects of having a morality: the acknowledgment of moral principles must show itself in accepting a reference to them as reasons for limiting one's claims, in acknowledging the burden of providing a special explanation, or excuse, when one acts contrary to them, or else in showing shame and remorse and a desire to make amends, and so on. It is sufficient to remark here that having a morality is analogous to having made a firm commitment in advance; for one must acknowledge the principles of morality even when to one's disadvantage. A man whose moral judgments always coincided with his interests could be suspected of having no morality at all.

Thus the two parts of the foregoing account are intended to mirror the kinds of circumstances in which questions of justice arise and the constraints of having a morality would impose upon persons so situated. In this way one can see how the acceptance of the principles of justice might come about, for given all these conditions as described, it would be natural if the two principles of justice were to be acknowledged. Since there is no way for anyone to win special advantages for himself, each might consider it reasonable to acknowledge equality as an initial principle. There is, however, no reason why they should regard this position as final: for if there are inequalities which satisfy the second principle, the immediate gain which equality would allow can be considered as intelligently invested in view of its future return. If, as is quite likely, these inequalities work as incentives to draw out better efforts, the members of this society may look upon them as concessions to human nature: they, like us, may think that people ideally should want to serve one another. But as they are mutually self-interested, their acceptance of these inequalities is merely the acceptance of the relations in which they actually stand, and a recognition of the motives which lead them to engage in their common practices. *They* have no title to complain of one another. And so provided that the conditions of the principle are met, there is no reason why they should not allow such inequalities. Indeed, it would be short-sighted of them not to do so, and could result, in most cases, only from their being dejected by the bare knowledge, or perception, that others are better situated. Each person will, however, insist on an advantage to himself, and so on a common advantage, for none is willing to sacrifice anything for the others.

These remarks are not offered as a rigorous proof that persons conceived and situated as the conjectural account supposes, and required to adopt the procedures described, would settle on the two principles of justice. For such a proof a more elaborate and formal argument would have to be given: there remain certain details to be filled in, and various alternatives to be ruled out. The argument should, however, be taken as a proof, or a sketch of a proof; for the proposition I seek to establish is a necessary one, that is, it is intended as a theorem: namely, that when mutually self-interested and rational persons confront one another in typical circumstances of justice, and when they are required by a procedure expressing the constraints of having a morality to jointly acknowledge principles by which their claims on the design of their common practices are to be judged, they will settle on these two principles as restrictions governing the assignment of rights and duties, and thereby accept them as limiting their rights against one another. It is this theorem which accounts for these principles as principles of justice, and explains how they come to be associated with this moral concept. Moreover, this theorem is analogous to those about human conduct in other branches of social thought. That is, a simplified situation is described in which rational persons pursuing certain ends and related to one another in a definite way, are required to act subject to certain limitations; then, given this situation, it is shown that they will act in a certain manner. Failure so to act would imply that one or more of the assumptions does not obtain. The foregoing account aims to establish, or to sketch, a theorem in this sense; the aim of the argument is to show the basis for saying that the principles of justice may be regarded as those principles which arise when the constraints of having a morality are imposed upon rational persons in typical circumstances of justice.

IV

These ideas are, of course, connected with a familiar way of thinking about justice which goes back at least to the Greek Sophists, and which regards the acceptance of the principles of justice as a compromise between persons of roughly equal power who enforce their will on each other if they could, but who, in view of the equality of forces amongst them and for the sake of their own peace and security acknowledge certain forms of conduct in so far as prudence seems to require. Justice is thought of as a pact between rational egoists the stability of which is dependent on a balance of power and a similarity of circumstances. While the previous account is connected with this tradition, and with its most recent variant, the theory of games, it differs from it in several important respects which, to forestall misinterpretations, I will set out here.

First, I wish to use the previous conjectural account of the background of justice as a way of analyzing the concept. I do not want, therefore, to be interpreted as assuming a general theory of human motivation: when I suppose that the parties are mutually self-interested, and are not willing to have their (substantial) interests sacrificed to others, I am referring to their conduct and motives as they are taken for granted in cases where questions of justice ordinarily arise. Justice is the virtue of practices where there are assumed to be competing interests and conflicting claims, and where it is supposed that persons will press their rights on each other. That persons are mutually self-interested in certain situations and for certain purposes is what gives rise to the question of justice in practices covering those circumstances. Among an association of saints, if such a community could really exist, the disputes about justice could hardly occur; for they would all work selflessly together for one end, the glory of God as defined by their common religion, and reference to this end would settle every question of right. The justice of practices does not come up until there are several different parties (whether we think of them as individuals, associations, or nations, and so on, is irrelevant) who do press their claims on one another, and who do regard themselves as representatives of interests which deserve to be considered. Thus the previous account involves no general theory of human motivation. Its intent is simply to incorporate into the conception of justice the relations of men to one another which set the stage for questions of justice. It makes no difference how wide or general these relations are, as this matter does not bear on the analysis of the concept.

Again, in contrast to the various conceptions of the social contract, the several parties do not establish any particular society or practice; they do not covenant to obey a particular sovereign body or to accept a given constitution. Nor do they, as in the theory of games (in certain respects a marvelously sophisticated development of this tradition), decide on individual strategies adjusted to their respective circumstances in the game. What the parties do is to *jointly* acknowledge certain *principles* of appraisal relating to their common *practices* either as already established or merely proposed. They accede to standards of judgment, not to a given practice; they do not make any specific agreement, or bargain, or adopt a particular strategy. The subject of their acknowledgment is, therefore, very general indeed; it is simply the acknowledgment of certain principles of judgment, fulfilling certain general conditions, to be used in criticizing the arrangement of their common affairs. The relations of mutual self-interest between the parties who are similarly circumstanced mirror the conditions under which questions of justice arise, and the procedure by which the principles of judgment are proposed and acknowledged reflects the constraints of having a morality. Each aspect, then, of the preceding hypothetical account serves the purpose of bringing out a feature of the notion of justice. One could, if one liked, view the principles of justice as the "solution" of this highest order "game" of adopting, subject to the procedure described, principles of argument for all coming particular "games" whose peculiarities one can in no way foresee. But this comparison, while no doubt helpful, must not obscure the fact that this highest order "game" is of a special sort. Its significance is that its various pieces represent aspects of the concept of justice.

Finally, I do not, of course, conceive the several parties as necessarily coming together to establish their common practices for the first time. Some institutions may, indeed, be set up *de novo;* but I have framed the preceding account so that it will apply when the full complement of social institutions already exists and represents the result of a long period of development. Nor is the account in any way fictitious. In any society where people reflect on their institutions they will have an idea of what principles of justice would be acknowledged under the conditions described, and there will be occasions when questions of justice are actually discussed in this way. Therefore if their practices do not accord with these principles, this will affect the quality of their social relations. For in this case there will be some recognized situations wherein the parties are mutually aware that one of them is forced to accept what the other would concede is unjust. The foregoing analysis may then be thought as representing the actual quality of relations between persons as defined by practices accepted as just. In such practices the parties will acknowledge the principles on which it is constructed, and the general recognition of this fact shows itself in the absence of resentment and in the sense of being justly treated. Thus one common objection to the theory of the social contract, its apparently historical and fictitious character, is avoided.

V

That the principles of justice may be regarded as arising in the manner described illustrates an important fact about them. Not only does it bring out the idea that justice is a primitive moral notion in that it arises once the concept of morality is imposed on mutually self-interested agents similarly circumstanced, but it emphasizes that, fundamental to justice, is the concept of fairness which relates to right dealing between persons who are cooperating with or competing against one another, as when one speaks of fair games, fair competition, and fair bargains. The question of fairness arises when free persons, who have no authority over one another, are engaging in a joint activity and amongst themselves settling or acknowledging the rules which define it and which determine the respective shares in its benefits and burdens. A practice will strike the parties as fair if none feels that, by participating in it, they or any of the others are taken advantage of, or forced to give in to claims which they do not regard as legitimate. This implies that each has a conception of legitimate claims which he thinks it reasonable for others as well as himself to acknowledge. If one thinks of the principles of justice as arising in the manner described, then they do define this sort of conception. A practice is just or fair, when it satisfies the principles which those who participate in it could propose to one another for mutual acceptance under the aforementioned circumstances. Persons engaged in just, or fair, practice can face one another openly and support their respective positions, should they appear questionable, by reference to principles which it is reasonable to expect each to accept.

It is this notion of the possibility of mutual acknowledgment of principles by free persons who have no authority over one another which makes the concept of fairness fundamental to justice. Only if such acknowledgment is possible can there be true community between persons in their common practices; otherwise their relations will appear to them as founded to some extent on force. If, in ordinary speech, fairness applies more particularly to practices in which there is a choice whether to engage or not (e.g., in games, business competition), and justice to practices in which there is no choice (e.g., in slavery), the element of necessity does not render the conception of mutual acknowledgment inapplicable, although it may make it much more urgent to change unjust than unfair institutions. For one activity in which one can always engage is that of proposing and acknowledging principles to one another supposing each to be similarly circumstanced; and to judge practices by the principles so arrived at is to apply the standard of fairness to them.

Now if the participants in a practice accept its rules as fair, and so have no complaint to lodge against it, there arises a *prima facie* duty (and a corresponding *prima facie* right) of the parties to each other to act in accordance with the practice when it falls upon them to comply. When any number of persons engage in a practice, or conduct a joint undertaking according to rules, and thus restrict their liberty, those who have submitted to these restrictions when required have the right to a similar acquiescence on the part of those who have benefited by their submission. These conditions will obtain if a practice is correctly acknowledged to be fair, for in this case all who participate in it will benefit from it. The rights and duties so arising are special rights and duties in that they depend on previous actions voluntarily undertaken, in this case on the parties having engaged in a common practice and knowingly accepted its benefits. It is not, however, an obligation which presupposes a deliberate performative act in the sense of a promise, or contract, and the like. An unfortunate mistake of proponents of the idea of the social contract was to suppose that political obligation does require some such act, or at least to use language which suggests it. It is sufficient that one has knowingly participated in and accepted the benefits of a practice acknowledged to be fair. This *prima facie* obligation may, of course, be overridden: it may happen, when it comes one's turn to follow a rule, that other considerations will justify not doing so. But one cannot, in general, be released from this obligation by denying the justice of the practice only when it falls on one to obey. If a person rejects a practice, he

should, so far as possible, declare his intention in advance, and avoid participating in it or enjoying its benefits.

This duty I have called that of fair play, but it should be admitted that to
refer to it in this way is, perhaps, to extend the ordinary notion of fairness.
Usually acting unfairly is not so much the breaking of any particular rule,
even if the infraction is difficult to detect (cheating), but taking advantage of
loopholes or ambiguities in rules, availing oneself of unexpected or special
circumstances which make it impossible to enforce them, insisting that rules
be enforced to one's advantage when they should be suspended, and more
generally, acting contrary to the notion of a practice. It is for this reason that
one speaks of the sense of fair play: acting fairly requires more than simply
being able to follow rules; what is fair must often be felt, or perceived, one
wants to say. It is not, however, an unnatural extension of the duty of fair
play to have it include the obligation which participants who have knowingly accepted the benefits of their common practice owe to each other to
act in accordance with it when their performance falls due; for it is usually
considered unfair if someone accepts the benefits of a practice but refuses to
do his part in maintaining it. Thus one might say of the tax-dodger that he
violates the duty of fair play: he accepts the benefits of government but will
not do his part in releasing resources to it; and members of labor unions
often say that fellow workers who refuse to join are being unfair; they refer
to them as "free riders," as persons who enjoy what are the supposed benefits of unionism, higher wages, shorter hours, job security, and the like, but
who refuse to share in its burdens in the form of paying dues, and so on.

The duty of fair play stands beside other *prima facie* duties such as
fidelity and gratitude as a basic moral notion; yet it is not to be confused
with them. These duties are all clearly distinct, as would be obvious from
their definitions. As with any moral duty, that of fair play implies a constraint
on self-interest in particular cases; on occasion it enjoins conduct which a
rational egoist strictly defined would not decide upon. So while justice does
not require of anyone that he sacrifice his interests in that *general position*
and procedure whereby the principles of justice are proposed and acknowledged, it may happen that in particular situations, arising in the context of
engaging in a practice, the duty of fair play will often cross his interests in
the sense that he will be required to forego particular advantages which the
peculiarities of his circumstances might permit him to take. There is, of
course, nothing surprising in this. It is simply the consequence of the firm
commitment which the parties may be supposed to have made, or which
they would make, in the general position, together with the fact that they
have participated in and accepted the benefits of a practice which they
regard as fair.

Now the acknowledgment of this constraint in particular cases, which is
manifested in acting fairly or wishing to make amends, feeling ashamed, and
the like, when one has evaded it, is one of the forms of conduct by which
participants in a common practice exhibit their recognition of each other as
persons with similar interests and capacities. In the same way that, failing a

special explanation, the criterion for the recognition of suffering is helping one who suffers, acknowledging the duty of fair play is a necessary part of the criterion for recognizing another as a person with similar interests and feelings as oneself. A person who never under any circumstances showed a wish to help others in pain would show, at the same time, that he did not recognize that they were in pain; nor could he have any feelings or affection or friendship for anyone; for having these feelings implies, failing special circumstances, that he comes to their aid when they are suffering. Recognition that another is a person in pain shows itself in sympathetic action; this primitive natural response is one of those responses upon which the various forms of moral conduct are built.

Similarly, the acceptance of the duty of fair play by participants in a common practice is a reflection in each person of the recognition of the aspirations and interests of the others to be realized by their joint activity. Failing a special explanation, their acceptance of it is a necessary part of the criterion for their recognizing one another as persons with similar interests and capacities, as the conception of their relations in the general position supposes them to be. Otherwise they would show no recognition of one another as persons with similar capacities and interests, and indeed, in some cases perhaps hypothetical, they would not recognize one another as persons at all, but as complicated objects involved in a complicated activity. To recognize another as a person one must respond to him and act towards him in certain ways; and these ways are intimately connected with the various *prima facie* duties. Acknowledging these duties in *some* degree, and so having the elements of morality, is not a matter of choice, or of intuiting moral qualities, or a matter of the expression of feelings or attitudes (the three interpretations between which philosophical opinion frequently oscillates); it is simply the possession of one of the forms of conduct in which the recognition of others as persons is manifested.

These remarks are unhappily obscure. Their main purpose here, however, is to forestall, together with the remarks in Section IV, the misinterpretation that, on the view presented, the acceptance of justice and the acknowledgment of the duty of fair play depends in everyday life solely on there being a *de facto* balance of forces between the parties. It would indeed be foolish to underestimate the importance of such a balance in securing justice; but it is not the only basis thereof. The recognition of one another as persons with similar interests and capacities engaged in a common practice must, failing a special explanation, show itself in the acceptance of the principles of justice and the acknowledgment of the duty of fair play.

The conception at which we have arrived, then, is that the principles of justice may be thought of as arising once the constraints of having a morality are imposed upon rational and mutually self-interested parties who are related and situated in a special way. A practice is just if it is in accordance with the principles which all who participate in it might reasonably be expected to propose or to acknowledge before one another when they are similarly circumstanced and required to make a firm commitment in advance without knowledge of what will be their peculiar condition, and thus when it meets standards which the parties could accept as fair should occasion arise for them to debate its merits. Regarding the participants themselves, once persons knowingly engage in a practice which they acknowledge to be fair and accept the benefits of doing so, they are bound by the duty of fair play to follow the rules when it comes their turn to do so, this implies a limitation on their pursuit of self-interest in particular cases.

Now one consequence of this conception is that, where it applies, there is no moral value in the satisfaction of a claim incompatible with it. Such a claim violates the conditions of reciprocity and community amongst persons, and he who presses it, not being willing to acknowledge it when pressed by another, has no grounds for complaint when it is denied; whereas he against whom it is pressed can complain. As it cannot be mutually acknowledged it is a resort to coercion; granting the claim is possible only if one party can compel acceptance of what the other will not admit. But it makes no sense to concede claims the denial of which cannot be complained of in preference to claims the denial of which can be objected to. Thus in deciding on the justice of a practice it is not enough to ascertain that it answers to wants and interests in the fullest and most effective manner. For if any of these conflict with justice, they should not be counted, as their satisfaction is no reason at all for having a practice. It would be irrelevant to say, even if true, that it resulted in the greatest satisfaction of desire. In tallying up the merits of a practice one must toss out the satisfaction of interests the claims of which are incompatible with the principles of justice.

VI

The discussion so far has been excessively abstract. While this is perhaps unavoidable, I should now like to bring out some of the features of the conception of justice as fairness by comparing it with the conception of justice in classical utilitarianism as represented by Bentham and Sidgwick, and its counterpart in welfare economics. This conception assimilates justice to benevolence and the latter in turn to the most efficient design of institutions to promote the general welfare. Justice is a kind of efficiency.

Now it is said occasionally that this form of utilitarianism puts no restrictions on what might be a just assignment of rights and duties in that there might be circumstances which, on utilitarian grounds, would justify institutions highly offensive to our ordinary sense of justice. But the classical utilitarian conception is not totally unprepared for this objection. Beginning with the notion that the general happiness can be represented by a social utility function consisting of a sum of individual utility functions with identical weights (this being the meaning of the maxim that each counts for one and no more than one), it is commonly assumed that the utility functions of individuals are similar in all essential respects. Differences between individuals are ascribed to accidents of education and upbringing, and they should not be taken into account. This assumption, coupled with that of diminishing marginal utility, results in a *prima facie* case for equality, for example, of equality in the distribution of income during any given period of time, laying aside indirect effects on the future. But even if utilitarianism is interpreted as having such restrictions built into the utility function, and even if it is supposed that these restrictions have in practice much the same result as the application of the principles of justice (and appear, perhaps, to be ways of expressing these principles in the language of mathematics and psychology), the fundamental idea is very different from the conception of justice as fairness. For one thing, that the principles of justice should be accepted is interpreted as the contingent result of a higher order administrative decision. The form of this decision is regarded as being similar to that of an entrepreneur deciding how much to produce of this or that commodity in view of its marginal revenue, or to that of someone distributing goods to needy persons according to the relative urgency of their wants. The choice between practices is thought of as being made on the basis of the allocation of benefits and burdens to individuals (these being measured by the present capitalized value of their utility over the full period of the practice's existence), which results from the distribution of rights and duties established by a practice.

Moreover, the individuals receiving these benefits are not conceived as being related in any way; they represent so many different directions in which limited resources may be allocated. The value of assigning resources to one direction rather than another depends solely on the preferences and interests of individuals as individuals. The satisfaction of desire has its value irrespective of the moral relations between persons, say as members of a joint undertaking, and of the claims which, in the name of these interests, they are prepared to make on one another: and it is this value which is to be taken into account by the (ideal) legislator who is conceived as adjusting the rules of the system from the center so as to maximize the value of the social utility function.

It is thought that the principles of justice will not be violated by a legal system so conceived provided these executive decisions are correctly made. In this fact the principles of justice are said to have their derivation and explanation; they simply express the most important general features of social institutions in which the administrative problem is solved in the best way. These principles have, indeed, a special urgency because, given the facts of human nature, so much depends on them; and this explains the peculiar quality of the moral feelings associated with justice. This assimilation of justice to a higher order executive decision, certainly a striking conception, is central to classical utilitarianism; and it also brings out its profound individualism, in one sense of this ambiguous word. It regards persons as so many *separate* directions in which benefits and burdens may be assigned; and the value of the satisfaction or dissatisfaction of desire is not thought to depend in any way on the moral relations in which individuals stand, or on the kinds of claims which they are willing, in the pursuit of their interests, to press on each other.

VII

Many social decisions are, of course, of an administrative nature. Certainly this is so when it is a matter of social utility in what one may call its ordinary sense: that is, when it is a question of the efficient design of social institutions for the use of common means to achieve common ends. In this case either the benefits and burdens may be assumed to be impartially distributed, or the question of distribution is misplaced, as in the instance of maintaining public order and security or national defense. But as an interpretation of the basis of the principles of justice, classical utilitarianism is mistaken. It *permits* one to argue, for example, that slavery is unjust on the grounds that the advantages to the slaveholder as slaveholder do not counterbalance the disadvantages to the slave and to society at large burdened by a comparatively inefficient system of labor. Now the conception of justice as fairness, when applied to the practice of slavery with its offices of slaveholder and slave, would not allow one to consider the advantages of the slaveholder in the first place. As that office is not in accordance with principles which could be mutually acknowledged, the gains accruing to the slaveholder, assuming them to exist, cannot be counted as in *any* way mitigating the injustice of the practice. The question whether these gains outweigh the disadvantages to the slave and to society cannot arise, since in considering the justice of slavery these gains have no weight at all which requires that they be overridden. Where the conception of justice as fairness applies, slavery is *always* unjust.

I am not, of course, suggesting the absurdity that the classical utilitarians approved of slavery. I am only rejecting a type of argument which their view allows them to use in support of their disapproval of it. The conception of justice as derivative from efficiency implies that judging the justice of a practice is always, in principle at least, a matter of weighing up advantages and disadvantages, each having an intrinsic value or disvalue as the satisfaction of interests, irrespective of whether or not these interests necessarily involve acquiescence in principles which could not be mutually acknowledged. Utilitarianism cannot account for the fact that slavery is always unjust, nor for the fact that it would be recognized as irrelevant in defeating the accusation of injustice for one person to say to another, engaged with him in a common practice and debating its merits, that nevertheless it allowed of the greatest satisfaction of desire. The charge of injustice cannot be rebutted in this way. If justice were derivative from a higher order executive efficiency, this would not be so.

But now, even if it is taken as established that, so far as the ordinary conception of justice goes, slavery is always unjust (that is, slavery by definition violates commonly recognized principles of justice), the classical utilitarian would surely reply that these principles, as other moral principles subordinate to that of utility, are only generally correct. It is simply for the most part true that slavery is less efficient than other institutions; and while common sense may define the concept of justice so that slavery is unjust, nevertheless, where slavery would lead to the greatest satisfaction of desire, it is not wrong. Indeed, it is then right, and for the very same reason that justice, as ordinarily understood, is usually right. If, as ordinarily understood, slavery is always unjust, to this extent the utilitarian conception of justice might be admitted to differ from that of common moral opinion. Still the utilitarian would want to hold that, as a matter of moral principle, his view is correct in giving no special weight to considerations of justice beyond that allowed for by the general presumption of effectiveness. And this, he claims, is as it should be. The everyday opinion is morally in error, although, indeed, it is a useful error, since it protects rules of general high utility.

The question, then, relates not simply to the analysis of the concept of justice as common sense defines it, but the analysis of it in the wider sense as to how much weight considerations of justice, as defined, are to have when laid against other kinds of moral considerations. Here again I wish to argue that reasons of justice have a *special* weight for which only the conception of justice as fairness can account. Moreover, it belongs to the concept of justice that they do have this special weight. While Mill recognized that this was so, he thought that it could be accounted for by the special urgency of the moral feelings which naturally support principles of such high utility. But it is a mistake to resort to the urgency of feeling; as with the appeal to intuition, it manifests a failure to pursue the question far enough. The special weight of considerations of justice can be explained from the conception of justice as fairness. It is only necessary to elaborate a bit what has already been said as follows.

If one examines the circumstances in which a certain tolerance of slavery is justified, or perhaps better, excused, it turns out that these are of a rather special sort. Perhaps slavery exists as an inheritance from the past and it proves necessary to dismantle it piece by piece; at times slavery may conceivably be an advance on previous institutions. Now while there may be some excuse for slavery in special conditions, it is never an excuse for it that it is sufficiently advantageous to the slaveholder to outweigh the disadvantages to the slave and to society. A person who argues in this way is not perhaps making a wildly irrelevant remark; but he is guilty of a moral fallacy. There is disorder in his conception of the ranking of moral principles. For the slaveholder, by his own admission, has no moral title to the advantages which he receives as a slaveholder. He is no more prepared than the slave to acknowledge the principle upon which is founded the respective positions in which they both stand. Since slavery does not accord with principles which they could mutually acknowledge, they each may be supposed to agree that it is unjust: it grants claims which it ought not to grant and in doing so denies claims which it ought not to deny. Amongst persons in a general position who are debating the form of their common practices, it cannot, therefore, be offered as a reason for a practice that, in conceding these very claims that ought to be denied, it nevertheless meets existing interests more effectively. By their very nature the satisfaction of these claims is without weight and cannot enter into any tabulation of advantages and disadvantages.

Furthermore, it follows from the concept of morality that, to the extent that the slaveholder recognizes his position vis-à-vis the slave to be unjust, he would not choose to press his claims. His not wanting to receive his special advantages is one of the ways in which he shows that he thinks slavery is unjust. It would be fallacious for the legislator to suppose, then, that it is a ground for having a practice that it brings advantage greater than disadvantages, if those for whom the practice is designed, to whom the advantages flow, acknowledge that they have no moral title to them and do not wish to receive them.

For these reasons the principles of justice have a special weight; and with respect to the principle of the greatest satisfaction of desire, as cited in the general position among those discussing the merits of their common practices, the principles of justice have an absolute weight. In this sense they are not contingent; and this is why their force is greater than can be accounted for by the general presumption (assuming that there is one) of the effectiveness, in the utilitarian sense, of practices which in fact satisfy them.

If one wants to continue using the concepts of classical utilitarianism, one will have to say, to meet this criticism, that at least the individual or social utility functions must be so defined that no value is given to the satisfaction of interests the representative claims of which violate the principles of justice. In this way it is no doubt possible to include these principles within the form of the utilitarian conception; but to do so is, of course, to change its inspiration altogether as a moral conception. For it is to incorporate within its principles which cannot be understood on the basis of a higher order executive decision aiming at the greatest satisfaction of desire.

It is worth remarking, perhaps, that this criticism of utilitarianism does not depend on whether or not the two assumptions, that of individuals having similar utility functions and that of diminishing marginal utility, are interpreted as psychological propositions to be supported or refuted by experience, or as moral and political principles expressed in a somewhat technical language. There are, certainly, several advantages in taking them in the latter fashion. For one thing, one might say that this is what Bentham and others really meant by them, at least as shown by how they were used in arguments for social reform. More importantly, one could hold that the best way to defend the classical utilitarian view is to interpret these assumptions as moral and political principles. It is doubtful whether, taken as psychological propositions, they are true of men in general as we know them under normal conditions. On the other hand, utilitarians would not have wanted to propose them merely as practical working principles of legislation, or as expedient maxims to guide reform, given the egalitarian sentiments of modern society. When pressed they might well have invoked the idea of a more or less equal capacity of men in relevant respects if given an equal chance in a just society. But if the argument above regarding slavery is correct, then granting these assumptions as moral and political principles makes no difference. To view individuals as equally fruitful lines for the allocation of benefits, even as a matter of moral principle, still leaves the mistaken notion that the satisfaction of desire has value in itself irrespective of the relations between persons as members of a common practice, and irrespective of the claims upon one another which the satisfaction of interests represents. To see the error of this idea one must give up the conception of justice as an executive decision altogether and refer to the notion of justice as fairness: that participants in a common practice be regarded as having an original and equal liberty and that their common practices be considered unjust unless they accord with principles which persons so circumstanced and related could freely acknowledge before one another, and so could accept as fair. Once the emphasis is put upon the concept of the mutual recognition of principles by participants in a common practice the rules of which are to define their several relations and give form to their claims on one another, then it is clear that the granting of a claim the principle of which could not be acknowledged by each in the general position (that is, in the position in which the parties propose and acknowledge principles before one another) is not a reason for adopting a practice. Viewed in this way, the background of the claim is seen to exclude it from consideration; that it can represent a value in itself arises from the conception of individuals as separate lines for the assignment of benefits, as isolated persons who stand as claimants on an administrative or benevolent largesse. Occasionally persons do so stand to one another; but this is not the general case, nor, more importantly, is it the case when it is a matter of the justice of practices themselves in which participants stand in various relations to be appraised in accordance with standards which they may be expected to acknowledge before one another. Thus however mistaken the notion of the social contract may be as history, and however far it may overreach itself as a general theory of social and political obligation, it does express, suitably interpreted, an essential part of the concept of justice.

VIII

By way of conclusion I should like to make two remarks: first, the original modification of the utilitarian principle (that it require of practices that the offices and positions defined by them be equal unless it is reasonable to suppose that the representative man in *every* office would find the inequality to his advantage), slight as it may appear at first sight, actually has a different conception of justice standing behind it. I have tried to show how this is so by developing the concept of justice as fairness and by indicating how this notion involves the mutual acceptance, from a general position, of the principles on which a practice is founded, and how this in turn requires the exclusion from consideration of claims violating the principles of justice. Thus the slight alteration of principle reveals another family of notions, another way of looking at the concept of justice.

Second, I should like to remark also that I have been dealing with the *concept* of justice. I have tried to set out the kinds of principles upon which judgments concerning the justice of practices may be said to stand. The analysis will be successful to the degree that it expresses the principles involved in these judgments when made by competent persons upon deliberation and reflection. Now every people may be supposed to have the concept of justice, since in the life of every society there must be at least some relations in which the parties consider themselves to be circumstanced and related as the concept of justice as fairness requires. Societies will differ from one another not in having or in failing to have this notion but in the range of cases to which they apply it and in the emphasis which they give to it as compared with other moral concepts.

A firm grasp of the concept of justice itself is necessary if these variations, and the reasons for them, are to be understood. No study of the development of moral ideas and of the differences between them is more sound than the analysis of the fundamental moral concepts upon which it must depend. I have tried, therefore, to give an analysis of the concept of justice which should apply generally, however large a part the concept may have in a given morality, and which can be used in explaining the course of men's thoughts about justice and its relations to other moral concepts. How it is to be used for this purpose is a large topic which I cannot, of course, take up here. I mention it only to emphasize that I have been dealing with the concept of justice itself and to indicate what use I consider such an analysis to have.

VIRTUE ETHICS

Philippa Foot

I

For many years the subject of the virtues and vices was strangely neglected by moralists working within the school of analytic philosophy. The tacitly accepted opinion was that a study of the topic would form no part of the fundamental work of ethics; and since this opinion was apparently shared by philosophers such as Hume, Kant, Mill, G. E. Moore, W. D. Ross, and H. A. Prichard, from whom contemporary moral philosophy has mostly been derived, perhaps the neglect was not so surprising after all. However that may be, things have recently been changing. During the past ten or fifteen years several philosophers have turned their attention to the subject; notably G. H. von Wright and Peter Geach. Von Wright devoted a not at all perfunctory chapter to the virtues in his book *The Varieties of Goodness* published in 1963, and Peter Geach's book called *The Virtues* appeared in 1977. Meanwhile a number of interesting articles on the topic have come out in the journals.

In spite of this recent work, it is best when considering the virtues and vices to go back to Aristotle and Aquinas. I myself have found Plato less helpful, because the individual virtues and vices are not so clearly or consistently distinguished in his work. It is certain, in any case, that the most systematic account is found in Aristotle, and in the blending of Aristotelian and Christian philosophy found in St. Thomas. By and large Aquinas followed Aristotle—sometimes even heroically—where Aristotle gave an opinion, and where St. Thomas is on his own, as in developing the doctrine of the theological virtues of faith, hope and charity, and in his theocentric doctrine of happiness, he still uses an Aristotelian framework where he can: as for instance in speaking of happiness as man's last end. However, there are different emphases and new elements in Aquinas's ethics: often he works things out in far more detail than Aristotle did, and it is possible to learn a great deal from Aquinas that one could not have got from Aristotle. It is my opinion that the *Summa Theologica* is one of the best sources we have for moral philosophy, and moreover that St. Thomas's ethical writings are as useful to the atheist as to the Catholic or other Christian believer.

There is, however, one minor obstacle to be overcome when one goes back to Aristotle and Aquinas for help in constructing a theory of virtues,

---

namely a lack of coincidence between their terminology and our own. For when we talk about the virtues we are not taking as our subject everything to which Aristotle gave the name *aretē* or Aquinas *virtus,* and consequently not everything called a virtue in translations of these authors. "The virtues" to us are the moral virtues whereas *aretē* and *virtus* refer also to arts, and even to excellences of the speculative intellect whose domain is theory rather than practice. And to make things more confusing we find some dispositions called moral virtues in translations from the Greek and Latin, although the class of virtues that Aristotle calls *aretē ēthikai* and Aquinas *virtutes morales* does not exactly correspond with our class of moral virtues. For us there are four cardinal moral virtues: courage, temperance, wisdom and justice. But Aristotle and Aquinas call only three of these virtues moral virtues; practical wisdom (Aristotle's *phronēsis* and Aquinas's *prudentia*) they class with the intellectual virtues, though they point out the close connexions between practical wisdom and what they call moral virtues; and sometimes they even use *aretē* and *virtus* very much as we use "virtue."

I will come back to Aristotle and Aquinas, and shall indeed refer to them frequently in this paper. But I want to start by making some remarks, admittedly fragmentary, about the concept of a moral virtue as we understand the idea.

First of all it seems clear that virtues are, in some general way, beneficial. Human beings do not get on well without them. Nobody can get on well if he lacks courage, and does not have some measure of temperance and wisdom, while communities where justice and charity are lacking are apt to be wretched places to live, as Russia was under the Stalinist terror, or Sicily under the Mafia. But now we must ask to whom the benefit goes, whether to the man who has the virtue or rather to those who have to do with him? In the case of some of the virtues the answer seems clear. Courage, temperance and wisdom benefit both the man who has these dispositions and other people as well; and moral failings such as pride, vanity, worldliness, and avarice harm both their possessor and others, though chiefly perhaps the former. But what about the virtues of charity and justice? These are directly concerned with the welfare of others, and with what is owed to them; and since each may require sacrifice of interest on the part of the virtuous man both may seem to be deleterious to their possessor and beneficial to others. Whether in fact it is so has, of course, been a matter of controversy since Plato's time or earlier. It is a reasonable opinion that on the whole a man is better off being charitable and just, but this is not to say that circumstances may not arise in which he will have to sacrifice everything for charity and justice.

Nor is this the only problem about the relation between virtue and human good. For one very difficult question concerns the relation between justice and the common good. Justice, in the wide sense in which it is understood in discussions of the cardinal virtues, and in this paper, has to do with that to which someone has a right—that which he is owed in respect of non-interference and positive service—and rights may stand in the way of the pursuit of the common good. Or so at least it seems to those who reject utilitarian doctrines. This dispute cannot be settled here, but I shall treat justice as a virtue independent of charity, and standing as a possible limit on the scope of that virtue.

Let us say then, leaving unsolved problems behind us, that virtues are in general beneficial characteristics, and indeed ones that a human being needs to have, for his own sake and that of his fellows. This will not, however, take us far towards a definition of a virtue, since there are many other qualities of a man that may be similarly beneficial, as for instance bodily characteristics such as health and physical strength, and mental powers such as those of memory and concentration. What is it, we must ask, that differentiates virtues from such things?

As a first approximation to an answer we might say that while health and strength are excellences of the body, and memory and concentration of the mind, it is the will that is good in a man of virtue. But this suggestion is worth only as much as the explanation that follows it. What might we mean by saying that virtue belongs to the will?

In the first place we observe that it is primarily by his intentions that a man's moral dispositions are judged. If he does something unintentionally this is usually irrelevant to our estimate of his virtue. But of course this thesis must be qualified, because failures in performance rather than intention may show a lack of virtue. This will be so when, for instance, one man brings harm to another without realising he is doing it, but where his ignorance is itself culpable. Sometimes in such cases there will be a previous act or omission to which we can point as the source of the ignorance. Charity requires that we take care to find out how to render assistance where we are likely to be called on to do so, and thus, for example, it is contrary to charity to fail to find out about elementary first aid. But in an interesting class of cases in which it seems again to be performance rather than intention that counts in judging a man's virtue there is no possibility of shifting the judgement to previous intentions. For sometimes one man succeeds where another fails not because there is some specific difference in their previous conduct but rather because his heart lies in a different place; and the disposition of the heart is part of virtue.

Thus it seems right to attribute a kind of moral failure to some deeply discouraging and debilitating people who say, without lying, that they mean to be helpful; and on the other side to see virtue *par excellence* in one who is prompt and resourceful in doing good. In his novel *A Single Pebble* John Hersey describes such a man, speaking of a rescue in a swift flowing river:

> It was the head tracker's marvellous swift response that captured my admiration at first, his split second solicitousness when he heard a cry of pain, his finding in mid-air, as it were, the only way to save the injured boy. But there was more to it than that. His action, which could not have been mulled over in his mind, showed a deep, instinctive love of life, a compassion, an optimism, which made me feel very good . . .

What this suggests is that a man's virtue may be judged by his innermost desires as well as by his intentions; and this fits with our idea that a virtue such as generosity lies as much in someone's attitudes as in his actions. Pleasure in the good fortune of others is, one thinks, the sign of a generous spirit; and small reactions of pleasure and displeasure often the surest signs of a man's moral disposition.

None of this shows that it is wrong to think of virtues as belonging to the will; what it does show is that "will" must here be understood in its widest sense, to cover what is wished for as well as what is sought.

A different set of considerations will, however, force us to give up any simple statement about the relation between virtue and will, and these considerations have to do with the virtue of wisdom. Practical wisdom, we said, was counted by Aristotle among the intellectual virtues, and while our *wisdom* is not quite the same as *phronēsis* or *prudentia* it too might seem to belong to the intellect rather than the will. Is not wisdom a matter of knowledge, and how can knowledge be a matter of intention or desire? The answer is that it isn't, so that there is good reason for thinking of wisdom as an intellectual virtue. But on the other hand wisdom has special connexions with the will, meeting it at more than one point.

In order to get this rather complex picture in focus we must pause for a little and ask what it is that we ourselves understand by wisdom: what the wise man knows and what he does. Wisdom, as I see it, has two parts. In the first place the wise man knows the means to certain good ends; and secondly he knows how much particular ends are worth. Wisdom in its first part is relatively easy to understand. It seems that there are some ends belonging to human life in general rather than to particular skills such as medicine or boatbuilding, ends having to do with such matters as friendship, marriage, the bringing up of children, or the choice of ways of life; and it seems that knowledge of how to act well in these matters belongs to some people but not to others. We call those who have this knowledge wise, while those who do not have it are seen as lacking wisdom. So, as both Aristotle and Aquinas insisted, wisdom is to be contrasted with cleverness because cleverness is the ability to take the right steps to any end, whereas wisdom is related only to good ends, and to human life in general rather than to the ends of particular arts.

Moreover, we should add, there belongs to wisdom only that part of knowledge which is within the reach of any ordinary human being: knowledge that can be acquired only by someone who is clever or who has access to special training is not counted as part of wisdom, and would not be so counted even if it could serve the ends that wisdom serves. It is therefore quite wrong to suggest that wisdom cannot be a moral virtue because virtue must be within the reach of anyone who really wants it and some people are too stupid to be anything but ignorant even about the most fundamental matters of human life. Some people are wise without being clever or well informed: they make good decisions and they know, as we say, "what's what."

In short wisdom, in what we called its first part, is connected with the will in the following ways. To begin with it presupposes good ends: the man who is wise does not merely know *how* to do good things such as looking after his children well, or strengthening someone in trouble, but must also want to do them. And then wisdom, in so far as it consists of knowledge which anyone can gain in the course of an ordinary life, is available to anyone who really wants it. As Aquinas put it, it belongs "to a power under the direction of the will."

The second part of wisdom, which has to do with values, is much harder to describe, because here we meet ideas which are curiously elusive, such as the thought that some pursuits are more worthwhile than others, and some matters trivial and some important in human life. Since it makes good sense to say that most men waste a lot of their lives in ardent pursuit of what is trivial and unimportant it is not possible to explain the important and the trivial in terms of the amount of attention given to different subjects by the average man. But I have never seen, or been able to think out, a true account of this matter, and I believe that a complete account of wisdom, and of certain other virtues and vices must wait until this gap can be filled. What we can see is that one of the things a wise man knows and a foolish man does not is that such things as social position, and wealth, and the good opinion of the world, are too dearly bought at the cost of health or friendship or family ties. So we may say that a man who lacks wisdom "has false values," and that vices such as vanity and worldliness and avarice are contrary to wisdom in a special way. There is always an element of false judgement about these vices, since the man who is vain for instance sees admiration as more important than it is, while the worldly man is apt to see the good life as one of wealth and power. Adapting Aristotle's distinction between the weak-willed man (the *akratēs*) who follows pleasure though he knows, in some sense, that he should not, and the licentious man (the *akolastos*) who sees the life of pleasure as the good life, we may say that moral failings such as these are never purely "*akratic.*" It is true that a man may criticise himself for his worldliness or vanity or love of money, but then it is his values that are the subject of his criticism.

Wisdom in this second part is, therefore, partly to be described in terms of apprehension, and even judgement, but since it has to do with a man's attachments it also characterises his will.

The idea that virtues belong to the will, and that this helps to distinguish them from such things as bodily strength or intellectual ability has, then, survived the consideration of the virtue of wisdom, albeit in a fairly complex and slightly attenuated form. And we shall find this idea useful again if we turn to another important distinction that must be made, namely that between virtues and other practical excellences such as arts and skills.

Aristotle has sometimes been accused, for instance by von Wright, of failing to see how different values are from arts or skills; but in fact one finds, among the many things that Aristotle and Aquinas say about this difference, the observation that seems to go to the heart of the matter. In the matter of arts and skills, they say, voluntary error is preferable to involuntary error, while in the matter of virtues (what we call virtues) it is the reverse. The last part of the thesis is actually rather hard to interpret, because it is not clear what is meant by the idea of involuntary viciousness. But we can leave this aside and still have all we need in order to distinguish arts or skills from virtues. If we think, for instance, of someone who deliberately makes a spelling mistake (perhaps when writing on the blackboard in order to explain this particular point) we see that this does not in any way count against his skill as a speller: "I did it deliberately" rebuts an accusation of this kind. And what can we say without running into any difficulties is that there is no comparable rebuttal in the case of an accusation relating to lack of virtue. If a man acts unjustly or uncharitably, or in a cowardly or intemperate manner, "I did it deliberately" cannot on any interpretation lead to exculpation. So, we may say, a virtue is not, like a skill or art, a mere capacity: it must actually engage the will.

II

I shall now turn to another thesis about the virtues, which I might express by saying that they are *corrective*, each one standing at a point at which there is some temptation to be resisted or deficiency of motivation to be made good. As Aristotle puts it, virtues are about what is difficult for men, and I want to see in what sense this is true, and then to consider a problem in Kant's moral philosophy in the light of what has been said.

Let us first think about courage and temperance.

Aquinas contrasted these virtues with justice in the following respect. Justice was concerned with operations, and courage and temperance with passions. What he meant by this seems to have been, primarily, that the man of courage does not fear immoderately nor the man of temperance have immoderate desires for pleasure, and that there was no corresponding moderation of a passion implied in the idea of justice. This particular account of courage and temperance might be disputed on the ground that a man's courage is measured by his action and not by anything as uncontrollable as fear; and similarly that the temperate man who must on occasion refuse pleasures need not *desire* them any less than the intemperate man. Be that as it may (and something will be said about it later) it is obviously true that courage and temperance have to do with particular springs of action as justice does not. Almost any desire can lead a man to act unjustly, not even excluding the desire to help a friend or to save a life, whereas a cowardly act must be motivated by fear or a desire for safety, and an act of intemperance by a desire for pleasure, perhaps even for a particular range of pleasures such as those of eating or drinking or sex. And now, going back to the idea of virtues as correctives, one may say that it is only because fear and the desire for pleasure often operate as temptations that courage and temperance exist as virtues at all. As things are we often want to run away not only where that is the right thing to do but also where we should stand firm; and we want pleasure not only where we should seek pleasure but where we should not. If human nature had been different there would have been no need of a corrective disposition in either place, as fear and pleasure would have been good guides to conduct throughout life. So Aquinas says, about the passions

> They may incite us to something against reason, and so we need a curb, which we name *temperance*. Or they may make us shirk a course of action dictated by reason, through fear of dangers or hardships. Then a person needs to be steadfast and not run away from what is right; and for this *courage* is named.

As with courage and temperance so with many other virtues: there is, for instance, a virtue of industriousness only because idleness is a temptation; and of humility only because men tend to think too well of themselves. Hope is a virtue because despair too is a temptation; it might have been that no one cried that all was lost except where he could really see it to be so, and in this case there would have been no virtue of hope.

With virtues such as justice and charity it is a little different, because they correspond not to any particular desire or tendency that has to be kept in check but rather to a deficiency of motivation; and it is this that they must make good. If people were as much attached to the good of others as they are to their own good there would no more be a general virtue of benevolence than there is a general virtue of self-love. And if people cared about the rights of others as they care about their own rights no virtue of justice would be needed to look after the matter, and rules about such things as contracts and promises would only need to be made public, like the rules of a game that everyone was eager to play.

On this view of the virtues and vices everything is seen to depend on what human nature is like, and the traditional catalogue of the two kinds of dispositions is not hard to understand. Nevertheless it may be defective, and anyone who accepts the thesis that I am putting forward will feel free to ask himself where the temptations and deficiencies that need correcting are really to be found. It is possible, for example, that the theory of human nature lying behind the traditional list of the virtues and vices puts too much emphasis on hedonistic and sensual impulses, and does not sufficiently take account of less straightforward inclinations such as the desire to be put upon and dissatisfied, or the unwillingness to accept good things as they come along.

It should now be clear why I said that virtues should be seen as correctives; and part of what is meant by saying that virtue is about things that are difficult for men should also have appeared. The further application of this idea is, however, controversial, and the following difficulty presents itself: that we both are and are not inclined to think that the harder a man finds it to act virtuously the more virtue he shows if he does act well. For on the one hand great virtue is needed where it is particularly hard to act virtuously; yet on the other it could be argued that difficulty in acting virtuously shows that the agent is imperfect in virtue: according to Aristotle, to take pleasure in virtuous action is the mark of true virtue, with the self-mastery of the one who finds virtue difficult only a second best. How then is this conflict to be decided? Who shows most courage, the one who wants to run away but does not, or the one who does not even want to run away? Who shows most charity, the one who finds it easy to make the good of others his object, or the one who finds it hard?

What is certain is that the thought that virtues are corrective does not constrain us to relate virtue to difficulty in each individual man. Since men in general find it hard to face great dangers or evils, and even small ones, we may count as courageous those few who without blindness or indifference are nevertheless fearless even in terrible circumstances. And when someone has a natural charity or generosity it is at least part of the virtue that he has; if natural virtue cannot be the whole of virtue this is because a kindly or fearless disposition could be disastrous without justice and wisdom, and because these virtues have to be learned, not because natural virtue is too easily acquired. I have argued that the virtues can be seen as correctives in relation to human nature in general but not that each virtue must present a difficulty to each and every man.

Nevertheless many people feel strongly inclined to say that it is for moral effort that moral praise is to be bestowed, and that in proportion as a man finds it easy to be virtuous so much the less is he to be morally admired for his good actions. The dilemma can be resolved only when we stop talking about difficulties standing in the way of virtuous action as if they were of only one kind. The fact is that some kinds of difficulties do indeed provide an occasion for much virtue, but that others rather show that virtue is incomplete.

To illustrate this point I shall first consider an example of honest action. We may suppose for instance that a man has an opportunity to steal, in circumstances where stealing is not morally permissible, but that he refrains. And now let us ask our old question. For one man it is hard to refrain from stealing and for another man it is not: which shows the greater virtue in acting as he should? Is it not difficult to see in this case that it makes all the difference whether the difficulty comes from circumstances, as that a man is poor, or that his theft is unlikely to be detected, or whether it comes from something that belongs to his own character. The fact that a man is *tempted* to steal is something about him that shows a certain lack of honesty; of the thoroughly honest man we say that it "never entered his head" meaning that it was never a real possibility for him. But the fact that he is poor is something that makes the occasion more *tempting,* and the difficulties of this kind make honest action all the more virtuous.

A similar distinction can be made between different obstacles standing in the way of charitable action. Some circumstances, as that great sacrifice is needed, or that the one to be helped is a rival, give an occasion on which a man's charity is severely tested. Yet in given circumstances of this kind it is the man who acts easily rather than the one who finds it hard who shows the most charity. Charity is a virtue of attachment, and that sympathy for others which makes it easier to help them is part of the virtue itself.

These are fairly simple cases, but I am not supposing that it is always easy to say where the relevant distinction is to be drawn. What, for instance, should we say about the emotion of fear as an obstacle to action? Is a man more courageous if he fears much and nevertheless acts, or if he is relatively fearless? Several things must be said about this. In the first place it seems that the emotion of fear is not a necessary condition for the display of courage; in the face of a great evil such as death or injury a man may show courage even if he does not tremble. On the other hand even irrational fears may give an occasion for courage: if someone suffers from claustrophobia or a dread of heights he may require courage to do that which would not be a courageous action for others. But not all fears belong from this point of view to the circumstances rather than to a man's character. For while we do not think of claustrophobia or a dread of heights as features of character, a general timorousness may be. Thus, although pathological fears are not the result of a man's choices and values some fears may be. The fears that count against a man's courage are those we think he could overcome, and among them, in a special class, those that reflect the fact that he values safety too much.

In spite of problems such as these, which have certainly not all been solved, both the distinction between different kinds of obstacles to virtuous action and the general idea that virtues are correctives will be useful in resolving a difficulty in Kant's moral philosophy closely related to the issues discussed in the preceding paragraphs. In a passage in the first section of the *Groundwork of the Metaphysics of Morals* Kant notoriously tied himself into a knot in trying to give an account of those actions which have as he put it "positive moral worth." Arguing that only actions done out of a sense of duty have this worth he contrasts a philanthropist who "takes pleasure in spreading happiness around him" with one who acts out of respect for duty, saying that the actions of the latter but not the former have moral worth. Much scorn has been poured on Kant for this curious doctrine, and indeed it does seem that something has gone wrong, but perhaps we are not in a position to scoff unless we can give our own account of the idea on which Kant is working. After all it does seem that he is right in saying that some actions are in accordance with duty, and even required by duty, without being the subjects of moral praise, like those of the honest trader who deals honestly in a situation in which it is in his interest to do so.

It was this kind of example that drove Kant to his strange conclusion. He added another example, however, in discussing acts of self-preservation; these he said, while they normally have no positive moral worth, may have it when a man preserves his life not from inclination but without inclination and from a sense of duty. Is he not right in saying that acts of self-preservation normally have no moral significance but that they may have it, and how do we ourselves explain this fact?

To anyone who approaches this topic from a consideration of the virtues the solution readily suggests itself. Some actions are in accordance with virtue without requiring virtue for their performance, whereas others are both in accordance with virtue and such as to show possession of a virtue. So Kant's trader was dealing honestly in a situation in which the virtue of honesty is not required for honest dealing, and it is for this reason that his action did not have "positive moral worth." Similarly, the care that one ordinarily takes for one's life, as for instance on some ordinary morning in eating one's breakfast and keeping out of the way of a car on the road, is something for which no virtue is required. As we said earlier there is no general virtue of self-love as there is a virtue of benevolence or charity, because men are generally attached sufficiently to their own good. Nevertheless in special circumstances virtues such as temperance, courage, fortitude, and hope may be needed if someone is to preserve his life. Are these circumstances in which the preservation of one's own life is a duty? Sometimes it is so, for sometimes it is what is owed to others that should keep a man from destroying himself, and then he may act out of a sense of duty. But not all cases in which acts of self-preservation show virtue are like this. For a man may display each of the virtues just listed even where he does not do any harm to others if he kills himself or fails to preserve his life. And it is this that explains why there may be a moral aspect to suicide which does not depend on possible injury to other people. It is not that suicide is "always wrong," whatever that would mean, but that suicide is *sometimes* contrary to virtues such as courage and hope.

Let us now return to Kant's philanthropists, with the thought that it is action that is in accordance with virtue and also displays a virtue that has moral worth. We see at once that Kant's difficulties are avoided, and the happy philanthropist reinstated in the position which belongs to him. For charity is, as we said, a virtue of attachment as well as action, and the sympathy that makes it easier to act with charity is part of the virtue. The man who acts charitably out of a sense of duty is not to be undervalued, but it is the other who most shows virtue and therefore to the other that most moral worth is attributed. Only a detail of Kant's presentation of the case of the dutiful philanthropist tells on the other side. For what he actually said was that this man felt no sympathy and took no pleasure in the good of others because "his mind was clouded by some sorrow of his own," and this is the kind of circumstance that increases the virtue that is needed if a man is to act well.

III

It was suggested above that an action with "positive moral worth," or as we might say a positively good action, was to be seen as one which was in accordance with virtue, by which I mean contrary to no virtue, and moreover one for which a virtue was required. Nothing has so far been said about another case, excluded by the formula, in which it might seem that an act displaying one virtue was nevertheless contrary to another. In giving this last description I am thinking not of two virtues with competing claims, as if what were required by justice could nevertheless be demanded by charity, or something of that kind, but rather of the possibility that a virtue such as courage or temperance or industry which overcomes a special temptation, might be displayed in an act of folly or villainy. Is this something that we must allow for, or is it only good or innocent actions which can be acts of these virtues? Aquinas, in his definition of virtue, said that virtues can produce only good actions, and that they are dispositions "of which no one can make bad use," except when they are treated as objects, as in being the subject of hatred or pride. The common opinion nowadays is, however, quite different. With the notable exception of Peter Geach hardly anyone sees any difficulty in the thought that virtues may sometimes be displayed in bad actions. Von Wright, for instance, speaks of the courage of the villain as if this were a quite unproblematic idea, and most people take it for granted that the virtues of courage and temperance may aid a bad man in his evil work. It is also supposed that charity may lead a man to act badly, as when someone does what he has no right to do, but does it for the sake of a friend.

There are, however, reasons for thinking that the matter is not so simple as this. If a man who is willing to do an act of injustice to help a friend, or for the common good, is supposed to act out of charity, and he so acts where a just man will not, it should be said that the unjust man has more charity than the just man. But do we not think that someone not ready to act unjustly may yet be perfect in charity, the virtue having done its whole work in prompting him to do the acts that are permissible? And is there not more difficulty than might appear in the idea of an act of injustice which is nevertheless an act of courage? Suppose for instance that a sordid murder were in question, say a murder done for gain or to get an inconvenient person out of the way, but that this murder had to be done in alarming circumstances or in the face of real danger; should we be happy to say that such an action was an act of courage or a courageous act? Did the murderer, who certainly acted boldly, or with intrepidity, if he did the murder, also act courageously? Some people insist that they are ready to say this, but I have noticed that they like to move over to a murder for the sake of conscience, or to some other act done in the course of a villainous enterprise but whose immediate end is innocent or positively good. On their hypothesis, which is that bad acts can easily be seen as courageous acts or acts of courage, my original example should be just as good.

What are we to say about this difficult matter? There is no doubt that the murderer who murdered for gain was *not a coward:* he did not have a second moral defect which another villain might have had. There is no difficulty about this because it is clear that one defect may neutralise another. As Aquinas remarked, it is better for a blind horse if it is slow. It does not follow, however, that an act of villainy can be courageous; we are inclined to say that it "took courage," and yet it seems wrong to think of courage as equally connected with good actions and bad.

One way out of this difficulty might be to say that the man who is ready to pursue bad ends does indeed have courage, and shows courage in his action, but that in him courage is not a virtue. Later I shall consider some cases in which this might be the right thing to say, but in this instance it does not seem to be. For unless the murderer consistently pursues bad ends his courage will often result in good; it may enable him to do many innocent or positively good things for himself or for his family and friends. On the strength of an individual bad action we can hardly say that in him courage is not a virtue. Nevertheless there is something to be said even about the individual action to distinguish it from one that would readily be called an act of courage or a courageous act. Perhaps the following analogy may help us to see what it is. We might think of words such as "courage" as naming characteristics of human beings in respect of a certain power, as words such as "poison" and "solvent" and "corrosive" so name the properties of physical things. The power to which virtue-words are so related is the power of producing good action, and good desires. But just as poisons, solvents and corrosives do not always operate characteristically, so it could be with virtues. If P (say arsenic) is a poison it does not follow that P acts as a poison wherever it is found. It is quite natural to say on occasion "P does not act as a poison here" though P is a poison and it is P that is acting here. Similarly courage is not operating as a virtue when the murderer turns his courage, which is a virtue, to bad ends. Not surprisingly the resistance that some of us registered was not to the expression "the courage of the murderer" or to the assertion that what he did "took courage" but rather to the description of that action as an act of courage or a courageous act. It is not that the action *could* not be so described, but that the fact that courage does not here have its characteristic operation is a reason for finding the description strange.

In this example we were considering an action in which courage was not operating as a virtue, without suggesting that in that agent it generally failed to do so. But the latter is also a possibility. If someone is both wicked and foolhardy this may be the case with courage, and it is even easier to find examples of a general connexion with evil rather than good in the case of some other virtues. Suppose, for instance, that we think of someone who is over-industrious, or too ready to refuse pleasure, and this is characteristic of him rather than something we find on one particular occasion. In this case the virtue of industry, or the virtue of temperance, has a systematic connexion with defective action rather than good actions; and it might be said in either case that the virtue did not operate as a virtue in this man. Just as we might say in a certain setting "P is not a poison here" though P is a poison and P is here, so we might say that industriousness, or temperance, is not a virtue in some. Similarly in a man habitually given to wishful thinking, who clings to false hopes, hope does not operate as a virtue and we may say that it is not a virtue in him.

The thought developed in the last paragraph, to the effect that not every man who has a virtue has something that is a virtue in him, may help to explain a certain discomfort that one may feel when discussing the virtues. It is not easy to put one's finger on what is wrong, but it has something to do with a disparity between the moral ideals that may seem to be implied in our talk about the virtues, and the moral judgement that we actually make. Someone reading the foregoing pages might, for instance, think that the author of this paper always admired most those people who had all the virtues, being wise and temperate as well as courageous, charitable, and just. And indeed it is sometimes so. There are some people who do possess all these virtues and who are loved and admired by all the world, as Pope John XXIII was loved and admired. Yet the fact is that many of us look up to some people whose chaotic lives contain rather little of wisdom or temperance, rather than to some others who possess these virtues. And while it may be that this is just romantic nonsense I suspect that it is not. For while wisdom always operates as a virtue, its close relation prudence does not, and it is prudence rather than wisdom that inspires many a careful life. Prudence is not a virtue in everyone, any more than industriousness is, for some it is rather an over-anxious concern for safety and propriety, and a determination to keep away from people or situations which are apt to bring trouble with them; and by such defensiveness much good is lost. It is the same with temperance. Intemperance can be an appalling thing, as it was with Henry VIII of whom Wolsey remarked that

> rather than he will miss or want any part of his will or appetite, he will put the loss of one half of his realm in danger.

Nevertheless in some people temperance is not a virtue, but is rather connected with timidity or with a grudging attitude to the acceptance of good things. Of course what is best is to live boldly yet without imprudence or intemperance, but the fact is that rather few can manage that.

*F*EMINIST ETHICS

Annette Baier

When I finished reading Carol Gilligan's *In a Different Voice,* I asked myself the obvious question for a philosopher reader: what differences should one expect in the moral philosophy done by women, supposing Gilligan's sample of women to be representative and supposing her analysis of their moral attitudes and moral development to be correct? Should one expect women to want to produce moral theories, and if so, what sort of moral theories? How will any moral theories they produce differ from those produced by men?

Obviously one does not have to make this an entirely a priori and hypothetical question. One can look and see what sort of contributions women have made to moral philosophy. Such a look confirms, I think, Gilligan's findings. What one finds *is* a bit different in tone and approach from the standard sort of moral philosophy as done by men following in the footsteps of the great moral philosophers (all men). Generalizations are extremely rash, but when I think of Phillipa Foot's work on the moral virtues, Elizabeth Anscombe's work on intention and on modern moral philosophy, Iris Murdoch's philosophical writings, Ruth Barcan Marcus's work on moral dilemmas, the work of the radical feminist moral philosophers who are not content with orthodox Marxist lines of thought, Jenny Teichman's book on illegitimacy, Susan Wolf's articles, Claudia Card's essay on mercy, Sabina Lovibond's writings, Gabriele Taylor's work on pride, love, and on integrity, Cora Diamond's and Mary Midgeley's work on our attitude toward animals, Sissela Bok's work on lying and on secrecy, Virginia Held's work, the work of Alison Jaggar, Marilyn Frye, and many others, I seem to hear a different voice from the standard moral philosophers' voice. I hear the voice Gilligan heard, made reflective and philosophical. What women want in moral philosophy is what they are providing. And what they are providing seems to me to confirm Gilligan's theses about women. One has to be careful here, of course, for not all important contributions to moral philosophy by women fall easily into the Gilligan stereotype or its philosophical extension. Nor has it been only women who have been proclaiming discontent with the standard approach in moral philosophy and trying new approaches. Michael Stocker, Alasdair MacIntyre, and Ian Hacking when he assesses the game-theoretic approach to morality, all should be given the status of honorary women, if we accept the hypothesis that there are some moral insights for whatever reason women seem to attain more easily or more reliably than men do. Still, exceptions confirm the rule, so I shall proceed undaunted by these important exceptions to my generalizations.

If Hacking is right, preoccupation with prisoner's and prisoners' dilemmas is a big boys' game, and a pretty silly one too. It is, I think, significant that women have not rushed into the field of game-theoretic moral philosophy, and that those who have dared enter that male locker room have said distinctive things there. Edna Ullmann Margalit's book *The Emergence of Norms* put prisoner's dilemma in its limited moral place. Supposing that at least part of the explanation for the relatively few women in this field is disinclination rather than disability, one might ask if this disinclination also extends to the construction of moral theories. For although we find out what sort of moral philosophy women want by looking to see what they have provided, if we do that for moral theory, the answer we get seems to be "none." None of the contributions to moral philosophy by women really counts as a moral theory, nor is seen as such by its author.

Is it that reflective women, when they become philosophers, want to do without moral theory, want no part in the construction of such theories? To conclude this at this early stage, when we have only a few generations of women moral philosophers to judge from, would be rash indeed. The term "theory" can be used in wider and narrower ways, and in its widest sense a moral theory is simply an internally consistent fairly comprehensive account of what morality is and when and why it merits our acceptance and support. In that wide sense, a moral theory is something it would take a skeptic, or one who believes that our intellectual vision is necessarily blurred or distorted when we let it try to take in too much, to be an antitheorist. Even if there were some truth in the latter claim, one might compatibly with it still hope to build up a coherent total account by a mosaic method, assembling a lot of smaller-scale works until one had built up a complete account—say, taking the virtues or purported virtues one by one until one had a more or less complete account. But would that sort of comprehensiveness in one's moral philosophy entitle one to call the finished work a moral theory? If it would, then many women moral philosophers today can be seen as engaged in moral theory construction. In the weakest sense of "theory," as a coherent near-comprehensive account, there are plenty of incomplete theories to be found in the works of women moral philosophers. And in *that* sense of theory, most of what are recognized as the current moral theories are also incomplete, because they do not yet purport to be really comprehensive. Wrongs to animals and wrongful destruction of our physical environment are put to one side by John Rawls, and in most "liberal" theories there are only hand waves concerning our proper attitude toward our children, toward the ill, toward our relatives, friends, and lovers.

Is comprehensiveness too much to ask of a moral theory? The paradigm examples of moral theories—those that are called by their authors "moral theories"—are distinguished not by the comprehensiveness of their internally coherent account but by the *sort* of coherence which is aimed at over a fairly broad area. Their method is not the mosaic method but the broad brushstroke method. Moral theories, as we know them, are, to change the art form, vaults rather than walls—they are not built by assembling painstakingly made brick after brick. In *this* sense of theory—a fairly tightly systematic account of a large area of morality, with a keystone supporting all the rest—women moral philosophers have not yet, to my knowledge, produced moral theories or claimed that they have.

Leaving to one side the question of what purpose (other than good clean intellectual fun) is served by such moral theories, and supposing for the sake of argument that women can, if they wish, systematize as well as the next man and, if need be, systematize in a mathematical fashion as well as the next mathematically minded moral philosopher, then what key concept or guiding motif might hold together the structure of a moral theory hypothetically produced by a reflective woman, Gilligan-style, who has taken up moral theorizing as a calling? What would be a suitable central question, principle, or concept to structure a moral theory which might accommodate those moral insights which women tend to have more readily than men, and to answer those moral questions which, it seems, worry women more than men? I hypothesized that the women's theory, expressive mainly of women's insights and concerns, would be an ethics of love, and this hypothesis seems to be Gilligan's too, since she has gone on from *In a Different Voice* to write about the limitations of Freud's understanding of love as women know it. But presumably women theorists will be like enough to men to want their moral theory to be acceptable to all, so acceptable both to reflective women and reflective men. Like any good theory, it will need not to ignore the partial truth of previous theories. It must therefore accommodate both the insights men have more easily than women and those women have more easily than men. It should swallow up its predecessor theories. Women moral theorists, if any, will have this very great advantage over the men whose theories theirs supplant, that they can stand on the shoulders of male moral theorists, as no man has yet been able to stand on the shoulders of any female moral theorist. There can be advantages as well as handicaps in being latecomers. So women theorists will need to connect their ethics of love with what has been the men theorists' preoccupation, namely, obligation.

The great and influential moral theorists have in the modern era taken *obligation* as the key and the problematic concept, and have asked what justifies treating a person as morally bound or obliged to do a particular thing. Since to be bound is to be unfree, by making obligation central one at the same time makes central the question of the justification of coercion, of forcing or trying to force someone to act in a particular way. The concept of obligation as justified limitation of freedom does just what one wants a good theoretical concept to do—to divide up the field (as one looks at different ways one's freedom may be limited, freedom in different spheres, different sorts and versions and levels of justification) and at the same time to hold the subfields together. There must in a theory be some generalization and some speciation or diversification, and a good rich key concept guides one both in recognizing the diversity and in recognizing the unity in it. The concept of obligation has served this function very well for the area of morality it covers, and so we have some fine theories about that area. But as Aristotelians and Christians, as well as women, know, there is a lot of morality *not* covered by that concept, a lot of very great importance even for the area where there are obligations.

This is fairly easy to see if we look at what lies behind the perceived obligation to keep promises. Unless there is some good moral reason why someone should assume the responsibility of rearing a child to be *capable* of taking promises seriously, once she understands what a promise is, the obligation to obey promises will not effectively tie her, and any force applied to punish her when she breaks promises or makes fraudulent ones will be of questionable justice. Is there an *obligation* on someone to make the child into a morally competent promisor? If so, on whom? Who has failed in his or her obligations when, say, war orphans who grew up without parental love or any other love arrive at legal adulthood very willing to be untrue to their word? Who failed in what obligation in all those less extreme cases of attempted but unsuccessful moral education? The parents who didn't produce promise-keeping offspring? Those who failed to educate the parents in how to educate their children (whoever it might be who could plausibly be thought to have the responsibility for training parents to fulfill their obligations)? The liberal version of our basic moral obligations tends to be fairly silent on who has what obligations to new members of the moral community, and it would throw most theories of the justification of obligations into some confusion if the obligation to rear one's children lovingly were added to the list of obligations. Such evidence as we have about the conditions in which children do successfully "learn" the morality of the community of which they are members suggests that we cannot substitute "conscientiously" for "lovingly" in this hypothetical extra needed obligation. But an obligation to love, in the strong sense needed, would be an embarrassment to the theorist, given most accepted versions of "ought implies can."

It is hard to make fair generalizations here, so I shall content myself with indicating how this charge I am making against the current men's moral theories, that their version of the justified list of obligations does not ensure the proper care of the young and so does nothing to ensure the stability of the morality in question over several generations, can be made against what I regard as the best of the men's recent theories, Rawls's theory of justice. One of the great strengths of Rawls's theory is the careful attention given to the question of how just institutions produce the conditions for their continued support, across generations, and in particular of how the sense of justice will arise in children, once there are minimally just institutions structuring the social world into which they are born. Rawls, more than most moral theorists, has attended to the question of the stability of his just society, given what we know about child development. But Rawls's sensitive account of the conditions for the development of that sense of justice needed for the maintenance of his version of a just society takes it for granted that there will be loving parents rearing the children in whom the sense of justice is to develop. "The parents, we may suppose, love the child, and in time the child comes to love and trust the parents." Why may we suppose this? Not because compliance with Rawls's verison of our obligations and duties will ensure it. Rawls's theory, like so many other theories of obligation, in the end must take out a loan not only on the natural duty of parents to care for children (which he will have no trouble including) but on the natural *virtue* of parental love (or even a loan on the maternal instinct?). The virtue of being a *loving* parent must supplement the natural duties and obligations of justice, if the just society is to last beyond the first generation. And as Nancy Chodorow's work indicates, the loving parents must also accept a certain division of child-care responsibility if their version of the obligations and virtues of men and women is, along with their version of the division of labor accompanying that allocation of virtues, to be passed on.

Reliance on a recognized obligation to turn oneself into a good parent or else to avoid becoming a parent would be a problematic solution. Good parents tend to be the children of good parents, so this obligation would collapse into the obligation to avoid parenthood unless one expected to be a good parent. That, given available methods of contraception, may itself convert into the obligation, should one expect not to be a good parent, to sexual abstinence, or sterilization, or resolute resort to abortion when contraception fails. The conditional obligation to abort, and in effect also the conditional obligation to sterilization, falls on the women. There may be conditions in which the rational moral choice is between obligatory sexual abstinence and obligatory sterilization, but obligatory abortion, such as women in China now face, seems to me a moral monster. I do not believe that liberal moral theorists will be able to persuade reflective women that a morality that in any conditions makes abortion obligatory, as distinct from permitted or advisable or, on occasion, best, is in their own as well as their male fellows' long-term self-interest. It would be tragic if such moral questions in the end came to the question of whose best interests to sacrifice, men's or women's. I do not believe that they *do* come to this, but should they, then justice would require that, given the long history of the subordination of women's to men's interests, men's interests be sacrificed. Justice, of course, never decides these issues unless power reinforces justice, so I am not predicting any victory for women, should it ever come to a fight over obligatory abortion or over who is to face obligatory sterilization.

No liberal moral theorist, as far as I know, is advocating obligatory abortion or obligatory sterilization when necessary to prevent the conception of children whose parents do not expect to love them. My point rather is that they escape this conclusion only by avoiding the issue of what is to ensure that new members of the moral community do get the loving care they need to become morally competent persons. Liberal moral theories assume that women either will provide loving maternal care, or will persuade their mates to provide loving paternal care, or when pregnant will decide for abortion, encouraged by their freedom-loving men. These theories, in other words, exploit the culturally encouraged maternal instinct and/or the culturally encouraged docility of women. The liberal system would receive a nasty spanner in its works should women use their freedom of choice as regards abortion to choose *not* to abort, and then leave their newborn children on their fathers' doorsteps. That would test liberal morality's ability to provide for its own survival.

At this point it may be objected that every moral theory must make some assumptions about the natural psychology of those on whom obligations are imposed. Why shouldn't the liberal theory count on a continuing sufficient supply of good loving mothers, as it counts on continuing self-interest and, perhaps, on a continuing supply of pugnacious men who are able and willing to become good soldiers, without turning any of these into moral *obligations?* Why waste moral resources recognizing as obligatory or as virtuous what one can count on getting without moral pressure? If, in the moral economy, one can get enough good mothers and good warriors "for free," why not gladly exploit what nature and cultural history offer? I cannot answer this question fully here, but my argument does depend upon the assumption that a decent morality will *not* depend for its stability on forces to which it gives no moral recognition. Its account books should be open to scrutiny, and there should be no unpaid debts, no loans with no prospect of repayment. I also assume that once we are clear about these matters and about the interdependencies involved, our principles of justice will not allow us to recognize either a special obligation on every woman to initiate the killing of the fetus she has conceived, should she and her mate be, or think they will be, deficient in parental love, or a special obligation on every young man to kill those his elders have labeled enemies of his country. Both such "obligations" are prima facie suspect, and difficult to make consistent with any of the principles supposedly generating obligations in modern moral theories. I also assume that, on reflection, we will not want to recognize as *virtues* the character traits of women and men which lead them to supply such life and death services "for free." Neither maternal servitude, nor the resoluteness needed to kill off one's children to prevent their growing up unloved, nor the easy willingness to go out and kill when ordered to do so by authorities seems to me to be a character trait a decent morality will encourage by labeling a virtue. But the liberals' morality must somehow encourage such traits if its stability depends on enough people showing them. There is, then, understandable motive for liberals' avoidance of the question of whether such qualities are or are not morally approved of, and of whether or not there is any obligation to act as one with such character traits would act.

It is symptomatic of the bad faith of liberal morality as understood by many of those who defend it that issues such as whether to fight or not to fight, to have or not to have an abortion, or to be or not to be an unpaid maternal drudge are left to individual conscience. Since there is no coherent guidance liberal morality can give on these issues, which clearly are *not* matters of moral indifference, liberal morality tells each of us, "the choice is yours," hoping that enough will choose to be self-sacrificial life providers and self-sacrificial death dealers to suit the purposes of the rest.

Rawls's theory does explicitly face the question of the moral justification of refusal to bear arms, and how a just society justly provides for its own defense. The hardships imposed on conscripted soldiers are, he says, a necessary evil, and the most that just institutions can do is to "make sure that the risks of suffering from those misfortunes are more or less evenly shared by all members of society over the course of their life, and that there is no avoidable class bias in selecting those who are called for duty." What of sex/gender bias? Or is that assumed to be unavoidable? Rawls's principles seem to me to imply that women should be conscripted, if anyone is (and I think that is right), but since he avoids the questions of justice between men and women one does not know whether he intended this implication. His suggestion that one argument in favor of a conscripted army is that it is less likely to be an instrument of unjustified foreign adventures will become even stronger, I believe, if half the conscripts are women. Like most male moral theorists, Rawls does not discuss the morality of having children, refusing to have them, refusing to care for them, nor does he discuss how just institutions might equalize the responsibilities involved in ensuring that there be new members of society and that they become morally competent members of it, so one does not know whether he accepts a gender-based division of social service here, leaving it to the men to do the dangerous defensive destruction of life and cities, while the support of new life, and any costs going or contrived to go with that, are left to the women. I hope that is not what he meant.

I do not wish, by having myself spoken of these two traditionally gender-based allocations of responsibility (producing and caring for new human life and the destruction of the lives of those officially labeled enemies) together, to leave the impression that I see any parallel between them except that they have both been treated as gender based and that both present embarrassments for liberal moral theory. Not all allocations of responsibility are allocations of burdens, and parenthood, unlike unchosen military life, need not be seen as essentially burden bearing. Good mothers and good soldiers make contributions of [very different sorts and sort of importance] to the ongoing life of a moral community, and they should not be seen, as they sometimes are, as fair mutual substitutes, as forms of social service. Good mothers will always be needed by a moral community, in the best conditions as well as the worst; the need for good military men, though foreseeably permanent, is a sign of some failure of our morality, a failure of our effectively acted upon moral laws to be valid theorems for the conservation of men in multitudes. Nor do the burdens of soldiering have any real analogue in the case of motherhood, which today *need* not impose real costs on the mother. If there are significant costs—loss of career opportunity, improperly recompensed drudgery in the home, or health risks—this is due to bad but largely remediable social arrangements, as the failure of parents to experience any especially parental satisfactions may be also due to bad but remediable socially produced attitudes toward parental responsibility. We do not, I think, want our military men to enjoy killing the enemy and destroying their cities, and any changes we made in social customs and institutions to make such pleasures more likely would be deplorable ones. Military life in wartime should always be seen as a sacrifice, while motherhood should never need to be seen as self-sacrificial service. If it is an honor and a privilege to bear arms for one's country, as we understandably tell our military conscripts and volunteers, part of the honor is being trusted with activities that are a necessary evil, being trusted not to enjoy their evil aspects, and being trusted to see the evil as well as the necessity. Only if we contrive to make the bringing into the world of new persons as nasty a business as killing already present persons will there be any just reason to exclude young women from conscripted armies or to exclude men from equal parental responsibility.

Granted that the men's theories of obligation need supplementation, to have much chance of integrity and coherence, and that the women's hypothetical theories will want to cover obligation as well as love, then what concept brings them together? My tentative answer is—the concept of appropriate trust, oddly neglected in moral theory. This concept also nicely mediates between reason and feeling, those tired old candidates for moral authority, since to trust is neither quite to believe something about the trusted nor necessarily to feel any emotion toward them—but to have a belief-informed and action-influencing attitude. To make it plausible that the neglected concept of appropriate trust is a good one for the enlightened moral theorist to make central, I need to show, or begin to show, how it could include obligation, indeed shed light on obligations and their justification, as well as include love, the other moral concerns of Gilligan's women, and many of the topics women moral philosophers have chosen to address, mosaic fashion. I would also need to show that it could connect all of these in a way which holds out promise both of synthesis and of comprehensive moral coverage. A moral theory which looked at the conditions for proper trust of all the various sorts we show, and at what sorts of reasons justify inviting such trust, giving it, and meeting it, would, I believe, not have to avoid turning its gaze on the conditions for the survival of the practices it endorses, so it could avoid that unpleasant choice many current liberal theories seem to have—between incoherence and bad faith. I do not pretend that we will easily agree once we raise the questions I think we should raise, but at least we may have a language adequate to the expression of both men's and women's moral viewpoints.

My trust in the concept of trust is based in part on my own attempts to restate and consider what is right and what wrong with men's theories, especially Hume's, which I consider the best of the lot. I have found myself reconstructing his account of the artifices of justice as an account of the progressive enlargement of a climate of trust, and have found that a helpful way to see it. It has some textual basis, but it is nevertheless a reconstruction, and one I have found, immodestly, an improvement. So it is because I have tried the concept and explored its dimensions a bit—the variety of goods we may trust others not to take from us, the sort of security or insurance we have when we do, the sorts of defenses or potential defenses we lay down when we trust, the various conditions for reasonable trust of various types—that I am hopeful about its power as a theoretical, and not just an exegetical, tool. I also found myself needing to use it when I made a brief rash attempt at that women's topic, caring (invited in by a male philosopher, I should say). I am reasonably sure that trust does generalize some central moral features of the recognition of binding obligations and moral virtues and of loving, as well as of other important relations between persons such as teacher-pupil, confider-confidante, worker to co-worker in the same cause, and professional to client. Indeed it is fairly obvious that love, the main moral phenomenon women want attended to, involves trust, so I anticipate little quarrel when I claim that, if we had a moral theory spelling out the conditions for appropriate trust and distrust, that would include a morality of love in all its variants—parental love, love of children for their parents, love of family members, love of friends, of lovers in the strict sense, of co-workers, of one's country and its figureheads, of exemplary heroines and heroes, of goddesses and gods.

Love and loyalty demand maximal trust of one sort, and maximal trustworthiness, and in investigating the conditions for maximal trust and maximal risk we must think about the ethics of love. More controversial may be my claim that the ethics of obligation will also be covered. I see it as covered because to recognize a set of obligations is to trust some group of persons to instill them, to demand that they be met, possibly to levy sanctions if they are not, and this is to trust persons with very significant coercive power over others. Less coercive but still significant power is possessed by those shaping our conception of the virtues and expecting us to display them, approving when we do, disapproving and perhaps shunning us when we do not. Such coercive and manipulative power over others requires justification, and is justified only if we have reason to trust those who have it to use it properly and to use the discretion which is always given when trust is given in a way which serves the purpose of the whole system of moral control, and not merely self-serving or morally improper purposes. Since the question of the justification of coercion becomes, at least in part, the question of the wisdom of trusting the coercers to do their job properly, the morality of obligation, in as far as it reduces to the morality of coercion, is covered by the morality of proper trust. Other forms of trust may also be involved, but trusting enforcers with the use of force is the most problematic form of trust involved.

The coercers and manipulators are, to some extent, all of us, so to ask what our obligations are and what virtues we should exhibit is to ask what it is reasonable to trust us to demand, expect, and contrive to get from one another. It becomes, in part, a question of what powers we can in reason trust ourselves to exercise properly. But self-trust is a dubious or limit case of trust, so I prefer to postpone the examination of the concept of proper self-trust at least until proper trust of others is more clearly understood. Nor do we distort matters too much if we concentrate on those cases where moral sanctions and moral pressure and moral manipulation is not self-applied but applied to others, particularly by older persons to younger persons. Most moral pressuring that has any effect goes on in childhood and early youth. Moral sanctions may continue to be applied, formally and informally, to adults, but unless the criminal courts apply them it is easy enough for adults to ignore them, to brush them aside. It is not difficult to become a sensible knave, and to harden one's heart so that one is insensible to the moral condemnation of one's victims and those who sympathize with them. Only if the pressures applied in the morally formative stage have given one a heart that rebels against the thought of such ruthless independence of what others think will one see any reason *not* to ignore moral condemnation, not to treat it as mere powerless words and breath. Condemning sensible knaves is as much a waste of breath as arguing with them—all we can sensibly do is to try to protect children against their criminal influence, and ourselves against their knavery. Adding to the criminal law will not be the way to do the latter, since such moves will merely challenge sensible knaves to find new knavish exceptions and loopholes, not protect us from sensible knavery. Sensible knaves are precisely those who exploit us without breaking the law. So the whole question of when moral pressure of various sorts, formative, reformative, and punitive, ought to be brought to bear by whom is subsumed under the question of whom to trust when and with what, and for what good reasons.

In concentrating on obligations, rather than virtues, modern moral theorists have chosen to look at the cases where more trust is placed in enforcers of obligations than is placed in ordinary moral agents, the bearers of obligations. In taking, as contractarians do, contractual obligations as the model of obligations, they concentrate on a case where the very minimal trust is put in the obligated person, and considerable punitive power entrusted to the one to whom the obligation is owed (I assume here that Hume is right in saying that when we promise or contract, we formally subject ourselves to the penalty, in case of failure, of never being trusted as a promisor again). This is an interesting case of the allocation of trust of various sorts, but it surely distorts our moral vision to suppose that *all* obligations, let alone all morally pressured expectations we impose on others, conform to that abnormally coercive model. It takes very special conditions for it to be safe to trust persons to inflict penalties on other persons, conditions in which either we can trust the penalizers to have the virtues necessary to penalize wisely and fairly, or else we can rely on effective threats to keep virtuous penalizers from abusing their power—that is to say, rely on others to coerce the first coercers into proper behavior. But that reliance too will either be trust or will have to rely on threats from coercers of the coercers of coercers, and so on. Morality on this model becomes a nasty, if intellectually intriguing, game of mutual mutually corrective threats. The central question of who should deprive whom of what freedom soon becomes the question of whose anger should be dreaded by whom (the theory of obligation), supplemented perhaps by an afterthought on whose favor should be courted by whom (the theory of the virtues).

Undoubtedly some important part of morality does depend in part on a system of threats and bribes, at least for its survival in difficult conditions when normal goodwill and normally virtuous dispositions may be insufficient to motivate the conduct required for the preservation and justice of the moral network of relationships. But equally undoubtedly life will be nasty, emotionally poor, and worse than brutish (even if longer), if that is all morality is, or even if that coercive structure of morality is regarded as the backbone, rather than as an available crutch, should the main support fail. For the main support has to come from those we entrust with the job of rearing and training persons so that they can be trusted in various ways, some trusted with extraordinary coercive powers, some with public decision-making powers, all trusted as parties to promise, most trusted by some who love them and by one or more willing to become co-parents with them, most trusted by dependent children, dependent elderly relatives, sick friends, and so on. A very complex network of a great variety of sorts of trust structures our moral relationships with our fellows, and if there is a *main* support to this network it is the trust we place in those who respond to the trust of new members of the moral community, namely, children, and prepare them for new forms of trust.

A theory which took as its central question "Who should trust whom with what, and why?" would not have to forego the intellectual fun and games previous theorists have had with the various paradoxes of morality—curbing freedom to increase freedom, curbing self-interest the better to satisfy self-interest, not aiming at happiness in order to become happier. For it is easy enough to get a paradox of trust to accompany or, if I am right, to generalize the paradoxes of freedom, self-interest, and hedonism. To trust is to make oneself or to let oneself be more vulnerable than one might have been to harm from others—to give them an opportunity to harm one, in the confidence that they will not take it, because they have no good reason to. Why would one take such a risk? For risk it always is, given the partial opaqueness to us of the reasoning and motivation of those we trust and with whom we cooperate. Our confidence may be, and quite often is, misplaced. That is what we risk when we trust. If the best reason to take such a risk is the expected gain in security which comes from a climate of trust, then in trusting we are always giving up security to get greater security, exposing our throats so that others become accustomed to not biting. A moral theory which made proper trust its central concern could have its own categorical imperative, could replace obedience to self-made laws and freely chosen restraint on freedom with security-increasing sacrifice of security, distrust in the promoters of a climate of distrust, and so on.

Such reflexive use of one's central concept, negative or affirmative, is an intellectually satisfying activity which is bound to have appeal to those system lovers who want to construct moral theories, and it may help them design their theory in an intellectually pleasing manner. But we should beware of becoming hypnotized by our slogans or of sacrificing truth to intellectual elegance. Any theory of proper trust should not *prejudge* the question of when distrust is proper. We might find more objects of proper distrust than just the contributors to a climate of reasonable distrust, just as freedom should be restricted not just to increase human freedom but to protect human life from poisoners and other killers. I suspect, however, that all the objects of reasonable distrust are more reasonably seen as falling into the category of ones who contribute to a decrease in the scope of proper trust than can all who are reasonably coerced be seen as themselves guilty of wrongful coercion. Still, even if all proper trust turns out to be for such persons and on such matters as will increase the scope or stability of a climate of reasonable trust, and all proper distrust for such persons and on such matters as increase the scope of reasonable distrust, overreliance on such nice reflexive formulae can distract us from asking all the questions about trust which need to be asked if an adequate moral theory is to be constructed around that concept. These questions should include when to *respond* to trust with *un*trustworthiness, when and when not to invite trust, as well as when to give and refuse trust. We should not assume that promiscuous trustworthiness is any more a virtue than is undiscriminating distrust. It is appropriate trustworthiness, appropriate trustingness, appropriate encouragement to trust which will be virtues, as will be judicious untrustworthiness, selective refusal to trust, discriminatng discouragement of trust.

Women are particularly well placed to appreciate these last virtues, since they have sometimes needed them to get into a position even to consider becoming moral theorizers. The long exploitation and domination of women by men depended on men's trust in women and women's trustworthiness to play their allotted role and so to perpetuate their own and their daughters' servitude. However keen women now are to end the lovelessness of modern moral philosophy, they are unlikely to lose sight of the cautious virtue of appropriate distrust or of the tough virtue of the principled betrayal of the exploiters' trust.

Gilligan's girls and women saw morality as a matter of preserving valued ties to others, of preserving the conditions for that care and mutual care without which human life becomes bleak, lonely, and after a while, as the mature men in her study found, not self-affirming, however successful in achieving the egoistic goals which had been set. The boys and men saw morality as a matter of finding workable traffic rules for self-assertors, so that they not needlessly frustrate one another and so that they could, should they so choose, cooperate in more positive ways to mutual advantage. Both for the women's sometimes unchosen and valued ties with others and for the men's mutual respect as sovereigns and subjects of the same minimal moral traffic rules (and for their more voluntary and more selective associations of profiteers), trust is important. Both men and women are concerned with cooperation, and the dimensions of trust-distrust structure the different cooperative relations each emphasize. The various considerations which arise when we try to defend an answer to any question about the appropriateness of a particular form of cooperation with its distinctive form of trust or distrust, that is, when we look into the terms of all sorts of cooperation, at the terms of trust in different cases of trust, at what are fair terms and what are trust-enhancing and trust-preserving terms, are suitably many and richly interconnected. A moral theory (or family of theories) that made trust its central problem could do better justice to men's and women's moral intuitions than do the going men's theories. Even if we don't easily agree on the answer to the question of who should trust whom with what, who should accept and who should meet various sorts of trust, and why, these questions might enable us better to reason morally together than we can when the central moral questions are reduced to those of whose favor one must court and whose anger one must dread. But such programmatic claims as I am making will be tested only when women standing on the shoulders of men, or men on the shoulders of women, or some theorizing Tiresias actually works out such a theory. I am no Tiresias, and have not foresuffered all the labor pains of such a theory. I aim here only to fertilize.

QUESTIONS FOR DISCUSSION

1. According to Robert Mortimer, moral rules are commands of God. Discuss the relation between rules and commands. Is the rule that we ought to obey the commands of God itself a command of God? Would there be any point in an officer issuing certain commands to his men and then commanding them to obey his previous commands?

2. Discuss the philosophical significance of the story of Job in the Old Testament. Was Job wrong to question God? Were Job's three friends wrong in the way they defended God? What dangers do you see in the concept of a divine authority whose decisions are above ethical criticism? Some religious philosophers have argued that such a conception of God is of great moral value because it reduces moral fanaticism. Do you agree?

3. A contemporary philosopher, Bernard Mayo, in *Ethics and the Moral Life,* distinguishes between "conscience" and conscience as follows: "Conscience" urges us to do what we believe to be right, while conscience requires us to do what is in fact right. Does this distinction seem sound to you? How would you judge whether an action is prompted by "conscience" or by conscience? Does Robert Mortimer allow for such a distinction between real and apparent conscience? If so, how?

4. "We are handicapped," writes Ruth Benedict, "in dealing with ethical problems so long as we hold to an absolute definition of morality." Does she mean that in a society that honors a Hitler or a Nero, their actions may be considered morally correct? If not, then what does she mean by a "definition of morality" that is not "absolute"?

5. "The Puritan divines of New England in the eighteenth century were the last persons whom contemporary opinion in the colonies regarded as psychopathic. . . . Yet to a modern observer it is they, not the confused and tormented women they put to death as witches, who were the psychoneurotics of Puritan New England." Which opinion does Benedict think more correct? Do you agree? Why?

6. Discuss Kant's distinction between practical or rational love and pathological or emotional love. Does such a distinction make sense to you?

7. Aristotle remarks that one who takes pleasure in doing what is right is morally superior to one who finds right action painful, but does it grudgingly. Compare this with Kant's claim that only action contrary to natural inclination deserves moral credit.

8. Smart's doctrine of act-utilitarianism employs benefit for the greatest number affected as the sole standard of right action. But how is benefit to be determined? Ronald Dworkin has argued that one of the greatest social benefits is an increase of social justice. But Smart contends that justice may be sacrificed to achieve social benefits such as avoiding a

race riot. Apparently philosophers disagree about how important a benefit justice is compared, say, to alleviation of suffering. Some, like Kant, believe that justice should never be sacrificed for other kinds of benefit. As British judges like to say, "Let justice be done though the heavens fall." Do you agree?

9. What does Richard Hare mean by the "inverted-commas" use of value terms like "good"? Can you give an example of an ironically evaluative use, where the very opposite is meant, and a purely descriptive use, where one means only to identify what other people consider good?

10. Are there really any cases of a purely commendatory use of value terms like "good," where no claim is intended that any criteria are satisfied, so that the descriptive component is absent?

11. What is Rawls's "Principle of Equality"? What is his "general position"? Why might some people in the original position reject the equality principle as formulated by Rawls?

12. According to Philippa Foot, the acquisition of moral virtues like courage and justice is highly beneficial to the individual as well as to society, although there are some situations in which the exercise of the virtue may be harmful to the agent. She considers such conflicts to be rare. Is she right? Or do you think, as Kant seems to, that conflicts between self-interest and moral virtue are all too common?

13. Do you agree with Annette Baier's contention that the past emphasis of philosophical ethics on moral obligation, rather than on love or trust, was due to the fact that until recently almost all philosophers were men and that such emphasis is typically masculine? Could it be rather that ethics is essentially the knowledge of obligations, while love and trust are properly subjects of psychology rather than ethics? One can command oneself to fulfill an obligation, but can one command oneself to love or to trust? Kant said "ought implies can," meaning that morally significant conduct is voluntary, within the agent's power to control. Is this true of love and trust?

SUGGESTED READINGS

Religious Absolutism

AQUINAS, ST., *Summa Theologica,* Book I, Part I, Questions LX–LXIII, trans. Dominican Fathers, Benziger Brothers, New York, 1925.

AUGUSTINE, ST., *The City of God,* Books XII–XIV, XXI, trans. M. Dods, Modern Library, New York, 1950.

BRANDT, R. B., *Ethical Theory,* Chap. 4, Prentice-Hall, Englewood Cliffs, N. J., 1959.

BRUNNER, E., *The Divine Imperative,* Hutchinson, London, 1950.

DONAGAN, A., *The Theory of Morality,* University of Chicago Press, Chicago, 1978.

HEPBURN, R. W., *Christianity and Paradox,* Watts, London, 1958.

MARTIN, C. B., *Religious Belief,* Cornell University Press, Ithaca, N.Y., 1959.

MAYO, B. *Ethics and the Moral Life,* Chap. 8, St. Martin's Press, New York, 1958.

NIEBUHR, R., *An Interpretation of Christian Ethics,* Harper, New York, 1935.

RAMSEY, P., *Basic Christian Ethics,* Scribner's, New York, 1950.

Cultural Relativism

BENEDICT, R., *Patterns of Culture,* Houghton Mifflin, Boston, 1961.

HARMAN, G. *The Nature of Morality,* Oxford University Press, New York, 1978.

HEGEL, G. W. F., *Philosophy of Right,* trans. T. M. Knox, Clarendon Press, Oxford, 1953.

HUME, D., *An Inquiry Concerning the Principles of Morals,* Liberal Arts Press, New York, 1957.

LEVY-BRUHL, L., *Ethics and Moral Science,* trans. E. Lee, Constable, London, 1905.

MACKIE, J., *Ethics: Inventing Right and Wrong,* Penguin Books, Baltimore, 1977.

NIETZSCHE, F., *The Genealogy of Morals,* in *The Philosophy of Nietzsche,* Modern Library, New York, 1950.

PETERS, R. S., *Hobbes,* Chap. 7, Penguin Books, Baltimore, 1956.

ROUSSEAU, J. J., *The Social Contract,* trans. G. D. H. Cole, Dutton, New York, 1938.

STACE, W. T., *The Concept of Morals,* Macmillan, New York, 1937.

SUMNER, W. G., *Folkways,* Ginn, Boston, 1934.

TOULMIN, S. E., *An Examination of the Place of Reason in Ethics, Part III,* Cambridge University Press, London, 1950.

WESTERMARCK, E., *The Origin and Development of the Moral Ideas,* Macmillan, New York, 1906–08.

————, *Ethical Relativity,* reprinted by Greenwood Press, 1970.

Rational Absolutism

BAIER, K., *The Moral Point of View: A Rational Basis of Ethics,* Chaps. 1, 8–10, 12, Cornell University Press, Ithaca, N.Y., 1958.

BLANSHARD, B., *The Nature of Thought,* George Allen & Unwin, London, 1939.

BUTLER, J., *Sermons,* Liberal Arts Press, New York, 1950.

CUDWORTH, R., *Treatise Concerning Eternal and Immutable Morality,* London, 1731.

GEWIRTH, A., *Reason and Morality,* University of Chicago Press, Chicago, 1978.

KORNER, S., *Kant,* Penguin Books, Baltimore, 1955.

MORE, H., *Enchiridion Ethicum,* London, 1667.

PRICHARD, H. A., *Moral Obligation,* Clarendon Press, Oxford, 1949.

————, "Does Moral Philosophy Rest on a Mistake?" *Mind,* 1905.

SINGER, M. G., *Generalization in Ethics,* Knopf, New York, 1961.

Utilitarianism

BENTHAM, J., *An Introduction to the Principles of Morals and Legislation,* Hafner, New York, 1948.

BRANDT, R.B., *Ethical Theory,* Prentice-Hall, Englewood Cliffs, N. J., 1959.

BROAD, C. D., *Five Types of Ethical Theory,* Harcourt, Brace, New York, 1930.

DEWEY, J., *Human Nature and Conduct,* Chaps. 3–4, Modern Library, New York, 1957.

EWING, A. C., *Ethics,* Chap. 5, English Universities Press, London, 1953.

FOOT, P., *Virtues and Vices and Other Essays in Moral Philosophy,* University of California Press, Berkeley, 1979.

GRIFFIN, J., "The Human Good and the Ambitions of Consequentialism," *The Journal of Social Philosophy and Policy,* 9, 2, Jan. 1992.

HAMPSHIRE, S., *Two Theories of Morality,* Oxford University Press, New York, 1977.

HOSPERS, J., *Human Conduct,* Chaps. 4–5, Harcourt, Brace & World, New York, 1961.

KAGAN, S., *The Limits of Morality,* Oxford University Press, 1989.

LOCKE, J., *Essay Concerning Human Understanding,* Book I, ed. A. C. Fraser, Clarendon Press, Oxford, 1894.

MOORE, G. E., *Ethics,* Oxford University Press, London, 1912.

———, *Principia Ethica,* Cambridge University Press, London, 1959.

SCHEFFLER, S., *The Rejection of Consequentialism,* Oxford University Press, London, 1989.

———, *Human Morality,* Oxford University Press, 1992.

SIDGWICK, H., *The Methods of Ethics,* Macmillan, London, 1922.

SMART, J. and B. WILLIAMS, *Utilitarianism: For and Against,* Cambridge University Press, London, 1973.

SPINOZA, B., *Ethics,* trans. R. Elwes, Bell, London, 1906.

STACE, W. T., *The Concept of Morals,* Macmillan, New York, 1937.

Prescriptivism

EDWARDS, P., *The Logic of Moral Discourse,* Free Press, Glencoe, 1955.

HARE, R. M., *The Language of Morals,* Clarendon, Oxford, 1950.

———, *Freedom and Reason,* Clarendon, Oxford, 1963.

HARMAN, G., *The Nature of Morality,* Oxford University Press, New York, 1977.

HUME, D., *Inquiry Concerning the Principles of Morals,* Clarendon, Oxford, 1975.

MACKIE, J. L., *Ethics,* Penguin Books, New York, 1977.

NOWELL-SMITH, P., *Ethics,* Penguin Books, London, 1954.

STEVENSON, C. L., *Ethics and Language,* Yale University Press, New Haven, 1943.

URMSON, J., *The Emotive Theory of Ethics,* Hutchinson, London, 1968.

WELLMAN, C., *The Language of Ethics,* Harvard University Press, Cambridge, 1961.

Contractarianism

ARISTOTLE, *Nichomachean Ethics,* Book V, trans. J. A. K. Thomson, Penguin Books, Baltimore, 1955.

BARRY, B. M., *The Liberal Theory of Justice,* Clarendon Press, Oxford, 1973.

BEDAU, H. A., ed., *Justice and Equality,* Prentice-Hall, Englewood Cliffs, N.J., 1971.

BRANDT, R.B., ed., *Social Justice,* Prentice-Hall, Englewood Cliffs, N.J., 1962.

BRYSON, L., ed., *Aspects of Human Equality,* Harper, New York, 1956.

FISHER, D., "Why should I Be Just?," *Proceedings of Aristotelian Society,* 77, 1977.

FLEW, A., "Equality or Justice?," *Midwestern Studies in Philosophy,* 3, 1978.

FRIEDRICH, C. J., and J. W. CHAPMAN, eds., *Justice,* Atherton Press, New York, 1963.

GINSBERG, M., *On Justice in Society,* Cornell University Press, 1965.

HAYEK, F., *Law, Legislation and Liberty: The Mirage of Social Justice,* University of Chicago Press, Chicago, 1977.

HOSPERS, J., "Free Enterprise as the Embodiment of Justice," in De George, R., and J. Pichler, eds., *Ethics, Free Enterprise and Public Policy.*

KELSEN, H., *What Is Justice?* University of California Press, Berkeley, 1957.

NOZICK, R., *Anarchy, State and Utopia,* Basic Books, New York, 1974.

OLAFSON, F., ed., *Justice and Social Policy,* Prentice-Hall, Englewood Cliffs, N.J., 1961.

RAWLS, J., *A Theory of Justice,* Harvard University Press, Cambridge, 1971.

SMART, J., "The Subjects of Justice," *Ethics,* 90, 1980.

STERBA, J., *The Demands of Justice,* Notre Dame University Press, South Bend, Ind., 1980.

WOLFF, R., "A Refutation of Rawls' Theorum on Justice," *Journal of Philosophy,* 63, 1966.

Virtue Ethics

DENT, N. J. H., *The Moral Psychology of the Virtues,* Cambridge, Mass.: Cambridge University Press, 1984.

FOOT, P., *Virtues and Vices,* Berkeley: University of California, 1978.

GEACH, P., *The Virtues,* Cambridge, Mass.: Cambridge University Press, 1977.

MACINTYRE, A. C., *After Virtue,* South Bend: University of Notre Dame Press, 1984.

PINCOFFS, E., *Quandaries and Virtues,* Lawrence: University of Kansas Press, 1986.

SLOTE, MICHAEL, *Goods and Virtues,* New York: Oxford University Press, 1984.

SLOTE, M., *From Morality to Virtue,* New York: Oxford University, 1992.

WALLACE, J. D., *Virtues and Vices,* Ithaca: Cornell University Press, 1978.

Feminist Ethics

BELL, L., *Rethinking Ethics,* Lanham, Md., Rowland and Littlefield, 1993.

CARD, C., ed., *Feminist Ethics,* Lawrence: University of Kansas Press, 1981.

FOOT, P., *Virtues and Vices,* Berkeley: University of California Press, 1978.

GILLIGAN, C., *In a Different Voice,* Cambridge: Harvard University Press, 1982.

JAGGAR, A., *Feminist Politics and Human Nature,* Totowa, N.J.: Rowman and Allanheld, 1983.

WYSCHOGROD, E., *Saints and Postmodernism,* Chicago: University of Chicago Press, 1990.

General

CASTANEDA, H., *The Structure of Morality,* Thomas, Springfield, 1973.

DONAGAN, A., *The Theory of Morality,* University of Chicago Press, 1977.

FEINBERG, J., *Moral Concepts,* Oxford University Press, London, 1969.

FRANKENA, W., *Ethics,* Prentice-Hall, Englewood Cliffs, 1963.

FRENCH, P., *The Scope of Morality,* University of Minnesota Press, Minneapolis, 1979.

GERT, B., *The Moral Rules,* Harper & Row, New York, 1966.

HARRISON, J., *Our Knowledge of Right and Wrong,* Allen & Unwin, London, 1971.

KAGAN, S., *The Limits of Morality,* Clarendon, Oxford, 1989.

NAGEL, T., *The Possibility of Altruism,* Clarendon, Oxford, 1970.

PARFIT, D., *Reasons and Persons,* Oxford, New York, 1984.

RAWLS, J., *A Theory of Justice,* Harvard University Press, Cambridge, 1971.

THOMSON, J. J., "On Some Ways in Which a Thing Can Be Good," *The Journal of Social Philosophy and Policy,* 9, 2, Summer, 1992, 98–117.

WARNOCK, G., *The Object of Morality,* Methuen, London, 1971.

WILLIAMS, B., *Morality, An Introduction to Ethics,* Harper & Row, New York, 1972.

———, *Ethics and the Limits of Philosophy,* Fantana, London, 1985.

2

THE GROUNDS
FOR MORAL RESPONSIBILITY

HARD DETERMINISM

Paul Edwards

In his essay "The Dilemma of Determinism," William James makes a distinction that will serve as a point of departure for my remarks. He there distinguishes between the philosophers he calls "hard" determinists and those he
labels "soft" determinists. The former, the hard determinists, James tells us,
"did not shrink from such words as fatality, bondage of the will, necessitation
and the like." He quotes a famous stanza from Omar Khayyám as representing this kind of determinism:

> With earth's first clay they did the last man knead,
> And there of the last harvest sowed the seed.
> And the first morning of creation wrote
> What the last dawn of reckoning shall read.

Another of Omar's verses expresses perhaps even better the kind of theory
that James has here in mind:

> Tis all a checker-board of nights and days,
> Where destiny with men for pieces plays;
> Thither and thither moves, and metes, and slays,
> And one by one back to the closet lays.

James mentioned no names other than Omar Khayyám. But there is little doubt that among the hard determinists he would have included Jonathan Edwards, Anthony Collins, Holbach, Priestley, Robert Owen, Schopenhauer, Freud, and also, if he had come a little earlier, Clarence Darrow.

James of course rejected both hard and soft determinism, but for hard determinism he had a certain respect: the kind of respect one sometimes has for an honest, straightforward adversary. For soft determinism, on the other hand, he had nothing but contempt, calling it a "quagmire of evasion." "Nowadays," he writes, "we have a *soft* determinism which abhors harsh words, and repudiating fatality, necessity, and even predeterminism, says that its real name is 'freedom.'" From his subsequent observations it is clear that he would include among the evasionists not only neo-Hegelians like Green and Bradley but also Hobbes and Hume and Mill; and if he were alive today James would undoubtedly include Schlick and Ayer and Stevenson and Noel-Smith. . . .

The theory James calls soft determinism, especially the Hume-Mill-Schlick variety of it, has been extremely fashionable during the last twenty-five years, while hardly anybody can be found today who has anything good to say for hard determinism. In opposition to this contemporary trend, I should like to strike a blow on behalf of hard determinism in my talk today. I shall also try to bring out exactly what is really at issue between hard and soft determinism. I think the nature of this dispute has frequently been misconceived chiefly because many writers, including James, have a very inaccurate notion of what is maintained by actual hard determinists, as distinct from the bogey men they set up in order to score an easy victory.

To begin with, it is necessary to spell more fully the main contentions of the soft determinists. Since it is the dominant form of soft determinism at the present time, I shall confine myself to the Hume-Mill-Schlick theory. According to this theory there is in the first place no contradiction whatsoever between determinism and the proposition that human beings are sometimes free agents. When we call an action "free" we never in any ordinary situation mean that it was uncaused; and this emphatically includes the kind of action about which we pass moral judgments. By calling an action "free" we mean that the agent was not compelled or constrained to perform it. Sometimes people act in a certain way because of threats or because they have been drugged or because of a posthypnotic suggestion or because of an irrational overpowering urge such as the one that makes a kleptomaniac steal something he does not really need. On such occasions human beings are not free agents. But on other occasions they act in certain ways because of their own unimpeded efforts, because they have chosen to act in these ways. On these occasions they are free agents although their actions are just as much caused by actions that are not deemed free. In distinguishing between free and unfree actions we do not try to mark the presence and absence of causes but attempt to indicate the *kind* of causes that are present.

Secondly there is no antithesis between determinism and moral responsibility. When we judge a person morally responsible for a certain action, we do indeed presuppose that he was a free agent at the time of the action. But the freedom presupposed is not the contracausal freedom about which indeterminists go into such ecstatic raptures. It is nothing more than the freedom already mentioned—the ability to act according to one's choices or desires. Since determinism is compatible with freedom in this sense, it is also compatible with moral responsibility. In other words, the world is after all wonderful: we can be determinists and yet go on punishing our enemies and our children, and we can go on blaming ourselves, all without a bad intellectual conscience.

Mill, who was probably the greatest moralizer among the soft determinists, recognized with particular satisfaction the influence or alleged influence of one class of human desires. Not only, for example, does such lowly desire as my desire to get a new car influence my conduct. It is equally true, or so at least Mill believed, that my desire to become a more virtuous person does on occasion influence my actions. By suitable training and efforts my desire to change my character may in fact bring about the desired changes. If Mill were alive today he might point to contemporary psychiatry as an illustration of his point. Let us suppose that I have an intense desire to be famous, but that I also have an intense desire to become a happier and more lovable person who, among other things, does not greatly care about fame. Let us suppose, furthermore, that I know of a therapy that can transform fame-seeking and unlovable into lovable and fame-indifferent character structures. If, now, I have enough money, energy, and courage, and if a few other conditions are fulfilled, my desire may actually lead to a major change in my character. Since we can, therefore, at least to some extent, form our own character, determinism according to Mill is compatible not only with judgments of moral responsibility about this or that particular *action* flowing from an unimpeded desire, but also, within limits, with moral judgments about the *character* of human beings.

I think that several of Mill's observations were well worth making and that James's verdict on his theory as a "quagmire of evasion" is far too derogatory. I think hard determinists have occasionally written in such a way as to suggest that they deny the casual efficacy of human desires and efforts. Thus Holbach wrote:

> You will say that I feel free. This is an illusion, which may be compared to that of the fly in the fable, who, lighting upon the pole of a heavy carriage, applauded himself for directing its course. Man, who thinks himself free, is a fly who imagines he has power to move the universe, while he is himself unknowingly carried along by it.

There is also the following passage in Schopenhauer:

> Every man, being what he is and placed in the circumstances which for the moment obtain, but which on their part also arise by strict necessity, can absolutely never do anything else than just what at that moment he does do. Accordingly, the whole course of a man's life, in all its incidents great and small, is as necessarily predetermined as the course of a clock.

Voltaire expresses himself in much the same way in the article on "Destiny" in the *Philosophical Dictionary:*

> Everything happens through immutable laws... everything is necessary.... "There are," some persons say, "some events which are necessary and others which are not." It would be very comic that one part of the world was arranged, and the other were not; that one part of what happens had to happen and that another part of what happens did not have to happen. If one looks closely at it, one sees that the doctrine contrary to that of destiny is absurd; but there are many people destined to reason badly; others not to reason at all, others to persecute those who reason....
>
> ... I necessarily have the passion for writing this, and you have the passion for condemning me; both of us are equally fools, equally the toy of destiny. Your nature is to do harm, mine is to love truth, and to make it public in spite of you.

Furthermore there can be little doubt that Hume and Mill and Schlick were a great deal clearer about the relation between motives and actions than the hard determinists, who either conceived it, like Collins, as one of logical necessity or, like Priestley and Voltaire and Schopenhauer, as necessarily involving coercion or constraint.

But when all is said and done, there remains a good deal of truth in James's charge that soft determinism is an evasion. For a careful reading of their works shows that none of the hard determinists really denied that human desires, efforts, and choices make a difference in the course of events. Any remarks to the contrary are at most temporary lapses. This, then, is hardly the point at issue. If it is not the point at issue, what is? Let me at this stage imagine a hard determinist replying to a champion of the Hume-Mill theory: "You are right," he would say, "in maintaining that some of our actions are caused by our desires and choices. But you do not pursue the subject far enough. You arbitrarily stop at the desires and volitions. We must not stop there. We must go on to ask where *they* come from: and if determinism is true there can be no doubt about the answer to this question. Ultimately our desires and our whole character are derived from our inherited equipment and the environmental influences to which we were subjected at the beginning of our lives. It is clear that we had no hand in shaping either of these." A hard determinist could quote a number of eminent supporters. "Our volitions and our desires," wrote Holbach in his little book *Good Sense,* "are never in our power. You think yourself free, because you do what you will: but are you free to will or not to will; to desire or not to desire?" And Schopenhauer expressed the same thought in the following epigram: "A man can surely do what he wills to do, but he cannot determine what he wills."

Let me turn once more to the topic of character transformation by means of psychiatry to bring out this point with full force. Let us suppose that both *A* and *B* are compulsive and suffer intensely from their neuroses. Let us assume that there is a therapy that could help them, which could materially change their character structure, but that it takes a great deal of energy and courage to undertake the treatment. Let us suppose that *A* has the necessary energy and courage while *B* lacks it. *A* undergoes the therapy and changes in the desired way. *B* just gets more and more compulsive and more and more miserable. Now, it is true that *A* helped form his own later character. But his starting point, his desire to change, his energy and courage, were already there. They may or may not have been the result of previous efforts on his own part. But there must have been a first effort, and the effort at that time was the result of factors that were not of his making.

The fact that a person's character is ultimately the product of factors over which he had no control is not denied by the soft determinists, though many of them don't like to be reminded of it when they are in a moralizing mood. Since the hard determinists admit that our desires and choices do on occasion influence the course of our lives, there is thus no disagreement between the soft and the hard determinists about the empirical facts. However, some hard determinists infer from some of these facts that human beings are never morally responsible for their actions. The soft determinists, as already stated, do not draw any such inference. In the remainder of my paper I shall try to show just what it is that hard determinists are inferring and why, in my opinion, they are justified in their conclusion.

I shall begin by adopting for my purposes a distinction introduced by C. A. Campbell in his extremely valuable article "Is Free Will a Pseudo-Problem?" in which he distinguishes between two conceptions of moral responsibility. Different persons, he says, require different conditions to be fulfilled before holding human beings morally responsible for what they do. First, there is what Campbell calls the ordinary unreflective person, who is rather ignorant and who is not greatly concerned with the theories of science, philosophy, and religion. If the unreflective person is sure that the agent to be judged was acting under coercion or constraint, he will not hold him responsible. If, however, he is sure that the action was performed in accordance with the agent's unimpeded rational desire, if he is sure that the action would not have taken place but for the agent's decision, then the unreflective person will consider ascription of moral responsibility justified. The fact that the agent did not ultimately make his own character will either not occur to him, or else it will not be considered a sufficient ground for withholding a judgment of moral responsibility.

In addition to such unreflective persons, continues Campbell, there are others who have reached "a tolerably advanced level of reflection."

> Such a person will doubtless be acquainted with the claims advanced in some quarters that causal law operates universally; or/and with the theories of some philosophies that the universe is throughout the expression of a single supreme principle; or/and with the doctrines of some theologians that the world is created, sustained and governed by an Omniscient and Omnipotent Being.

Such a person will tend to require the fulfillment of a further condition before holding anybody morally responsible. He will require not only that the agent was not coerced or constrained but also—and this is taken to be an additional condition—that he "could have chosen otherwise than he actually did." I should prefer to put this somewhat differently, but it will not affect the main conclusion drawn by Campbell, with which I agree. The reflective person, I should prefer to express it, requires not only that the agent was not coerced; he also requires that the agent *originally chose his own character*—the character that now displays itself in his choices and desires and efforts. Campbell concludes that determinism is indeed compatible with judgments of moral responsibility in the unreflective sense, but that it is incompatible with judgments of moral responsibility in the reflective sense.

Although I do not follow Campbell in rejecting determinism, I agree basically with his analysis, with one other qualification. I do not think it is a question of the different senses in which the term is used by ignorant and unreflective people, on the one hand, and by those who are interested in science, religion, and philosophy, on the other. The very same persons, whether educated or uneducated, use it in certain contexts in the one sense and in other contexts in the other. Practically all human beings, no matter how much interested they are in science, religion, and philosophy, employ what Campbell calls the unreflective conception when they are dominated by violent emotions like anger, indignation, or hate, and especially when the conduct they are judging has been personally injurious to them. On the other hand, a great many people, whether they are educated or not, will employ what Campbell calls the reflective conception when they are not consumed with hate or anger—when they are judging a situation calmly and reflectively and when the fact that the agent did not ultimately shape his own character has been vividly brought to their attention. Clarence Darrow in his celebrated pleas repeatedly appealed to the jury on precisely this ground. If any of you, he would say, had been reared in an environment like that of the accused or had to suffer from his defective heredity, *you* would now be standing in the dock. I cannot refrain at this stage from reading a poem written by the hard determinist, A. E. Housman, which Darrow recited on such occasions. Its title is "The Culprit," and it is the soliloquy of a boy about to be hanged.

> The night my father got me
> His mind was not on me;
> He did not plague his fancy
> To muse if I should be
> The son you see.
>
> The day my mother bore me
> She was a fool and glad,
> For all the pain I cost her,
> That she had borne the lad
> That borne she had.

My mother and my father
 Out of the light they lie;
The warrant could not find them,
 And here 'tis only I
 Shall hang so high.

Oh let not man remember
 The soul that God forgot,
But fetch the county kerchief
 And noose me in the knot,
 And I will rot.

For so the game is ended
 That should not have begun.
My father and my mother
 They had a likely son,
 And I have none.

Darrow nearly always convinced the jury that the accused could not be held morally responsible for his acts; and certainly the majority of the jurors were relatively uneducated.

I have so far merely distinguished between two concepts of moral responsibility. I now wish to go a step farther and claim that only one of them can be considered, properly speaking, a moral concept. This is not an easy point to make clear, but I can at least indicate what I mean. We do not normally consider just any positive or negative feeling a "moral" emotion. Nor do we consider just any sentence containing the words "good" or "bad" expressions of "moral" judgment. For example, if a man hates a woman because she rejected him, this would not be counted as a moral emotion. If, however, he disapproves, say, of Senator McCarthy's libelous speech against Adlai Stevenson before the 1952 election because he disapproves of slander in general and not merely because he likes Stevenson and dislikes McCarthy, his feeling would be counted as moral. A feeling or judgment must in a certain sense be "impersonal" before we consider it moral. To this I would add that it must also be a judgment of violent emotions. Confining myself to judgments, I would say that a judgment was "moral" only if it was formulated in a calm and reflective mood, or at least if it was supported in a calm and reflective state of mind. If this is so, it follows that what Campbell calls the reflective sense of "moral responsibility" is the only one that qualifies as a properly moral use of the term.

Before I conclude I wish to avoid a certain misunderstanding of my remarks. From the fact that human beings do not ultimately shape their own character, I said, it *follows* that they are never morally responsible. I do not mean that by reminding people of the ultimate causes of their character one makes them more charitable and less vengeful. Maybe one does, but that is not what I mean. I mean "follow" or "imply" in the same sense as, or in a sense closely akin to, that in which the conclusion of a valid syllogism follows from the premises. The effectiveness of Darrow's pleas does not merely show, I am arguing, how powerfully he could sway the emotions of the jurors. His pleas also brought into the open one of the conditions the jurors, like others, consider necessary on reflection before they hold an agent morally responsible. Or perhaps I should say that Darrow *committed* the jurors in their reflective nature to a certain ground for the ascription of moral responsibility.

*L*IBERTARIANISM

Roderick M. Chisholm

> *A staff moves a stone, and is moved by a hand, which is moved by a man.*
>
> —ARISTOTLE, *Physics,* 256a

I

The metaphysical problem of human freedom might be summarized in the following way: "Human beings are responsible agents; but this fact appears to conflict with a deterministic view of human action (the view that every event that is involved in an act is caused by some other event); and it *also* appears to conflict with an indeterministic view of human action (the view that the act, or some event that is essential to the act, is not caused at all)." To solve the problem, I believe, we must make somewhat far-reaching assumptions about the self of the agent—about the man who performs the act.

Perhaps it is needless to remark that, in all likelihood, it is impossible to say anything significant about this ancient problem that has not been said before.

Let us consider some deed, or misdeed, that may be attributed to a responsible agent: one man, say, shot another. If the man *was* responsible for what he did, then, I would urge, what was to happen at the time of the shooting was something that was entirely up to the man himself. There was a moment at which it was true, both that he could have fired the shot and also that he could have refrained from firing it. And if this is so, then, even though he did fire it, he could have done something else instead. (He didn't find himself firing the shot "against his will," as we say.) I think we can say, more generally, then, that if a man is responsible for a certain event or a certain state of affairs (in our example, the shooting of another man), then that event or state of affairs was brought about by some act of his, and the act was something that was in his power either to perform or not to perform.

But now, if the act which he *did* perform was an act that was also in his power *not* to perform, then *it* could not have been caused or determined by any event that was not itself within his power either to bring about or not to bring about. For example, if what we say he did was really something that was brought about by a second man, one who forced his hand upon the

---

"Libertarianism," by Roderick M. Chisholm, from *Freedom & Determinism,* ed. K. Lehrer.

trigger, say, or who, by means of hypnosis, compelled him to perform the act, then, since the act was caused by the *second* man, it was nothing that was within the power of the *first* man to prevent. And precisely the same thing is true, I think, if instead of referring to a second man who compelled the first one, we speak instead of the *desires* and *beliefs* which the first man happens to have had. For if what we say he did was really something that was brought about by his own beliefs and desires, if these beliefs and desires in the particular situation in which he happened to have found himself caused him to do just what it was they say he did do, then, since *they* caused it, *he* was unable to do anything other than just what he did do. It makes no difference whether the cause of the deed was internal or external: if the cause was some state or event for which the man himself was not responsible, then he was not responsible for what we have been mistakenly calling his act. If a flood caused the poorly structured dam to break, then, given the flood and the constitution of the dam, the break, we may say, *had* to occur and nothing could have happened in its place. And if the flood of desire caused the weak-willed man to give in, then he too, had to do just what it was that he did do and he was no more responsible than was the dam for the results that followed. (It is true, of course, that if the man is responsible for the beliefs and desires that he happens to have, then he may also be responsible for the things they lead him to do. But the question now becomes: *is* he responsible for the beliefs and desires he happens to have? If he is, then there was a time when they were within his power either to acquire or not to acquire, and we are left, therefore, with our general point.)

One may object: But surely if there were such a thing as a man who is really *good,* then he would be responsible for things that he would do; yet, he would be unable to do anything other than just what he does do, since, being good, he will always choose to do what is best. The answer, I think, is suggested by a comment that Thomas Reid makes upon an ancient author. The author had said of Cato, "He was good because he could not be otherwise," and Reid observes: "This saying, if understood literally and strictly, is not the praise of Cato, but of his constitution which was no more the work of Cato than his existence." If Cato was himself responsible for the good things that he did, then Cato, as Reid suggests, was such that, although he had the power to do what was not good, he exercised his power only for that which was good.

All of this, if it is true, may give a certain amount of comfort to those who are tender-minded. But we should remind them that it also conflicts with a familiar view about the nature of God—with the view that St. Thomas Aquinas expresses by saying that "every movement both of the will and of nature proceeds from God as the Prime Mover." If the act of the sinner *did* proceed from God as the Prime Mover, then God was in the position of the second agent we just discussed—the man who forced the trigger finger, or the hypnotist—and the sinner, so-called, was *not* responsible for what he did. (This may be a bold assertion, in view of the history of western theology, but I must say that I have never encountered a single good reason for denying it.)

There is one standard objection to all of this and we should consider it briefly.

The objection takes the form of a stratagem—one designed to show that determinism (and divine providence) is consistent with human responsibility. The stratagem is one that was used by Jonathan Edwards and by many philosophers in the present century, most notably, G. E. Moore.

One proceeds as follows: The expression

(a) He could have done otherwise,

it is argued, means no more nor less than

(b) If he had chosen to do otherwise, then he would have done otherwise.

(In place of "chosen," one might say "tried," "set out," "decided," "undertaken," or "willed.") The truth of statement (b), it is then pointed out, is consistent with determinism (and with divine providence); for even if all of the man's actions were causally determined, the man could still be such that, *if* he had chosen otherwise, then he would have done otherwise. What the murderer saw, let us suppose, along with his beliefs and desires, *caused* him to fire the shot; yet he was such that *if,* just then, he had chosen or decided *not* to fire the shot, then he would not have fired it. All of this is certainly possible. Similarly, we could say, of the dam, that the flood caused it to break and also that the dam was such that, *if* there had been no flood or similar pressure, then the dam would have remained intact. And therefore, the argument proceeds, if (b) is consistent with determinism, and if (a) and (b) say the same thing, then (a) is also consistent with determinism; hence we can say that the agent *could* have done otherwise, even though he was caused to do what he did do; and therefore determinism and moral responsibility are compatible.

Is the argument sound? The conclusion follows from the premises, but the catch, I think, lies in the first premise—the one saying that statement (a) tells us no more nor less than what statement (b) tells us. For (b), it would seem, could be true while (a) is false. That is to say, our man might be such that, if he had chosen to do otherwise, then he would have done otherwise, and yet *also* such that he could not have done otherwise. Suppose, after all, that our murderer could not have *chosen,* or could not have *decided,* to do otherwise. Then the fact that he happens also to be a man such that, if he had chosen not to shoot he would not have shot, would make no difference. For if he could *not* have chosen *not* to shoot, then he could not have done anything other than just what it was that he did do. In a word: from our statement (b) above ("If he had chosen to do otherwise, then he would have done otherwise"), we cannot make an inference to (a) above ("He could have done otherwise"), unless we can *also* assert:

(c) He could have chosen to do otherwise.

And therefore, if we must reject this third statement (c), then, even though we may be justified in asserting (b), we are not justified in asserting (a). If the man could not have chosen to do otherwise, then he would not have done otherwise—*even if* he was such that, if he *had* chosen to do otherwise, then he would have done otherwise.

The stratagem in question, then, seems to me not to work, and I would say, therefore, that the ascription of responsibility conflicts with a deterministic view of action.

Perhaps there is less need to argue that the ascription of responsibility also conflicts with an indeterministic view of action—with the view that the act, or some event that is essential to the act, is not caused at all. If the act—the firing of the shot—was not caused at all, if it was fortuitous or capricious, happening so to speak "out of the blue," then, presumably, no one—and nothing—was responsible for the act. Our conception of action, therefore, should be neither deterministic nor indeterministic. Is there any other possibility?

We must not say that every event involved in the act is caused by some other event, and we must not say that the act is something that is not caused at all. The possibility that remains, therefore, is this: We should say that at least one of the events that are involved in the act is caused, not by any other events, but by something else instead. And this something else can only be the agent—the man. If there is an event that is caused, not by other events, but by the man, then there are some events involved in the act that are not caused by other events. But if the event in question is caused by the man, then it *is* caused and we are not committed to saying that there is something involved in the act that is not caused at all.

But this, of course, is a large consequence, implying something of considerable importance about the nature of the agent or the man.

If we consider only inanimate natural objects, we may say that causation, if it occurs, is a relation between *events* or *states of affairs.* The dam's breaking was an event that was caused by a set of other events—the dam being weak, the flood being strong, and so on. But if a man is responsible for a particular deed, then, if what I have said is true, there is some event, or set of events, that is caused, *not* by other events or states of affairs, but by the man himself, by the agent, whatever he may be.

I shall borrow a pair of medieval terms, using them, perhaps, in a way that is slightly different from that for which they were originally intended. I shall say that when one event or state of affairs (or set of events or states of affairs) causes some other event or state of affairs, then we have an instance of *transeunt* causation. And I shall say that when an *agent,* as distinguished from an event, causes an event or state of affairs, then we have an instance of *immanent* causation.

The nature of what is intended by the expression "immanent causation" may be illustrated by this sentence from Aristotle's *Physics:* "Thus, a staff moves a stone, and is moved by a hand, which is moved by a man." (VII, 5, 256a, 6–8) If the man was responsible, then we have in this illustration a number of instances of causation—most of them transeunt, but at least one of them immanent. What the staff did to the stone was an instance of transeunt causation, and thus we may describe it as a relation between events: "the motion of the staff caused the motion of the stone." And similarly for what the hand did to the staff: "the motion of the hand caused the motion of the staff." And, as we know from physiology, there are still other events which caused the motion of the hand. Hence we need not introduce the agent at this particular point, as Aristotle does—we *need* not, though we *may.* We *may* say that the hand was moved by the man, but we may *also* say that the motion of the hand was caused by the motion of certain muscles; and we may say the motion of the muscles was caused by certain events that took place within the brain. But some event, and presumably one of those that took place within the brain, was caused by the agent and not by any other events.

There are, of course, objections to this way of putting the matter; I shall consider the two that seem to me to be the most important.

One may object, firstly: "If the *man* does anything, then, as Aristotle's remark suggests, what he does is to move the *hand.* But he certainly does not *do* anything to his brain—he may not even know that he *has* a brain. And if he doesn't do anything to the brain, and if, as physiology seems to tell us, the motion of the hand was caused by something that happened within the brain, then there is no point in appealing to 'immanent causation' as being something incompatible with 'transeunt causation'—for the whole thing, after all, is a matter of causal relations among events or states of affairs. The motion of the hand was caused by the brain and not by the man."

The answer to this objection, I think, is this: It is true that the agent does not *do* anything with his brain, or to his brain, in the sense in which he *does* something with his hand and does something to the staff. But from this it does not follow that the agent was not the immanent cause of something that happened within his brain.

We should note a useful distinction that has been proposed by Professor A. I. Melden—namely, the distinction between "making something A happen" and "doing A." If I reach for the staff and pick it up, then one of the things that I *do* is just that—reach for the staff and pick it up. And if it is something that I do, then there is a very clear sense in which it may be said to be something that I know that I do. If you ask me, "Are you doing something, or trying to do something, with the staff?," I will have no difficulty in finding an answer. But in doing something with the staff, I also make various things happen which are not in the same sense things that I do: I will make various air-particles move; I will free a number of blades of grass from the pressure that had been upon them; and I may cause a shadow to move from one place to another. If these are merely things that I make happen, as distinguished from things that I do, then I may know nothing whatever about them; I may not have the slightest idea that, in moving the staff, I am bringing about any such thing as the motion of air-particles, shadows, and blades of grass.

We may say, in answer to the first objection, therefore, that it is true that our agent does nothing to his brain or with his brain; but from this it does not follow that the agent is not the immanent cause of some event within his brain, for the brain event may be something which, like the motion of the air-particles, he made happen in picking up the staff. The only difference between the two cases is this: in each case, he made something happen when he picked up the staff; but in the one case—the motion of the air-particles or of the shadows—it was the motion of the staff that caused the event to happen; and in the other case—the event that took place in the brain—it was this event that caused the motion of the staff.

The point is, in a word, that whenever a man does something A, then (by "immanent causation") he makes a certain cerebral event happen, and this cerebral event (by "transeunt causation") makes A happen.

The second objection is more difficult, and it concerns the very concept of "immanent causation," or causation by an agent, as this concept is to be interpreted here. The concept is subject to a difficulty which has long been associated with that of the prime mover unmoved. We have said that there must be some event A, presumably some cerebral event, which is caused not by any other event, but by the agent. Since A was not caused by any other event, then the agent himself cannot be said to have undergone any change or produced any other event (such as "an act of will" or the like) which brought A about. For if the cerebral event is caused by some change *within* the agent, then it *is* caused by an event and we have lost the solution to our problem. But now: if, when the agent made A happen, there was no event involved other than A itself, no event which could be described as *making* A happen, what did the agent's causation consist of? What, for example, is the difference between A's just happening, and the agent's *causing* A to happen? We cannot attribute the difference to any event that took place within the agent. And so far as the event A itself is concerned, there would seem to be no discernible difference—no discernible difference between A just happening and the agent causing A to happen. Thus Aristotle said that the activity of the prime mover is nothing in addition to the motion that it produces, and Suarez said that "the action is in reality nothing but the effect as it flows from the agent." Must we conclude, then, that there is no more to the man's action in causing event A then there is to the event A's happening by itself? Here we would seem to have a distinction without a difference—in which case we have failed to find a *via media* between a deterministic and an indeterministic view of action.

The only answer, I think, can be this: that the difference between the man's causing A, on the one hand, and the event A just happening, on the other, lies in the fact that, in the first case but not the second, the event A *was* caused and was caused by the man. There was a brain event A; the agent did, in fact, cause the brain event; but there was nothing that he did to cause it.

This answer may not entirely satisfy and it will be likely to provoke the following question: "But what are you really *adding* to the assertion that A happened when you utter the words 'The agent *caused* A to happen'?" As soon as we have put the question this way, we see, I think, that whatever difficulty we may have encountered is one that may be traced to the concept of causation generally—whether "immanent" or "transeunt." The problem, in other words, is not a problem that is peculiar to our conception of human action. It is a problem that must be faced by anyone who makes use of the concept of causation at all and therefore, I would say, it is a problem for everyone but the complete indeterminist.

For the problem, as we put it, referring just to "immanent causation," or causation by an agent, was this: "What is the difference between saying, of an event A, that A just happened and saying that someone caused A to happen?" The analogous problem, which holds for "transeunt causation," or causation by an event, is this: "What is the difference between saying, of two events A and B, that B happened and then A happened, and saying that B's happening was the *cause* of A's happening?" And the only answer that one can give is this—that in the one case the agent was the cause of A's happening, and in the other case event B was the cause of A's happening. The nature of transeunt causation is no more clear than is that of immanent causation. In short, as long as we talk about causation at all (and we cannot avoid it) the difficulty is one that we will have on our hands. It is not a difficulty that is peculiar, therefore, to our treatment of the problem of freedom.

But we may plausibly say—and there is a respectable philosophical tradition to which we may appeal—that the notion of immanent causation, or causation by an agent, is in fact more clear than that of transeunt causation, or causation by an event, and that it is only by understanding our own causal efficacy, as agents, that we can grasp the concept of *cause* at all. Hume may be said to have shown that we do not derive the concept of *cause* from what we perceive of external things. How, then, do we derive it? The most plausible suggestion, it seems to me, is that of Reid, once again: namely, that "the conception of an efficient cause may very probably be derived from the experience we have had . . . of our own power to produce certain effects." If we did not understand the concept of immanent causation, we would not understand that of transeunt causation.

It may have been noted that I have avoided the term "free will" in all of this. For even if there is such a faculty as "the will," which somehow sets our acts a-going, the question of freedom, as John Locke said, is not "the question whether the will be free"; it is the question "whether a man be free." For if there is a "will," as a moving faculty, the question is whether the man is free to will to do those things that he does will to do—and also whether he is free *not* to will any of those things that he does will to do, and, again, whether he is free to will any of those things that he does not will to do. Jonathan Edwards tried to restrict himself to the question—"Is the man free to do what it is that he wills?"—but the answer to this question will not tell us whether the man is responsible for what it is that he *does* will to do. Using still another pair of medieval terms, we may say that the metaphysical problem of freedom does not concern the *actus imperatus:* it does not concern the question whether we are free to accomplish whatever it is that we will or set out to do; it concerns the *actus elicitus,* the question whether we are free to will or to set out to do those things that we will or set out to do. It is one thing to ask whether the things that a man wills are things that are within his power: this is the problem of the *actus imperatus.* It is quite a different thing to ask whether his willing itself is something that is within his power: this is the problem of the *actus elicitus.* And this latter—the problem of the *actus elicitus*—is the problem, not of the freedom of the will, but of the freedom of the man.

If we are responsible, and if what I have been trying to say is true, then we have a prerogative which some would attribute only to God: each of us, when we act, is a prime mover unmoved. In doing what we do, we cause certain events to happen, and nothing—or no one—causes us to cause those events to happen.

If we are thus prime movers unmoved and if our actions, or those for which we are responsible, are not causally determined, then they are not causally determined by our *desires.* And this means that the relation between what we want or what we desire, on the one hand, and what it is that we do, on the other, is not as simple as most philosophers would have it.

We may distinguish between what we might call the "Hobbist approach" and what we might call the "Kantian approach" to this question. The Hobbist approach is the one that is generally accepted at the present time, but the Kantian approach, I believe, is the one that is true. According to Hobbism, if we *know,* of some man, what his beliefs and desires happen to be and how strong they are, if we know what he feels certain of, what he desires more than anything else, and if we know the state of his body and what stimuli he is being subjected to, then we may *deduce,* logically, just what it is that he will do—or, more accurately, just what it is that he will try, set out, or undertake to do. Thus Professor Melden has said that "the connection between wanting and doing is logical."

But according to the Kantian approach to our problem, and this is the one that I would take, there is no such logical connection between wanting and doing, nor need there even be a causal connection. No set of statements about a man's desires, beliefs, and stimulus situation at any time implies any statement, telling us what the man will try, set out, or undertake to do at that time. As Reid put it, "Though we may reason from men's motives to their actions and, in many cases, with great probability," we can never do so "with absolute certainty."

This means that, in one very strict sense of the terms, there can be no complete science of man. If we think of science as a matter of finding out what laws happen to hold, and if the statement of a law tells us what kinds of events are caused by what other kinds of events, then there will be human actions that we cannot explain by subsuming them under any laws. We cannot say, "It is causally necessary that, given such and such desires and beliefs, and being subject to such and such stimuli, the agent will do so and so." For at times the agent, if he chooses, may rise above his desires and do something else instead.

But all of this is consistent with saying that, perhaps more often than not, our desires do exist under conditions such that those conditions necessitate us to act. And we may also say, with Leibniz, that at other times our desires may "incline without necessitating."

Leibniz's phrase presents us with still another philosophical problem. What does it mean to say that a desire, or a motive, might "incline without necessitating"? There is a temptation, certainly, to say that "to incline" means to cause and that "not to necessitate" means not to cause, but obviously we cannot have it both ways.

Nor will Leibniz's own solution do. In his letter to Coste, he puts the problem as follows: "When a choice is proposed, for example to go out or not to go out, it is a question whether, with all the circumstances, internal and external, motives, perceptions, dispositions, impressions, passions, inclinations taken together, I am still in a contingent state, or whether I am necessitated to make the choice, for example, to go out; that is to say, whether this proposition, true and determined in fact, *In all these circumstances taken together I shall choose to go out,* is contingent or necessary." Leibniz's answer might be put as follows: in one sense of the terms "necessary" and "contingent," the proposition "In all these circumstances taken together I shall choose to go out," may be said to be contingent and not necessary, and in another sense of these terms, it may be said to be necessary, and not contingent. But the sense in which the proposition may be said to be contingent, according to Leibniz, is only this: there is no logical contradiction involved in denying the proposition. And the sense in which it may be said to be necessary is this: since "nothing ever occurs without cause of determining reason," the proposition is causally necessary. "Whenever all the circumstances taken together are such that, the balance of deliberation is heavier on one side than on the other, it is certain and infallible that that is the side that is going to win out." But if what we have been saying is true, the proposition "In all these circumstances taken together I shall choose to go out" may be causally as well as logically contingent. Hence we must find another interpretation for Leibniz's statement that our motives and desires may incline us, or influence us, to choose without thereby necessitating us to choose.

Let us consider a public official who has some moral scruples but who also, as one says, "could be had." Because of the scruples that he does have, he would never take any positive steps to receive a bribe—he would not actively solicit one. But morality has its limits and he is also such that, if we were to confront him with a *fait accompli* or to let him see what is about to happen ($10,000 in cash is being deposited behind the garage), then he would succumb and be unable to resist. The general situation is a familiar one and this is one reason that people pray to be delivered from temptation. (And it also justifies Kant's remark: "How many there are who may have led a long blameless life, who are only *fortunate* in having escaped so many temptations.") Our relation to the misdeed that we contemplate may not be a matter simply of our being able to bring it about or not to bring it about. As St. Anselm noted, there are at least four possibilities. We may illustrate them, by reference to our public official and the event which is his receiving the bribe, in the following way: (i) he may be able to bring the event about himself (*facere esse*), in which case he would actively cause himself to receive the bribe; (ii) he may be able to refrain from bringing it about himself (*non facere esse*), in which case he would not himself do anything to insure that he receive the bribe; (iii) he may be able to do something to prevent the event from occurring (*facere non esse*), in which case he would make sure that the $10,000 was *not* left behind the garage; or (iv) he may be unable to do anything to prevent the event from occurring (*non facere non esse*), in which case, though he may not solicit the bribe, he would allow himself to keep it. We have envisaged our official as a man who can resist the temptation to (i) but cannot resist the temptation to (iv): he can refrain from bringing the event about himself, but he cannot bring himself to do anything to prevent it.

Let us think of "inclination without necessitation," then, in such terms as these. First we may contrast the two propositions:

(1) He can resist the temptation to do something in order to make A happen;

(2) He can resist the temptation to allow A to happen (i.e., to do nothing to prevent A from happening).

We may suppose that the man has some desire to have A happen and thus has a motive for making A happen. His motive for making A happen, I suggest, is one that *necessitates,* provided that, because of the motive, (1) is false: he cannot resist the temptation to do something in order to make A happen. His motive for making A happen is one that *inclines,* provided that, because of the motive, (2) is false: like our public official, he cannot bring himself to do anything to prevent A from happening. And therefore we can say that his motive for making A happen is one that *inclines* but does not *necessitate,* provided that, because of the motive, (1) is true and (2) is false; he can resist the temptation to make it happen but he cannot resist the temptation to allow it to happen.

Let us now consider the concept of an act, or a deed, in more detail.

II

The concept of an act, or a deed, is both imputative and descriptive. When we say of a man that he *did* something, we may be declaring, by way of imputation, that the man is to be held responsible for making a certain thing happen; that is to say, we may be pronouncing a verdict, notifying our hearers that forthwith we are holding this man responsible. But we are also making a descriptive statement; we are saying that the man was a causal factor in making something happen, or in keeping something from happening. Let us now try to lay bare this descriptive element in the concept of an act, stripping from it all implications of moral and legal responsibility. The point of doing this is to throw light upon the interrelations among several important and perplexing concepts and to contribute toward the solution of certain additional philosophical puzzles.

H. L. A. Hart has suggested that the descriptive facts we presuppose in applying our action concepts might consist simply of facts about the state of the agent's body and what it causes or fails to cause ("His arm went up and knocked over the lamp" as distinguished from "He knocked over the lamp with his arm"). But this suggestion, it seems to me, is clearly mistaken. If we ask ourselves, for example, "What facts, in the absence of defeating considerations, would warrant our saying that one man has killed another?" we will find, I think, that these facts cannot be described merely by reference to what is caused by some state of the agent's body; similarly for some, at least, of those facts that would defeat the ascription of killing.

What more is there, then, to the concept of an act? First, there is the fact that the agent himself, as we have seen, is a causal factor. We must say that at least one of the events that is involved in any act is caused, not by any other event, but by the agent, by the man. Causation is a relation that holds, not only between states or events, but also between agents, as causes, and states or events, as effects. And, secondly, there is the fact that the concept of an act is essentially teleological. Action involves *endeavor* or *purpose,* one thing occurring *in order that* some other thing may occur. And this concept of endeavor, or purpose, must be distinguished from that of *want* or *desire.* A man may endeavor, or undertake, to bring about what he does not desire and what he does not even believe to be a means to anything that he desires; and he may refrain from undertaking to bring about what he does desire.

Some philosophers, however, have attempted to define purpose, or endeavor, in terms of belief, causation, and desire. It has been suggested, for example, that a man might be said to bring about something X *for the purpose of* bringing about something Y, provided that the following three conditions hold: (i) he desires Y; (ii) he believes that, if he brings about X, then he will bring about Y; and (iii) this belief and desire jointly cause him to bring about X. But this type of definition is too broad and does not in fact capture the concept of purpose. Suppose, for example: (i) a certain man desires to inherit a fortune; (ii) he believes that, if he kills his uncle, then he will inherit a fortune; and (iii) this belief and this desire agitate him so severely that he drives excessively fast, with the result that he accidentally runs over and kills a pedestrian who, unknown to the nephew, was none other than the uncle. The proposed definition of purpose would require us to say, incorrectly, that the nephew killed the uncle in order to inherit the fortune.

Let us attempt to set forth the descriptive element in the concept of action by an undefined locution, one indicating both that the agent is a cause and that the action is purposive or teleological. I propose the following:

> There is a state of affairs A and a state of affairs B, such that, at time *t*, he makes B happen in the endeavor to make A happen.

As an alternative for the English expression, "He makes B happen," we might use "He realizes B," "He brings it about that B," or, if "state of affairs" is replaced by "proposition," then "He makes it true that B." The letters may be replaced, in obvious ways, by propositional clauses. The relation of "making happen" is transitive and asymmetrical: if A makes B happen, then B does not make A happen. The states of affairs to which our locution refers may be "unchanges" as well as changes; they may also be complex (e.g., "He makes B happen with an end to making it happen that A and that A makes C happen"). And the subject term of "makes happen" may designate either a state of affairs or a person.

"Make happen" is to be taken in such a way that we may say, of a man who raises his arm, not only that he makes it happen that his arm goes up, but also that he makes it happen, just before, that certain other physiological events occur inside his body, and that he makes it happen, just subsequently, that air particles move in various ways.

The teleological component of our locution (viz., "in the endeavor to make A happen") should be taken as intentional. This means, for example, that a man may make something happen in the endeavor to make A happen without thereby actually making A happen. It also means that, from "He made something happen in the endeavor to make A happen and he did thereby make A happen" and "A is the same concrete event as B," we may not infer "He made something happen in the endeavor to make B happen." And it also means that, if a man makes something B happen in the endeavor to make something A happen, then he can *know,* directly or immediately, that he is making something happen in the endeavor to make A happen, but, as the example from the previous paragraph will indicate, he may not know at all that he is making B happen.

Since we are attempting to describe *action* in terms of *making happen*—or, more accurately, in terms of making things happen *in the endeavor* to make things happen—the "A's" and "B's" of our formulae will not normally be replaceable by expressions which themselves refer to actions. If I am right, the man who raises his arm under ordinary circumstances will make something happen in the endeavor to make it happen, *not* that he raises his arm, but that his arm goes up. (But the paralytic, in the course of his exercises, may make things happen now in the endeavor to make it happen that later he raises his arm.) To act, therefore, is to endeavor to make happen. But from this it does not follow that when a man acts he therefore endeavors to act. What the liar endeavors to do, for example, is not to *lie,* but to make it happen that his hearers are deceived.

SOFT DETERMINISM

P. H. Nowell-Smith

In the last chapter I tried to show that "could have" sentences in non-moral contexts can be analyzed in terms of "would have ... if ..."; and we must now see whether the application of this analysis to moral cases is consistent with our ordinary use of moral language.

The first question to be considered is the question of what sorts of if-clauses are in fact allowed to excuse a man from blame. Clearly "I could not have kept my promise because I was kidnapped" will exculpate me while "I could not have kept my promise because I am by nature a person who takes promises very lightly" will not. Translated into the hypothetical form, these become respectively "I would have kept my promise if I had not been kidnapped" and "I would have kept my promise if I had been a more conscientious person." Again it is clear that the first exculpates while the second does not. The philosophical difficulties, however, are to decide just why some "would ... ifs" excuse while others do not and to provide a criterion for distinguishing the exculpating from the non-exculpating cases. Forcible seizure exculpates; but do threats or psychological compulsion? And if, as some suggest, desires are internal forces which operate on the will, do they exculpate in the way in which external forces do? The problem of free-will is puzzling because it seems impossible, without indulging in sheer dogmatism to know just where to stop treating desires as "compelling forces."

Now before tackling this difficulty it will be prudent to examine what goes on in a place where questions of responsibility are settled every day and have been settled daily for hundreds of years, namely, a court of law. Lawyers have evolved a terminology of remarkable flexibility, refinement, and precision and, although there may be a difference between moral and legal verdicts, it would be strange if the logic of lawyers' talk about responsibility were very different from our ordinary moral talk.

To establish a verdict of "guilty" in a criminal case it is necessary to establish that the accused did that which is forbidden by the law or, in technical language, commited the *actus reus,* and also that he had what is called *mens rea.* This last phrase is sometimes translated "guilty mind" and in many modern textbooks of jurisprudence it is supposed to consist of two elements, (a) foresight of the consequences and (b) voluntariness. But, whatever the textbooks may say, in actual practice lawyers never look for a positive ingredient called volition or voluntariness. A man is held to have *mens rea,* and therefore to be guilty, if the *actus reus* is proved, *unless* there are certain specific conditions which preclude a verdict of guilty. "What is meant by the mental element in criminal liability (*mens rea*) is only to be understood by considering certain defenses or exceptions, such as Mistake of Fact, Accident, Coercion, Duress, Provocation, Insanity, Infancy." The list of pleas that can be put up to rebut criminal liability is different in different cases; but in the case of any given offense there is a restricted list of definite pleas which will preclude a verdict of guilty.

This is not to say that the burden of proof passes to the defense. In some cases, such as murder, it is necessary for the prosecution to show that certain circumstances were not present which would, if present, defeat the accusation. The essential point is that the concept of a "voluntary action" is a negative, not a positive one. To say that a man acted voluntarily is in effect to say that he did something when he was not in one of the conditions specified in the list of conditions which preclude responsibility. The list of pleas is not exhaustive; we could, if we wished, add to it; and in making moral judgments we do so. For example, we sometimes allow the fact that a man acted impulsively to exonerate him morally or at least to mitigate his offense in a case in which the law would not allow this. But it remains true that, in deciding whether an action was voluntary or not, we do not look for a positive ingredient but rather for considerations that would preclude its being voluntary and thereby exonerate the agent. In moral cases the most important types of plea that a man can put forward are (a) that he was the victim of certain sorts of ignorance, and (b) that he was the victim of certain sorts of compulsion.

IGNORANCE

A man may be ignorant of many elements in the situation in which he acts. For example he may not know that it was a policeman who told him to stop, that the stuff he put in the soup was arsenic, that the money he took was not his own. In such cases he would be blamed only if it was thought that he ought to have known or taken the trouble to find out. And his vicious trait of character was not contumacy or callousness or greed or disregard for any moral principle, but carelessness; and carelessness can amount to a vice. Firearms are so notoriously dangerous that the excuse "I didn't know it was loaded" will not do. The reason why he is blamed for carelessness and not for the specific vice for which he would have been blamed if he had done any of these things intentionally, is that, although he intended to do what he did, he did not intend to break a moral rule. He intended to take the money but not to steal. His action was not, therefore, a manifestation of the particular vice that the actions of thieves manifest. Ignorance of fact excuses or reduces the seriousness of an offense; but there is one type of ignorance that never excuses; and that is, in legal contexts, ignorance of the law and, in moral contexts, ignorance of right and wrong.

Now why should ignorance of fact excuse while ignorance of rules does not? Why should a man who takes someone else's money thinking it to be his own, be guiltless of anything (except possibly carelessness), while a man who takes it, knowing it not to be his own, but because he sees nothing wrong in taking other people's money, be held guilty and therefore blameworthy? We are not here concerned with the question of why some types of action should be stigmatized as "wrong," but solely with the question of why ignorance of what is wrong should not be held to exculpate.

The reason is that while the man who thought the money was his own did not intend to act on the maxim "It is permitted to take other people's money," the thief does act on this maxim. If a man does something because he does not think it is wrong he cannot plead that he did not choose to do it, and it is for choosing to do what is *in fact* wrong, whether he knows it or not, that a man is blamed. The situation is exactly analogous to that in which some non-moral capacity is concerned. "I would have solved the problem, if I had known all the data" would, if substantiated, allow me to get full marks. But "I would have solved the problem if I had known more mathematics" would not. Since competence at mathematics is not a moral trait of character, men are not blamed for lack of it; but they are given low marks and denied prizes.

COMPULSION

So long as "compulsion" is used in the literal sense it is not difficult to see why it should be held to exonerate. If a man is compelled to do something, he does not choose to do it, and his action is not a manifestation of his moral character or principles. Now, since the purpose of blame and punishment is to change a man's character and principles, neither blame nor punishment is called for in such a case. It would be unjust to punish him since the rules for punishing lay down that a man who acts under compulsion is not to be punished; and the rules lay this down because, with due allowance for superstition and stupidity, we do not have pointless rules. Once more we must be careful to avoid the mistake of saying that the justice of a sentence turns on the question of whether the accused is likely to be reformed by it. What is at issue here is not our reason for exonerating this accused, but our reason for making a *general* exception in the case of men whose actions are not expressions of their moral character. Physical compulsion is an obvious case where this is so.

But what if the source of compulsion is within the man himself? It is not an accident that we use "compulsion" in a psychological way and exonerate compulsives. There are two questions that are relevant here. In the first place we ask whether the man could have resisted the "compulsion"; and we decide this in the way that we decide all "could have" questions. We look for evidence of his past behavior in this, and also in related matters; for the behavior of the compulsive is usually odd in matters unconnected with his special compulsion, and we compare his case with other known cases. Once the capacity to resist the compulsion is established beyond reasonable doubt, we do not allow unsupported sceptical doubts about his capacity to resist it in a particular case to rebut the conclusion that he could have helped it. And we do not allow this because there is no way of establishing or refuting the existence of a capacity except by appeal to general evidence. If the capacity has been established and all the necessary conditions were present, we would not say that, in this case, he was the victim of a compulsion. Indeed, a "compulsion" is not something that could be said to operate in a particular case only; for to say that a man has psychological compulsion is to say something about his behavior over a long period. A compulsion is more like a chronic disorder than like a cold; and it is still less like a sneeze.

It is also relevant to raise the question whether he had any motive for doing what he did. Part of the difference between a kleptomaniac and a thief lies in the fact that the former has no motive for what he does; and he escapes blame because the point of blame is to strengthen some motives and weaken others. We are sometimes inclined to take the psychologists' talk about compulsions too seriously. We think that a man is excused because he has a "compulsion," as if the compulsion could be pointed to in the way that an external object which pushed him could be pointed to. But compulsions are not objects inside us; and we use the word "compulsion," not because we have isolated and identified the object which caused him to do what he did, but because we want to excuse him in the same sort of way we excuse someone who is literally pushed; and we want to excuse him for the same sort of reason. We know that it will do no good to punish him.

DESIRES

A man might plead that he would have acted otherwise if he had not had a strong desire to do what he did; but the desire was so strong that, as things were, he could not have acted otherwise. Would this plea be allowed to exonerate him? In some cases it would; for there are, as we have seen, cases of addiction in which we allow that a man is not to blame, since his craving was too strong for him. But in most cases it would be considered frivolous to say "I would have done the right thing if I hadn't wanted to do the wrong thing"; for it is just for this that men are blamed.

To distinguish an overwhelming desire from one that the agent could have resisted is not always easy; but the criterion that we in fact use for making the distinction is not difficult to understand. We know from experience that most men can be trained to curb some desires, but not others; and we assume that what is true in most cases is true in a given case unless special reasons are given for doubting this. Now it might seem that, although this evidence enables us to predict that we shall be able to train the man to curb his desire in future, it sheds no light on the question whether he could have curbed it on the occasion in question. I shall say more about this question of moral training later; here I only wish to point out that we have no criterion for deciding whether a man could have resisted a desire on a given occasion other than general evidence of his capacity and the capacity of others like him. We do not, because we cannot, try to answer this question as if it referred solely to the given occasion; we treat it as a question about a capacity.

CHARACTER

Finally a man might plead that he could not help doing what he did because that's the sort of man he is. He would not have done it if he had been more honest or less cowardly or less mean and so on. This sort of plea is paradoxical in the same sort of way that the plea of ignorance of moral rules and the plea that he did it because he wanted to are paradoxical. And all three paradoxes stem from the same source, the uncritical extension of "ought implies can" and of the exculpatory force of "he could not have acted otherwise" to cases which they will not cover. We know that these pleas are not in fact accepted; the puzzle is to see why.

The plea "I could not help it because I am that sort of person" might be backed up by an explanation of how I came to be that sort of person. Just as the discovery of a compelling cause exonerates, so, it might be argued, to reveal the causes of my character being what it is to show that I could not help being what I am and thus to exonerate me. But this argument is fallacious. In the first place to discover the cause of something is not to prove that it is inevitable. On the contrary the discovery of a disease is often the first step towards preventing it.

Now it is logically impossible to prevent something happening if we know the cause of it, since it could not have a cause unless it occurred and therefore it was not prevented. So when we talk of preventing diseases or accidents we are not talking about preventing cases which have occurred but about ensuring that there are no future cases. Similarly, if I know how Jones came to be a dishonest man, I cannot prevent him from being dishonest now; but it may be possible to prevent others from becoming dishonest and to cure Jones of his dishonesty.

Secondly, the discovery of a cause of something has no necessary bearing on a verdict about that thing. We know that a man has come to be what he is because of three main types of cause, heredity, education, and his own past actions. These three factors are not independent of each other and it is not the business of a philosopher to say exactly what is the effect of each or which is the most important for moral training. The question "Granted that we want people to be better and that we have fairly clear ideas about what 'being better' means, should we try to breed a superior race or pay more attention to education?" is not a philosophical question. But it is the business of a philosopher to show in what ways these "causes" are related to responsibility.

Now these three factors also play a part in situations in which non-moral verdicts are given. Leopold Mozart was a competent musician; his son Wolfgang was given a good musical education and practiced his art assiduously.

Each of these facts helps to explain how he was able to compose and play so well. There is plenty of evidence that musical ability runs in families and still more of the effects of teaching and practice. But, having learnt these facts, we do not have the slightest tendency to say that, because Mozart's abilities were "due" to heredity, teaching, and practice, his compositions were not "really" his own, or to abate one jot of our admiration. In the same way, however a man came by his moral principles, they are still *his* moral principles and he is praised or blamed for them. The plea that, being what he is he cannot help doing what he does, will no more save the wicked man than it will save the bad pianist or actor who has the rashness to expose his incompetence in public. Nor is he saved by being able to explain how he has come to be what he is.

Hereditary tendencies are not causes and do not compel, although a man may inherit a tendency to some form of psychological compulsion. In general to say that a man has a tendency to do something is to say that his father also used to do the same sort of thing; and neither of these facts has any tendency to exculpate.

The belief that heredity or a bad upbringing excuse a man's present character is partly due to the false belief that to explain something is to assign an antecedent cause to it, and that, to be voluntary, an action must be uncaused. But there is also a good reason for this belief. In fact we do sometimes allow these factors to exculpate, and if the question of explanation was as irrelevant to the question of responsibility as I have suggested, it would be hard to understand why we do this. Why do we tend to deal less harshly with juvenile delinquents who come from bad homes than with those who have had every chance? The question is not one of justice, since it is not a question whether Jones ought to be punished, but whether the law should lay down that people whose bad characters are due to certain causes should be punished. We must therefore ask what is our reason for differentiating between two boys whose characters and actions are the same but who come respectively from bad and good homes. And the reason is that in the first case we have not had a chance to see what kindness and a good education could do, while in the second we know that they have failed. Since punishment involves the infliction of pain and since it is a moral rule that unnecessary pain should not be inflicted, there is a general presumption that people should not be punished if the same end could be achieved without the infliction of pain. This consideration is, of course, irrelevant to the question whether Jones should be punished; but it is highly relevant to the question whether a distinction should be made between those whose characters have come to be what they are because of a bad education and those whose characters are bad in spite of a good one.

But suppose a man should plead that he cannot now help doing what he does because his character was formed by his own earlier actions? This also will not excuse him. The logic of this plea is that he did X because he was, at the time, the sort of man to do X and that he became this sort of man because he did Y and Z in the past. But if he cannot be blamed for doing X now, can he be blamed for having done Y and Z in the past? It would seem that he cannot, for he will exculpate himself in exactly the same way.

Once again the argument presupposes that if his present character can be explained in terms of what happened in the past he necessarily escapes blame. The assumption is that a man's actions form a chain in which each necessitates the next. Now, if we suppose that, to be free, an action must be uncaused, either we shall find a genuinely uncaused action at the beginning of the chain or we shall not. If we do not, then no action is culpable; and if we do, then we must suppose that, while most of our actions are caused and therefore blameless, there was in the past some one uncaused action for which alone a man can be held responsible. This theory has in fact been held, although even in the history of philosophy it would be hard to find another so bizarre. The objections to it are clear. In the first place we praise and blame people for what they do now, not for what they might have done as babies; and secondly this hypothetical infantile action could hardly be said to be an action of the agent at all, since it is *ex hypothesi* inexplicable in terms of his character.

The conclusion of the foregoing argument is that "He could not have acted otherwise" does not always exculpate and, in particular, that it does not exculpate if the reason which is adduced to explain just why he could not have acted otherwise is that he was a man of a certain moral character. We have seen that "He could not have acted otherwise" is to be construed as "he would have acted otherwise, if . . ." and we have seen which types of "if" are not allowed to exculpate. We must now see why they are not. . . .

Moral traits of character are tendencies or dispositions to behave in certain ways. How are they to be distinguished from other tendencies? If any tendency were to count as "moral" we should have to say that conformity to physical laws was a universal trait of human character and that susceptibility to colds was part of the moral character of a particular man.

The first and most obvious limitation lies in the fact that the names of virtues and vices are not purely descriptive words. They are terms of praise and blame used to express approval and disapproval and to influence the conduct of the person whose character is appraised and also of others. These three functions are tied together in a way that should by now be familiar. Appraising, praising, and blaming are things that men *do,* and can only be understood on the assumption that they do them for a purpose and use means adapted to their purpose. The logic of virtue-and-vice-words is tailor-made to fit the purposes and conditions of their use.

Men would not employ a special form of speech for changing the character and conduct of others, unless they had a pro-attitude towards those changes; so that the first limitation that can be put on "moral character" is that traits of character are tendencies to do things that arouse approval or disapproval. But moral verdicts do not just express the attitudes of the speaker; they are couched in impersonal language and imply accepted standards because the traits of character that a given man wants to strengthen or inhibit in others are usually those that other men also want to strengthen and inhibit. The impersonal language of morals implies a rough community of pro-and-con attitudes. Moreover men would not have adopted the moral language they have unless it was likely to achieve its purpose; and its purpose is achieved because most men dislike disapprobation. The power of moral language is greatly enhanced by the very facts which make impersonal moral language possible. No one likes to be universally condemned and most men are willing to take considerable pains to avoid it.

But this limitation is not enough. There are many things for which men are applauded and condemned which do not count as parts of their moral character. A great musician, mathematician, actor, or athlete is applauded and rewarded for what he does and his ability may be called a "virtue," but not a moral virtue. Conversely, if a man fails to save a life because he cannot swim, we may regret his incapacity and urge him to learn, but his incapacity is not called a vice.

A man may fail to achieve some worthy object because he is physically or intellectually incompetent, too weak or too stupid. But he may also fail because he is too cowardly or too dishonest or has too little regard for the welfare of others. Why do we call the first set of traits "non-moral" and never condemn them while the second are called "moral" and condemned? It is clear that it will not help to say that we intuit a non-natural relation of fittingness which holds between blame-worthiness and dishonesty or meanness but not between blameworthiness and physical weakness or stupidity. For this is only to say that the former traits deserve blame while the latter do not and that we cannot understand why. To discover why we draw the line in the way that we do we must first ask exactly where we draw it; and all that is necessary for this purpose is to construct two lists, the one of moral traits, the other of non-moral. Cowardice, avarice, cruelty, selfishness, idleness, would go into the first list; clumsiness, physical weakness, stupidity, and anaemia into the second. The second list, will, of course, contain items of many different sorts, since we are interested, not in the way in which non-moral characteristics differ from each other, but in the distinction between moral and non-moral.

If we construct these two lists we shall find that the items in list one have two properties in common which the items in list two do not have. (a) We believe that if a man's action can be explained by reference to a "list one" characteristic he could have acted otherwise. And it would appear at first sight that this is the crucial feature which distinguishes moral from non-moral characteristics. Why does a schoolmaster punish a lazy boy but not a stupid one for equally bad work if not because he believes that the lazy boy could have done better while the stupid boy could not? But why does the schoolmaster believe this? In fact he appeals to the evidence of past performance. On the libertarian view this would scarcely be relevant, since the boy might not have been lazy in the past but was lazy at just that moment. And perhaps his momentary laziness was no more under his control than the stupid boy's stupidity? An analysis on these lines could hardly fail to lead to the paradoxical conclusion that no one has any reason whatever for ascribing responsibility. And even if it were possible to answer the question whether he could have acted otherwise, we should be left with the question why this is considered relevant to the propriety of holding him responsible.

Moreover it would be circular to make the phrase "he could have acted otherwise" the distinguishing criterion of moral characteristics; since, as we have seen, it is necessary to make use of the distinction between actions explained by reference to moral, and actions explained by reference to non-moral characteristics in order to elucidate the phrase "he could have acted otherwise."

(b) There is, however, another element which all the characteristics in list one have and those in list two do not. It is an empirical fact that list one characteristics can be strengthened or weakened by the fear of punishment or of an adverse verdict or the hope of a favorable verdict. And when we remember that the purpose of moral verdicts and of punishment is to strengthen or weaken certain trends of character it is not difficult to see that this feature, so far from being synthetically connected with the notion of a "moral" characteristic, a virtue or a vice, is just what constitutes it. What traits of character can be strengthened or weakened in this way is a matter of empirical fact. Knives can be sharpened, engines decarbonized, fields fertilized, and dogs trained to do tricks. And men also can be trained, within certain limits, to behave in some ways and not in others. Pleasure and pain, reward and punishment are the rudders by which human conduct is steered, the means by which moral character is molded; and "moral" character is just that set of dispositions that can be molded by these means. Moral approval and disapproval play the same role. It is not just an accident that they please and hurt and that they are used only in cases in which something is to be gained by pleasing or hurting.

We might therefore say that moral traits of character are just those traits that are known to be amenable to praise or blame; and this would explain why we punish idle boys but not stupid ones, thieves but not kleptomaniacs, the sane but not the insane. This is not to say that amenability to praise and blame is what justifies either of these in a particular case; that, as we have seen, is a question to be decided by reference to the rule. But a breach of moral rule is only considered to be culpable when it is attributable to the agent's character, his vice or moral weakness; and our theory is intended to explain just what is included in and what excluded from "moral character" and to explain why this distinction should be considered relevant to responsibility. . . .

. . . The whole weight of the analysis is now seen to rest on the proposition that people only do those things which are either objects of a direct pro-attitude (i.e. that they want to do or enjoy doing for their own sake) or are believed to produce results towards which they have pro-attitudes. It is absurd to ask why a man who thinks that praise and blame will alter certain dispositions which he wishes to alter should praise and blame them. For this is a special case of the question "Why do people adopt means that they believe to be the best means of achieving their ends?"; and this is an absurd question in a way in which "Why does a man deserve blame only if he acted voluntarily and has broken a moral rule?" is not.

Nevertheless this way of tracing the connections between pro-attitudes, moral rules, verdicts on character, and ascriptions of responsibility is obviously too simple and schematic. It is more like an account of the way in which moral language would be used by people who knew all the facts and thoroughly understood what they were doing than like a description of the way in which moral language is actually used. In practice these connections are much looser than the theory suggests; and there are two reasons for this. In the first place there is the inveterate conservatism of moral language. Even when it is known that a certain type of conduct, for example homosexuality, is not amenable to penal sanctions or moral disapproval, it is difficult to persuade people that it is not morally wrong.

The second reason is more respectable. We are still very ignorant of the empirical facts of human nature, and this ignorance both makes it wise for us to make moral judgments in accordance with a more or less rigid system of rules and also infects the logic of moral language. Our moral verdicts do not, therefore, always imply that the person condemned has in fact done something "bad" or "undesirable" in a non-moral sense. An act of cowardice or dishonesty might, by chance, be attended with the happiest consequences; but it would still be blamed. But this fact does not involve any major modification in the theory that bad traits of character are those which (a) tend to bring about undesirable results in most cases, and (b) are alterable by praise and blame. For, in deciding whether a trait of character is vicious or not, we consider its effects in the majority of cases. We do not want to reinforce a tendency to behave in a certain way just because it turns out, on rare occasions, to be beneficial. And, in making a moral judgment, we do not consider the actual consequences of the action concerned. Nor do we even need to consider the consequences that such actions usually have. A man has broken faith or been cowardly or mean; we condemn him forthwith without considering why such actions are condemned. The fact that deceitful, cowardly, and mean actions are, by and large, harmful is relevant, not to the questions "Has Jones done wrong? Is he a bad man? Does he deserve to be blamed?" but to the question "Why are deceitfulness, cowardice and meanness called 'vices' and condemned?"

This theory enables us to understand why it is not only moral weakness that is blamed, but also wickedness; and it also enables us to distinguish between moral weakness and addiction in a way that the libertarian theory could not. A wicked character can be improved by moral censure and punishment; and if we really thought that a man was so bad as to be irremediable we should, I think, cease to blame him, though we might impose restraints on him as we would on a mad dog. Moral weakness is considered to be a less culpable state, since the morally weak man has moral principles which are good enough, but fails to live up to them. He is therefore more likely to be improved by encouragement than the wicked man is. What he needs is the confidence which comes from knowing that others are on the side of his principles. But both he and the wicked man differ from the addict or compulsive in that the latter will respond neither to threats nor to encouragement.

HARD AND SOFT DETERMINISM

Susan Wolf

In order for a person to be morally responsible, two conditions must be satisfied. First, he must be a free agent—an agent, that is, whose actions are under his own control. For if the actions he performs are not up to him to decide, he deserves no credit or discredit for doing what he does. Second, he must be a moral agent—an agent, that is, to whom moral claims apply. For if the actions he performs can be neither right nor wrong, then there is nothing to credit or discredit him with. I shall call the first condition, *the condition of freedom,* and the second, *the condition of value.* Those who fear that the first condition can never be met worry about the problem of free will. Those who fear that the second condition can never be met worry about the problem of moral skepticism. Many people believe that the condition of value is dependent on the condition of freedom—that moral prescriptions make sense only if the concept of free will is coherent. In what follows, I shall argue that the converse is true—that the condition of freedom depends on the condition of value. Our doubts about the existence of true moral values, however, will have to be left aside.

I shall say that an agent's action is *psychologically determined* if his action is determined by his interests—that is, his values or desires—and his interests are determined by his heredity or environment. If all our actions are so determined, then the thesis of psychological determinism is true. This description is admittedly crude and simplistic. A more plausible description of psychological determination will include among possible determining factors a wider range of psychological states. There are, for example, some beliefs and emotions which cannot be analyzed as values or desires and which clearly play a role in the psychological explanations of why we act as we do. For my purposes, however, it will be easier to leave the description of psychological determinism uncluttered. The context should be sufficient to make the intended application understood.

Many people believe that if psychological determinism is true, the condition of freedom can never be satisfied. For if an agent's interests are determined by heredity and environment, they claim, it is not up to the agent to have the interests he has. And if his actions are determined by his interests as well, then he cannot but perform the actions he performs. In order for an agent to satisfy the condition of freedom, then, his actions must not be

"Hard and Soft Determinism," by Susan Wolf, reprinted from the *Journal of Philosophy* LXXVII, 3 (March 1980). Reprinted by permission of the author and publisher.

psychologically determined. Either his actions must not be determined by his interests, or his interests must not be determined by anything external to himself. They therefore conclude that the condition of freedom requires the absence of psychological determinism. And they think this is what we mean to express when we state the condition of freedom in terms of the requirement that the agent "could have done otherwise."

Let us imagine, however, what an agent who satisfied this condition would have to be like. Consider first what it would mean for the agent's actions not to be determined by his interests—for the agent, in other words, to have the ability to act despite his interests. This would mean, I think, that the agent has the ability to act against everything he cares about. It would mean, for example, that if the agent's son were inside a burning building, the agent could just stand there and watch the house go up in flames. Or that the agent, though he thinks his neighbor a fine and agreeable fellow, could just go up one day, ring the doorbell, and punch him in the nose. One might think such pieces of behavior should not be classified as actions at all—that they are rather more like spasms that the agent cannot control. If they are actions, at least, they are very bizarre, and an agent who performed them would have to be insane. Indeed, one might think he would have to be insane if he had even the ability to perform them. For the rationality of an agent who could perform such irrational actions as these must be hung by a dangerously thin thread.

So let us assume that his actions are determined by his interests, but that his interests are not determined by anything external to himself. Then of any of the interests he happens to have, it must be the case that he does not have to have them. Though perhaps he loves his wife, it must be possible for him not to love her. Though perhaps he cares about people in general, it must be possible for him not to care. This agent, moreover, could not have reasons for his interests—at least no reasons of the sort we normally have. He cannot love his wife, for example, because of the way his wife is—for the way his wife is is not up to him to decide. Such an agent, presumably, could not be much committed to anything; his interests must be something like a matter of whim. Such an agent must be able not to care about the lives of others, and, I suppose, he must be able not to care about his own life as well. An agent who didn't care about these things, one might think, would have to be crazy. And again, one might think he would have to be crazy if he had even the ability not to care.

In any case, it seems, if we require an agent to be psychologically undetermined, we cannot expect him to be a moral agent. For if we require that his actions not be determined by his interests, then *a fortiori* they cannot be determined by his moral interests. And if we require that his interests not be determined by anything else, then *a fortiori* they cannot be determined by his moral reasons.

When we imagine an agent who performs right actions, it seems, we imagine an agent who is rightly determined: whose actions, that is, are determined by the right sorts of interests, and whose interests are determined by the right sorts of reasons. But an agent who is not psychologically determined cannot perform actions that are right in this way. And if his actions can never be appropriately right, then in not performing right actions, he can never be wrong. The problem seems to be that the undetermined agent is so free as to be free *from moral reasons.* So the satisfaction of the condition of freedom seems to rule out the satisfaction of the condition of value.

This suggests that the condition of freedom was previously stated too strongly. When we require that a responsible agent "could have done otherwise" we cannot mean that it was determined that he did what he did. It has been proposed that "he could have done otherwise" should be analyzed as a conditional instead. For example, we might say that "he could have done otherwise" means that he would have done otherwise, if he had tried. Thus the bank robber is responsible for robbing the bank, since he would have restrained himself if he had tried. But the man he locked up is not responsible for letting him escape, since he couldn't have stopped him even if he had tried.

Incompatibilists, however, will quickly point out that such an analysis is insufficient. For an agent who would have done otherwise if he had tried cannot be blamed for his action if he could not have tried. The compatibilist might try to answer this objection with a new conditional analysis of "he could have tried." He might say, for example, that "he could have tried to do otherwise" be interpreted to mean he would have tried to do otherwise, if he had chosen. But the incompatibilist now has a new objection to make: namely, what if the agent could not have chosen?

It should be obvious that this debate might be carried on indefinitely with a proliferation of conditionals and a proliferation of objections. But if an agent is determined, no conditions one suggests will be conditions that an agent could have satisfied.

Thus, any conditional analysis of "he could have done otherwise" seems too weak to satisfy the condition of freedom. Yet if "he could have done otherwise" is not a conditional, it seems too strong to allow the satisfaction of the condition of value. We seem to think of ourselves one way when we are thinking about freedom, and to think of ourselves another way when we are thinking about morality. When we are thinking about the condition of freedom, our intuitions suggest that the incompatibilists are right. For they claim that an agent can be free only insofar as his actions are not psychologically determined. But when we are thinking about the condition of value, our intuitions suggest that the compatibilists are right. For they claim that an agent can be moral only insofar as his actions are psychologically determined. If our intuitions require that both of these claims are right, then the concept of moral responsibility must be incoherent. For then a free agent can never be moral, and a moral agent can never be free.

In fact, however, I believe that philosophers have generally got our intuitions wrong. There is an asymmetry in our intuitions about freedom which has generally been overlooked. As a result, it has seemed that the answer to the problem of free will can lie in only one of two alternatives: Either the fact that an agent's action was determined is always compatible with his being responsible for it, or the fact that the agent's action was determined will always rule his responsibility out. I shall suggest that the solution lies elsewhere—that both compatibilists and incompatibilists are wrong. What we need in order to be responsible beings, I shall argue, is a suitable combination of determination and indetermination.

When we try to call up our intuitions about freedom, a few stock cases come readily to mind. We think of the heroin addict and the kleptomaniac, of the victim of hypnosis, and the victim of a deprived childhood. These cases, I think, provide forceful support for our incompatibilist intuitions. For of the kleptomaniac it may well be true that he would have done otherwise if he had tried. The kleptomaniac is not responsible because he could not have tried. Of the victim of hypnosis it may well be true that he would have done otherwise if he had chosen. The victim of hypnosis is not responsible because he could not have chosen.

The victim of the deprived childhood who, say, embezzles some money, provides the most poignant example of all. For this agent is not coerced nor overcome by an irresistible impulse. He is in complete possession of normal adult faculties of reason and observation. He seems, indeed, to have as much control over his behavior as we have of ours. He acts on the basis of his choice, and he chooses on the basis of his reasons. If there is any explanation of why this agent is not responsible, it would seem that it must consist simply in the fact that his reasons are determined.

These examples are all peculiar, however, in that they are examples of people doing bad things. If the agents in these cases were responsible for their actions, this would justify the claim that they deserve to be blamed. We seldom look, on the other hand, at examples of agents whose actions are morally good. We rarely ask whether an agent is truly responsible if his being responsible would make him worthy of praise.

There are a few reasons why this might be so which go some way in accounting for the philosophers' neglect. First, acts of moral blame are more connected with punishment than acts of moral praise are connected with reward. So acts of moral blame are likely to be more public, and examples will be readier to hand. Second, and more important, I think, we have stronger reasons for wanting acts of blame to be justified. If we blame someone or punish him, we are likely to be causing him some pain. But if we praise someone or reward him, we will only add to his pleasures. To blame someone undeservedly is, in any case, to do him an injustice. Whereas to praise someone undeservedly is apt to be just a harmless mistake. For this reason, I think, our intuitions about praise are weaker and less developed than our intuitions about blame. Still, we do have some intuitions about cases of praise, and it would be a mistake to ignore them entirely.

When we ask whether an agent's action is deserving of praise, it seems we do not require that he could have done otherwise. If an agent does the right thing for just the right reasons, it seems absurd to ask whether he could have done the wrong. "I cannot tell a lie," "He couldn't hurt a fly" are not exemptions from praiseworthiness but testimonies to it. If a friend presents you with a gift and says "I couldn't resist," this suggests the strength of his friendship and not the weakness of his will. If one feels one "has no choice" but to speak out against injustice, one ought not to be upset about the depth of one's commitment. And it seems I should be grateful for the fact that if I were in trouble, my family "could not help" but come to my aid.

Of course, these phrases must be given an appropriate interpretation if they are to indicate that the agent is deserving of praise. "He couldn't hurt a fly" must allude to someone's gentleness—it would be perverse to say this of someone who was in an iron lung. It is not admirable in George Washington that he cannot tell a lie, if it is because he has a tendency to stutter that inhibits his attempts. "He could not have done otherwise" as it is used in the context of praise, then, must be taken to imply something like "because he was too good." An action is praiseworthy only if it is done for the right reasons. So it must be only in light of and because of these reasons that the praiseworthy agent "could not help" but do the right thing.

But when an agent does the right thing for the right reasons, the fact that, having the right reasons, he *must* do the right should surely not lessen the credit he deserves. For presumably the reason he cannot do otherwise is that his virtue is so sure or his moral commitment so strong.

One might fear that if the agent really couldn't have acted differently, his virtue must be *too* sure or his commitment *too* strong. One might think, for example, that if someone literally couldn't *resist* buying a gift for a friend, his generosity would not be a virtue—it would be an obsession. For one can imagine situations in which it would be better if the agent did resist—if, for example, the money that was spent on the gift was desperately needed for some other purpose. Presumably, in the original case, though, the money was not desperately needed—we praise the agent for buying a gift for his friend rather than, say, a gift for himself. But from the fact that the man could not resist in this situation it doesn't follow that he couldn't resist in another. For part of the explanation of why he couldn't resist in this situation is that in this situation he has no reason to try to resist. This man, we assume, has a generous nature—a disposition, that is, to perform generous acts. But, then, if he is in a situation that presents a golden opportunity, and has no conflicting motive, how could he act otherwise?

One might still be concerned that if his motives are determined, the man cannot be truly deserving of praise. If he cannot help but have a generous character, then the fact that he is generous is not up to him. If a man's motives are determined, one might think, then *he* cannot control them, so it cannot be to his credit if his motives turn out to be good. But whether a man is in control of his motives cannot be decided so simply. We must know not only whether his motives are determined, but how they are determined as well.

We can imagine, for example, a man with a generous mother who became generous as a means of securing her love. He would not have been generous had his mother been different. Had she not admired generosity, he would not have developed this trait. We can imagine further that once this man's character had been developed, he would never subject it to question or change. His character would remain unthinkingly rigid, carried over from a childhood over which he had no control. As he developed a tendency to be generous, let us say, he developed other tendencies—a tendency to brush his teeth twice a day, a tendency to avoid the company of Jews. The explanation for why he developed any one of these traits is more or less the same as the explanation for why he has developed any other. And the explanation for why he has retained some of these tendencies is more or less the same as the explanation for why he has retained any other. These tendencies are all, for him, merely habits which he has never thought about breaking. Indeed, they are habits which, by hypothesis, it was determined he would never think about breaking. Such a man, perhaps, would not deserve credit for his generosity, for his generosity might be thought to be senseless and blind. But we can imagine a different picture in which no such claim is true, in which a generous character might be determined and yet under the agent's control.

We might start again with a man with a generous mother who starts to develop his generosity out of a desire for her love. But his reasons for developing a generous nature need not be his reasons for retaining it when he grows more mature. He may notice, for example, that his generous acts provide an independent pleasure, connected to the pleasure he gives the person on whom his generosity is bestowed. He may find that being generous promotes a positive fellow feeling and makes it easier for him to make friends than it would otherwise be. Moreover, he appreciates being the object of the generous acts of others, and he is hurt when others go to ungenerous extremes. All in all, his generosity seems to cohere with his other values. It fits in well with his ideals of how one ought to live.

Such a picture, I think, might be determined as the former one. But it is compatible with the exercise of good sense and an open frame of mind. It is determined, because the agent does not create his new reasons for generosity any more than he created his old ones. He does not *decide* to feel an independent pleasure in performing acts of generosity, or decide that such acts will make it easier for him to make friends. He discovers that these are consequences of a generous nature—and if he is observant and perceptive, he cannot help but discover this. He does not choose to be the object of the generous acts of others, or to be the victim of less generous acts of less virtuous persons. Nor does he choose to be grateful to the one and hurt by the other. He cannot help but have these experiences—they are beyond his control. So it seems that what reasons he *has* for being generous depends on what reasons there *are*.

If the man's character is determined in this way, however, it seems absurd to say that it is not under his control. His character is determined on the basis of his reasons, and his reasons are determined by what reasons there are. What is not under his control, then, is that generosity be a virtue, and it is only because he realizes this that he remains a generous man. But one cannot say for *this* reason that his generosity is not praiseworthy. This is the best reason for being generous that a person could have.

So it seems that an agent can be morally praiseworthy even though he is determined to perform the action he performs. But we have already seen that an agent cannot be morally blameworthy if he is determined to perform the action he performs. Determination, then, is compatible with an agent's responsibility for a good action, but incompatible with an agent's responsibility for a bad action. The metaphysical conditions required for an agent's responsibility will vary according to the value of the action he performs.

The condition of freedom, as it is expressed by the requirement that an agent could have done otherwise, thus appears to demand a conditional analysis after all. But the condition must be one that separates the good actions from the bad—the condition, that is, must be essentially value-laden. An analysis of the condition of freedom that might do the trick is:

He could have done otherwise if there had been good and sufficient reason.

where the "could have done otherwise" in the analysans is not a conditional at all. For presumably an action is morally praiseworthy only if there are no good and sufficient reasons to do something else. And an action is morally blameworthy only if there are good and sufficient reasons to do something else. Thus, when an agent performs a good action, the condition of freedom is a counterfactual: though it is required that the agent would have been able to do otherwise *had there been* good and sufficient reason to do so, the situation in which the good-acting agent actually found himself is a situation in which there was no such reason. Thus, it is compatible with the satisfaction of the condition of freedom that the agent in this case could not actually have done other than what he actually did. When an agent performs a bad action, however, the condition of freedom is not a counterfactual. The bad-acting agent does what he does in the face of good and sufficient reasons to do otherwise. Thus the condition of freedom requires that the agent in this case could have done otherwise in just the situation in which he was actually placed. An agent, then, can be determined to perform a good action and still be morally praiseworthy. But if an agent is to be blameworthy, he must unconditionally have been able to do something else.

It may be easier to see how this analysis works, and how it differs from conditional analyses that were suggested before, if we turn back to the case in which these previous analyses failed—namely, the case of the victim of a deprived childhood.

We imagined a case, in particular, of a man who embezzled some money, fully aware of what he was doing. He was neither coerced nor overcome by an irresistible impulse, and he was in complete possession of normal adult faculties of reason and observation. Yet it seems he ought not to be blamed for committing his crime, for, from his point of view, one cannot reasonably expect him to see anything wrong with his action. We may suppose that in childhood he was given no love—he was beaten by his father, neglected by his mother. And that the people to whom he was exposed when he was growing up gave him examples only of evil and selfishness. From his point of view, it is natural to conclude that respecting other people's property would be foolish. For presumably no one had ever respected his. And it is natural for him to feel that he should treat other people as adversaries.

In light of this, it seems that this man shouldn't be blamed for an action we know to be wrong. For if we had had his childhood, we wouldn't have known it either. Yet this agent seems to have as much control over his life as we are apt to have over ours: he would have done otherwise, if he had tried. He would have tried to do otherwise, if he had chosen. And he would have chosen to do otherwise, if he had had reason. It is because he couldn't have had reason that this agent should not be blamed.

Though this agent's childhood was different from ours, it would seem to be neither more nor less binding. The good fortune of our childhood is no more to our credit than the misfortune of his is to his blame. So if he is not free because of the childhood he had, then is would appear that we are not free either. Thus it seems no conditional analysis of freedom will do—for there is nothing internal to the agent which distinguishes him from us.

My analysis, however, proposes a condition that is not internal to the agent. And it allows us to state the relevant difference: namely that, whereas our childhoods fell within a range of normal decency, his was severely deprived. The consequence this has is that he, unlike us, could not have had reasons even though there were reasons around. The problem is not that his reason was functioning improperly, but that his data were unfortuitously selective. Since the world for him was not suitably cooperating, his reason cannot attain its appropriate goal.

The goal, to put it bluntly, is the True and the Good. The freedom we want is the freedom to find it. But such a freedom requires not only that we, as agents, have the right sorts of abilities—the abilities, that is, to direct and govern our actions by our most fundamental selves. It requires as well that the world cooperate in such a way that our most fundamental selves have the opportunity to develop into the selves they ought to be.

If the freedom necessary for moral responsibility is the freedom to be determined by the True and the Good, then obviously we cannot know whether we have such a freedom unless we know, on the one hand, that there *is* a True and a Good and, on the other, that there *are* capacities for finding them. As a consequence of this, the condition of freedom cannot be stated in purely metaphysical terms. For we cannot know which capacities and circumstances are necessary for freedom unless we know which capacities and circumstances will enable us to form the *right* values and perform the *right* actions. Strictly speaking, I take it, the capacity to reason is not enough—we need a kind of sensibility and perception as well. But these are capacities, I assume, that most of us have. So when the world cooperates, we are morally responsible.

I have already said that the condition of freedom cannot be stated in purely metaphysical terms. More specifically, the condition of freedom cannot be stated in terms that are value-free. Thus, the problem of free will has been misrepresented insofar as it has been thought to be a purely metaphysical problem. And, perhaps, this is why the problem of free will has seemed for so long to be hopeless.

That the problem should have seemed to be a purely metaphysical problem is not, however, unnatural or suprising. For being determined by the True and the Good is very different from being determined by one's garden variety of causes, and I think it is not unnatural to feel as if one rules out the other. For to be determined by the Good is not to be determined by the Past. And to do something because it is the right thing to do is not to do it because one has been taught to do it. One might think, then, that one can be determined only by one thing or the other. For if one is going to do whatever it is right to do, then it seems one will do it whether or not one has been taught. And if one is going to do whatever one has been taught to do, then it seems one will do it whether or not it is right.

In fact, however, such reasoning rests on a category mistake. These two explanations do not necessarily compete, for they are explanations of different kinds. Consider, for example, the following situation: you ask me to name the capital of Nevada, and I reply "Carson City." We can explain why I give the answer I do give in either of the following ways: First, we can point out that when I was in the fifth grade I had to memorize the capitals of the fifty states. I was taught to believe that Carson City was the capital of Nevada, and was subsequently positively reinforced for doing so. Second, we can point out that Carson City *is* the capital of Nevada, and that this was, after all, what you wanted to know. So on the one hand, I gave my answer because I was taught. And on the other, I gave my answer because it was right.

Presumably, these explanations are not unrelated. For if Carson City were not the capital of Nevada, I would not have been taught that it was. And if I hadn't been taught that Carson City was the capital of Nevada, I wouldn't have known that it was. Indeed, one might think that if the answer I gave weren't right, I *couldn't* have given it because I was taught. For no school board would have hired a teacher who got such facts wrong. And if I hadn't been taught that Carson City was the capital of Nevada, perhaps I couldn't have given this answer because it was right. For that Carson City is the capital of Nevada is not something that can be known a priori.

Similarly, we can explain why a person acts justly in either of the following ways: First, we can point out that he was taught to act justly, and was subsequently positively reinforced for doing so. Second, we can point out that it is right to act justly, and go on to say why he knows this is so. Again, these explanations are likely to be related. For if it weren't right to act justly, the person may well have been taught that it was. And if the person hadn't been taught that he ought to act justly, the person may not have discovered this on his own. Of course, the explanations of both kinds in this case will be more complex than the explanations in the previous case. But what is relevant here is that these explanations are compatible: that one can be determined by the Good and determined by the Past.

In order for an agent to be morally free, then, he must be capable of being determined by the Good. Determination by the Good is, as it were, the goal we need the freedom to pursue. We need the freedom *to* have our actions determined by the Good, and the freedom to be or to become the sorts of persons whose actions will continue to be so determined. In light of this, it should be clear that no standard incompatibilist views about the conditions of moral responsibility can be right, for, according to these views, an agent is free only if he is the sort of agent whose actions are not causally determined at all. Thus, an agent's freedom would be incompatible with the realization of the goal for which freedom is required. The agent would be, in the words, though not in the spirit, of Sartre, "condemned to be free"—he could not both be free and realize a moral ideal.

Thus, views that offer conditional analyses of the ability to do otherwise, views that, like mine, take freedom to consist in the ability *to be determined* in a particular way, are generally compatibilist views. For insofar as an agent *is* determined in the right way, the agent can be said to be acting freely. Like the compatibilists, then, I am claiming that whether an agent is morally responsible depends not on whether but on how that agent is determined. My view differs from theirs only in what I take the satisfactory kind of determination to be.

However, since on my view the satisfactory kind of determination is determination by reasons that an agent ought to have, it will follow that an agent can be both determined and responsible only insofar as he performs actions that he ought to perform. If an agent performs a morally bad action, on the other hand, then his actions can't be determined in the appropriate way. So if an agent is ever to be responsible for a bad action, it must be the case that his action is not psychologically determined at all. According to my view, then, in order for both moral praise and moral blame to be justified, the thesis of psychological determinism must be false.

Is it plausible that this thesis is false? I think so. For though it appears that some of our actions are psychologically determined, it appears that others are not. It appears that some of our actions are not determined by our interests, and some of our interests are not determined at all. That is, it seems that some of our actions are such that no set of psychological facts are sufficient to explain them. There are occasions on which a person takes one action, but there seems to be no reason why he didn't take another.

For example, we sometimes make arbitrary choices—to wear the green shirt rather than the blue, to have coffee rather than tea. We make such choices on the basis of no reason—and it seems that we might, in these cases, have made a different choice instead.

Some less trivial and more considered choices may also be arbitrary. For one may have reasons on both sides which are equally strong. Thus, one may have good reasons to go to graduate school and good reasons not to; good reasons to get married, and good reasons to stay single. Though we might want, in these cases, to choose on the basis of reasons, our reasons simply do not settle the matter for us. Other psychological events may be similarly undetermined, such as the chance occurrence of thoughts and ideas. One is just struck by an idea, but for no particular reason—one might as easily have had another idea or no idea at all. Or one simply forgets an appointment one has made, even though one was not particularly distracted by other things at the time.

On retrospect, some of the appearance of indetermination may turn out to be deceptive. We decide that unconscious motives dictated a choice that seemed at the time to be arbitrary. Or a number of ideas that seemed to occur to us at random reveal a pattern too unusual to be the coincidence we thought. But if some of the appearances of indetermination are deceptive, I see no reason to believe that all of them should be.

Let us turn, then, to instances of immoral behavior, and see what the right kind of indetermination would be. For indetermination, in this context, is indetermination among some number of fairly particular alternatives—and if one's alternatives are not of the appropriate kind, indetermination will not be sufficient to justify moral blame. It is not enough, for example, to know that a criminal who happened to rob a bank might as easily have chosen to hold up a liquor store instead. What we need to know, in particular, is that when an agent performs a wrong action, he could have performed the right action for the right reasons instead. That is, first, the agent could have had the interests that the agent ought to have had, and second, the agent could have acted on the interests on which he ought to have acted.

Corresponding to these two possibilities, we can imagine two sorts of moral failure: the first corresponds to a form of negligence, the second to a form of weakness. Moral negligence consists in a failure to recognize the existence of moral reasons that one ought to have recognized. For example, a person hears that his friend is in the hospital, but fails to attend to this when planning his evening. He doesn't stop to think about how lonely and bored his friend is likely to be—he simply reaches for the *TV Guide* or for his novel instead. If the person could have recognized his friend's sorry predicament, he is guilty of moral negligence. Moral weakness, on the other hand, consists in the failure to act on the reasons that one knows one ought, for moral reasons, to be acting on. For example, a person might go so far as to conclude that he really ought to pay his sick friend a visit, but the thought of the drive across town is enough to convince him to stay at home with his book after all. If the person could have made the visit, he is guilty of moral weakness.

There is, admittedly, some difficulty in establishing that an agent who performs a morally bad action satisfies the condition of freedom. It is hard to know whether an agent who did one thing could have done another instead. But presumably we decide such questions now on the basis of statistical evidence—and if, in fact, these actions are not determined, this is the best method there can be. We decide, in other words, that an agent could have done otherwise if others in his situation have done otherwise, and these others are like him in apparently relevant ways. Or we decide that an agent could have done otherwise if he himself has done otherwise in situations that are like this one in all apparently relevant ways.

It should be emphasized that the indetermination with which we are here concerned is indetermination only at the level of psychological explanation. Such indetermination is compatible with determination at other levels of explanation. In particular, a sub-psychological, or physiological, explanation of our behavior may yet be deterministic. Some feel that if this is the case, the nature of psychological explanations of our behavior cannot be relevant to the problem of free will. Though I am inclined to disagree with this view, I have neither the space nor the competence to argue this here.

Restricting the type of explanation in question appropriately, however, it is a consequence of the condition of freedom I have suggested that the explanation for why a responsible agent performs a morally bad action must be, at some level, incomplete. There must be nothing that made the agent perform the action he did, nothing that prevented him from performing a morally better one. It should be noted that there may be praiseworthy actions for which the explanations are similarly incomplete. For the idea that an agent who could have performed a morally bad action actually performs a morally good one is no less plausible than the idea that an agent who could have performed a morally good action actually performs a morally bad one. Presumably, an agent who does the right thing for the right reasons deserves praise for his action whether it was determined or not. But whereas indetermination is compatible with the claim that an agent is deserving of praise, it is essential to the justification of the claim that an agent is deserving of blame.

Seen from a certain perspective, this dealing out of praise and blame may seem unfair. In particular, we might think that if it is truly undetermined whether a given agent in a given situation will perform a good action or a bad one, then it must be a matter of chance that the agent ends up doing what he does. If the action is truly undetermined, then it is not determined by the agent himself. One might think that in this case the agent has no more control over the moral quality of his action than does anything else.

However, the fact that it is not determined whether the agent will perform a good action or a bad one does not imply that which action he performs can properly be regarded as a matter of chance. Of course, in some situations an agent might choose to make it a matter of chance. For example, an agent struggling with the decision between fulfilling a moral obligation and doing something immoral that he very much wants to do might ultimately decide to let the toss of a coin settle the matter for him. But, in normal cases, the way in which the agent makes a decision involves no statistical process or randomizing event. It appears that the claim that there is no complete explanation of why the agent who could have performed a better action performed a worse one or of why the agent who could have performed a worse action performed a better one rules out even the explanation that it was a matter of chance.

In order to have control over the moral quality of his actions, an agent must have certain requisite abilities—in particular, the abilities necessary to see and understand the reasons and interests he ought to see and understand

and the abilities necessary to direct his actions in accordance with his reasons and interests. And if, furthermore, there is nothing that interferes with the agent's use of these abilities—that is, no determining cause that prevents him from using them and no statistical process that, as it were, takes out of his hands the control over whether or not he uses them—then it seems that these are all the abilities that the agent needs to have. But it is compatible with the agent's having these abilities and with there being no interferences to their use that it is not determined whether the agent will perform a good action or a bad one. The responsible agent who performs a bad action fails to exercise these abilities sufficiently, though there is no complete explanation of why he fails. The responsible agent who performs a good action does exercise these abilities—it may or may not be the case that it is determined that he exercise them.

The freedom required for moral responsibility, then, is the freedom to be good. Only this kind of freedom will be neither too much nor too little. For then the agent is not so free as to be free from moral reasons, nor so unfree as to make these reasons ineffective.

QUESTIONS FOR DISCUSSION

1. In the view expressed by Paul Edwards in this chapter (in later years he changed somewhat toward soft determinism), the statements "My greed made me rob the bank," said by a thief, and "A loaded gun pointed at me made me hand over the money," said by a bank teller, involve the same degree of moral responsibility—that is, either both actions are excusable because they are causally inescapable, or neither is. Do you see any important differences between these two cases?

2. What two conceptions of moral responsibility does Edwards take over from Campbell, and how does he rephrase the second conception? Is any question begged by his rephrasing?

3. According to Chisholm, what is the importance of the way we interpret the phrase "could have done otherwise"? What is the interpretation suggested by Jonathan Edwards and G. E. Moore, and why does Chisholm reject it?

4. What is the difference, for Chisholm, between "transeunt" causation and "immanent" causation, and how does it help solve the problem of free will?

5. Our desires, says Chisholm, sometimes necessitate us to act, but at other times merely "incline" us to act. What does he seem to mean by "incline," and how does it affect determinism?

6. What is Nowell-Smith's proposed interpretation of "could have done otherwise," and how does it differ from Chisholm's?

7. According to Nowell-Smith, what are the main "excusing conditions" that relieve a person of responsibility for his or her action? Why, for Nowell-Smith, is being causally necessitated by overwhelming desire not a valid excusing condition? That is, what makes certain excuses (such as lack of talent) acceptable and others (such as laziness or greed) unacceptable?

8. What does Wolf mean by "psychological determination"? Does a motive or a reason determine an action in so strong a way that the agent cannot refrain from performing it? Should phrases like "I could not help stealing the money" or "Logic compels me to vote guilty" be taken at face value, or are they exaggerations like "I'm dying to meet her"?

9. According to Wolf, when would it be fair to blame someone for wrongdoing and when would it be unfair?

SUGGESTED READINGS

ABELSON, R., *Lawless Mind,* St. Martin's Press, New York, 1988.

ARISTOTLE, *Nichomachean Ethics,* Book III, trans. J. A. K. Thomson, Penguin Books, Baltimore, 1955.

AUGUSTINE, ST., *The Problem of Free Choice,* trans. M. Pontifex, Newman Press, Westminster, 1955.

AYER, A. J., *Philosophical Essays,* St. Martin's Press, New York, 1954.

BERLIN, I., *Historical Inevitability,* Oxford University Press, London, 1954.

BEROFSKY, B., *Determinism,* Princeton University Press, Princeton, N.J., 1971.

———, ed., *Free Will and Determinism,* Harper & Row, New York, 1966.

BRADLEY, F. H., *Ethical Studies,* Essay I, Clarendon Press, Oxford, 1927.

BRAND, M., ed., *The Nature of Human Action,* Scott, Foresman, Glenview, Ill., 1970.

BRANDT, R. B., *Ethical Theory,* Chap. 20, Prentice-Hall, Englewood Cliffs, N.J., 1959.

BRUNTON, A., "A Definitive Non-solution of the Free Will Problem," *Philosophical Investigations,* 16, 3 (1993), 231–42.

CAMPBELL, C. A., *On Selfhood and Godhood,* Macmillan, New York, 1957.

———, *In Defense of Free Will,* Humanities Press, New York, 1967.

CHISHOLM, R. M., *Human Freedom and the Self,* University of Kansas Press, Lawrence, 1964.

CLARKE, R., "Free Will and the Conditions of Moral Responsibility," *Philosophical Studies,* 66, 1 (April 1992), 53–72.

DENNETT, D. K., *Elbow Room,* MIT Press, Cambridge, 1984.

DWORKIN, G., ed., *Determinism, Free Will and Moral Responsibility,* Prentice-Hall, Englewood Cliffs, N.J., 1970.

EDWARDS, J., *Freedom of the Will,* Vol. I, ed. P. Ramsey, Yale University Press, New Haven, Conn., 1957.

ELLIS, R., "Agent Causation, Chance and Determinism," *Philosophical Inquiry,* 5 (1983), 29–42.

FEINBERG, J., *Doing and Deserving: Essays in the Theory of Responsibility,* Princeton University Press, Princeton, N.J., 1970.

FOLEY, R., "Compatibilism," *Mind,* 87 (1978).

FRANKFURT, H., "Freedom of the Will and the Concept of a Person," *Journal of Philosophy,* 68 (1971).

FRENCH, P., *The Spectrum of Responsibility,* St. Martin's Press, New York, 1991.

FRIQUEGNON, M., "The Paradoxes of Determinism," *Philosophy and Phenomenological Research,* 33 (1972).

GLOVER, J., *Responsibility,* Humanities Press, New York, 1970.

GOMBERG, P., "Free Will as Ultimate Responsibility," *American Philosophical Quarterly,* 15 (1978).

HAMPSHIRE, S., *Freedom of Mind and Other Essays,* Princeton University Press, Princeton, N.J., 1971.

HARE, R. M., "Prediction and Moral Appraisal," *Midwestern Studies in Philosophy,* 3 (1978).

HOBBES, T., *Leviathan,* Chap. XXI. Liberal Arts Press, New York, 1958.

HOOK, S., ed., *Determinism and Freedom in the Age of Modern Science,* New York University Press, New York, 1958.

HOSPERS, J., *Human Conduct,* Chap. 10, Harcourt, Brace & World, New York, 1961.

HUME, D. A., *A Treatise of Human Nature,* Book II, Part III, Clarendon Press, Oxford, 1928.

JAMES, W., *The Will to Believe and Other Essays in Popular Philosophy,* Longmans Green, New York, 1896.

KAUFMAN, A., "Responsibility," *Encyclopedia of Philosophy,* ed. P. Edwards, Macmillan, New York, 1967.

KENNY, A., *Free Will and Moral Responsibility: Four Lectures,* Routledge and Kegan Paul, London, 1978.

LOCKE, J., *Essay Concerning Human Understanding,* Book II, Chap. 21, ed. A. C. Fraser, Clarendon Press, Oxford, 1894.

MCKERNEY, P., "Self-Determination and the Project," *Journal of Philosophy,* 76 (1979).

MELDEN, A. I., *Free Action,* Humanities Press, New York, 1961.

————, ed., *Essays in Moral Philosophy,* University of Washington Press, Seattle, 1958.

MILL, J. S., *A System of Logic,* Chap. II, Book 6, London, 1843.

MORGENBESSER, S., and J. L. WALSH, eds., *Free Will,* Prentice-Hall, Englewood Cliffs, N.J., 1962.

NOWELL-SMITH, P. H., *Ethics,* Chaps. 19–20, Pelican Books, Baltimore, 1954.

PETERS, R. S., *The Concept of Motivation,* Humanities Press, New York, 1960.

ROSS, W. D., *Foundations of Ethics,* Chap. 10, Clarendon Press, Oxford, 1938.

RYLE, G., *The Concept of Mind,* Chap. III, Barnes & Noble, New York, 1962.

————, *Dilemmas,* Chaps. I–II, Cambridge University Press, London, 1960.

SARTRE, J.-P., *Being and Nothingness,* trans. H. E. Barnes, Philosophical Library, New York, 1956.

SELLERS, W., and J. HOSPERS, eds., *Readings in Ethical Theory,* Appleton-Century-Crofts, New York, 1952.

SIDGWICK, H., *The Methods of Ethics,* Macmillan, London, 1922. 56–66.

SLOTE, M., "Understanding Free Will," *Journal of Philosophy,* 77 (1980).

SPINOZA, B., *Ethics,* Parts III–IV, Hafner, New York, 1949.

STAMPE, D., and M. GILSON, "Of One's Own Free Will," *Philosophy and Phenomenological Research,* 52, 3 (Summer 1992), 529–55.

STEIN, L., "Freedom, Blame and Moral Community," *Journal of Philosophy,* 71 (1974).

STRAWSON, G., *Freedom and Belief,* Oxford University Press, New York, 1986.

VAN INGARTEN, P., *Essay on Free Will,* Oxford University Press, New York, 1983.

WATSON, G., ed., *Free Will,* New York: Oxford University Press, 1986.

WOLF, S., *Freedom Within Reason,* New York: Oxford University Press, 1990.

PART TWO

*T*HE MORALITY
OF TAKING LIFE

We begin our study of applied ethics with perhaps the most dramatic and difficult question one must face: when, if ever, is it morally right to kill a human being? Of all our moral convictions, the belief that human life is sacred is most deeply rooted in our nature and traditions. If there are permissible exceptions to this principle, then it may seem doubtful that any moral principles are immune from exceptions, and we seem led inexorably toward moral skepticism. Yet occasions arise—such as a desperately unwanted pregnancy, the unbearable suffering of the terminally ill, a dangerous aggression against oneself or one's nation—that seem to call for the taking of life through abortion, suicide, euthanasia, or capital punishment. Are there values that take precedence over the value of human life in some circumstances, or is human life "sacred" in the sense that it should never be sacrificed for any purpose? If life is not sacred, then perhaps nothing else is, and do we not slide down a "slippery slope" toward the conclusion that no standards of moral judgment are or need be universally accepted?

SUICIDE

We begin in chapter 3 with that act of taking life that is least subject to moral criticism because, for one reason, the perpetrator has removed himself from vulnerability to criticism and also because the "right to life" to which we appeal in prohibiting murder seems not to be violated by voluntary renunciation.

It might be argued that ethical discussion of suicide is pointless. The decision to take one's own life is a private and socially uncontrollable matter. The uninvolved, disinterested spectator cannot appreciate the feelings of the person he is judging, nor can the anguished person contemplating suicide be expected to worry about the propriety of so desperate an action. This liberal attitude toward suicide, a rather popular one outside religious circles, rests on the assumption that any self-destructive action is *prima facie* evidence of mental derangement—a state of illness, to be treated, if possible, rather than condemned. This modern tendency to excuse suicide on grounds of insanity is matched, at the other extreme, by the traditional Judaeo-Christian condemnation of it as a mortal sin. Both extremes refuse to distinguish rational suicide, committed for more or less weighty reasons, from irrational, hysterical suicide whose explanation requires psychiatric expertise. If suicide relieves one of unbearable and incurable pain, frees one's family of the burden of caring for the terminally ill, protects the prisoner awaiting torture from informing on his comrades, or, as in the Japanese tradition of hara-kiri, is required as a matter of honor, then surely it is a rational, responsible action and an appropriate subject for moral evaluation. On the other hand, irrational suicide committed in a state of hysteria, as in the case of the jilted lover or the despondent child, calls for sympathetic explanation rather than moral judgment. The arguments that follow apply, therefore, only to rational suicide.

An act of suicide has uniquely paradoxical features. It contradicts the most powerful tendency in animal nature—that of self-preservation. It requires a high degree of momentary physical courage, which we ordinarily admire, combined with the will to destroy life, which we ordinarily condemn. In primitive cultures, social attitudes toward suicide vary considerably: suicide simply never happens in some, is rare and shameful in others, and in still others is the customary penance for violating a taboo. Even in advanced cultures, religious and philosophical views of suicide range from denunciation to commendation. The Koran condemns suicide as worse than murder; the Talmud makes it a crime that deprives the perpetrator of burial rites; Christianity considers it a form of murder. From the eleventh century on, civil laws in Europe made it a crime punishable by confiscation of property and denial of Christian burial. Yet prior to the rise of Christianity, the Greeks and Romans admired rational suicide as a form of heroism. Seneca and Epicetus maintained that a person is morally obliged to take his own life if he cannot bear his suffering with dignity. Ancient Greek legends are so replete with accounts of heroic self-destruction that we can say that Greeks admired their heroes as much for the way they died as for the way they lived. Suicide is sanctioned by Far Eastern religions as a way of releasing the soul from its bodily prison. The Hindu custom of *suttee,* whereby a wife throws herself on the funeral pyre of her dead husband, and the Shinto tradition of hara-kiri invest suicide with honor and embellish it with ritual.

Clearly, then, very different and incompatible ethical standards have been at work in determining attitudes toward ending one's own life. Our task is to make these standards explicit and to judge their relative merits. St. Thomas Aquinas (1225–1274) employs the standard of conformity to natural and divine law in arguing that self-preservation is a universal natural tendency and that human life is sacred because it belongs to God, not man. He also appeals to the standard of social welfare, maintaining that every person owes it to his society to remain alive and continue to contribute to it. Aquinas considers sympathetically some of the main reasons that motivate suicide, such as incurable suffering and the wish to escape dishonor, but he insists that such reasons are inadequate to justify the act. The evils that suicide may help to avert, he maintains, are always less serious than the evil of taking life.

David Hume (1711–1776), one of the major figures of the eighteenth-century Enlightenment, rejects the Thomistic standards of natural law and divine authority, arguing that man is a part of a system of nature completely governed by causal laws, so that no action, no matter how odd or abnormal, can be "contrary to nature." And since God acts only through nature, no action can be contrary to the will of God. Nor can it be ungrateful to destroy the gift of life, since in doing so one is exercising another divine gift—the power of terminating one's life. Comparing Hume's discussion with that of Aquinas, we can see how scientific determinism tends to undermine religious ethics. Against the Thomistic principle that the life of the individual belongs to society, Hume defends the more democratic and individualistic belief that one's life is entirely one's own to do with as one wishes. Hume employs, as his basic standard of ethical judgment, the utilitarian principle that one ought to do whatever increases happiness or decreases suffering. Whether suicide is right or wrong depends on whether, in the particular case, it satisfies this principle. But, in general, Hume admires rational suicide as a courageous act. Perhaps his dislike of the religious tradition that condemns suicide as sinful provokes him to a less qualified defense than his utilitarian relativism entails.

Joyce Carol Oates, the distinguished contemporary novelist, takes a view of suicide somewhere in between those of Aquinas and Hume. Unlike Aquinas, she does not condemn it as immoral, but she does criticize it as (in most cases) foolish. In contrast with Hume, who asserts "I believe that no man ever threw away life while it was worth keeping," thus assuming suicide to be almost always a rational action, Oates maintains that it is seldom rational, that is, that most suicides do throw away their lives when they are worth keeping. She condemns writers like Sylvia Plath and Anne Sexton, and the novelist-philosopher Albert Camus, who romanticize self-destruction as an act of supreme freedom. This view, she maintains, is intellectually and aesthetically objectionable because it is supported by false metaphors that misdescribe death as if it were a positively desirable state. "To so desperately confuse the terms of our finite contract as to invent a liberating Death when it is really brute, inarticulateness that awaits—the 'artist' of suicide is a groping, blundering, failed artist, and his artwork a mockery of genuine achievement."

Oates does not deny that some acts of self-destruction are rational, and even heroic, namely those performed for reasons of principle, such as the partially self-inflicted martyrdoms of Socrates and Jesus, or when suicide is "the necessary next move that will preserve one's dignity" when one is a burden to others or in unbearable and unending pain. But most suicidal actions are due to neurotic motives, where what one really wants is not one's death, but to punish others, or to express one's disappointment with the world. "Rationally," she asserts, "one cannot 'choose' Death because Death is an unknown experience, and perhaps it isn't even an 'experience'— perhaps it is simply nothing and one cannot imagine nothing." One can choose to die as a means of achieving some greater purpose, such as relieving one's family of the burden of caring for one, but one cannot choose death for its own sake, as a better state to be in than life, since death is not a state one can be in. Thus while most suicides do not call for condemnation, they may well be criticized and deplored as foolish mistakes.

EUTHANASIA

Medical science and economic abundance have increased the average life span to the point where the most poignant social problem of our time has become that of caring for the grievously incapacitated. The "right to die" has become a popular slogan among those, like Dr. Jack Kevorkian, who believe that euthanasia, the topic of Chapter 4, is the humane solution to this problem, provided that it be permitted only when no doubt exists about the subject's preference for a quick and painless death over a long and painful one. Those who insist on the sanctity of life on religious grounds maintain that we have no more right to "solve" the problem of slow dying by quickly terminating life than Hitler had to carry out his "final solution" to the so-called "Jewish problem." But while the victims of the Holocaust did not want to be exterminated, many terminally ill patients do ask, even beg, to be released from their suffering, and so the analogy seems unfair. Nevertheless, critics of euthanasia may reply that a patient who is of sufficiently sound mind to make a rational decision about life and death by that very fact has reason to prefer life, while the one who is really ill enough to prefer death is too far gone to make a rational decision. Thus, begging to die is never rational. Rather, it is a hysterical cry, calling for sympathy, but not for lethal action. This line of reasoning shifts the issue from a moral ground to a factual one of whether there are reliable means of ensuring that a person's decision to end his or her life is a rational one.

The medical profession generally accepts the principle that a doctor may refrain from extraordinary measures to keep a terminally ill patient alive (such as surgery, intravenous feeding, using a respirator), which many writers call "passive euthanasia." However, a doctor may not deliberately terminate the patient's life, no matter how painlessly—that is, the doctor may not perform active euthanasia. In a now-famous essay first published in the *New England Journal of Medicine,* James Rachels argues that in the case of infants affected by extreme Down's syndrome or spina bifida with intestinal blockage, the passive euthanasia often practiced by allowing the child to die of starvation and dehydration is far less humane than a painless but lethal injection. Rachels's general conclusion was that there is no moral difference ("per se," that is, independent of other factors) between active and passive euthanasia, between killing and letting die. Either course may be better or worse, depending on the circumstances.

Thomas Sullivan, a professor of philosophy at a Catholic college, argues that the traditional distinction between active and passive euthanasia is a pertinent one and supports the American Medical Association's prohibition on active killing, as contrasted with passive letting die. Sullivan criticizes the use of the term "passive euthanasia," as if not using extraordinary means to keep a patient alive were a passive way of killing. It isn't killing at all, he insists. The important distinction, he argues, is not between activity and passivity, but between ordinary means of preserving life and extraordinary means, and between the intention to bring about a patient's death as contrasted with the intention not to make an unusual effort to keep the patient alive.

Rachels replies to Sullivan first by pointing out that Sullivan has not disputed his major claim—that there is no moral difference between active killing and passive letting die—but merely claims it to be irrelevant to the actual medical practices employed with respect to defective infants who require surgery to be kept alive. Rather than debating the question of relevance, Rachels focuses his reply on Sullivan's claim that the difference between wrongful killing and permissible letting die is to be located in the intention of the agent (usually the doctor), in deciding what to do about a terminally ill patient. Does the doctor intend the patient's death? Then, whether active or passive, the doctor is committing murder, in the sense that he or she is wrongfully bringing about death. Rachels contends that this position confuses the judgment of an action as right or wrong with the judgment of the agent's character as good or evil. Jack and Jill perform the same action of visiting their grandmother. Jill intends thereby to inherit money, while Jack intends to comfort the old woman. This, claims Rachels, doesn't make Jill's action wrong; rather it shows us that Jill is not as good a person as Jack.

Neither is Sullivan's emphasis on the distinction between ordinary and extraordinary treatment decisive in these matters, according to Rachels. Insulin injections and antibiotic pills would seem to rank as quite ordinary measures, yet they may be withheld from patients suffering from terminal illness so as not to prolong the process of dying. The relevant question for Rachels is not "do we intend that the patient die?" since it is already settled that the patient will die, but "what is the least painful way of dying?"

ABORTION

Abortion and infanticide were regularly practiced in ancient Greece and Rome, where children were regarded as the property of their parents, and the same is still true in some parts of the world. With the rise of Judaeo-Christian-Islamic consciousness, Western civilization became committed to the appreciation of all human life as God's most valuable gift to humankind. As long as state and church were considered the terrestrial agents of divine authority the principle of the sanctity of human life was not thought to prohibit war or execution, but only individual, private killing, with the exception of self-defense, in which case taking life also saves life. It was believed that the soul, which was the essence of humanity, is infused into the human fetus at conception, or shortly thereafter. Consequently, abortion came to be regarded by some as the worst form of murder, because it deprives the fetus of baptismal purgation of original sin. Religious opinion has been divided over whether therapeutic abortion to save the mother's life can be justified on the grounds of self-defense. With the decline of orthodoxy in this century, there has been a mounting tendency to rescind legal prohibitions of abortion and to regard the issue as a practical rather than a moral one, to be decided according to the needs of parents and society.

The anti-abortion position is often called "conservative" and the pro-abortion position "liberal"; the former has been the traditional view, while the latter represents a break with religious and cultural tradition in favor of individual liberty of action. However, there is considerable tension within the liberal position, which also emphasizes human rights, central among which is the right to life. Thus, people opposed to abortion need not base their argument on religious doctrine. They can oppose abortion on the liberal ground that the fetus has a right to life that cannot be overridden. Perhaps the only way out of this liberal dilemma is that taken by Mary Anne Warren, which denies that human rights such as the right to life apply to a fetus; however, this position is fraught with problems, such as the permissibility of infanticide.

John T. Noonan, a Catholic theologian, defends the present position of the Catholic church, which prohibits abortion under any circumstances with the possible exception of therapeutic abortion to save the mother's life. Doctors may perform surgery on a pregnant woman when it is necessary to save her life, even when the probable result is the death of the fetus, only on the condition that fetal death is not intended even if foreseen. The principle involved has come to be called the "principle of double effect." According to this principle, an action may be performed in order to achieve a desired result with the knowledge that harm will also result, as long as the harm itself is not desired and is not chosen as a necessary means to the desired effect. Thus, it would be permissible to remove a fetus by cesarean section even when it is probable that the fetus will not survive; however, it would not be permissible to crush the fetus in a craniotopic abortion, for in this case fetal death is the necessary means of saving the mother's life.

Noonan's central argument against nontherapeutic abortion under any conditions is this: there is no point in the development of a human embryo into a full-fledged person when it is reasonable to draw a line and claim that, on one side, the fetus is insufficiently human to have the right to life, while on the other side of the line it is fully human, a person endowed with full moral rights, including the right to life. On the theological assumption that the soul is created at, or soon after, conception, that moment seems the only reasonable point at which to draw such a line; later developments, such as the appearance of brain waves, quickening, viability, and even birth are not, because the difference in the fetus just before and just after these developments is so slight that it cannot support so serious a distinction. One need not even accept the theological doctrine of ensoulment in order to arrive at the same conclusion, since it is a fact established by the sciences of genetics and embryology that, at the moment of conception, a "sharp shift in probability" occurs—that is, an overwhelming likelihood that the fertilized cell will develop into a normal human being. In the light of this extraordinarily high potentiality for personhood, the fetus should be regarded as tantamount to a person and treated as such.

Mary Anne Warren takes the diametrically opposite position from Noonan, namely, that a woman has a right to rid herself of a fetus under any circumstances, even for trivial reasons, because her right to terminate her pregnancy overrides any right the fetus might be claimed to have, even its right to life. Her argument is that a human fetus is only a potential person, not an actual person, and only actual persons have full moral rights. Potential persons have only partial rights, easily overriden by the more robust rights of actual persons. This same point, she admits, holds of newborn infants in the first month or so of postnatal life, so that, in her view, infanticide is also permissible, a consequence that many will find unpalatable.

Taking a position somewhere in between these two extremes, Jane English denies that a sharp line can be drawn at any point between actual person and potential person, and concludes that the issue of abortion should be decided on different grounds, primarily those of defending the mother's vital interests. Unlike Warren, English does not consider the mother's rights over her body to override automatically the right to life of the fetus. For English, this may be so in the early stages of the pregnancy, when the fetus is no more like a human person than a fish, but not later on, when only the defense of the mother's life or sanity can justify killing the fetus. She argues, against both Noonan and Warren, that abortion is clearly not as objectionable as infanticide, because the mother can protect her interests against the baby without killing it—for example, by giving it up for adoption. This fact, she holds, makes birth a crucial dividing line for moral judgment, even if it does not distinguish a person from a nonperson.

CAPITAL PUNISHMENT

Is capital punishment a vestige of primitive brutality, or is it a justifiable response to crimes that threaten society? We have been admonished "Thou shall not kill" ever since Moses ascended Mount Sinai, and yet strong objections to legal execution were not voiced until the eighteenth century. The Judaeo-Christian emphasis on mercy and on the sanctity of human life had little effect on penal institutions prior to the Enlightenment, perhaps because of man's religious preoccupation with salvation in the next world and disregard for diminishing pain in this world. Indeed, it was difficult to reconcile the belief in an omnipotent Lawgiver, fearfully punishing those who broke His commandments, with opposition to executions by the state and the church, particularly when these were considered to be agents of God.

Anticlerical writers of the late eighteenth and early nineteenth centuries were the first to denounce cruel and excessive punishment. Beccaria, Voltaire, Diderot, Rousseau, and even Robespierre demanded a humane and rational penal system. Russia, under Catherine the Great, who was influenced by Beccaria's book *Crimes and Punishments,* was the first nation to respond to the protests against capital punishment, and in 1750 abolished the death penalty for all crimes except treason. During the nineteenth century, religious groups as well as utilitarian freethinkers in Great Britain agitated successfully to reduce the number of crimes punishable by death from over 200, including petty theft, to only two, premeditated murder and treason; and some American states abolished the death penalty. The trend of the last two centuries has been toward limiting capital punishment, but grounds remain, as the reader will see, for doubting whether it should be abolished for the most serious crimes. The execution of Adolph Eichmann by the State of Israel was a particularly challenging test for those who believe that no crime should be punished by death.

Anthony Amsterdam, a defense attorney and professor of criminal law, strongly condemns capital punishment as official murder of a particularly cruel sort, because the victim is kept prisoner, helplessly awaiting his or her predicted and inevitable moment of death. Amsterdam considers the two main reasons usually offered for the death penalty, namely, retribution ("an eye for an eye") and deterrence of other would-be murderers. In rebuttal of the first reason, he points out that it is unworkable: "We do not burn down arsonists' houses or cheat back at bunco artists." Further, he argues, the death penalty cannot be fairly and evenly applied, because different states have different rules and because the well-to-do can afford better legal defense than the poor. Against the second reason, deterrence, Amsterdam argues that statistical studies overwhelmingly indicate that execution has no greater value in reducing violent crime rates than life imprisonment. Only three such studies have ever supported the greater deterrent value of capital punishment and these, he argues, were poorly conducted and incorrectly interpreted.

Ernest Van den Haag, a professor of sociology and a practicing psychotherapist, argues for the reestablishment of the death penalty in states where is has been abolished and its maintenance in states where it already exists, on two grounds: (1) that it is a just mode of punishment for the gravest crimes, such as premeditated homicide, espionage, and terrorism, and (2) that it is needed as a deterrent to such crimes. According to Van den Haag, punishment has two primary functions: the achievement of justice and the social benefit of deterring crime. By "justice" he seems to mean that for lawbreakers to be made to suffer their transgressions is a good thing in itself, regardless of whether it promotes the social benefit of preventing further crimes. He argues that those who deny that justice is a purpose of punishment and yet denounce the death penalty on the ground that it is unjustly applied more to the poor than to the wealthy are inconsistent. Insofar as the latter claim is true, Van den Haag contends, the fault lies in the way the courts apply the penalty but not in the penalty itself. On the other hand, once the issue of injustice is raised, it follows that the carrying out of justice is conceded to be a primary purpose of punishment. "If justice is not a purpose of penalties, injustice cannot be an objection to the death penalty, or to any other; if it is, justice cannot be ruled out as an argument for any penalty." Just how Van den Haag would argue positively that justice is fulfilled by capital punishment, he does not say. Perhaps he would cite the scriptural retributive principle, "an eye for an eye," or the modern equivalent cited in the Gilbert and Sullivan operetta *The Mikado:* "Let the punishment fit the crime." (On this issue, compare Amsterdam's essay above.)

Most of Van den Haag's essay is devoted to the argument for the deterrent value of the death penalty. Van den Haag is aware of the voluminous statistical evidence in modern criminology which seems to tell against the deterrent value of capital punishment, but he attempts to deflect the force of this evidence by pointing out that factors other than the maintenance or abolition of capital punishment may be responsible for the failure of the homicide rate to rise in abolition states and fall in death penalty states. Such factors include general cultural climate, effectiveness of law enforcement, reliability of crime records, and homogeneity of population. Surprisingly, for a sociologist, he denies that poverty and the degradation of slum ghettos are among these other causal factors. In this denial he seems to be demanding that to qualify as causal factors, poverty and ghetto conditions must be *in themselves* sufficient conditions for crime, rather than factors which, *together with others,* produce crime, although he criticizes opponents of the death penalty for making this demand of capital punishment. Holding that the available evidence fails to prove that the death penalty has no more deterrent value than life imprisonment and that, for certain cases, such as prisoners already serving life sentences, it is the only possible deterrent to further killing, Van den Haag reasons that abolition of the death penalty where it exists, or failure to reinstate it where it has been abolished, risks the lives of future innocent victims of the murders that the death penalty might have prevented, in order to avoid taking the life of convicted murderers. He considers this choice to be morally perverse.

3

SUICIDE

*T*HE SIN OF SUICIDE

St. Thomas Aquinas

We proceed thus to the Fifth Article:

Objection 1. It would seem lawful for a man to kill himself. For murder is a sin in so far as it is contrary to justice. But no man can do an injustice to himself, as is proved in *Ethic.* v. 11. Therefore no man sins by killing himself.

Obj. 2. Further, It is lawful, for one who exercises public authority, to kill evildoers. Now he who exercises public authority is sometimes an evildoer. Therefore he may lawfully kill himself.

Obj. 3. Further, It is lawful for a man to suffer spontaneously a lesser danger that he may avoid a greater. Thus it is lawful for a man to cut off a decayed limb even from himself, that he may save his whole body. Now sometimes a man, by killing himself, avoids a greater evil, for an example an unhappy life, or the shame of sin. Therefore a man may kill himself.

Obj. 4. Further, Samson killed himself, as related in Judges xvi, and yet he is numbered among the saints (Heb. xi). Therefore it is lawful for a man to kill himself.

Obj. 5. Further, It is related (2 Mach. xiv. 42) that a certain Razias killed himself, *choosing to die nobly rather than to fall into the hands of the wicked, and to suffer abuses unbecoming his noble birth.* Now nothing that is done nobly and bravely is unlawful. Therefore suicide is not unlawful.

On the contrary, Augustine says (*De Civ. Dei* i. 20): *Hence it follows that the words "Thou shall not kill" refer to the killing of a man; not another man; therefore, not even thyself. For he who kills himself, kills nothing else than a man.*

I answer that, It is altogether unlawful to kill oneself, for three reasons. First, because everything naturally loves itself, the result being that everything naturally keeps itself in being, and resists corruption so far as it can. Wherefore suicide is contrary to the inclination of nature and to charity, whereby every man should love himself. Hence suicide is always a mortal sin, as being contrary to the natural law and to charity.

Secondly, because every part, as such, belongs to the whole. Now every man is part of the community, and so, as such, he belongs to the community. Hence by killing himself he injures the community, as the Philosopher declares (*Ethic* v. ii).

Thirdly, because life is God's gift to man, and is subject to His power, Who kills and makes to live. Hence whoever takes his own life sins against God, even as he who kills another's slave sins against that slave's master, and as he who usurps himself judgment of a matter not entrusted to him. For it belongs to God alone to pronounce sentence of death and life, according to Deut. xxxii. 39, *I will kill and I will make to live.*

Reply Obj. 1. Murder is a sin, not only because it is contrary to justice, but also because it is opposed to charity, which a man should have towards himself; in this respect suicide is a sin in relation to oneself. In relation to the community and God, it is sinful, by reason also to its opposition to justice.

Reply Obj. 2. One who exercises public authority may lawfully put to death an evildoer, since he can pass judgment on him. But no man is judge of himself. Wherefore it is not lawful for one who exercises public authority to put himself to death for any sin whatsoever, although he may lawfully commit himself to the judgment of others.

Reply Obj. 3. Man is made master of himself through his free will: wherefore he can lawfully dispose of himself as to those matters which pertain to this life, which is ruled by man's free will. But the passage from this life to another and happier one is subject not to man's free will but to the power of God. Hence it is not lawful for man to take his own life that he may pass to a happier life, nor that he may escape any unhappiness whatsoever to the present life, because the ultimate and most fearsome evil of this life is death, as the Philosopher states (*Ethic.* iii. 6). Therefore to bring death upon oneself in order to escape the other afflictions of this life is to adopt a greater evil in order to avoid a lesser. In like manner it is unlawful to take one's own life on account of one's having committed a sin, both because by so doing one does oneself a very great injury, by depriving oneself of the time needful for repentance, and because it is not lawful to slay an evildoer except by the sentence of the public authority. Again it is unlawful for a woman to kill herself lest she be violated, because she ought not to commit on herself the very great sin of suicide to avoid the lesser sin of another. For she commits no sin in being violated by force, provided she does not consent, since *without consent of the mind there is no stain on the body,* as the Blessed Lucy declared. Now it is evident that fornication and adultery are less grievous sins than taking a man's, especially one's own, life, since the latter is most grievous, because one injures oneself, to whom one owes the greatest love. Moreover it is most dangerous since no time is left wherein to expiate it by repentance. Again it is not lawful for anyone to take his own life for fear he should consent to sin, because *evil must not be done that good may come* (Rom. iii. 8) or that evil may be avoided, especially if the evil be of small account and an uncertain event, for it is uncertain whether one will at some future time consent to a sin, since God is able to deliver man from sin under any temptation whatever.

Reply Obj. 4. As Augustine says (*De Civ. Dei* i. 21), *not even Samson is to be excused that he crushed himself together with his enemies under the ruins of the house, except that the Holy Ghost, Who had wrought many wonders through him, had secretly commanded him to do this.* He assigns the same reason in the case of certain holy women who at the time of persecution took their own lives and are commemorated by the Church.

Reply Obj. 5. It belongs to fortitude that a man does not shrink from being slain by another, for the sake of the good of virtue and that he may avoid sin. But that a man take his own life in order to avoid penal evils has indeed an appearance of fortitude (for which reason some . . . have killed themselves, thinking to act from fortitude), yet it is not true fortitude, but rather a weakness of soul unable to bear penal evils, as the Philosopher (*Ethic.* iii. 7) and Augustine (*De Civ. Dei* i. 22, 23) declare.

*T*HE RIGHT OF SUICIDE

David Hume

One considerable advantage that arises from Philosophy consists in the sovereign antidote which it affords to superstition and false religion. All other remedies against that pestilent distemper are in vain, or at least uncertain. Plain good sense and the practice of the world, which alone serve most purposes of life, are here found ineffectual: History as well as daily experience furnish instances of men endowed with the strongest capacity for business and affairs, who have all their lives crouched under slavery to the grossest superstition. Even gaiety and sweetness of temper, which infuse a balm into every other wound, afford no remedy to so virulent a poison, as we may particularly observe of the fair sex, who, though commonly possessed of these rich presents of nature, feel many of their joys blasted by this importunate intruder. But when sound Philosophy has once gained possession of the mind, superstition is effectually excluded; and one may fairly affirm that her triumph over this enemy is more complete than over most of the vices and imperfections incident to human nature. Love or anger, ambition or avarice, have their root in the temper and affections, which the soundest reason is scarce ever able fully to correct; but superstition, being founded on false opinion, must immediately vanish when true philosophy has inspired juster sentiments of superior powers. The contest is here more equal between the distemper and the medicine, and nothing can hinder the latter from proving effectual but its being false and sophisticated.

It will here be superfluous to magnify the merits of philosophy by displaying the pernicious tendency of that vice of which it cures the human mind. The superstitious man, says Tully, is miserable in every scene, in every incident of life; even sleep itself, which banishes all cares of unhappy mortals, affords him matter of new terror while he examines his dreams and finds in those visions of the night prognostications of future calamities. I may add that though death alone can put a full period to this misery, he dares not fly to this refuge but still prolongs a miserable existence from a vain fear lest he offend his maker by using the power with which that beneficient being has endowed him. The presents of God and nature are ravished from us by this cruel enemy; and notwithstanding that one step would remove us from the regions of pain and sorrow, her menaces still chain us down to a hated being which she herself chiefly contributes to render miserable.

It is observed by such as have been reduced by the calamities of life to the necessity of employing this fatal remedy that if the unseasonable care of their friends deprive them of that species of Death which they proposed to

---

From Hume's "Of Suicide," first published in 1898.

themselves, they seldom venture upon any other or can summon up so much resolution a second time as to execute their purpose. So great is our horror of death that when it presents itself under any form besides that to which a man has endeavored to reconcile his imagination, it acquires new terrors and overcomes his feeble courage. But when the menaces of superstition are joined to this natural timidity, no wonder it quite deprives men of all power over their lives, since even many pleasures and enjoyments to which we are carried by a strong propensity are torn from us by this inhuman tyrant. Let us here endeavor to restore men to their native liberty by examining all the common arguments against Suicide and showing that the action may be free from every imputation of guilt or blame, according to the sentiments of all the ancient philosophers.

If Suicide be criminal, it must be a transgression of our duty either to God, our neighbor, or ourselves.—To prove that suicide is not transgression of our duty to God, the following considerations may perhaps suffice. In order to govern the material world, the almighty Creator has established general and immutable laws by which all bodies, from the greatest planet to the smallest particle of matter, are maintained in their proper sphere and function. To govern the animal world, he has endowed all living creatures with bodily and mental powers, with senses, passions, appetites, memory, and judgment, by which they are impelled or regulated in that course of life to which they are destined. These two distinct principles of the material and animal world continually encroach upon each other, and mutually retard or forward each other's operations. The powers of men and of all other animals are restrained and directed by the nature and qualities of the surrounding bodies, and the modifications and actions of these bodies are incessantly altered by the operation of all animals. Man is stopped by rivers in his passage over the surface of the earth; and rivers, when properly directed, lend their force to the motion of machines, which serve to the use of man. But though the provinces of material and animal powers are not kept entirely separate, there results from thence *no* discord or disorder in the creation; on the contrary, from the mixture, union, and contrast of all the various powers of inanimate bodies and living creatures arises that surprising harmony and proportion which affords the surest argument of supreme wisdom. The providence of the Deity appears not immediately in any operation, but governs everything by those general and immutable laws which have been established from the beginning of time. All events, in one sense, may be pronounced the action of the Almighty; they all proceed from those powers with which he has endowed his creatures. A house which falls by its own weight is not brought to ruin by his providence more than one destroyed by the hands of men; nor are the human faculties less his workmanship than the laws of motion and gravitation. When the passions play, when the judgment dictates, when the limbs obey, this is all the operation of God, and upon these animate principles, as well as upon the inanimate, has he established the government of the universe. Every event is alike important in the eyes of that infinite being, who takes in at one glance the more distant regions of space and remotest periods of time. There is no event, however important to us, which he has exempted from the general laws that govern the universe or which he has peculiarly reserved for his own immediate action and operation. The revolution of states and empires depends upon the smallest caprice or passion of single men; and the lives of men are shortened or extended by the smallest accident of air or diet, sunshine or tempest. Nature still continues her progress and operation; and if general laws be ever broke by particular volitions of the Deity, it is after a manner which entirely escapes human observation. As, on the one hand, the elements and other inanimate parts of the creation carry on their action without regard to the particular interest and situation of men, so men are entrusted to their judgment and discretion in the various shocks of matter and may employ every faculty with which they are endowed in order to provide for their ease, happiness, or preservation. What is the meaning then of that principle that a man who, tired of life and haunted by pain and misery, bravely overcomes all the natural terrors of death and makes his escape from this cruel scene, that such a man, I say, has incurred the indignation of his Creator by encroaching on the office of divine providence and disturbing the order of the universe? Shall we assert that the Almighty has reserved to himself in any peculiar manner the disposal of the lives of men and has not submitted that event, in common with others, to the general laws by which the universe is governed? This is plainly false; the lives of men depend upon the same laws as the lives of all other elements, and these are subjected to the general laws of matter and motion. The fall of a tower or the infusion of poison will destroy a man equally with the meanest creature; an inundation sweeps away everything without distinction that comes within the reach of its fury. Since therefore the lives of men are forever dependent on the general laws of matter and motion, is a man's disposing of his life criminal because in every case it is criminal to encroach upon these laws or disturb their operation? But this seems absurd; all animals are entrusted to their own prudence and skill for their conduct in the world and have full authority, as far as their power extends, to alter all the operations of nature. Without the exercise of this authority they could not subsist a moment; every action, every motion of a man, innovates on the order of some parts of matter and diverts from their ordinary course the general laws of motion. Putting together, therefore, these conclusions, we find that human life depends upon the general laws of matter and motion and that it is no encroachment on the office of providence to disturb or alter these general laws. Has not everyone, of consequence, the free disposal of his own life? And may he not lawfully employ that power with which nature has endowed him? In order to destroy the evidence of this conclusion, we must show a reason why this particular case is excepted. Is it because human life is of so great importance that it is a presumption for human prudence to dispose of it? But the life of a man is of no greater importance to the universe than that of an oyster. And were it of ever so great importance, the order of nature has actually submitted it to human prudence and reduced us to a necessity in every incident of determining concerning it. Were the disposal of human life so much reserved as the peculiar province of the Almighty that it were an encroachment of his right for men to dispose of their own lives, it would be equally criminal to act for the preservation of life as for its destruction. If I turn aside a stone which is falling upon my head, I disturb the course of nature, and I invade the peculiar province of the Almighty by lengthening out my life beyond the period which by the general laws of matter and motion he has assigned it.

A hair, a fly, an insect is able to destroy this mighty being whose life is of such importance. It is an absurdity to suppose that human prudence may lawfully dispose of what depends on such insignificant causes? It would be no crime in me to divert the Nile or Danube from its course, were I able to effect such purposes. Where then is the crime of turning a few ounces of blood from their natural channel?—Do you imagine that I repine at Providence or curse my creation because I go out of life and put a period to a being which, were it to continue, would render me miserable? Far be such sentiments from me; I am only convinced of a matter of fact, which you yourself acknowledge possible, that human life may be unhappy and that my existence, if further prolonged, would become ineligible; but I thank providence both for the good which I have already enjoyed and for the power with which I am endowed of escaping the ill that threatens me. To you it belongs to repine providence, who foolishly imagine that you have no such power and who must still prolong a hated life, though loaded with pain and sickness, with shame and poverty.—Do you not teach that when any ill befalls me, though by the malice of my enemies, I ought to be resigned to providence and that the actions of men are the operations of the Almighty as much as the actions of inanimate beings? When I fall upon my own sword, therefore, I receive my death equally from the hands of the Deity as if it had proceeded from a lion, a precipice, or a fever. The submission which you require to providence in every calamity that befalls me excludes not human skill and industry, if possibly by their means I can avoid or escape the calamity. And why may I not employ one remedy as well as another?—If my life be not my own, it were criminal for me to put it in danger, as well as to dispose of it; nor could one man deserve the appellation of *hero* whom glory or friendship transports into the greatest dangers, and another merit the reproach of *wretch* or *miscreant* who puts a period to his life for like motives.—There is no being which possesses any power or faculty that it receives not from its Creator, nor is there any one which by ever so irregular an action can encroach upon the plan of his providence or disorder the universe. Its operations are his works equally with that chain of events which it invades, and whichever principle prevails, we may for that very reason conclude it to be most favoured by him. Be it animate or inanimate, rational or irrational, it is all a case: its power is still derived from the supreme creator and is alike comprehended in the order of his providence. When the horror of pain prevails over the love of life, when a voluntary action anticipates the effects of blind causes, it is only in consequence of those powers and principles which he has implanted in his creatures. Divine providence is still inviolate and placed far beyond the reach of human injuries. It is impious, says the old Roman superstition, to divert rivers from their course or invade the prerogatives of nature. It is impious, says the French superstition, to inoculate for the small pox, or usurp the business of providence, by voluntarily producing distempers and maladies. It is impious, says the modern European superstition, to put a period to our own life and thereby rebel against our creator. And why not impious, say I, to build houses, cultivate the ground, or sail upon the ocean? In all these actions we employ our powers of mind and body to produce some innovation in the course of nature; and in none of them do we any more. They are all of them therefore equally innocent or equally criminal.—*But you are placed by providence, like a sentinel in a particular station, and when you desert it without being recalled, you are equally guilty of rebellion against your almighty sovereign and have incurred his displeasure.*—I ask, why do you conclude that providence has placed me in this station? For my part I find that I owe my birth to a long chain of causes, of which many depend upon voluntary actions of men. *But Providence guided all these causes, and nothing happens in the universe without its consent and cooperation.* If so, then neither does my death, however voluntary, happen without its consent; and whenever pain or sorrow so far overcome my patience as to make me tired of life, I may conclude that I am recalled from my station in the clearest and most express terms. It is Providence surely that has placed me at this present moment in this chamber, but may I not leave it when I think proper, without being liable to the imputation of having deserted my post or station? When I shall be dead, the principles of which I am composed will still perform their part in the universe and will be equally useful in the grand fabric as when they composed this individual creature. The difference to the whole will be no greater than between my being in a chamber and in the open air. The one change is of more importance to me than the other, but not more so to the universe.

It is a kind of blasphemy to imagine that any created being can disturb the order of the world or invade the business of providence! It supposes that that being possesses powers and faculties which it received not from its creator and which are not subordinate to his government and authority. A man may disturb society, no doubt, and thereby incur the displeasure of the Almighty; but the government of the world is placed far beyond his reach and violence. And how does it appear that the Almighty is displeased with those actions that disturb society? By the principles which he has implanted in human nature and which inspire us with a sentiment of remorse if we ourselves have been guilty of such actions and with that of blame and disapprobation if we ever observe them in others.—Let us now examine, according to the method proposed, whether Suicide be of this kind of actions, and be a breach of our duty to our *neighbor* and to *society*.

A man who retires from life does no harm to society; he only ceases to do good, which, if it is an injury, is of the lowest kind. All our obligations to do good to society seem to imply something reciprocal. I receive the benefits of society and therefore ought to promote its interests, but when I withdraw myself altogether from society, can I be bound any longer? But, allowing that our obligations to do good were perpetual, they have certainly some bounds. I am not obliged to do a small good to society at the expense of a great harm to myself; why then should I prolong a miserable existence because of some frivolous advantage which the public may perhaps receive from me? If upon account of age and infirmities I may lawfully resign any office and employ my time altogether in fencing against these calamities and alleviating as much as possible the miseries of my future life, why may I not cut short these miseries at once by an action which is no more prejudicial to society?—But suppose that it is no longer in my power to promote the interest of society; suppose that I am a burden to it; suppose that my life hinders some person from being much more useful to society. In such cases my resignation of life must not only be innocent but laudable. And most people who lie under any temptation to abandon existence are in some such situation; those who have health, or power, or authority, have commonly better reason to be in humor with the world.

A man is engaged in a conspiracy for the public interest, is seized upon suspicion, is threatened with the rack, and knows from his own weakness that the secret will be extorted from him. Could such a one consult the public interest better than by putting a quick period to a miserable life? This was the case of the famous and brave Strozi of Florence.—Again, suppose a malefactor is condemned to a shameful death; can any reason be imagined why he may not anticipate his punishment and save himself all the anguish of thinking on its dreadful approaches? He invades the business of providence no more than the magistrate did who ordered his execution, and his voluntary death is equally advantageous to society by ridding it of a pernicious member.

That suicide may often be consistent with interests and with our duty to ourselves, no one can question who allows that age, sickness, or misfortune may render life a burden and make it worse even than annihilation. I believe that no man ever threw away life while it was worth keeping. For such is our natural horror of death that small motives will never be able to reconcile us to it; and though perhaps the situation of a man's health or fortune did not seem to require this remedy, we may at least be assured that any one who, without apparent reason, has had recourse to it was cursed with such an incurable depravity or gloominess of temper as must poison all enjoyment and render him equally miserable as if he had been loaded with the most grievous misfortunes.—If suicide be supposed a crime it is only cowardice can impel us to it. If it be no crime, both prudence and courage should engage us to rid ourselves at once of existence when it becomes a burden. It is the only way that we can then be useful to society—by setting an example which, if imitated, would preserve to everyone his chance for happiness in life and would effectually free him from all danger of misery.

*T*HE FALSE ART OF SUICIDE

Joyce Carol Oates

> *In the morning of life the son tears himself loose from the mother,*
> *from the domestic hearth, to rise through battle to his destined heights.*
> *Always he imagines his worst enemy in front of him, yet he carries the*
> *enemy within himself—a deadly longing for the abyss, a longing to*
> *drown in his own source, to be sucked down to the realm of the*
> *Mothers. His life is a constant struggle against extinction, a violent yet*
> *fleeting deliverance from ever-lurking night. This death is no external*
> *enemy, it is his own inner longing for the stillness and profound*
> *peace of all-knowing non-existence, for all-seeing sleep in the ocean*
> *of coming-to-be and passing away.*
>
> C. G. Jung, *Symbols of Transformation*

Not only the artist, that most deliberate of persons, but all human beings
employ metaphor: the conscious or unconscious creation of concrete, literal terms that seek to express the abstract, the not-at-hand, the ineffable. Is
the suicide an artist? Is Death-by-Suicide an art form, the employment of a
metaphor so vast, so final, that it obliterates and sweeps into silence all
opposition? But there are many suicides, there are many deaths, some highly
conscious and others groping, perplexed, perhaps murderous, hardly conscious at all: a succumbing to the gravitational pull of which Jung speaks in
the quotation above, which takes him away from the "realm of the
Mothers"—but only for a while, until his life's energy runs its course, and he
is drawn down into what Jung calls, in metaphorical language that is beautiful, even seductive, the "profound peace of all-knowing non-existence." Yet
if we were to push aside metaphor, if we were no longer even to speak in a
reverential tone of Death, but instead of Deadness—mere, brute, flat, distinctly unseductive Deadness—how artistic a venture is it, how meaningfully can it engage our deepest attention?

My thesis is a simple one: apart from circumstances which insist upon
self-destruction as the inevitable next move, the necessary next move that
will preserve one's dignity, the act of suicide itself is a consequence of the
employment of false metaphors. It is a consequence of the atrophying of the

creative imagination: the failure of the imagination, not to be confused with gestures of freedom, or rebellion, or originality, or transcendence. To so desperately confuse the terms of our finite contract as to invent a liberating Death when it is really brute, inarticulate Deadness that awaits—the "artist" of suicide is a groping, blundering, failed artist, and his art-work a mockery of genuine achievement.

The "artistic" suicide—in contrast to the suicide who acts in order to hasten an inevitable end, perhaps even to alleviate terrible pain—is always mesmerized by the imaginative act of self-destruction, *as if it were a kind of creation.* It is a supreme gesture of the will, an insistence upon one's absolute freedom; that it is "contrary to nature," a dramatic violation of the life-force, makes the gesture all the more unique. One can determine one's self, one's identity, by choosing to put an end to that identity—which is to say, an end to finitude itself. The suicide who deliberates over his act, who very likely has centered much of his life around the possibility of the act, rejects our human condition of finitude (all that we are not, as well as all that we are); his self-destruction is a disavowal, in a sense, of what it means to *be* human. But does the suicide who is transfixed by metaphor suffer a serious derangement of perception, so that he contemplates the serene, transcendental, Platonic "all-knowing non-existence" while what awaits him is merely a biological death—that is, deadness?

In Sylvia Plath's famous poem "Lady Lazarus" the young woman poet boasts of her most recent suicide attempt in language that, though carefully restrained by the rigorous formal discipline of the poem, strikes us as very close to hysteria. She is a "smiling woman," only thirty; and like the cat she has nine times to die. (Though in fact Plath's next attempt, an attempt said not to have been altogether serious, was to be her last.) She is clearly proud of herself, though self-mocking as well, and her angry contempt for the voyeurs crowding around is beautifully expressed:

What a million filaments.
The peanut-crunching crowd
Shoves in to see

Them unwind me hand and foot—
The big strip tease.
Gentlemen, ladies

These are my hands
My knees
I may be skin and bone,

Nevertheless I am the same, identical woman.

Dying
Is an art, like everything else.
I do it exceptionally well.
I do it so it feels like hell.

I do it so it feels real.
I guess you could say I've a call.

In this poem and in numerous others from the collection *Ariel* and *Winter Trees* the poet creates vivid images of self-loathing, frequently projected onto other people or onto nature, and consequently onto life itself. It is Sylvia Plath whom Sylvia Plath despises, and by confusing her personality with the deepest layer of being, her own soul, she makes self-destruction inevitable. It is not *life* that has become contaminated, and requires a radical exorcism; it is the temporal personality, the smiling thirty-year-old woman trapped in a failing marriage and over-burdened with the responsibilities of motherhood, in one of the coldest winters in England's recorded history. Unable to strike out at her ostensible enemies (her husband Ted Hughes, who had left her for another woman; her father, long dead, who had "betrayed" her by dying when she was a small child), Plath strikes out at the enemy within, and murders herself in her final shrill poems before she actually turns on the gas oven and commits suicide. If her death, and even many of her poems, strike us as adolescent gestures it is perhaps because she demonstrated so little self-knowledge; her anguish was sheer emotion, never translated into coherent images. Quite apart from the surreal figures of speech Plath employs with such frenzied power, her work exhibits a curious deficiency of imagination, most evident in the autobiographical novel *The Bell Jar,* in which the suicidal narrator speaks of her consciousness as trapped inside a bell-jar, forced to breathe again and again the same stale air.

"There is but one truly serious philosophical question," Camus has said in a statement now famous, "and that is suicide." Camus exaggerates, certainly, and it is doubtful whether, strictly speaking, suicide is a "philosophical" problem at all. It may be social, moral, even economic, even political— especially political; but is it "philosophical"? Marcus Aurelius noted in his typically prudent manner: "In all that you do or say or think, recollect that at any time the power of withdrawal from life is in your hands," and Nietzsche said, perhaps less sombrely, "The thought of suicide is a strong consolation; one can get through many a bad night with it." But these are *problems,* they are *thoughts;* that they are so clearly conceptualized suggests their detachment from the kind of anguish, raw and undifferentiated, that drove Sylvia Plath to her premature death. The poet Anne Sexton liked to claim that suicides were a special people. "Talking death" for suicides is "life." In Sexton's third collection of poems, *Live or Die,* she included a poem characterized by remarkable restraint and dignity, one of the most intelligent (and despairing) works of what is loosely called the "confessional mode." Is suicide a philosophical problem? Is it intellectual, abstract, cerebral? Hardly:

Since you ask, most days I cannot remember.
I walk in my clothing, unmarked by that voyage.
Then the almost unnameable lust returns.

Even then I have nothing against life.
I know well the grass blades you mention,
the furniture you have placed under the sun.

But suicides have a special language.
Like carpenters they want to know *which tools.*
They never ask *why build.*

In Sexton the gravitational pull toward death seems to preclude, or exclude, such imaginative speculations as those of Camus; *that* death is desirable is never questioned.

Of course there are the famous suicides, the noble suicides, who do not appear to have been acting blindly, out of a confused emotional state: there is Socrates who acquiesced courteously, who did not choose to flee his execution; there is Cato; Petronius; Jesus of Nazareth. In literature, there are, famously, Shakespeare's Othello, who *rises* to his death, and Shakespeare's Antony and Cleopatra, both of whom outwit their conquerors by dying, the latter an "easy" death, the former an awkward, ghastly Roman death, poorly executed. Macbeth's ferocious struggle with Macduff is a suicidal gesture, and a perfect one, as is Hamlet's final combat with the enemy most like himself in age and spirit. The Hamlet-like Stavrogin of Dostoyevsky's monumental *The Possessed* worries that he may lack the "magnanimity" to kill himself, and to rid the world of such a loathsome creature as he; but he acquires the necessary strength and manages to hang himself, a symbolic gesture tied up clearly with Dostoyevsky's instinct for the logic of self-destruction as a consequence of modern man's "freedom" (i.e., alienation) from his nation.

Is the subjective act, then, nursed and groomed and made to bring forth its own sort of sickly fruit, really a public, political act? "Many die too late, and a few die too early," Nietzsche says boldly. "The doctrine still sounds strange: *Die at the right time!*" Nietzsche does not address himself to the less-than-noble; he is speaking, perhaps, not to individuals at all but to trans-individual values that, once healthy, are now fallen into decay, and must be hastened to their inevitable historical end. If until recent times death has been a taboo subject in our culture, suicide has been nothing short of an obscenity: a sudden raucous jeering shout in a genteel gathering. The suicide does not play the game, does not observe the rules; he leaves the party too soon, and leaves the other guests painfully uncomfortable. The world which has struck them as tolerable, even enjoyable, is, perhaps to a more discerning temperament, simply impossible: like Dostoyevsky's Ivan Karamazov, he respectfully returns his ticket to his Creator. The private gesture becomes violently and unmistakably public, which accounts for the harsh measures taken to punish suicides—or the bodies of suicides—over the centuries.

It is possible to reject society's extreme judgment, I think, without taking up an unqualified cause for the "freedom" of suicide, particularly if one makes sharp distinctions between kinds of suicides—the altruistic, the pathological, and the metaphorical. It is in metaphorical self-murder that what is murdered is an aspect of the self, and what is attained is a fictitious "transcendence" of physical circumstance.

But can one freely choose a condition, a state of being, that has never been experienced except in the imagination and, even there, *only in metaphor?* The wish "I want to die" might be a confused statement masking any number of unarticulated wishes: "I want to punish you, and you, and you"; "I want to punish the loathsome creature that appears to be myself"; "I want to be taken up by my Creator, and returned to the bliss of my first home"; "I want to alter my life because it is so disappointing, or painful, or boring"; "I want to silence the voices that are always shouting instructions"; "I want—I know not what." Rationally one cannot "choose" Death because Death is an unknown experience, and perhaps it isn't even an "experience"—perhaps it is simply nothing; and one cannot imagine nothing. The brain simply cannot fathom it, however glibly its thought-clusters may verbalize *non-existence, negation of being, Death,* and other non-referential terms. There is a curious heckling logic to the suicide's case, but his initial premise may be totally unfounded. *I want to die* may in fact be an empty statement expressing merely an emotion: *I am terribly unhappy at the present time.*

Still, people commit suicide because it is their deepest, most secret wish, and if the wish is too secret to be consciously admitted it will manifest itself in any number of metaphorical ways. We can list some of them— alcoholism, accidents, self-induced malnutrition, wretched life-choices, a cultivation of melancholy. The world is there, the world *is,* not awaiting our interpretations but unresisting when we compose them, and it may be that the mere semblance of the world's acquiescence to our metaphor-making leads us deeper and deeper into illusion. Because passion, even misdirected and self-pitying and claustrophobic, is always appealing, and has the power to drown out quieter, more reasonable voices, we will always be confronted by the fascination an intelligent public will feel for the most skillfully articulated of death-wishes.

QUESTIONS FOR DISCUSSION

1. Do you accept the distinction, suggested in the introduction to Part Two, between "rational" and "hysterical" suicide?

2. Does suicide raise a moral or a practical issue? Does your answer depend on the circumstances of the suicide? If so, indicate what kinds of suicide you regard as subject to moral criticism and what kinds as subject to purely practical evaluation.

3. Do you agree with St. Thomas Aquinas's assumption that what is morally wrong for the individual should always be prohibited by law? Can you think of any seriously wrong actions which are *not* prohibited by law and which hardly anyone would claim should be prohibited? What factors, if any, other than immorality should be present to justify legal prohibition of a mode of action?

4. Catholic authorities recently declared that the captain of a ship "going down with the ship" is committing suicide, which is equivalent to murder and therefore a mortal sin. Do you agree that such an action is, strictly speaking, suicidal? If an aviator flies a plane loaded with bombs directly into an enemy ship, is he committing suicide? Or the soldier who throws himself on a hand grenade to save his fellow men?

5. In Jean-Paul Sartre's play *Morts sans sepultures,* members of the Resistance movement captured by the Nazis and awaiting torture murder a comrade who they are sure will be unable to resist the torture and will reveal important information to the enemy. Discuss the ethics of this action. Is it on the same level as suicide, or is it worse than suicide?

6. Discuss whether euthanasia (mercy killing) is an act of the same moral quality as altruistic suicide for the benefit of others or whether it is morally worse, and why.

7. Comment on Hume's assertion: "I believe that no man ever threw away life while it was worth keeping."

8. What metaphors does Joyce Carol Oates criticize as falsely romanticizing suicide? Does she herself describe death metaphorically? If so, are her metaphors more appropriate, and why?

9. What does Joyce Carol Oates mean by writing: "Rationally one cannot 'choose' Death because Death is an unknown experience, and perhaps it isn't even an 'experience'—perhaps it is simply nothing; and one cannot imagine nothing." Cannot one choose nothing over something, if the something is very bad? Epicurus said that because death is not a state one can be in, it need not be feared. Was he right about that?

SUGGESTED READINGS

ARISTOTLE, *Nichomachean Ethics,* 1138 a7, trans. J. A. K. Thomson, Penguin Books, Baltimore, 1955.

AUGUSTINE, ST., *The City of God,* Books I, XVI–XXVI, trans. M. Dods, Modern Library, New York, 1950.

BILLIMORIA, P., "The Jaina Ethic of Voluntary Death," *Bioethics,* 6, 14 (1992), 331–55.

BRADY, B., *Suicide and Euthanasia,* Boston, Kluwer, 1989.

CHORON, J., *Suicide,* Scribner's, New York, 1972.

CICERO, *De Finibus,* Book III, 60, trans. H. Rackham, Loeb Classical Library, Harvard University Press, Cambridge, Mass., 1914.

DAUBE, D., "The Linguistics of Suicide," *Philosophy & Public Affairs,* I (1972).

DONNE, J., *Biothanatus,* Facsimile Text Society, New York, 1930.

DOUGLAS, J. D., *Social Meanings of Suicide,* Princeton University Press, Princeton, N.J., 1967.

DURKHEIM, E., *Suicide,* trans. J. A. Spaulding and G. Simpson, ed. G. Simpson, Free Press, New York, 1960.

EPICTETUS, *Discourses,* trans. W. A. Oldfather, Harvard University Press, Cambridge, Mass., 1959.

GIBBS, J. P., ed., *Suicide,* Harper & Row, New York, 1968.

HILLMAN, J., *Suicide and the Soul,* Harper & Row, New York, 1973.

HOLLAND, R., "Suicide as a Social Problem," *Ratio,* 12 (1970).

KOBLER, A. L., "Suicide: Right and Reason," *Bioethics Quarterly,* 2 (1980).

LESSER, H., "Suicide and Self-Murder," *Philosophy,* 55 (1980).

MAYO, D., and B. PABST, eds., *Suicide: The Philosophical Issues,* St. Martin's Press, New York, 1980.

MCCARRICK, P., "Active Euthanasia and Assisted Suicide," *Kennedy Institute of Ethics Journal,* 2, 1 (1992), 79–100.

MORTON, M., "The Discovery of Death: Dying and Suicide," *Kinesis,* 7 (1976).

ST. JOHN-STEVAS, N., *Life, Death and the Law,* Indiana University Press, Bloomington, Ind., 1961.

SCHOPENHAUER, A., *Studies in Pessimism,* trans. T. B. Saunders, George Allen & Unwin, London, 1903.

SENECA, *Epistles,* XII, trans. E. Barker, Clarendon Press, Oxford, 1932.

SHNEIDMAN, E. S., ed., *Essays in Self-Destruction,* Science House, New York, 1967.

———, ed., *On the Nature of Suicide,* Jossey Bass, San Francisco, 1969.

SPROTT, S. E., *Suicide,* Open Court, Chicago, 1973.

SZASZ, T., "The Ethics of Suicide," *The Antioch Review,* 31 (1971).

WESTERMARCK, E. A., *The Origin and Development of the Moral Ideas,* Mac Millan, London, 1926.

WILLIAMS, G., *The Sanctity of Life and the Criminal Law,* Knopf, New York, 1957.

WOLF, S., "Final Exit: The End of Argument," *Hastings Center Review,* 22, 1 (1992), 30–33.

SEE ALSO articles on suicide in *The Jewish Encyclopedia, The Catholic Encyclopedia, The Encyclopaedia of the Social Sciences,* and *The Encyclopaedia of Religion and Ethics.*

4

*E*UTHANASIA

*A*CTIVE AND PASSIVE EUTHANASIA: AN IMPERTINENT DISTINCTION?

Thomas D. Sullivan

Because of recent advances in medical technology, it is today possible to save or prolong the lives of many persons who in an earlier era would have quickly perished. Unhappily, however, it is often impossible to do so without committing the patient and his family to a future filled with sorrows. Modern methods of neurosurgery can successfully close the opening at the base of the spine of a baby born with severe myelomeningocoele, but do nothing to relieve the paralysis that afflicts it from the waist down or to remedy the patient's incontinence of stool and urine. Antibiotics and skin grafts can spare the life of a victim of severe and massive burns, but fail to eliminate the immobilizing contractions of arms and legs, the extreme pain, and the hideous disfigurement of the face. It is not surprising, therefore, that physicians and moralists in increasing number recommend that assistance should not be given to such patients, and that some have even begun to advocate the deliberate hastening of death by medical means, provided informed consent has been given by the appropriate parties.

The latter recommendation consciously and directly conflicts with what might be called the "traditional" view of the physician's role. The traditional view, as articulated, for example, by the House of Delegates of the American Medical Association in 1973, declared:

> The intentional termination of the life of one human being by another—mercy killing—is contrary to that for which the medical profession stands and is contrary to the policy of the American Medical Association.

> The cessation of the employment of extra-ordinary means to prolong the life of the body when there is irrefutable evidence that biological death is imminent is the decision of the patient and/or his immediate family. The advice and judgment of the physician should be freely available to the patient and/or his immediate family.

Basically this view involves two points: (1) that it is impermissible for the doctor or anyone else to terminate intentionally the life of a patient, but (2) that it is permissible in some cases to cease the employment of "extra-ordinary means" of preserving life, even though the death of the patient is a foreseeable consequence.

Does this position really make sense? Recent criticism charges that it does not. The heart of the complaint is that the traditional view arbitrarily rules out all cases of intentionally acting to terminate life, but permits what is in fact the moral equivalent, letting patients die. This accusation has been clearly articulated by James Rachels in a widely-read article that appeared in a recent issue of the *New England Journal of Medicine,* entitled "Active and Passive Euthanasia." By "active euthanasia" Rachels seems to mean *doing something* to bring about a patient's death, and by "passive euthanasia," not doing anything, i.e., just letting the patient die. Referring to the A.M.A. statement, Rachels sees the traditional position as always forbidding active euthanasia, but permitting passive euthanasia. Yet, he argues, passive euthanasia may be in some cases morally indistinguishable from active euthanasia, and in other cases even worse. To make his point he asks his readers to consider the case of a Down's syndrome baby with an intestinal obstruction that easily could be remedied through routine surgery. Rachels comments:

> I can understand why some people are opposed to all euthanasia and insist that such infants must be allowed to live. I think I can also understand why other people favor destroying these babies quickly and painlessly. But why should anyone favor letting 'dehydration and infection wither a tiny being over hours and days?' The doctrine that says that a baby may be allowed to dehydrate and wither, but may not be given an injection that would end its life without suffering, seems so patently cruel as to require no further refutation.

Rachels' point is that decisions such as the one he describes as "patently cruel" arise out of a misconceived moral distinction between active and passive euthanasia, which in turn rests upon a distinction between killing and letting die that itself has no moral importance.

> One reason why so many people think that there is an important difference between active and passive euthanasia is that they think killing someone is morally worse than letting someone die. But is it? . . . To investigate this issue two cases may be considered that are exactly alike except that one involves killing whereas the other involves letting someone die. Then, it can be asked whether this difference makes any difference to the moral assessments. . . .
>
> In the first, Smith stands to gain a large inheritance if anything should

happen to his six-year-old cousin. One evening while the child is taking his bath, Smith sneaks into the bathroom and drowns the child, and then arranges things so that it will look like an accident.

In the second, Jones also stands to gain if anything should happen to his six-year-old cousin. Like Smith, Jones sneaks in planning to drown the child in his bath. However, just as he enters the bathroom Jones sees the child slip and hit his head, and fall face down in the water. Jones is delighted; he stands by, ready to push the child's head back under if it is necessary, but it is not necessary. With only a little thrashing about, the child drowns all by himself, "accidentally," as Jones watches and does nothing.

Rachels observes that Smith killed the child, whereas Jones "merely" let the child die. If there's an important moral distinction between killing and letting die, then, we should say that Jones' behavior from a moral point of view is less reprehensible than Smith's. But while the law might draw some distinctions here, it seems clear that the acts of Jones and Smith are not different in any important way, or, if there is a difference, Jones' action is even worse.

In essence, then, the objection to the position adopted by the A.M.A. of Rachels and those who argue like him is that it endorses a highly question-able moral distinction between killing and letting die, which, if accepted, leads to indefensible medical decisions. Nowhere does Rachels quite come out and say that he favors active euthanasia in some cases, but the implica-tion is clear. Nearly everyone holds that it is sometimes pointless to prolong the process of dying and that in those cases it is morally permissible to let a patient die even though a few hours or days could be salvaged by proce-dures that would also increase the agonies of the dying. But if it is impossible to defend a general distinction between letting people die and acting to terminate their lives directly, then it would seem that active euthanasia also may be morally permissible.

Now what shall we make of all this? It *is* cruel to stand by and watch a Down's baby die an agonizing death when a simple operation would remove the intestinal obstruction, but to offer the excuse that in failing to operate we didn't *do* anything to bring about death is an example of moral evasive-ness comparable to the excuse Jones would offer for his action of "merely" letting his cousin die. Furthermore, it is true that if someone is trying to bring about the death of another human being, then it makes little difference from the moral point of view if his purpose is acheived by action or by malevolent omission, as in the cases of Jones and Smith.

But if we acknowledge this, are we obliged to give up the traditional view expressed by the A.M.A. statement? Of course not. To begin with, we are hardly obliged to assume the Jones-like role Rachels assigns the defender of the traditional view. We have the option of operating on the Down's baby and saving its life. Rachels mentions that possibility only to hurry past it as if that is not what his opposition would do. But, of course, that is precisely the course of action most defenders of the traditional position would choose.

Secondly, while it may be that the reason some rather confused people give for upholding the traditional view is that they think killing someone is always worse than letting them die, nobody who gives the matter much thought puts it that way. Rather they say that killing someone is clearly morally worse than not killing them, and killing them can be done by acting to bring about their death or by refusing ordinary means to keep them alive in order to bring about the same goal.

What I am suggesting is that Rachels' objections leave the position he sets out to criticize untouched. It is worth noting that the jargon of active and passive euthanasia—and it is jargon—does not appear in the resolution. Nor does the resolution state or imply the distinction Rachels attacks, a distinction that puts a moral premium on overt behavior—moving or not moving one's parts—while totally ignoring the intentions of the agent. That no such distinction is being drawn seems clear from the fact that the A.M.A. resolution speaks approvingly of ceasing to use extra-ordinary means in certain cases, and such withdrawals might easily involve bodily movement, for example unplugging an oxygen machine.

In addition to saddling his opposition with an indefensible distinction it doesn't make, Rachels proceeds to ignore one that it does make—one that is crucial to a just interpretation of the view. Recall the A.M.A. allows the withdrawal of what it calls extra-ordinary means of preserving life; clearly the contrast here is with ordinary means. Though in its short statement those expressions are not defined, the definition Paul Ramsey refers to as standard in his book, *The Patient as Person,* seems to fit.

> Ordinary means of preserving life are all medicines, treatments, and operations, which offer a reasonable hope of benefit for the patient and which can be obtained and used without excessive expense, pain, and other inconveniences.
>
> Extra-ordinary means of preserving life are all those medicines, treatments, and operations which cannot be obtained without excessive expense, pain, or other inconvenience, or which, if used, would not offer a reasonable hope of benefit.

Now with this distinction in mind, we can see how the traditional view differs from the position Rachels mistakes for it. The traditional view is that the intentional termination of human life is impermissible, irrespective of whether this goal is brought about by action or inaction. Is the action or refraining *aimed at* producing a death? Is the termination of life *sought, chosen or planned?* Is the intention deadly? If so, the act or omission is wrong.

But we all know it is entirely possible that the unwillingness of a physician to use extra-ordinary means for preserving life may be prompted not by a determination to bring about death, but by other motives. For example, he may realize that further treatment may offer little hope of reversing the dying process and/or be excruciating, as in the case when a massively necrotic bowel condition in a neonate is out of control. The doctor who does what he can to comfort the infant but does not submit it to further treatment or surgery may foresee that the decision will hasten death, but it certainly doesn't follow from that fact that he intends to bring about its death. It is, after all, entirely possible to foresee that something will come about as a result of one's conduct without intending the consequence or side effect. If I drive downtown, I can foresee that I'll wear out my tires a little, but I don't drive downtown with the intention of wearing out my tires. And if I choose to forego my exercises for a few days, I may think that as a result my physical condition will deteriorate a little, but I don't omit my exercise with a view to running myself down. And if you have to fill a position and select Green, who is better qualified for the post than her rival Brown, you needn't appoint Mrs. Green with the intention of hurting Mr. Brown, though you may foresee that Mr. Brown will feel hurt. And if a country extends its general education programs to its illiterate masses, it is predictable the suicide rate will go up, but even if the public officials are aware of this fact, it doesn't follow that they initiate the program with a view to making the suicide rate go up. In general, then, it is not the case that all the foreseeable consequences and side effects of our conduct are necessarily intended. And it is because the physician's withdrawal of extra-ordinary means can be otherwise motivated than by a desire to bring about the predictable death of the patient that such action cannot categorically be ruled out as wrong.

But the refusal to use ordinary means is an altogether different matter. After all, what is the point of refusing assistance which offers reasonable hope of benefit to the patient without involving excessive pain or other inconvenience? How could it be plausibly maintained that the refusal is not motivated by a desire to bring about the death of the patient? The traditional position, therefore, rules out not only direct actions to bring about death, such as giving a patient a lethal injection, but malevolent omissions as well, such as not providing minimum care for the newborn.

The reason the A.M.A. position sounds so silly when one listens to arguments such as Rachels' is that he slights the distinction between ordinary and extra-ordinary means and then drums on cases where *ordinary* means are refused. The impression is thereby conveyed that the traditional doctrine sanctions omissions that are morally indistinguishable in a substantive way from direct killings, but then incomprehensibly refuses to permit quick and painless termination of life. If the traditional doctrine would approve of Jones' standing by with a grin on his face while his young cousin drowned in a tub, or letting a Down's baby wither and die when ordinary means are available to preserve its life, it would indeed be difficult to see how anyone could defend it. But so to conceive the traditional doctrine is simply to misunderstand it. It is not a doctrine that rests on some supposed distinction between "active" and "passive euthanasia," whatever those words are supposed to mean, nor on a distinction between moving and not moving our bodies. It is simply a prohibition against intentional killing, which includes both direct actions and malevolent omissions.

To summarize—the traditional position represented by the A.M.A. statement is not incoherent. It acknowledges, or more accurately, insists upon the fact that withholding ordinary means to sustain life may be tantamount to killing. The traditional position can be made to appear incoherent only by imposing upon it a crude idea of killing held by none of its more articulate advocates.

Thus the criticism of Rachels and other reformers, misapprehending its target, leaves the traditional position untouched. That position is simply a prohibition of murder. And it is good to remember, as C. S. Lewis once pointed out:

> No man, perhaps, ever at first described to himself the act he was about to do as Murder, or Adultery, or Fraud, or Treachery. . . . And when he hears it so described by other men he is (in a way) sincerely shocked and surprised. Those others "don't understand." If they knew what it had really been like for him, they would not use those crude "stock" names. With a wink or a titter, or a cloud of muddy emotion, the thing has slipped into his will as something not very extraordinary, something of which, rightly understood in all of his peculiar circumstances, he may even feel proud.

I fully realize that there are times when those who have the noble duty to tend the sick and the dying are deeply moved by the sufferings of their patients, especially of the very young and the very old, and desperately wish they could do more than comfort and companion them. Then, perhaps, it seems that universal moral principles are mere abstractions having little to do with the agony of the dying. But of course we do not see best when our eyes are filled with tears.

*I*N DEFENSE OF BOTH

James Rachels

Many thinkers, including almost all orthodox Catholics, believe that euthanasia is immoral. They oppose killing patients in any circumstances whatever. However, they think it is all right, in some special circumstances, to allow patients to die by withholding treatment. The American Medical Association's policy statement on mercy killing supports this traditional view. In my paper "Active and Passive Euthanasia" I argued, against the traditional view, that there is in fact no moral difference between killing and letting die—if one is permissible, then so is the other.

Professor Sullivan does not dispute my argument; instead he dismisses it as irrelevant. The traditional doctrine, he says, does not appeal to or depend on the distinction between killing and letting die. Therefore, arguments against that distinction "leave the traditional position untouched."

Is my argument really irrelevant? I don't see how it can be. As Sullivan himself points out,

> Nearly everyone holds that it is sometimes pointless to prolong the process of dying and that in those cases it is morally permissible to let a patient die even though a few more hours or days could be salvaged by procedures that would also increase the agonies of the dying. But if it is impossible to defend a general distinction between letting people die and acting to terminate their lives directly, then it would seem that active euthanasia also may be morally permissible.

But traditionalists like Professor Sullivan hold that active euthansia—the direct killing of patients—is *not* morally permissible; so, if my argument is sound, their view must be mistaken. I cannot agree, then, that my argument "leaves the traditional position untouched."

However, I shall not press this point. Instead I shall present some further arguments against the traditional position, concentrating on those elements of the position which Professor Sullivan himself thinks most important. According to him, what is important is, first, that we should never *intentionally* terminate the life of a patient, either by action or omission, and second, that we may cease or omit treatment of a patient, knowing that this will result in death, only if the means of treatment involved are *extraordinary.*

INTENTIONAL AND NONINTENTIONAL TERMINATION OF LIFE

We can, of course, distinguish between what a person does and the intention with which he does it. But what is the significance of this distinction for ethics?

> The traditional view [says Sullivan] is that the intentional termination of human life is impermissible irrespective of whether this goal is brought about by action or inaction. Is the action or refraining *aimed at* producing death? Is the termination of life *sought, chosen, or planned?* Is the intention deadly? If so, the act or omission is wrong.

Thus on the traditional view there is a very definite sort of moral relation between act and intention. An act which is otherwise permissible may become impermissible if it is accompanied by a bad intention. The intention makes the act wrong.

There is reason to think that this view of the relation between act and intention is mistaken. Consider the following example. Jack visits his sick and lonely grandmother, and entertains her for the afternoon. He loves her and his only intention is to cheer her up. Jill also visits the grandmother, and provides an afternoon's cheer. But Jill's concern is that the old lady will soon be making her will; Jill wants to be included among the heirs. Jack also knows that his visit might influence the making of the will, in his favor, but that is not part of his plan. Thus Jack and Jill do the very same thing—they both spend an afternoon cheering up their sick grandmother—and what they do may lead to the same consequences, namely influencing the will. But their intentions are quite different.

Jack's intention was honorable and Jill's was not. Could we say on that account that what Jack did was right, but what Jill did was wrong? No; for Jack and Jill did the very same thing, and if they did the same thing, we cannot say that one acted rightly and the other wrongly. Consistency requires that we assess similar actions similarly. Thus if we are trying to evaluate their *actions,* we must say about one what we say about the other.

However, if we are trying to assess Jack's *character,* or Jill's, things are very different. Even though their actions were similar, Jack seems admirable for what he did, while Jill does not. What Jill did—comforting an elderly sick relative—was a morally good thing, but we would not think well of her for it since she was only scheming after the old lady's money. Jack, on the other hand, did a good thing *and* he did it with an admirable intention. Thus we think well, not only of what Jack did, but of Jack.

The traditional view, as presented by Professor Sullivan, says that the intention with which an act is done is relevant to determining whether the act is right. The example of Jack and Jill suggests that, on the contrary, the intention is not relevant to deciding whether the *act* is right or wrong, but instead it is relevant to assessing the character of the person who does the act, which is very different.

Now let us turn to an example that concerns more important matters of life and death. This example is adapted from one used by Sullivan himself. A massively necrotic bowel condition in a neonate is out of control. Dr. White realizes that further treatment offers little hope of reversing the dying process and will only increase the suffering; so, he does not submit the infant to further treatment—even though he knows that this decision will hasten death. However, Dr. White does not seek, choose, or plan that death, so it is not part of his intention that the baby dies.

Dr. Black is faced with a similar case. A massively necrotic bowel condition in a neonate is out of control. He realizes that further treatment offers little hope of saving the baby and will only increase its suffering. He decides that it is better for the baby to die a bit sooner than to go on suffering pointlessly; so, with the intention of letting the baby die, he ceases treatment.

According to the traditional position, Dr. White's action was acceptable, but Dr. Black acted wrongly. However, this assessment faces the same problem we encountered before. Dr. White and Dr. Black did *the very same thing:* their handing of the cases was identical. Both doctors ceased treatment, knowing that the baby would die sooner, and both did so because they regarded continued treatment as pointless, given the infants' prospects. So how could one's action be acceptable and the other's not? There was, of course, a subtle difference in their *attitudes* toward what they did. Dr. Black said to himself, "I want this baby to die now, rather than later, so that it won't suffer more; so I won't continue the treatment." A defender of the traditional view might choose to condemn Dr. Black for this, and say that his character is defective (although I would not say that); but the traditionalist should not say that Dr. Black's *action* was wrong on that account, at least not if he wants to go on saying that Dr. White's action was right. A pure heart cannot make a wrong act right: neither can an impure heart make a right act wrong. As in the case of Jack and Jill, the intention is relevant, not to determining the rightness of actions, but to assessing the character of the people who act.

There is a general lesson to be learned here. The rightness or wrongness of an act is determined by the reasons for or against it. Suppose you are trying to decide, in this example, whether treatment should be continued. What are the reasons for and against this course of action? On the one hand, if treatment is ceased the baby will die very soon. On the other hand, the baby will die eventually anyway, even if treatment is continued. It has no chance of growing up. Moreover, if its life is prolonged, its suffering will be prolonged as well, and the medical resources used will be unavailable to others who would have a better chance of a satisfactory cure. In light of all this, you may well decide against continued treatment. But notice that there is no mention here of anybody's intentions. The intention you would have, if you decided to cease treatment, is not one of the things you need to consider. It is not among the reasons either for or against the action. That is why it is irrelevant to determining whether the action is right.

In short, a person's intention is relevant to an assessment of his character. The fact that a person intended so-and-so by his action may be a reason for thinking him a good or a bad person. But the intention is not relevant to determining whether the act itself is morally right. The rightness of the act must be decided on the basis of the objective reasons for or against it. It is permissible to let the baby die, in Sullivan's example, because of the facts about the baby's condition and its prospects—not because of anything having to do with anyone's intentions. Thus the traditional view is mistaken on this point.

ORDINARY AND EXTRAORDINARY MEANS OF TREATMENT

The American Medical Association policy statement says that life-sustaining treatment may sometimes be stopped if the means of treatment are "extraordinary"; the implication is that "ordinary" means of treatment may not be withheld. The distinction between ordinary and extraordinary treatments is crucial to orthodox Catholic thought in this area, and Professor Sullivan reemphasizes its importance: he says that, while a physician may sometimes rightly refuse to use extraordinary means to prolong life, "the refusal to use ordinary means is an altogether different matter."

However, upon reflection it is clear that it is sometimes permissible to omit even very ordinary sorts of treatments.

> Suppose that a diabetic patient long accustomed to self-administration of insulin falls victim to terminal cancer, or suppose that a terminal cancer patient suddenly develops diabetes. Is he in the first case obliged to continue, and in the second case obliged to begin, insulin treatment and die painfully of cancer, or in either or both cases may the patient choose rather to pass into diabetic coma and an earlier death? . . . What of the conscious patient suffering from a painful incurable disease who suddenly gets pneumonia? Or an old man slowly deteriorating who from simply being inactive and recumbent gets pneumonia: Are we to use antibiotics in a likely successful attack upon this disease which from time immemorial has been called "the old man's friend"?

These examples are provided by Paul Ramsey, a leading theological ethicist. Even so conservative a thinker as Ramsey is sympathetic with the idea that, in such cases, life-prolonging treatment is not mandatory: the insulin and the antibiotics need not be used. Yet surely insulin and antibiotics are "ordinary" treatments by today's medical standards. They are common, easily administered, and cheap. There is nothing exotic about them. So it appears that the distinction between ordinary and extraordinary means does not have the significance traditionally attributed to it.

But what of the *definitions* of "ordinary" and "extraordinary" means which Sullivan provides? Quoting Ramsey, he says that

> Ordinary means of preserving life are all medicines, treatments, and operations, which offer a reasonable hope of benefit for the patient and which

can be obtained and used without excessive expense, pain, and other inconveniences.

Extra-ordinary means of preserving life are all those medicines, treatments, and operations which cannot be obtained without excessive expense, pain, or other inconvenience, or which, if used, would not offer a reasonable hope of benefit.

Do these definitions provide us with a useful distinction—one that can be used in determining when a treatment is mandatory and when it is not?

The first thing to notice is the way the word "excessive" functions in these definitions. It is said that a treatment is extraordinary if it cannot be obtained without *excessive* expense or pain. But when is an expense "excessive"? Is a cost of $10,000 excessive? If it would save the life of a young woman and restore her to perfect health, $10,000 does not seem excessive. But if it would only prolong the life of Ramsey's cancer-stricken diabetic a short while, perhaps $10,000 is excessive. The point is not merely that what is excessive changes from case to case. The point is that what is excessive *depends on* whether it would be a good thing for the life in question to be prolonged.

Second, we should notice the use of the word "benefit" in the definitions. It is said that ordinary treatments offer a reasonable hope of *benefit* for the patient; and that treatments are extraordinary if they will not benefit the patient. But how do we tell if a treatment will benefit the patient? Remember that we are talking about life-prolonging treatments; the "benefit," if any, is the continuation of life. Whether continued life is a benefit depends on the details of the particular case. For a person with a painful terminal illness, a temporarily continued life may not be a benefit. For a person in an irreversible coma, such as Karen Quinlan, continued biological existence is almost certainly not a benefit. On the other hand, for a person who can be cured and resume a normal life, life-sustaining treatment definitely is a benefit. Again, the point is that in order to decide whether life-sustaining treatment is a benefit we must *first* decide whether it would be a good thing for the life in question to be prolonged.

Therefore, these definitions do not mark out a distinction that can be used to help us decide when treatment may be omitted. We cannot by using the definitions identify which treatments are extraordinary, and then use that information to determine whether the treatment may be omitted. For the definitions require that we must *already* have decided the moral questions of life and death *before* we can answer the question of which treatments are extraordinary!

We are brought, then, to this conclusion about the distinction between ordinary and extraordinary means. If we apply the distinction in a straightforward, commonsense way, the traditional doctrine is false, for it is clear that it is sometimes permissible to omit ordinary treatments. On the other hand, if we define the terms as suggested by Ramsey and Sullivan, the distinction is useless in practical decision-making. In either case, the distinction provides no help in formulating an acceptable ethic of letting die.

SUMMARY

The distinction between killing and letting die has no moral importance; on that Professor Sullivan and I agree. He, however, contends that the distinctions between intentional and nonintentional termination of life, and ordinary and extraordinary means, must be at the heart of a correct moral view. I believe that the arguments given above refute this view. Those distinctions are no better than the first one. The traditional view is mistaken.

In my original paper I did not argue in favor of active euthanasia. I merely argued that active and passive euthanasia are equivalent: *if* one is acceptable, so is the other. However, Professor Sullivan correctly inferred that I do endorse active euthanasia: I believe that it is in some instances morally justified, and that it ought to be made legal. This he believes to be pernicious. In his penultimate paragraph he says that the traditional doctrine "is simply a prohibition of murder," and that those of us who think otherwise are confused, teary-eyed sentimentalists. But the traditional doctrine is not that. It is a muddle of indefensible claims, backed by tradition but not by reason.

QUESTIONS FOR DISCUSSION

1. If relatives can commit a person to a mental institution or to dangerous surgery, then why not also to euthanasia? What are the differences in these actions that might lead one to answer no?

2. Is intense and unending pain a good enough reason for suicide? If it is, is it also a good enough reason for euthanasia?

3. What is the distinction between active and passive euthanasia that Sullivan criticizes? According to James Rachels, there is no moral difference between the two. Do you agree, or do you agree with the American Medical Association that active euthanasia is impermissible but passive euthanasia is permissible? Why so?

4. Supporters of euthanasia argue that it is cruel to the close relatives of a terminal patient to keep the patient alive. How important is this consideration?

5. What standards of right action that were argued for in Chapter 1, such as minimizing suffering, obedience to moral law, obedience to divine command, or conformity to social tradition are appealed to by Sullivan and Rachels? Which of these standards do you think best applies to euthanasia?

6. If, as Rachels claims, "letting die" is as bad as killing, are we as bad as murderers if we do not contribute to famine relief?

7. Sullivan claims that what justifies or condemns an action is the intention or goal of the action. Rachels maintains that it is the consequences of the action that matter most. What do you think?

SUGGESTED READINGS

ABRAMS, N., "Active and Passive Euthanasia," *Philosophy,* 53 (1978).

BEAUCHAMP, T. and A. DAVIDSON, "The Definition of Euthanasia," *Journal of Medical Philosophy,* 4 (1979).

BROCK, D., "Voluntary Active Euthanasia," *Hastings Center Report,* 22, 2 (1992), 10–22.

BRODY, B., *Suicide and Euthanasia,* Kluwer, Boston, 1989.

CHESTERTON, G. K., "Euthanasia and Murder," *American Law Review,* 8 (1937).

CUTLER, D., ed., *Updating Life and Death,* Beacon Press, Boston, 1969.

DOWNING, A., ed., *Euthanasia and the Right to Die,* Owen, London, 1969.

FEINBERG, J., "Overlooking the Merits of the Individual Case," *Ratio Juris,* 4, 2 (1991), 131–51.

FLETCHER, J., *Morals and Medicine,* Beacon Press, Boston, 1960.

FOOT, P., "Euthanasia," *Philosophy and Public Affairs,* 6 (1977).

GOODRICH, T., "The Morality of Killing," *Philosophy,* 44 (1969).

HARE, R. M., "Euthanasia: A Christian View," *Philosophic Exchange,* 2 (1975).

HUSAK, D., "Killing, Letting Die and Euthanasia," *Journal of Medical Ethics,* 5 (1979).

KAMM, F., *Morality, Mortality,* Oxford: Oxford University Press, 1993.

———, "The Doctrine of Double Effect," *Journal of Medicine and Philosophy,* 16, 5 (1991), 571–85.

KASS, L., "Is There a Right To Die?," *Hastings Center Report,* 23, 1 (1993), 34–43.

KUBLER-ROSS, E., *Questions and Answers on Death and Dying,* Macmillan, New York, 1974.

LAPPE, M., "Dying While Living: A Critique of Allowing-to-Die Legislation," *Journal of Medical Ethics,* 4 (1978).

MC CLOSKEY, H., "The Right to Life," *Mind,* 84 (1975).

NAGEL, T., "Death," *Nous,* 4 (1971).

PELLEGRINO, E., "Doctors Must Not Kill," *Journal of Clinical Ethics,* 7, 1 (1993), 71–84.

RACHELS, J., "Active and Passive Euthanasia," *New England Journal of Medicine,* 292 (1975).

ST. JOHN-STEVAS, N., *Life, Death and the Law,* Indiana University Press, Bloomington, 1961.

STEINBOCK, B., ed., *Killing and Letting Die,* Prentice-Hall, Englewood Cliffs, N.J., 1979.

VAUX, K., *Who Shall Live?,* Fortress Press, 1970.

WEIR, R., *Ethical Issues in Death and Dying,* Columbia University Press, New York, 1986.

WILLIAMS, G., *The Sanctity of Life and the Criminal Law,* Knopf, New York, 1957.

5

ABORTION

THE IMMORALITY OF ABORTION
John T. Noonan, Jr.

The most fundamental question involved in the long history of thought on abortion is: How do you determine the humanity of a being? To phrase the question that way is to put in comprehensive humanistic terms what the theologians either dealt with as an explicitly theological question under the heading of "ensoulment" or dealt with implicitly in their treatment of abortion. The Christian position as it originated did not depend on a narrow theological or philosophical concept. It had no relation to theories of infant baptism. It appealed to no special theory of instantaneous ensoulment. It took the world's view on ensoulment as that view changed from Aristotle to Zacchia. There was, indeed, theological influence affecting the theory of ensoulment finally adopted, and, of course, ensoulment itself was a theological concept, so that the position was always explained in theological terms. But the theological notion of ensoulment could easily be translated into humanistic language by substituting "human" for "rational soul"; the problem of knowing when a man is a man is common to theology and humanism.

If one steps outside the specific categories used by the theologians, the answer they gave can be analyzed as a refusal to discriminate among human beings on the basis of their varying potentialities. Once conceived, the being was recognized as man because he had man's potential. The criterion for humanity, thus, was simple and all-embracing: if you are conceived by human parents, you are human.

The strength of this position may be tested by a review of some of the other distinctions offered in the contemporary controversy over legalizing abortion. Perhaps the most popular distinction is in terms of viability. Before an age of so many months, the fetus is not viable, that is, it cannot be removed from the mother's womb and live apart from her. To that extent, the life of the fetus is absolutely dependent on the life of the mother. This dependence is made the basis of denying recognition to its humanity.

There are difficulties with this distinction. One is that the perfection of artificial incubation may make the fetus viable at any time: it may be removed and artifically sustained. Experiments with animals already show that such a procedure is possible. This hypothetical extreme case relates to an actual difficulty: there is considerable elasticity to the idea of viability. Mere length of life is not an exact measure. The viability of the fetus depends on the extent of its anatomical and functional development. The weight and length of the fetus are better guides to the state of its development than age, but weight and length vary. Moreover, different racial groups have different ages at which their fetuses are viable. Some evidence, for example, suggests that Negro fetuses mature more quickly than white fetuses. If viability is the norm, the standard would vary with race and with many individual circumstances.

The most important objection to this approach is that dependence is not ended by viability. The fetus is still absolutely dependent on someone's care in order to continue existence; indeed a child of one or three or even five years of age is absolutely dependent on another's care for existence; uncared for, the older fetus or the younger child will die as surely as the early fetus detached from the mother. The unsubstantial lessening in dependence at viability does not seem to signify any special acquisition of humanity.

A second distinction has been attempted in terms of experience. A being who has had experience, has lived and suffered, who possesses memories, is more human than one who has not. Humanity depends on formation by experience. The fetus is thus "unformed" in the most basic human sense.

This distinction is not serviceable for the embryo which is already experiencing and reacting. The embryo is responsive to touch after eight weeks and at least at that point is experiencing. At an earlier stage the zygote is certainly alive and responding to its environment. The distinction may also be challenged by the rare case where aphasia has erased adult memory: has it erased humanity? More fundamentally, this distinction leaves even the older fetus or the younger child to be treated as an unformed inhuman thing. Finally, it is not clear why experience as such confers humanity. It could be argued that certain central experiences such as loving or learning are necessary to make a man human. But then human beings who have failed to love or to learn might be excluded from the class called man.

A third distinction is made by appeal to the sentiments of adults. If a fetus dies, the grief of the parents is not the grief they would have for a living child. The fetus is an unnamed "it" till birth, and is not perceived as personality until at least the fourth month of existence when movement in the womb manifests a vigorous presence demanding joyful recognition by the parents.

Yet feeling is notoriously an unsure guide to the humanity of others. Many groups of humans have had difficulty in feeling that persons of another tongue, color, religion, sex, are as human as they. Apart from reactions to alien groups, we mourn the loss of a ten-year-old boy more than the loss of his one-day-old brother or his 90-year-old grandfather. The difference felt and the grief expressed vary with the potentialities extinguished, or the experience wiped out; they do not seem to point to any substantial difference in the humanity of baby, boy, or grandfather.

Distinctions are also made in terms of sensation by the parents. The embryo is seen only at birth. What can be neither seen nor felt is different from what is tangible. If the fetus cannot be seen or touched at all, it cannot be perceived as man.

Yet experience shows that sight is even more untrustworthy than feeling in determining humanity. By sight, color became an appropriate index for saying who was a man, and the evil of racial discrimination was given foundation. Nor can touch provide the test; a being confined by sickness, "out of touch" with others, does not thereby seem to lose his humanity. To the extent that touch still has appeal as a criterion, it appears to be a survival of the old English idea of "quickening"—a possible mistranslation of the Latin *animatus* used in the canon law. To that extent touch as a criterion seems to be dependent on the Aristotelian notion of ensoulment, and to fall when this notion is discarded.

Finally, a distinction is sought in social visibility. The fetus is not socially perceived as human. It cannot communicate with others. Thus, both subjectively and objectively, it is not a member of society. As moral rules are rules for the behavior of members of society to each other, they cannot be made for behavior toward what is not yet a member. Excluded from the society of men, the fetus is excluded from the humanity of men.

By force of the argument from the consequences, this distinction is to be rejected. It is more subtle than that founded on an appeal to physical sensation, but it is equally dangerous in its implications. If humanity depends on social recognition, individuals or whole groups may be dehumanized by being denied any status in their society. Such a fate is fictionally portrayed in *1984* and has actually been the lot of many men in many societies. In the Roman empire, for example, condemnation to slavery meant the practical denial of most human rights; in the Chinese Communist world, landlords have been classified as enemies of the people and so treated as nonpersons by the state. Humanity does not depend on social recognition, though often the failure of society to recognize the prisoner, the alien, the heterodox as human has led to the destruction of human beings. Anyone conceived by a man and a woman is human. Recognition of this condition by society follows a real event in the objective order, however imperfect and halting the recognition. Any attempt to limit humanity to exclude some group runs the risk of furnishing authority and precedent for excluding other groups in the name of the consciousness or perception of the controlling group in the society.

A philosopher may reject the appeal to the humanity of the fetus because he views "humanity" as a secular view of the soul and because he doubts the existence of anything real and objective which can be identified as humanity. One answer to such a philosopher is to ask how he reasons about moral questions without supposing that there is a sense in which he and the others of whom he speaks are human. Whatever group is taken as the society which determines who may be killed is thereby taken as human. A second answer is to ask if he does not believe that there is a right and wrong way of deciding moral questions. If there is such a difference, experience may be appealed to: to decide who is human on the basis of the sentiment of a given society has led to consequences which rational men would characterize as monstrous.

The rejection of the attempted distinctions based on viability and visibility, experience and feeling, may be buttressed by the following considerations: Moral judgments often rest on distinctions, but if the distinctions are not to appear arbitrary fiat, they should relate to some real difference in probabilities. There is a kind of continuity in all life, but the earlier stages of the elements of human life possess tiny probabilities of development. Consider for example, the spermatozoa in any normal ejaculate: There are about 200,000,000 in any single ejaculate, of which one has a chance of developing into a zygote. Consider the oocytes which may become ova: there are 100,000 to 1,000,000 oocytes in a female infant, of which a maximum of 390 are ovulated. But once spermatozoon and ovum meet and the conceptus is formed, such studies as have been made show that roughly in only 20 percent of the cases will spontaneous abortion occur. In other words, the chances are about 4 out of 5 that this new being will develop. At this stage in the life of the being there is a sharp shift in probabilities, an immense jump in potentialities. To make a distinction between the rights of spermatozoa and the right of the fertilized ovum is to respond to an enormous shift in possibilities. For about twenty days after conception the egg may split to form twins or combine with another egg to form a chimera, but the probability of either event happening is very small.

It may be asked, What does a change in biological probabilities have to do with establishing humanity? The argument from probabilities is not aimed at establishing humanity but at establishing an objective discontinuity which may be taken into account in moral discourse. As life itself is a matter of probabilities, as most moral reasoning is an estimate of probabilities, so it seems in accord with the structure of reality and the nature of moral thought to found a moral judgment on the change in probabilities at conception. The appeal to probabilities is the most commensensical of arguments, to a greater or smaller degree all of us base our actions on probabilities, and in morals, as in law, prudence and negligence are often measured by the account one has taken of the probabilities. If the chance is 200,000,000 to 1 that the movement in the bushes into which you shoot is a man's, I doubt if many persons would hold you careless in shooting; but if the chances are 4 out of 5 that the movement is a human being's, few would acquit you of blame. Would the argument be different if only one out of ten children conceived came to term? Of course this argument would be different. This argument is an appeal to probabilities that actually exist, not to any and all states of affairs which may be imagined.

The probabilities as they do exist do not show the humanity of the embryo in the sense of a demonstration in logic any more than the probabilities of the movement in the bush being a man demonstrate beyond all doubt that the being is a man. The appeal is a "buttressing" consideration, showing the plausibility of the standard adopted. The argument focuses on the decisional factor in any moral judgment and assumes that part of the business of a morality is drawing lines. One evidence of the nonarbitrary character of the line drawn is the difference of probabilities on either side of it. If a spermatozoon is destroyed, one destroys a being which had a chance of far less than 1 in 200 billion of developing into a reasoning being, possessed of the genetic code, a heart and other organs, and capable of pain. If a fetus is destroyed, one destroys a being already possessed of the genetic code, organs, and sensitivity to pain, and one which had an 80 percent chance of developing further into a baby outside the womb who, in time, would reason.

The positive argument for conception as the decisive moment of humanization is that at conception the new being receives the genetic code. It is this genetic information which determines his characteristics, which is the biological carrier of the possibility of human wisdom, which makes him a self-evolving being. A being with a human genetic code is man.

This review of current controversy over the humanity of the fetus emphasizes what a fundamental question the theologians resolved in asserting the inviolability of the fetus. To regard the fetus as possessed of equal rights with other humans was not, however, to decide every case where abortion might be employed. It did decide the case where the argument was that the fetus should be aborted for its own good. To say a being was human was to say it had a destiny to decide for itself which could not be taken from it by another man's decision. But human beings with equal rights often come in conflict with each other, and some decision must be made as whose claims are to prevail. Cases of conflict involving the fetus are different only in two respects: the total inability of the fetus to speak for itself and the fact that the right of the fetus regularly at stake is the right to life itself.

The approach taken by the theologians to these conflicts was articulated in terms of "direct" and "indirect." Again, to look at what they were doing from outside their categories, they may be said to have been drawing lines or "balancing values." "Direct" and "indirect" are spatial metaphors; "line-drawing" is another. "To weigh" or "to balance" values is a metaphor of a more complicated mathematical sort hinting at the process which goes on in moral judgments. All the metaphors suggest that, in the moral judgments made, comparisons were necessary, that no value completely controlled. The principle of double effect was no doctrine fallen from heaven, but a method of analysis appropriate where two relative values were being compared. In Catholic moral theology, as it developed, life even of the innocent was not taken as an absolute. Judgments on acts affecting life issued from a process of weighing. In the weighing, the fetus was always given a value greater than zero, always a value separate and independent from its parents. This valuation was crucial and fundamental in all Christian thought on the subject and marked it off from any approach which considered that only the parents' interests needed to be considered.

Even with the fetus weighed as human, one interest could be weighed as equal or superior: that of the mother in her own life. The casuists between 1450 and 1895 were willing to weigh this interest as superior. Since 1895, that interest was given decisive weight only in the two special cases of the cancerous uterus and the ectopic pregnancy. In both of these cases the fetus itself had little chance of survival even if the abortion were not performed. As the balance was once struck in favor of the mother whenever her life was endangered, it could be so struck again. The balance reached between 1895 and 1930 attempted prudentially and pastorally to forestall a multitude of exceptions for interests less than life.

The perception of the humanity of the fetus and the weighing of fetal rights against other human rights constituted the work of the moral analysts. But what spirit animated their abstract judgments? For the Christian community it was the injunction of Scripture to love your neighbor as yourself. The fetus as human was a neighbor; his life had parity with one's own. The commandment gave life to what otherwise would have been only rational calculation.

The commandment could be put in humanistic as well as theological terms: Do not injure your fellow man without reason. In these terms, once the humanity of the fetus is perceived, abortion is never right except in self-defense. When life must be taken to save life, reason alone cannot say that a mother must prefer a child's life to her own. With this exception, now of great rarity, abortion violates the rational humanist tenet of the equality of human lives.

For Christians the commandment to love had received a special imprint in that the exemplar proposed of love was the love of the Lord for his disciples. In the light given by this example, self-sacrifice carried to the point of death seemed in the extreme situations not without meaning. In the less extreme cases, preference for one's own interests to the life of another seemed to express cruelty or selfishness irreconcilable with the demands of love.

*T*HE RIGHT TO ABORTION

Mary Anne Warren

We will be concerned with both the moral status of abortion, which for our purposes we may define as the act which a woman performs in voluntarily terminating, or allowing another person to terminate, her pregnancy, and the legal status which is appropriate for this act. I will argue that, while it is not possible to produce a satisfactory defense of a woman's right to obtain an abortion without showing that a fetus is not a human being, in the morally relevant sense of that term, we ought not to conclude that the difficulties involved in determining whether or not a fetus is human make it impossible to produce any satisfactory solution to the problem of the moral status of abortion. For it is possible to show that, on the basis of intuitions which we may expect even the opponents of abortion to share, a fetus is not a person, and hence not the sort of entity to which it is proper to ascribe full moral rights.

Of course, while some philosophers would deny the possibility of any such proof, others will deny that there is any need for it, since the moral permissibility of abortion appears to them to be too obvious to require proof. But the inadequacy of this attitude should be evident from the fact that both the friends and the foes of abortion consider their position to be morally self-evident. Because proabortionists have never adequately come to grips with the conceptual issues surrounding abortion, most if not all, of the arguments which they advance in opposition to laws restricting access to abortion fail to refute or even weaken the traditional antiabortion argument, i.e., that a fetus is a human being, and therefore abortion is murder.

These arguments are typically of one of two sorts. Either they point to the terrible side effects of the restrictive laws, e.g., the deaths due to illegal abortions, and the fact that it is poor women who suffer the most as a result of these laws, or else they state that to deny a woman access to abortion is to deprive her of her right to control her own body. Unfortunately, however, the fact that restricting access to abortion has tragic side effects does not, in itself, show that the restrictions are unjustified, since murder is wrong regardless of the consequences of prohibiting it; and the appeal to the right to control one's body, which is generally construed as a property right, is at best a rather feeble argument for the permissibility of abortion. Mere ownership does not give me the right to kill innocent people whom I find on my property, and indeed I am apt to be held responsible if such people injure themselves while on my property. It is equally unclear that I have any moral right to expel an innocent person from my property when I know that doing so will result in his death.

Furthermore, it is probably inappropriate to describe a woman's body as her property, since it seems natural to hold that a person is something distinct from her property, but not from her body. Even those who would object to the identification of a person with his body, or with the conjunction of his body and his mind, must admit that it would be very odd to describe, say, breaking a leg, as damaging one's property, and much more appropriate to describe it as injuring one*self.* Thus it is probably a mistake to argue that the right to obtain an abortion is in any way derived from the right to own and regulate property.

But however we wish to construe the right to abortion, we cannot hope to convince those who consider abortion a form of murder of the existence of any such right unless we are able to produce a clear and convincing refutation of the traditional antiabortion argument, and this has not, to my knowledge, been done. With respect to the two most vital issues which that argument involves, i.e., the humanity of the fetus and its implication for the moral status of abortion, confusion has prevailed on both sides of the dispute.

Thus, both proabortionists and antiabortionists have tended to abstract the question of whether abortion is wrong to that of whether it is wrong to destroy a fetus, just as though the rights of another person were not necessarily involved. This mistaken abstraction has led to the almost universal assumption that if a fetus is a human being, with a right to life, then it follows immediately that abortion is wrong (except perhaps when necessary to save the woman's life), and that it ought to be prohibited. It has also been generally assumed that unless the question about the status of the fetus is answered, the moral status of abortion cannot possibly be determined.

Two recent papers, one by B. A. Brody, and one by Judith Thomson, have attempted to settle the question of whether abortion ought to be prohibited apart from the question of whether or not the fetus is human. Brody examines the possibility that the following two statements are compatible: (1) that abortion is the taking of innocent human life, and therefore wrong; and (2) that nevertheless it ought not to be prohibited by law, at least under the present circumstances. Not surprisingly, Brody finds it impossible to reconcile these two statements, since, as he rightly argues, none of the unfortunate side effects of the prohibition of abortion is bad enough to justify legalizing the *wrongful* taking of human life. He is mistaken, however, in concluding that the incompatibility of (1) and (2), in itself, shows that "the legal problem about abortion cannot be resolved independently of the status of the fetus problem."

What Brody fails to realize is that (1) embodies the questionable assumption that if a fetus is a human being, then of course abortion is morally wrong, and that an attack on *this* assumption is more promising, as a way of reconciling the humanity of the fetus with the claim that laws prohibiting abortion are unjustified, than is an attack on the assumption that if abortion is the wrongful killing of innocent human beings then it ought to be prohibited. He thus overlooks the possibility that a fetus may have a right to life and abortion still be morally permissible, in that the right of a woman to terminate an unwanted pregnancy might override the right of the fetus to be kept alive. The immorality of abortion is no more demonstrated by the humanity of the fetus, in itself, than the immorality of killing in self-defense is demonstrated by the fact that the assailant is a human being. Neither is it demonstrated by the *innocence* of the fetus, since there may be situations in which the killing of innocent human beings is justified.

It is perhaps not surprising that Brody fails to spot this assumption, since it has been accepted with little or no argument by nearly everyone who has written on the morality of abortion. John Noonan is correct in saying that "the fundamental question in the long history of abortion is, How do you determine the humanity of a being?" He summarizes his own antiabortion argument, which is a version of the official position of the Catholic Church, as follows:

> . . . it is wrong to kill humans, however poor, weak, defenseless, and lacking in opportunity to develop their potential they may be. It is therefore morally wrong to kill Biafrans. Similarly, it is morally wrong to kill embryos.

Noonan bases his claim that fetuses are human upon what he calls the theologians' criterion of humanity: that whoever is conceived of human beings is human. But although he argues at length for the appropriateness of this criterion, he never questions the assumption that if a fetus is human then abortion is wrong for exactly the same reason that murder is wrong.

Judith Thomson is, in fact, the only writer I am aware of who has seriously questioned this assumption; she has argued that, even if we grant the antiabortionist his claim that a fetus is a human being, with the same right to life as any other human being, we can still demonstrate that, in at least some and perhaps most cases, a woman is under no moral obligation to complete an unwanted pregnancy. Her argument is worth examining, since if it holds up it may enable us to establish the moral permissibility of abortion without becoming involved in problems about what entitles an entity to be considered human, and accorded full moral rights. To be able to do this would be a great gain in the power and simplicity of the proabortion position, since, although I will argue that these problems can be solved at least as decisively as can any other moral problem, we should certainly be pleased to be able to avoid having to solve them as part of the justification of abortion.

On the other hand, even if Thomson's argument does not hold up, her insight, i.e., that it requires *argument* to show that if fetuses are human then abortion is properly classified as murder, is an extremely valuable one. The assumption she attacks is particularly invidious, for it amounts to the decision that it is appropriate, in deciding the moral status of abortion, to leave the rights of the pregnant woman out of consideration entirely, except possibly when her life is threatened. Obviously, this will not do; determining what moral rights, if any, a fetus possesses is only the first step in determining the moral status of abortion. Step two, which is at least equally essential, is finding a just solution to the conflict between whatever rights the fetus may have, and the rights of the woman who is unwillingly pregnant. While the historical error has been to pay far too little attention to the second step, Ms. Thomson's suggestion is that if we look at the second step first we may find that a woman has a right to obtain an abortion *regardless* of what rights the fetus has.

Our own inquiry will also have two stages. In Section I, we will consider whether or not it is possible to establish that abortion is morally permissible even on the assumption that a fetus is an entity with a full-fledged right to life. I will argue that in fact this cannot be established, at least not with the conclusiveness which is essential to our hopes of convincing those who are skeptical about the morality of abortion, and that we therefore cannot avoid dealing with the question of whether or not a fetus really does have the same right to life as a (more fully developed) human being.

In Section II, I will propose an answer to this question, namely, that a fetus cannot be considered a member of the moral community, the set of beings with full and equal moral rights, for the simple reason that it is not a person, and that it is personhood, and not genetic humanity, i.e., humanity as defined by Noonan, which is the basis for membership in this community. I will argue that a fetus, whatever its stage of development, satisfies none of the basic criteria of personhood, and is not even enough *like* a person to be accorded even some of the same rights on the basis of this resemblance. Nor, as we will see, is a fetus's *potential* personhood a threat to the morality of abortion, since, whatever the rights of potential people may be, they are invariably overridden in any conflict with the moral rights of actual people.

I

We turn now to Professor Thomson's case for the claim that even if a fetus has full moral rights, abortion is still morally permissible, at least sometimes, and for some reasons other than to save the woman's life. Her argument is based upon a clever, but I think faulty, analogy. She asks us to picture ourselves waking up one day, in bed with a famous violinist. Imagine that you have been kidnapped, and your bloodstream hooked up to that of the violinist, who happens to have an ailment which will certainly kill him unless he is permitted to share your kidneys for a period of nine months. No one else can save him, since you alone have the right type of blood. He will be unconscious all that time, and you will have to stay in bed with him, but after the nine months are over he may be unplugged, completely cured, that is provided that you have cooperated.

Now then, she continues, what are your obligations in this situation? The antiabortionist, if he is consistent, will have to say that you are obligated to stay in bed with the violinist: for all people have a right to life, and

violinists are people, and therefore it would be murder for you to discon-
nect yourself from him and let him die. But this is outrageous, and so there
must be something wrong with the same argument when it is applied to
abortion. It would certainly be commendable of you to agree to save the
violinist, but it is absurd to suggest that your refusal to do so would be
murder. His right to life does not obligate you to do whatever is required to
keep him alive; nor does it justify anyone else in forcing you to do so. A law
which required you to stay in bed with the violinist would clearly be an
unjust law, since it is no proper function of the law to force unwilling people
to make huge sacrifices for the sake of other people toward whom they have
no such prior obligation.

Thomson concludes that, if this analogy is an apt one, then we can grant
the antiabortionist his claim that a fetus is a human being, and still hold that
it is at least sometimes the case that a pregnant woman has the right to
refuse to be a Good Samaritan towards the fetus, i.e., to obtain an abortion.
For there is a great gap between the claim that x has a right to life, and the
claim that y is obligated to do whatever is necessary to keep x alive, let alone
that he ought to be forced to do so. It is y's duty to keep x alive only if he has
somehow contracted a *special* obligation to do so; and a woman who is
unwillingly pregnant, e.g., who was raped, has done nothing which obligates
her to make the enormous sacrifice which is necessary to preserve the
conceptus.

This argument is initially quite plausible, and in the extreme case of
pregnancy due to rape it is probably conclusive. Difficulties arise, however,
when we try to specify more exactly the range of cases in which abortion is
clearly justifiable even on the assumption that the fetus is human. Professor
Thomson considers it a virtue of her argument that it does not enable us to
conclude that abortion is *always* permissible. It would, she says, be "indecent" for a woman in her seventh month to obtain an abortion just to avoid
having to postpone a trip to Europe. On the other hand, her argument
enables us to see that "a sick and desperately frightened schoolgirl pregnant
due to rape may *of course* choose abortion, and that any law which rules this
out is an insane law." So far, so good; but what are we to say about the
woman who becomes pregnant not through rape but as a result of her own
carelessness, or because of contraceptive failure, or who gets pregnant intentionally and then changes her mind about wanting a child? With respect to
such cases, the violinist analogy is of much less use to the defender of the
woman's right to obtain an abortion.

Indeed, the choice of a pregnancy due to rape, as an example of a case in
which abortion is permissible even if a fetus is considered a human being, is
extremely significant; for it is only in the case of pregnancy due to rape that
the woman's situation is adequately analogous to the violinist case for our
intuitions about the latter to transfer convincingly. The crucial difference
between a pregnancy due to rape and the *normal* case of an unwanted
pregnancy is that in the normal case we cannot claim that the woman is in
no way responsible for her predicament; she could have remained chaste, or

taken her pills more faithfully, or abstained on dangerous days, and so on. If, on the other hand, you are kidnapped by strangers, and hooked up to a strange violinist, then you are free of any shred of responsibility for the situation, on the basis of which it could be argued that you are obligated to keep the violinist alive. Only when her pregnancy is due to rape is a woman clearly just as nonresponsible.

Consequently, there is room for the antiabortionist to argue that in the normal case of unwanted pregnancy a woman has, by her own actions, assumed responsibility for the fetus. For if x behaves in a way which he could have avoided, and which he knows involves, let us say, a 1 percent chance of bringing into existence a human being, with a right to life, and does so knowing that if this should happen then that human being will perish unless x does certain things to keep him alive, then it is by no means clear that when it does happen x is free of any obligation to what he knew in advance would be required to keep that human being alive.

The plausibility of such an argument is enough to show that the Thomson analogy can provide a clear and persuasive defense of a woman's right to obtain an abortion only with respect to those cases in which the woman is in no way responsible for her pregnancy, e.g., where it is due to rape. In all other cases, we would almost certainly conclude that it was necessary to look carefully at the particular circumstances in order to determine the extent of the woman's responsibility, and hence the extent of her obligation. This is an extremely unsatisfactory outcome, from the viewpoint of the opponents of restrictive abortion laws, most of whom are convinced that a woman has a right to obtain an abortion regardless of how and why she got pregnant.

Of course a supporter of the violinist analogy might point out that it is absurd to suggest that forgetting her pill one day might be sufficient to obligate a woman to complete an unwanted pregnancy. And indeed it *is* absurd to suggest this. As we will see, the moral right to obtain an abortion is not in the least dependent upon the extent to which the woman is responsible for her pregnancy. But unfortunately, once we allow the assumption that a fetus has full moral rights, we cannot avoid taking this absurd suggestion seriously. Perhaps we can make this point more clear by altering the violinist story just enough to make it more analogous to a normal unwanted pregnancy and less to a pregnancy due to rape, and then seeing whether it is still obvious that you are not obligated to stay in bed with the fellow.

Suppose, then, that violinists are peculiarly prone to the sort of illness the only cure for which is the use of someone else's bloodstream for nine months, and that because of this there has been formed a society of music lovers who agree that whenever a violinist is stricken they will draw lots and the loser will, by some means, be made the one and only person capable of saving him. Now then, would you be obligated to cooperate in curing the violinist if you had voluntarily joined this society, knowing the possible consequences, and then your name had been drawn and you had been kidnapped? Admittedly, you did not promise ahead of time that you would, but you did deliberately place yourself in a position in which it might happen that a human life would be lost if you did not. Surely this is at least a prima facie reason for supposing that you have an obligation to stay in bed with the violinist. Suppose that you had gotten your name drawn deliberately; surely *that* would be quite a strong reason for thinking that you had such an obligation.

It might be suggested that there is one important disanalogy between the modified violinist case and the case of an unwanted pregnancy, which makes the woman's responsibility significantly less, namely, the fact that the fetus *comes into existence* as the result of the result of the woman's actions. This fact might give her a right to refuse to keep it alive, whereas she would not have had this right had it existed previously, independently, and then as a result of her actions become dependent upon her for its survival.

My own intuition, however, is that x has no more right to bring into existence, either deliberately or as a foreseeable result of actions he could have avoided, a being with full moral rights (y), and then refuse to do what he knew beforehand would be required to keep that being alive, than he has to enter into an agreement with an existing person, whereby he may be called upon to save that person's life, and then refuse to do so when so called upon. Thus, x's responsibility for y's existence does not seem to lessen his obligation to keep y alive, if he is also responsible for y's being in a situation in which only he can save him.

Whether or not this intuition is entirely correct, it brings us back once again to the conclusion that once we allow the assumption that a fetus has full moral rights it becomes an extremely complex and difficult question whether and when abortion is justifiable. Thus the Thomson analogy cannot help us produce a clear and persuasive proof of the moral permissibility of abortion. Nor will the opponents of the restrictive laws thank us for anything less; for their conviction (for the most part) is that abortion is obviously *not* a morally serious and extremely unfortunate, even though sometimes justified act, comparable to killing in self-defense or to letting the violinist die, but rather is closer to being a morally neutral act, like cutting one's hair.

The basis of this conviction, I believe, is the realization that a fetus is not a person, and thus does not have a full-fledged right to life. Perhaps the reason why this claim has been so inadequately defended is that it seems self-evident to those who accept it. And so it is, insofar as it follows from what I take to be perfectly obvious claims about the nature of personhood, and about the proper grounds for ascribing moral rights, claims which ought, indeed, to be obvious to both the friends and foes of abortion. Nevertheless, it is worth examining these claims, and showing how they demonstrate the moral innocuousness of abortion, since this apparently has not been adequately done before.

II

The question which we must answer in order to produce a satisfactory solution to the problem of the moral status of abortion is this: How are we to define the moral community, the set of beings with full and equal moral rights, such that we can decide whether a human fetus is a member of this community or not? What sort of entity, exactly, has the inalienable rights to life, liberty, and the pursuit of happiness? Jefferson attributed these rights to all *men,* and it may or may not be fair to suggest that he intended to attribute them *only* to men. Perhaps he ought to have attributed them to all human beings. If so, then we arrive, first, at Noonan's problem of defining what makes a being human, and, second, at the equally vital question which Noonan does not consider, namely, What reason is there for identifying the moral community with the set of all human beings, in whatever way we have chosen to define that term?

1. On the Definition of "Human"

One reason why this vital second question is so frequently overlooked in the debate over the moral status of abortion is that the term "human" has two distinct, but not often distinguished, senses. This fact results in a slide of meaning, which serves to conceal the fallaciousness of the traditional argument that since (1) it is wrong to kill innocent human beings, and (2) fetuses are innocent human beings, then (3) it is wrong to kill fetuses. For if "human" is used in the same sense in both (1) and (2) then, whichever of the two senses is meant, one of these premises is question-begging. And if it is used in two different senses then of course the conclusion doesn't follow.

Thus, (1) is a self-evident moral truth, and avoids begging the question about abortion, only if "human being" is used to mean something like "a full-fledged member of the moral community." (It may or may not also be meant to refer exclusively to members of the species *Homo sapiens.*) We may call this the *moral* sense of "human." It is not to be confused with what we will call the *genetic* sense, i.e., the sense in which *any* member of the species is a human being, and no member of any other species could be. If (1) is acceptable only if the moral sense is intended, (2) is non–question-begging only if what is intended is the genetic sense.

In "Deciding Who is Human," Noonan argues for the classification of fetuses with human beings by pointing to the presence of the full genetic code, and the potential capacity for rational thought. It is clear that what he needs to show, for his version of the traditional argument to be valid, is that fetuses are human in the moral sense, the sense in which it is analytically true that all human beings have full moral rights. But, in the absence of any argument showing that whatever is genetically human is also morally human, and he gives none, nothing more than genetic humanity can be demonstrated by the presence of the human genetic code. And, as we will see, the *potential* capacity for rational thought can at most show that an entity has the potential for *becoming* human in the moral sense.

2. Defining the Moral Community

Can it be established that genetic humanity is sufficient for moral humanity? I think that there are very good reasons for not defining the moral community in this way. I would like to suggest an alternative way of defining the moral community, which I will argue for only to the extent of explaining why it is, or should be, self-evident. The suggestion is simply that the moral community consists of all and only *people,* rather than all and only human beings; and probably the best way of demonstrating its self-evidence is by considering the concept of personhood, to see what sorts of entity are and are not persons, and what the decision that a being is or is not a person implies about its moral rights.

What characteristics entitle an entity to be considered a person? This is obviously not the place to attempt a complete analysis of the concept of personhood, but we do not need such a fully adequate analysis just to determine whether and why a fetus is or isn't a person. All we need is a rough and approximate list of the most basic criteria of personhood, and some idea of which, or how many, of these an entity must satisfy in order to properly be considered a person.

In searching for such criteria, it is useful to look beyond the set of people with whom we are acquainted, and ask how we would decide whether a totally alien being was a person or not. (For we have no right to assume that genetic humanity is necessary for personhood.) Imagine a space traveler who lands on an unknown planet and encounters a race of beings utterly unlike any he has ever seen or heard of. If he wants to be sure of behaving morally toward these beings, he has to somehow decide whether they are people, and hence have full moral rights, or whether they are the sort of thing which he need not feel guilty about treating as, for example, a source of food.

How should he go about making this decision? If he has some anthropological background, he might look for such things as religion, art, and the manufacturing of tools, weapons, or shelters, since these factors have been used to distinguish our human from our prehuman ancestors, in what seems to be closer to the moral than the genetic sense of "human." And no doubt he would be right to consider the presence of such factors as good evidence that the alien beings were people, and morally human. It would, however, be overly anthropocentric of him to take the absence of these things as adequate evidence that they were not, since we can imagine people who have progressed beyond, or evolved without ever developing, these cultural characteristics.

I suggest that the traits which are most central to the concept of personhood, or humanity in the moral sense, are, very roughly, the following:

1. consciousness (of objects and events external and/or internal to the being), and in particular the capacity to feel pain;
2. reasoning (the *developed* capacity to solve new and relatively complex problems);

3. self-motivated activity (activity which is relatively independent of either genetic or direct external control);

4. the capacity to communicate, by whatever means, messages of an indefinite variety of types, that is, not just with an indefinite number of possible contents, but on indefinitely many possible topics;

5. the presence of self-concepts, and self-awareness, either individual or racial, or both.

Admittedly, there are apt to be a great many problems involved in formulating precise definitions of these criteria, let alone in developing universally valid behavioral criteria for deciding when they apply. But I will assume that both we and our explorer know approximately what (1)–(5) mean, and that he is also able to determine whether or not they apply. How, then, should he use his findings to decide whether or not the alien beings are people? We needn't suppose that an entity must have *all* of these attributes to be properly considered a person; (1) and (2) alone may well be sufficient for personhood, and quite probably (1)–(3) are sufficient. Neither do we need to insist that any one of these criteria is *necessary* for personhood, although once again (1) and (2) look like fairly good candidates for necessary conditions, as does (3), if "activity" is construed so as to include the activity of reasoning.

All we need to claim, to demonstrate that a fetus is not a person, is that any being which satisfies *none* of (1)–(5) is certainly not a person. I consider this claim to be so obvious that I think anyone who denied it, and claimed that a being which satisfied none of (1)–(5) was a person all the same, would thereby demonstrate that he had no notion at all of what a person is—perhaps because he had confused the concept of a person with that of genetic humanity. If the opponents of abortion were to deny the appropriateness of these five criteria, I do not know what further arguments would convince them. We would probably have to admit that our conceptual schemes were indeed irreconcilably different, and that our dispute could not be settled objectively.

I do not expect this to happen, however, since I think that the concept of a person is one which is very nearly universal (to people), and that it is common to both proabortionists and antiabortionists, even though neither group has fully realized the relevance of this concept to the resolution of their dispute. Furthermore, I think that on reflection even the antiabortionists ought to agree not only that (1)–(5) are central to the concept of personhood, but also that it is a part of this concept that all and only people have full moral rights. The concept of a person is in part a moral concept; once we have admitted that *x* is a person we have recognized, even if we have not agreed to respect, *x*'s right to be treated as a member of the moral community. It is true that the claim that *x* is a *human being* is more commonly voiced as part of an appeal to treat *x* decently than is the claim that *x* is a person, but this is either because "human being" is here used in the sense which implies personhood, or because the genetic and moral senses of "human" have been confused.

Now if (1)–(5) are indeed the primary criteria of personhood, then it is clear that genetic humanity is neither necessary nor sufficient for establishing that an entity is a person. Some human beings are not people, and there may well be people who are not human beings. A man or woman whose consciousness has been permanently obliterated but who remains alive is a human being which is no longer a person; defective human beings, with no appreciable mental capacity, are not and presumably never will be people; and a fetus is a human being which is not yet a person, and which therefore cannot coherently be said to have full moral rights. Citizens of the next century should be prepared to recognize highly advanced, self-aware robots or computers, should such be developed, and intelligent inhabitants of other worlds, should such be found, as people in the fullest sense, and to respect their moral rights. But to ascribe full moral rights to an entity which is not a person is as absurd as to ascribe moral obligations and responsibilities to such an entity.

3. Fetal Development and the Right to Life

Two problems arise in the application of these suggestions for the definition of the moral community to the determination of the precise moral status of a human fetus. Given that the paradigm example of a person is a normal adult human being, then (1) How like this paradigm, in particular how far advanced since conception, does a human being need to be before it begins to have a right to life by virtue, not of being fully a person as of yet, but of being *like* a person? and (2) To what extent, if any, does the fact that a fetus has the *potential* for becoming a person endow it with some of the same rights? Each of these questions requires some comment.

In answering the first question, we need not attempt a detailed consideration of the moral rights of organisms which are not developed enough, aware enough, intelligent enough, etc., to be considered people, but which resemble people in some respects. It does seem reasonable to suggest that the more like a person, in the relevant respects, a being is, the stronger is the case for regarding it as having a right to life, and indeed the stronger its right to life is. Thus we ought to take seriously the suggestion that, insofar as "the human individual develops biologically in a continuous fashion . . . the rights of a human person might develop in the same way." But we must keep in mind that the attributes which are relevant in determining whether or not an entity is enough like a person to be regarded as having some of the same moral rights are no different from those which are relevant to determining whether or not it is fully a person—i.e., are no different from (1)–(5)—and that being genetically human, or having recognizably human facial and other physical features, or detectable brain activity, or the capacity to survive outside the uterus, are simply not among these relevant attributes.

Thus it is clear that even though a seven- or eight-month fetus has features which make it apt to arouse in us almost the same powerful protective instinct as is commonly aroused by a small infant, nevertheless it is not significantly more personlike than is a very small embryo. It is *somewhat* more personlike; it can apparently feel and respond to pain, and it may even have a rudimentary form of consciousness, insofar as its brain is quite active. Nevertheless, it seems safe to say that it is not fully conscious, in the way that an infant of a few months is, and that it cannot reason, or communicate messages of indefinitely many sorts, does not engage in self-motivated activity, and has no self-awareness. Thus, in the *relevant* respects, a fetus, even a fully developed one, is considerably less personlike than is the average mature mammal, indeed the average fish. And I think that a rational person must conclude that if the right to life of a fetus is to be based upon its resemblance to a person, then it cannot be said to have any more right to life than, let us say, a newborn guppy (which also seems to be capable of feeling pain), and that a right of that magnitude could never override a woman's right to obtain an abortion, at any stage of her pregnancy.

There may, of course, be other arguments in favor of placing legal limits upon the stage of pregnancy in which an abortion may be performed. Given the relative safety of the new techniques of artificially inducing labor during the third trimester, the danger to the woman's life or health is no longer such an argument. Neither is the fact that people tend to respond to the thought of abortion in the later stages of pregnancy with emotional repulsion, since mere emotional responses cannot take the place of moral reasoning in determining what ought to be permitted. Nor, finally, is the frequently heard argument that legalizing abortion, especially late in the pregnancy, may erode the level of respect for human life, leading, perhaps, to an increase in unjustified euthanasia and other crimes. For this threat, if it is a threat, can be better met by educating people to the kinds of moral distinctions which we are making here than by limiting access to abortion (which limitation may, in its disregard for the rights of women, be just as damaging to the level of respect for human rights).

Thus, since the fact that even a fully developed fetus is not personlike enough to have any significant right to life on the basis of its personlikeness shows that no legal restrictions upon the stage of pregnancy in which an abortion may be performed can be justified on the grounds that we should protect the rights of the older fetus; and since there is no other apparent justification for such restrictions, we may conclude that they are entirely unjustifed. Whether or not it would be *indecent* (whatever that means) for a woman in her seventh month to obtain an abortion just to avoid having to postpone a trip to Europe, it would not, in itself, be *immoral,* and therefore it ought to be permitted.

4. Potential Personhood and the Right to Life

We have seen that a fetus does not resemble a person in any way which can support the claim that it has even some of the same rights. But what about its *potential,* the fact that if nurtured and allowed to develop naturally it will very probably become a person? Doesn't that alone give it at least some right to life? It is hard to deny that the fact that an entity is a potential person is a strong prima facie reason for not destroying it; but we need not conclude from this that a potential person has a right to life, by virtue of that potential. It may be that our feeling that it is better, other things being equal, not to destroy a potential person is better explained by the fact that potential people are still (felt to be) an invaluable resource, not to be lightly squandered. Surely, if every speck of dust were a potential person, we would be much less apt to conclude that every potential person has a right to become actual.

Still, we do not need to insist that a potential person has no right to life whatever. There may well be something immoral, and not just imprudent, about wantonly destroying potential people, when doing so isn't necessary to protect anyone's rights. But even if a potential person does have some prima facie right to life, such a right could not possibly outweigh the right of a woman to obtain an abortion, since the rights of any actual person invariably outweigh those of any potential person, whenever the two conflict. Since this may not be immediately obvious in the case of a human fetus, let us look at another case.

Suppose that our space explorer falls into the hands of an alien culture, whose scientists decide to create a few hundred thousand or more human beings, by breaking his body into its component cells, and using these to create fully developed human beings, with, of course, his genetic code. We may imagine that each of these newly created men will have all of the original man's abilities, skills, knowledge, and so on, and also have an individual self-concept, in short that each of them will be a bona fide (though hardly unique) person. Imagine that the whole project will take only seconds, and that its chances of success are extremely high, and that our explorer knows all of this, and also knows that these people will be treated fairly. I maintain that in such a situation he would have every right to escape if he could, and thus to deprive all of these potential people of their potential lives; for his right to life outweighs all of theirs together, in spite of the fact that they are all genetically human, all innocent, and all have a very high probability of becoming people very soon, if only he refrains from acting.

Indeed, I think he would have a right to escape even if it were not his life which the alien scientists planned to take, but only a year of his freedom, or, indeed, only a day. Nor would he be obligated to stay if he had gotten captured (thus bringing all these people-potentials into existence) because of his own carelessness, or even if he had done so deliberately, knowing the consequences. Regardless of how he got captured, he is not morally obligated to remain in captivity for *any* period of time for the sake of permitting any number of potential people to come into actuality, so great is the margin by which one actual person's right to liberty outweighs whatever right to life even a hundred thousand potential people have. And it seems reasonable to conclude that the rights of a woman will outweigh by a similar margin whatever right to life a fetus may have by virtue of its potential personhood.

Thus, neither a fetus's resemblance to a person, nor its potential for becoming a person provides any basis whatever for the claim that it has any significant right to life. Consequently, a woman's right to protect her health, happiness, freedom, and even her life, by terminating an unwanted pregnancy, will always override whatever right to life it may be appropriate to ascribe to a fetus, even a fully developed one. And thus, in the absence of any overwhelming social need for every possible child, the laws which restrict the right to obtain an abortion, or limit the period of pregnancy during which an abortion may be performed, are a wholly unjustified violation of a woman's most basic moral and constitutional rights.

POSTSCRIPT ON INFANTICIDE

Since the publication of this article, many people have written to point out that my argument appears to justify not only abortion, but infanticide as well. For a new-born infant is not significantly more person-like than an advanced fetus, and consequently it would seem that if the destruction of the latter is permissible so too must be that of the former. Inasmuch as most people, regardless of how they feel about the morality of abortion, consider infanticide a form of murder, this might appear to represent a serious flaw in my argument.

Now, if I am right in holding that it is only people who have a full-fledged right to life, and who can be murdered, and if the criteria of personhood are as I have described them, then it obviously follows that killing a new-born infant isn't murder. It does *not* follow, however, that infanticide is permissible, for two reasons. In the first place, it would be wrong, at least in this country and in this period of history, and other things being equal, to kill a new-born infant, because even if its parents do not want it and would not suffer from its destruction, there are other people who would like to have it, and would, in all probability, be deprived of a great deal of pleasure by its destruction. Thus, infanticide is wrong for reasons analogous to those which make it wrong to wantonly destroy natural resources, or great works of art.

Secondly, most people, at least in this country, value infants and would much prefer that they be preserved, even if foster parents are not immediately available. Most of us would rather be taxed to support orphanages than allow unwanted infants to be destroyed. So long as there are people who want an infant preserved, and who are willing and able to provide the means of caring for it, under reasonably humane conditions, it is, *ceteris parabis,* wrong to destroy it.

But, it might be replied, if this argument shows that infanticide is wrong, at least at this time and in this country, doesn't it also show that abortion is wrong? After all, many people value fetuses, are disturbed by their destruction, and would much prefer that they be preserved, even at some cost to themselves. Furthermore, as a potential source of pleasure to some foster family, a fetus is just as valuable as an infant. There is, however, a crucial difference between the two cases: so long as the fetus is unborn, its preservation, contrary to the wishes of the pregnant woman, violates her rights to freedom, happiness, and self-determination. Her rights override the rights of those who would like the fetus preserved, just as if someone's life or limb is threatened by a wild animal, his right to protect himself by destroying the animal overrides the rights of those who would prefer that the animal not be harmed.

The minute the infant is born, however, its preservation no longer violates any of its mother's rights, even if she wants it destroyed, because she is free to put it up for adoption. Consequently, while the moment of birth does not mark any sharp discontinuity in the degree to which an infant possesses the right to life, it does mark the end of its mother's to determine its fate. Indeed, if abortion could be performed without killing the fetus, she would never possess the right to have the fetus destroyed, for the same reasons that she has no right to have an infant destroyed.

On the other hand, it follows from my argument that when an unwanted or defective infant is born into a society which cannot afford and/or is not willing to care for it, then its destruction is permissible. This conclusion will, no doubt, strike many people as heartless and immoral; but remember that the very existence of people who feel this way, and who are willing and able to provide care for unwanted infants, is reason enough to conclude that they should be preserved.

Wrongs and Rights

Jane English

The abortion debate rages on. Yet the two most popular positions seem to be clearly mistaken. Conservatives maintain that a human life begins at conception and that therefore abortion must be wrong because it is murder. But not all killings of humans are murders. Most notably, self-defense may justify even the killing of an innocent person.

Liberals, on the other hand, are just as mistaken in their argument that since a fetus does not become a person until birth, a woman may do whatever she pleases in and to her own body. First, you cannot do as you please with your own body if it affects other people adversely. Second, if a fetus is not a person, that does not imply that you can do to it anything you wish. Animals, for example, are not persons, yet to kill or torture them for no reason at all is wrong.

At the center of the storm has been the issue of just when it is between ovulation and adulthood that a person appears on the scene. Conservatives draw the line at conception, liberals at birth. In this paper I first examine our concept of a person and conclude that no single criterion can capture the concept of a person and no sharp line can be drawn. Next I argue that if a fetus is a person, abortion is still justifiable in many cases; and if a fetus is not a person, killing it is still wrong in many cases. To a large extent, these two solutions are in agreement. I conclude that our concept of a person cannot and need not bear the weight that the abortion controversy has thrust upon it.

I

The several factions in the abortion argument have drawn battle lines around various proposed criteria for determining what is and what is not a person. For example, Mary Anne Warren lists five features (capacities for reasoning, self-awareness, complex communications, etc.) as her criteria for personhood and argues for the permissibility of abortion because a fetus falls outside this concept. Baruch Brody uses brain waves. Michael Tooley picks having-a-concept-of-self as his criterion and concludes that infanticide and abortion are justifiable, while the killing of adult animals is not. On the other side, Paul Ramsey claims a certain gene structure is the defining characteris-

Jane English, "Wrongs and Rights," *The Canadian Journal of Philosophy,* Vol. V, No. 2 (October, 1975), pp. 233–243. Reprinted by permission.

tic. John Noonan prefers conceived-of-humans and presents counterexamples to various other candidate criteria. For instance, he argues against viability as the criterion because the newborn and infirm would then be nonpersons, since they cannot live without the aid of others. He rejects any criterion that calls upon the sorts of sentiments a being can evoke in adults on the grounds that this would allow us to exclude other races as nonpersons if we could just view them sufficiently unsentimentally.

These approaches are typical: foes of abortion propose sufficient conditions for personhood which fetuses satisfy, while friends of abortion counter with necessary conditions for personhood which fetuses lack. But these both presuppose that the concept of a person can be captured in a straitjacket of necessary and/or sufficient conditions. Rather, "person" is a cluster of features, of which rationality, having a self-concept, and being conceived of humans are only part.

What is typical of persons? Within our concept of a person we include, first, certain biological factors: descended from humans, having a certain genetic make-up, having a head, hands, arms, eyes, capable of locomotion, breathing, eating, sleeping. There are psychological factors: sentience, perception, having a concept of self and of one's own interests and desires, the ability to use tools, the ability to use language or symbol systems, the ability to joke, to be angry, to doubt. There are rationality factors: the ability to reason and draw conclusions, the ability to generalize and to learn from past experience, the ability to sacrifice present interests for greater gains in the future. There are social factors: the ability to work in groups and respond to peer pressures, the ability to recognize and consider as valuable the interests of others, seeing oneself as one among "other minds," the ability to sympathize, encourage, love, the ability to evoke from others the responses of sympathy, encouragement, love, the ability to work with others for mutual advantage. Then there are legal factors: being subject to the law and protected by it, having the ability to sue and enter contracts, being counted in the census, having a name and citizenship, the ability to own property, inherit, and so forth.

Now the point is not that this list is incomplete, or that you can find counterinstances to each of its points. People typically exhibit rationality, for instance, but someone who was irrational would not thereby fail to qualify as a person. On the other hand, something could exhibit the majority of these features and still fail to be a person, as an advanced robot might. There is no single core of necessary and sufficient features which we can draw upon with the assurance that they constitute what really makes a person; there are only features that are more or less typical.

This is not to say that no necessary or sufficient conditions can be given. Being alive is a necessary condition for being a person, and being a U.S. Senator is sufficient. But rather than falling inside a sufficient condition or outside a necessary one, a fetus lies in the penumbra region where our concept of a person is not so simple. For this reason I think a conclusive answer to the question whether a fetus is a person is unattainable.

Here we might note a family of simple fallacies that proceed by stating a necessary condition for personhood and showing that a fetus has that characteristic. This is a form of the fallacy of affirming the consequent. For example, some have mistakenly reasoned from the premise that a fetus is human (after all, it is a human fetus rather than, say, a canine fetus), to the conclusion that it is a human. Adding an equivocation on "being," we get the fallacious argument that since a fetus is something both living and human, it is a human being.

Nonetheless, it does seem clear that a fetus has very few of the above family of characteristics, whereas a newborn baby exhibits a much larger proportion of them—and a two-year-old has even more. Note that one traditional antiabortion argument has centered on pointing out the many ways in which a fetus resembles a baby. They emphasize its development ("It already has ten fingers...") without mentioning its dissimilarities to adults (it still has gills and a tail). They also try to evoke the sort of sympathy on our part that we only feel toward other persons ("Never to laugh... or feel the sunshine?"). This all seems to be a relevant way to argue, since its purpose is to persuade us that a fetus satisfies so many of the important features on the list that it ought to be treated as a person. Also note that a fetus near the time of birth satisfies many more of these factors than a fetus in the early months of development. This could provide reason for making distinctions among the different stages of pregnancy, as the U.S. Supreme Court has done.

Historically, the time at which a person had been said to come into existence has varied widely. Muslims date personhood from fourteen days after conception. Some medievals followed Aristotle in placing ensoulment at forty days after conception for a male fetus and eighty days for a female fetus. In European common law since the seventeenth century, abortion was considered the killing of a person only after quickening, the time when a pregnant woman first feels the fetus move on its own. Nor is this variety of opinions surprising. Biologically, a human being develops gradually. We shouldn't expect there to be any specific time or sharp dividing point when a person appears on the scene.

For these reasons I believe our concept of a person is not sharp or decisive enough to bear the weight of a solution to the abortion controversy. To use it to solve that problem is to clarify *obscurum per obscurius.*

II

Next let us consider what follows if a fetus is a person after all. Judith Jarvis Thomson's landmark article, "A Defense of Abortion," correctly points out that some additional argumentation is needed at this point in the conservative argument to bridge the gap between the premise that a fetus is an innocent person and the conclusion that killing it is always wrong. To arrive at this conclusion, we would need the additional premise that killing an innocent person is always wrong. But killing an innocent person is sometimes permissible, most notably in self-defense. Some example may help draw out our intuitions or ordinary judgments about self-defense.

Suppose a mad scientist, for instance, hypnotized innocent people to jump out of the bushes and attack innocent passersby with knives. If you are so attacked, we agree you have a right to kill the attacker in self-defense, if killing him is the only way to protect your life or to save yourself from serious injury. It does not seem to matter here that the attacker is not malicious but himself an innocent pawn, for your killing of him is not done in a spirit of retribution but only in self-defense.

How severe an injury may you inflict in self-defense? In part this depends upon the severity of the injury to be avoided: you may not shoot someone merely to avoid having your clothes torn. This might lead one to the mistaken conclusion that the defense may only equal the threatened injury in severity; that to avoid death you may kill, but to avoid a black eye you may only inflict a black eye or the equivalent. Rather, our laws and customs seem to say that you may create an injury somewhat, but not enormously greater than the injury to be avoided. To fend off an attack whose outcome would be as serious as rape, a severe beating or the loss of a finger, you may shoot; to avoid having your clothes torn, you may blacken an eye.

Aside from this, the injury you may inflict should only be the minimum necessary to deter or incapacitate the attacker. Even if you know he intends to kill you, you are not justified in shooting him if you could equally well save yourself by the simple expedient of running away. Self-defense is for the purpose of avoiding harms rather than equalizing harms.

Some cases of pregnancy present a parallel situation. Though the fetus is itself innocent, it may pose a threat to the pregnant woman's well-being, life prospects, or health, mental or physical. If the pregnancy presents a slight threat to her interests, it seems self-defense cannot justify abortion. But if the threat is on a part with a serious beating or the loss of a finger, she may kill the fetus that poses such a threat, even if it is an innocent person. If a lesser harm to the fetus could have the same defensive effect, killing it would not be justified. It is unfortunate that the only way to free the woman from the pregnancy entails the death of the fetus (except in very late stages of pregnancy). Thus a self-defense model supports Thomson's point that the woman has a right only to be freed from the fetus, not a right to demand its death.

The self-defense model is most helpful when we take the pregnant woman's point of view. In the pre-Thomson literature, abortion is often framed as a question for a third party: do you, a doctor, have a right to choose between the life of the woman and that of the fetus? Some have claimed that if you were a passerby who witnessed a struggle between the innocent hypnotized attacker and his equally innocent hypnotized victim, you would have no reason to kill either in defense of the other. They have concluded that the self-defense model implies that a woman may attempt to abort herself, but that a doctor should not assist her. I think the position of the third party is somewhat more complex. We do feel some inclination to intervene on behalf of the victim rather than the attacker, other things equal. But if both parties are innocent, other factors come into consideration. You would rush to the aid of your husband whether he was attacker or attackee. If a hypnotized famous violinist were attacking a skid row bum, we would try to save the individual who is of more value to society. These considerations would tend to support abortion in some cases.

But suppose you are a frail senior citizen who wishes to avoid being knifed by one of these innocent hypnotics, so you have hired a bodyguard to accompany you. If you are attacked, it is clear we believe that the bodyguard, acting as your agent, has a right to kill the attacker to save you from a serious beating. Your rights of self-defense are transferred to your agent. I suggest that we should similarly view the doctor as the pregnant woman's agent in carrying out a defense she is physically incapable of accomplishing herself.

Thanks to modern technology, the cases are rare in which a pregnancy poses as clear a threat to a woman's bodily health as an attacker brandishing a switchblade. How does self-defense fare when more subtle, complex, and long-range harms are involved?

To consider a somewhat fanciful example, suppose you are a highly trained surgeon when you are kidnapped by the hypnotic attacker. He says he does not intend to harm you but to take you back to the mad scientist who, it turns out, plans to hypnotize you to have a permanent mental block against all your knowledge of medicine. This would automatically destroy your career which would in turn have a serious adverse impact on your family, your personal relationships, and your happiness. It seems to me that if the only way you can avoid this outcome is to shoot the innocent attacker, you are justified in so doing. You are defending yourself from a drastic injury to your life prospects. I think it is no exaggeration to claim that unwanted pregnancies (most obviously among teenagers) often have such adverse lifelong consequences as the surgeon's loss of livelihood.

Several parallels arise between various views on abortion and the self-defense model. Let's suppose further that these hypnotized attackers only operate at night, so that it is well known that they can be avoided completely by the considerable inconvenience of never leaving your house after dark. One view is that since you could stay home at night, therefore if you go out and are selected by one of these hypnotized people, you have no right to defend yourself. This parallels the view that abstinence is the only acceptable way to avoid pregnancy. Others might hold that you ought to take along some defense such as Mace which will deter the hypnotized person without killing him, but that if this defense fails, you are obliged to submit to the resulting injury, no matter how severe it is. This parallels the view that contraception is all right but abortion is always wrong, even in cases of contraceptive failure.

A third view is that you may kill the hypnotized person only if he will actually kill you, but not if he will only injure you. This is like the position that abortion is permissible only if it is required to save a woman's life.

Finally we have the view that it is all right to kill the attacker, even if only to avoid a very slight inconvenience to yourself and even if you knowingly walked down the very street where all these incidents have been taking place without taking along any Mace or protective escort. If we assume that a fetus is a person, this is the analogue of the view that abortion is always justifiable, "on demand."

The self-defense model allows us to see an important difference that exists between abortion and infanticide, even if a fetus is a person from conception. Many have argued that the only way to justify abortion without justifying infanticide would be to find some characteristic of personhood that is acquired at birth. Michael Tooley, for one, claims infanticide is justifiable because the really significant characteristics of person are acquired some time after birth. But all such approaches look to characteristics of the developing human and ignore the relation between the fetus and the woman. What if, after birth, the presence of an infant or the need to support it posed a grave threat to the woman's sanity or life prospects? She could escape this threat by the simple expedient of running away. So a solution that does not entail the death of the infant is available. Before birth, such solutions are not available because of the biological dependence of the fetus on the woman. Birth is the crucial point not because of any characteristics the fetus gains, but because after birth the woman can defend herself by a means less drastic than killing the infant. Hence self-defense can be used to justify abortion without necessarily thereby justifying infanticide.

III

On the other hand, supposing a fetus is not after all a person, would abortion always be morally permissible? Some opponents of abortion seem worried that if a fetus is not a full-fledged person, then we are justified in treating it in any way at all. However, this does not follow. Nonpersons do get some consideration in our moral code, though of course they do not have the same rights as persons have (and in general they do not have moral responsibilities), and though their interests may be overridden by the interests of persons. Still, we cannot just treat them in any way at all.

Treatment of animals is a case in point. It is wrong to torture dogs for fun or to kill wild birds for no reason at all. It is wrong Period, even though dogs and birds do not have the same rights persons do. However, few people think it is wrong to use dogs as experimental animals, causing them considerable suffering in some cases, provided that the resulting research will probably bring discoveries of great benefit to people. And most of us think it all right to kill birds for food or to protect our crops. People's rights are different from the consideration we give to animals, then, for it is wrong to experiment on people, even if others might later benefit a great deal as a result of their suffering. You might volunteer to be a subject, but this would be supererogatory; you certainly have a right to refuse to be a medical guinea pig.

But how do we decide what you may or may not do to nonpersons? This is a difficult problem, one for which I believe no adequate account exists. You do not want to say, for instance, that torturing dogs is all right whenever the sum of its effects on people is good—when it doesn't warp the sensibilities of the torturer so much that he mistreats people. If that were the case, it would be all right to torture dogs if you did it in private, or if the torturer lived on a desert island or died soon afterward, so that his actions had no effect on people. This is an inadequate account, because whatever moral consideration animals get, . . . it will have to be a general proscription of certain actions, not merely a weighing of the impact on people on a case-by-case basis. . . .

It is crucial that psychological facts play a role here. Our psychological constitution makes it the case that for our ethical theory to work, it must prohibit certain treatment of nonpersons which are significantly personlike. If our moral rules allowed people to treat some personlike nonpersons in ways we do not want people to be treated, this would undermine the system of sympathies and attitudes that makes the ethical system work. For this reason, we would choose in the original position to make mistreatment of some sorts of animals wrong in general (not just wrong in the cases with public impact). Thus it makes sense that it is those animals whose appearance and behavior are most like those of people that get the most consideration in our moral scheme.

It is because of "coherence of attitudes," I think, that the similarity of a fetus to a baby is very significant. A fetus one week before birth is so much like a newborn baby in our psychological space that we cannot allow any cavalier treatment of the former while expecting full sympathy and nurturative support for the latter. Thus, I think that antiabortion forces are indeed giving their strongest arguments when they point to the similarities between a fetus and a baby, and when they try to evoke our emotional attachment to and sympathy for the fetus. An early horror story from New York about nurses who were expected to alternate between caring for six-month premature infants and disposing of viable 24-week aborted fetuses is just that—a horror story. These beings are so much alike that no one can be asked to draw a distinction and treat them so very differently.

Remember, however, that in the early weeks after conception, a fetus is very much unlike a person. It is hard to develop these feelings for a set of genes which doesn't yet have a head, hands, beating heart, response to touch or the ability to move by itself. Thus it seems to me that the alleged "slippery slope" between conception and birth is not so very slippery. In the early stages of pregnancy, abortion can hardly be compared to murder for psychological reasons, but in the latest stages it is psychologically akin to murder.

Another source of similarity is the bodily continuity between fetus and adult. Bodies play a surprisingly central role in our attitudes toward persons. One has only to think of the philosophical literature on how far physical identity suffices for personal identity or Wittgenstein's remark that the best picture of the human soul is the human body. Even after death, when all agree the body is no longer a person, we still observe elaborate customs of respect for the human body; like people who torture dogs, necrophiliacs are not to be trusted with people. So it is appropriate that we show respect to a fetus as the body continuous with the body of a person. This is a degree of resemblance to persons that animals cannot rival.

Michael Tooley also utilizes a parallel with animals. He claims that it is always permissible to drown newborn kittens and draws conclusions about infanticide. But it is only permissible to drown kittens when their survival would cause some hardship. Perhaps it would be a burden to feed and house six more cats or to find other homes for them. The alternative of letting them starve produces even more suffering than the drowning. Since the kittens get their rights secondhand, so to speak, *via* the need for coherence in our attitudes, their interests are often overridden by the interests of full-fledged persons. But if their survival would be no inconvenience to people at all, then it is wrong to drown them, *contra* Tooley.

Tooley's conclusions about abortion are wrong for the same reason. Even if a fetus is not a person, abortion is not always permissible, because of the resemblance of a fetus to a person. I agree with Thomson that it would be wrong for a woman who is seven months pregnant to have an abortion to avoid having to postpone a trip to Europe. In the early months of pregnancy when the fetus hardly resembles a baby at all, then, abortion is permissible whenever it is in the interests of the pregnant woman or her family. The reasons would only need to outweigh the pain and inconvenience of the abortion itself. In the middle months, when the fetus comes to resemble a person, abortion would be justifiable only when the continuation of the pregnancy or the birth of the child would cause harms—physical, psychological, economic, or social—to the woman. In the late months of pregnancy, even on our current assumption that a fetus is not a person, abortion seems to be wrong except to save a woman from significant injury or death.

The Supreme Court has recognized similar gradations in the alleged slippery slope stretching between conception and birth. To this point, the present paper has been a discussion of the moral status of abortion only, not its legal status. In view of the great physical, financial, and sometimes psychological costs of abortion, perhaps the legal arrangement most compatible with the proposed moral solution would be the absence of restrictions, that is, so-called abortion "on demand."

So I conclude, first, that application of our concept of a person will not suffice to settle the abortion issue. After all, the biological development of a human being is gradual. Second, whether a fetus is a person or not, abortion is justifiable early in pregnancy to avoid modest harms and seldom justifiable late in pregnancy except to avoid significant injury or death.

QUESTIONS FOR DISCUSSION

1. Do we recognize the same rights for the mentally retarded and the insane as we recognize for normal people? If not, why must we nevertheless recognize and respect their right to life? Does an unborn fetus or a newborn infant have more or fewer rights than a severely retarded human being? Explain your view.

2. What is Noonan's main argument? Why we should draw the line for recognizing the right to life at conception, rather than at quickening or viability or birth?

3. What is the "principle of double effect" cited by Noonan, and how does it apply to therapeutic abortion?

4. Why does Mary Anne Warren reject the argument offered by some pro-choice writers, that the mother's body is her property and she may expel any trespasser from it?

5. What does Warren mean in criticizing pro-life writers like Noonan for confusing the concept of a human being with the concept of a person? What, for her, is the difference?

6. In a celebrated essay in defense of abortion, Professor Judith Thomson compared an unwanted fetus in its mother's womb to a violinist secretly—without her knowledge or consent—connected to a woman's kidneys. What criticism does Warren make of this analogy?

7. How serious is the difference between Warren and English's views on when abortion is permissible? On what ground does English believe that abortion at a later stage of fetal development is morally more objectionable than at an early stage?

SUGGESTED READINGS

BAIRD, R., *The Ethics of Abortion,* Prometheus, Buffalo, New York, 1989.

BAJEMA, C., *Abortion and the Meaning of Personhood,* Baker Books, 1974.

BOK, S., "Ethical Problems of Abortion," *Hastings Center Studies,* 2 (1974).

BRANDT, R., "The Morality of Abortion," *Monist,* 56 (1972).

BRODY, B., "Abortion and the Sanctity," *American Philosophical Quarterly,* 10 (1973).

CALLAHAN, D., *Abortion Law, Choice and Morality,* Macmillan, New York, 1970.

CALLAHAN, D., and S. CALLAHAN, *Abortion: Understanding Differences,* Plenum Press, New York, 1984.

DEDEK, J., *Human Life: Some Moral Issues,* Sheed & Ward, 1972.

ENGELHARDT, H., "The Ontology of Abortion," *Ethics,* 84 (1974).

ENGLISH, J., "Abortion and the Concept of a Person," *Canadian Journal of Philosophy,* 5 (1975).

FEINBERG, J., *The Problem of Abortion,* Wadsworth, 1973.

FINNIE, J., J. THOMSON, M. TOOLEY, and R. WERTHEIMER, eds., *The Rights and Wrongs of Abortion*, Princeton University Press, Princeton, N.J., 1974.

FOST, N., "Our Curious Attitude Toward the Fetus," *Hastings Center Report*, 4 (1974).

GALLAGHER, K., "Abortion and Choice," *Public Affairs Quarterly*, 7, 1 (1993). 13–17.

GATENS-ROBINSON, E., "A Defense of Women's Choice," *Southern Journal of Philosophy*, 30, 3 (1992), 39–66.

GILLESPIE, N., "Abortion and Human Rights," *Ethics*, 87 (1977).

GOLDMAN, A., "Abortion and the Right to Die," *Personalist*, 60 (1979).

HILGERS, T. and D. HORAN, eds., *Abortion and Social Justice*, Sheed & Ward, 1973.

JAGGAR, A., "Abortion and a Woman's Right to Decide," *Philosophical Forum*, 5 (1973).

KAMM, F., *Creation and Abortion*, Oxford University Press, New York, 1992.

KENYON, E., *The Dilemma of Abortion*, Faber, Boston, 1986.

KOHL, M., *The Morality of Killing: Euthanasia, Abortion and Transplants*, Humanities Press, 1974.

LANGER, R., "Abortion and the Right to Privacy," *Journal of Social Philosophy*, 23, 2 (1992), 23–51.

MARGOLIS, J., "Abortion," *Ethics*, 84 (1973).

MATHIEU, D., "Crime and Punishment: Abortion or Murder?," *Journal of Social Philosophy*, 23, 2 (1992), 5–22.

MATTHEWS, G., "Life and Death or the Arrival and Departure of the Psyche," *American Philosophical Quarterly*, 16 (1979).

MEYERS, C., "Maintaining the Violinist," *Journal of Social Philosophy*, 23, 2 (1992), 52–64.

MONTAGUE, P., "The Moral Status of Human Zygotes," *Canadian Journal of Philosophy*, 8 (1978).

NOONAN, J., ed., *The Morality of Abortion: Legal and Historical Perspectives*, Harvard University Press, Cambridge, Mass., 1970.

PAUL, E., "Self-Ownership, Abortion and Infanticide," *Journal of Medical Ethics*, 5 (1979).

PIUS XI, *Casti Connubi*, Paulist Press, 1941.

REED, E., and C. MORIARTY, *Abortion and the Catholic Church: Two Feminists Defend Women's Rights*, Pathfinder Press, 1973.

ST. JOHN-STEVAS, N., *Life, Death and the Law*, Indiana University Press, Bloomington, 1961.

SARVIS, B., and H. RODMAN, *The Abortion Controversy*, Columbia University Press, New York, 1974.

SCHWARTZ, L., *Arguing about Abortion*, Belmont: Wadsworth, 1992.

STERBER, J., "Abortion, Distant Peoples and Future Generations," *The Journal of Philosophy*, 77 (1980).

SUMNER, L. *Abortion and Moral Theory*, Princeton University Press, Princeton, N.J., 1981.

THOMSON, J. J., "Killing, Letting Die and the Trolley Problem," *Monist*, 59 (1976).

WEISS, R., "The Perils of Personhood," *Ethics*, 89 (1978).

WILLIAMS, G., *The Sanctity of Life and the Criminal Law*, Knopf, New York, 1957.

6

CAPITAL PUNISHMENT

THE FOLLY OF CAPITAL PUNISHMENT

Anthony G. Amsterdam

My discussion of capital punishment will proceed in three stages.

First, I would like to set forth certain basic factual realities about capital punishment, like the fact that capital punishment is a fancy phrase for legally killing people. Please forgive me for beginning with such obvious and ugly facts. Much of our political and philosophical debate about the death penalty is carried on in language calculated to conceal these realities and their implications. The implications, I will suggest, are that capital punishment is a great evil—surely the greatest evil except for war that our society can intentionally choose to commit.

This does not mean that we should do away with capital punishment. Some evils, like war, are occasionally necessary, and perhaps capital punishment is one of them. But the fact that it is a great evil means that we should not choose to do it without some very good and solid reason of which we are satisfactorily convinced upon sufficient evidence. The conclusion of my first point simply is that the burden of proof upon the question of capital punishment rightly rests on those who are asking us to use our laws to kill people with, and that this is a very heavy burden.

Second, I want to review the justifications that have been advanced to support capital punishment. I want to explore with you concepts such as retribution and deterrence, and some of the assumptions and evidence about them. The conclusion of my second point will be that none of these reasons which we like to give ourselves for executing criminals can begin to sustain the burden of proof that rightfully rests upon them.

Third, I would like to say a word about history—about the slow but absolutely certain progress of maturing civilization that will bring an inevitable end to punishment by death. That history does not give us the choice between perpetuating and abolishing capital punishment, because we could not perpetuate it if we wanted to. A generation or two within a single nation can retard but not reverse a long-term, worldwide evolution of this magnitude. Our choice is narrower although it is not unimportant: whether we shall be numbered among the last generations to put legal killing aside. I will end by asking you to cast your choice for life instead of death. But, first, let me begin with some basic facts about the death penalty.

I. The most basic fact, of course, is that capital punishment means taking living, breathing men and women, stuffing them into a chair, strapping them down, pulling a lever, and exterminating them. We have almost forgotten this fact because there have been no executions in this country for more than ten years, except for Gary Gilmore whose combined suicide and circus were so wildly extravagant as to seem unreal. For many people, capital punishment has become a sanitized and symbolic issue: Do you or do you not support your local police? Do you or do you not care enough about crime to get tough with criminals? These abstractions were never what capital punishment was about, although it was possible to think so during the ten-year moratorium on executions caused by constitutional challenges to the death penalty in the courts. That is no longer possible. The courts have now said that we can start up executions again, if we want to. Today, a vote for capital punishment is a vote to kill real, live people.

What this means is, first, that we bring men or women into court and put them through a trial for their lives. They are expected to sit back quietly and observe decent courtroom decorum throughout a proceeding whose purpose is systematically and deliberately to decide whether they should be killed. The jury hears evidence and votes; and you can always tell when a jury has voted for death because they come back into court and they will not look the defendant or defense counsel in the eyes. The judge pronounces sentence and the defendant is taken away to be held in a cell for two to six years, hoping that his appeals will succeed, not really knowing what they are all about, but knowing that if they fail, he will be taken out and cinched down and put to death. Most of the people in prison are reasonably nice to him, and even a little apologetic; but he realizes every day for that 700 or 2,100 days that they are holding him there helpless for the approaching slaughter; and that, once the final order is given, they will truss him up and kill him, and that nobody in that vast surrounding machinery of public officials and servants of the law will raise a finger to save him. This is why Camus once wrote that an execution

> is not simply death. It is just as different . . . from the privation of life as a concentration camp is from prison. . . . It adds to death a rule, a public premeditation known to the future victim, an organization . . . which is itself a source of moral sufferings more terrible than death . . . [Capital

punishment] is . . . the most premeditated of murders, to which no criminal's deed, however calculated . . . can be compared. . . . For there to be an equivalency, the death penalty would have to punish a criminal who had warned his victim of the date at which he would inflict a horrible death on him and who, from the moment onward, had confined him at his mercy for months. Such a monster is not encountered in private life.

I will spare you descriptions of the execution itself. Apologists for capital punishment commonly excite their readers with descriptions of extremely gruesome, gory murders. All murders are horrible things, and executions are usually a lot cleaner physically—although, like Camus, I have never heard of a murderer who held his victim captive for two or more years waiting as the minutes and hours ticked away toward his preannounced death. The clinical details of an execution are as unimaginable to me as they are to most of you. We have not permitted public executions in this country for over 40 years. The law in every state forbids more than a few people to watch the deed done behind prison walls. In January of 1977, a federal judge in Texas ruled that executions could be photographed for television, but the attorneys general of 25 states asked the federal Court of Appeals to set aside that ruling, and it did. I can only leave to your imagination what they are trying so very hard to hide from us. Oh, of course, executions are too hideous to put on television; we all know that. But let us not forget that it is the same hideous thing, done in secret, which we are discussing under abstract labels like "capital punishment" that permit us to talk about the subject in after-dinner conversation instead of spitting up.

In any event, the advocates of capital punishment can and do accentuate their arguments with descriptions of the awful physical details of such hideous murders as that of poor Sharon Tate. All of us naturally and rightly respond to these atrocities with shock and horror. You can read descriptions of executions that would also horrify you (for example, in Byron Eshelman's 1962 book, *Death Row Chaplain,* particularly pages 160–61), but I prefer not to insult your intelligence by playing "can you top this" with issues of life and death. I ask you only to remember two things, if and when you are exposed to descriptions of terrifying murders.

First, the murders being described are not murders that are being done by us, or in our name, or with our approval; and our power to stop them is exceedingly limited even under the most exaggerated suppositions of deterrence, which I shall shortly return to question. Every execution, on the other hand, is done by our paid servants, in our collective name, and we can stop them all. Please do not be bamboozled into thinking that people who are against executions are in favor of murders. If we had the individual or the collective power to stop murders, we would stop them all—and for the same basic reason that we want to stop executions. Murders and executions are both ugly, vicious things, because they destroy the same sacred and mysterious gift of life which we do not understand and can never restore.

Second, please remember therefore that descriptions of murders are relevant to the subject of capital punishment only on the theory that two wrongs make a right, or that killing murderers can assuage their victims' sufferings or bring them back to life, or that capital punishment is the best deterrent to murder. The first two propositions are absurd, and the third is debatable—although, as I shall latter show, the evidence is overwhelmingly against it. My present point is only that deterrence *is* debatable, whereas we *know* that persons whom we execute are dead beyond recall, no matter how the debate about deterrence comes out. That is a sufficient reason, I believe, why the burden of proof on the issue of deterrence should be placed squarely upon the executioners.

There are other reasons too. Let me try to state them briefly.

Capital punishment not merely kills people, it also kills some of them in error, and these are errors which we can never correct. When I speak about legal error, I do not mean only the question whether "they got the right man" or killed somebody who "didn't do it." Errors of that sort do occur: Timothy Evans, for example, an innocent man whose execution was among the reasons for the abolition of the death penalty in Great Britain. If you read Anthony Scaduto's recent book, *Scapegoat,* you will come away with unanswerable doubts whether Bruno Richard Hauptmann was really guilty of the kidnapping of the Lindbergh infant for which he was executed, or whether we killed Hauptmann, too, for a crime he did not commit.

In 1975, the Florida Cabinet pardoned two black men, Freddie Lee Pitts and Wilbert Lee, who were twice tried and sentenced to death and spent 12 years apiece on death row for a murder committed by somebody else. This one, I am usually glibly told, "does not count," because Pitts and Lee were never actually put to death. Take comfort if you will but I cannot, for I know that only the general constitutional attack which we were then mounting upon the death penalty in Florida kept Pitts and Lee alive long enough to permit discovery of the evidence of their innocence. Our constitutional attack is now dead, and so would Pitts and Lee be if they were tried tomorrow. Sure, we catch some errors. But we often catch them by extremely lucky breaks that could as easily not have happened. I represented a young man in North Carolina who came within a hair's breadth of being the Gary Gilmore of his day. Like Gilmore, he became so depressed under a death sentence that he tried to dismiss his appeal. He was barely talked out of it, his conviction was reversed, and on retrial a jury acquitted him in 11 minutes.

We do not know how many "wrong men" have been executed. We think and pray that they are rare—although we can't be sure because, after a man is dead, people seldom continue to investigate the possibility that he was innocent. But that is not the biggest source of error anyway.

What about *legal* error? In 1968, the Supreme Court of the United States held that it was unconstitutional to exclude citizens from capital trial juries simply because they had general conscientious or religious objections to the death penalty. That decision was held retroactive; and I represented 60 or 70 men whose death sentences were subsequently set aside for constitutional errors in jury selection. While researching their cases, I found the cases of at least as many more men who had already been executed on the basis of trials infected with identical errors. On June 29, 1977, we finally won a decision from the Supreme Court of the United States that the death penalty is excessively harsh and therefore unconstitutional for the crime of rape. Fine, but it comes too late for the 455 men executed for rape in this country since 1930—405 of them black.

In 1975, the Supreme Court held that the constitutional presumption of innocence forbids a trial judge to tell the jury that the burden of proof is on a homicide defendant to show provocation which reduces murder to manslaughter. On June 17, 1977, the Court held that this decision was also retroactive. Jury charges of precisely that kind were standard forms for more than a century in many American states that punished murder with death. Can we ever begin to guess how many people were unconstitutionally executed under this so-called retroactive decision?

Now what about errors of fact that go to the degree of culpability of a crime? In almost every state, the difference between first- and second-degree murder—or between capital and noncapital murder—depends on whether the defendant acted with something called "premeditation" as distinguished from intent to kill. Premeditation means intent formed beforehand, but no particular amount of time is required. Courts tell juries that premeditation "may be as instantaneous as successive thoughts in the mind." Mr. Justice Cardozo wrote that *he* did not understand the concept of premeditation after several decades of studying and trying to apply it as a judge. Yet this is the kind of question to which a jury's answer spells out life or death in a capital trial—this, and the questions whether the defendant had "malice aforethought," or "provocation and passion," or "insanity," or the "reasonableness" necessary for killing in self-defense.

I think of another black client, Johnny Coleman, whose conviction and death sentence for killing a white truck driver named "Screwdriver" Johnson we twice got reversed by the Supreme Court of the United States. On retrial a jury acquitted him on the grounds of self-defense upon exactly the same evidence that an earlier jury had had when it sentenced him to die. When ungraspable legal standards are thus applied to intangible mental states, there is not merely the possibility but the actuarial certainty that juries deciding substantial volumes of cases are going to be wrong in an absolutely large number of them. If you accept capital punishment, you must accept the reality—not the risk, but the reality—that we shall kill people whom the law says that it is not proper to kill. No other outcome is possible when we presume to administer an infallible punishment through a fallible system.

You will notice that I have taken examples of black defendants as some of my cases of legal error. There is every reason to believe that discrimination on grounds of race and poverty fatally infect the administration of capital justice in this country. Since 1930, an almost equal number of white and black defendants has been executed for the crime of murder, although blacks constituted only about a tenth of the nation's population during this period. No sufficiently careful studies have been done of these cases, controlling variables other than race, so as to determine exactly what part race played in the outcome. But when that kind of systematic study *was* done in rape cases, it showed beyond the statistical possibility of a doubt that black men who raped white women were disproportionately sentenced to die on the basis of race alone. Are you prepared to believe that juries which succumbed to conscious or unconscious racial prejudices in rape cases were or are able to put those prejudices wholly aside where the crime charged is murder? Is it not much more plausible to believe that even the most conscientious juror—or judge, or prosecuting attorney—will be slower to want to inflict the death penalty on a defendant with whom he can identify as a human being; and that the process of identification in our society is going to be very seriously affected by racial identity?

I should mention that there have been a couple of studies—one by the *Stanford Law Review* and the other by the Texas Judicial Council—which found no racial discrimination in capital sentencing in certain murder cases. But both of these studies had methodological problems and limitations; and both of them also found death-sentencing discrimination against the economically poor, who come disproportionately from racial minorities. The sum of the evidence still stands where the National Crime Commission found it ten years ago, when it described the following discriminatory patterns. "The death sentence," said the Commission, "is disproportionately imposed and carried out on the poor, the Negro, and members of unpopular groups."

Apart from discrimination, there is a haphazard, crazy-quilt character about the administration of capital punishment that every knowledgeable lawyer or observer can describe but none can rationally explain. Some juries are hanging juries, some counties are hanging counties, some years are hanging years; and men live or die depending on these flukes.

However atrocious the crime may have been for which a particular defendant is sentenced to die, "[e]xperienced wardens know many prisoners serving life or less whose crimes were equally, or more atrocious." That is a quotation, by the way, from former Attorney General Ramsey Clark's statement to a congressional subcommittee; and wardens Lewis Lawes, Clinton Duffy, and others have said the same thing.

With it I come to the end of my first point. I submit that the deliberate judicial extinction of human life is intrinsically so final and so terrible an act as to cast the burden of proof for its justification upon those who want us to do it. But certainly when the act is executed through a fallible system which assures that we kill some people wrongly, others because they are black or poor or personally unattractive or socially unacceptable, and all of them quite freakishly in the sense that whether a man lives or dies for any particular crime is a matter of luck and happenstance, *then,* at the least, the burden of justifying capital punishment lies fully and heavily on its proponents.

II. Let us consider those justifications. The first and the oldest is the concept of *retribution:* an eye for an eye, a life for a life. You may or may not believe in this kind of retribution, but I will not waste your time debating it because it cannot honestly be used to justify the only form of capital punishment that this country has accepted for the past half-century. Even before the judicial moratorium, executions in the United States had dwindled to an average of about 30 a year. Only a rare, sparse handful of convicted murderers was being sentenced to die or executed for the selfsame crimes for which many, many times as many murderers were sent away to prison. Obviously, as Professor Herbert Wechsler said a generation ago, the issue of capital punishment is no longer "whether it is fair or just that one who takes another person's life should lose his own. . . . [W]e do not and cannot act upon . . . [that proposition] generally in the administration of the penal law. The problem rather is whether a small and highly random sample of people who commit murder . . . ought to be despatched, while most of those convicted of . . . [identical] crimes are dealt with by imprisonment."

Sometimes the concept of retribution is modernized a little with a notion called *moral reinforcement*—the ideal that we should punish very serious crimes very severely in order to demonstrate how much we abhor them. The trouble with *this* justification for capital punishment, of course, is that it completely begs the question, which is *how severely* we ought to punish any particular crime to show appropriate abhorrence for it. The answer can hardly be found in a literal application of the eye-for-an-eye formula. We do not burn down arsonists' houses or cheat back at bunco artists. But if we ought not punish all crimes exactly according to their kind, then what is the fit moral reinforcement for murder? You might as well say burning at the stake or boiling in oil as simple gassing or electrocution.

Or is it not more plausible—if what we really want to say is that the killing of a human being is wrong and ought to be condemned as clearly as we can—that we should choose the punishment of prison as the fitting means to make this point? So far as moral reinforcement goes, the difference between life imprisonment and capital punishment is precisely that imprisonment continues to respect the value of human life. The plain message of capital punishment, on the other hand, is that life ceases to be sacred whenever someone with the power to take it away decides that there is a sufficiently compelling pragmatic reason to do so.

But there is still another theory of a retributive sort which is often advanced to support the death penalty, particularly in recent years. This is the argument that *we*—that is, the person making the argument—we no longer believe in the outworn concept of retribution, but the *public*—they believe in retribution, and so we must let them have their prey or they will lose respect for law. Watch for this argument because it is the surest sign of demagogic depravity. It is disgusting in its patronizing attribution to "the public" of a primitive, uneducable bloodthirstiness which the speaker is unprepared to defend but is prepared to exploit as a means of sidestepping the rational and moral limitations of a *just* theory of retribution. It outpilates Pilate in its abnegation of governmental responsibility to respond to popular misinformation with enlightenment, instead of seizing on it as a pretext for atrocity. This argument asserts that the proper way to deal with a lynch mob is to string its victim up before the mob does.

I don't think "the public" is a lynch mob or should be treated as one. People today are troubled and frightened by crime, and legitimately so. Much of the apparent increase of violent crime in our times is the product of intensified statistics keeping, massive and instantaneous and graphic news reporting, and manipulation of figures by law enforcement agencies which must compete with other sectors of the public economy for budget allocations. But part of the increase is also real, and very disturbing. Murders ought to disturb us all, whether or not they are increasing. Each and every murder is a terrible human tragedy. Nevertheless, it is irresponsible for public officials—particularly law enforcement officials whom the public views as experts—first to exacerbate and channel legitimate public concern about crime into public support for capital punishment by advertising unsupportable claims that capital punishment is an answer to the crime problem, and then to turn around and cite public support for capital punishment as justification when all other justifications are shown to be unsupportable. Politicians do this all the time, for excellent political reasons. It is much easier to advocate simplistic and illusory solutions to the crime problem than to find real and effective solutions. Most politicians are understandably afraid to admit that our society knows frighteningly little about the causes or cure of crime, and will have to spend large amounts of taxpayers' money even to begin to find out. The facile politics of crime do much to explain our national acceptance of capital punishment, but nothing to justify it.

Another supposed justification for capital punishment that deserves equally brief treatment is the notion of *isolation* or *specific deterrence*—the idea that we must kill a murderer to prevent him from murdering ever again. The usual forms that this argument takes are that a life sentence does not mean a life sentence—it means parole after 7, or 12, or 25 years; and that, within prisons themselves, guards and other prisoners are in constant jeopardy of death at the hands of convicted but unexecuted murderers.

It amazes me that these arguments can be made or taken seriously. Are we really going to kill a human being because we do not trust other people—the people whom we have chosen to serve on our own parole boards—to make a proper judgment in his case at some future time? We trust this same parole board to make far more numerous, difficult, and dangerous decisions: hardly a week passes when they do not consider the cases of armed robbers, for example, although armed robbers are much, much more likely statistically to commit future murders than any murderer is to repeat his crime. But if we really do distrust the public agencies of law—if we fear that they may make mistakes—then surely that is a powerful argument *against* capital punishment. Courts which hand out death sentences because they predict that a man will still be criminally dangerous 7 or 25 years in the future cannot conceivably make fewer mistakes than parole boards who release a prisoner after 7 or 25 years of close observation in prison have convinced them that he is reformed and no longer dangerous.

But pass this point. If we refuse to trust the parole system, then let us provide by law that the murderers whose release we fear shall be given sentences of life imprisonment without parole which *do* mean life imprisonment without parole. I myself would be against that, but it is far more humane than capital punishment, and equally safe.

As for killings inside prisons, if you examine them you will find that they are very rarely done by convicted murderers, but are almost always done by people imprisoned for crimes that no one would think of making punishable by death. Warden Lawes of Sing Sing and Governor Wallace of Alabama, among others, regularly employed murder convicts as house servants because they were among the very safest of prisoners. There are exceptions, of course; but these can be handled by adequate prison security. You cannot tell me or believe that a society which is capable of putting a man on the moon is incapable of putting a man in prison, keeping him there, and keeping him from killing while he is there. And if anyone says that this is costly, and that we should kill people in order to reduce government expenditures, I can only reply that the cost of housing a man for life in the most physically secure conditions imaginable is considerably less than the cost of putting the same man through all of the extraordinary legal proceedings necessary to kill him.

That brings me to the last supposed justification for the death penalty: *deterrence.* This is the subject that you most frequently hear debated, and many people who talk about capital punishment talk about nothing else. I have done otherwise here, partly for completeness, partly because it is vital to approach the subject of deterrence knowing precisely what question you want to ask and have answered. I have suggested that the proper question is *whether there is sufficiently convincing evidence that the death penalty deters murder better than does life imprisonment so that you are willing to accept responsibility for doing the known evil act of killing human beings—with all of the attending ugliness that I have described—on the faith of your conviction in the superior deterrent efficacy of capital punishment.*

If this is the question, then I submit that there is only one fair and reasonable answer. When the Supreme Court of the United States reviewed the evidence in 1976, it described that evidence as "inconclusive." Do not let anybody tell you—as death-penalty advocates are fond of doing—that the Supreme Court held the death penalty justifiable as a deterrent. What the Court's plurality opinion said, exactly, was that "there is no convincing evidence *either supporting or refuting . . .* [the] view" that "the death penalty may not function as a significantly greater deterrent than lesser penalties." *Because* the evidence was inconclusive, the Court held that the Constitution did not forbid judgment either way. But if the evidence is inconclusive, is it *your* judgment that we should conclusively kill people on a factual theory that the evidence does not conclusively sustain?

I hope not. But let us examine the evidence more carefully because— even though it is not conclusive—it is very, very substantial; and the overwhelming weight of it refutes the claims of those who say that capital punishment is a better deterrent than life imprisonment for murder.

For more than 40 years, criminologists have studied this question by a variety of means. They have compared homicide rates in countries and states that did and did not have capital punishment, or that actually executed people more and less frequently. Some of these studies compared large aggregates of abolitionist and retentionist states; others compared geographically adjacent pairs or triads of states, or states that were chosen because they were comparable in other socioeconomic factors that might affect homicide. Other studies compared homicide rates in the same country or state before and after the abolition or reinstatement of capital punishment, or they compared homicide rates for the same geographic area during periods preceding and following well publicized executions. Special comparative studies were done relating to police killings and prison killings. All in all, there were dozens of studies. Without a single exception, *none* of them found that the death penalty had any statistically significant effect upon the rate of homicide or murder. Often I have heard advocates of capital punishment explain away its failures by likening it to a great lighthouse: "We count the ships that crash," they say, "but we never know how many saw the light and were saved." What these studies show, however, is that coastlines of the same shape and depth and tidal structure, with and without lighthouses, invariably have the same number of shipwrecks per year. On that evidence, would you invest your money in a lighthouse, or would you buy a sonar if you really wanted to save lives?

In 1975, the first purportedly scientific study ever to find that capital punishment *did* deter homicides was published. This was done by Isaac Ehrlich of Chicago, who is not a criminologist but an economist. Using regression analysis involving an elaborate mathematical model, Ehrlich reported that every execution deterred something like eight murders. Naturally, supporters of capital punishment hurriedly clambered on the Ehrlich bandwagon.

Unhappily, for them, the wagon was a factory reject. Several distinguished econometricians—including a team headed by Lawrence Klein, president of the American Economic Association—reviewed Ehrlich's work and found it fatally flawed with numerous methodological errors. Some of these were technical: it appeared, for example, that Ehrlich had produced his results by the unjustified and unexplained use of a logarithmic form of regression equation instead of the more conventional linear form—which made his findings of deterrence vanish. Equally important, it was shown that Ehrlich's findings depended entirely on data from the post-1962 period, when executions declined and the homicide rate rose *as a part of a general rise, in the overall crime rate that Ehrlich incredibly failed to consider.*

Incidentally, the nonscientific proponents of capital punishment are also fond of suggesting that the rise in homicide rates in the 1960s and the 1970s, when executions were halted, proves that executions used to deter homicides. This is ridiculous when you consider that crime as a whole has increased during this period; that homicide rates have increased about *half* as much as the rates for all other FBI Index crimes; and that whatever factors are affecting the rise of most noncapital crimes (which *cannot* include cessation of executions) almost certainly affect the homicide-rate rise also.

In any event, Ehrlich's study was discredited and a second, methodologically inferior study by a fellow named Yunker is not even worth criticizing here. These are the only two scientific studies in 40 years, I repeat, which have ever purported to find deterrence. On the other hand, several recent studies have been completed by researchers who adopted Ehrlich's basic regression-analysis approach but corrected its defects. Peter Passell did such a study finding no deterrence. Kenneth Avio did such a study finding no deterrence. Brian Forst did such a study finding no deterrence. If you want to review all of these studies yourselves, you may find them discussed and cited in an excellent article in the 1976 *Supreme Court Review* by Hans Zeisel, at page 317. The conclusion you will have to draw is that—during 40 years and today—the scientific community has looked and looked and looked for any reliable evidence that capital punishment deters homicide better than does life imprisonment, and it has found no such evidence at all.

Proponents of capital punishment frequently cite a different kind of study, one that was done by the Los Angeles Police Department. Police officers asked arrested robbers who did not carry guns, or did not use them, *why* they did not; and the answers, supposedly, were frequently that the robber "did not want to get the death penalty." It is noteworthy that the Los Angeles Police Department has consistently refused to furnish copies of this study and its underlying data to professional scholars, apparently for fear of criticism. I finally obtained a copy of the study from a legislative source, and I can tell you that it shows two things. First, an arrested person will tell a police officer anything that he thinks the officer wants to hear. Second, police officers, like all other human beings, hear what they want to hear. When a robber tries to say that he did not carry or use a gun because he did not wish to risk the penalties for homicide, he will describe those penalties in terms of whatever the law happens to be at the time and place. In Minnesota, which has no death penalty, he will say, "I didn't want to get life imprisonment." In Los Angeles, he will say, "I didn't want to get the death penalty." Both responses mean the same thing; neither tells you that death is a superior deterrent to life imprisonment.

The real mainstay of the deterrence thesis, however, is not evidence but intuition. You and I ask ourselves: Are we not afraid to die? Of course! Would the threat of death, then, not intimidate us to forbear from a criminal act? Certainly! *Therefore,* capital punishment must be a deterrent. The trouble with this intuition is that the people who are doing the reasoning and the people who are doing the murdering are not the same people. You and I do not commit murder for a lot of reasons other than the death penalty. The death penalty might perhaps also deter us from murdering—but altogether needlessly, since we would not murder with it or without it. Those who are sufficiently dissocialized to murder and are not responding to the world in the way that we are, and we simply cannot "intuit" their thinking processes from ours.

Consider, for example, the well-documented cases of persons who kill *because* there is a death penalty. One of these was Pamela Watkins, a babysitter in San Jose who had made several unsuccessful suicide attempts and was frightened to try again. She finally strangled two children so that the state of California would execute her. In various bizarre forms, this "suicide-murder" syndrome is reported by psychiatrists again and again. (Parenthetically, Gary Gilmore was probably such a case.) If you intuit that somewhere, sometime, the death penalty *does* deter some potential murders, are you also prepared to intuit that their numbers mathematically exceed the numbers of these wretched people who are actually induced to murder by the existence of capital punishment?

Here, I suggest, our intuition does—or should—fail, just as the evidence certainly does fail, to establish a deterrent justification for the death penalty. There is simply no credible evidence, and there is no rational way of reasoning about the real facts once you know them, which can sustain this or any other justification with the degree of confidence that should be demanded before a civilized society deliberately extinguishes human life.

III.   I have only a little space for my final point, but it is sufficient because the point is perfectly plain. Capital punishment is a dying institution in this last quarter of the twentieth century. It has already been abandoned in law or in fact throughout most of the civilized world. England, Canada, the Scandinavian countries, virtually all of Western Europe except for France and Spain have abolished the death penalty. The vast majority of countries in the Western Hemisphere have abolished it. Its last strongholds in the world—apart from the United States—are in Asia and Africa, particularly South Africa. Even the countries which maintain capital punishment on the books have almost totally ceased to use it in fact. In the United States, considering only the last half century, executions have plummeted from 199 in 1935 to approximately 29 a year during the decade before 1967, when the ten-year judicial moratorium began.

Do you doubt that this development will continue? Do you doubt that it will continue because it is the path of civilization—the path up out of fear and terror and the barbarism that terror breeds, into self-confidence and decency in the administration of justice? The road, like any other built by men, has its detours, but over many generations it has run true, and will run true. And there will therefore come a time—perhaps in 20 years, perhaps in 50 or 100, but very surely and very shortly as the lifetime of nations is measured—when our children will look back at us in horror and unbelief because of what we did in their names and for their supposed safety, just as we look back in horror and unbelief at the thousands of crucifixions and beheadings and live disembowelments that our ancestors practiced for the supposed purpose of making our world safe from murderers and robbers, thieves, shoplifters, and pickpockets.

All of these kinds of criminals are still with us, and will be with our children—although we can certainly decrease their numbers and their damage, and protect ourselves from them a lot better, if we insist that our politicians stop pounding on the whipping boy of capital punishment and start coming up with some real solutions to the real problems of crime. Our children will cease to execute murderers for the same reason that we have ceased to string up pickpockets and shoplifters at the public crossroads, although there are still plenty of them around. Our children will cease to execute murderers because executions are a self-deluding, self-defeating, self-degrading, futile, and entirely stupid means of dealing with the crime of murder, and because our children will prefer to be something better than murderers themselves. Should we not—can we not—make the same choice now?

*T*HE WISDOM
OF CAPITAL PUNISHMENT

Ernest Van den Haag

I

If rehabilitation and protection of society from unrehabilitated offenders were the only purposes of legal punishment the death penalty could be abolished: it cannot attain the first end, and is not needed for the second. No case for the death penalty can be made unless "doing justice," or "deterring others," are among our penal aims. Each of these purposes can justify capital punishment by itself; opponents, therefore, must show that neither actually does, while proponents can rest their case on either.

Although the argument from justice is intellectually more interesting, and, in my view, decisive enough, utilitarian arguments have more appeal: the claim that capital punishment is useless because it does not deter others, is most persuasive. I shall, therefore, focus on this claim. Lest the argument be thought to be unduly narrow, I shall show, nonetheless, that some claims of injustice rest on premises which the claimants reject when arguments for capital punishment are derived therefrom; while other claims of injustice have no independent standing: their weight depends on the weight given to deterrence.

II

Capital punishment is regarded as unjust because it may lead to the execution of innocents, or because the guilty poor (or disadvantaged) are more likely to be executed than the guilty rich.

Regardless of merit, these claims are relevant only if "doing justice" is one purpose of punishment. Unless one regards it as good, or, at least, better, that the guilty be punished rather than the innocent, and that the equally guilty be punished equally, unless, that is, one wants penalties to be just, one cannot object to them because they are not. However, if one does include justice among the purpose of punishment, it becomes possible to justify any one punishment—even death—on grounds of justice. Yet, those who object to the death penalty because of its alleged injustice, usually deny not only

FROM "On Deterrence and the Death Penalty," *Journal of Criminal Law, Criminology and Political Science,* vol. 60, no. 2, published by Northwestern University School of Law, reprinted with permission of the author.

the merits, or the sufficiency, of specific arguments based on justice, but the propriety of justice as an argument: they exclude "doing justice" as a purpose of legal punishment. If justice is not a purpose of penalties, injustice cannot be an objection to the death penalty, or to any other; if it is, justice cannot be ruled out as an argument for any penalty.

Consider the claim of injustice on its merits now. A convicted man may be found to have been innocent; if he was executed, the penalty cannot be reversed. Except for fines, penalties never can be reversed. Time spent in prison cannot be returned. However, a prison sentence may be remitted once the prisoner serving it is found innocent; and he can be compensated for the time served (although compensation ordinarily cannot repair the harm). Thus, though (nearly) all penalties are irreversible, the death penalty, unlike others, is irrevocable as well.

Despite all precautions, errors will occur in judicial proceedings: the innocent may be found guilty; or the guilty rich may more easily escape conviction, or receive lesser penalties than the guilty poor. However, these injustices do not reside in the penalties inflicted but in their maldistribution. It is not the penalty—whether death or prison—which is unjust when inflicted on the innocent, but its imposition on the innocent. Inequity between poor and rich also involves distribution, not the penalty distributed. Thus injustice is not an objection to the death penalty but to the distributive process—the trial. Trials are more likely to be fair when life is at stake—the death penalty is probably less often unjustly inflicted than others. It requires special consideration not because it is more, or more often, unjust than other penalties, but because it is always irrevocable.

Can any amount of deterrence justify the possibility of irrevocable injustice? Surely injustice is unjustifiable in each actual individual case; it must be objected to whenever it occurs. But we are concerned here with the process that may produce injustice, and with the penalty that would make it irrevocable—not with the actual individual cases produced, but with the general rules which may produce them. To consider objections to a general rule (the provision of any penalties by law) we must compare the likely net result of alternative rules and select the rule (or penalty) likely to produce the least injustice. For however one defines justice, to support it cannot mean less than to favor the least injustice. If the death of innocents because of judicial error is unjust, so is the death of innocents by murder. If some murders could be avoided by a penalty conceivably more deterrent than others—such as the death penalty—then the question becomes: which penalty will minimize the number of innocents killed (by the crime and by punishment)? It follows that the irrevocable injustice sometimes inflicted by the death penalty would not significantly militate against it, if capital punishment deters enough murders to reduce the total number of innocents killed so that fewer are lost than would be lost without it.

In general, the possibility of injustice argues against penalization of any kind only if the expected usefulness of penalization is less important than the probable harm (particularly to innocents) and the probable inequities.

The possibility of injustice argues against the death penalty only inasmuch as the added usefulness (deterrence) expected from irrevocability is thought less important than the added harm. (Were my argument specifically concerned with justice, I could compare the injustice inflicted by the courts with the injustice—outside the courts—avoided by the judicial process. *I.e.,* "important" here may be used to include everything to which importance is attached.)

We must briefly examine now the general use and effectiveness of deterrence to decide whether the death penalty could add enough deterrence to be warranted.

III

Does any punishment "deter others" at all? Doubts have been thrown on this effect because it is thought to depend on the incorrect rationalistic psychology of some of its eighteenth- and nineteenth-century proponents. Actually deterrence does not depend on rational calculation, on rationality or even on capacity for it; nor do arguments for it depend on rationalistic psychology. Deterrence depends on the likelihood and on the regularity—not on the rationality—of human responses to danger; and further on the possibility of reinforcing internal controls by vicarious external experiences.

Responsiveness to danger is generally found in human behavior; the danger can, but need not, come from the law or from society; nor need it be explicitly verbalized. Unless intent on suicide, people do not jump from high mountain cliffs, however tempted to fly through the air; and they take precautions against falling. The mere risk of injury often restrains us from doing what is otherwise attractive; we refrain even when we have no direct experience, and usually without explicit computation of probabilities, let alone conscious weighing of expected pleasure against possible pain. One abstains from dangerous acts because of vague, inchoate, habitual and, above all, preconscious fears. Risks and rewards are more often felt than calculated; one abstains without accounting to oneself, because "it isn't done," or because one literally does not conceive of the action one refrains from. Animals as well refrain from painful or injurious experiences presumably without calculation; and the threat of punishment can be used to regulate their conduct.

Unlike natural dangers, legal threats are constructed deliberately by legislators to restrain actions which may impair the social order. Thus legislation transforms social into individual dangers. Most people further transform external into internal danger: they acquire a sense of moral obligation, a conscience, which threatens them, should they do what is wrong. Arising originally from the external authority of rulers and rules, conscience is internalized and becomes independent of external forces. However, conscience is constantly reinforced in those whom it controls by the coercive imposition of external authority on recalcitrants and on those who have not acquired it. Most people refrain from offenses because they feel an obligation to behave lawfully. But this obligation would scarcely be felt if those who do not feel or follow it were not to suffer punishment.

Although the legislators may calculate their threats and the responses to be produced, the effectiveness of the threats neither requires nor depends on calculations by those responding. The predictor (or producer) of effects must calculate; those whose responses are predicted (or produced) need not. Hence, although legislation (and legislators) should be rational, subjects, to be deterred as intended, need not be: they need only be responsive.

Punishments deter those who have not violated the law for the same reasons—and in the same degrees (apart from internalization: moral obligation) as do natural dangers. Often natural dangers—all dangers not deliberately created by legislation (*e.g.,* injury of the criminal inflicted by the crime victim) are insufficient. Thus, the fear of injury (natural danger) does not suffice to control city traffic; it must be reinforced by the legal punishment meted out to those who violate the rules. These punishments keep most people observing the regulations. However, where (in the absence of natural danger) the threatened punishment is so light that the advantage of violating rules tends to exceed the disadvantage of being punished (divided by the risk), the rule is violated (*e.g.,* parking fines are too light). In this case the feeling of obligation tends to vanish as well. Elsewhere punishment deters.

To be sure, not everybody responds to threatened punishment. Nonresponsive persons may be (a) self-destructive or (b) incapable of responding to threats, or even of grasping them. Increases in the size, or certainty, of penalties would not affect these two groups. A third group (c) might respond to more certain or more severe penalties. If the punishment threatened for burglary, robbery, or rape were a $5 fine in North Carolina, and five years in prison in South Carolina, I have no doubt that the North Carolina treasury would become quite opulent until vigilante justice would provide the deterrence not provided by law. Whether to increase penalties (or improve enforcement) depends on the importance of the rule to society, the size and likely reaction of the group that did not respond before, and the acceptance of the added punishment and enforcement required to deter it. Observation would have to locate the points—likely to differ in different times and places—at which diminishing, zero, and negative returns set in. There is no reason to believe that all present and future offenders belong to the *a priori* nonresponsive groups, or that all penalties have reached the point of diminishing, let alone zero returns.

IV

Even though its effectiveness seems obvious, punishment as a deterrent has fallen into disrepute. Some ideas which help explain this progressive heedlessness were uttered by Lester Pearson, then Prime Minister of Canada, when, in opposing the death penalty, he proposed that instead "the state seek to eradicate the causes of crime—slums, ghettos, and personality disorders."

"Slums, ghettos, and personality disorders" have not been shown, singly or collectively, to be "the causes" of crime.

(1)   The crime rate in the slums is indeed higher than elsewhere; but so is the death rate in hospitals. Slums are no more "causes" of crime, than hospitals are of death; they are locations of crime, as hospitals are of death. Slums and hospitals attract people selectively; neither is it the "cause" of the condition (disease in hospitals, poverty in slums) that leads to the selective attraction.

As for poverty which draws people into slums, and, sometimes, into crime, any relative disadvantage may lead to ambition, frustration, resentment and, if insufficiently restrained, to crime. Not all relative disadvantages can be eliminated; indeed very few can be, and their elimination increases the resentment generated by the remaining ones; not even relative poverty can be removed altogether. (Absolute poverty—whatever that may be— hardly affects crime.) However, though contributory, relative disadvantages are not a necessary or sufficient cause of crime: most poor people do not commit crimes, and some rich people do. Hence, "eradication of poverty" would, at most, remove one (doubtful) cause of crime.

In the United States, the decline in poverty has not been associated with a reduction of crime. Poverty measured in dollars of constant purchasing power, according to present government standards and statistics, was the condition of one-half of all our families in 1920; of one-fifth in 1962; and of less than one-sixth in 1966. In 1967, 5.3 million families out of 49.8 million were poor—one-ninth of all families in the United States. If crime has been reduced in a similar manner, it is a well kept secret.

Those who regard poverty as a cause of crime often draw a wrong inference from a true proposition: the rich will not commit certain crimes— Rockefeller never riots; nor does he steal. (He mugs, but only on T.V.) Yet while wealth may be the cause of not committing (certain) crimes, it does not follow that poverty (absence of wealth) is the cause of committing them. Water extinguishes or prevents fire; but its absence is not the cause of fire. Thus, if poverty could be abolished, if everybody had all "necessities" (I don't pretend to know what this would mean), crime would remain, for, in the words of Aristotle, "the greatest crimes are committed not for the sake of basic necessities but for the sake of superfluities." Superfluities cannot be provided by the government; they would be what the government does not provide.

(2)   Negro ghettos have a high, Chinese ghettos have a low, crime rate. Ethnic separation, voluntary or forced, obviously has little to do with crime; I can think of no reason why it should.

(3)   I cannot see how the state could "eradicate" personality disorders even if all causes and cures were known and available. (They are not.) Further, the known incidence of personality disorders within the prison population does not exceed the known incidence outside—though our knowledge of both is tenuous. Nor are personality disorders necessary, or

sufficient causes for criminal offenses, unless these be identified by means of (moral, not clinical) definition with personality disorders. In this case, Mr. Pearson would have proposed to "eradicate" crime by eradicating crime—certainly a sound, but not a helpful idea.

Mr. Pearson's views are part as well of the mental furniture of the former U.S. Attorney General, Ramsey Clark, who told a congressional committee that "... only the elimination of the causes of crime can make a significant and lasting difference in the incidence of crime." Uncharitably interpreted, Mr. Clark revealed that only the elimination of causes eliminates effects—a sleazy cliché and wrong to boot. Given the benefit of the doubt, Mr. Clark probably meant that the causes of crime are social; and that therefore crime can be reduced "only" by non-penal (social) measures.

This view suggests a fireman who declines firefighting apparatus by pointing out that "in the long run only the elimination of the causes" of fire "can make a significant and lasting difference in the incidence" of fire, and that firefighting equipment does not eliminate "the causes"—except that such a fireman would probably not rise to fire chief. Actually, whether fires are checked, depends on equipment and on the efforts of the firemen using it no less than on the presence of "the causes": inflammable materials. So with crimes. Laws, courts and police actions are no less important in restraining them, than "the causes" are in impelling them. If firemen (or attorneys general) pass the buck and refuse to use the means available, we may all be burned while waiting for "the long run" and "the elimination of the causes."

Whether any activity—be it lawful or unlawful—takes place depends on whether the desire for it, or for whatever is to be secured by it, is stronger than the desire to avoid the costs involved. Accordingly people work, attend college, commit crimes, go to the movies—or refrain from any of these activities. Attendance at a theatre may be high because the show is entertaining and because the price of admission is low. Obviously the attendance depends on both—on the combination of expected gratification and cost. The wish, motive or impulse for doing anything—the experienced, or expected, gratification—is the cause of doing it; the wish to avoid the cost is the cause of not doing it. One is no more or no less "cause" than the other. (Common speech supports this use of "cause" no less than logic: "Why did you go to Jamaica?" "*Because* it is such a beautiful place." "Why didn't you go to Jamaica?" "*Because* it is too expensive."—"Why do you buy this?" "*Because* it is so cheap." "Why don't you buy that?" "*Because* it is too expensive.") Penalties (costs) are causes of lawfulness, or (if too low or uncertain) of unlawfulness, of crime. People do commit crimes because, given their conditions, the desire for the satisfaction sought prevails. They refrain if the desire to avoid the cost prevails. Given the desire, low cost (penalty) causes the action, and high cost restraint. Given the cost, desire becomes the causal variable. Neither is intrinsically more causal than the other. The crime rate increases if the cost is reduced or the desire raised. It can be decreased by raising the cost or by reducing the desire.

The cost of crime is more easily and swiftly changed than the conditions producing the inclination to it. Further, the costs are very largely within the power of the government to change, whereas the conditions producing propensity to crime are often only indirectly affected by government action, and some are altogether beyond the control of the government. Our unilateral emphasis on these conditions and our undue neglect of costs may contribute to an unnecessarily high crime rate.

V

The foregoing suggests the question posed by the death penalty: is the deterrence added (return) sufficiently above zero to warrant irrevocability (or other, less clear, disadvantages)? The question is not only whether the penalty deters, but whether it deters more than alternatives and whether the difference exceeds the cost of irrevocability. (I shall assume that the alternative is actual life imprisonment so as to exclude the complication produced by the release of the unrehabilitated.)

In some fairly infrequent but important circumstances the death penalty is the only possible deterrent. Thus, in case of acute *coups d'état,* or of acute substantial attempts to overthrow the government, prospective rebels would altogether discount the threat of any prison sentence. They would not be deterred because they believe the swift victory of the revolution will invalidate a prison sentence and turn it into an advantage. Execution would be the only deterrent because, unlike prison sentences, it cannot be revoked by victorious rebels. The same reasoning applies to deterring spies or traitors in wartime. Finally, men who, by virtue of past acts, are already serving, or are threatened, by a life sentence, could be deterred from further offenses only by the threat of the death penalty.

What about criminals who do not fall into any of these (often ignored) classes? Prof. Thorsten Sellin has made a careful study of the available statistics: he concluded that they do not yield evidence for the deterring effect of the death penalty. Somewhat surprisingly, Prof. Sellin seems to think that this lack of evidence for deterrence is evidence for the lack of deterrence. It is not. It means that deterrence has not been demonstrated statistically—not that nondeterrence has been.

It is entirely possible, indeed likely (as Prof. Sellin appears willing to concede), that the statistics used, though the best available, are nonetheless too slender a reed to rest conclusions on. They indicate that the homicide rate does not vary greatly between similar areas with or without the death penalty, and in the same area before and after abolition. However, the similar areas are not similar enough; the periods are not long enough; many social differences and changes, other than the abolition of the death penalty, may account for the variation (or lack of) in homicide rates with and without, before and after abolition; some of these social differences and changes are likely to have affected homicide rates. I am unaware of any statistical analysis which adjusts for such changes and differences. And logically, it is quite consistent with the postulated deterrent effect of capital punishment that there be less homicide after abolition: with retention there might have been still less.

Homicide rates do not depend exclusively on penalities any more than do other crime rates. A number of conditions which influence the propensity to crime, demographic, economic, or generally social, changes or differences—even such matters as changes of the divorce laws or of the cotton price—may influence the homicide rate. Therefore variation or constancy cannot be attributed to variations or constancy of the penalties, unless we know that no other factor influencing the homicide rate has changed. Usually we don't. To believe the death penalty deterrent does not require one to believe that the death penalty, or any other, is the only, or the decisive causal variable; this would be as absurd as the converse mistake that "social causes" are the only, or always the decisive factor. To favor capital punishment, the efficacy of neither variable need be denied. It is enough to affirm that the severity of the penalty may influence some potential criminals, and that the added severity of the death penalty adds to deterrence, or may do so. It is quite possible that such a deterrent effect may be offset (or intensified) by non-penal factors which affect propensity; its presence or absence therefore may be hard, and perhaps impossible to demonstrate.

Contrary to what Prof. Sellin *et al.* seem to presume, I doubt that offenders are aware of the absence or presence of the death penalty state by state or period by period. Such unawareness argues against the assumption of a calculating murderer. However, unawareness does not argue against the death penalty if by deterrence we mean a preconscious, general response to a severe, but not necessarily specifically and explicitly apprehended, or calculated threat. A constant homicide rate, despite abolition, may occur because of unawareness and not because of lack of deterrence: people remain deterred for a lengthy interval by the severity of the penalty in the past, or by the severity of penalties used in similar circumstances nearby.

I do not argue for a version of deterrence which would require me to believe that an individual shuns murder while in North Dakota, because of the death penalty; and merrily goes to it in South Dakota since it has been abolished there; or that he will start the murderous career from which he had hitherto refrained, after abolition. I hold that the generalized threat of the death penalty may be a deterrent, and the more so, the more generally applied. Deterrence will not cease in the particular areas of abolition or at particular times of abolition. Rather, general deterrence will be somewhat weakened, through local (partial) abolition. Even such weakening will be hard to detect owing to changes in many offsetting, or reinforcing, factors.

For all these reasons, I doubt that the presence or absence of a deterrent effect of the death penalty is likely to be demonstrable by statistical means. The statistics presented by Prof. Sellin *et al.* show only that there is no statistical proof for the deterrent effect of the death penalty. But they do not show that there is no deterrent effect. Not to demonstrate presence of the effect is not the same as to demonstrate its absence; certainly not when there are plausible explanations for the nondemonstrability of the effect.

It is on our uncertainty that the case for deterrence must rest.

VI

If we do not know whether the death penalty will deter others, we are confronted with two uncertainties. If we impose the death penalty, and achieve no deterrent effect thereby, the life of a convicted murderer has been expended in vain (from a deterrent viewpoint). There is a net loss. If we impose the death sentence and thereby deter some future murderers, we spared the lives of some future victims (the prospective murderers gain too; they are spared punishment because they were deterred). In this case, the death penalty has led to a net gain, unless the life of a convicted murderer is valued more highly than that of the unknown victim, or victims (and the non-imprisonment of the deterred nonmurderer).

The calculation can be turned around, of course. The absence of the death penalty may harm no one and therefore produce a gain—the life of the convicted murderer. Or it may kill future victims of murderers who could have been deterred, and thus produce a loss—their life.

To be sure, we must risk something certain—the death (or life) of the convicted man, for something uncertain—the death (or life) of the victims of murderers who may be deterred. This is in the nature of uncertainty—when we invest, or gamble, we risk the money we have for an uncertain gain. Many human actions, most commitments—including marriage and crime—share this characteristic with the deterrent purpose of any penalization, and with its rehabilitative purpose (and even with the protective).

More proof is demanded for the deterrent effect of the death penalty than is demanded for the deterrent effect of other penalties. This is not justified by the absence of other utilitarian purposes such as protection and rehabilitation; they involve no less uncertainty than deterrence.

Irrevocability may support a demand for some reason to expect more deterrence than revocable penalties might produce, but not a demand for more proof of deterrence, as has been pointed out above. The reason for expecting more deterrence lies in the greater severity; the terrifying effect inherent in finality. Since it seems more important to spare victims than to spare murderers, the burden of proving that the greater severity inherent in irrevocability adds nothing to deterrence lies on those who oppose capital punishment. Proponents of the death penalty need show only that there is no more uncertainty about it than about greater severity in general.

The demand that the death penalty be proved more deterrent than alternatives can not be satisfied any more than the demand that six years in prison be proved to be more deterrent than three. But the uncertainty which confronts us favors the death penalty as long as by imposing it we might save future victims of murder. This effect is as plausible as the general idea that penalties have deterrent effects which increase with their severity.

Though we have no proof of the positive deterrence of the penalty, we also have no proof of zero, or negative effectiveness. I believe we have no right to risk additional future victims of murder for the sake of sparing convicted murderers; on the contrary; our moral obligation is to risk the possible ineffectiveness of executions. However rationalized, the opposite view appears to be motivated by the simple fact that executions are more subjected to social control than murder. However, this applies to all penalties and does not argue for the abolition of any.

QUESTIONS FOR DISCUSSION

1. How significant is the statistical evidence cited by Amsterdam against the claim that capital punishment deters violent crime? Is Van den Haag right in claiming that the lack of evidence FOR deterrence is not a good argument AGAINST deterrence? Is the lack of evidence, after years of research, for the success value of a cancer-treatment substance a good argument or a poor argument for the Federal Drug Administration to authorize sale of that substance as a cure for cancer?

2. Is the principle of the sanctity of human life violated more grievously by executing a convicted murderer, or by failing to prevent the murder of an innocent victim?

3. Why does Amsterdam think that capital punishment is morally worse than most criminal acts of murder?

4. Does the fact that it is the state and not the private citizen who carries out the death penalty relieve the private citizen (that is, you and me) of moral responsibility for killing?

5. Is Amsterdam right that the brutalizing effect on society of institutionalized killing outweighs whatever positive value capital punishment might have? For example, would you mind living next door to a professional executioner?

6. Do you think it proper for doctors to provide lethal injections to ensure minimum pain for the condemned?

7. Discuss Van den Haag's claim that not putting convicted murderers to death unfairly risks the lives of future victims of murder. Is it unfair to risk the lives of future victims of automobile accidents by raising the speed limit?

8. Some who condemn capital punishment condone political assassination. Is it more consistent to condemn the political assassination of brutal dictators while supporting capital punishment?

9. Many people support capital punishment on the ground that it is unfair to tax innocent citizens in order to support murderers in prison. Do you agree?

SUGGESTED READINGS

AQUINAS, ST., *Summa Theologica,* Book II, Part II, trans. Dominican Fathers, Benziger Brothers, New York, 1925.

ARISTOTLE, *Nichomachean Ethics,* Book V, trans. J. A. K. Thomson, Penguin Books, Baltimore, 1955.

BEDAU, H. A., ed., *The Death Penalty in America,* Anchor Books, Garden City, 1964.

BENTHAM, J., *An Introduction to the Principles of Morals and Legislation,* Hafner, New York, 1948.

BOWERS, W., *Executions in America,* Lexington Books, Lexington, Mass., 1974.

CALVERT, B., "Retribution, Arbitrariness and the Death Penalty," *Journal of Social Philosophy,* 23, 3 (1992), 140–65.

CAMUS, A., *Reflections on the Guillotine,* trans. R. Howard, Fridtjof-Karla, Michigan City, 1959.

COOPER, D., *The Lesson of the Scaffold,* Ohio State University Press, Columbus, 1974.

DARROW, C., and A. J. TALLEY, *Debate, Resolved: That Capital Punishment Is a Wise Public Policy,* League for Public Discussion, New York, 1924.

DAVIS, M., "Death, Deterrence, and the Method of Common Sense," *Social Theory and Practice,* 7, 2 (1981).

DISALLE, M. V., and L. G. BLOCHMAN, *The Power of Life and Death,* Random House, New York, 1965.

FANNING, C. E., *Capital Punishment,* Wilson, New York, 1913.

GOTTLIEB, G. H., *Capital Punishment,* Center for the Study of Democratic Institutions, Santa Barbara, Calif., 1967.

KOESTLER, A. and C. ROLPH, *Hanged by the Neck,* Penguin Books, Baltimore, 1961.

LAWES, L. E., *Man's Judgment of Death,* Putnam, New York, 1924.

LEWIS, C. S., et al., *Essays on the Death Penalty,* ed. T. R. Ingram, St. Thomas, Houston, Tex., 1971.

MC CAFFERTY, J., ed., *Capital Punishment,* Lieber-Atherton, New York, 1972.

MC CLELLAN, G. S., ed., *Capital Punishment,* Wilson, New York, 1961.

MALONE, P., "Death Row and the Medical Model," *Hastings Center Report,* 9 (1979).

MELTSNER, M., *Cruel and Unusual: The Supreme Court and Capital Punishment,* Random House, New York, 1973.

MORELAND, J. P. and N. L. GEISLER, *Moral Issues of Our Times,* Prager, New York, 1991.

———, "Human Dignity and Capital Punishment," *Journal of Philosophical Research,* 16 (1991), 233–50.

NATHANSON, S., *An Eye for an Eye?,* Rowman & Littlefield, Totowa, N.J., 1987.

SCHEDLER, G., "Capital Punishment and Its Deterrent Effect," *Social Theory and Practice,* 4 (1976).

SCOTT, G. R., *The History of Capital Punishment,* Torchstream Books, London, 1950.

WILLIAMS, G., *The Sanctity of Life and the Criminal Law,* Knopf, New York, 1957.

PART THREE

*T*HE GOOD SOCIETY

Our explorations in previous chapters of the standards of morality and their bearings on issues of life and death, punishment and responsibility, were concerned mainly with what ought and ought not to be done by an individual person. We shall now address the structure of social institutions and how such structures contribute to or detract from the ideal form of a just and harmonious society. In the five chapters that follow, we will examine five hotly disputed issues reflecting our concerns about how best to live and interact with others—namely famine relief, population control, affirmative action, the right to privacy versus legislative paternalism, and the rights of nonhuman animals.

THE ETHICS OF FAMINE RELIEF

One of the most poignant moral dilemmas that confronts people in affluent societies is what to do about the poverty and suffering that are endemic in underdeveloped areas throughout the world. To what extent should we contribute money, food, clothing, and technical assistance to alleviate the misery of those less fortunate than ourselves? Peter Singer argues persuasively that we have as strong a moral obligation to contribute as much as we can spare (on the average, he suggests, at least half our income) to famine relief as we do to refrain from theft and murder. Garrett Hardin argues to the contrary, that we are morally obliged *not* to give such assistance, on the ground that the foreseeable consequences of doing so would be greater suffering in the future due to overpopulation and failure to improve local methods of food production.

Singer's plea for maximum aid to the less fortunate is derived from a strictly utilitarian ethical theory. The fundamental moral principle that should govern our actions, he holds, is that "If it is in our power to prevent something bad (e.g., suffering and death) from happening, without thereby sacrificing anything of comparable moral importance, we ought, morally, to do it." This principle defines what has been called "negative utilitarianism," as contrasted with J. S. Mill's more positive Greatest Happiness Principle, that we ought always to act to bring about maximum happiness for the greatest number. The duty to alleviate suffering seems to most people considerably more compelling than the alleged duty to promote happiness, if only because our best efforts to make even one other person happy are so frequently unsuccessful.

One might expect a utilitarian moralist to be less demanding of self-sacrifice than one who holds either a religious ethical view like Mortimer's Christian ethics, or a rational absolutist (deontological) view like that of Kant (cf. Chapter 1). For the utilitarian requires us to calculate benefits in a detached and unsentimental way, rather than be moved by sympathy at the sight of desperate poverty and hunger. The rather coldly tough-minded argument of Hardin against famine relief seems more in accordance with the popular image of utilitarian counsel, of the kind we often receive from the political economists, who speak of cost-benefit analysis and fiscal responsibility, than does Singer's appeal to moral duty, an appeal that people commonly associate with missionary zeal. But Singer points out that both the Christian ideal of charity and the Kantian notion of a meritorious duty to help others in need fail to make assistance to the less fortunate as rigorously obligatory as refraining from felonious assault. It is, he argues, commonly but mistakenly believed that while it is praiseworthy to help others, it is not so seriously blameworthy to fail to do so as to warrant punishment. He challenges this common moral attitude on the ground that (as James Rachels argues in Chapter 4) failing to save life is as culpable as actively taking life.

Hardin does not quarrel with this negative utilitarian outlook, but he maintains, on the basis of the same principles, that we ought to steel ourselves to allow people in underdeveloped areas to suffer and die of hunger and disease, so as to prevent overpopulation and excessive reliance on external aid which, he claims, will surely result in even greater suffering on the part of future generations.

Singer considers this kind of counterargument to his position and acknowledges that it has force. But he warns us not to conclude that we need do nothing to ameliorate poverty and famine. "The conclusion that should be drawn is that . . . one ought to be doing all one can to promote population control" (and, one might add, to improve local methods of food production and distribution). This, in fact, is precisely Hardin's proposed substitute for direct famine relief. But the moral dilemma remains: should we refrain from ameliorating the terrible suffering of people in famine-stricken areas now for the sake of avoiding even greater suffering for their descendants—no matter how thorough our efforts to encourage population control and agricultural improvements, or does our duty toward the suffering now take precedence over our duty to future generations? A Christian or a Kantian would support present duty over future, but a utilitarian, who considers this emphasis on proximity to be sentimental and irrational, must say no. It is not clear what Singer would reply to this specific question. But his point is well taken that those who say we need do nothing at all to alleviate famine so that people will learn to help themselves are merely excusing their own selfishness.

ENVIRONMENTAL ETHICS: POPULATION CONTROL

At least since World War II, humanity has become increasingly aware of itself as an interdependent and fragile global community in grave danger of annihilation as a result of the malevolence of its own quarreling subgroups and the often greedy depletion and pollution of its natural environment. The threat of thermonuclear war, the spread of radioactive wastes, the rapid exhaustion of fossil fuels such as coal and oil, the gradual wearing away of the protective ozone layer of the upper atmosphere, and the destruction of our rain forests are dangers to human survival that have come to the attention of statesmen, scientists, public interest groups, and concerned individuals all over the globe.

Unlike the threat of thermonuclear war, resource depletion and pollution do not menace the present generation. For this reason many people refuse to concern themselves about the problem. They would rather not confront one especially crucial aspect of the depletion problem: the shortage of the world food supply due to overpopulation. This danger threatens future generations to an increasing degree. The underlying ethical problem is to what extent should we, in this present generation, sacrifice some of our well being and comforts to ensure the minimal well being of our descendants? And how strong of a moral obligation does this involve when compared to the obligations we normally try to meet?

The Canadian philosopher, Jan Narveson, considers how best to identify and fulfill our moral obligations with respect to procreation and the correlative rights, if any, of our potential children and their contemporaries, such as the right to be born or, for that matter, to be kept from being born, and the right not to have to compete with too many contemporaries for a dwindling share of the earth's resources.

Narveson proposes a utilitarian criterion for determining our obligations to our descendants in terms of the amount of benefit or amelioration of suffering we produce for later generations and the degree of sacrifice required of our present interests. But, as he points out, there is more than one utilitarian criterion: total benefit, which is measured by some additive method given a constant size of population; total benefit with increasing population; or average well being with either constant or increasing population. Narveson considers it intuitively obvious that the second of these criteria is unacceptable, since it would support the conclusion that we could deplete and pollute at will provided that we produce so few children that, even if their average well being is so low as to make life barely livable, their total well being will exceed ours. Derek Parfit has aptly named this the "repugnant conclusion," and Narveson agrees. Narveson proposes to escape such absurd consequences by insisting on what Parfit calls a "person affecting" criterion: maximizing benefit for just those people whom we expect to bring into the world. The good we should aim at is not the mere existence of benefit, whosoever it is, but the benefit of particular persons.

Parfit finds this approach problematic and seeks to avoid the so-called "total view." This is the belief that we should maximize the total amount of well being, even if it involves creating millions of people who will live in misery—a view which Narveson, Parfit, and most other people consider repugnant. Narveson suggests that utilitarianism should be understood in a "person-affecting" way. We should try to maximize the welfare of certain people, namely, those whom we intend to bring into existence. And we should intend to produce only as many people as can occupy the earth comfortably.

Parfit finds this proposed solution inadequate because of the "identity problem." If we refrain from producing some descendants in favor of others, we do not render the first group (those we refrain from creating) better off, because they won't exist at all. Nor can we applaud ourselves for making the second group better off than they would otherwise have been. If we had acted differently they would not have been the ones who came into existence. For example, if we deplete and pollute at will, many children will die and be replaced by others. Different children will be born than those who would have been born if we had lived more thriftily. It follows that our happy descendants will be well off at the expense of the billions of possible people who won't be born. For example, a woman suffers from an illness that might result in a defective baby and she postpones becoming pregnant until after her recovery. That doesn't help the baby she would have had—it simply won't exist. Nor can the child she does have be said to be better off than had she not waited, for it would not have come into existence. The identity problem is that people conceived at one time cannot be identical to people conceived at another time, so that no particular future individuals can be either benefited or harmed by anything we do now. Perhaps there is no such animal as a "particular future individual"? But in that case, Parfit has proved his point against Narveson: Utilitarian principles that can be applied effectively to what we should do for our descendants cannot take the form of "person-affecting" principles of the kind Narveson suggested. Parfit has no solution of his own to offer—in fact, he also criticizes a solution proposed by Peter Singer—but he obviously believes that we have utilitarian obligations to future generations and he hopes for a coherent way to formulate them.

AFFIRMATIVE ACTION: IS IT UNJUST DISCRIMINATION IN REVERSE?

For the last several decades, beginning with the historic Supreme Court decision of 1954, the United States has been engaged in the effort to solve what the sociologist Gunnar Myrdal has called the American Dilemma, that is, the conflict between the commitment to equality of individual rights on which the nation was founded and which is expressed in its Constitution, and its history of mistreatment of native Americans, blacks, women, Jews, Hispanics, and other minorities. It is not easy to undo the effects of centuries of injustice. The very attempt is bound to produce new injustices and considerable resentment on the part of those who are required to pay the costs of compensation for the misdeeds of their ancestors. The slaughter of the native American peoples by the white colonists and pioneers and the importation into America of black African slaves, followed by centuries of exploitation of their descendants, have finally come to be generally recognized as conduct unworthy of a nation that prides itself on its belief in freedom, democracy, and the brotherhood of man. That question is no longer a matter of serious dispute. The new question is how best to undo the terrible damage of the past. The decade of the sixties was a time of social and political struggles over de jure desegregation of schools, theaters, restaurants, swimming pools, and housing. In the subsequent decade, strenuous efforts were made to achieve de facto desegregation by means of compulsory busing of children away from racially unbalanced neighborhood schools. Movements arose that demanded similar amelioration of the condition of women, children, the physically handicapped, and other disadvantaged groups.

The governmental policy for rectifying past injustices that has aroused the most controversy in recent years is the policy called "affirmative action" by its supporters and "reverse discrimination" by its detractors. Chapter 9 examines this policy. Its avowed purpose has been to improve the racial, ethnic, and sexual balance in prestigious and lucrative professions by giving preference to disadvantaged groups in admissions and hiring procedures. The federal government has formulated admissions and hiring guidelines for universities, professional schools, business organizations, and government bureaus, and has utilized its power of financial subsidy to enforce compliance. This policy has been met with considerable resistance by conservatives and also by many liberals, for it threatens the entrenched prerogatives of the middle class intelligentsia, the very social group that in the past has provided leadership of movements for greater social and economic equality and for the recognition of universal human rights.

The issue of affirmative action is particularly divisive because it seems to require abandonment, or at least qualification, of two principles that have long been thought essential to social justice: the principles of equal opportunity and selection according to merit. Throughout the first half of this century, liberal social reforms were demanding that Jews, blacks, and women be granted equal opportunities to compete for prestigious jobs and social positions, and that such positions be awarded solely on the basis of merit, without regard to race, creed, color, or sex. Affirmative action seems to require that selection processes no longer be color-blind or sex-blind, but employ racial, sexual, and ethnic criteria in addition to that of merit. It is hard for old-fashioned liberals to swallow this new medicine. Hard or not, does social justice require that they do so?

Lisa Newton says no. She maintains that it is contrary to the liberal tradition of supporting equal opportunity for all and contrary to the long respected political and juridical principle, first formulated by Aristotle, of equal treatment under the law, to favor any one group over others for social benefits and honors. She warns that everyone may regard himself or herself as belonging to some particular minority group and on that ground claim compensation for past discrimination, so that once the precedent is set for acknowledging such claims, society will become a battleground of all sorts of groups competing for special consideration. Fair adjudication of such claims, she argues, is impossible when laws defining the precise rights of citizens cannot be cited as objective criteria for claims to compensation. How much compensation to grant to which groups claiming past discrimination becomes a "free for all" decided by political muscle rather than by impartial adjudication, and the democratic ideal of a "rule of law" is seriously undermined.

Newton grants that the moral ideal of equality is wider than that of political justice (equality under the law), but she maintains that this moral ideal cannot be realized by preferential treatment of minorities, because such a procedure would violate the narrower ideal of political justice, with which it should remain consistent. Thus the only way to realize moral equality is to establish and enforce better laws that will ensure equality of treatment for all groups and individuals in the future.

Ronald Dworkin answers yes. The purpose of affirmative action, he maintains, is to compensate members of disadvantaged groups for the cultural deprivation from which they have suffered, by offering them special assistance and opportunities to improve their conditions of life and, indirectly, the conditions of life of their fellow victims. Such a policy will, he concedes, have the effect of frustrating the interests of those candidates for prestigious positions who would otherwise have won out in the competition. Dworkin argues, however, that they are not thereby being punished or deprived of any rights, because no one has a right to a privileged social position, that is, a privilege is not the same thing as a right. Newton and other critics of reverse discrimination insist that only proven merit provides a fair basis for selection of the professional elite. Dworkin disputes this claim and also denies the presupposition on which it rests, that such positions have, in the past, been decided purely, or even mainly, on proven merit. He points out that professional schools and universities have traditionally weighed merit against other criteria, such as social standing, regional balance, character and fitness, and personality traits thought most likely to serve the professional and the community. Few who now denounce affirmative action have ever complained about the traditional employment of these nonmerit criteria. In any case, Dworkin argues, the general purpose of establishing any criteria for awarding special social privileges is to benefit society. Examination grades are an important criterion because they correlate well with high performance, which in turn serves the community. But so also does it serve the community to have races, religions, ethnic groups, and sexes proportionately represented in the most prestigious positions and offices. Therefore the employment of the latter criteria is not intended as punishment, nor does it violate anyone's right to equal treatment, for there is no such right. Dworkin introduces an interesting distinction between treating people equally and treating people as equals, arguing that only the latter can be insisted upon as a right, although critics of affirmative action mistakenly insist upon the former. That it is not morally obligatory to treat people equally, Dworkin reasons, is clear from the fact that a parent, one of whose children is gravely ill and the other mildly ill of the same ailment, is not morally required to divide the medicine equally between them.

If Dworkin is correct in claiming that affirmative action does not violate anyone's rights, but only withholds privileges, then the soundness of the policy becomes a matter of whether, in the long run, it is likely to do more good than harm. Clearly, the policy is divisive, since its implementation has already engendered considerable resistance and hostility on the part of those who consider it unjust. But almost any innovative social policy is bound to meet with strong denunciation by those who must pay its costs. The question is, are we more likely to achieve social harmony by paying no attention to differences of race, sex, and ethnic origin (the liberal ideal of the past) or by taking note of such factors where they constitute serious disadvantages and compensating for those disadvantages, as in handicapped sports events? This would seem to be less a matter of basic moral principles than a practical question to which only future social experience can provide the clear answer.

PRIVACY AND PATERNALISM

One of the most bitterly disputed issues of political ethics has been where to draw the line between governmental power and individual liberty. What may society legitimately require of its members, and what must it leave to their personal initiative? John Stuart Mill, in his classic *Essay on Liberty*, draws that line in a remarkably clear and simple way that has influenced many people ever since. He distinguishes the "private domain" of individual liberty, where the state must never intrude (except for vital emergencies), from the "public domain," which is the proper area of governmental regulation. Mill defines the private domain as all those individual actions that affect only the persons who perform them, and the public domain as all actions that may affect prejudicially the interests of others. Over the latter area, he asserts, "society has jurisdiction ... and the question whether the general welfare will or will not be promoted by interfering with it becomes open to discussion."

As Gerald Dworkin points out, Mill offers two main arguments for his division between these two domains, a utilitarian argument and what is, in effect, a deontological argument appealing to a right to privacy and autonomy that must not be infringed upon. The utilitarian argument, while plausible, is of course open to refutation, since it depends on all sorts of variable factors. Mill argues that it is to the long-range benefit of a society that its members be entrusted with the liberty to make their own decisions, including mistakes from which they learn to do better. Moreover, each individual knows what is in his or her own interest better than any governmental official, and so will, on the whole, make better decisions of that nature than can be imposed by the state.

Mill's deontological argument is that a person has an almost absolute right to act in accordance with his own conception of what is best for him, because that is what it means to be an autonomous person rather than a slave. The one exception Mill makes to noninterference with self-harming individual action is that the state may forbid a person to sell himself into slavery, since such an action destroys the very autonomy that defines the private domain. The interference of the state in the private domain, on the ground that the state may prevent its citizens from harming themselves, is denounced as paternalism, in the sense that the state pretends to have the authority of a parent to make decisions for his child.

Gerald Dworkin agrees with Mill's utilitarian argument that *in general* it is best for a society to grant its members autonomy of action where it is clearly not harmful to others, but he brings attention to the many possible situations in which exceptions can be made to so general a rule, in addition to the few exceptions recognized by Mill. As for the second, more stringent argument of Mill to the effect that the right of privacy must (almost) never be violated, the wealth of exceptions indicated earlier, he claims, shows that this deontological position of Mill's is mistaken and inconsistent with Mill's general utilitarian point of view. Dworkin offers a list of kinds of paternalistic laws, such as requiring motorcycle helmets and automobile seatbelts, prohibiting the sale or use of dangerous drugs, protecting the consumer from false advertising, and compelling workers to save for their old age, which can be justified as necessary limitations on individual autonomy, the necessity of which is recognized by the very citizens whose liberty is thereby curtailed, like Ulysses ordering himself to be bound to the mast so that he won't jump overboard as his ship passes the Sirens.

David Richards, a professor of constitutional law at New York University Law School, defends the more libertarian position of Mill against the somewhat more authoritarian view of Dworkin, with particular reference to one kind of interference in the private domain that most people think is justified: the prohibition of the sale and use of dangerous drugs like cocaine, crack, heroin, and LSD. This seems to be the overwhelmingly majority view in most countries of the world, including this country, despite its strong tradition of individual autonomy stemming from its early history of pioneer life. Richards, like Mill, believes this to be an unfortunate view that should be remedied by improved philosophical clarity. He notes that not all dangerous drugs are forbidden, for example, tobacco and alcohol are not forbidden (at least since the repeal of Prohibition in the early 1930s). Which drugs are and which are not prohibited seems to depend more on which companies spend the most money bribing government officials than on the degree of danger involved in their use. In any case, if people want to take risks to their health for the sake of enhanced perception or mere amusement, they should have that right in a democratic society that respects the constitutional right to privacy.

ANIMAL RIGHTS

As we have seen in the previous chapter, the rights of future persons are a controversial matter, because of their present nonexistence. The issue of animal rights is also a matter of heated controversy, but for a different reason. Animals exist, but of course they are different from us. The question is, how relevant those differences are to moral rights and obligations owed by and to nonhuman animals. It is by now almost universally agreed that, among humans, race, religion, gender, and ethnic origin are not relevant factors in acknowledging rights and duties. But other factors are sometimes relevant, such as age, disabilities, mental retardation, and criminal record. What then of the salient differences between dogs, cats, deer, birds, and humans? Are they morally relevant or not? Peter Singer speaks for those who say no, and Ruth Cigman for those who say yes.

Peter Singer proposes that the social goal of animal liberation be added to the goals of black, Hispanic, women's, and gay liberation, on the ground that acknowledging moral rights as due only to human beings is "speciesism," a type of snobbish and unjust discrimination analogous to racism and antisemitism. He grants that nonhuman animals are intellectually inferior to most (but not all) humans, but he argues that intellectual differences do not justify inequality of treatment. If they did, then most of the human race would be in serious trouble. Singer quotes with appreciation the early nineteenth-century British founder of the utilitarian movement, Jeremy Bentham, to the effect that, in deciding how we should treat animals, "The question is not, Can they reason? nor Can they talk? but, Can they suffer?"

Singer appears to be assuming that animals not only can suffer, but can suffer as intensely as humans, an assumption that Ruth Cigman seriously questions.

After powerfully rebutting the traditional Cartesian reasons for doubting that animals have any states of consciousness at all (Descartes claimed they were automata devoid of any genuinely mental features), Singer concludes that animals' lack of linguistic and related mental skills (such as reasoning) is irrelevant to their right not to have pain inflicted on them and not to be killed. He denounces animal experimentation for either scientific or commercial purposes, and cruel treatment of animals ("factory farming") in preparation for killing them to be sold as food. These activities, he claims, are morally analogous to racist pogroms and genocide. In consequence, he recommends vegetarianism.

Ruth Cigman grants that it is morally wrong to mistreat animals by inflicting unnecessary pain on them, as in nonvital laboratory experimentation and in the factory-farming described by Singer. But she denies that we violate animals' right to life on the grounds that, as Mary Anne Warren argued with respect to abortion (see Chapter 5), a creature with no concept of itself as an enduring subject of experience and no concept of its future cannot hope for a long life and therefore does not suffer a genuine "misfortune" when it is killed. As for being made to suffer, she agrees that causing "gratuitous" suffering of animals, as in hunting or cosmetic experimentation, is cruel and immoral, but she surmises that the term "gratuitous" is vague and subject to varying standards. She sees no reason why humans owe animals equality of concern or treatment (thus no reason why "speciesism" is immoral), and she quotes the renowned Austrian philosopher, Ludwig Wittgenstein, to the effect that, while animals obviously do suffer from pain and terror, as one can clearly see from their behavior, it is doubtful whether they can suffer as intensely as we in experiencing the total defeat of our life's goals that we call "tragedy." Therefore the suffering of animals is less deep and serious than that of normally sensitive humans.

To Cigman's arguments against animal rights others have added the consideration that having rights entails the capacity to reciprocate by acknowledging the rights of others, which nonlanguage-using animals could not possibly possess. Opponents of this view can, however, reply, as Singer does, that infants and retarded humans cannot reciprocate either, yet we acknowledge their rights. Why not do the same for animals? And so the debate goes on.

7

*F*AMINE RELIEF

*T*HE DUTY OF FAMINE RELIEF

Peter Singer

As I write this, in November 1971, people are dying in East Bengal from lack of food, shelter, and medical care. The suffering and death that are occurring there now are not inevitable, not unavoidable in any fatalistic sense of the term. Constant poverty, a cyclone, and a civil war have turned at least nine million people into destitute refugees; nevertheless, it is not beyond the capacity of the richer nations to give enough assistance to reduce any further suffering to very small proportions. The decisions and actions of human beings can prevent this kind of suffering. Unfortunately, human beings have not made the necessary decisions. At the individual level, people have, with very few exceptions, not responded to the situation in any significant way. Generally speaking, people have not given large sums to relief funds; they have not written to their parliamentary representatives demanding increased government assistance; they have not demonstrated in the streets, held symbolic fasts, or done anything else directed toward providing the refugees with the means to satisfy their essential needs. At the government level, no government has given the sort of massive aid that would enable the refugees to survive for more than a few days. Britain, for instance, has given rather more than most countries. It has, to date, given £14,750,000. For comparative purposes, Britain's share of the nonrecoverable development costs of the Anglo-French Concorde project is already in excess of £275,000,000, and on present estimates will reach £440,000,000. This implication is that the British government values a supersonic transport more than thirty times as highly as it values the lives of the nine million refugees. Australia is another country which, on a per capita basis, is well up in the "aid to Bengal" table. Australia's aid, however, amounts to less than one-twelfth of the cost of Sydney's new opera house. The total amount given, from all sources, now stands at about £65,000,000. The estimated cost of keeping the refugees alive for one year is £464,000,000. Most of the refugees have now been in the camps for more than six months. The World Bank has said that India needs a minimum of £300,000,000 in assistance from other countries before the end of the year. It seems obvious that assistance on this scale will not be forthcoming. India will be forced to choose between letting the refugees starve or diverting funds from her own development program, which will mean that more of her own people will starve in the future.

These are the essential facts about the present situation in Bengal. So far as it concerns us here, there is nothing unique about this situation except its magnitude. The Bengal emergency is just the latest and most acute of a series of major emergencies in various parts of the world, arising both from natural and from man-made causes. There are also many parts of the world in which people die from malnutrition and lack of food independent of any special emergency. I take Bengal as my example only because it is the present concern, and because the size of the problem has ensured that it has been given adequate publicity. Neither individuals nor governments can claim to be unaware of what is happening there.

What are the moral implications of a situation like this? In what follows, I shall argue that the way people in relatively affluent countries react to a situation like that in Bengal cannot be justified; indeed, the whole way we look at moral issues—our moral conceptual scheme—needs to be altered, and with it, the way of life that has come to be taken for granted in our society.

In arguing for this conclusion I will not, of course, claim to be morally neutral. I shall, however, try to argue for the moral position that I take, so that anyone who accepts certain assumptions, to be made explicit, will, I hope, accept my conclusion.

I begin with the assumption that suffering and death from lack of food, shelter, and medical care are bad. I think most people will agree about this, although one may reach the same view by different routes. I shall not argue for this view. People can hold all sorts of eccentric positions, and perhaps from some of them it would not follow that death by starvation is in itself bad. It is difficult, perhaps impossible, to refute such positions, and so for brevity I will henceforth take this assumption as accepted. Those who disagree need read no further.

My next point is this: if it is in our power to prevent something bad from happening, without thereby sacrificing anything of comparable moral importance, we ought, morally, to do it. By "without sacrificing anything of comparable moral importance" I mean without causing anything else comparably bad to happen, or doing something that is wrong in itself, or failing to promote some moral good, comparable in significance to the bad thing that we can prevent. This principle seems almost as uncontroversial as the last one. It requires us only to prevent what is bad, and not to promote what is good, and it requires this of us only when we can do it without sacrificing anything that is, from the moral point of view, comparably important. I could even, as far as the application of my argument to the Bengal emergency is concerned, qualify the point so as to make it: if it is in our power to prevent something very bad from happening, without thereby sacrificing anything morally significant, we ought, morally, to do it. An application of this principle would be as follows: if I am walking past a shallow pond and see a child drowning in it, I ought to wade in and pull the child out. This will mean getting my clothes muddy, but this is insignificant, while the death of the child would presumably be a very bad thing.

The uncontroversial appearance of the principle just stated is deceptive. If it were acted upon, even in its qualified form, our lives, our society, and our world would be fundamentally changed. For the principle takes, firstly, no account of proximity or distance. It makes no moral difference whether the person I can help is a neighbor's child ten yards from me or a Bengali whose name I shall never know, ten thousand miles away. Secondly, the principle makes no distinction between cases in which I am the only person who could possibly do anything and cases in which I am just one among millions in the same position.

I do not think I need to say much in defense of the refusal to take proximity and distance into account. The fact that a person is physically near to us, so that we have personal contact with him, may make it more likely that we *shall* assist him, but this does not show that we *ought* to help him rather than another who happens to be further away. If we accept any principle of impartiality, universalizability, equality, or whatever, we cannot discriminate against someone merely because he is far away from us (or we are far away from him). Admittedly, it is possible that we are in a better position to judge what needs to be done to help a person near to us than one far away, and perhaps also to provide the assistance we judge to be necessary. If this were the case, it would be a reason for helping those near to us first. This may once have been a justification for being more concerned with the poor in one's own town than with famine victims in India. Unfortunately for those who like to keep their moral responsibilities limited, instant communication and swift transportation have changed the situation. From the moral point of view, the development of the world into a "global village" has made an important, though still unrecognized, difference to our moral situation. Expert observers and supervisors, sent out by famine relief organizations or permanently stationed in famine-prone areas, can direct our aid to a refugee in Bengal almost as effectively as we could get it to someone on our own block. There would seem, therefore, to be no possible justification for discriminating on geographical grounds.

There may be a greater need to defend the second implication of my principle—that the fact that there are millions of other people in the same position, in respect to the Bengal refugees, as I am, does not make the situation significantly different from a situation in which I am the only person who can prevent something very bad from occurring. Again, of course, I admit that there is a psychological difference between the cases; one feels less guilty about doing nothing if one can point to others, similarly placed, who have also done nothing. Yet this can make no real difference to our moral obligations. Should I consider that I am less obliged to pull the drowning child out of the pond if on looking around I see other people, no further away than I am, who have also noticed the child but are doing nothing? One has only to ask this question to see the absurdity of the view that numbers lessen obligation. It is a view that is an ideal excuse for inactivity; unfortunately most of the major evils—poverty, overpopulation, pollution—are problems in which everyone is almost equally involved.

The view that numbers do make a difference can be made plausible if stated in this way: if everyone in circumstances like mine gave £5 to the Bengal Relief Fund, there would be enough to provide food, shelter, and medical care for the refugees; there is no reason why I should give more than anyone else in the same circumstances as I am; therefore I have no obligation to give more than £5. Each premise in this argument is true, and the argument looks sound. It may convince us, unless we notice that it is based on a hypothetical premise, although the conclusion is not stated hypothetically. The argument would be sound if the conclusion were: if everyone in circumstances like mine were to give £5, I would have no obligation to give more than £5. If the conclusion were so stated, however, it would be obvious that the argument has no bearing on a situation in which it is not the case that everyone else gives £5. This, of course, is the actual situation. It is more or less certain that not everyone in circumstances like mine will give £5. So there will not be enough to provide the needed food, shelter, and medical care. Therefore by giving more than £5 I will prevent more suffering than I would if I gave just £5.

It might be thought that this argument has an absurd consequence. Since the situation appears to be that very few people are likely to give substantial amounts, it follows that I and everyone else in similar circumstances ought to give as much as possible, that is, at least up to the point at which by giving more one would begin to cause serious suffering for oneself and one's dependents—perhaps even beyond this point to the point of marginal utility, at which by giving more one would cause oneself and one's dependents as much suffering as one would prevent in Bengal. If everyone does this, however, there will be more than can be used for the benefit of the refugees, and some of the sacrifice will have been unnecessary. Thus, if everyone does what he ought to do, the result will not be as good as it would be if everyone did a little less than he ought to do, or if only some do all that they ought to do.

The paradox here arises only if we assume that the actions in question—sending money to the relief funds—are performed more or less simultaneously, and are also unexpected. For if it is to be expected that everyone is going to contribute something, then clearly each is not obliged to give as much as he would have been obliged to had others not been giving too. And if everyone is not acting more or less simultaneously, then those giving later will know how much more is needed, and will have no obligation to give more than is necessary to reach this amount. To say this is not to deny the principle that people in the same circumstances have the same obligations, but to point out that the fact that others have given or may be expected to give, is a relevant circumstance: those giving after it has become known that many others are giving and those giving before are not in the same circumstances. So the seemingly absurd consequence of the principle I have put forward can occur only if people are in error about the actual circumstances—that is, if they think they are giving when others are not, but in fact they are giving when others are. The result of everyone doing what he really ought to do cannot be worse than the result of everyone doing less than he ought to do, although the result of everyone doing what he reasonably believes he ought to do could be.

If my argument so far has been sound, neither our distance from a preventable evil nor the number of other people who, in respect to the evil, are in the same situation as we are, lessens our obligation to mitigate or prevent that evil. I shall therefore take as established the principle I asserted earlier. As I have already said, I need to assert it only in its qualified form: if it is in our power to prevent something very bad from happening, without thereby sacrificing anything else morally significant, we ought, morally, to do it.

The outcome of this argument is that our traditional moral categories are upset. The traditional distinction between duty and charity cannot be drawn, or at least, not in the place we normally draw it. Giving money to the Bengal Relief Fund is regarded as an act of charity in our society. The bodies which collect money are known as "charities." These organizations see themselves in this way—if you send them a check, you will be thanked for your "generosity." Because giving money is regarded as an act of charity, it is not thought that there is anything wrong with not giving. The charitable man may be praised, but the man who is not charitable is not condemned. People do not feel in any way ashamed or guilty about spending money on new clothes or a new car instead of giving it to famine relief. (Indeed, the alternative does not occur to them.) This way of looking at the matter cannot be justified. When we buy new clothes not to keep ourselves warm but to look "well-dressed" we are not providing for any important need. We would not be sacrificing anything significant if we were to continue to wear our old clothes, and give the money to famine relief. By doing so, we would be preventing another person from starving. It follows from what I have said earlier that we ought to give money away, rather than spend it on clothes which we do not need to keep us warm. To do so is not charitable, or generous. Nor is it the kind of act which philosophers and theologians have called "supererogatory"—an act which it would be good to do, but not wrong not to do. On the contrary, we ought to give the money away, and it is wrong not to do so.

I am not maintaining that there are no acts which are charitable, or that there are no acts which it would be good to do but not wrong not to do. It may be possible to redraw the distinction between duty and charity in some other place. All I am arguing here is that the present way of drawing the distinction, which makes it an act of charity for a man living at the level of affluence which most people in the "developed nations" enjoy to give money to save someone else from starvation, cannot be supported. It is beyond the scope of my argument to consider whether the distinction should be redrawn or abolished altogether. There would be many other possible ways of drawing the distinction—for instance, one might decide that it is good to make other people as happy as possible, but not wrong not to do so.

Despite the limited nature of the revision in our moral conceptual scheme which I am proposing, the revision would, given the extent of both affluence and famine in the world today, have radical implications. These implications may lead to further objections, distinct from those I have already considered. I shall discuss two of these.

One objection to the position I have taken might be simply that it is too drastic a revision of our moral scheme. People do not ordinarily judge in the way I have suggested they should. Most people reserve their moral condemnation for those who violate some moral norm, such as the norm against taking another person's property. They do not condemn those who indulge in luxury instead of giving to famine relief. But given that I did not set out to present a morally neutral description of the way people make moral judgments, the way people do in fact judge has nothing to do with the validity of my conclusion. My conclusion follows from the principle which I advanced earlier, and unless that principle is rejected, or the arguments shown to be unsound, I think the conclusion must stand, however strange it appears.

It might, nevertheless, be interesting to consider why our society, and most other societies, do judge differently from the way I have suggested they should. In a well-known article, J. O. Urmson suggests that the imperatives of duty, which tell us what we must do, as distinct from what it would be good to do but not wrong not to do, function so as to prohibit behavior that is intolerable if men are to live together in society. This may explain the origin and continued existence of the present division between acts of duty and acts of charity. Moral attitudes are shaped by the needs of society, and no doubt society needs people who will observe the rules that make social existence tolerable. From the point of view of a particular society, it is essential to prevent violations of norms against killing, stealing, and so on. It is quite inessential, however, to help people outside one's own society.

If this is an explanation of our common distinction between duty and supererogation, however, it is not a justification of it. The moral point of view requires us to look beyond the interests of our own society. Previously, as I have already mentioned, this may hardly have been feasible, but it is quite feasible now. From the moral point of view, the prevention of the starvation of millions of people outside our society must be considered at least as pressing as the upholding of property norms within our society.

It has been argued by some writers, among them Sidgwick and Urmson, that we need to have a basic moral code which is not too far beyond the capacities of the ordinary man, for otherwise there will be a general breakdown of compliance with the moral code. Crudely stated, this argument suggests that if we tell people that they ought to refrain from murder and give everything they do not really need to famine relief, they will do neither, whereas if we tell them that they ought to refrain from murder and that it is good to give to famine relief but not wrong not to do so, they will at least refrain from murder. The issue here is: Where should we draw the line between conduct that is required and conduct that is good although not required, so as to get the best possible result? This would seem to be an empirical question, although a very difficult one. One objection to the Sidgwick-Urmson line of argument is that it takes insufficient account of the effect that moral standards can have on the decisions we make. Given a society in which a wealthy man who gives five percent of his income to famine relief is regarded as most generous, it is not surprising that a proposal that we all ought to give away half our incomes will be thought to be absurdly unrealistic. In a society which held that no man should have more than enough while others have less than they need, such a proposal might seem narrow-minded. What it is possible for a man to do and what he is likely to do are both, I think, very greatly influenced by what people around him are doing and expecting him to do. In any case, the possibility that by spreading the idea that we ought to be doing very much more than we are to relieve famine we shall bring about a general breakdown of moral behavior seems remote. If the stakes are an end to widespread starvation, it is worth the risk. Finally, it should be emphasized that these considerations are relevant only to the issue of what we should require from others, and not to what we ourselves ought to do.

The second objection to my attack on the present distinction between duty and charity is one which has from time to time been made against utilitarianism. It follows from some forms of utilitarian theory that we all ought, morally, to be working full time to increase the balance of happiness over misery. The position I have taken here would not lead to this conclusion in all circumstances, for if there were no bad occurrences that we could prevent without sacrificing something of comparable moral importance, my argument would have no application. Given the present conditions in many parts of the world, however, it does follow from my argument that we ought, morally, to be working full time to relieve great suffering of the sort that occurs as a result of famine or other disasters. Of course, mitigating circumstances can be adduced—for instance, that if we wear ourselves out through overwork, we shall be less effective than we would otherwise have been. Nevertheless, when all considerations of this sort have been taken into account, the conclusion remains: we ought to be preventing as much suffering as we can without sacrificing something else of comparable moral importance. This conclusion is one which we may be reluctant to face. I cannot see, though, why it should be regarded as a criticism of the position for which I have argued, rather than a criticism of our ordinary standards of behavior. Since most people are self-interested to some degree, very few of us are likely to do everything that we ought to do. It would, however, hardly be honest to take this as evidence that it is not the case that we ought to do it.

It may still be thought that my conclusions are so wildly out of line with what everyone else thinks and has always thought that there must be something wrong with the argument somewhere. In order to show that my conclusions, while certainly contrary to contemporary Western moral standards, would not have seemed so extraordinary at other times and in other places, I would like to quote a passage from a writer not normally thought of as a way-out radical, Thomas Aquinas.

> Now, according to the natural order instituted by divine providence, material goods are provided for the satisfaction of human needs. Therefore the division and appropriation of property, which proceeds from human law, must not hinder the satisfaction of man's necessity from such goods. Equally, whatever a man has in superabundance is owed, of natural right, to the poor for their sustenance. So Ambrosius says, and it is also to be found in the *Decretum Gratiani:* "The bread which you withhold belongs to the hungry; the clothing you shut away, to the naked; and the money you bury in the earth is the redemption and freedom of the penniless."

I now want to consider a number of points, more practical than philosophical, which are relevant to the application of the moral conclusion we have reached. These points challenge not the idea that we ought to be doing all we can to prevent starvation, but the idea that giving away a great deal of money is the best means to this end.

It is sometimes said that overseas aid should be a government responsibility, and that therefore one ought not to give to privately run charities. Giving privately, it is said, allows the government and the noncontributing members of society to escape their responsibilities.

This argument seems to assume that the more people there are who give to privately organized famine relief funds, the less likely it is that the government will take over full responsibility for such aid. This assumption is unsupported, and does not strike me as at all plausible. The opposite view—that if no one gives voluntarily, a government will assume that its citizens are uninterested in famine relief and would not wish to be forced into giving aid—seems more plausible. In any case, unless there were a definite probability that by refusing to give one would be helping to bring about massive government assistance, people who do refuse to make voluntary contributions are refusing to prevent a certain amount of suffering without being able to point to any tangible beneficial consequence of their refusal. So the onus of showing how their refusal will bring about government action is on those who refuse to give.

I do not, of course, want to dispute the contention that governments of affluent nations should be giving many times the amount of genuine, no-strings-attached aid that they are giving now. I agree, too, that giving privately is not enough, and that we ought to be campaigning actively for entirely new standards for both public and private contributions to famine relief. Indeed, I would sympathize with someone who thought that campaigning was more important than giving oneself, although I doubt whether preaching what one does not practice would be very effective. Unfortunately, for many people the idea that "it's the government's responsibility" is a reason for not giving which does not appear to entail any political action either.

Another, more serious reason for not giving to famine relief funds is that until there is effective population control, relieving famine merely postpones starvation. If we save the Bengal refugees now, others, perhaps the children of these refugees, will face starvation in a few years' time. In support of this, one may cite the now well-known facts about the population explosion and the relatively limited scope for expanded production.

This point, like the previous one, is an argument against relieving suffering that is happening now, because of a belief about what might happen in the future; it is unlike the previous point in that very good evidence can be adduced in support of this belief about the future. I will not go into the evidence here. I accept that the earth cannot support indefinitely a population rising at the present rate. This certainly poses a problem for anyone who thinks it important to prevent famine. Again, however, one could accept the argument without drawing the conclusion that it absolves one from any obligation to do anything to prevent famine. The conclusion that should be drawn is that the best means of preventing famine, in the long run, is population control. It would then follow from the position reached earlier that one ought to be doing all one can to promote population control (unless one held that all forms of population control were wrong in themselves, or would have significantly bad consequences). Since there are organizations working specifically for population control, one would then support them rather than more orthodox methods of preventing famine.

A third point raised by the conclusion reached earlier relates to the question of just how much we all ought to be giving away. One possibility, which has already been mentioned, is that we ought to give until we reach the level of marginal utility—that is, the level at which, by giving more, I would cause as much suffering to myself or my dependents as I would relieve by my gift. This would mean, of course, that one would reduce oneself to very near the material circumstances of a Bengali refugee. It will be recalled that earlier I put forward both a strong and a moderate version of the principle of preventing bad occurrences. The strong version, which required us to prevent bad things from happening unless in doing so we would be sacrificing something of comparable moral significance, does seem to require reducing ourselves to the level of marginal utility. I should also say that the strong version seems to me to be the correct one. I proposed the more moderate version—that we should prevent bad occurrences unless, to do so, we had to sacrifice something morally significant—only in order to show that even on this surely undeniable principle a great change in our way of life is required. On the more moderate principle, it may not follow that we ought to reduce ourselves to the level of marginal utility, for one might hold that to reduce oneself and one's family to this level is to cause something significantly bad to happen. Whether this is so I shall not discuss, since, as I have said, I can see no good reason for holding the moderate version of the principle rather than the strong version. Even if we accepted the principle only in its moderate form, however, it should be clear that we would have to give away enough to ensure that the consumer society, dependent as it is on people spending on trivia rather than giving to famine relief, would slow down and perhaps disappear entirely. There are several reasons why this would be desirable in itself. The value and necessity of economic growth are now being questioned not only by conservationists, but by economists as well. There is no doubt, too, that the consumer society has had a distorting effect on the goals and purposes of its members. Yet looking at the matter purely from the point of view of overseas aid, there must be a limit to the extent to which we should deliberately slow down our economy; for it might be the case that if we gave away, say, forty percent of our Gross National Product, we would slow down the economy so much that in absolute terms we would be giving less than if we gave twenty-five percent of the much larger GNP that we would have if we limited our contribution to this smaller percentage.

I mention this only as an indication of the sort of factor that one would have to take into account in working out an ideal. Since Western societies generally consider one percent of the GNP an acceptable level for overseas aid, the matter is entirely academic. Nor does it affect the question of how much an individual should give in a society in which very few are giving substantial amounts.

It is sometimes said, though less often now than it used to be, that philosophers have no special role to play in public affairs, since most public issues depend primarily on an assessment of facts. On questions of fact, it is said, philosophers as such have no special expertise, and so it has been possible to engage in philosophy without committing oneself to any position on major public issues. No doubt there are some issues of social policy and foreign policy about which it can truly be said that a really expert assessment of the facts is required before taking sides or acting, but the issue of famine is surely not one of these. The facts about the existence of suffering are beyond dispute. Nor, I think, is it disputed that we can do something about it, either through orthodox methods of famine relief or through population control or both. This is therefore an issue on which philosophers are competent to take a position. The issue is one which faces everyone who has more money than he needs to support himself and his dependents, or who is in a position to take some sort of political action. These categories must include practically every teacher and student of philosophy in the universities of the Western world. If philosophy is to deal with matters that are relevant to both teachers and students, this is an issue that philosophers should discuss.

Discussion, though, is not enough. What is the point of relating philosophy to public (and personal) affairs if we do not take our conclusions seriously? In this instance, taking our conclusion seriously means acting upon it. The philosopher will not find it any easier than anyone else to alter his attitudes and way of life to the extent that, if I am right, is involved in doing everything that we ought to be doing. At the very least, though, one can make a start. The philosopher who does so will have to sacrifice some of the benefits of the consumer society, but he can find compensation in the satisfaction of a way of life in which theory and practice, if not yet in harmony, are at least coming together.

*T*HE ERROR OF FAMINE RELIEF

Garrett Hardin

Environmentalists use the metaphor of the earth as a "spaceship" in trying to persuade countries, industries and people to stop wasting and polluting our natural resources. Since we all share life on this planet, they argue, no single person or institution has the right to destroy, waste, or use more than a fair share of its resources.

But does everyone on earth have an equal right to an equal share of its resources? The spaceship metaphor can be dangerous when used by misguided idealists to justify suicidal policies for sharing our resources through uncontrolled immigration and foreign aid. In their enthusiastic but unrealistic generosity, they confuse the ethics of a spaceship with those of a lifeboat.

A true spaceship would have to be under the control of a captain, since no ship could possibly survive if its course were determined by committee. Spaceship Earth certainly has no captain; the United Nations is merely a toothless tiger, with little power to enforce any policy upon its bickering members.

If we divide the world crudely into rich nations and poor nations, two thirds of them are desperately poor, and only one third comparatively rich, with the United States the wealthiest of all. Metaphorically each rich nation can be seen as a lifeboat full of comparatively rich people. In the ocean outside each lifeboat swim the poor of the world, who would like to get in, or at least to share some of the wealth. What should the lifeboat passengers do?

First, we must recognize the limited capacity of any lifeboat. For example, a nation's land has a limited capacity to support a population and as the current energy crisis has shown us, in some ways we have already exceeded the carrying capacity of our land.

ADRIFT IN A MORAL SEA

So here we sit, say fifty people in our lifeboat. To be generous, let us assume it has room for ten more, making a total capacity of sixty. Suppose the fifty of us in the lifeboat see 100 others swimming in the water outside, begging for admission to our boat or for handouts. We have several options: we may be tempted to live by the Christian ideal of being "our brother's keeper," or by the Marxist ideal of "to each according to his needs." Since the needs of all in the water are the same, and since they can all be seen as "our brothers," we could take them all into our boat, making a total of 150 in a boat designed for sixty. The boat swamps, everyone drowns. Complete justice, complete catastrophe.

Since the boat has an unused excess capacity of ten more passengers, we could admit just ten more to it. But which ten do we let in? How do we choose? Do we pick the best ten, the neediest ten, "first come, first served"? And what do we say to the ninety we exclude? If we do let an extra ten into our lifeboat, we will have lost our "safety factor," an engineering principle of critical importance. For example, if we don't leave room for excess capacity as a safety factor in our country's agriculture, a new plant disease or a bad change in the weather could have disastrous consequences.

Suppose we decide to preserve our small safety factor and admit no more to the lifeboat. Our survival is then possible, although we shall have to be constantly on guard against boarding parties.

While this last solution clearly offers the only means of our survival, it is morally abhorrent to many people. Some say they feel guilty about their good luck. My reply is simple: "Get out and yield your place to others." This may solve the problem of the guilt-ridden person's conscience, but it does not change the ethics of the lifeboat. The needy person to whom the guilt-ridden person yields his place will not himself feel guilty about this good luck. If he did, he would not climb aboard. The net result of conscience-stricken people giving up their unjustly held seats is the elimination of that sort of conscience from the lifeboat.

This is the basic metaphor within which we must work out our solutions. Let us now enrich the image, step by step, with substantive additions from the real world, a world that must solve real and pressing problems of overpopulation and hunger.

The harsh ethics of the lifeboat become even harsher when we consider the reproductive differences between the rich nations and the poor nations. The people inside the lifeboats are doubling in numbers every eighty-seven years; those swimming around outside are doubling, on the average, every thirty-five years, more than twice as fast as the rich. And since the world's resources are dwindling, the difference in prosperity between the rich and the poor can only increase.

As of 1973, the United States had a population of 210 million people, who were increasing by 0.8 percent per year. Outside our lifeboat, let us imagine another 210 million people (say the combined populations of Colombia, Ecuador, Venezuela, Morocco, Pakistan, Thailand and the Philippines), who are increasing at a rate of 3.3 percent per year. Put differently, the doubling time for this aggregate population is twenty-one years, compared to eighty-seven years of the United States.

MULTIPLYING THE RICH AND THE POOR

Now suppose the United States agreed to pool its resources with those seven countries, with everyone receiving an equal share. Initially the ratio of

Americans to non-Americans in this model would be one-to-one. But consider what the ratio would be after eighty-seven years, by which time the Americans would have doubled to a population of 420 million. By then, doubling every twenty-one years, the other group would have swollen to 3.54 billion. Each American would have to share the available resources with more than eight people.

But, one could argue, this discussion assumes that current population trends will continue, and they may not. Quite so. Most likely the rate of population increase will decline much faster in the United States than it will in the other countries and there does not seem to be much we can do about it. In sharing with "each according to his needs," we must recognize that needs are determined by population size, which is determined by the rate of reproduction, which at present is regarded as a sovereign right of every nation, poor or not. This being so, the philanthropic load created by the sharing ethic of the spaceship can only increase.

THE TRAGEDY OF THE COMMONS

The fundamental error of spaceship ethics, and the sharing it requires, is that it leads to what I call "the tragedy of the commons." Under a system of private property, the men who own property recognize their responsibility to care for it, for if they don't they will eventually suffer. A farmer, for instance, will allow no more cattle in a pasture than its carrying capacity justifies. If he overloads it, erosion sets in, weeds take over, and he loses the use of the pasture.

If a pasture becomes a commons open to all, the right of each to use it may not be matched by a corresponding responsibility to protect it. Asking everyone to use it with discretion will hardly do, for the considerate herdsman who refrains from overloading the commons suffers more than a selfish one who says his needs are greater. If everyone would restrain himself, all would be well; but it takes only one less than everyone to ruin a system of voluntary restraint. In a crowded world of less than perfect human beings, mutual ruin is inevitable if there are no controls. This is the tragedy of the commons.

One of the major tasks of education today should be the creation of such an acute awareness of the dangers of the commons that people will recognize its many varieties. For example, the air and water have become polluted because they are treated as commons. Further growth in the population or per capita conversion of natural resources into pollutants will only make the problem worse. The same holds true for the fish of the oceans. Fishing fleets have nearly disappeared in many parts of the world, technological improvements in the art of fishing are hastening the day of complete ruin. Only the replacement of the system of the commons with a responsible system of control will save the land, air, water and oceanic fisheries.

THE WORLD FOOD BANK

In recent years there has been a push to create a new commons called a World Food Bank, an international depository of food reserves to which nations would contribute according to their abilities and from which they would draw according to their needs. This humanitarian proposal has received support from many liberal international groups, and from such prominent citizens as Margaret Mead, U.N. Secretary General Kurt Waldheim, and senators Edward Kennedy and George McGovern.

A world food bank appeals powerfully to our humanitarian impulses. But before we rush ahead with such a plan, let us recognize where the greatest political push comes from, lest we be disillusioned later. Our experience with the "Food for Peace program," or Public Law 480, gives us the answer. This program moved billions of dollars worth of U.S. surplus grain to food-short, population-long countries during the past two decades. But when P.L. 480 first became law, a headline in the business magazine *Forbes* revealed the real power behind it: "Feeding the World's Hungry Millions: How It will Mean Billions for U.S. Business."

And indeed it did. In the years 1960 to 1970, U.S. taxpayers spent a total of $7.9 billion on the Food for Peace program. Between 1948 and 1970, they also paid an additional $50 billion for other economic-aid programs, some of which went for food and food-producing machinery and technology. Though all U.S. taxpayers were forced to contribute to the cost of P.L. 480, certain special interest groups gained handsomely under the program. Farmers did not have to contribute the grain; the Government, or rather the taxpayers, bought it from them at full market prices. The increased demand raised prices of farm products generally. The manufacturers of farm machinery, fertilizers and pesticides benefited by the farmers' extra efforts to grow more food. Grain elevators profited from storing the surplus until it could be shipped. Railroads made money hauling it to ports, and shipping lines profited from carrying it overseas. The implementation of P.L. 480 required the creation of a vast Government bureaucracy, which then acquired its own vested interest in continuing the program regardless of its merits.

EXTRACTING DOLLARS

Those who proposed and defended the Food for Peace program in public rarely mentioned its importance to any of these special interests. The public emphasis was always on its humanitarian effects. The combination of silent selfish interests and highly humanitarian apologists made a powerful and successful lobby for extracting money from taxpayers. We can expect the same lobby to push now for the creation of a World Food Bank.

However great the potential benefit to selfish interests, it should not be a decisive argument against a truly humanitarian program. We must ask if such a program would actually do more good than harm, not only momentarily but also in the long run. Those who propose the food bank usually refer to a current "emergency" or "crisis" in terms of world food supply. But what is an emergency? Although they may be infrequent and sudden, everyone knows that emergencies will occur from time to time. A well-run family, company, organization or country prepares for the likelihood of accidents and emergencies. It expects them, it budgets for them, it saves for them.

LEARNING THE HARD WAY

What happens if some organizations or countries budget for accidents and others do not? If each country is solely responsible for its own well-being, poorly managed ones will suffer. But they can learn from experience. They may mend their ways, and learn to budget for infrequent but certain emergencies. For example, the weather varies from year to year, and periodic crop failures are certain. A wise and competent government saves out of the production of the good years in anticipation of bad years to come. Joseph taught this policy to Pharaoh in Egypt more than 2,000 years ago. Yet the great majority of the governments in the world today do not follow such a policy. They lack either the wisdom or the competence, or both. Should those nations that do manage to put something aside be forced to come to the rescue each time an emergency occurs among the poor nations?

"But it isn't their fault!" some kindhearted liberals argue. "How can we blame the poor people who are caught in an emergency? Why must they suffer for the sins of their governments?" The concept of blame is simply not relevant here. The real question is, what are the operational consequences of establishing a world food bank? If it is open to every country every time a need develops, slovenly rulers will not be motivated to take Joseph's advice. Someone will always come to their aid. Some countries will deposit food in the world food bank, and others will withdraw it. There will be almost no overlap. As a result of such solutions to food shortage emergencies, the poor countries will not learn to mend their ways, and will suffer progressively greater emergencies as their populations grow.

POPULATION CONTROL THE CRUDE WAY

On the average, poor countries undergo a 2.5 percent increase in population each year; rich countries, about 0.8 percent. Only rich countries have anything in the way of food reserves set aside, and even they do not have as much as they should. Poor countries have none. If poor countries received no food from the outside, the rate of their population growth would be periodically checked by crop failures and famines. But if they can always draw on a world food bank in time of need, their population can continue to grow unchecked, and so will their "need" for aid. In the short run, a world food bank may diminish that need, but in the long run it actually increases the need without limit.

Without some system of worldwide food sharing, the proportion of people in the rich and poor nations might eventually stabilize. The over-populated poor countries would decrease in numbers, while the rich countries that had room for more people would increase. But with a well-meaning system of sharing, such as a world food bank, the growth differential between the rich and the poor countries will not only persist, it will increase. Because of the higher rate of population growth in the poor countries of the world, 88 percent of today's children are born poor, and only 12 percent rich. Year by year the ratio becomes worse, as the fast-reproducing poor outnumber the slow-reproducing rich.

A world food bank is thus a commons in disguise. People will have more motivation to draw from it than to add to any common store. The less provident and less able will multiply at the expense of the abler and more provident, bringing eventual ruin upon all who share in the commons. Besides, any system of "sharing" that amounts to foreign aid from the rich nations to the poor nations will carry the taint of charity, which will contribute little to the world peace so devoutly desired by those who support the idea of a world food bank.

As past U.S. foreign-aid programs have amply and depressingly demonstrated, international charity frequently inspires mistrust and antagonism rather than gratitude on the part of the recipient nation.

CHINESE FISH AND MIRACLE RICE

The modern approach to foreign aid stresses the export of technology and advice, rather than money and food. As an ancient Chinese proverb goes: "Give a man a fish and he will eat for a day; teach him how to fish and he will eat for the rest of his days." Acting on this advice, the Rockefeller and Ford Foundations have financed a number of programs for improving agriculture in the hungry nations. Known as the "Green Revolution," these programs have led to the development of "miracle rice" and "miracle wheat," new strains that offer bigger harvests and greater resistance to crop damage. Norman Borlaug, the Nobel Prize winning agronomist who, supported by the Rockefeller Foundation, developed "miracle wheat," is one of the most prominent advocates of a world food bank.

Whether or not the Green Revolution can increase food production as much as its champions claim is a debatable but possibly irrelevant point. Those who support this well-intended humanitarian effort should first consider some of the fundamentals of human ecology. Ironically, one man who did was the late Alan Gregg, a vice president of the Rockefeller Foundation. Two decades ago he expressed strong doubts about the wisdom of such attempts to increase food production. He likened the growth and spread of humanity over the surface of the earth to the spread of cancer in the human body, remarking that "cancerous growths demand food; but, as far as I know, they have never been cured by getting it."

OVERLOADING THE ENVIRONMENT

Every human born constitutes a draft on all aspects of the environment: food, air, water, forests, beaches, wildlife, scenery, and solitude. Food can, perhaps, be significantly increased to meet a growing demand. But what about clean beaches, unspoiled forests, and solitude? If we satisfy a growing population's need for food, we necessarily decrease its per capita supply of the other resources needed by men.

India, for example, now has a population of 600 million, which increases by 15 million each year. This population already puts a huge load on a relatively impoverished environment. The country's forests are now only a small fraction of what they were three centuries ago, and floods and erosion continually destroy the insufficient farmland that remains. Every one of the 15 million new lives added to India's population puts an additional burden on the environment, and increases the economic and social costs of crowding. However humanitarian our intent, every Indian life saved through medical or nutritional assistance from abroad diminishes the quality of life for those who remain, and for subsequent generations. If rich countries make it possible, through foreign aid, for 600 million Indians to swell to 1.2 billion in a mere twenty-eight years, as their current growth rate threatens, will future generations of Indians thank us for hastening the destruction of their environment? Will our good intentions be sufficient excuse for the consequences of our actions?

My final example of a commons in action is one for which the public has the least desire for rational discussion—immigration. Anyone who publicly questions the wisdom of current U.S. immigration policy is promptly charged with bigotry, prejudice, ethnocentrism, chauvinism, isolationism or selfishness. Rather than encounter such accusations, one would rather talk about other matters, leaving immigration policy to wallow in the crosscurrents of special interests that take no account of the good of the whole, or the interests of posterity.

Perhaps we still feel guilty about things we said in the past. Two generations ago the popular press frequently referred to Dagos, Wops, Polacks, Chinks, and Krauts in articles about how America was being "overrun" by foreigners of supposedly inferior genetic stock. But because the implied inferiority of foreigners was used then as justification for keeping them out, people now assume that restrictive policies could only be based on such misguided notions. There are other grounds.

A NATION OF IMMIGRANTS

Just consider the numbers involved. Our Government acknowledges a net inflow of 400,000 immigrants a year. While we have no hard data on the extent of illegal entries, educated guesses put the figure at about 600,000 a year. Since the natural increase (excess of births over deaths) of the resident population now runs about 1.7 million per year, the yearly gain from immigration amounts to at least 19 percent of the total annual increase, and may be as much as 37 percent if we include the estimate for illegal immigrants. Considering the growing use of birth control devices, the potential effect of educational campaigns by such organizations as Planned Parenthood Federation of America and Zero Population Growth, and the influence of inflation and the housing shortage, the fertility rate of American women may decline so much that immigration could account for all the yearly increase in population. Should we not at least ask if that is what we want?

For the sake of those who worry about whether the "quality" of the average immigrant compares favorably with the quality of the average resident, let us assume that immigrants and nativeborn citizens are of exactly equal quality, however one defines that term. We will focus here only on quantity; and since our conclusions will depend on nothing else, all charges of bigotry and chauvinism become irrelevant.

IMMIGRATION VS. FOOD SUPPLY

World food banks *move food to the people,* hastening the exhaustion of the environment of the poor countries. Unrestricted immigration, on the other hand, *moves people to the food,* thus speeding up the destruction of the environment of the rich countries. We can easily understand why poor people should want to make this latter transfer, but why should rich hosts encourage it?

As in the case of foreign-aid programs, immigration receives support from selfish interests and humanitarian impulses. The primary selfish interest in unimpeded immigration is the desire of employers for cheap labor, particularly in industries and trades that offer degrading work. In the past, one wave of foreigners after another was brought into the United States to work at wretched jobs for wretched wages. In recent years the Cubans, Puerto Ricans and Mexicans have had this dubious honor. The interests of the employers of cheap labor mesh well with the guilty silence of the country's liberal intelligentsia. White Anglo-Saxon Protestants are particularly reluctant to call for a closing of the doors to immigration for fear of being called bigots.

But not all countries have such reluctant leadership. Most educated Hawaiians, for example, are keenly aware of the limits of their environment, particularly in terms of population growth. There is only so much room on the islands, and the islanders know it. To Hawaiians, immigrants from the other forty-nine states present as great a threat as those from other nations. At a recent meeting of Hawaiian government officials in Honolulu, I had the ironic delight of hearing a speaker, who like most of his audience was of Japanese ancestry, ask how the country might practically and constitutionally close its doors to further immigration. One member of the audience countered: "How can we shut the doors now? We have many friends and relatives in Japan we'd like to bring here some day so that they can enjoy Hawaii too." The Japanese-American speaker smiled sympathetically and answered; "Yes, but we have children now, and someday we'll have grandchildren too. We can bring people here from Japan only by giving away some of the land that we hope to pass on to our grandchildren some day. What right do we have to do that?"

At this point, I can hear U.S. liberals asking: "How can you justify slamming the door once you're inside? You say that immigrants should be kept out. But aren't we all immigrants, or the descendents of immigrants? If we insist on staying, must we not admit all others?" Our craving for intellectual order leads us to seek and prefer symmetrical rules and morals: a single rule for me and everybody else; the same rule yesterday, today, and tomorrow. Justice, we feel, should not change with time and place.

We Americans of non-Indian ancestry can look upon ourselves as the descendants of thieves who are guilty morally, if not legally, of stealing this land from its Indian owners. Should we then give back the land to the now living American descendants of those Indians? However morally or logically sound this proposal may be, I, for one, am unwilling to live by it and I know no one else who is. Besides, the logical consequence would be absurd. Suppose that, intoxicated with a sense of pure justice, we should decide to turn our land over to the Indians. Since all our wealth has also been derived from the land, wouldn't we be morally obliged to give that back to the Indians too?

PURE JUSTICE VS. REALITY

Clearly, the concept of pure justice produces an infinite regression to absurdity. Centuries ago, wise men invented statutes of limitations to justify the rejection of such pure justice, in the interest of preventing continual disorder. The law zealously defends property rights, but only relatively recent property rights. Drawing a line after an arbitrary time has elapsed may be unjust, but the alternatives are worse.

We are all the descendants of thieves, and the world's resources are inequitably distributed. But we must begin the journey to tomorrow from the point where we are today. We cannot remake the past. We cannot safely divide the wealth equitably among all peoples so long as people reproduce at different rates. To do so would guarantee that our grandchildren, and everyone else's grandchildren, would have only a ruined world to inhabit.

To be generous with one's own possessions is quite different from being generous with those of posterity. We should call this point to the attention of those who, from a commendable love of justice and equality, would institute a system of the commons, either in the form of a world food bank, or of unrestricted immigration. We must convince them if we wish to save at least some parts of the world from environmental ruin.

Without a true world government to control reproduction and the use of available resources, the sharing ethic of the spaceship is impossible. For the foreseeable future, our survival demands that we govern our actions by the ethics of a lifeboat, harsh though they may be. Posterity will be satisfied with nothing less.

QUESTIONS FOR DISCUSSION

1. Of the four general ethical theories discussed in chapter 1, which would you say best supports the arguments of Singer and Hardin for their views on famine relief?

2. Do you agree with Singer that we have as strong a moral duty to prevent the suffering and death of others as our duty not to cause it? Compare to James Rachels's essay "In Defense of Both" in Chapter 4.

3. If contributing half one's income to famine relief requires a parent to forgo music lessons and summer camp for her children, is she morally obligated to do so, according to Singer? What are his "strong" and "moderate" versions of how much a person should sacrifice for others, and which version does he favor?

4. Is Singer right that we are morally obliged to contribute more than our fair share to famine relief when too many others fail to contribute at all? What if giving more would directly influence others to give less?

5. Explain the distinction between duty and "supererogatory" charity made by writers like Sidgwick and Urmson and criticized by Singer. What are his criticisms?

6. What is Singer's reply to the argument raised by Hardin that famine relief does more harm than good because it increases population? Do you agree?

7. Is Hardin right that "lifeboat ethics" demands different rules of conduct from ordinary ethics? Can people be expected to follow different moral principles in different situations, or do emergencies require coercive intervention by a higher authority such as a ship's officer in a lifeboat, or a government in times of drought or flood?

8. Why is the World Food Bank plan criticized by Hardin? Why is he opposed to it? Would his argument support private charities as against government programs?

9. What forms of assistance does Hardin claim should be given by affluent nations to disadvantaged nations? To what extent does Singer agree?

SUGGESTED READINGS

DENUYL, D., "The Right to Welfare and the Virtue of Charity," *Social Philosophy and Policy,* 10, 1 (1993), 192–224.

DORJAL, L. and J. GOUGH, *A Theory of Human Need,* New York: Guilford, 1991.

ERLICH, P., *The Population Bomb,* New York: Ballantine, 1968.

GARTH, J., *No Need for Hunger,* New York: Random House, 1963.

KENT, G., *The Political Economy of Hunger,* New York: Praeger, 1984.

LUCAS, G. and T. OGLETREE, eds., *Lifeboat Ethics,* New York: Harper & Row, 1976.

MALTHUS, T. R., *Essay on the Principles of Population,* ed. D. Winch, Cambridge University Press, 1992.

OSBORN, F., *The Limits of the Earth,* Boston: Little, Brown, 1953.

PADDOCK, W., *Time of Famines,* Boston: Little, Brown, 1976.

SMITH, T., "Why a Teleological Defense of Rights Needn't Yield Welfare Rights," *Journal of Social Philosophy,* 23, 3 (1992), 35–50.

TYDINGS, J., *Born to Starve,* New York: William Morrow, 1970.

WHELAN, J., "Contractualism and the Right to Aid," *Journal of Philosophical Research,* 17 (1992), 427–42.

8

*E*NVIRONMENTAL ETHICS

*M*ORAL PROBLEMS OF POPULATION

Jan Narveson

I

My subject is: how do we decide—to whose interests or rights or what sort of values can we appeal in trying to determine—how *many* people there ought to be? There is a general feeling in many quarters that there are already too many, while others hotly deny it. On what basis is that question to be resolved? . . .

A cautionary note, . . . is this: a view about population *can* be dictated by one's views about other matters. . . . For example, if one believes, say, that contraception and abortion are absolutely wrong, and also that people ought to get married and have sexual relations, then one is effectively saddled with a population "policy," and any consideration of the issues to be discussed below would be relegated to the status of academic questions. Most readers, I take it, do not have any such beliefs, and even if they think that there are some moral weights to be attached to such things on their own, they will nevertheless want to know how much weight to attach to population problems as such, thus to strike an intelligent balance. It is not the purpose of this paper to attempt to strike that balance, but rather to try to determine—or rather, more modestly, to examine some of the major questions relevant to determining—what the situation is regarding population problems by themselves.

Let us begin by making two distinctions, the first of which is crucial, I think, to the question, the second of which is of some importance, especially for focusing intuitions about certain issues. The first distinction is that between a problem essentially concerned with justice and rights, or "perfect" duties and obligations, and one which is purely a matter of better and worse. The other distinction is one of points of view, in particular that of an administrator or legislator, concerned only to secure the best public policy and effective administration thereof, and that of the concerned parent or would-be parent or involved citizen who stands to gain or lose by one policy or another. These distinctions, of course, cut across each other, since persons occupying either sort of viewpoint could and normally would be inclined to use the language of either rights or values in various situations. The reason why the former distinction may be essential here is that rights and duties can hold only between persons, whereas there is no comparable restriction in the language of values. The latter distinction makes some difference because of the likelihood that we will make different judgments from these different viewpoints, and these differences might affect one's total judgment on the question. I will be more precise about these points in the course of the discussion.

II

If population policy is determined by rights, then whose rights are involved? And which of their rights are relevant? If we assume, as we are nowadays inclined to do, that every human being, just as such, has some fundamental rights, then it follows that every addition to the population of the world makes a certain additional, undeniable claim upon some of the world's resources, and therefore upon the rest of us who happen to control those resources. These claims must then be balanced against our right to pursue the good life in whatever way we please. In a situation where the existing population is very substantial, the likelihood arises that there will be over-population, not simply in the sense that there are too many people for the world's resources to be able to keep them all alive at all, but rather in the narrower and, I think much more important sense, that those resources are insufficient to provide for a successful, rich, and interesting life, a life at a high standard which we think people have a right to attempt to attain. If newcomers are too numerous, then those already on hand may complain, if population control is practically possible, that their right to the pursuit of happiness is being infringed. They might direct those complaints against any or all of three classes of people: the newcomers themselves, the parents of the newcomers, or the political agencies which could have, but did not, impose a policy of population limitation. But to put the blame on members of the first class would surely be unreasonable, for of course they cannot help being born, and either to blame them or, worse, to exclude them from some of the benefits to which we think every human is entitled, would be accordingly unjust. The blame, if blame there is, must fall on one of the other classes.

Blame might suitably fall upon the second class, the parents of the newcomers, if they were in a position to appreciate the situation and to do something about it, both of which require a level of education which they may well not have had. And it might fall upon administrators who could, but did not, make the relevant populations aware of the situation or make available to them the technical means to do something about it. But in turn, these administrators may have been restrained by political pressures from their constituencies who oppose population control on religious grounds, for instance. But let us suppose that neither sort of excuse is applicable. Then what kind of reply could such parents or administrators make? They might, of course, challenge the claim that there is not enough room or insufficient resources to enable the new ones to attain a high standard of life. They might, for example, successfully argue that resources are being ineffi-ciently allocated or utilized at present. Indian Communists, for instance, could point out that the Chinese are neither starving nor miserable despite their actual inferiority in material resources to India, and conclude that it is the social and political organization of the subcontinent which was at fault. Or in a still more philosophical vein, it could be argued that the notion of a high standard of life which we are arguing from is faulty and that in fact only trivial material resources are necessary for the good life. These replies would require one kind of response. We should have to say, for instance, that the Chinese are losing more than they gain becuase of the reduction in political and social rights which their system entails. Or we could argue that some may be able to live well, according to their rights, on practically nothing, but that we should be depriving the newcomers of the chance to choose between that conception of a good life and others which would require more material resources. But all of these views and counterviews may be felt to miss the essential point. For it may be argued, not that we the living do or do not have this or that right but that, in fact, the unborn have a right to life and that beside this right, the others are of less or no account.

It is suggestions of this last kind that raise a quite different kind of philo-sophical issue from any of the other possible replies. To see this, we must carefully distinguish two possible interpretations of the claim that the unborn have rights. One interpretation is that it is those who are not *yet* born, but *will* be, who have rights. And if this is the point, then I think it is undeniable. If we think that all men have certain rights, then it follows that we think that people living in the year 2469 have them, just as much as we do now, and that people living six millennia ago had them, although not much of anything could, perhaps, be done about them at the time. In short, time as such would seem to be quite irrelevant to the attribution of fundamental rights, however much it may be that circumstances, which change with time, might affect the practica-bility of securing them, or the less fundamental ones which follow from the fundamental ones in various circumstances. Indeed, it is just this perception of the irrelevance of time that makes us concede rights to the newcomers, for instance. Alternatively, however, the point may be that people who could have been born, indeed who would have been if it weren't for the operation of (say) contraceptives, whose very right to be born is what is in question. What about this suggestion?

It is at this point that the temptation is strong to invoke points of logic. For to argue in this latter way is to assert rights without bearers: it is, ex hypothesi, not possible to specify any of the supposed rightholders if they are merely possible individuals. To say that they are "possible individuals," after all, is not to say that they are a certain *sort* of individuals, but to say that they are not individuals at all. Indeed, to say that "they" are is a misleading way of putting it, for that is also a referring term without a referent. And if the doctrine in question requires such use of referring terms, then it may be dismissed on logical grounds. According to one view of the matter, sentences whose subject terms lack reference are false, since they entail an assertion that there are things to which they refer; according to another view, such sentences (or statements made with them) presuppose the existence of their referents and in their absence simply have no truth-value at all. In either case, the views expressed by their means cannot be true, which is all that matters in the present case.

The question arises whether the view in question can be reformulated so as not to violate these canons of reference. I can think of only two ways to do this, one of which leads to absurdities, though not the same kind of absurdities; and the other of which changes the subject. The first way is to find something other than persons for the doctrine to refer to. (I dismiss the suggestion that the rightholders are parents, e.g., for that simply isn't an interpretation of the view we are considering at all, but a misunderstanding. That it is parents whose rights are at stake is what we were discussing before, and will be again.) What other candidates might there be? Some might point to, say, embryos. But that would only be relevant to the cases in which abortion rather than contraception was the method employed, even if embryos are capable of having rights. Again, it could be held, just conceivably, in addition to the insoluble awkwardnesses to which they give rise (what of the offspring which one's offspring would have had if one had had them? Which existing germ plasm could we identify them with?), any such view meets with a simple but unanswerable objection: viz., that it makes no sense to attribute *rights* to anything which is not a person or group of persons. To argue that children, idiots, or animals have rights, one must show they are sufficiently like adult humans to be accounted as persons themselves. But "possible individuals" and germ plasms, etc., are too far from having the relevant qualities to be serious candidates. So any such effort to reformulate the position that it is, somehow, the unborn (or unconceived) who have the rights which ground population policy must fail.

The other way to try reformulating the view in question is to argue that the existence of people, either as many as possible or, at least, as many as possible who would meet a certain standard of, say, happiness, is a good in itself and should therefore be brought about. This certainly makes sense, but it involves a change of subject, for it has nothing essentially to do with rights. Accordingly, I shall table discussion of this view until later.

Meanwhile, we should consider another aspect of the subject as it has been raised so far. I have argued, in effect, that no positive argument for promoting world population can be coherently founded on a notion of the rights of the possible people who are not born if a policy of limitation is adopted. Can we argue, though, that a negative argument can be constructed on the basis of violation of rights of those who are born into circumstances which give them no chance of leading a satisfactory life? Here the situation is a little more complicated. If you have a child, then of course he has rights. And if he is born in circumstances where it is inevitable that the things to which he has rights will not be supplied him, then what?

On the one hand, it may be said that the foregoing arguments established that a person cannot be said to have had a right to be born, and therefore to have a right to have been born; and therefore, by parity of reasoning, that he cannot have had a right to remain unborn or therefore to have now a right not to have been born. These would no doubt be picturesque ways of putting the point. Yet it seems, on the other hand, abundantly clear that the person on account of whom we would charge a parent, or perhaps a policy maker or administrator, with irresponsibility at the least when a child is born disfigured, then spends a brief life of pain before dying of starvation, is that child himself. We would say of a person who was disfigured by an act of violence and allowed to starve that his rights as a human being had been violated: so why not say the same of our hypothetical starveling? Notice that there is no failure of reference here, at least: our victim is all too real—there is, so to say, too much reference rather than too little. However, it must also be admitted that if we were to say that people have a right not to have been born, then this is one which nobody can ever have fulfilled. Still, we can say that everyone has a right to a decent life, and that the parents (or others who can be held responsible, if any) of people born in circumstances which make it impossible to lead such a life have in effect violated it. Since others who do have the chance at a decent life have had it fulfilled, we do not have the same oddity in putting it this way. And I therefore see no reason to deny that a concern for people's rights can dictate a restrictive population policy even though they are the very people who would not have existed had it been in effect. But no parallel argument can support a promotive population policy. To argue for a larger population on the score of rights, we can only appeal to the rights of those who already exist.

This latest argument raises the question of how high a standard of life we are going to set before we begin accusing people of violating rights by having children. After all, if we set it too high and maintain, e.g., that people have a right to expect perfect happiness, then since nobody could be said to have even a long-short chance of being born into circumstances which would enable him to achieve it, it would follow that we all have a duty to refrain from having any children at all. But then, this seems an extremely unreasonable standard; and that it is, seems a sufficient reply to the argument. It is enough to say that everyone has a right to have children provided that they have a reasonable chance of living a good life, and that having them would not deprive any other parent of his chance to have children on the same basis.

What this objective does accomplish, though, is the raising of the question of the rationale of rights, at least of this type. Why, e.g., set the standard alluded to at one point rather than another? What is the point of extending rights to have children, or indeed any rights, to anyone? Some may view this as a question needing no answer. They may feel that we simply recognize rights which are there, and that their being there to recognize is simply a fact of an ultimate kind. But most theorists, along with the present one, see nothing but darkness and confusion in such a view, and will want to press on to the reasons for allowing and disallowing rights and their correlative duties and obligations. For this purpose, we need a theory of moral values, or if this is different, a theory of reasons for moral rules and statutes. Perhaps we should just be considering how much good is done by adopting one population policy rather than another. And of theories of this kind, the utilitarian theory seems to me much the most plausible, as well as the presently most popular one. So, with apologies to any who may feel that I shall now be considering everything except the truth, I turn to that view.

III

There are, of course, a number of different theories called "utilitarian," and some of the divergences of interpretation are relevant to the present question, though some others are not. For that matter, it is not clear that all of the divergences are due to differences in interpretation of a single generically stated idea; some may, in the end, simply be different theories, grouped with the others by virtue of being rather more similar to them than to distinctively nonutilitarian views. My reference to "the" utilitarian theory, therefore, may be inappropriate. Still, I hope to supply reasons for giving a certain preference to one general characterization, and to argue from that one. By so doing, I hope to reduce the feeling of intractable oddity which, I shall argue, results from overlooking these essential features.

On any view which unqualifiedly deserves the name "utilitarian," the only ultimate considerations on the basis of which moral appraisals are properly made are those concerning the welfare of sentient beings; and the aim of morality is to maximize such welfare all around. On one popular interpretation of that view, it is each person's duty to bring about the maximum balance of welfare over illbeing that he can. The reason for this is assumed to be that we have as our sole ultimate duty that of maximizing the intrinsic value in the world, and happiness or welfare is the only thing which has it. This, we should note, is a teleological view expressed in deontic language: it is a view about our duty, but the content of that duty is expressed in terms of value, which in turn is assumed to be possessed only by happiness. It is rather a breathtaking theory, not only in the (no doubt deceptive) simplicity with which it can be stated, but also in the drastic character of its consequences. Applied to the present question, for example, it is clear that this formulation sweeps aside any objections of the kind raised in the previous section to an "expansive" population policy. There is no need to worry about quantification over nonexistent people, because the theory is not essentially concerned with their rights or interests. To increase human happiness by increasing the number of happy people is just as desirable as to do it by any other means; and if a greater such increase may be brought about by producing new people than by improving the lives of those already on hand, then that is not only the preferable thing to do, but positively the duty of those in a position to effect the increase.

One score on which one might object to this theory is its use, or at least its application, of the term "duty." If the assumption behind the theory was that "it is one's duty to do *x*" meant something like "the best thing one could do is *x*," then that would be a clear misuse of the term. Whether it is one's duty to do the very best thing possible is a substantive question, not a linguistic one. Assuming that the theorist propounding this version of utilitarianism accepts this point but sticks to his last, then I think it could be argued that the standard of duty proposed is simply far too high, and almost certainly self-defeating. Our duty is what we may be properly blamed, held to account, for not performing. If the standard is set so high that we are certain to fail, then normal people are likely to chuck the whole project: if we are always in the wrong, then let us at least indulge ourselves in the most enjoyable sins, and ignore the fact that there are degrees of right and wrong and that the less than best may still be worth doing, certainly more worth doing than the worst, for example. Other considerations of this general sort may also be advanced: for instance, in the case of the population question, the deplorable effects on people's emotional and sexual lives if they labor under the necessity of producing as many children as possible provided only that they will be at least modestly happy. Such arguments, of course, may show that the idea is self-defeating: for if the classification of something as a duty increases misery more than the happiness resulting from performing it, then it is, on the present view, our duty not to classify it as a duty, literally, but rather a criterion for determining the best, or most recommended, thing to do, from the moral point of view.

The objection about "duty" may be taken care of by introducing a subsidiary theory about the range of cases in which, say, enough utility is at stake to constitute something a duty properly so called. For example, it might be held that our duty is only to refrain from increasing misery and to prevent or rectify it to some suitable standard, further humanitarian activity being accounted supererogatory. This is a complicated business but not, I think, an insuperably complicated one. Supposing that can be done, however, it still leaves us with a theory according to which it is a moral matter whether or not to add members to the population, and the previously mentioned consequences, only now stated in terms of what is morally preferable or less preferable instead of in terms of duty, would still obtain. It would still follow that it might be morally preferable to have some more children rather than devoting the resources they would require to improving the lives of those already in being. This still seems to me difficult to accept. Let us, at any rate, look into the matter further.

The version of utilitarianism we have been exploring proposes that we promote human happiness on the ground that happiness is intrinsically valuable, and that we should promote what is intrinsically valuable. Now, if we agree that something is intrinsically valuable, then no doubt we should do something to promote it, or anyway there is something to be said for promoting it. But is this the sort of ground on which we should promote human happiness? This seems to me very doubtful. I am inclined to say instead that we should promote people's happiness, and reduce their unhappiness, where possible, because they are people and that is the way people should be treated. It is not, as it were, because people are nice things to have around, still less that happiness is a nice thing to have around, although that is probably true enough. Intrinsic value is the particular home, one supposes, of the aesthetic. And we can well imagine people discussing the question of what sort of world is nicest or most interesting, some extolling the virtues of vast barren wastelands and rugged mountains, with a smallish and hardy populace to do combat with its challenges, others favoring a more social sort of place with lots of cities full of varied people with diverse tastes and customs, and so on. Suppose, now, a third contingent arguing for plenty of war, poverty, sadism, and disease. We should certainly be inclined to rate the third view as, among other things, thoroughly immoral. As between the first and second, however, I find it overwhelmingly plausible to say that the issue between them, hence the choice between them, was a matter of taste. Morally speaking, so far as the descriptions go, there seems nothing to choose between them. No doubt there is, in an obvious sense, more happiness in the second than in the first, supposing that the people in each "possible world" are comparably happy. But it seems to me simply odd to count that as a reason for thinking that the second situation is morally better than the first. And this in either the sense that the people in one of them are necessarily better or worse people or, more important, the sense that there is any moral reason for attempting to bring about, supposing one had the power to influence the matter, one of them rather than the other. The third choice, on the other hand, seems evil in both senses, that it would be full of evil people, and that it would be full of misery, which we should avoid bringing about if we can. I imagine that these intuitions of mine are shared by many. Do they make sense?

What I am suggesting is this. Morality has to do with how we treat whatever people there are. Utilitarianism, construed as a moral theory, says that we should aim at maximizing the happiness of people, the balance of their desirable over their undesirable experience. To the extent that a person is less happy than he could have been, where we could have done what would have made him better off, at no or anyway less cost to ourselves or third parties, he has not gotten as good treatment, morally, as would have been desirable. On this view, moral questions *presuppose* the existence of people. If we are contemplating an increase in the population, then we may consider how well or badly the new people would be likely to be in the circumstances they would occupy. But suppose we decide, in the end, not to bring them into existence. Then even if they would have been perfectly happy, still, nobody misses anything; or anyway, it is only we, the people he would have had desirable effects upon, who are missing something. But there isn't any loss of anything by the contemplated party, since he doesn't exist. On the other hand, if we actually do bring him into existence, then of course we must be as concerned for his welfare as anyone else's. Suppose we could foresee that his life would be miserable. Then it seems obvious that a way to avoid that would be to avoid conceiving him in the first place, and that that, accordingly, is what we should do. The suggestion, in other words, is that we can have a moral reason, arising from concern for the welfare of actual persons, for not having children, but not, arising from the same considerations, for having them, so long as the persons in question are those who would be brought into existence by the contemplated acts. There is no moral objection to having children who would be happy, for the duties we would then have to them would be discharged satisfactorily. But if it would be impossible to fulfill the duty to promote their welfare, then we ought to avoid conception.

My previous efforts to press the above argument have met with serious objections. According to one such objection, my view has the consequence that nobody should ever have any children. For we can never be quite certain that any new child will be happy, but we can always be certain that new children will not be unhappy, viz., by never having any new children. The result, of course, is that after awhile there would not be any people left, but then, that would not bother anybody, for there would be nobody to be bothered by it. The author of this objection, Hermann Vetter, professes to welcome this result, but I must confess that I do not. But I don't see why it must be accepted either. If the only relevant considerations in conduct were considerations of duty, or for that matter of morals, then perhaps it would. But this is far from true. On the contrary, nearly everything we do is and quite rightly, done for reasons having no special connection with morals. We enjoy, for example, playing games. In doing so, our reason is usually enjoyment. One runs, of course, the risk that tempers will be inflamed and that someone will be made miserable by arguments about rules, or by losing; or someone might even be moved to mayhem. If you are quite certain that this will happen, that is a good reason for not playing at all, but if it is reasonably unlikely to happen, then the likelihood that you will enjoy the game is sufficient justification for running that risk. There is no need to assume that there is a moral duty to enjoy oneself, or even that there is anything moral about the whole thing. In the case of having children, the benefits we see in it, including the fact that we like having them around and think that the world would be a better place for it, have the same effect: they justify the risk that one might not be able to fulfill the duties which, of course, will be generated when you have the child. But the fact that you would do well by a child if you had one does not mean that there is a reason, arising from the principle that we ought to do well by people, for bringing him into existence at all. If you don't have him, the subject of how to treat him simply doesn't arise.

Another objection, from Timothy Sprigge's penetrating discussion of my earlier treatments, goes as follows. My argument, in effect, is that the cases where we are contemplating producing children are asymmetrical as regards moral considerations. If you don't have a child who would have been happy, then nobody can reproach you for having deprived him of happiness, for there simply won't be anyone to do it. But if you do do it, and he's unhappy, then he can reproach you for having done it. Well, Sprigge points out, it is equally true, is it not, that if I don't have the unhappy child, nobody can thank me for having spared him the misery of life. So "in the first case, there cannot be anyone to reproach you if you don't so act, but there may be someone to thank you if you do. In the second case there can be someone to reproach you if you do do it, but there cannot be anyone to thank you if you don't." Similarly, to my argument that a person cannot be said to be happier than he would have been if he hadn't existed, Sprigge points out that a person cannot be said to be unhappier than he would have been if he hadn't existed. If anything followed from that, it would have to be that "procreation can neither increase nor decrease the happiness of the person thus brought into existence and that his interests cannot be considered as those of "a party whose interests are in question." If this seems ridiculous, as it surely does, we must interpret the utilitarian formula so as to count both cases as cases where happiness is relevantly affected." Does this establish the symmetry which I have been concerned to deny?

One thing which must be borne in mind is that the issue is not to be identified with the other issue of whether our duties, strictly speaking, concern only (say) the reduction of suffering and not the increase of well-being. Rather, the question is whether we are to take the having of (happy) children as a morally commendable thing, something which we ought (morally) to do, rather than just another activity which we may do if we please but with nothing special to be said for it from the moral point of view. It is difficult to keep this question distinct from the other one, and I will not attest as beyond peradventure that I did not mix the two up somewhat in my previous treatments, although I claimed not to be doing so. Nevertheless, I am inclined to think that I was barking up the right tree, at least, and propose to keep at it here.

Let us look at the thing in the following way. When we contemplate embarking on any course of action, it is prudent to look ahead and consider what sort of problems one will encounter as one goes along. Suppose one can foresee that these problems will be insoluble. Then that seems an incontrovertible objection to starting out at all. This is to evade, or avoid, the problems and not, of course, to solve them. But it is the insolubility of those very problems that constitutes the reason for not starting out, even though, by prudently not doing so, one never in fact encounters those problems at all. On the other hand, suppose that one can foresee that the problems would in fact be soluble, perhaps with very little effort. Is that, in itself, a point in favor of embarking on the course of action? Well, surely not! It seems to me in itself absolutely no positive recommendation of a course of action that the problems it would pose are capable of solution. There would have to be something else to be said for it, in its own right; solubility of operational problems is a point in favor only in the sense that it is not a point against. And I am inclined to suggest that the same holds true of increase of population. If you bring people into existence, then of course you must treat them in accordance with their moral status as human beings. And if you can foresee that it will not be possible to do that, or that no matter how much you or anyone tries, you won't be able to succeed in enabling them to live a worthwhile life, then that is a reason for not starting on the project in the first place. Like the avoidance of the course of action with insoluble problems, it is not of course a solution to the problems, exactly: yet the fact that it would avoid them, whereas they would arise and be insoluble if one went ahead, seems a conclusive reason for such avoidance, arising entirely from internal considerations. But like the solubility of such problems, the fact that one would be able to treat, and that others would treat, the newcomer in a satisfactory way does not seem of itself any reason at all for having him. For such a reason we need to turn to such facts as that his parents want children, or that his addition would add to the happiness of the existing community, or that people just like the idea of having more people around. If there is this analogy between the two sorts of cases, then the feeling that there is an asymmetry of the kind I have been advocating seems to be borne out.

I hope, without feeling entirely confident about it, that this argument at least makes the position I am arguing for tenable. At the intuitive level, there seem to me further reasons to think that it is the right line to take. It is widely felt, for instance, that there is something bogus about pointing to the claims of newcomers to benefits which will be at the expense of those already around, in cases where the new ones need not have appeared, given restraint by appropriate parties. There is resentment against certain classes of people who increase their political power by outbreeding the others. The point is not that the newborn ought to inherit the sins of their parents and suffer relative decrement of rights: on the contrary, it is precisely that once on hand, the newcomers cannot be denied the same treatment as everyone else. It is the claim that the unborn who need not have been born deserve as much consideration, so to speak, as those already here which is objected to. To reply to such claims by asserting that the presently existing are simply being "selfish," as is sometimes done, is simple blackmail: for the people with respect to whom the present populace is accused of selfishness don't even exist and won't if their parents exercise appropriate restraint.

The point is not one which can be handled by the reminder that if newcomers create a hardship on present populace, then there may be a net loss in overall utility even when we count the new ones, because of these bad effects on persons now on hand. For regardless of supposed net gains, people will object to *any* real diminution of their standard of life by the avoidable influx of new people. When this is a matter of objecting to immigrants, say, then this attitude is no doubt a selfish one, to some degree. But if it is perfectly possible for there to be no newcomers to worry about, then that seems quite another matter.

If these arguments carry weight, then, people are morally within their rights in objecting to increments in the population if such increments would cause any decrement at all in their present standards of well-being. The well-being of the new people who would be brought into existence if the proposed expansion is carried through cannot be considered at all as a point counting morally in favor of the expansion, to be balanced against the costs to those already here. Morally, we are quite free to decide on any policy we want, short of one which would entail suffering on the part of anyone, including the newcomers themselves. In practice, of course, people do want to have children and are willing to go to trouble and expense to have them. But the same is true of new cars, and yet no one, I suppose, regards the acquisition of cars as a *moral* goal. Increment of population is, no doubt, a community goal in most communities, save monastic ones. But celibates are not depriving people of happiness by refusing to have children, except perhaps themselves: there is nothing immoral, or even slightly unbenevolent, about having no children when one could have had them and the resulting children would have been happy ones.

IV

Still, after all this, a community might be concerned to try to decide just what an optimum population would be. Perhaps this is not a moral question, but it may still be a perfectly askable, and in some cases quite relevant, question. And here it may seem reasonable to use a utilitarian principle, even if it is not assumed that there is any moral compulsion to bring new people into existence. For one might reason as follows. We do, anyway, want to keep the human race going, indeed, to keep our particular strand of it going. But given that we want to do that, we also want the best lives possible for our children. The quality of their lives will, of course, be affected by all sorts of things, but one of the things which may affect it is how many of them there are. For example, the available resources which on our present view are necessary to make a good life, are finite in quantity; have too many people around, and they may be exhausted quickly unless each person's share is reduced, with consequent reduction in his level of well-being. Space to live in is constant, more or less, though it does not get used up through time; there might be an optimum density of population from this point of view too. And so on. How, and on what grounds, do we proceed if we want the best possible community?

Assuming that we have, somehow, a measure of well-being, and that well-being is the relevant variable, then there have traditionally been two interpretations of classical utilitarianism, taken as a view relevant to expansionary population policy, viz., the "total" and the "average." According to the "total" view, one version of which was described at the beginning of the previous section, the optimum community is the one with the greatest total amount of happiness, that is to say, the greatest balance of happiness over misery, or pleasure over pain. According to the "average" view, on the other hand, that community is best, whatever its size, which has the highest average happiness per person. Obviously, the two views are indistinguishable if applied to a constant population, since the average is simply the total divided by the number of persons in question. Applied to population problems of the kind we are discussing, however, the difference between the two is in principle considerable, as we shall see in detail below. But it is worth bearing in mind that any number of other possible views may be defined if we bring distributional constraints into the picture. Some might argue for a community with the highest minimum, or the highest maximum, or the highest median, or the most equal distribution above some minimum level, and so on and so on. I shall suggest some points about the "total" and "average" views, and then argue that on this issue, the other distributive principles may be irrelevant. But mostly I shall be showing how extraordinarily difficult and intractable an issue this seems to be, pending some wholly novel way of looking at it.

If we think that happiness is simply a good thing to have around, then the "total" view is an inevitable consequence. Each addition to the population, provided only that he is on balance happy and that his addition does not subtract materially from the well-being of those already present, must be reckoned an improvement. The best community is, it would seem, quite likely to be the largest, short of conditions in which considerable deprivation sets in. On this view, then, the old examination-question case of two communities, one twice as numerous but with half the average happiness compared with the other, arises, and there would be nothing to choose between them.

If the "total" view is unpopular, I should think there would be two reasons for it, one accounted for in my preceding discussion. It is that we do not, in the required way, think that happiness is an intrinsically good thing. We are in favor of making people happy, but neutral about making happy people. Or rather, neutral as a public policy, regarding it as a matter for private decision. Provided the children produced have a good chance at a good life, we think people should have them if they want them. The other reason is that it seems repulsive to think that the goodness of a community is a function of its size, e.g., that America is a happier country than Canada because it is so much bigger, demographically. If we substitute "better" for "happier," the result is at least as intuitively repugnant. If either of these objections applies at all, then it is hard to doubt that it has a lot of force. The first seems to me quite decisive, if it is true, for it is surely the foundation of the whole idea. The second may be just a consequence of the first. If it is not, then it may just be a reflection of ordinary usage, or of popular opinion; in either case, it would not carry much weight in the present issue.

But the "average" theory, though it accounts rather well for the two objections against the "total" one, has some awkward consequences of its own. Let us consider two in particular. (1) Suppose that we have a particular population of quite happy people. And suppose that an addition is made to this community of people who are just slightly less happy than the others. No decrement of the standard of life of those already present is incurred: it is a sheer addition. Well, on the average approach, we should have to say that the resulting community, even though it has everything that the old one did, and a bit more besides, is a less desirable one. This seems surprising, at least: for normally one would think that if you add something good to a good thing, without altering what was already there, then the result would be even better. (2) The other point might be regarded as an ad hominem, but if so one of considerable force. Suppose that I am considering having a child. I have reason to suppose that it would be a reasonably happy child, one who could lead a reasonably satisfying life. However, I happen to live in an extraordinarily blessed community, so my child would be rather below average. My particular addition would lower the community average, just slightly. Am I then doing something wrong in having it?

The second of these objections may be persuasive only because the theory is too strongly stated. On the formulation that it is wrong to do anything that would not make the greatest possible contribution to average happiness, this consequence would ensue. But if, more innocuously, it was merely said that this would be less than the best thing to do, but not actually wrong, then perhaps the consequence would be less paradoxical. And if the first objection is answerable, then it would also be true. That is, to produce this child would—very slightly—reduce the goodness of the community. But in the individual case, would this matter? What we have here is, perhaps, a conflict between the viewpoint of the impersonal administrator or, for that matter, bystander, and that of the concerned participant. Perhaps we should say here that such considerations might be good reason for adopting public measures which would make it less likely that people would have children who could be foreseen to be unlikely to lead good lives, but not very good reasons for would-be parents who very much want to have children to forego the pleasure of having them. After all, it seems absurd, especially on utilitarian grounds, to deny the very great happiness of parenthood to those who want it for the reason that their child might be slightly less happy than average.

At this point, I wish to reinforce a distinction which I have been mentioning here and there. This might enable us to effect a sort of working compromise between the two views. The distinction is between consideration of the effects of additions to population on the already existing members, and those concerning only the well-being of the new population, together with whatever purely arithmetical consequences this has for the population as a whole. Thus suppose that the new population would actually reduce the dietary intake of everyone because there was only enough to go round and no marginal increase of food resources was available to feed the newcomers: then that would be an effect on existing populace. And as argued in the preceding section, I don't think that any actual decrement of living standards of preexisting population is necessarily justified on moral grounds. Now, it would be possible for both the total and the average views to yield consequences of this type. On the total view, this is obvious, for the addition of each new member would justify the loss of almost as much well-being as the new member himself would enjoy. On the average view, it is less obvious, but still possible. For some newcomer might be so greatly superior to the average that even if his presence made for a slight decline in some presently existing members' standard of life, he might improve the average more than their loss decreases it. If my previous arguments are correct, *neither* of these cases would be justified. We need consider only the cases where previous populace would not lose at all. Of course, they may gain, and indeed, this is prima facie to be expected, simply because people who have children normally enjoy having them. They are made happier by the increase.

If we do confine ourselves to such cases, then I don't think we can really object to the implication of the "total" view, that so long as each new person has good prospects, it is not wrong to produce him. Nevertheless, I don't see why we can't also say that it would be better if his chances were at least as good as average. But that, of course, is a truism: to do better is preferable to doing worse.

Another important set of possibilities has not yet been considered. Imagine the case where a new person would improve the happiness of those already present, but his own happiness would be below average, though not so low as to cancel out the gain. Both the total and the average view could approve cases of this kind, even if the new person were thoroughly miserable. The case conceivably might be that of a slave, for example, of extraordinary capacity; or of a monarch who had great ability but hated his job and suffered miserably from it. This is exactly the same kind of problem as the "innocent man" problem in general utilitarian theory, of course, and invites much the same kind of responses. If it is accepted that this is intolerable, then we must either reject utilitarianism as thus far conceived, or interpret it in a way which will avoid this result. I am inclined toward reinterpretation. We should accept neither the sacrifice of the existing for the sake of those who need not come, nor the sacrifice of those who do come to those already here. If such a restriction is accepted, then the total and average views again divide, and the average view has a slight additional question to resolve. On the total view, any addition above the minimum, who produces no or good effects on previous people, is welcome. (But there could still be some sacrifice: suppose we can choose between producing A, who would be quite happy but produce less benefit for those already here, and B who would be less happy than A but would produce more for the community than the difference between him and A. Presumably this would be acceptable on the total view.) On the amended average view, on the other hand, the new person would have to be of at least average happiness whatever the amount of benefit the population derived from his presence. But which average? The higher average resulting from his contributions, or the average before he came on the scene? It is difficult to support the average view against the total view in amended form. If we accept some sacrifice of existing people to other existing people in a community, then why not some sacrifice from a new person?

As suggested at the outset of this section, it is possible to produce any number of other formulae on this subject, calling for populations with various distributions of happiness. But I am inclined to think that there is no basis for accepting any such formula that would not provide a still better reason for accepting either the average or the total view. Put rather roughly, the reason is as follows. Newly produced people may be arranged in serial order according to the time at which they are born. Thus we can consider each case one at a time, and, we suppose, can control the flow of new cases as required, in the light of available resources plus the effects of the preceding one. Now surely we want each new addition to be as happy as possible, other things being neglected. The only reasonable question can be where to draw the line: below what point of expected utility do we exercise restraint and not have the person at all? Wherever we set it, it is hard to see how we could set it differently for different cases. Either we set it at some absolute minimum, e.g., the point where the person in question would agree that his life was better than none, was worth going on with. Or at the maximum compatible with sustaining the human race at all—or not even that, but just the maximum compatible with that maximum being socially attainable. Or if we allow the point to vary from case to case, it must be because of effects on previous population (or on further population in the light of available resources). If the latter, though, it must surely be to maximize the happiness of those concerned. So it seems impossible to justify the selection of some sort of distribution as an end in itself: to say that in the optimum situation, we want so many people to be this happy, so many more to be rather less so (though they could have been more so), and so on. To suppose that some such result might be justified would be, I think, to confuse the question of distribution of happiness with that of distribution of resources. It is possible that altering the distribution of resources in some particular way would have effects on the general happiness. For example, an equal distribution might generate less envy and competition of a destructive kind. Or an unequal distribution might provide incentives which improved production for the community as a whole. Or an unequal distribution might be preferred because most people enjoyed seeing a few very rich people even if they were not rich themselves. But no such considerations could apply to distributions of happiness, unless we suppose a population of envious, sadistic, jealous, or malevolent people. But if we are to assume anything of that sort, it should surely be that everyone is either good-willed or else simply normal, so far as we know what that is.

V

All of this brings up the question: how do we *decide* among these alternative views of what constitutes an optimum? Indeed, just what do we think we are deciding about? Simple benevolence is a possible answer; but the trouble is, we don't know what constitutes benevolence in cases like this, where it seems as though we are asking how to be benevolent toward nonexistent people, or perhaps towards humanity in the abstract. And of course, there are many concrete questions about the capability of a given area of sustaining people at one or another level of diet, conveniences, etc., and of just which conveniences are preferable, which are comparable to ordinary questions about the treatment of the present population, whatever it may be. But the population question as we are raising it here concerns questions too fundamental to be compared with those. Or so it may seem.

There is one method which comes to mind fairly readily these days. This is the one proposed by Professor Rawls, wherein we are asked to make choices between different possible communities. In his case, the questions raised had to do with principles of justice: would we rather, if we had no idea just who or where we would be in a given community, live in this one, governed by one sort of laws, or that one, ruled by another sort? Analogously, then, we might try asking whether we would rather live in a community with one sort of population policy, or which exemplified the result of long application of one sort, or in another? For example, would I rather live in a community where the average happiness is greater, or in which the total is higher but the average lower?

But as soon as we set up the problem in this way, we reach a snag of monumental proportions. The effect of the requirement that I am not to know where I will end up in the particular community contemplated presumably is that I am to suppose that I have an equal chance of being anybody in it. This by definition will favor the average view against the total view, *unless* we also make some sort of allowance for the fact that there are more people in the community with the total policy (let us suppose). And am I to reckon not only the chances that I would be this or that person in a given society, but also the chances of my being a member of it at all? The chances, in other words, of my existing, given the one case or the other? And if so, what would it mean for me to say that I'd rather take my chances of not existing at all so that, if I did exist, my happiness would probably be greater than if I chose to live in the other community? This seems a perfectly mindboggling question. Yet if we don't allow it, or something like it, then the dice are loaded quite perfectly in favor of the "average" view, bearing in mind my points about distributive views.

Or so it seems, until we remember a further fact about this method. We are choosing between various possible communities, we suppose. But are we choosing not only between communities with different policies, but also between communities with different *levels* of well-being? If so, of course, we should want the highest rather than the lowest. But now we are making choices in a complete vacuum. For how do you make use of the fact that everybody wants to live as good a life as possible as a basis for population policy? Unless at some point we say, "and I'd rather not live at all than live in *that* community," we don't, it seems, know what to do. Suppose that in the community we have, newborn people have such and such a chance of living a life of such and such quality: how does it help us to know that a rational chooser would prefer this to a community where he had a greater chance of living a less good life, and on the other hand, would prefer another community where he had a better chance of living a better life?

Perhaps it could be suggested that at any rate, a person will have no complaint against his parents or community if he finds himself with as good a life as the average of his fellows. But why should he complain if it were below average, but still good? Or why not complain if it were above average, but not perfect? "I did not choose to be born: a pox on you for bringing me into this miserable world" is a complaint with no sensible reply, if it is made at all.

So perhaps all we can do is base our policy on the chances of its not being made, which in turn will be a function of the expectations and hopes, the capacities for adaptation and acceptance, which we instill into the young and which we develop in ourselves as we go through life. This is a hybrid of the amended total and average views. Let us encourage to be born as many as are wanted and who will find life at least tolerable, by the standards we have come to accept, provided that their appearance does not significantly lower the standard of life of those now alive. But this standard of tolerability will go up as the average quality of life improves. As for what in particular makes a life at least tolerable, or better, that is a problem which must be left to each of those who live it. And as to the question of what the point is of having people around at all, with however enjoyable lives, that too is one which may be left to each of us now alive, who can pass it on to our children, if we decide to have them.

With this rather indecisive result, I shall let the problem rest for the time being, secure in the confidence that the mistakes in the foregoing will be spotted by many, and in hopes—less secure—that some among my readers will come up with that "wholly novel way of looking at the matter" which seems rather sorely needed.

ON DOING THE BEST
FOR OUR CHILDREN

Derek Parfit

The ethics of population really are, as Narveson says, "extraordinarily difficult." All that I shall do here is sketch some of the difficulties still facing Narveson and Peter Singer.

I start with a general remark. Such difficulties may seem to face only utilitarians. This is not so. They face most of those who give any weight to a utilitarian principle.

Narveson's main claim is about the form of this principle. He believes that it should not be "impersonal"—for example, it should not run: "We ought to increase happiness." It should rather be "person-affecting"—for example, it might run: "It is better to do what affects people for the better."

Why does Narveson claim this? Partly because the "impersonal" form leads to some version of the "Total View"—which he finds repugnant. The "person-affecting" form seems to provide an alternative.

The first problem is that it only does so on the assumption that conceiving a person cannot affect him for the better. Without this assumption, the "person-affecting" form may itself lead to the Total View. The assumption can be challenged; but for the purpose of argument I shall take it for granted throughout this paper.

A second problem can be presented in a pair of cases. The first involves a woman who intends to become pregnant as soon as possible. She learns that she has an illness which would give to any child she conceives now a certain handicap. If she waits for two months, the illness would have passed, and she would then conceive a normal child.

Suppose she decides not to wait—suppose that she knowingly conceives a handicapped rather than a normal child. Has she thereby harmed her child, or affected him for the worse?

We must first ask: "When her child grows up, could he truly say, 'If my mother had waited, I would have been born later, and been a normal child'?" The answer is "No." If she had waited, he would not have been born at all; she would have had a different child. (What I have just claimed would be judged true on either of the main views about the subject. According to one view, the particular pair of cells from which a child sprang are essential to his identity—and a child conceived two months later would in fact have

---

sprung from different cells. According to the rival view, the handicapped child *could* have sprung from different cells—or even different parents—provided that the child who (it is claimed) *would* have been him would have been sufficiently *like* him. The handicapped child and a child conceived two months later would in fact *not* have been sufficiently similar; they would have been as unlike as ordinary siblings. So it is also true on this other view that if the child's mother had waited, she would have had a different child.

It seems, then, that the handicapped child is not worse off than he would otherwise have been—for he *wouldn't* otherwise have been. Might we still claim that, in knowingly conceiving a handicapped child, the woman harms this child? We might perhaps claim this if the child's life would be worse than nothing—would be worth *not* living. But we can assume that the handicap is not so severe—that the child's life, though impaired, is still worth living. And, in his case, being handicapped is the only way in which he can receive life. When a person's leg is removed to save his life, it is not true, at least in any morally relevant sense, that this harms the person. We seem bound to say the same about our case. The handicapped child is not affected for the worse. So—as far as the child is concerned—we are not told by any "person-affecting" principle that his mother acted wrongly.

Now in this first case there will presumably be worse effects on other people—on her husband, or her other children. So there are some "person-affecting" grounds for condemning what she does. But we cannot *rely* on "side-effects." They can point the other way.

Suppose we have a choice between two social policies. These will alter the standard of living—or, more broadly, the quality of life. The effects of one policy would, in the short term, be slightly better, but, in the long term, be much worse. Since there clearly could be such a difference between two policies, we need not specify details. It is enough to assume that, on the "Short Term Policy," the quality of life would be slightly higher for (say) the next three generations, but be lower for the fourth generation, and be *much* lower for several later generations.

We can next note a second fact about the difference between the policies. The particular members of the fourth and later generations, on the Short Term Policy, would not have been born at all if instead we had pursued the Long Term Policy. Given the effects of the policies on the details of people's lives, different marriages would increasingly be made. More simply, even in the same marriages, the children would increasingly be conceived at different times. As we argued, this would be enough to make them different children.

We can now apply a "person-affecting" principle. The members of the later generations would be different on the different policies. So if we pursue the Short Term Policy there will never be anyone who is worse off than he would otherwise have been. The Short Term Policy harms no one. Since it benefits certain people (those who exist now), it is the policy chosen by our principle.

What is most disturbing is not this conclusion, but the way in which it has been reached. The example shows that the long-term effects of social policies, even if clearly disastrous—even if it clearly affects for the worse—won't be worse for particular people. They are thus ignored by our principle. (As Narveson writes, without "effects on certain people . . . we can do as we like.") The predictable collapse in the quality of life is, moreover, *totally* ignored. We might claim that we should grant *less* weight to the further future, or that we have special duties to our children. But a "person-affecting" principle gives to the further future *no* weight.

This seems indefensible. If it is, population policies, which all have long-term effects, ought not to be chosen by appealing to such a principle.

This objection may not seem decisive. If so, we can advance others. For example: a "person-affecting" principle can have self-contradictory implications. I shall argue this elsewhere; but the objection sketched here—the "Identity Objection"—seems to me sufficient. Narveson's main claim is that population policy should be determined by the rights and interests of the affected people. I conclude that this is not so.

The objection may seem to have rested on a quibble. Could we not have claimed, in our first case, "The woman's child would be worse off born now than he would be if he were born later"? This claim is, in a sense, true. But in this sense it is not about the different possible states of the same particular person. It is like the claim, "Children are taller now than they were 100 years ago." "They," here, does not mean "they themselves," it merely substitutes for the word "children."

We might now reinterpret the "person-affecting" form of principle. We might say: "It is worse to do what makes the resulting people worse off than they—i.e. "the resulting people"—would otherwise have been." We allow that "the resulting people" can be *different* people.

When our choice involves the *same number* of resulting people, we shall now get good advice. Thus the Reinterpreted Principle implies directly—without an appeal to "side-effects"—that our woman ought to wait, so as to have a normal child. (Notice how it does this. She is told to do the best for "her child," where this covers *all* of the people who might be "her child." The principle treats a whole group of possible people as if it were a single ["honorary"] actual person.)

Even in these cases, the Reinterpreted Principle seems a cheat. But we are here concerned with population policy, where the choice involves *different numbers* of resulting people. There are two ways of applying the principle to such cases. We can allow the phrase "the resulting people" to cover *all* of the people in the different outcomes. This yields the "Concertina Principle," which I criticize elsewhere. We can instead revise the principle so that it covers the *same* number—or "core." This is the line explored by Peter Singer.

Singer works with two "Core Principles"—which, confusingly, he fails to distinguish. Singer's principles can be reached by revising the following axioms:

(1) It is worse to do one of two things if this makes those who exist now, or who will exist *whichever* we do, worse off than they would have been if we had done the other thing,

and

(2) The same as (1), except that for "*whichever* we do" we substitute "*whatever* we do."

The difference between these axioms can be shown in the case of a second woman. She intends to become pregnant in a few months' time, but learns that, unless she receives treatment now, any child she then conceives would be handicapped. Her treatment would not postpone her intended pregnancy, so we can assume that it would not affect the *identity* of the child she later conceives—it would only affect whether or not this child is handicapped.

According to axiom (1), it would be worse for this woman to refuse the treatment; she would be affecting her future child for the worse. What does (2) imply? Is her future child someone who will exist *whatever* she does? No—for she could remain childless. So if instead, though intending pregnancy, she refuses treatment—if she gives her future child the handicap—(2) fails to imply that she acts for the worse.

This may seem enough ground for rejecting (2). Its defenders might appeal to "side-effects." This child, though, is made to be worse off than he *himself* would have been. This fact (2) ignores. The example shows that only (1) is a full "person-affecting" axiom; (2) is less generous. And we might say, "Surely an axiom ought at least to cover all those whom we affect for the worse?" But the subject is so difficult that I shall consider what can be achieved by revising (2).

The axioms need to be revised to meet the Identity Objection. To use an ambiguous phrase, they cover "those who will exist anyway." The objection is that on different policies different people would increasingly be born—so the axioms cover no one in the further future. They ignore long-term effects, however disastrous.

Singer's answer runs: "Phrases like 'those who will exist anyway' need not be used to imply a relation of personal identity between those who [would] exist if one policy is adopted, and those who [would] exist if the other policy is adopted. Instead, we should take the phrase to refer to the number of lives that will be in the course of being lived . . . whatever policy is adopted."

This suggestion needs to be filled out. A phrase like "the resulting people" *can* be used without implying personal identity; it can instead be taken to refer to the different people who, on different policies, would *be* "the resulting people." This cannot be done with the phrase "those who will exist anyway." This phrase cannot be taken to refer to the different people who would *be* "those who would have existed anyway"—for if the people would, on the different policies, be *different,* there will be no such people.

Nor can the phrase be simply taken to refer to the *number* of people that will exist anyway—for, if we call this number 'P', how do we know, when policies produce more than P people, to *which* P people our phrase refers? We can only answer this—we can only select our "core"—if we choose some further phrase.

QUESTIONS FOR DISCUSSION

1. How do orthodox Western religious institutions, which prohibit birth control and abortion, attempt to deal with overpopulation, insofar that they acknowledge that there is a problem? Do they, as Narveson suggests, "relegate such issues to the status of academic questions, or do they offer practical solutions"?

2. The claim that the unborn have rights that must be respected has two possible interpretations, according to Narveson. Which one does he accept as valid? Which one does he reject as absurd?

3. What is the difference, according to both Narveson and Parfit, between the "total view" form of utilitarianism and the "person-affecting" view? Which does Narveson support?

4. Discuss Parfit's criticism of the person-affecting view. Does he have anything better to offer?

5. What is the "identity problem" that Parfit brings to the reader's attention? Does he have a solution to it? What consequence does he draw from it?

6. Distinguish between the short-term policy and long-term policy as discussed by Parfit. From which point of view does it follow that "the Short Term Policy harms no one"? Which policy do you consider morally superior?

SUGGESTED READINGS

BAIER, K., "Justice and Procreation," *Journal of Social Philosophy*, 22, 3 (1991), 5–17.

BARRY, B. and R. SIKORA, *Obligations to Future Generations*, Temple University Press, Philadelphia, 1978.

BAYLES, M., *Ethics and Population*, Schenkman, Cambridge, Mass., 1976.

COOPER, D. and J. PALMER, *The Environment in Question*, New York: Routledge, 1992.

DEGEORGE, R., and J. PICHLER, *Ethics, Free Enterprise and Public Policy*, Oxford University Press, New York, 1978.

DELATTRE, E., "Rights, Responsibilities and Future Persons," *Ethics* (April 1972).

DESHALIT, A., "Community and the Rights of Future Generations," *Journal of Applied Philosophy*, 9, 1 (1992), 105–15.

GOODPASTER, K., and K. SAYRE, eds., *Ethics and Problems of the Twenty-first Century*, University of Notre Dame Press, 1979.

GRAHAM, G., and E. GRAHAM, "The Crisis of Population Growth," *Journal of Moral and Social Studies*, 7, 3 (1992), 205–36.

GREEN, R., *Population Growth and Justice*, Scholars Press, Missoula, Mont., 1976.

MARSHALL, P., "Thinking for Tomorrow," *Journal of Applied Philosophy,* 10, 1 (1993), 105–13.

PARFIT, D., *Reasons and Persons,* Part IV, Oxford University Press, New York, 1987.

PARTRIDGE, E., ed., *Responsibilities to Future Generations,* Prometheus Books, Buffalo, New York, 1981.

PULVERTAFT, W. R., "Population Ethics," *Danish Yearbook of Philosophy,* Copenhagen, 1991, 36–50.

RAWLS, J., *A Theory of Justice,* section 44, Harvard University Press, Cambridge, Mass., 1971.

SCHERER, D., ed., *Upstream, Downstream: Issues in Environmental Ethics,* Philadelphia: Temple University Press, 1990.

STEARNS, J., "Ecology and the Indefinite Unborn," *Monist* (October 1972).

WOGAMEN, J., ed., *The Population Crisis and Moral Responsibility,* Public Affairs Press, Washington, D.C., 1973.

9

AFFIRMATIVE ACTION

THE INJUSTICE
OF AFFIRMATIVE ACTION
Lisa H. Newton

I have heard it argued that "simple justice" requires that we favor women and blacks in employment and educational opportunities, since women and blacks were "unjustly" excluded from such opportunities for so many years in the not so distant past. It is a strange argument, an example of a possible implication of a true proposition advanced to dispute the proposition itself, like an octopus absent-mindedly slicing off his head with a stray tentacle. A fatal confusion underlies this argument, a confusion fundamentally relevant to our understanding of the notion of the rule of law.

Two senses of justice and equality are involved in this confusion. The root notion of justice, progenitor of the other, is the one that Aristotle (*Nichomachean Ethics* 5. 6; *Politics* 1.2; 3. 1) assumes to be the foundation and proper virtue of the political association. It is the condition which free men establish among themselves when they "share a common life in order that their association bring them self-sufficiency"—the regulation of their relationship by law, and the establishment, by law, of equality before the law. Rule of law is the name and pattern of this justice; its equality stands against the inequalities—of wealth, talent, etc.—otherwise obtaining among its participants, who by virtue of that equality are called "citizens." It is an achievement—complete, or, more frequently, partial—of certain people in certain concrete situations. It is fragile and easily disrupted by powerful individuals who discover that the blind equality of rule of law is inconve-

---

"Against Affirmative Action," by Lisa H. Newton, from *Ethics* Vol. 83, #4 (1973), pp. 308–312. Reprinted by permission of The University of Chicago Press.

nient for their interests. Despite its obvious instability, Aristotle assumed that the establishment of justice in this sense, the creation of citizenship, was a permanent possibility for men and that the resultant association of citizens was the natural home of the species. At levels below the political association, this rule-governed equality is easily found; it is exemplified by any group of children agreeing together to play a game. At the level of the political association, the attainment of this justice is more difficult, simply because the stakes are so much higher for each participant. The equality of citizenship is not something that happens of its own accord, and without the expenditure of a fair amount of effort it will collapse into the rule of a powerful few over an apathetic many. But at least it has been achieved, at some times in some places; it is always worth trying to achieve, and eminently worth trying to maintain, wherever and to whatever degree it has been brought into being.

Aristotle's parochialism is notorious; he really did not imagine that persons other than Greeks could associate freely in justice, and the only form of association he had in mind was the Greek *polis*. With the decline of the *polis* and the shift in the center of political thought, his notion of justice underwent a sea change. To be exact, it ceased to represent a political type and became a moral ideal: the ideal of equality as we know it. This ideal demands that all men be included in citizenship—that one Law govern all equally, that all men regard all other men as fellow citizens, with the same guarantees, rights, and protections. Briefly, it demands that the circle of citizenship achieved by any group be extended to include the entire human race. Properly understood, its effect on our associations can be excellent: it congratulates us on our achievement of rule of law as a process of government but refuses to let us remain complacent until we have expanded the associations to include others within the ambit of the rules, as often and as far as possible. While one man is a slave, none of us may feel truly free. We are constantly prodded by this ideal to look for possible unjustifiable discrimination, for inequalities not absolutely required for the functioning of the society and advantageous to all. And after twenty centuries of pressure, not at all constant, from this ideal, it might be said that some progress has been made. To take the cases in point for this problem, we are now prepared to assert, as Aristotle would never have been, the equality of sexes and of persons of different colors. The ambit of American citizenship, once restricted to white males of property, has been extended to include all adult free men, then all adult males including ex-slaves, then all women. The process of acquisition of full citizenship was for these groups a sporadic trail of half-measures, even now not complete; the steps on the road to full equality are marked by legislation and judicial decisions which are only recently concluded and still often not enforced. But the fact that we can now discuss the possibility of favoring such groups in hiring shows that over the area that concerns us, at least, full equality is presupposed as a basis for discussion. To that extent, they are full citizens, fully protected by the law of the land.

It is important for my argument that the moral ideal of equality be recognized as logically distinct from the condition (or virtue) of justice in the political sense. Justice in this sense exists *among* a citizenry, irrespective of the number of the populace included in that citizenry. Further, the moral ideal is parasitic upon the political virtue, for "equality" is unspecified—it means nothing until we are told in what respect that equality is to be realized. In a political context, "equality" is specified as "equal rights"— equal access to the public realm, public goods and offices, equal treatment under the law—in brief, the equality of citizenship. If citizenship is not a possibility, political equality is unintelligible. The ideal emerges as a generalization of the real condition and refers back to that condition for its content.

Now, if justice (Aristotle's justice in the political sense) is equal treatment under law for all citizens, what is injustice? Clearly, injustice is the violation of that equality, discriminating for or against a group of citizens, favoring them with special immunities and privileges or depriving them of those guaranteed to the others. When the southern employer refuses to hire blacks in white-collar jobs, when Wall Street will only hire women as secretaries with new titles, when Mississippi high schools routinely flunk all black boys above ninth grade, we have examples of injustice, and we work to restore the equality of the public realm by ensuring that equal opportunity will be provided in such cases in the future. But of course, when the employers and the schools *favor* women and blacks, the same injustice is done. Just as the previous discrimination did, this reverse discrimination violates the public equality which defines citizenship and destroys the rule of law for the areas in which these favors are granted. To the extent that we adopt a program of discrimination, reverse or otherwise, justice in the political sense is destroyed, and none of us, specifically affected or not, is a citizen, a bearer of rights—we are all petitioners for favors. And to the same extent, the ideal of equality is undermined, for it has content only where justice obtains, and by destroying justice we render the ideal meaningless. It is, then, an ironic paradox, if not a contradiction in terms, to assert that the ideal of equality justifies the violation of justice; it is as if one should argue, with William Buckley, that an ideal of humanity can justify the destruction of the human race.

Logically, the conclusion is simple enough: all discrimination is wrong *prima facie* because it violates justice, and that goes for reverse discrimination too. No violation of justice among the citizens may be justified (may overcome the *prima facie* objection) by appeal to the ideal of equality, for that ideal is logically dependent upon the notion of justice. Reverse discrimination, then, which attempts no other justification than an appeal to equality, is wrong. But let us try to make the conclusion more plausible by suggesting some of the implications of the suggested practice of reverse discrimination in employment and education. My argument will be that the problems raised there are insoluble, not only in practice but in principle.

We may argue, if we like, about what "discrimination" consists of. Do I discriminate against blacks if I admit none to my school when none of the black applicants are qualified by the tests I always give? How far must I go to root out cultural bias from my application forms and tests before I can say that I have not discriminated against those of different cultures? Can I assume that women are not strong enough to be roughnecks on my oil rigs, or must I test them individually? But this controversy, the most popular and well-argued aspect of the issue, is not as fatal as two others which cannot be avoided: if we are regarding the blacks as a "minority" victimized by discrimination, what is a "minority"? And for any group—blacks, women, whatever—that has been discriminated against, what amount of reverse discrimination wipes out the initial discrimination? Let us grant as true that women and blacks were discriminated against, even when laws forbade such discrimination, and grant for the sake of argument that a history of discrimination must be wiped out by reverse discrimination. What follows?

First, are there other groups which have been discriminated against? For they should have the same right of restitution. What about American Indians, Chicanos, Appalachian Mountain whites, Puerto Ricans, Jews, Cajuns, and Orientals? And if these are to be included, the principle according to which we specify a "minority" is simply the criterion of "ethnic (sub) group," and we're stuck with every hyphenated American in the lower-middle class clamoring for special privileges for *his* group—and with equal justification. For be it noted, when we run down the Harvard roster, we find not only a scarcity of blacks (in comparison with the proportion in the population) but an even more striking scarcity of those second-, third-, and fourth-generation ethnics who make up the loudest voice of Middle America. Shouldn't they demand *their* share? And eventually, the WASPs will have to form their own lobby, for they too are a minority. The point is simply this: there is no "majority" in America who will not mind giving up just a bit of their rights to make room for a favored minority. There are only other minorities, each of which is discriminated against by the favoring. The initial injustice is then repeated dozens of times, and if each minority is granted the same right of restitution as the others, an entire area of rule governance is dissolved into a pushing and shoving match between self-interested groups. Each works to catch the public eye and political popularity by whatever means of advertising and power politics lend themselves to the effort, to capitalize as much as possible on temporary popularity until the restless mob picks another group to feel sorry for. Hardly an edifying spectacle, and in the long run no one can benefit: the pie is no larger—it's just that instead of setting up and enforcing rules for getting a piece, we've turned the contest into a free-for-all, requiring much more effort for no larger a reward. It would be in the interest of all the participants to reestablish an objective rule to govern the process, carefully enforced and the same for all.

Second, supposing that we do manage to agree in general that women and blacks (and all the others) have some right of restitution, some right to a privileged place in the structure of opportunities for a while, how will we know when that while is up? How much privilege is enough? When will the guilt be gone, the price paid, the balance restored? What recompense is right for centuries of exclusion? What criterion tells us when we are done? Our experience with the Civil Rights movement shows us that agreement on these terms cannot be presupposed: a process that appears to some to be going at a mad gallop into a black takeover appears to the rest of us to be at a standstill. Should a practice of reverse discrimination be adopted, we may safely predict that just as some of us begin to see "a satisfactory start toward righting the balance," others of us will see that we "have already gone too far in the other direction" and will suggest that the discrimination ought to be reversed again. And such disagreement is inevitable, for the point is that we could not *possibly* have any criteria for evaluating the kind of recompense we have in mind. The context presumed by any discussion of restitution is the context of rule of law: law sets the rights of men and simultaneously sets the method for remedying the violation of those rights. You may exact suffering from others and/or damage payments for yourself if and only if the others have violated your rights; the suffering you have endured is not sufficient reason for them to suffer. And remedial rights exist only where there is law: primary human rights are useful guides to legislation but cannot stand as reasons for awarding remedies for injuries sustained. But then, the context presupposed by any discussion of restitution is the context of preexistent full citizenship. No remedial rights could exist for the excluded; neither in law nor in logic does there exist a right to *sue* for a standing to sue.

From these two considerations, then, the difficulties with reverse discrimination become evident. Restitution for a disadvantaged group whose rights under the law have been violated is possible by legal means, but restitution for a disadvantaged group whose grievance is that there was no law to protect them simply is not. First, outside of the area of justice defined by the law, no sense can be made of "the group's rights," for no law recognizes that group or the individuals in it, qua members, as bearers of rights (hence *any* group can constitute itself as a disadvantaged minority in some sense and demand similar restitution). Second, outside of the area of protection of law, no sense can be made of the violation of rights (hence the amount of the recompense cannot be decided by any objective criterion). For both reasons, the practice of reverse discrimination undermines the foundation of the very ideal in whose name it is advocated; it destroys justice, law, equality, and citizenship itself, and replaces them with power struggles and popularity contests.

THE JUSTICE OF AFFIRMATIVE ACTION

Ronald Dworkin

I

In 1945 a black man named Sweatt applied to the University of Texas Law School, but was refused admission because state law provided that only whites could attend. The Supreme Court declared that this law violated Sweatt's rights under the Fourteenth Amendment to the United States Constitution, which provides that no state shall deny any man the equal protection of its laws. In 1971 a Jew named DeFunis applied to the University of Washington Law School; he was rejected although his test scores and college grades were such that he would have been admitted if he had been a black or a Filipino or a Chicano or an American Indian. DeFunis asked the Supreme Court to declare that the Washington practice, which required less exacting standards of minority groups, violated his rights under the Fourteenth Amendment.

The Washington Law School's admission procedures were complex. Applications were divided into two groups. The majority—those not from the designated minority groups—were first screened so as to eliminate all applicants whose predicted average, which is a function of college grades and aptitude test scores, fell below a certain level. Majority applicants who survived this initial cut were then placed in categories that received progressively more careful consideration. Minority-group applications, on the other hand, were not screened; each received the most careful consideration by a special committee consisting of a black professor of law and a white professor who had taught in programs to aid black law students. Most of the minority applicants who were accepted in the year in which DeFunis was rejected had predicted averages below the cutoff level, and the law school conceded that any minority applicant with his average would certainly have been accepted.

The *DeFunis* case split those political action groups that have traditionally supported liberal causes. The B'nai B'rith Anti-Defamation League and the AFL-CIO, for example, filed briefs as amici curiae in support of DeFunis's claim, while the American Hebrew Women's Council, the UAW, and the UMWA filed briefs against it.

These splits among old allies demonstrate both the practical and the philosophical importance of the case. In the past liberals held, within one set of attitudes, three propositions: that racial classification is an evil in itself; that every person has a right to an educational opportunity commensurate with his abilities; and that affirmative state action is proper to remedy the serious inequalities of American society. In the last decade, however, the opinion has grown that these three liberal propositions are in fact not compatible, because the most effective programs of state action are those that give a competitive advantage to minority racial groups.

That opinion has, of course, been challenged. Some educators argue that benign quotas are ineffective, even self-defeating, because preferential treatment will reinforce the sense of inferiority that many blacks already have. Others make a more general objection. They argue that any racial discrimination, even for the purpose of benefiting minorities, will in fact harm those minorities, because prejudice is fostered whenever racial distinctions are tolerated for any purpose whatever. But these are complex and controversial empirical judgments, and it is far too early, as wise critics concede, to decide whether preferential treatment does more harm or good. Nor is it the business of judges, particularly in constitutional cases, to overthrow decisions of other officials because the judges disagree about the efficiency of social policies. This empirical criticism is therefore reinforced by the moral argument that even if reverse discrimination does benefit minorities and does reduce prejudice in the long run, it is nevertheless wrong because distinctions of race are inherently unjust. They are unjust because they violate the rights of individual members of groups not so favored, who may thereby lose a place, as DeFunis did.

DeFunis presented this moral argument, in the form of a constitutional claim, to the courts. The Supreme Court did not, in the end, decide whether the argument was good or bad. DeFunis had been admitted to the law school after one lower court had decided in his favor, and the law school said that he would be allowed to graduate however the case was finally decided. The Court therefore held that the case was moot and dismissed the appeal on that ground. But Justice Douglas disagreed with this neutral disposition of the case; he wrote a dissenting opinion in which he argued that the Court should have upheld DeFunis's claim on the merits. Many universities and colleges have taken Justice Douglas's opinion as handwriting on the wall, and have changed their practices in anticipation of a later Court decision in which his opinion prevails. In fact, his opinion pointed out that law schools might achieve much the same result by a more sophisticated policy than Washington used. A school might stipulate, for example, that applicants from all races and groups would be considered together, but that the aptitude tests of certain minority applicants would be graded differently, or given less weight in overall predicted average, because experience had shown that standard examinations were for different reasons a poorer test of the actual ability of these applicants. But if this technique is used deliberately to achieve the same result, it is devious, and it remains to ask why the candid program used by the University of Washington was either unjust or unconstitutional.

II

DeFunis plainly has no constitutional right that the state provide him a legal education of a certain quality. His rights would not be violated if his state did not have a law school at all, or if it had a law school with so few places that he could not win one on intellectual merit. Nor does he have a right to insist that intelligence be the exclusive test of admission. Law schools do rely heavily on intellectual tests for admission. That seems proper, however, not because applicants have a right to be judged in that way, but because it is reasonable to think that the community as a whole is better off if its lawyers are intelligent. That is, intellectual standards are justified, not because they reward the clever, but because they seem to serve a useful social policy.

Law schools sometimes serve that policy better, moreover, by supplementing intelligence tests with other sorts of standards: they sometimes prefer industrious applicants, for example, to those who are brighter but lazier. They also serve special policies for which intelligence is not relevant. The Washington Law School, for example, gave special preference not only to minority applicants but also to veterans who had been at the school before entering the military, and neither DeFunis nor any of the briefs submitted in his behalf complained of that preference.

DeFunis does not have an absolute right to a law school place, nor does he have a right that only intelligence be used as a standard for admission. He says he nevertheless has a right that race *not* be used as a standard, no matter how well a racial classification might work to promote the general welfare or to reduce social and economic inequality. He does not claim, however, that he has this right as a distinct and independent political right that is specifically protected by the Constitution, as is his right to freedom of speech and religion. The Constitution does not condemn racial classification directly, as it does condemn censorship or the establishment of a state religion. DeFunis claims that his right that race not be used as a criterion of admission follows from the more abstract right of equality that is protected by the Fourteenth Amendment, which provides that no state shall deny to any person the equal protection of the law.

But the legal arguments made on both sides show that neither the text of the Constitution nor the prior decisions of the Supreme Court decisively settle the question whether, as a matter of law, the Equal Protection Clause makes all racial classifications unconstitutional. The Clause makes the concept of equality a test of legislation, but it does not stipulate any particular conception of that concept. Those who wrote the clause intended to attack certain consequences of slavery and racial prejudice, but it is unlikely that they intended to outlaw all racial classifications, or that they expected such a prohibition to be the result of what they wrote. They outlawed whatever policies would violate equality, but left it to others to decide, from time to time, what that means. There cannot be a good legal argument in favor of DeFunis, therefore, unless there is a good moral argument that all racial classifications, even those that make society as a whole more equal, are inherently offensive to an individual's right to equal protection for himself.

There is nothing paradoxical, of course, in the ideal that an individual's right to equal protection may sometimes conflict with an otherwise desirable social policy, including the policy of making the community more equal overall. Suppose a law school were to charge a few middle-class students, selected by lot, double tuition in order to increase the scholarship fund for poor students. It would be serving a desirable policy—equality of opportunity— by means that violated the right of the students selected by lot to be treated equally with other students who could also afford the increased fees. It is, in fact, part of the importance of DeFunis's case that it forces us to acknowledge the distinction between equality as a policy and equality as a right, a distinction that political theory has virtually ignored. He argues that the Washington Law School violated his individual right to equality for the sake of a policy of greater equality overall, in the same way that double tuition for arbitrarily chosen students would violate their rights for the same purpose.

We must therefore concentrate our attention on that claim. We must try to define the central concept on which it turns, which is the concept of an individual right to equality made a constitutional right by the Equal Protection Clause. What rights to equality do citizens have as individuals which might defeat programs aimed at important economic and social policies, including the social policy of improving equality overall?

There are two different sorts of rights they may be said to have. The first is the right to *equal treatment,* which is the right to an equal distribution of some opportunity or resource or burden. Every citizen, for example, has a right to an equal vote in a democracy; that is the nerve of the Supreme Court's decision that one person must have one vote even if a different and more complex arrangement would better secure the collective welfare. The second is the right to *treatment as an equal,* which is the right, not to receive the same distribution of some burden or benefit, but to be treated with the same respect and concern as anyone else. If I have two children, and one is dying from a disease that is making the other uncomfortable, I do not show equal concern if I flip a coin to decide which should have the remaining dose of a drug. This example shows that the right to treatment as an equal is fundamental, and the right to equal treatment, derivative. In some circumstances the right to treatment as an equal will entail a right to equal treatment, but not, by any means, in all circumstances.

DeFunis does not have a right to equal treatment in the assignment of law school places; he does not have a right to a place just because others are given places. Individuals may have a right to equal treatment in elementary education, because someone who is denied elementary education is unlikely to lead a useful life. But legal education is not so vital that everyone has an equal right to it.

DeFunis does have the second sort of right—a right to treatment as an equal in the decision as to which admissions standards should be used. That is, he has a right that his interests be treated as fully and sympathetically as the interests of any others when the law school decides whether to count race as a pertinent criterion for admission. But we must be careful not to overstate what that means.

Suppose an applicant complains that his right to be treated as an equal is violated by tests that place the less intelligent candidates at a disadvantage against the more intelligent. A law school might properly reply in the following way. Any standard will place certain candidates at a disadvantage as against others, but an admission policy may nevertheless be justified if it seems reasonable to expect that the overall gain to the community exceeds the overall loss, and if no other policy that does not provide a comparable disadvantage would produce even roughly the same gain. An individual's right to be treated as an equal means that his potential loss must be treated as a matter of concern, but that loss may nevertheless be outweighed by the gain to the community as a whole. If it is, then the less intelligent applicant cannot claim that he is cheated of his right to be treated as an equal just because he suffers a disadvantage others do not.

Washington may make the same reply to DeFunis. Any admissions policy must put some applicants at a disadvantage, and a policy of preference for minority applicants can reasonably be supposed to benefit the community as a whole, even when the loss to candidates such as DeFunis is taken into account. If there are more black lawyers, they will help to provide better legal services to the black community, and so reduce social tensions. It might well improve the quality of legal education for all students, moreover, to have a greater number of blacks as classroom discussants of social problems. Further, if blacks are seen as successful law students, then other blacks who do meet the usual intellectual standards might be encouraged to apply and that, in turn, would raise the intellectual quality of the bar. In any case, preferential admissions of blacks should decrease the difference in wealth and power that now exists between different racial groups, and so make the community more equal overall. It is, as I said, controversial whether a preferential admissions program will in fact promote these various policies, but it cannot be said to be implausible that it will. The disadvantage to applicants such as DeFunis is, on that hypothesis, a cost that must be paid for a greater gain; it is in that way like the disadvantage to less intelligent students that is the cost of ordinary admissions policies.

We now see the difference between DeFunis's case and the case we imagined, in which a law school charged students selected at random higher fees. The special disadvantage to these students was not necessary to achieve the gain in scholarship funds, because the same gain would have been achieved by a more equal distribution of the cost amongst all the students who could afford it. That is not true of DeFunis. He did suffer from the Washington policy more than those majority applicants who were accepted. But that discrimination was not arbitrary; it was a consequence of the meritocratic standards he approves. DeFunis's argument therefore fails. The Equal Protection Clause gives constitutional standing to the right to be treated as an equal, but he cannot find, in that right, any support for his claim that the clause makes all racial classification illegal.

III

If we dismiss DeFunis's claim in this straightforward way, however, we are left with this puzzle. How can so many able lawyers, who supported his claim both in morality and law, have made that mistake? These lawyers all agree that intelligence is a proper criterion for admission to law schools. They do not suppose that anyone's constitutional right to be treated as an equal is compromised by that criterion. Why do they deny that race, in the circumstances of this decade, may also be a proper criterion?

They fear, perhaps, that racial criteria will be misused; that such criteria will serve as an excuse for prejudice against the minorities that are not favored, such as Jews. But that cannot explain their opposition. Any criteria may be misused, and in any case they think that racial criteria are wrong in principle and not simply open to abuse.

Why? The answer lies in their belief that, in theory as well as in practice, *DeFunis* and *Sweatt* must stand or fall together. They believe that it is illogical for liberals to condemn Texas for raising a color barrier against Sweatt, and then applaud Washington for raising a color barrier against DeFunis. The difference between these two cases, they suppose, must be only the subjective preference of liberals for certain minorities now in fashion. If there is something wrong with racial classifications, then it must be something that is wrong with racial classifications as such, not just classifications that work against those groups currently in favor. That is the inarticulate premise behind the slogan, relied on by defendants of DeFunis, that the Constitution is colorblind. That slogan means, of course, just the opposite of what it says: it means that the Constitution is so sensitive to color that it makes any institutional racial classification invalid as a matter of law.

It is of the greatest importance, therefore, to test the assumption that Sweatt and DeFunis must stand or fall together. If that assumption is sound, then the straightforward argument against DeFunis must be fallacious after all, for no argument could convince us that segregation of the sort practiced against Sweatt is justifiable or constitutional. Superficially, moreover, the arguments against DeFunis do indeed seem available against Sweatt, because we can construct an argument that Texas might have used to show that segregation benefits the collective welfare, so that the special disadvantage to blacks is a cost that must be paid to achieve an overall gain.

Suppose the Texas admissions committee, though composed of men and women who themselves held no prejudice, decided that the Texas economy demanded more white lawyers than they could educate, but could find no use for black lawyers at all. That might have been, after all, a realistic assessment of the commercial market for lawyers in Texas just after World War II. Corporate law firms needed lawyers to serve booming business but could not afford to hire black lawyers, however skillful, because the firms' practices would be destroyed if they did. It was no doubt true that the black community in Texas had great need of skillful lawyers, and would have preferred to use black lawyers if they were available. But the committee might well have thought that the commercial needs of the state as a whole outweighed that special need.

Or suppose the committee judged, no doubt accurately, that alumni gifts to the law school would fall off drastically if it admitted a black student.

The committee might deplore that fact, but nevertheless believe that the consequent collective damage would be greater than the damage to black candidates excluded by the racial restriction.

It may be said that these hypothetical arguments are disingenuous, because any policy of excluding blacks would in fact be supported by a prejudice against blacks as such, and arguments of the sort just described would be accepted by men who do not have the prejudices the objection assumes. It therefore does not follow from the fact that the admissions officers were prejudiced, if they were, then they would have rejected these arguments if they had not been.

In any case, arguments such as those I describe were in fact used by officials who might have been free from prejudice against those they excluded. Many decades ago, as the late Professor Bickel reminds us in his brief for the B'nai B'rith, President Lowell of Harvard University argued in favor of a quota limiting the number of Jews who might be accepted by his university. He said that if Jews were accepted in numbers larger than their proportion of the population, as they certainly would have been if intelligence were the only test, then Harvard would no longer be able to provide to the world men of the qualities and temperament it aimed to produce, men, that is, who were more well-rounded and less exclusively intellectual than Jews tended to be, and who, therefore, were better and more likely leaders of other men, both in and out of government. It was no doubt true, when Lowell spoke, that Jews were less likely to occupy important places in government or at the heads of large public companies. If Harvard wished to serve the general welfare by improving the intellectual qualities of the nation's leaders, it was rational not to allow its classes to be filled up with Jews. The men who reached that conclusion might well prefer the company of Jews to that of the Wasps who were more likely to become senators. Lowell suggested he did, though perhaps the responsibilities of his office prevented him from frequently indulging his preference.

It might now be said, however, that discrimination against blacks, even when it does serve some plausible policy, is nevertheless unjustified because it is invidious and insulting. The briefs opposing DeFunis make just that argument to distinguish his claim from Sweatt's. Because blacks were the victims of slavery and legal segregation, they say, any discrimination that excludes blacks will be taken as insulting by them, whatever arguments of general welfare might be made in its support. But it is not true, as a general matter, that any social policy is unjust if those whom it puts at a disadvantage feel insulted. Admission to law school by intelligence is not unjust because those who are less intelligent feel insulted by their exclusion. Everything depends upon whether the feeling of insult is produced by some more objective feature that would disqualify the policy even if the insult were not felt. If segregation does improve the general welfare, even when the disadvantage to blacks is fully taken into account, and if no other reason can be found why segregation is nevertheless unjustified, then the insult blacks feel, while understandable, must be based on misperception.

It would be wrong, in any case, to assume that men in the position of DeFunis will not take *their* exclusion to be insulting. They are very likely to think of themselves, not as members of some large majority group that is privileged overall, but as members of some other minority, such as Jews or Poles or Italians, whom comfortable and successful liberals are willing to sacrifice in order to delay more violent social change. If we wish to distinguish *DeFunis* from *Sweatt* on some argument that uses the concept of an insult, we must show that the treatment of the one, but not the other, is in fact unjust.

IV

So these familiar arguments that might distinguish the two cases are unconvincing. That seems to confirm that Sweatt and DeFunis must be treated alike, and therefore that racial classification must be outlawed altogether. But fortunately a more successful ground of distinction can be found to support our initial sense that the cases are in fact very different. This distinction does not rely, as these unconvincing arguments do, on features peculiar to issues of race or segregation, or even on features peculiar to issues of educational opportunity. It relies instead on further analysis of the idea, which was central to my argument against DeFunis, that in certain circumstances a policy which puts many individuals at a disadvantage is nevertheless justified because it makes the community as a whole better off.

Any institution which uses that idea to justify a discriminatory policy faces a series of theoretical and practical difficulties. There are, in the first place, two distinct senses in which a community may be said to be better off as a whole, in spite of the fact that certain of its members are worse off, and any justification must specify which sense is meant. It may be better off in a *utilitarian* sense, that is, because the average or collective level of welfare in the community is improved even though the welfare of some individuals falls. Or it may be better off in an *ideal* sense, that is, because it is more just, or in some other way closer to an ideal society, whether or not average welfare is improved. The University of Washington might use either utilitarian or ideal arguments to justify its racial classification. It might argue, for example, that increasing the number of black lawyers reduces racial tensions, which improves the welfare of almost everyone in the community. That is a utilitarian argument. Or it might argue that, whatever effect minority preference will have on average welfare, it will make the community more equal and therefore more just. That is an ideal, not a utilitarian, argument.

The University of Texas, on the other hand, cannot make an ideal argument for segregation. It cannot claim that segregation makes the community more just whether it improves the average welfare or not. The arguments it makes to defend segregation must therefore all be utilitarian arguments. The arguments I invented, like the argument that white lawyers could do more than black lawyers to improve commercial efficiency in Texas, are utilitarian, since commercial efficiency makes the community better off only if it improves average welfare.

Utilitarian arguments encounter a special difficulty that ideal arguments do not. What is meant by average or collective welfare? How can the welfare of an individual be measured, even in principle, and how can gains in the welfare of different individuals be added and then compared with losses, so as to justify the claim that gains outweigh losses overall? The utilitarian argument that segregation improves average welfare presupposes that such calculations can be made. But how?

Jeremy Bentham, who believed that only utilitarian arguments could justify political decisions, gave the following answer. He said that the effect of a policy on an individual's welfare could be determined by discovering the amount of pleasure or pain the policy brought him, and that effect of the policy on the collective welfare could be calculated by adding together all the pleasure and subtracting all of the pain it brought to everyone. But, as Bentham's critics insisted, it is doubtful whether there exists a simple psychological state of pleasure common to all those who benefit from a policy or of pain common to all those who lose by it; in any case it would be impossible to identify, measure, and add the different pleasures and pains felt by vast numbers of people.

Philosophers and economists who find utilitarian arguments attractive, but who reject Bentham's psychological utilitarianism, propose a different concept of individual and overall welfare. They suppose that whenever an institution or an official must decide upon a policy, the members of the community will each prefer the consequences of one decision to the consequences of others. DeFunis, for example, prefers the consequences of the standard admissions policy to the policy of minority preference Washington used, while the blacks in some urban ghetto might each prefer the consequences of the latter policy to the former. If it can be discovered what each individual prefers, and how intensely, then it might be shown that a particular policy would satisfy on balance more preferences, taking into account their intensity, than alternative policies. On this concept of welfare, a policy makes the community better off in a utilitarian sense if it satisfies the collection of preferences better than alternative policies would, even though it dissatisfies the preferences of some.

Of course, a law school does not have available any means of making accurate judgments about the preferences of all those whom its admissions policies will affect. It may nevertheless make judgments which, though speculative, cannot be dismissed as implausible. It is, for example, plausible to think that in postwar Texas, the preferences of the people were overall in favor of the consequences of segregation in law schools, even if the intensity of the competing preference for integration, and not simply the number of those holding that preference, is taken into account. The officials of the Texas law school might have relied upon voting behavior, newspaper editorials, and simply their own sense of their community in reaching that decision. Though they might have been wrong, we cannot now say, even with the benefit of hindsight, that they were.

So even if Bentham's psychological utilitarianism is rejected, law schools may appeal to preference utilitarianism to provide at least a rough and speculative justification for admissions policies that put some classes of applicants at a disadvantage. But once it is made clear that these utilitarian arguments are based on judgments about the actual preferences of members of the community, a fresh and much more serious difficulty emerges.

The utilitarian argument, that a policy is justified if it satisfies more preferences overall, seems at first sight to be an egalitarian argument. It seems to observe strict impartiality. If the community has only enough medicine to treat some of those who are sick, the argument seems to recommend that those who are sickest be treated first. If the community can afford a swimming pool or a new theater, but not both, and more people want the pool, then it recommends that the community build the pool, unless those who want the theater can show that their preferences are so much more intense that they have more weight in spite of the numbers. One sick man is not to be preferred to another because he is worthier of official concern: the tastes of the theater audience are not to be preferred because they are more admirable. In Bentham's phrase, each man is to count as one and no man is to count as more than one.

These simple examples suggest that the utilitarian argument not only respects, but embodies, the right of each citizen to be treated as the equal of any other. The chance that each individual's preferences have to succeed, in the competition for social policy, will depend upon how important his preference is to him, and how many others share it, compared to the intensity and number of competing preferences. His chance will not be affected by the esteem or contempt of either officials or fellow citizens, and he will therefore not be subservient or beholden to them.

But if we examine the range of preferences that individuals in fact have, we shall see that the apparent egalitarian character of a utilitarian argument is often deceptive. Preference utilitarianism asks officials to attempt to satisfy people's preferences so far as this is possible. But the preferences of an individual for the consequences of a particular policy may be seen to reflect, on further analysis, either a *personal* preference for his own enjoyment of some goods or opportunities, or an *external* preference for the assignment of goods and opportunities to others, or both. A white law school candidate might have a personal preference for the consequences of segregation, for example, because the policy improves his own chances of success, or an external preference for those consequences because he has contempt for blacks and disapproves social situations in which the races mix.

The distinction between personal and external preferences is of great importance for this reason. If a utilitarian argument counts external preferences along with personal preferences, then the egalitarian character of that argument is corrupted, because the chance that anyone's preferences have to succeed will then depend, not only on the demands that the personal preferences of others make on scarce resources, but on the respect or affection they have for him or for his way of life. If external preferences tip the balance, then the fact that a policy makes the community better off in a utilitarian sense would *not* provide a justification compatible with the right of those it disadvantages to be treated as equals.

This corruption of utilitarianism is plain when some people have external preferences because they hold political theories that are themselves contrary to utilitarianism. Suppose many citizens, who are not themselves sick, are racists in political theory, and therefore prefer that scarce medicine be given to a white man who needs it rather than a black man who needs it more. If utilitarianism counts these political preferences at face value, then it will be, from the standpoint of personal preferences, self-defeating, because the distribution of medicine will then not be, from that standpoint, utilitarian at all. In any case, self-defeating or not, the distribution will not be egalitarian in the sense defined. Blacks will suffer, to a degree that depends upon the strength of the racist preference, from the fact that others think them less worthy of respect and concern.

There is a similar corruption when the external preferences that are counted are altruistic or moralistic. Suppose many citizens, who themselves do not swim, prefer the pool to the theater because they approve of sports and admire athletes, or because they think that the theater is immoral and ought to be repressed. If the altruistic preferences are counted, so as to reinforce the personal preferences of swimmers, the result will be a form of double counting: each swimmer will have the benefit not only of his own preference, but also of the preference of someone else who takes pleasure in his success. If the moralistic preferences are counted, the effect will be the same: actors and audiences will suffer because their preferences are held in lower respect by citizens whose personal preferences are not themselves engaged.

In these examples, external preferences are independent of personal preferences. But of course political, altruistic, and moralistic preferences are often not independent, but grafted on to the personal preferences they reinforce. If I am white and sick, I may also hold a racist political theory. If I want a swimming pool for my own enjoyment I may also be altruistic in favor of my fellow athlete, or I may also think that the theater is immoral. The consequences of counting these external preferences will be as grave for equality as if they were independent of personal preference, because those against whom the external preferences run might be unable or unwilling to develop reciprocal external preferences that would right the balance.

External preferences therefore present a great difficulty for utilitarianism. That theory owes much of its popularity to the assumption that it embodies the right of citizens to be treated as equals. But if external preferences are counted in overall preferences, then this assumption is jeopardized. That is, in itself, an important and neglected point in political theory; it bears, for example, on the liberal thesis, first made prominent by Mill, that the government has no right to enforce popular morality by law. It is often said that this liberal thesis is inconsistent with utilitarianism, because if the preferences of the majority that homosexuality should be repressed, for example, are sufficiently strong, utilitarianism must give way to their wishes.

But the preference against homosexuality is an external preference, and the present argument provides a general reason why utilitarians should not count external preferences of any form. If utilitarianism is suitably reconstituted so as to count only personal preferences, then the liberal thesis is a consequence, not an enemy, of that theory.

It is not always possible, however, to reconstitute a utilitarian argument so as to count only personal preferences. Sometimes personal and external preferences are so inextricably tied together, and so mutually dependent, that no practical test for measuring preferences will be able to discriminate the personal and external elements in any individual's overall preference. That is especially true when preferences are affected by prejudice. Consider, for example, the associational preference of a white law student for white classmates. This may be said to be a personal preference for an association with one kind of colleague rather than another. But it is a personal preference that is parasitic upon external preferences: except in very rare cases a white student prefers the company of other whites because he has racist social and political convictions, or because he has contempt for blacks as a group. If these associational preferences are counted in a utilitarian argument used to justify segregation, then the egalitarian character of the argument is destroyed just as if the underlying external preferences were counted directly. Blacks would be denied their right to be treated as equals because the chance that their preferences would prevail in the design of admissions policy would be crippled by the low esteem in which others hold them. In any community in which prejudice against a particular minority is strong, then the personal preferences upon which a utilitarian argument must fix will be saturated with that prejudice; it follows that in such a community no utilitarian argument purporting to justify a disadvantage to the minority can be fair.

This final difficulty is therefore fatal to Texas' utilitarian arguments in favor of segregation. The preferences that might support any such argument are either distinctly external, like the preferences of the community at large for racial separation, or are inextricably combined with and dependent upon external preferences, like the associational preferences of white students for white classmates and white lawyers for white colleagues. These external preferences are so widespread that they must corrupt any such argument. Texas' claim, that segregation makes the community better off in a utilitarian sense, is therefore incompatible with Sweatt's right to treatment as an equal guaranteed by the Equal Protection Clause.

It does not matter, to this conclusion, whether external preferences figure in the justification of a fundamental policy, or in the justification of derivative policies designed to advance a more fundamental policy. Suppose Texas justifies segregation by pointing to the apparently neutral economic policy of increasing community wealth, which satisfies the personal preferences of everyone for better homes, food, and recreation. If the argument that segregation will improve community wealth depends upon the fact of external preference; if the argument notices, for example, that because of prejudice industry will run more efficiently if factories are segregated; then the argument has the consequence that the black man's personal preferences are defeated by what others think of him. Utilitarian arguments that justify a disadvantage to members of a race against whom prejudice runs will always be unfair arguments, unless it can be shown that the same disadvantage would have been justified in the absence of the prejudice. If the prejudice is widespread and pervasive, as in fact it is in the case of blacks, that can never be shown. The preferences on which any economic argument justifying segregation must be based will be so intertwined with prejudice that they cannot be disentangled to the degree necessary to make any such contrary-to-fact hypothesis plausible.

We now have an explanation that shows why any form of segregation that disadvantages blacks is, in the United States, an automatic insult to them, and why such segregation offends their right to be treated as equals. The argument confirms our sense that utilitarian arguments purporting to justify segregation are not simply wrong in detail but displaced in principle. This objection to utilitarian arguments is not, however, limited to race or even prejudice. There are other cases in which counting external preferences would offend the rights of citizens to be treated as equals, and it is worth briefly noticing these, if only to protect the argument against the charge that it is constructed ad hoc for the racial case. I might have a moralistic preference against professional women, or an altruistic preference for virtuous men. It would be unfair for any law school to count preferences like these in deciding whom to admit to law schools; unfair because these preferences, like racial prejudices, make the success of the personal preferences of an applicant depend on the esteem and approval, rather than on the competing personal preferences, of others.

The same objection does not hold, however, against a utilitarian argument used to justify admission based on intelligence. That policy need not rely, directly or indirectly, on any community sense that intelligent lawyers are intrinsically more worthy of respect. It relies instead upon the law school's own judgment, right or wrong, that intelligent lawyers are more effective in satisfying personal preferences of others, such as the preference for wealth or winning law suits. It is true that law firms and clients prefer the services of intelligent lawyers; that fact might make us suspicious of any utilitarian argument that is said not to depend upon that preference, just as we are suspicious of any argument justifying segregation that is said not to depend upon prejudice. But the widespread preference for intelligent lawyers is, by and large, not parasitic on external preferences: law firms and clients prefer intelligent lawyers because they also hold the opinion that such lawyers will be more effective in serving their personal preferences. Instrumental preferences, of that character, do not themselves figure in utilitarian arguments, though a law school may accept, on its own responsibility, the instrumental hypothesis upon which such preferences depend.

V

We therefore have the distinctions in hand necessary to distinguish *DeFunis* from *Sweatt*. The arguments for an admissions program that discriminates against blacks are all utilitarian arguments, and they are all utilitarian arguments that rely upon external preferences in such a way as to offend the constitutional right of blacks to be treated as equals. The arguments for an admissions program that discriminates in favor of blacks are both utilitarian and ideal. Some of the utilitarian arguments do rely, at least indirectly, on external preferences, such as the preference of certain blacks for lawyers of their own race; but the utilitarian arguments that do not rely on such preferences are strong and may be sufficient. The ideal arguments do not rely upon preferences at all, but on the independent argument that a more equal society is a better society even if its citizens prefer inequality. That argument does not deny anyone's right to be treated as an equal himself.

We are therefore left, in *DeFunis,* with the simple and straightforward argument with which we began. Racial criteria are not necessarily the right standards for deciding which applicants should be accepted by law schools. But neither are intellectual criteria, nor indeed, any other set of criteria. The fairness—and constitutionality—of any admissions program must be tested in the same way. It is justified if it serves a proper policy that respects the right of all members of the community to be treated as equals, but not otherwise. The criteria used by schools that refused to consider blacks failed that test, but the criteria used by the University of Washington Law School do not.

We are all rightly suspicious of racial classifications. They have been used to deny, rather than to respect, the right of equality, and we are all conscious of the consequent injustice. But if we misunderstand the nature of that injustice because we do not make the simple distinctions that are necessary to understand it, then we are in danger of more injustice still. It may be that preferential admissions programs will not, in fact, make a more equal society, because they may not have the effects their advocates believe they will. That strategic question should be at the center of debate about these programs. But we must not corrupt the debate by supposing that these programs are unfair even if they do work. We must take care not to use the Equal Protection Clause to cheat ourselves of equality.

QUESTIONS FOR DISCUSSION

1. What are the two senses of "justice" distinguished by Newton? Why, according to her, is the political sense the only one relevant to the issue of affirmative action?

2. Is there an important ethical difference between social programs such as Head Start that provide special assistance to disadvantaged groups, and affirmative action legislation that requires professional schools and businesses to set aside a proportionate number of positions for minorities?

3. Why, according to Newton, does the attempt to compensate victims of past discrimination that was not illegal undermine the ideal of equality before the law?

4. What does Dworkin mean by "treating people as equals" as distinct from "equal treatment of people"? Why is the latter not always desirable or just?

5. Is affirmative action as justifiable for women as for racial and ethnic minorities? Do the same arguments apply to both?

6. Affirmative action programs sometimes generate resentment or backlash. Is this an argument against them or is it further evidence of the need for them?

SUGGESTED READINGS

AXELSEN, D., "With all Deliberate Delay: On Justifying Preferential Policies in Education and Employment," *Philosophical Forum,* 9 (1977–8).

BARMER, W., "Reverse Discrimination: Misconception and Confusion," *Journal of Social Philosophy,* 10 (1979).

BENSON, R., "Defining Quality in Education," *Educational Studies,* 8 (1977).

BLACKSTONE, W., "Reverse Discrimination and Compensatory Justice," *Social Theory and Practice,* 3 (1975).

CORLETT, J. A., "Racism and Affirmative Action," *Journal of Social Philosophy,* 24, 1 (1993), 163–75.

DE MARCO, J., "Compensatory Justice and Equal Opportunity," *Journal of Social Philosophy,* 6 (1975).

EZORSKY, G., "Hiring Women Faculty," *Philosophy and Public Affairs,* 7 (1977).

———, *Reason and Justice,* Ithaca: Cornell University Press, 1991.

FRIED, M., "The Invisibility of Oppression," *Philosophical Forum,* 11 (1979).

GOLDMAN, A., "The Principle of Equal Opportunity," *Southern Journal of Philosophy,* 15 (1977).

GROSS, B., *Reverse Discrimination,* Buffalo: Prometheus, 1977.

HARWOOD, S., "Affirmative Action Is Justified," *Contemporary Philosophy,* 13, 2 (1990), 14–17.

KETCHUM, S., "Evidence, Statistics and Rights: A Reply to Simon," *Analysis,* 39 (1979).

NEWTON, L., "Corruptions of Thought, Word and Deed," *Contemporary Philosophy,* 13, 7 (1991), 14–16.

ROSENFELD, M., *Affirmative Action and Justice,* New Haven: Yale University Press, 1991.

SAPADIN, E., "Race Isn't Merit," *Reason Papers,* 15 (1990), 1412–48.

SASSEEN, R., "Affirmative Action and the Principle of Equality," *Studies in the Philosophy of Education,* 9 (1976).

SHER, G., "Groups and Justice," *Ethics,* 87 (1977).

SIMON, R., "Preferential Treatment for Groups or for Individuals," *National Forum,* 58 (1978).

STORER, M., "The Enigma of Human Equality," *Religious Humanism,* 37 (1977).

TAYLOR, B., *Affirmative Action at Work,* Pittsburgh: University of Pittsburgh Press, 1991.

WASSERSTROM, R., "A Defense of Programs of Preferential Treatment," *National Forum,* 58 (1978).

WATRAS, J., "Affirmative Action and the *Bakke* Decision," *Thought,* 14 (1979).

10

PRIVACY AND ITS LIMITS

THE PRIVATE DOMAIN

John Stuart Mill

What, then, is the rightful limit to the sovereignty of the individual over himself? Where does the authority of society begin? How much of human life should be assigned to individuality, and how much to society?

Each will receive its proper share if each has that which more particularly concerns it. To individuality should belong the part of life in which it is chiefly the individual that is interested; to society, the part which chiefly interests society.

Though society is not founded on a contract, and though no good purpose is answered by inventing a contract in order to deduce social obligations from it, everyone who receives the protection of society owes a return for the benefit, and the fact of living in society renders it indispensable that each should be bound to observe a certain line of conduct toward the rest. This conduct consists, first, in not injuring the interests of one another, or rather certain interests which, either by express legal provision or by tacit understanding, ought to be considered as rights; and secondly, in each person's bearing his share (to be fixed on some equitable principle) of the labors and sacrifices incurred for defending the society or its members from injury and molestation. These conditions society is justified in enforcing at all costs to those who endeavor to withhold fulfillment. Nor is this all that society may do. The acts of an individual may be hurtful to others or wanting in due consideration for their welfare, without going to the length of violating any of their constituted rights. The offender may then be justly punished by opinion, though not by law. As soon as any part of a person's conduct affects prejudicially the interests of others, society has jurisdiction over it, and the question whether the general welfare will or will not be promoted by interfering with it becomes open to discussion. But there is no

FROM *On Liberty,* first published in 1859.

room for entertaining any such question when a person's conduct affects the interests of no persons besides himself, or needs not affect them unless they like (all the persons concerned being of full age and the ordinary amount of understanding). In all such cases, there should be perfect freedom, legal and social, to do the action and stand the consequences.

It would be a great misunderstanding of this doctrine to suppose that it is one of selfish indifference which pretends that human beings have no business with each other's conduct in life, and that they should not concern themselves about the well-doing or well-being of one another, unless their own interest is involved. Instead of any diminution, there is need of a great increase of disinterested exertion to promote the good of others. But disinterested benevolence can find other instruments to persuade people to their good than whips and scourges, either of the literal or the metaphysical sort. I am the last person to undervalue the self-regarding virtues; they are only second in importance, if even second, to the social. It is equally the business of education to cultivate both. But even education works by conviction and persuasion as well as by compulsion, and it is by the former only that, when the period of education is passed, the self-regarding virtues should be inculcated. Human beings owe to each other help to distinguish the better from the worse, and encouragement to choose the former and avoid the latter. They should be forever stimulating each other to increased exercise of their higher faculties and increased direction of their feelings and aims toward wise instead of foolish, elevating instead of degrading, objects and contemplations. But neither one person, nor any number of persons, is warranted in saying to another human creature of ripe years that he shall not do with his life for his own benefit what he chooses to do with it. He is the person most interested in his own well-being: the interest which any other person, except in cases of strong personal attachment, can have in it is trifling compared with that which he himself has; the interest which society has in him individually (except as to his conduct to others) is fractional and altogether indirect, while with respect to his own feelings and circumstances the most ordinary man or woman has means of knowledge immeasurably surpassing those that can be possessed by anyone else. The interference of society to overrule his judgment and purposes in what only regards himself must be grounded on general presumptions which may be altogether wrong and, even if right, are as likely as not to be misapplied to individual cases, by persons no better acquainted with the circumstances of such cases than those who look at them merely from without. In this department, therefore, of human affairs, individuality has its proper field of action. In the conduct of human beings toward one another it is necessary that general rules should for the most part be observed in order that people may know what they have to expect; but in each person's own concerns his individual spontaneity is entitled to free exercise. Considerations to aid his judgment, exhortations to strengthen his will may be offered to him, even obtruded on him, by others; but he himself is the final judge. All errors which he is likely to commit against advice and warning are far outweighed by the evil of allowing others to constrain him to what they deem his good.

I do not mean that the feelings with which a person is regarded by others ought not to be in any way affected by his self-regarding qualities or deficiencies. This is neither possible nor desirable. If he is eminent in any of the qualities which conduce to his own good, he is, so far, a proper object of admiration. He is so much the nearer to the ideal perfection of human nature. If he is grossly deficient in those qualities, a sentiment the opposite of admiration will follow. There is a degree of folly, and a degree of what may be called (though the phrase is not unobjectionable) lowness or depravation of taste, which, though it cannot justify doing harm to the person who manifests it, renders him necessarily and properly a subject of distaste, or, in extreme cases, even of contempt: a person could not have the opposite qualities in due strength without entertaining these feelings. Though doing no wrong to anyone, a person may so act as to compel us to judge him, and feel to him, as a fool or as a being of an inferior order; and since this judgment and feeling are a fact which he would prefer to avoid, it is doing him a service to warn him of it beforehand, as of any other disagreeable consequence to which he exposes himself. It would be well, indeed, if this good office were much more freely rendered than the common notions of politeness at present permit, and if one person could honestly point out to another that he thinks him in fault, without being considered unmannerly or presuming. We have a right, also, in various ways, to act upon our unfavorable opinion of anyone, not to the oppression of his individuality, but in the exercise of ours. We are not bound, for example, to seek his society; we have a right to avoid it (though not to parade the avoidance), for we have a right to choose the society most acceptable to us. We have a right, and it may be our duty, to caution others against him if we think his example or conversation likely to have a pernicious effect on those with whom he associates. We may give others a preference over him in optional good offices, except those which tend to his improvement. In these various modes a person may suffer very severe penalties at the hands of others for faults which directly concern only himself; but he suffers these penalties only in so far as they are the natural and, as it were, the spontaneous consequences of the faults themselves, not because they are purposely inflicted on him for the sake of punishment. A person who shows rashness, obstinacy, self-conceit—who cannnot live within moderate means; who cannot restrain himself from hurtful indulgence; who pursues animal pleasures at the expense of those of feeling and intellect—must expect to be lowered in the opinion of others, and to have a less share of their favorable sentiments; but of this he has no right to complain unless he has merited their favor by special excellence in his social relations and has thus established a title to their good offices, which is not affected by his demerits toward himself.

What I contend for is that the inconveniences which are strictly inseparable from the unfavorable judgment of others are the only ones to which a person should ever be subjected for that portion of his conduct and character which concerns his own good, but which does not affect the interest of others in their relations with him. Acts injurious to others require a totally different treatment. Encroachment on their rights; infliction on them of any loss or damage not justified by his own rights; falsehood or duplicity in dealing with them; unfair or ungenerous use of advantages over them; even selfish abstinence from defending them against injury—these are fit objects of moral reprobation and, in grave cases, of moral retribution and punishment. And not only these acts, but the dispositions which lead to them, are properly immoral and fit subjects of disapprobation which may rise to abhorrence. Cruelty of disposition; malice and ill-nature; that most antisocial and odious of all passions, envy; dissimulation and insincerity, irascibility on insufficient cause, and resentment disproportion to the provocation; the love of domineering over others; the desire to engross more than one's share of advantages (the *pleonexia* of the Greeks); the pride which derives gratification from the abasement of others; the egotism which thinks self and its concerns more important than everything else, and decides all doubtful questions in its own favor—these are moral vices and constitute a bad and odious moral character; unlike the self-regarding faults previously mentioned, which are not properly immoralities and, to whatever pitch they may be carried, do not constitute wickedness. They may be proofs of any amount of folly or want of personal dignity and self-respect, but they are only a subject of moral reprobation when they involve a breach of duty to others, for whose sake the individual is bound to have care for himself. What are called duties to ourselves are not socially obligatory unless circumstances render them at the same time duties to others. The term duty to oneself, when it means anything more than prudence, means self-respect or self-development, and for none of these is anyone accountable to his fellow creatures, because for none of them is it for the good of mankind that he be held accountable to them.

The distinction between the loss of consideration which a person may rightly incur by defect of prudence or of personal dignity, and the reprobation which is due to him for an offense against the rights of others, is not a merely nominal distinction. It makes a vast difference both in our feelings and in our conduct toward him whether he displeases us in things in which we think we have a right to control him or in things in which we know that we have not. If he displeases us, we may express our distaste, and we may stand aloof from a person as well as from a thing that displeases us; but we shall not therefore feel called on to make his life uncomfortable. We shall reflect that he already bears, or will bear, the whole penalty of his error; if he spoils his life by mismanagement, we shall not, for that reason, desire to spoil it still further; instead of wishing to punish him, we shall rather endeavor to alleviate his punishment by showing him how he may avoid or cure the evils his conduct tends to bring upon him. He may be to us an object of pity, perhaps of dislike, but not of anger or resentment; we shall not treat him like an enemy of society; the worst we shall think ourselves justified in doing is leaving him to himself, if we do not interfere benevolently by showing interest or concern for him. It is far otherwise if he has infringed the rules necessary for the protection of his fellow creatures, individually or collectively. The evil consequences of his acts do not then fall on himself, but on others; and society, as the protector of all its members, must retaliate on him, must inflict pain on him for the express purpose of punishment, and must take care that it be sufficiently severe. In the one case, he is an offender at our bar, and we are called on not only to sit in judgment on him, but, in one shape or another, to execute our own sentence; in the other case, it is not our part to inflict any suffering on him, except what may incidentally follow from our using the same liberty in the regulation of our own affairs which we allow to him in his.

The distinction here pointed out between the part of a person's life which concerns only himself and that which concerns others, many persons will refuse to admit. How (it may be asked) can any part of the conduct of a member of society be a matter of indifference to the other members? No person is an entirely isolated being; it is impossible for a person to do anything seriously or permanently hurtful to himself without mischief reaching at least to his near connections, and often far beyond them. If he injures his property, he does harm to those who directly or indirectly derived support from it, and usually diminishes, by a greater or less amount, the general resources of the community. If he deteriorates his bodily or mental faculties, he not only brings evil upon all who depended on him for any portion of their happiness, but disqualifies himself for rendering the services which he owes to his fellow creatures generally, perhaps becomes a burden on their affection or benevolence; and if such conduct were very frequent hardly any offense that is committed would detract more from the general sum of good. Finally, if by his vices or follies a person does no direct harm to others, he is nevertheless (it may be said) injurious by his example, and ought to be compelled to control himself for the sake of those whom the sight or knowledge of his conduct might corrupt or mislead.

And even (it will be added) if the consequences of misconduct could be confined to the vicious or thoughtless individual, ought society to abandon to their own guidance those who are manifestly unfit for it? If protection against themselves is confessedly due to children and persons under age, is not society equally bound to afford it to persons of mature years who are equally incapable of self-government? If gambling, or drunkenness, or incontinence, or idleness, or uncleanliness are as injurious to happiness, and as great a hindrance to improvement, as many or most of the acts prohibited by law, why (it may be asked) should not law, as far as is consistent with practicability and social convenience, endeavor to repress these also? And as a supplement to the unavoidable imperfections of law, ought not opinion at least to organize a powerful police against these vices and visit rigidly with social penalties those who are known to practice them? There is no question here (it may be said) about restricting individuality, or impeding the trial of new and original experiments in living. The only things it is sought to prevent are things which have been tried and condemned from the beginning of the world until now—things which experience has shown not to be useful or suitable to any person's individuality. There must be some length of time and amount of experience after which a moral or prudential truth may be regarded as established; and it is merely desired to prevent generation after generation from falling over the same precipice which has been fatal to their predecessors.

I fully admit that the mischief which a person does to himself may seriously affect, both through their sympathies and their interests, those nearly connected with him and, in a minor degree, society at large. When, by conduct of this sort, a person is led to violate a distinct and assignable obligation to any other person or persons, the case is taken out of the self-regarding class and becomes amenable to moral disapprobation in the proper sense of the term. If, for example, a man, through intemperance or extravagance, becomes unable to pay his debts, or, having undertaken the moral responsibility of a family, becomes from the same cause incapable of supporting or educating them, he is deservedly reprobated and might be justly punished; but it is for the breach of duty to his family or creditors, not for the extravagance. If the resources which ought to have been devoted to them had been diverted from them for the most prudent investment, the moral culpability would have been the same. George Barnwell murdered his uncle to get money for his mistress, but if he had done it to set himself up in business, he would equally have been hanged. Again, in the frequent case of a man who causes grief to his family by addiction to bad habits, he deserves reproach for his unkindness or ingratitude; but so he may for cultivating habits not in themselves vicious, if they are painful to those with whom he passes his life, or who from personal ties are dependent on him for their comfort. Whoever fails in the consideration generally due to the interests and feelings of others, not being compelled by some more imperative duty, or justified by allowable self-preference, is a subject of moral disapprobation for that failure, but not for the cause of it, nor for the errors, merely personal to himself, which may have remotely led to it. In like manner, when a person disables himself, by conduct purely self-regarding, from the performance of some definite duty incumbent on him to the public, he is guilty of a social offense. No person ought to be punished simply for being drunk; but a soldier or a policeman should be punished for being drunk on duty. Whenever, in short, there is a definite damage, or a definite risk of damage, either to an individual or to the public, the case is taken out of the province of liberty and placed in that of morality or law.

But with regard to the merely contingent or, as it may be called, constructive injury which a person causes to society by conduct which neither violates any specific duty to the public, nor occasions perceptible hurt to any assignable individual except himself, the inconvenience is one which society can afford to bear, for the sake of the greater good of human freedom. If grown persons are to be punished for not taking proper care of themselves, I would rather it were for their own sake than under pretense of preventing them from impairing their capacity of rendering to society benefits which society does not pretend it has a right to exact. But I cannot consent to argue the point as if society had no means of bringing its weaker members up to its ordinary standard of rational conduct, except waiting till they do something irrational, and then punishing them, legally or morally, for it. Society has had absolute power over them during all the early portion of their existence; it has had the whole period of childhood and nonage in which to try whether it could make them capable of rational conduct in life. The existing generation is master both of the training and the entire circumstances of the generation to come; it cannot indeed make them perfectly wise and good, because it is itself so lamentably deficient in goodness and wisdom; and its best efforts are not always, in individual cases, its most successful ones; but it is perfectly well able to make the rising generation, as a whole, as good as, and a little better than, itself. If society lets any considerable number of its members grow up mere children, incapable of being acted on by rational consideration of distant motives, society has itself to blame for the consequences. Armed not only with all the powers of education, but with the ascendancy which the authority of a received opinion always exercises over the minds who are least fitted to judge for themselves, and aided by the *natural* penalties which cannot be prevented from falling on those who incur the distaste or the contempt of those who know them— let not society pretend that it needs, besides all this, the power to issue commands and enforce obedience in the personal concerns of individuals in which, on all principles of justice and policy, the decision ought to rest with those who are to abide the consequences. Nor is there anything which tends more to discredit and frustrate the better means of influencing conduct than a resort to the worse. If there be among those whom it is attempted to coerce into prudence or temperance any of the material of which vigorous and independent characters are made, they will infallibly rebel against the yoke. No such person will ever feel that others have a right to control him in his concerns, such as they have to prevent him from injuring them in theirs; and it easily comes to be considered a mark of spirit and courage to fly in the face of such usurped authority and do with ostentation the exact opposite of what it enjoins, as in the fashion of grossness which succeeded, in the time of Charles II, to the fanatical moral intolerance of the Puritans. With respect to what is said of the necessity of protecting society from the bad example set to others by the vicious or the self-indulgent, it is true that bad example may have a pernicious effect, especially the example of doing wrong to others with impunity to the wrongdoer. But we are now speaking of conduct which, while it does no wrong to others, is supposed to do great harm to the agent himself; and I do not see how those who believe this can think otherwise than that the example, on the whole, must be more salutary than hurtful, since, if it displays the misconduct, it displays also the painful or degrading consequences which, if the conduct is justly censured, must be supposed to be in all or most cases attendant on it.

But the strongest of all the arguments against the interference of the public with purely personal conduct is that, when it does interfere, the odds are that it interferes wrongly and in the wrong place. On questions of social morality, of duty to others, the opinion of the public, that is, of an overruling majority, though often wrong, is likely to be still oftener right, because on such questions they are only required to judge of their own interests, of the manner in which some mode of conduct, if allowed to be practiced, would affect themselves. But the opinion of a similar majority, imposed as a law on the minority, on questions of self-regarding conduct is quite as likely to be wrong as right, for in these cases public opinion means, at the best, some people's opinion of what is good or bad for other people, while very often it does not even mean that—the public, with the most perfect indifference, passing over the pleasure or convenience of those whose conduct they censure and considering only their own preference. There are many who consider as an injury to themselves any conduct which they have a distaste for, and resent it as an outrage to their feelings; as a religious bigot, when charged with disregarding the religious feelings of others, has been known to retort that they disregard his feelings by persisting in their abominable worship or creed. But there is not parity between the feeling of a person for his own opinion and the feeling of another who is offended at his holding it, no more than between the desire of a thief to take a purse and the desire of the right owner to keep it. And a person's taste is as much his own peculiar concern as his opinion or his purse. It is easy for anyone to imagine an ideal public which leaves the freedom and choice of individuals in all uncertain matters undisturbed and only requires them to abstain from modes of conduct which universal experience has condemned. But where has there been seen a public which set any such limit to its censorship? Or when does the public trouble itself about universal experience? In its interferences with personal conduct it is seldom thinking of anything but the enormity of acting or feeling differently from itself; and this standard of judgment, thinly disguised, is held up to mankind as the dictate of religion and philosophy by nine-tenths of all moralists and speculative writers. These teach that things are right because they are right; because we feel them to be so. They tell us to search in our own minds and hearts for laws of conduct binding on ourselves and on all others. What can the poor public do but apply these instructions and make their own personal feelings of good and evil, if they are tolerably unanimous in them, obligatory on all the world?

The evil here pointed out is not one which exists only in theory; and it may perhaps be expected that I should specify the instances in which the public of this age and country improperly invests its own preferences with the character of moral laws. I am not writing an essay on the aberrations of existing moral feeling. That is too weighty a subject to be discussed parenthetically, and by way of illustration. Yet examples are necessary to show that the principle I maintain is of serious and practical moment, and that I am not endeavoring to erect a barrier against imaginary evils. And it is not difficult to show, by abundant instances, that to extend the bounds of what may be called moral police until it encroaches on the most unquestionably legitimate liberty of the individual is one of the most universal of all human propensities.

As a first instance, consider the antipathies which men cherish on no better grounds than that persons whose religious opinions are different from theirs do not practice their religious observances, especially their religious abstinences. To cite a rather trivial example, nothing in the creed or practice of Christians does more to envenom the hatred of Mohammedans against them than the fact of their eating pork. There are few acts which Christians and Europeans regard with more unaffected disgust than Mussulmans regard this particular mode of satisfying hunger. It is in the first place, an offense against their religion; but this circumstance by no means explains either the degree or the kind of their repugnance; for wine also is forbidden by their religion, and to partake of it is by all Mussulmans accounted wrong, but not disgusting. Their aversion to the flesh of the "unclean beast" is, on the contrary, of that peculiar character, resembling an instinctive antipathy, which the idea of uncleanness, when once it thoroughly sinks into the feelings, seems always to excite even in those whose personal habits are anything but scrupulously clean, and of which the sentiment of religious impurity, so intense in the Hindus, is a remarkable example. Suppose now that in a people of whom the majority were Mussulmans, that majority should insist upon not permitting pork to be eaten within the limits of the country. This would be nothing new in Mohammedan countries. Would it be a legitimate exercise of the moral authority of public opinion, and if not, why not? The practice is really revolting to such a public. They also sincerely think that it is forbidden and abhorred by the Deity. Neither could the prohibition be censured as religious persecution. It might be religious in its origin, but it would not be persecution for religion, since nobody's religion makes it a duty to eat pork. The only tenable ground of condemnation would be that with the personal tastes and self-regarding concerns of individuals the public has no business to interfere.

To come somewhat nearer home: the majority of Spaniards consider it a gross impiety, offensive in the highest degree to the Supreme Being, to worship him in any other manner than the Roman Catholic; and no other public worship is lawful on Spanish soil. The people of all southern Europe look upon a married clergy as not only irreligious, but unchaste, indecent, gross, disgusting. What do Protestants think of these perfectly sincere feelings, and of the attempt to enforce them against non-Catholics? Yet, if mankind are justified in interfering with each other's liberty in things which do not concern the interests of others, on what principle is it possible consistently to exclude these cases? Or who can blame people for desiring to suppress what they regard as a scandal in the sight of God and man? No stronger case can be shown for prohibiting anything which is regarded as a personal immorality than is made out for suppressing these practices in the eyes of those who regard them as impieties; and unless we are willing to adopt the logic of persecutors, and to say that we may persecute others because we are right, and that they must not persecute us because they are wrong, we must beware of admitting a principle of which we should resent as a gross injustice the application to ourselves.

The preceding instances may be objected to, although unreasonably, as drawn from contingencies impossible among us—opinion, in this country, not being likely to enforce abstinence from meats or to interfere with people for worshiping and for either marrying or not marrying, according to their creed or inclination. The next example, however, shall be taken from an interference with liberty which we have by no means passed all danger of. Wherever the Puritans have been sufficiently powerful, as in New England, and in Great Britain at the time of the Commonwealth, they have endeavored, with considerable success, to put down all public, and nearly all private, amusements: especially music, dancing, public games, or other assemblages for purposes of diversion, and the theater. There are still in this country large bodies of persons by whose notions of morality and religion these recreations are condemned; and those persons belonging chiefly to the middle class, who are the ascendant power in the present social and political condition of the kingdom, it is by no means impossible that persons of these sentiments may at some time or other command a majority in Parliament. How will the remaining portion of the community like to have the amusements that shall be permitted to them regulated by the religious and moral sentiments of the stricter Calvinists and Methodists? Would they not, with considerable peremptoriness, desire these intrusively pious members of society to mind their own business? This is precisely what should be said to every government and every public who have the pretension that no person shall enjoy any pleasure which they think wrong. But if the principle of the pretension be admitted, no one can reasonably object to its being acted on in the sense of the majority, or other preponderating power in the country; and all persons must be ready to conform to the idea of a Christian commonwealth as understood by the early settlers in New England, if a religious profession similar to theirs should ever succeed in regaining its lost ground, as religions supposed to be declining have so often been known to do.

To imagine another contingency, perhaps more likely to be realized than the one last mentioned. There is confessedly a strong tendency in the modern world toward a democratic constitution of society, accompanied or not by popular political institutions. It is affirmed that in the country where this tendency is most completely realized—where both society and the government are most democratic: the United States—the feeling of the majority, to whom any appearance of a more showy or costly style of living than they can hope to rival is disagreeable, operates as a tolerably effectual sumptuary law, and that in many parts of the Union it is really difficult for a person possessing a very large income to find any mode of spending it which will not incur popular disapprobation. Though such statements as these are doubtless much exaggerated as a representation of existing facts, the state of things they describe is not only a conceivable and possible, but a probable result of democratic feeling combined with the notion that the public has a right to a veto on the manner in which individuals shall spend their incomes.

We have only further to suppose a considerable diffusion of Socialist opinions, and it may become infamous in the eyes of the majority to possess more property than some very small amount, or any income not earned by manual labor. Opinions similar in principle to these already prevail widely among the artisan class and weigh oppressively on those who are amenable to the opinion chiefly of that class, namely, its own members. It is known that the bad workmen who form the majority of the operatives in many branches of industry are decidedly of the opinion that bad workmen ought to receive the same wages as good, and that no one ought to be allowed, through piecework or otherwise, to earn by superior skill or industry more than others can without it. And they employ a moral police, which occasionally becomes a physical one, to deter skillful workmen from receiving, and employers from giving, a larger remuneration for a more useful service. If the public have any jurisdiction over private concerns, I cannot see that these people are in fault, or that any individual's particular public can be blamed for asserting the same authority over his individual conduct which the general public asserts over people in general.

But, without dwelling upon suppositious cases, there are, in our own day, gross usurpations upon the liberty of private life actually practiced, and still greater ones threatened with some expectation of success, and opinions propounded which assert an unlimited right in the public not only to prohibit by law everything which it thinks wrong, but, in order to get at what it thinks wrong, to prohibit a number of things which it admits to be innocent.

Under the name of preventing intemperance, the people of one English colony, and of nearly half the United States, have been interdicted by law from making any use whatever of fermented drinks, except for medical purposes, for prohibition of their sale is in fact, as it is intended to be, prohibition of their use. And though the impracticability of executing the law has caused its repeal in several of the States which had adopted it, including the one from which it derives its name, an attempt has notwithstanding been commenced, and is prosecuted with considerable zeal by many of the professed philanthropists, to agitate for a similar law in this country. The association, or "Alliance," as it terms itself, which has been formed for this purpose, has acquired some notoriety through the publicity given to a correspondence between its secretary and one of the very few English public men who hold that a politician's opinion ought to be founded on principles. Lord Stanley's share in this correspondence is calculated to strengthen the hopes already built on him by those who know how rare such qualities as are manifested in some of his public appearances unhappily are among those who figure in political life. The organ of the Alliance, who would "deeply deplore the recognition of any principle which could be wrested to justify bigotry and persecution," undertakes to point out the "broad and impassable barrier" which divides such principles from those of the association. "All matters relating to thought, opinion, conscience, appear to me," he says, "to be without the sphere of legislation; all pertaining to social act, habit, relation, subject only to a discretionary power vested in the State itself, and not in the individual, to be within it." No mention is made of a third class, different from either of these, viz., acts and habits which are not social, but individual; although it is to this class, surely, that the act of drinking fermented liquors belongs. Selling fermented liquors, however, is trading, and trading is a social act. But the infringement complained of is not on the liberty of the seller, but on that of the buyer and consumer; since the State might just as well forbid him to drink wine as purposely make it impossible for him to obtain it. The secretary, however, says, "I claim, as a citizen, a right to legislate whenever my social rights are invaded by the social act of another." And now for the definition of these "social rights": "If anything invades my social rights, certainly the traffic in strong drink does. It destroys my primary right of security by constantly creating and stimulating social disorder. It invades my right of equality by deriving a profit from the creation of a misery I am taxed to support. It impedes my right to free moral and intellectual development by surrounding my path with dangers and by weakening and demoralizing society, from which I have a right to claim mutual aid and intercourse." A theory of "social rights" the like of which probably never before found its way into distinct language: being nothing short of this—that it is the absolute social right of every individual that every other individual shall act in every respect exactly as he ought; that whosoever fails thereof in the smallest particular violates my social right and entitles me to demand from the legislature the removal of the grievance. So monstrous a principle is far more dangerous than any single interference with liberty; there is no violation of liberty which it would not justify; it acknowledges no right to any freedom whatever, except perhaps to that of holding opinions in secret, without ever disclosing them; for the moment an opinion which I consider noxious passes anyone's lips, it invades all the "social rights" attributed to me by the Alliance. The doctrine ascribes to all mankind a vested interest in each other's moral, intellectual, and even physical perfection, to be defined by each claimant according to his own standard.

Another important example of illegitimate interference with the rightful liberty of the individual, not simply threatened, but long since carried into triumphant effect, is Sabbatarian legislation. Without doubt, abstinence on one day in the week, so far as the exigencies of life permit, from the usual daily occupation, though in no respect religiously binding on any except Jews, is a highly beneficial custom. And inasmuch as this custom cannot be observed without a general consent to that effect among the industrious classes, therefore, in so far as some persons by working may impose the same necessity on others, it may be allowable and right that the law should guarantee to each the observance by others of the custom, by suspending the greater operations of industry on a particular day. But this justification, grounded on the direct interest which others have in each individual's observance of the practice, does not apply to the self-chosen occupations in which a person may think fit to employ his leisure, nor does it hold good, in the smallest degree, for legal restrictions on amusements. It is true that the amusement of some is the day's work of others; but the pleasure, not to say the useful recreation, of many is worth the labor of a few, provided the occupation is freely chosen and can be freely resigned. The operatives are perfectly right in thinking that if all worked on Sunday, seven days' work would have to be given for six days' wages; but so long as the great mass of employments are suspended, the small number who for the enjoyment of others must still work to obtain a proportional increase of earnings; and they are not obliged to follow these occupations if they prefer leisure to emolument. If a further remedy is sought, it might be found in the establishment by custom of a holiday on some other day of the week for those particular classes of persons. The only ground, therefore, on which restrictions on Sunday amusements can be defended must be that they are religiously wrong—a motive of legislation which can never be too earnestly protested against. *"Deorum injuriae Diis curae."* It remains to be proved that society or any of its officers holds a commission from on high to avenge any supposed offense to Omnipotence which is not also a wrong to our fellow creatures. The notion that it is one man's duty that another should be religious was the foundation of all the religious persecutions ever perpetrated, and, if admitted, would fully justify them. Though the feeling which breaks out in the repeated attempts to stop railway traveling on Sunday, in the resistance to the opening of museums, and the like, has not the cruelty of the old persecutors, the state of mind indicated by it is fundamentally the same. It is a determination not to tolerate others in doing what is permitted by their religion, because it is not permitted by the persecutor's religion. It is a belief that God not only abominates the act of the misbeliever, but will not hold us guiltless if we leave him unmolested.

I cannot refrain from adding to these examples of the little account commonly made of human liberty the language of downright persecution which breaks out from the press of this country whenever it feels called on to notice the remarkable phenomenon of Mormonism. Much might be said on the unexpected and instructive fact that an alleged new revelation and a religion founded on it—the product of palpable imposture, not even supported by the *prestige* of extraordinary qualities in its founder—is believed by hundreds of thousands, and has been made the foundation of a society in the age of newspapers, railways, and the electric telegraph. What here concerns us is that this religion, like other and better religions, has its martyrs: that its prophet and founder was, for his teaching, put to death by a mob; that others of its adherents lost their lives by the same lawless violence; that they were forcibly expelled, in a body, from the country in which they first grew up, while, now that they have been chased into a solitary recess in the midst of a desert, many in this country openly declare that it would be right (only that it is not convenient) to send an expedition against them and compel them by force to conform to the opinions of other people. The article of the Mormonite doctrine which is the chief provocative to the antipathy which thus breaks through the ordinary restraints of religious tolerance is its sanction of polygamy; which, though permitted to Mohammedans, and Hindus, and Chinese, seems to excite unquenchable animosity when practiced by persons who speak English and profess to be a kind of Christians. No one has a deeper disapprobation than I have of this Mormon institution; both for other reasons and because, far from being in any way countenanced by the principle of liberty, it is a direct infraction of that principle, being a mere riveting of the chains of one half of the community, and an emancipation of the other from reciprocity of obligation toward them. Still, it must be remembered that this relation is as much voluntary on the part of the women concerned in it, and who may be deemed the sufferers by it, as is the case with any other form of the marriage institution; and however surprising this fact may appear, it has its explanation in the common ideas and customs of the world, which, teaching women to think marriage the one thing needful, make it intelligible that many a woman should prefer being one of several wives to not being a wife at all. Other countries are not asked to recognize such unions, or release any portion of their inhabitants from their own laws on the score of Mormonite opinions. But when the dissentients have conceded to the hostile sentiments of others far more than could justly be demanded; when they have left the countries to which their doctrines were unacceptable and established themselves in a remote corner of the earth, which they have been the first to render habitable to human beings, it is difficult to see on what principles but those of tyranny they can be prevented from living there under what laws they please, provided they commit no aggression on other nations and allow perfect freedom of departure to those who are dissatisfied with their ways. A recent writer, in some respects of considerable merit, proposes (to use his own words) not a crusade, but a *civilizade,* against this polygamous community, to put an end to what seems to him a retrograde step in civilization. It also appears so to me, but I am not aware that any community has a right to force another to be civilized. So long as the sufferers by the bad laws do not invoke assistance from other communities, I cannot admit that persons entirely unconnected with them ought to step in and require that a condition of things with which all who are directly interested appear to be satisfied should be put an end to because it is a scandal to persons some thousands of miles distant who have no part or concern in it. Let them send missionaries, if they please, to preach against it; and let them, by any fair means (of which silencing the teachers is not one), oppose the progress of similar doctrines among their own people. If civilization has got the better of barbarism when barbarism had the world to itself, it is too much to profess to be afraid lest barbarism, after having been fairly got under, should revive and conquer civilization. A civilization that can thus succumb to its vanquished enemy must first have become so degenerate that neither its appointed priests and teachers, nor anybody else, has the capacity, or will take the trouble, to stand up for it. If this be so, the sooner such a civilization receives notice to quit, the better. It can only go on from bad to worse until destroyed and regenerated (like the Western Empire) by energetic barbarians.

PATERNALISM

Gerald Dworkin

> *Neither one person, nor any number of persons, is warranted in say-*
> *ing to another human creature of ripe years, that he shall not do with*
> *his life for his own benefit what he chooses to do with it.*
>
> —MILL

> *I do not want to go along with a volunteer basis. I think a fellow*
> *should be compelled to become better and not let him use his discre-*
> *tion whether he wants to get smarter, more healthy or more honest.*
>
> —GENERAL HERSHEY

I take as my starting point the "one very simple principle" proclaimed by Mill in *On Liberty* . . . "That principle is, that the sole end for which mankind are warranted, individually or collectively, in interfering with the liberty of action of any of their number, is self-protection. That the only purpose for which power can be rightfully exercised over any member of a civilized community, against his will, is to prevent harm to others. He cannot right-fully be compelled to do or forbear because it will be better for him to do so, because it will make him happier, because, in the opinion of others, to do so would be wise, or even right."

This principle is neither "one" nor "very simple." It is at least two principles; one asserting that self-protection or the prevention of harm to others is sometimes a sufficient warrant and the other claiming that the individual's own good is *never* a sufficient warrant for the exercise of com-pulsion either by the society as a whole or by its individual members. I assume that no one, with the possible exception of extreme pacifists or anarchists, questions the correctness of the first half of the principle. This essay is an examination of the negative claim embodied in Mill's principle—the objection to paternalistic interferences with a man's liberty.

I

By paternalism I shall understand roughly the interference with a person's liberty of action justified by reasons referring exclusively to the welfare, good, happiness, needs, interests or values of the person being coerced. One

---

is always well-advised to illustrate one's definitions by examples but it is not easy to find "pure" examples or paternalistic interferences. For almost any piece of legislation is justified by several different kinds of reasons and even if historically a piece of legislation can be shown to have been introduced for purely paternalistic motives, it may be that advocates of the legislation with an anti-paternalistic outlook can find sufficient reasons justifying the legislation without appealing to the reasons which were originally adduced to support it. Thus, for example, it may be that the original legislation requiring motorcyclists to wear safety helmets was introduced for purely paternalistic reasons. But the Rhode Island Supreme Court recently upheld such legislation on the grounds that it was "not persuaded that the legislature is powerless to prohibit individuals from pursuing a course of conduct which could conceivably result in their becoming public charges," thus clearly introducing reasons of a quite different kind. Now I regard this decision as being based on reasoning of a very dubious nature but it illustrates the kind of problem one has in finding examples. The following is a list of the kinds of interferences I have in mind as being paternalistic.

II

1. Laws requiring motorcyclists to wear safety helmets when operating their machines.
2. Laws forbidding persons from swimming at a public beach when lifeguards are not on duty.
3. Laws making suicide a criminal offense.
4. Laws making it illegal for women and children to work at certain types of jobs.
5. Laws regulating certain kinds of sexual conduct, e.g. homosexuality among consenting adults in private.
6. Laws regulating the use of certain drugs which may have harmful consequences to the user but do not lead to antisocial conduct.
7. Laws requiring a license to engage in certain professions with those not receiving a license subject to fine or jail sentence if they do engage in the practice.
8. Laws compelling people to spend a specified fraction of their income on the purchase of retirement annuities (Social Security).
9. Laws forbidding various forms of gambling (often justified on the grounds that the poor are more likely to throw away their money on such activities than the rich who can afford to).
10. Laws regulating the maximum rates of interest for loans.
11. Laws against duelling.

In addition to laws which attach criminal or civil penalties to certain kinds of action there are laws, rules, regulations, decrees which make it either difficult or impossible for people to carry out their plans and which are also justified on paternalistic grounds. Examples of this are:

1. Laws regulating the types of contracts which will be upheld as valid by the courts, e.g. (an example of Mill's to which I shall return) no man may make a valid contract for perpetual involuntary servitude.

2. Not allowing assumption of risk as a defense to an action based on the violation of a safety statute.

3. Not allowing as a defense to a charge of murder or assault the consent of the victim.

4. Requiring members of certain religious sects to have compulsory blood transfusions. This is made possible by not allowing the patient to have recourse to civil suits for assault and battery and by means of injunctions.

5. Civil commitment procedures when these are specifically justified on the basis of preventing the person being committed from harming himself. The D.C. Hospitalization of the Mentally Ill Act provides for involuntary hospitalization of a person who "is mentally ill, and because of that illness, is likely to injure himself or others if allowed to remain at liberty." The term injure in this context applies to unintentional as well as intentional injuries.

All of my examples are of existing restrictions on the liberty of individuals. Obviously one can think of interferences which have not been imposed. Thus one might ban the sale of cigarettes, or require that people wear safety-belts in automobiles (as opposed to merely having them installed), enforcing this by not allowing motorists to sue for injuries even when caused by other drivers if the motorist was not wearing a seatbelt at the time of the accident.

I shall not be concerned with activities which though defended on paternalistic grounds are not interferences with the liberty of persons, e.g. the giving of subsidies in kind rather than in cash on the grounds that the recipients would not spend the money on the goods which they really need, or not including a $1,000 deductible provision in a basic protection automobile insurance plan on the ground that the people who would elect it could least afford it. Nor shall I be concerned with measures such as "truth-in-advertising" acts and Pure Food and Drug legislation which are often attacked as paternalistic but which should not be considered so. In these cases all that is provided—it is true by the use of compulsion—is information which it is presumed that rational persons are interested in having in order to make wise decisions. There is no interference with the liberty of the consumer unless one wants to stretch a point beyond good sense and say that his liberty to apply for a loan without knowing the true rate of interest is diminished. It is true that sometimes there is sentiment for going further than providing information, for example when laws against usurious interest are passed preventing those who might wish to contract loans at high rates of interest from doing so, and these measures may correctly be considered paternalistic.

III

Bearing these examples in mind, let me return to a characterization of paternalism. I said earlier that I meant by the term, roughly, interference with a person's liberty for his own good. But, as some of the examples show, the class of persons whose good is involved is not always identical with the class of persons whose freedom is restricted. Thus, in the case of professional licensing it is the practitioner who is directly interfered with but it is the would-be patient whose interests are presumably being served. Not allowing the consent of the victim to be a defense to certain types of crime primarily affects the would-be aggressor but it is the interests of the willing victim that we are trying to protect. Sometimes a person may fall into both classes as would be the case if we banned the manufacture and sale of cigarettes and a given manufacturer happened to be a smoker as well.

Thus we may first divide paternalistic interferences into "pure" and "impure" cases. In "pure" paternalism the class of persons whose freedom is restricted is identical with the class of persons whose benefit is intended to be promoted by such restrictions. Examples: the making of suicide a crime, requiring passengers in automobiles to wear seatbelts, requiring a Christian Scientist to receive a blood transfusion. In the case of "impure" paternalism in trying to protect the welfare of a class of persons we find that the only way to do so will involve restricting the freedom of other persons besides those who are benefited. Now it might be thought that there are no cases of "impure" paternalism since any case could always be justified on non-paternalistic grounds, i.e. in terms of preventing harm to others. Thus we might ban cigarette manufacturers from continuing to manufacture their product on the grounds that we are preventing them from causing illness to others in the same way that we prevent other manufacturers from releasing pollutants into the atmosphere, thereby causing danger to the members of the community. The difference is, however, that in the former but not the latter case the harm is of such a nature that it could be avoided by those individuals affected if they so chose. The incurring of the harm requires, so to speak, the active cooperation of the victim. It would be mistaken theoretically and hypocritical in practice to assert that our interference in such cases is just like our interference in standard cases of protecting others from harm. At the very least someone interfered with in this way can reply that no one is complaining about his activities. It may be that impure paternalism requires arguments or reasons of a stronger kind in order to be justified, since there are persons who are losing a portion of their liberty and they do not even have the solace of having it be done "in their own interest." Of course in some sense, if paternalistic justifications are ever correct, then we are protecting others, we are preventing some from injuring others, but it is important to see the differences between this and the standard case.

Paternalism then will always involve limitations on the liberty of some individuals in their own interest but it may also extend to interferences with the liberty of parties whose interests are not in question.

IV

Finally, by way of some more preliminary analysis, I want to distinguish paternalistic interference with liberty from a related type with which it is often confused. Consider, for example, legislation which forbids employees to work more than, say, 40 hours per week. It is sometimes argued that such legislation is paternalistic for if employees desired such a restriction on their hours of work they could agree among themselves to impose it voluntarily. But because they do not the society imposes its own conception of their best interests upon them by the use of coercion. Hence this is paternalism.

Now it may be that some legislation of this nature, is, in fact, paternalistically motivated. I am not denying that. All I want to point out is that there is another possible way of justifying such measures which is not paternalistic in nature. It is not paternalistic because, as Mill puts it in a similar context, such measures are "required not to overrule the judgment of individuals respecting their own interest, but to give effect to that judgment: they being unable to give effect to it except by concert, which concert again cannot be effectual unless it receives validity and sanction from the law." (*Principles of Political Economy*).

The line of reasoning here is a familiar one first found in Hobbes and developed with great sophistication by contemporary economists in the last decade or so. There are restrictions which are in the interests of a class of persons taken collectively but are such that the immediate interest of each individual is furthered by his violating the rule when others adhere to it. In such cases the individuals involved may need the use of compulsion to give effect to their collective judgment of their own interest by guaranteeing each individual compliance by the others. In these cases compulsion is not used to achieve some benefit which is not recognized to be a benefit by those concerned, but rather because it is the only feasible means of achieving some benefit which *is* recognized as such by all concerned. This way of viewing matters provides us with another characterization of paternalism in general. Paternalism might be thought of as the use of coercion to achieve a good which is not recognized as such by those persons for whom the good is intended. Again while this formulation captures the heart of the matter— it is surely what Mill is objecting to in *On Liberty*—the matter is not always quite like that. For example, when we force motorcyclists to wear helmets we are trying to promote a good—the protection of the person from injury—which is surely recognized by most of the individuals concerned. It is not that a cyclist doesn't value his bodily integrity; rather, as a supporter of such legislation would put it, he either places, perhaps irrationally, another value or good (freedom from wearing a helmet) above that of physical well-being, or, perhaps, while recognizing the danger in the abstract, he either does not fully appreciate it or he underestimates the likelihood of its occurring. But now we are approaching the question of possible justifications of paternalistic measures and the rest of this essay will be devoted to that question.

V

I shall begin for dialectical purposes by discussing Mill's objections to paternalism and then go on to discuss more positive proposals.

An initial feature that strikes one is the absolute nature of Mill's prohibitions against paternalism. It is so unlike the carefully qualified admonitions of Mill and his fellow Utilitarians on other moral issues. He speaks of self-protection as the *sole* end warranting coercion, of the individual's own goals as *never* being a sufficient warrant. Contrast this with his discussion of the prohibition against lying in *Utilitarianism:*

> Yet that even this rule, sacred as it is, admits of possible exception, is acknowledged by all moralists, the chief of which is where the withholding of some fact . . . would save an individual . . . from great and unmerited evil.

The same tentativeness is present when he deals with justice:

> It is confessedly unjust to break faith with any one: to violate an engagement, either express or implied, or disappoint expectations raised by our own conduct, at least if we have raised these expectations knowingly and voluntarily. Like all the other obligations of justice already spoken of, this one is not regarded as absolute, but as capable of being overruled by a stronger obligation of justice on the other side.

This anomaly calls for some explanation. The structure of Mill's argument is as follows:

1. Since restraint is an evil the burden of proof is on those who propose such restraint.
2. Since the conduct which is being considered is purely self-regarding, the normal appeal to the protection of the interests of others is not available.
3. Therefore we have to consider whether reasons involving reference to the individual's own good, happiness, welfare, or interests are sufficient to overcome the burden of justification.
4. We either cannot advance the interests of the individual by compulsion, or the attempt to do so involves evils which outweigh the good done.
5. Hence the promotion of the individual's own interests does not provide a sufficient warrant for the use of compulsion.

Clearly the operative premise here is (4), and it is bolstered by claims about the status of the individual as judge and appraiser of his welfare, interests, needs, etc.:

> With respect to his own feelings and circumstances, the most ordinary man or woman has means of knowledge immeasurably surpassing those that can be possessed by anyone else.
>
> He is the man most interested in his own well-being: the interest which any other person, except in cases of strong personal attachment, can have in it is trifling, compared to that which he himself has.

These claims are used to support the following generalizations concerning the utility of compulsion for paternalistic purposes.

> The interferences of society to overrule his judgment and purposes in what only regards himself must be grounded on general presumptions; which may be altogether wrong, and even if right, are as likely as not to be misapplied to individual cases.
>
> But the strongest of all the arguments against the interference of the public with purely personal conduct is that when it does interfere, the odds are that it interferes wrongly and in the wrong place.
>
> All errors which the individual is likely to commit against advice and warning are far outweighed by the evil of allowing others to constrain him to what they deem his good.

Performing the utilitarian calculation by balancing the advantages and disadvantages we find that: "Mankind are greater gainers by suffering each other to live as seems good to themselves, than by compelling each other to live as seems good to the rest." Ergo, (4).

This classical case of a utilitarian argument with all the premises spelled out is not the only line of reasoning present in Mill's discussion. There are asides, and more than asides, which look quite different and I shall deal with them later. But this is clearly the main channel of Mill's thought and it is one which has been subjected to vigorous attack from the moment it appeared— most often by fellow Utilitarians. The link that they have usually seized on is, as Fitzjames Stephen put it in *Liberty, Equality, Fraternity,* the absence of proof that the "mass of adults are so well acquainted with their own interests and so much disposed to pursue them that no compulsion or restraint put upon them by any others for the purpose of promoting their interest can really promote them." Even so sympathetic a critic as H. L. A. Hart is forced to the conclusion that:

> In Chapter 5 of his essay [On Liberty] Mill carried his protests against paternalism to lengths that may now appear to us as fantastic . . . No doubt if we no longer sympathise with this criticism this is due, in part, to a general decline in the belief that individuals know their own interest best.
>
> Mill endows the average individual with "too much of the psychology of a middle-aged man whose desires are relatively fixed, not liable to be artificially stimulated by external influences; who knows what he wants

and what gives him satisfaction or happiness; and who pursues these things when he can."

Now it is interesting to note that Mill himself was aware of some of the limitations on the doctrine that the individual is the best judge of his own interests. In his discussion of government intervention in general (even where the intervention does not interfere with liberty but provides alternative institutions to those of the market) after making claims which are parallel to those just discussed, e.g. "People understand their own business and their own interests better, and care for them more, than the government does, or can be expected to do." He goes on to an intelligent discussion of the "very large and conspicuous exceptions" to the maxim that:

> Most persons take a juster and more intelligent view of their own interest, and of the means of promoting it than can either be prescribed to them by a general enactment of the legislature, or pointed out in the particular case by a public functionary.

Thus there are things

> of which the utility does not consist in ministering to inclinations, nor in serving the daily uses of life, and the want of which is least felt where the need is greatest. This is peculiarly true of those things which are chiefly useful as tending to raise the character of human beings. The uncultivated cannot be competent judges of cultivation. Those who most need to be made wiser and better, usually desire it least, and, if they desired it, would be incapable of finding the way to it by their own lights.
>
> ...A second exception to the doctrine that individuals are the best judges of their own interest, is when an individual attempts to decide irrevocably now what will be best for his interest at some future and distant time. The presumption in favor of individual judgment is only legitimate, where the judgment is grounded on actual, and especially on present, personal experience; not where it is formed antecedently to experience, and not suffered to be reversed even after experience has condemned it.

The upshot of these exceptions is that Mill does not declare that there should never be government interference with the economy but rather that

> ...in every instance, the burden of making out a strong case should be thrown not on those who resist but on those who recommend government interference. Letting alone, in short, should be the general practice: every departure from it, unless required by some great good, is a certain evil.

In short, we get a presumption, not an absolute prohibition. The question is why doesn't the argument against paternalism go the same way?

I suggest that the answer lies in seeing that in addition to a purely utilitarian argument Mill uses another as well. As a Utilitarian, Mill has to show, in Fitzjames Stephen's words, that: "Self-protection apart, no good object can be attained by any compulsion which is not in itself a greater evil than the absence of the object which the compulsion obtains." To show this is impossible; one reason being that it isn't true. Preventing a man from selling himself into slavery (a paternalistic measure which Mill himself accepts as legitimate), or from taking heroin, or from driving a car without wearing seatbelts may constitute a lesser evil than allowing him to do any of these things. A consistent Utilitarian can only argue against paternalism on the grounds that it (as a matter of fact) does not maximize the good. It is always a contingent question that may be refuted by the evidence. But there is also a noncontingent argument which runs through *On Liberty*. When Mill states that "there is a part of the life of every person who has come to years of discretion, within which the individuality of that person ought to reign uncontrolled either by any other person or by the public collectively," he is saying something about what it means to be a person, an autonomous agent. It is because coercing a person for his own good denies this status as an independent entity that Mill objects to it so strongly and in such absolute terms. To be able to choose is a good that is independent of the wisdom of what is chosen. A man's "mode of laying out his existence is the best, not because it is the best in itself, but because it is his own mode." It is the privilege and proper condition of a human being, arrived at the maturity of his faculties, to use and interpret experience in his own way.

As further evidence of this line of reasoning in Mill, consider the one exception to his prohibition against paternalism.

> In this and most civilised countries, for example, an engagement by which a person should sell himself, or allow himself to be sold, as a slave, would be null and void; neither enforced by law nor by opinion. The ground for thus limiting his power of voluntarily disposing of his own lot in life, is apparent, and is very clearly seen in this extreme case. The reason for not interfering, unless for the sake of others, with a person's voluntary acts, is consideration for his own liberty. His voluntary choice is evidence that what he so chooses is desirable, or at least endurable, to him, and his good is on the whole best provided for by allowing him to take his own means of pursuing it. But by selling himself for a slave, he abdicates his liberty; he foregoes any future use of it beyond that single act. He therefore defeats, in his own case, the very purpose which is the justification of allowing him to dispose of himself. He is no longer free; but is thenceforth in a position which has no longer the presumption in its favour, that would be afforded by his voluntarily remaining in it. The principle of freedom cannot require that he should be free not to be free. It is not freedom to be allowed to alienate his freedom.

Now leaving aside the fudging on the meaning of freedom in the last line it is clear that part of this argument is incorrect. While it is true that *future* choices of the slave are not reasons for thinking that what he chooses then is desirable for him, what is at issue is limiting his immediate choice; and since this choice is made freely, the individual may be correct in thinking that his interests are best provided for by entering such a contract. But the main consideration for not allowing such a contract is the need to preserve the liberty of the person to make future choices. This gives us a principle—a very narrow one—by which to justify some paternalistic interferences. Paternalism is justified only to preserve a wider range of freedom for the individual in question. How far this principle could be extended, whether it can justify all the cases in which we are inclined upon reflection to think paternalistic measures justified, remains to be discussed. What I have tried to show so far is that there are two strains of argument in Mill—one a straightforward Utilitarian mode of reasoning and one which relies not on the goods which free choice leads to but on the absolute value of the choice itself. The first cannot establish any absolute prohibition but at most a presumption and indeed a fairly weak one given some fairly plausible assumptions about human psychology; the second, while a stronger line of argument, seems to me to allow on its own grounds a wider range of paternalism than might be suspected. I turn now to a consideration of these matters.

VI

We might begin looking for principles governing the acceptable use of paternalistic power in cases where it is generally agreed that it is legitimate. Even Mill intends his principles to be applicable only to mature individuals, not those in what he calls "non-age." What is it that justifies us in interfering with children? The fact that they lack some of the emotional and cognitive capacities required in order to make fully rational decisions. It is an empirical question to just what extent children have an adequate conception of their own present and future interests but there is not much doubt that there are many deficiencies. For example, it is very difficult for a child to defer gratification for any considerable period of time. Given these deficiencies and given the very real and permanent dangers that may befall the child it becomes not only permissible but even a duty of the parent to restrict the child's freedom in various ways. There is however an important moral limitation on the exercise of such parental power which is provided by the notion of the child eventually coming to see the correctness of his parent's interventions. Parental paternalism may be thought of as a wager by the parent on the child's subsequent recognition of the wisdom of the restrictions. There is an emphasis on what could be called future-oriented consent—on what the child will come to welcome, rather than on what he does welcome.

The essence of this idea has been incorporated by idealist philosophers into various types of "real-will" theory as applied to fully adult persons. Extensions of paternalism are argued for by claiming that in various respects, chronologically mature individuals share the same deficiencies in knowledge, capacity to think rationally, and the ability to carry out decisions that children possess. Hence in interfering with such people we are in effect doing what they would do if they were fully rational. Hence we are not really opposing their will, hence we are not really interfering with their freedom. The dangers of this move have been sufficiently exposed by Berlin in his *Two Concepts of Freedom.* I see no gain in theoretical clarity nor in practical advantage in trying to pass over the real nature of the interferences with liberty that we impose on others. Still the basic notion of consent is important and seems to me the only acceptable way of trying to delimit an area of justified paternalism.

Let me start by considering a case where the consent is not hypothetical in nature. Under certain conditions it is rational for an individual to agree that others should force him to act in ways which, at the time of action, the individual may not see as desirable. If, for example, a man knows that he is subject to breaking his resolves when temptation is present, he may ask a friend to refuse to entertain his requests at some later stage.

A classical example is given in the Odyssey when Odysseus commands his men to tie him to the mast and refuse all future orders to be set free, because he knows the power of the Sirens to enchant men with their songs. Here we are on relatively sound ground in later refusing Odysseus' request to be set free. He may even claim to have changed his mind but since it is *just* such changes that he wished to guard against we are entitled to ignore them.

A process analogous to this may take place on a social rather than individual basis. An electorate may mandate its representatives to pass legislation which when it comes time to "pay the price" may be unpalatable. I may believe that a tax increase is necessary to halt inflation though I may resent the lower pay check each month. However in both this case and that of Odysseus the measure to be enforced is specifically requested by the party involved and at some point in time there is genuine consent and agreement on the part of those persons whose liberty is infringed. Such is not the case of the paternalistic measures we have been speaking about. What must be involved here is not consent to specific measures but rather consent to a system of government, run by elected representatives, with an understanding that they may act to safeguard our interests in certain limited ways.

I suggest that since we are all aware of our irrational propensities, deficiencies in cognitive and emotional capacities, and avoidable and unavoidable ignorance it is rational and prudent for us to in effect take out "social insurance policies." We may argue for and against proposed paternalistic measures in terms of what fully rational individuals would accept as forms of protection. Now clearly, since the initial agreement is not about specific measures we are dealing with a more-or-less blank check and therefore there have to be carefully defined limits. What I am looking for are certain kinds of conditions which make it plausible to suppose that rational men could reach agreement to limit their liberty even when other men's interests are not affected.

Of course as in any kind of agreement schema there are great difficulties in deciding what rational individuals would or would not accept. Particularly in sensitive areas of personal liberty, there is always a danger of the dispute over agreement and rationality being a disguised version of evaluative and normative disagreement.

Let me suggest types of situations in which it seems plausible to suppose that fully rational individuals would agree to having paternalistic restrictions imposed upon them. It is reasonable to suppose that there are "goods" such as health which any person would want to have in order to pursue his own good—no matter how that good is conceived. This is an argument used in connection with compulsory education for children but it seems to me that it can be extended to other goods which have this character. Then one could agree that the attainment of such goods should be promoted even when not recognized to be such, at the moment, by the individuals concerned.

An immediate difficulty arises from the fact that men are always faced with competing goods and that there may be reasons why even a value such as health—or indeed life—may be overriden by competing values. Thus the problem with the Christian Scientist and blood transfusions. It may be more important for him to reject "impure substances" than to go on living. The difficult problem that must be faced is whether one can give sense to the notion of a person irrationally attaching weights to competing values.

Consider a person who knows the statistical data on the probability of being injured when not wearing seatbelts in an automobile and knows the types and gravity of the various injuries. He also insists that the inconvenience attached to fastening the belt every time he gets in and out of the car outweighs for him the possible risks to himself. I am inclined in this case to think that such a weighing is irrational. Given his life-plans, which we are assuming are those of the average person, his interests and commitments already undertaken, I think it is safe to predict that we can find inconsistencies in his calculations at some point. I am assuming that this is not a man who for some conscious or unconscious reasons is trying to injure himself nor is he a man who just likes to "live dangerously." I am assuming that he is like us in all the relevant respects but just puts an enormously high negative value on inconvenience—one which does not seem comprehensible or reasonable.

It is always possible, of course, to assimilate this person to creatures like myself. I, also, neglect to fasten my seatbelt and I concede such behavior is not rational but not because I weigh the inconvenience differently from those who fasten their belts. It is just that having made (roughly) the same calculation as everybody else I ignore it in my actions. [Note: a much better case of weakness of the will than those usually given in ethics texts.] A plausible explanation for this deplorable habit is that although I know in some intellectual sense what the probabilities and risks are I do not fully appreciate them in an emotionally genuine manner.

We have two distinct types of situation in which a man acts in a non-rational fashion. In one case he attaches incorrect weights to some of his values; in the other he neglects to act in accordance with his actual preferences and desires. Clearly there is a stronger and more persuasive argument for paternalism in the latter situation. Here we are really not—by assumption—imposing a good on another person. But why may we not extend our interference to what we might call evaluative delusions? After all, in the case of cognitive delusions we are prepared, often, to act against the expressed will of the person involved. If a man believes that when he jumps out the window he will float upwards—Robert Nozick's example—

would not we detain him, forcibly if necessary? The reply will be that this man doesn't wish to be injured and if we could convince him that he is mistaken as to the consequences of his action he would not wish to perform the action. But part of what is involved in claiming that the man who doesn't fasten his seatbelts is attaching an incorrect weight to the inconvenience of fastening them is that if he were to be involved in an accident and severely injured he would look back and admit that the inconvenience wasn't as bad as all that. So there is a sense in which if I could convince him of the consequences of his action he also would not wish to continue his present course of action. Now the notion of consequences being used here is covering a lot of ground. In one case it's being used to indicate what will or can happen as a result of a course of action and in the other it's making a prediction about the future evaluation of the consequences—in the first sense—of a course of action. And whatever the difference between facts and values—whether it be hard and fast or soft and slow—we are genuinely more reluctant to consent to interferences where evaluative differences are the issue. Let me now consider another factor which comes into play in some of these situations which may make an important difference in our willingness to consent to paternalistic restrictions.

Some of the decisions we make are of such a character that they produce changes which are in one or another way irreversible. Situations are created in which it is difficult or impossible to return to anything like the initial stage at which the decision was made. In particular, some of these changes will make it impossible to continue to make reasoned choices in the future. I am thinking specifically of decisions which involve taking drugs that are physically or psychologically addictive and those which are destructive of one's mental and physical capacities.

I suggest we think of the imposition of paternalistic interferences in situations of this kind as being a kind of insurance policy which we take out against making decisions which are far-reaching, potentially dangerous and irreversible. Each of these factors is important. Clearly there are many decisions we make that are relatively irreversible. In deciding to learn to play chess I could predict in view of my general interest in games that some portion of my free time was going to be preempted and that it would not be easy to give up the game once I acquired a certain competence. But my whole life-style was not going to be jeopardized in an extreme manner. Further it might be argued that even with addictive drugs such as heroin one's normal life plans would not be seriously interfered with if an inexpensive and adequate supply were readily available. So this type of argument might have a much narrower scope than appears to be the case at first.

A second class of cases concerns decisions which are made under extreme psychological and sociological pressures. I am not thinking here of the making of the decision as being something one is pressured into—e.g. a good reason for making duelling illegal is that unless this is done many people might have to manifest their courage and integrity in ways in which they would rather not do so—but rather of decisions, such as that to commit suicide, which are usually made at a point where the individual is not thinking clearly and calmly about the nature of his decision. In addition, of course, this comes under the previous heading of all-too-irrevocable decisions. Now there are practical steps which a society could take if it wanted to decrease the possibility of suicide—for example not paying social security benefits to the survivors or, as religious institutions do, not allowing persons to be buried with the same status as natural deaths. I think we may count these as interferences with the liberty of persons to attempt suicide and the question is whether they are justifiable.

Using my argument schema the question is whether rational individuals would consent to such limitations. I see no reason for them to consent to an absolute prohibition but I do think it is reasonable for them to agree to some kind of enforced waiting period. Since we are all aware of the possibility of temporary states, such as great fear or depression, that are inimical to the making of well-informed and rational decisions, it would be prudent for all of us if there were some kind of institutional arrangement whereby we were restrained from making a decision which is so irreversible. What this would be like in practice is difficult to envisage and it may be that if no practical arrangements were feasible we would have to conclude that there should be no restriction at all on this kind of action. But we might have a "cooling off" period, in much the same way that we now require couples who file for divorce to go through a waiting period. Or, more farfetched, we might imagine a Suicide Board composed of a psychologist and another member picked by the applicant. The Board would be required to meet and talk with the person proposing to take his life, though its approval would not be required.

A third class of decisions—these classes are not supposed to be disjointed—involves dangers which are either not sufficiently understood or appreciated correctly by the persons involved. Let me illustrate, using the example of cigarette smoking, a number of possible cases.

1. A man may not know the facts—e.g. smoking between 1 and 2 packs a day shortens life expectancy 6.2 years, the costs and pain of the illness caused by smoking, etc.
2. A man may know the facts, wish to stop smoking, but not have the requisite willpower.
3. A man may know the facts but not have them play the correct role in his calculation because, say, he discounts the danger psychologically since it is remote in time and/or inflates the attractiveness of other consequences of his decisions which he regards as beneficial.

In case 1 what is called for is education, the posting of warnings, etc. In case 2 there is no theoretical problem. We are not imposing a good on someone who rejects it. We are simply using coercion to enable people to carry out their own goals. (Note: There obviously is a difficulty in that only a subclass of the individuals affected wish to be prevented from doing what they are doing.) In case 3 there is a sense in which we are imposing a good on someone in that given his current appraisal of the facts he doesn't wish to be restricted. But in another sense we are not imposing a good since what is being claimed—and what must be shown or at least argued for—is that an accurate accounting on his part would lead him to reject his current course of action. Now we all know that such cases exist, that we are prone to disregarding dangers that are only possibilities, that immediate pleasures are often magnified and distorted.

If in addition the dangers are severe and far-reaching, we could agree to allow the state a certain degree of power to intervene in such situations. The difficulty is in specifying in advance, even vaguely, the class of cases in which intervention will be legitimate.

A related difficulty is that of drawing a line so that it is not the case that all ultrahazardous activities are ruled out, e.g. mountain climbing, bullfighting, sports-car racing, etc. There are some risks—even very great ones—which a person is entitled to take with his life.

A good deal depends on the nature of the deprivation—e.g. does it prevent the person from engaging in the activity completely or merely limit his participation—and how important to the nature of the activity is the absence of restriction when this is weighed against the role that the activity plays in the life of the person. In the case of automobile seatbelts, for example, the restriction is trivial in nature, interferes not at all with the use or enjoyment of the activity, and does, I am assuming, considerably reduce a high risk of serious injury. Whereas, for example, making mountain climbing illegal completely prevents a person from engaging in an activity which may play an important role in his life and his conception of the person he is.

In general, the easiest cases to handle are those which can be argued about in the terms which Mill thought to be so important—a concern not just for the happiness or welfare, in some broad sense, of the individual but rather a concern for the autonomy and freedom of the person. I suggest that we would be most likely to consent to paternalism in those instances in which it preserves and enhances for the individual his ability to rationally consider and carry out his own decisions.

I have suggested in this essay a number of types of situations in which it seems plausible that rational men would agree to granting the legislative powers of a society the right to impose restrictions on what Mill calls "self-regarding" conduct. However, rational men knowing something about the resources of ignorance, ill-will and stupidity available to the lawmakers of a society—a good case in point is the history of drug legislation in the United States—will be concerned to limit such intervention to a minimum. I suggest in closing two principles designed to achieve this end.

In all cases of paternalistic legislation there must be a heavy and clear burden of proof placed on the authorities to demonstrate the exact nature of the harmful effects (or beneficial consequences) to be avoided (or achieved) and the probability of their occurrence. The burden of proof here is twofold—what lawyers distinguish as the burden of going forward and the burden of persuasion. That the authorities have the burden of going forward means that it is up to them to raise the question and bring forward evidence of the evils to be avoided. Unlike the case of new drugs where the manufacturer must produce some evidence that the drug has been tested and found not harmful, no citizen has to show with respect to self-regarding conduct that it is not harmful or promotes his best interests. In addition the nature and cogency of the evidence for the harmfulness of the course of action must be set at a high level. To paraphrase a formulation of the burden of proof for criminal proceedings—better 10 men ruin themselves than one man be unjustly deprived of liberty.

Finally, I suggest a principle of the least restrictive alternative. If there is an alternative way of accomplishing the desired end without restricting liberty although it may involve great expense, inconvenience, etc., the society must adopt it.

SEX, DRUGS, AND PRIVACY

David A. J. Richards

It is initially important to distinguish two kinds of paternalism: interference on the basis of facts unknown to the agent, in order to save the agent from harms that he would wish to avoid, and interference on the basis of values that the agent does not himself share. Paternalism of the first kind, as applied in such laws as those securing the purity of drugs, is unobjectionable. Paternalism of the second kind, which underlies many laws currently criminalizing drug use, is not only objectionable, it is a violation of human rights.

On this basis, no good argument can be made that paternalistic considerations justify the kind of interference in choices to use drugs that is involved in the current criminalization of many forms of drug use. Indeed, in many cases, such choices seem all *too* rational.

Drug use serves many disparate purposes: therapeutic care and cure, the relief of pain or anxiety, the stimulation or depression of mood or levels of arousal, the exploration of imaginative experience for creative, aesthetic, religious, therapeutic, recreational, or other purposes, and sheer recreative pleasure. These purposes are not irrational. To the contrary, the pursuit of them may enable the person better to achieve his ends in general, or to explore aspects of experience or attitudes to living which he may reasonably wish to incorporate into his theory of ends. There is almost no form of drug use which, in a suitably supportive context and setting, may not advance important human goods, including the capacity of some poor and deprived people to work more comfortably, to endure adverse climatic and environmental circumstances, and in general to meet more robustly and pleasurably the demands on their lives. Some religions, like some artists, have centered themselves on drug use, finding in drugs a matrix of religious and imaginative experience in which to explore and sometimes realize their higher-order interests in giving life intelligible meaning and coherence. Some persons today find in the triumph of technological society the *reductio ad absurdum* of certain dynamics of Western culture and identify drug use as one organon for cultivating a saner and more balanced metaphysical orientation that expresses their most authentic and reasonable interests. Some find even in "addictive" drugs a way of life with more interest, challenge, and self-respect than the available alternatives. It is dogmatic to assert that these and other people do not, through drug use, more rationally advance their ends.

Sometimes the paternalistic argument is made that certain forms of drug use, even if carefully regulated, may result in certain clear harms to the user. For example, heroin use may lead to addiction, to impotence, to certain organic disorders, and sometimes, despite all proper precautions, to death. As long as any such irreparable harm to the person is in prospect, it is argued, paternalistic interference is justified. Even if certain of these alleged harms, for example, addiction, are morally problematic and question-begging, others, such as death, are not. The first requirement of just paternalism, however, is that judgments of irrationality must rest on a neutral theory of the good consistent with the agent's own higher-order interests in rationality and freedom. Even intentionally ending one's own life cannot, in all circumstances, be supposed irrational under this criterion. If intentional killing is not always irrational, neither, a fortiori, is drug use, in which the user makes trade-offs between valued forms of activity and higher risks of death that reasonable persons sometimes embrace. Certainly, the right of persons to engage in many high-risk occupations and activities is uncontroversial. Part of respect for human rights is the recognition of the right of persons, as free and rational beings, to determine the meanings of their own lives and projects, including the frame of such plans at the boundaries of life and death. The values that some persons place on drug use can be accorded no less respect. Certainly, drug use does not enable a person to realize more than is implicit in the interests and ambitions brought to the drug experience, but that indicates not the frivolity or pointlessness of the experience, but its potential seriousness for the kinds of spiritual exploration and risk-taking by independent-minded and rational persons that should be centrally protected in a free society.

At most, paternalistic concern for forms of irreparable harm might dictate appropriate forms of regulation to insure that drugs are available only to mature persons who understand, critically evaluate and voluntarily accept the risks. To minimize pointless risks, such regulations might insure that certain drugs, LSD, for example, are taken only under appropriate supervision. In general, however, there is no ground of just paternalism for an absolute prohibition of such drugs.

The radical vision of autonomy and mutual concern and respect is a vision of persons, as such, having human rights to create their own lives on terms fair to all. To view individuals in this way is to affirm basic intrinsic limits on the degree to which, even benevolently, one person may control the life of another. Within ethical constraints expressive of mutual concern and respect for autonomy, people are, in this conception, free to adopt a number of disparate and irreconcilable visions of the good life. Indeed, the adoption of different kinds of life plans, within these constraints, affords the moral good of different experiments in living by which people can more rationally assess such basic life choices. The invocation of inadequate moral and paternalistic arguments of the kind discussed violates these considerations of human rights, confusing unreflective personal ideology with the moral reasoning that alone can justify the deprivation of liberty by criminal penalty.

DRUG USE AND CONSTITUTIONAL PRIVACY

I have thus far set forth a number of negative arguments to show why various moral arguments condemning drug use are mistaken. The remainder of the chapter will consider the affirmative case for allowing forms of drug use, that is, for the existence of rights of the person that include the right to use drugs. In this way, the scope and limits of this right can be clarified, and its relation to the personal ideals secure from state intervention can be addressed.

As Chapter 2 argued, the constitutional right to privacy may be interpreted, consistent with the human rights perspective embodied in the Constitution, as subjecting the scope of the criminal law to constitutional assessment and criticism in terms of the autonomy-based interpretation of treating persons as equals. The United States is a constitutional democracy committed to the conception of human rights as an unwritten constitution, in terms of which the meaning of constitutional guaranties is to be construed. It is wholly natural and historically consistent with constitutional commitments to regard the autonomy-based interpretation of treating persons as equals as the regulative ideal in terms of which the public morality, which the criminal law expresses, is to be interpreted. Sometimes this thought has been expressed, as a rough first approximation, in terms of the harm principle, the principle that the state may impose criminal sanctions only on conduct which harms others. The present account has tried to reformulate the thought in terms of the autonomy-based interpretation of treating persons as equals, and has tried to show how this conception imposes specific constraints on the kinds of principles that may permissibly be enforced by the public morality. The traditional idea of "harm," for example, appears in the account, but is interpreted in terms of the rights of the person, in contrast to Mill's utilitarian reformulation.

A corollary of this way of thinking is that, when the scope of the criminal law exceeds such moral constraints, it violates human rights. The constitutional right to privacy expresses a form of this moral criticism of unjust overcriminalization, and may be understood as a convergence of three viewpoints. These include, first, the view that the traditional moral argument for criminalization is critically deficient, and, indeed, demonstrably fails to respect human rights. A second element is an antipaternalistic feature. The still extant force of the invalid traditional moral arguments distorts the capacity to see that certain traditionally condemned life choices may be rationally undertaken. Paternalistic interference is tolerated and even encouraged, when, in fact, such interference cannot be justified. Third, there is a strong autonomy-based liberty interest in protecting human dignity from the invasions of moralism and paternalism.

In light of this convergence of factors, it is natural to expect that the constitutional right to privacy would have been aggressively invoked to invalidate prohibitions on drug use, as it was in sexual and, more recently, right-to-die contexts. In fact, aside from a free exercise of religion case not directly relevant to constitutional privacy issues, in only one notable case, *Ravin v. State,* has a court unequivocally pursued such a privacy argument to strike down prohibitions of marijuana use in the home. Even the *Ravin* court, however, refused to attach the right to drug use in itself, finding the privacy right to arise out of the home context instead. In short, American courts seem disinclined to pursue privacy arguments in contexts of drug use because they fail to identify drug use as a basic life choice.

In my view, this judgment cannot withstand critical examination. In order to understand why decisions to use drugs are embraced by the constitutional right to privacy, it is necessary to draw together earlier observations regarding the idea of human rights, the values of dignity and moral personality that it encompasses and should protect, the unjust moral argument that often underlies prohibitions of drug use, and the necessary implications of these ideas and values for the protection of certain forms of drug use. Even if decisions to use drugs were, in fact, rarely or never made or acted on, the right to so decide is, for reasons now to be explained, fundamental.

I have interpreted the human rights perspective in terms of the autonomy-based interpretation of treating persons as equals, which includes respect for the higher-order interests of persons in freedom and rationality. One central component must be respect for the capacity of persons—beings capable of critical self-consciousness—to regulate and interpret their experiences in terms of their own standards of reasonable argument and evidence. Thus, both historically and as a matter of moral principle, respect for independent religious conscience and for principles of religious toleration have been at the heart of evolving ideas of human rights. Historically, respect for religious belief has expressed what is today regarded as the deeper principle of respect for individual conscience, the right of persons independently to evaluate and control their own experience.

Commitment to this basic moral principle requires a neutral respect for evaluative independence. But this principle is, as we have seen, violated by the moral perfectionism that has dominated the American approach to drug control. Indeed, this moral perfectionism attacks the very foundations of evaluative independence; for it seeks to inculcate through law a kind and quality of subjective human experience modeled after a religious ideal of rigid self-control dedicated selflessly to the good of others. In the place of independent control over and evaluation of one's own experience, we have a reigning orthodoxy. Majoritarian legislatures seek to enforce a kind of secularized version of the religious technology of self-mastery. The state, consistent with the autonomy-based interpretation of treating persons as equals, has no just role adjudicating among or preferring, let along enforcing, one such technology over another. Such a use of state power is precisely the form of content-based control over ways of life, thought, and experience against which constitutional morality rebels. Indeed, the enforcement of perfectionist ideals expresses precisely the contempt for autonomous evaluative independence and self-control that should trigger appropriate constitutional attack and remedy.

It may be objected that drug experience is not the kind of subjective experience protected by constitutional principles of toleration. This is not an argument; rather it is an expression of the long American tradition of the public morality. This tradition cannot, as has been shown, be sustained. It is based on untenable forms of moral argument and is, on examination, inconsistent with deeper constitutional values to which all espouse fundamental allegiance. It fails to observe constitutional constraints on the kind of harm that may be the object of criminal penalties; indeed, ideologically, it seeks supremacy for its own model of self-mastery through the criminal law in the way that consitutional morality clearly forbids. In short, since this common sense of public morality cannot be sustained, higher-order interests in freedom and rationality would identify respect for choices to use drugs as an aspect of personal dignity that is worthy of protection under the constitutional right to privacy, and call for its implementation by courts and legislatures.

A fair-minded respect for this right will assure respect for the pluralistic cultures and ways of life which different patterns of drug use embody and which have been heretofore lacking in America's cultural life. Patterns of drug use are implicitly ideological: alcohol use, for example, is often associated with cultural patterns in which aggressiveness plays a central role; use of marijuana, in contrast, is associated with more peaceful and inward ways of life. Respect for the right of drug use would preserve individual and subcultural experience and experiment from a majoritarian cultural hegemony, rooted in a crude and callously manipulative utilitarianism. There is no good reason why this utilitarian ideology has been permitted to go unchallenged as the governing American ideal in matters of drug policy; it trivializes our values into simplistic subservience to technological civilization and fails to take seriously American ideals of human rights and their implications for a pluralism of spiritual perspectives.

We may summarize the implications of this right to use drugs in terms of the background moral principles, expressive of the autonomy-based interpretation of treating persons as equals, which define its limits. The principle of autonomy in matters of drugs does not apply to persons presumably lacking rational capacities, such as young children, nor does it validate the use of particular drugs in circumstances where they would lead to the infliction on others of serious bodily harm. There is no objection, for example, to the prohibition of drugs whose use demonstrably leads to violence, or to limitations of drug use in certain contexts, such as before driving. In addition, the liberty of drug use includes the right of others to avoid involvement in the drug experience. There would be no objection, therefore, to reasonable regulations of the time, manner, and place of drug use, or of the obtrusive solicitation of drug use.

Finally, it is important to remind ourselves, yet again, that there are limits to an argument grounded in human rights of the kind here presented. To say that a person has a human right to do an act is to make a political and legal claim that certain conduct must be protected by the state from forms of coercive prohibition. To assert the existence of such a right is not to assert that it should be exercised. The latter question is an issue of personal morality. Its disposition may turn on considerations that have no proper place in questions of political and legal morality.

To say, therefore, that people have a human right to use drugs is not to conclude that everyone should exercise this right. For example, a person might justifiably invoke certain perfectionist ideals in declining to use drugs. These ideals might include religious dedications or purely secular conceptions that the control and cultivation of aspects of personal competence and subjectivity are inconsistent with drug use. Certainly, such ideals cannot justifiably be invoked to qualify our general rights of autonomy, for self-respect and fulfillment do not require conformity to such ideals. Even as personal moral ideas, however, perfectionist notions may be criticized as inhumanly rigid, masochistically manipulative, directed at questionable moral aims, and insensitive to the values of spontaneity and humanely varied experience. Nonetheless, an individual may justifiably espouse a moral ideal, regulate his or her life accordingly, and criticize others for not observing as humane an ideal in their personal lives. However, legal enforcement of such an ideal wrongly imposes a personal ideal upon persons who may find it unfulfilling or even oppressive and exploitative.

QUESTIONS FOR DISCUSSION

1. What is Mill's definition of the "private domain"? Does Mill's rule against state interference apply to children, to the mentally retarded? If not, why?

2. Describe the two main lines of Mill's argument against paternalistic legislation? Which argument is more persuasive? Give reasons for your choice.

3. Mill, according to Dworkin, discusses the main exceptions to his own anti-paternalism. Identify these as well as the additional exceptions that Dworkin finds reasonable. Do you agree or disagree?

4. Which of Mill's two lines of argument against paternalism does Dworkin reject, and on what grounds?

5. On the other hand, which of Mill's two lines of argument against paternalistic legislation does Richards accept and employ in his criticism of antidrug legislation?

6. Are enforced savings through social security and laws requiring automobile seatbelts and motorcycle helmets objectionable cases of paternalistic legislation, or can they be justified on nonpaternalistic grounds such as the protection of the interests of others?

SUGGESTED READINGS

CAPRON, A., "Privacy: Dead and Gone?," *Hastings Center Report,* 22, 1 (1992), 43–45.

FREDERICK, M. D., "Surrogate Motherhood: Politics and Privacy," *Journal of Clinical Ethics,* 4, 1 (1993), 82–91.

HUGHES, G. B., *Law, Reason and Justice,* New York University Press, 1989.

INNESS, J., *Privacy, Intimacy and Isolation,* New York: Oxford University Press, 1992.

JOHNSON, J., "A Theory of the Nature and Value of Privacy," *Public Affairs Quarterly,* 6, 3 (1992), 271–88.

KLEINIG, J., *Paternalism,* Totowa, N.J.: Rowman and Allenheld, 1984.

MACHAN, T., "The Right to Privacy vs. Uniformitarianism," *Journal of Social Philosophy* (Fall 1992), 75–84.

RESNICK, D., "Genetic Privacy in Employment," *Public Affairs Quarterly,* 7, 1 (1993), 82–91.

SCHOEMAN, F., *Privacy and Social Freedom,* New York: Cambridge University Press, 1992.

11

DO ANIMALS HAVE RIGHTS?

ANIMAL LIBERATION

Peter Singer

I

We are familiar with Black Liberation, Gay Liberation, and a variety of other movements. With Women's Liberation some thought we had come to the end of the road. Discrimination on the basis of sex, it has been said, is the last form of discrimination that is universally accepted and practiced without pretense, even in those liberal circles which have long prided themselves on their freedom from racial discrimination. But one should always be wary of talking of "the last remaining form of discrimination." If we have learned anything from the liberation movements, we should have learned how difficult it is to be aware of the ways in which we discriminate until they are forcefully pointed out to us. A liberation movement demands an expansion of our moral horizons, so that practices that were previously regarded as natural and inevitable are now seen as intolerable.

Animals, Men and Morals is a manifesto for an Animal Liberation movement. The contributors to the book may not all see the issue this way. They are a varied group. Philosophers, ranging from professors to graduate students, make up the largest contingent. There are five of them, including the three editors, and there is also an extract from the unjustly neglected German philosopher with an English name, Leonard Nelson, who died in 1927. There are essays by two novelist/critics, Brigid Brophy and Maureen Duffy, and another by Muriel the Lady Dowding, widow of Dowding of Battle of Britain fame and the founder of "Beauty Without Cruelty," a movement that cam-

---

paigns against the use of animals for furs and cosmetics. The other pieces are by a psychologist, a botanist, a sociologist, and Ruth Harrison, who is probably best described as a professional campaigner for animal welfare.

Whether or not these people, as individuals, would all agree that they are launching a liberation movement for animals, the book as a whole amounts to no less. It is a demand for a complete change in our attitudes to nonhumans. It is a demand that we cease to regard the exploitation of other species as natural and inevitable, and that, instead, we see it as a continuing moral outrage. Patrick Corbett, Professor of Philosophy at Sussex University, captures the spirit of the book in his closing words:

> ... We require now to extend the great principles of liberty, equality and fraternity over the lives of animals. Let animal slavery join human slavery in the graveyard of the past.

The reader is likely to be skeptical. "Animal Liberation" sounds more like a parody of liberation movements than a serious objective. The reader may think: We support the claims of blacks and women for equality because blacks and women really are equal to whites and males—equal in intelligence and in abilities, capacity for leadership, rationality, and so on. Humans and nonhumans obviously are not equal in these respects. Since justice demands only that we treat equals equally, unequal treatment of humans and nonhumans cannot be an injustice.

This is a tempting reply, but a dangerous one. It commits the nonracist and nonsexist to a dogmatic belief that blacks and women really are just as intelligent, able, etc., as whites and males—and no more. Quite possibly this happens to be the case. Certainly attempts to prove that racial or sexual differences in these respects have a genetic origin have not been conclusive. But do we really want to stake our demand for equality on the assumption that there are no genetic differences of this kind between the different races or sexes? Surely the appropriate response to those who claim to have found evidence for sure genetic differences is not to stick to the belief that there are no differences, whatever the evidence to the contrary; rather one should be clear that the claim to equality does not depend on IQ. Moral equality is distinct from factual equality. Otherwise it would be nonsense to talk of the equality of human beings, since humans, as individuals, obviously differ in intelligence and almost any ability one cares to name. If possessing greater intelligence does not entitle one human to exploit another, why should it entitle humans to exploit nonhumans?

Jeremy Bentham expressed the essential basis of equality in his famous formula: "Each to count for one and none for more than one." In other words, the interests of every being that has interests are to be taken into account and treated equally with the like interests of any other being. Other moral philosophers, before and after Bentham, have made the same point in different ways. Our concern for others must not depend on whether they possess certain characteristics, though just what that concern involves may, of course, vary according to such characteristics.

Bentham, incidentally, was well aware that the logic of the demand for racial equality did not stop at the equality of humans. He wrote:

> The day *may* come when the rest of the animal creation may acquire those rights which never could have been withholden from them but by the hand of tyranny. The French have already discovered that the blackness of the skin is no reason why a human being should be abandoned without redress to the caprice of a tormentor. It may one day come to be recognized that the number of the legs, the villosity of the skin, or the termination of the *os sacrum,* are reasons equally insufficient for abandoning a sensitive being to the same fate. What else is it that should trace the insuperable line? Is it the faculty of reason, or perhaps the faculty of discourse? But a full-grown horse or dog is beyond comparison a more rational, as well as a more conversable animal, than an infant of a day, or a week, or even a month, old. But suppose they were otherwise, what would it avail? The question is not, Can they *reason?* nor Can they *talk?* but, Can they *suffer?*

Surely Bentham was right. If a being suffers, there can be no moral justification for refusing to take that suffering into consideration, and, indeed, to count it equally with the like suffering (if rough comparisons can be made) of any other being.

So the only question is: Do animals other than man suffer? Most people agree unhesitatingly that animals like cats and dogs can and do suffer, and this seems also to be assumed by those laws that prohibit wanton cruelty to such animals. Personally, I have no doubt at all about this and find it hard to take seriously the doubts that a few people apparently do have. The editors and contributors of *Animals, Men and Morals* seem to feel the same way, for although the question is raised more than once, doubts are quickly dismissed each time. Nevertheless, because this is such a fundamental point, it is worth asking what grounds we have for attributing suffering to other animals.

It is best to begin by asking what grounds any individual human has for supposing that other humans feel pain. Since pain is a state of consciousness, a "mental event," it can never be directly observed. No observations, whether behavioral signs such as writhing or screaming or physiological or neurological recordings, are observations of pain itself. Pain is something one feels, and one can only infer that others are feeling it from various external indications. The fact that only philosophers are ever skeptical about whether other humans feel pain shows that we regard such inference as justifiable in the case of humans.

Is there any reason why the same inference should be unjustifiable for other animals? Nearly all the external signs which lead us to infer pain in other humans can be seen in other species, especially "higher" animals such as mammals and birds. Behavioral signs—writhing, yelping, or other forms of calling, attempts to avoid the source of pain, and many others—are present. We know, too, that these animals are biologically similar in the relevant respects, having nervous systems like ours which can be observed to function as ours do.

So the grounds for inferring that these animals can feel pain are nearly as good as the grounds for inferring other humans do. Only nearly, for there is one behavioral sign that humans have but nonhumans, with the exception of one or two specially raised chimpanzees, do not have. This, of course, is a developed language. As the quotation from Bentham indicates, this has long been regarded as an important distinction between man and other animals. Other animals may communicate with each other, but not in the way we do. Following Chomsky, many people now mark this distinction by saying that only humans communicate in a form that is governed by rules of syntax. (For the purposes of this argument, linguists allow those chimpanzees who have learned a syntactic sign language to rank as honorary humans.) Nevertheless, as Bentham pointed out, this distinction is not relevant to the question of how animals ought to be treated, unless it can be linked to the issue of whether animals suffer.

This link may be attempted in two ways. First, there is a hazy line of philosophical thought, stemming perhaps from some doctrines associated with Wittgenstein, which maintains that we cannot meaningfully attribute states of consciousness to beings without language. I have not seen this argument made explicit in print, though I have come across it in conversation. This position seems to me very implausible, and I doubt that it would be held at all if it were not thought to be a consequence of a broader view of the significance of language. It may be that the use of a public, rule-governed language is a precondition of conceptual thought. It may even be, although personally I doubt it, that we cannot meaningfully speak of a creature having an intention unless that creature can use a language. But states like pain, surely, are more primitive than either of these, and seem to have nothing to do with language.

Indeed, as Jane Goodall points out in her study of chimpanzees, when it comes to the expression of feelings and emotions, humans tend to fall back on nonlinguistic modes of communication which are often found among apes, such as a cheering pat on the back, an exuberant embrace, a clasp of hands, and so on. Michael Peters makes a similar point in his contribution to *Animals, Men and Morals* when he notes that the basic signals we use to convey pain, fear, sexual arousal, and so on are not specific to our species. So there seems to be no reason at all to believe that a creature without language cannot suffer.

The second, and more easily appreciated way of linking language and the existence of pain is to say that the best evidence that we can have that another creature is in pain is when he tells us that he is. This is a distinct line of argument, for it is not being denied that a non−language-user conceivably could suffer, but only that we could know that he is suffering. Still, this line of argument seems to me to fail, and for reasons similar to those just given. "I am in pain" is not the best possible evidence that the speaker is in pain (he might be lying) and it is certainly not the only possible evidence. Behavioral signs and knowledge of the animal's biological similarity to ourselves together provide adequate evidence that animals do suffer. After all, we would not accept linguistic evidence if it contradicted the rest of the evidence. If a man was severely burned, and behaved as if he were in pain, writhing, groaning, being very careful not to let his burned skin touch anything, and so on, but later said he had not been in pain at all, we would be more likely to conclude that he was lying or suffering from amnesia than that he had not been in pain.

Even if there were stronger grounds for refusing to attribute pain to those who do not have a language, the consequences of this refusal might lead us to examine these grounds unusually critically. Human infants, as well as some adults, are unable to use language. Are we to deny that a year-old infant can suffer? If not, how can language be crucial? Of course, most parents can understand the responses of even very young infants better than they understand the responses of other animals, and sometimes infant responses can be understood in the light of later development.

This, however, is just a fact about the relative knowledge we have of our own species and other species, and most of this knowledge is simply derived from closer contact. Those who have studied the behavior of other animals soon learn to understand their responses at least as well as we understand those of an infant. (I am not just referring to Jane Goodall's and other well-known studies of apes. Consider, for example, the degree of an understanding achieved by Tinbergen from watching herring gulls.) Just as we understand infant human behavior in the light of adult human behavior, so we can understand the behavior of other species in the light of our own behavior (and sometimes we can understand our own behavior better in the light of the behavior of other species).

The grounds we have for believing that other mammals and birds suffer are, then, closely analogous to the grounds we have for believing that other humans suffer. It remains to consider how far down the evolutionary scale this analogy holds. Obviously it becomes poorer when we get further away from man. To be more precise would require a detailed examination of all that we know about other forms of life. With fish, reptiles, and other vertebrates the analogy still seems strong, with molluscs like oysters it is much weaker. Insects are more difficult, and it may be that in our present state of knowledge we must be agnostic about whether they are capable of suffering.

If there is no moral justification for ignoring suffering when it occurs, and it does occur in other species, what are we to say of our attitudes toward these other species? Richard Ryder, one of the contributors to *Animals, Men and Morals,* uses the term "speciesism" to describe the belief that we are entitled to treat members of other species in a way in which it would be wrong to treat members of our own species. The term is not euphonious, but it neatly makes the analogy with racism. The nonracist would do well to bear the analogy in mind when he is inclined to defend human behavior toward nonhumans. "Shouldn't we worry about improving the lot of our own species before we concern ourselves with other species?" he may ask. If we substitute "race" for "species" we shall see that the question is better not asked. "Is a vegetarian diet nutritionally adequate?" resembles the slaveowner's claim that he and the whole economy of the South would be ruined without slave labor. There is even a parallel with skeptical doubts about whether animals suffer, for some defenders of slavery professed to doubt whether blacks really suffer in the way that whites do.

I do not want to give the impression, however, that the case for Animal Liberation is based on the analogy with racism and no more. On the contrary, *Animals, Men and Morals* describes the various ways in which humans exploit nonhumans, and several contributors consider the defenses that have been offered, including the defense of meat-eating mentioned in the last paragraph. Sometimes the rebuttals are scornfully dismissive, rather than carefully designed to convince the detached critic. This may be a fault, but it is a fault that is inevitable, given the kind of book this is. The issue is not one on which one can remain detached. As the editors state in their Introduction:

> Once the full force of moral assessment has been made explicit there can be no rational excuse left for killing animals, be they killed for food, science, or sheer personal indulgence. We have not assembled this book to provide the reader with yet another manual on how to make brutalities less brutal. Compromise, in the traditional sense of the term, is simply unthinking weakness when one considers the actual reasons for our crude relationships with the other animals.

The point is that on this issue there are few critics who are genuinely detached. People who eat pieces of slaughtered nonhumans every day find it hard to believe that they are doing wrong; and they also find it hard to imagine what else they could eat. So for those who do not place nonhumans beyond the pale of morality, there comes a stage when further argument seems pointless, a stage at which one can only accuse one's opponent of hypocrisy and reach for the sort of sociological account of our practices and the way we defend them that is attempted by David Wood in his contribution to this book. On the other hand, to those unconvinced by the arguments, and unable to accept that they are merely rationalizing their dietary preferences and their fear of being thought peculiar, such sociological explanations can only seem insultingly arrogant.

II

The logic of speciesism is most apparent in the practice of experimenting on nonhumans in order to benefit humans. This is because the issue is rarely obscured by allegations that nonhumans are so different from humans that we cannot know anything about whether they suffer. The defender of vivisection cannot use this argument because he needs to stress the similarities between man and other animals in order to justify the usefulness to the former of experiments on the latter. The researcher who makes rats choose between starvation and electric shocks to see if they develop ulcers (they do) does so because he knows that the rat has a nervous system very similar to man's, and presumably feels an electric shock in a similar way.

Richard Ryder's restrained account of experiments on animals made me angrier with my fellow men than anything else in this book. Ryder, a clinical psychologist by profession, himself experimented on animals before he came to hold the view he puts forward in his essay. Experimenting on animals is now a large industry, both academic and commercial. In 1969, more than 5 million experiments were performed in Britain, the vast majority without anesthetic (though how many of these involved pain is not known). There are no accurate U.S. figures, since there is no federal law on the subject, and in many cases no state law either. Estimates vary from 20 million to 200 million. Ryder suggests that 80 million may be the best guess. We tend to think that this is all for vital medical research, but of course it is not. Huge numbers of animals are used in university departments from Forestry to Psychology, and even more are used for commercial purposes, to test whether cosmetics can cause skin damage, or shampoos eye damage, or to test food additives or laxatives or sleeping pills or anything else.

A standard test for foodstuffs is the "LD50." The object of this test is to find the dosage level at which 50 percent of the test animals will die. This means that nearly all of them will become very sick before finally succumbing or surviving. When the substance is a harmless one, it may be necessary to force huge doses down the animals, until in some cases sheer volume or concentration causes death.

Ryder gives a selection of experiments, taken from recent scientific journals. I will quote two, not for the sake of indulging in gory details, but in order to give an idea of what normal researchers think they may legitimately do to other species. The point is not that the individual researchers are cruel men, but that they are behaving in a way that is allowed by our speciesist attitudes. As Ryder points out, even if only 1 percent of the experiments involve severe pain, that is 50,000 experiments in Britain each year, or nearly 150 every day (and about fifteen times as many in the United States, if Ryder's guess is right). Here then are two experiments:

> O. S. Ray and R. J. Barrett of Pittsburg gave electric shocks to the feet of 1,042 mice. They then caused convulsions by giving more intense shocks through cup-shaped electrodes applied to the animal's eyes or through pressure spring clips attached to their ears. Unfortunately some of the mice who "successfully completed Day One training were found sick or dead prior to testing on Day Two." [*Journal of Comparative and Physiological Psychology*, 1969, vol. 67, pp. 110–116]
>
> At the National Institute for Medical Research, Mill Hill, London, W. Feldberg and S. L. Sherwood injected chemicals into the brains of cats— "with a number of widely different substances, recurrent patterns of reaction were obtained. Retching, vomiting, defaecation, increased salivation and greatly accelerated respiration leading to panting were common features." . . .
>
> The injection into the brain of a large dose of Tubocuraine caused the

cat to jump "from the table to the floor and then straight into its cage, where it started calling more and more noisily whilst moving about restlessly and jerkily . . . finally the cat fell with legs and neck flexed, jerking in rapid clonic movements, the condition being that of a major [epileptic] convulsion . . . within a few seconds the cat got up, ran for a few yards at high speed and fell in another fit. The whole process was repeated several times within the next ten minutes, during which the cat lost faeces and foamed at the mouth."

This animal finally died thirty-five minutes after the brain injection. [*Journal of Physiology,* 1954, vol. 123, pp. 148–167]

There is nothing secret about these experiments. One has only to open any recent volume of a learned journal, such as the *Journal of Comparative and Physiological Psychology,* to find full descriptions of experiments of this sort, together with the results obtained—results that are frequently trivial and obvious. The experiments are often supported by public funds.

It is a significant indication of the level of acceptability of these practices that, although these experiments are taking place at this moment on university campuses throughout the country, there has, so far as I know, not been the slightest protest from the student movement. Students have been rightly concerned that their universities should not serve the purposes of the military or big business. Speciesism continues undisturbed, and many students participate in it. There may be a few qualms at first, but since everyone regards it as normal, and it may even be a required part of a course, the student soon becomes hardened and, dismissing his earlier feelings as "mere sentiment," comes to regard animals as statistics rather than sentient beings with interests that warrant consideration.

Argument about vivisection has often missed the point because it has been put in absolutist terms: Would the abolitionist be prepared to let thousands die if they could be saved by experimenting on a single animal? The way to reply to this purely hypothetical question is to pose another: Would the experimenter be prepared to experiment on a human orphan under six months old, if it were the only way to save many lives? (I say "orphan" to avoid the complication of parental feelings, although in doing so I am being overfair to the experimenter, since the nonhuman subjects of experiments are not orphans.) A negative answer to this question indicates that the experimenter's readiness to use nonhumans is simple discrimination, for adult apes, cats, mice, and other mammals are more conscious of what is happening to them, more self-directing, and, so far as we can tell, just as sensitive to pain as a human infant. There is no characteristic that human infants possess that adult mammals do not have to the same or a higher degree.

(It might be possible to hold that what makes it wrong to experiment on a human infant is that the infant will in time develop into more than the nonhuman, but one would then, to be consistent, have to oppose abortion, and perhaps contraception, too, for the fetus and the egg and sperm have the same potential as the infant. Moreover, one would still have no reason for experimenting on a nonhuman rather than a human with brain damage severe enough to make it impossible for him to rise above infant level.)

The experimenter, then, shows a bias for his own species whenever he carries out an experiment on a nonhuman for a purpose that he would not think justified him in using a human being at an equal or lower level of sentience, awareness, ability to be self-directing, etc. No one familiar with the kind of results yielded by these experiments can have the slightest doubt that if this bias were eliminated the number of experiments performed would be zero or very close to it.

III

If it is vivisection that shows the logic of speciesism most clearly, it is the use of other species for food that is at the heart of our attitudes toward them. Most of *Animals, Men and Morals* is an attack on meat-eating—an attack which is based solely on concern for nonhumans, without reference to arguments derived from consideration of ecology, macrobiotics, health, or religion.

The idea that nonhumans are utilities, means to our ends, pervades our thought. Even conservationists who are concerned about the slaughter of wild fowl but not about the vastly greater slaughter of chickens for our tables are thinking in this way—they are worried about what we would lose if there were less wildlife. Stanley Godlovitch, pursuing the Marxist idea that our thinking is formed by the activities we undertake in satisfying our needs, suggests that man's first classification of his environment was into Edibles and Inedibles. Most animals came into the first category, and there they have remained.

Man may always have killed other species for food, but he has never exploited them so ruthlessly as he does today. Farming has succumbed to business methods, the objective being to get the highest possible ratio of output (meat, eggs, milk) to input (fodder, labor costs, etc.). Ruth Harrison's essay "On Factory Farming" gives an account of some aspects of modern methods, and of the unsuccessful British campaign for effective controls, a campaign which was sparked off by her *Animal Machines* (Stuart: London, 1964).

Her article is in no way a substitute for her earlier book. This is a pity since, as she says, "Farm produce is still associated with mental pictures of animals browsing in the fields, . . . of hens having a last forage before going to roost. . . ." Yet neither in her article nor elsewhere in *Animals, Men and Morals* is this false image replaced by a clear idea of the nature and extent of factory farming. We learn of this only indirectly, when we hear of the code of reform proposed by an advisory committee set up by the British government.

Among the proposals, which the government refused to implement on the grounds that they were too idealistic, were: "*Any animal should at least have room to turn around freely.*"

Factory farm animals need liberation in the most literal sense. Veal calves are kept in stalls five feet by two feet. They are usually slaughtered when about four months old, and have been too big to turn in their stalls for at least a month. Intensive beef herds, kept in stalls only proportionately larger for much longer periods, account for a growing percentage of beef production. Sows are often similarly confined when pregnant, which, because of artificial methods of increasing fertility, can be most of the time. Animals confined in this way do not waste food by exercising, nor do they develop unpalatable muscle.

"A dry bedded area should be provided for all stock." Intensively kept animals usually have to stand and sleep on slatted floors without straw, because this makes cleaning easier.

"Palatable roughage must be readily available to all calves after one week of age." In order to produce the pale veal housewives are said to prefer, calves are fed on an all-liquid diet until slaughter, even though they are long past the age at which they would normally eat grass. They develop a craving for roughage, evidenced by attempts to gnaw wood from their stalls. (For the same reason, their diet is deficient in iron.)

"Battery cages for poultry should be large enough for a bird to be able to stretch one wing at a time." Under current British practice, a cage for four or five laying hens has a floor area of twenty inches by eighteen inches, scarcely larger than a double page of the *New York Review of Books*. In this space, on a sloping wire floor (sloping so the eggs roll down, wire so the dung drops through) the birds live for a year or eighteen months while artificial lighting and temperature conditions combine with drugs in their food to squeeze the maximum number of eggs out of them. Table birds are also sometimes kept in cages. More often they are reared in sheds, no less crowded. Under these conditions all the birds' natural activities are frustrated, and they develop "vices" such as pecking each other to death. To prevent this, beaks are often cut off, and the sheds kept dark.

How many of those who support factory farming by buying its produce know anything about the way it is produced? How many have heard something about it, but are reluctant to check up for fear that it will make them uncomfortable? To nonspeciesists, the typical consumer's mixture of ignorance, reluctance to find out the truth, and vague belief that nothing really bad could be allowed seems analogous to the attitudes of "decent Germans" to the death camps.

There are, of course, some defenders of factory farming. Their arguments are considered, though again rather sketchily, by John Harris. Among the most common: "Since they have never known anything else, they don't suffer." This argument will not be put by anyone who knows anything about animal behavior, since he will know that not all behavior has to be learned. Chickens attempt to stretch wings, walk around, scratch, and even dust-bathe or build a nest, even though they have never lived under conditions that allowed these activities. Calves can suffer from maternal deprivation no matter at what age they were taken from their mothers. "We need these intensive methods to provide protein for a growing population." As ecologists and famine relief organizations know, we can produce far more protein per acre if we grow the right vegetable crop, soy beans for instance, than if we use the land to grow crops to be converted into protein by animals who use nearly 90 percent of the protein themselves, even when unable to exercise.

There will be many readers of this book who will agree that factory farming involves an unjustifiable degree of exploitation of sentient creatures, and yet will want to say that there is nothing wrong with rearing animals for food, provided it is done "humanely." These people are saying, in effect, that although we should not cause animals to suffer, there is nothing wrong with killing them.

There are two possible replies to this view. One is to attempt to show that this combination of attitudes is absurd. Roslind Godlovitch takes this course in her essay, which is an examination of some common attitudes to animals. She argues that from the combination of "animal suffering is to be avoided" and "there is nothing wrong with killing animals" it follows that all animal life ought to be exterminated (since all sentient creatures will suffer to some degree at some point in their lives). Euthanasia is a contentious issue only because we place some value on living. If we did not, the least amount of suffering would justify it. Accordingly, if we deny that we have a duty to exterminate all animal life, we must concede that we are placing some value on animal life.

This argument seems to me valid, although one could still reply that the value of animal life is to be derived from the pleasures that life can have for them, so that, provided their lives have a balance of pleasure over pain, we are justified in rearing them. But this would imply that we ought to produce animals and let them live as pleasantly as possible, without suffering.

At this point, one can make the second of the two possible replies to the view that rearing and killing animals for food is all right so long as it is done humanely. This second reply is that so long as we think that a nonhuman may be killed simply so that a human can satisfy his taste for meat, we are still thinking of nonhumans as means rather than as ends in themselves. The factory farm is nothing more than the application of technology to this concept. Even traditional methods involve castration, the separation of mothers and their young, the breaking up of herds, branding or ear-punching, and of course transportation to the abattoirs and the final moments of terror when the animal smells blood and senses danger. If we were to try rearing animals so that they lived and died without suffering, we should find that to do so on anything like the scale of today's meat industry would be a sheer impossibility. Meat would become the prerogative of the rich.

I have been able to discuss only some of the contributions to this book, saying nothing about, for instance, the essays on killing for furs and for sport. Nor have I considered all the detailed questions that need to be asked once we start thinking about other species in the radically different way presented by this book. What, for instance, are we to do about genuine conflicts of interest like rats biting slum children? I am not sure of the answer, but the essential point is just that we *do* see this as a conflict of interests, that we recognize that rats have interests too. Then we may begin to think about other ways of resolving the conflict—perhaps by leaving out rat baits that sterilize the rats instead of killing them.

I have not discussed such problems because they are side issues compared with the exploitation of other species for food and for experimental purposes. On these central matters, I hope that I have said enough to show that this book, despite its flaws, is a challenge to every human to recognize his attitudes to nonhumans as a form of prejudice no less objectionable than racism or sexism. It is a challenge that demands not just a change of attitudes, but a change in our way of life, for it requires us to become vegetarians.

Can a purely moral demand of this kind succeed? The odds are certainly against it. The book holds out no inducements. It does not tell us that we will become healthier, or enjoy life more, if we cease exploiting animals. Animal Liberation will require greater altruism on the part of mankind than any other liberation movement, since animals are incapable of demanding it for themselves, or of protesting against their exploitation by votes, demonstrations, or bombs. Is man capable of such genuine altruism? Who knows? If this book does have a significant effect, however, it will be a vindication of all those who have believed that man has within himself the potential for more than cruelty and selfishness.

*N*O NEED FOR LIBERATION

Ruth Cigman

It has been argued that "speciesism"—unjust and discriminatory attitudes towards species other than our own—is a vice analogous to sexism and racism. Opposition to this phenomenon embraces two kinds of claims, one of them reasonable, the other by no means so. The weak claim, which I accept, is that we should treat many animals better than we do, and take whatever steps are necessary to oppose certain cruel practices toward them. The stronger claim is that, as women and blacks should have rights equal to those of men and whites, animals should have rights equal to those of persons, because difference of species does not constitute a morally relevant difference.

My view is that the stronger claim is sentimental and confused. Most important, it seriously misrepresents features of human experience such as attitudes to life and the misfortune of death. I shall attack it by exploring the relationship between (a) the kinds of obligations we have towards a creature (person, animal), and the corelative rights to which he or she is entitled; and (b) the kinds of misfortunes of which that creature may be a subject (or victim). In particular, I shall be concerned with the complex relationship between the right to life and the capacity to be a subject of the misfortune of death. This relationship is significant where human lives are concerned; it does not, I believe, carry over to the lives of other species. My claim will be that death is not, and cannot be, a misfortune for any creature other than a human; this is a reason for denying nonhumans the right to life and therefore for embracing a form of speciesism. I shall then consider some implications for vegetarianism.

I. SPECIES INEQUALITY

The phenomenon of speciesism must be described with care. One anti-speciesist has described it as the belief that it is justifiable "to treat a member of another species in a way in which it would be wrong to treat our own." This definition isn't quite right; nor does it parallel the definitions of racism and sexism. A school which received an application from a parent for admission of her child and pet monkey would be quite justified in accepting the child and rejecting the monkey, however dull the child and bright the monkey; just as a dramatic director would be justified in turning down the most talented actress in the world in favor of an inferior actor, to fill the role of King Lear. Neither school nor director would be guilty of the "ism" in question. The vice abhorred by anti-speciesists is not the denial that animals and persons are in all respects identical (whatever this would mean), and therefore entitled to identical treatment; it is rather a much more plausible claim about the possession across species (many, not all) of certain morally relevant *capacities*. Specifically, speciesism may be seen as a failure to acknowledge the equal capacities of persons and animals to *suffer,* and (it is claimed) the moral equality which is a corollary of this fact.

As such, speciesism bears at least a superficial resemblance to sexism and racism, the error of which consists in part in a failure to understand what Bernard Williams has called the "useful tautology" that all human beings are human beings. This phrase serves to remind anyone who believes that blacks or women are inherently inferior that these are not merely members of a certain species, but are also *human* or *persons.* The emphasis on these terms suggests certain capacities and related vulnerabilities which are more or less universally possessed by persons, and one is made to think of such truths as: all persons are able to suffer physical and mental pain, and to experience, and be frustrated in, affection for others. These truths give rise to certain moral claims which may be irrationally obscured by incidental characteristics such as skin color and sex.

Some anti-speciesists (notably Jeremy Bentham and, more recently, Peter Singer) have attacked speciesism along similar lines. Species equality, they argue, is typically overlooked by virtue of morally insignificant features such as the number of legs a creature possesses, or the inability to talk. Equal capacity to suffer is the only reasonable ground for moral equality; it has been shown, moreover, that many species are in possession of nervous systems of comparable complexity to those of humans, and that they therefore suffer pain of comparable intensity.

However the equal capacity to suffer physical pain is only part of what the antisexist or antiracist is getting at by emphasizing the humanity or personhood of all human beings. Implicit in this claim (the tautological status of which is, of course, more apparent than real) is an allusion to a *range* of vulnerabilities, or misfortunes, of which persons are able to be subjects, and by virtue of which they possess equal rights. Among these is the misfortune of death. Nothing that is said by the anti-speciesist about the suffering of physical pain suggests that animals are subject to the same range of misfortunes as persons, still less that death is a misfortune for an animal. Even if we grant that the equal capacity of persons and animals to suffer physical pain somehow yields equal rights not to be recipients of physical cruelty, it is far from clear why this should entail moral equality, that is, equality over a range of fundamental rights.

I want to suggest that a right to X entails the right to be protected from certain actions which will result in the misfortune, or possible misfortune, of not-X. A condition for being the subject of a right is therefore the *capacity* to be a subject of the corresponding misfortune. The relationship between capacity and desire in this context must be examined: for example, a creature may be a subject of the misfortune of death even if he or she doesn't *desire* not to die, so long as it is the case that he or she has the *capacity* to desire not to die. My suggestion is that, when we fill in the concept of desiring not to die in a way which is relevant to the misfortune of death and the right to life, we shall have to withhold this from animals.

I turn to these problems in subsequent sections. To conclude the present section, I want to clarify the distinction between the right to be protected from cruelty and the right to be protected from death with reference to a provocative example of Robert Nozick. Nozick asks us to imagine the following: someone derives a special, unsubstitutable pleasure from swinging a baseball bat, in circumstances where the regretted but unavoidable corollary of this act is the smashing of a cow's skull. We must consider whether the extra pleasure derived from this act, compared with a similar and harmless alternative act, could possibly justify the act morally. Nozick says that it cannot, thereby suggesting that the purely hedonistic justification for the (analogous) activity of meat-eating (and by implication, comparable activities which involve animal suffering and deaths) is inadequate.

What exactly does this example show? Its plausibility rests upon the suggested identification between, on the one hand, meat-eating and whimsical bat-swinging; and on the other, cow-skull—smashing and the taking of animal lives. The first pair are analogically but questionably related; it is arguable that meat-eating is unjustly viewed as a whimsical, essentially eccentric satisfaction. This is a relatively unimportant point which I shall set aside for now. The second identification is more serious, since it is hardly analogical (we are to assume that smashing the cow's skull is fatal), yet more liable to obscure the problem at hand. In particular, it obscures two claims which I want to distinguish:

(1) We have an obligation not to inflict gratuitous suffering on animals (or to refrain from gratuitous cruelty to animals).

(2) We have an obligation not to kill animals quickly and painlessly.

Claim (1) is, I take it, sufficiently vague to be self-evidently true, or at any rate, not hard to defend. I shall not attempt to do this, but I shall suggest that, while there is room for many divergences of opinion over what counts as "gratuitous" suffering or cruelty, these will generally, and reasonably, fall within an area embraced by whimsical satisfaction and the protection of fundamental human interests (life, health) as, respectively, inadequate and adequate justifications for causing animal suffering. (I shall return to this topic later in connection with vegetarianism.) Claim (2), which is more interesting, I believe to be false. If so, the moral justification for meat-eating would appear to depend above all upon the *manner* in which animals are killed. The force of Nozick's example then rests upon the question (setting aside for now the problematic analogy between meat-eating and whimsical bat-swinging) whether or not skull-smashing is a quick and painless death for a cow. I don't know whether it is or not, but I shall proceed with the assumption that it is *possible* to kill a cow quickly and painlessly. The moral significance of such a death may then be considered.

II. ANIMAL MISFORTUNE AND HUMAN MISFORTUNE

Of what kinds of misfortunes are animals subjects? A claim which may be rejected at the start is this: it is impossible to know exactly how much animals suffer, or what counts as a misfortune *for them;* it is therefore a form of speciesist arrogance to assume that their misfortunes are worthy of less concern than our own. Against this it must be said that the evidence we have that animals suffer *at all* is the same as the evidence which enables us to judge the nature and extent of this suffering. No philosopher has suggested this more powerfully than Wittgenstein, in his remarks about the deeply misunderstood relationship between behavior and the "inner life." It is worth quoting some of these:

> . . . only of a living human being and what resembles (behaves like) a living human being can one say: it has sensations; it sees; is blind; hears; is deaf; is conscious or unconscious.

Look at a stone and imagine it having sensations. One says to oneself: How could one so much as get the idea of ascribing a *sensation to a thing?* One might as well ascribe it to a number!—And now look at a wriggling fly and at once these difficulties vanish and pain seems to get a foothold here, where before everything was so to speak, too smooth for it.

> One can imagine an animal, angry, frightened, unhappy, happy, startled. But hopeful? And why not?
> A dog believes his master is at the door. But can he also believe his master will come the day after tomorrow?—And *what* can he not do here?

Wittgenstein is not merely concerned in these passages with the difficulty of *imagining* the truth of certain mental descriptions (for example, "This dog is hopeful"; "This stone has sensations"). Maybe one *can* (or thinks one can—it may be hard to distinguish these) imagine these being true; what one cannot do is sensibly *consider* the possibility that they may be true, for to do this (Wittgenstein suggests) would be to remove the concept of hope from the context in which it has sense—where human beings talk and behave in ways which reveal their sense of the future, of alternative prospects, of concern for themselves and others, and so on. These form part of the structure, so to speak, of hope; it does not make sense to ascribe hope to a creature which manifests no awareness of future possibilities. Wittgenstein's choice of example may be questioned here; I think there do exist a small number of animals which may express hope in their behavior. But the point is sound: the mental experience which is sensibly attributed to a creature is commensurate with the complexity and nature of its behavioral expression. A wriggling fly may be supposed to feel pain; here, though, hope definitely fails to find a foothold.

If this is correct, two further conclusions must be drawn: (1) The "useful tautology" discussed earlier does not merely suggest certain vulnerabilities to which more or less everyone is subject; it also suggests, I think, certain complexities of experience surrounding these vulnerabilities, which are not attributable to animals. I have in mind, for example, the fear of death, or of contracting a fatal disease; the desire for respect or esteem from others; the desire to lead a fulfilling life (for one's life to have a "point," or "meaning"); the desire to achieve certain goals and resolve certain problems; and, finally, corresponding fears and desires on behalf of others. (2) These thoughts or experiences suggest a reason why persons deserve greater moral concern than animals. The capacity to talk does not *itself* provide such a reason; rather this capacity is related to, and is a condition for, the capacity to suffer complex and severe misfortunes, which animals are logically unable to suffer. Among these are the kinds of misfortunes which we call "tragic." It is with great strain that we say of an animal that he suffers a tragedy, even, I think, when he is destined for a premature death. The failure of Bentham and others to recognize this results from a crude conception of what it is to suffer a misfortune. Let us consider this briefly.

This conception is narrowly utilitarian. If one thinks, with Bentham, that all the good and bad things that can happen to one in life are quantities of pleasurable and painful experience, the comparison between animal and human misfortune will appear quite reasonable; for it is plausible, given this conception, to suggest that one can distinguish degrees of *intensity* of animal pain as well as one can do this with human pain. But notice that this view suggests (a) that all misfortune involves unpleasant experiences; (b) that all unpleasant experiences are measurable against one another—which is most implausible where tragedies and many other severe misfortunes are concerned; and (c) that death (as opposed to dying) is not a misfortune at all, for it involves no unpleasant experience, but rather an *absence* of experience. In fact, (c) is part of a famous argument by Lucretius, to the effect that the fear of death grows out of an irrational conception of death as a state which we *endure,* in which the loss of life is in some sense experienced. Lucretius argues that death is not experienced at all, for it is complete annihilation; therefore there is no subject for *whom* death can be a misfortune, and hence death is not a misfortune at all.

I do not want to suggest that Bentham is committed to this Lucretian view, only that the identification of misfortune with unpleasant experience has this conception as a likely corollary. This identification seems to me *generally* adequate where animals are concerned; misfortunes for animals essentially consist in a rather limited range of unpleasant experiences (physical pain, emotional loss, and so on). To the extent that these are the kinds of misfortunes of which animals may be victims, I think it is correct to conclude that death is not a misfortune for an animal. For if the worst that can be said of the quick and painless death of an animal (of course suffering is another matter) is that it removes a quantity of pleasurable experience from the world, this does not justify calling that death a misfortune *for the animal who dies.* One may *prefer* that the death had not occurred, because one has a kind of utilitarian preference for a world containing as much pleasure as possible. This is very different from saying that it is the animal's misfortune. For this to make sense, it would have to be the case that the animal revealed a certain kind of *desire* to live, or was capable of having such a desire to live. What it is to have such a desire, and how this makes possible a very different kind of misfortune from that which we have discussed, will now be considered in connection with two recent articles on death and the Lucretian argument.

III. DEATH AS A MISFORTUNE

In the first, Thomas Nagel defends an Aristotelian conception of misfortune. This is as far from Bentham as one can imagine; Aristotle, we must remember, even included amongst a person's misfortunes the misfortunes of his or her descendants for an indefinite period of time beyond his or her death. It is very much in the Aristotelian spirit that Nagel says:

> It . . . seems to me worth exploring the position that most good and ill fortune has as its subject a person identified by his history and his possibilities, rather than merely by his categorical state of the moment. . . .

Nagel has in mind misfortunes such as deterioration to a "vegetable-like" condition, and betrayal in cases where the subject is ignorant that he has been betrayed. That these are not *experienced* as misfortunes does not prevent their being described as such. So it is also, Nagel suggests, with death, which is a misfortune for a clearly identified subject (contrary to Lucretius' argument) because it closes certain possibilities which would otherwise have been open to him or her. Nagel concludes that death is indeed a severe misfortune, even a tragedy, for most of us; for the experience of leading a life generally includes a sense of open-ended possibility which appears fortuitously circumscribed by the prospect of death at age eighty or so.

The concept of misfortune as something which befalls a subject "identified by his history and his possibilities" is unquestionably one which we possess. Yet this is rather vague, and should be considered briefly. Nagel appears to think that one's "history and possibilities" *may* be independent of one's desires, and that betrayal may be a misfortune for a person even though he is indifferent to whether he has ever been betrayed. Again, if desires are of negligible importance in deciding whether someone is the subject of a misfortune, an aborted fetus must, it seems to me, be seen as the victim of a terrible misfortune, being denied a possible life. This does not seem quite right—at least it is not obviously right. This is because what counts as a misfortune often depends not merely upon one's possibilities, but upon how these are viewed, how they are related to one's desires. (It is possible that Nagel had something like this in mind when he talked of a person's "history.") That this qualification is necessary is shown by the fact that most of us have many "possibilities" the nonfulfillment of which may wrongly be regarded as our misfortune, if our desires are ignored. It is very irritating, for example, to see parents bemoan their child's failure to become a concert pianist or a doctor because, despite his or her desire to do something else, this was a "possibility." One could in this way become the victim of all sorts of misfortunes, viewed differently by various anxious devotees, while leading a life with which one is perfectly content.

In the face of this, one may experience a kind of existentialist indignation, expressible in the words: "I am free to choose what counts as a misfortune *for me.*" Yet this isn't right either, and it brings out an important truth in Nagel's position. The concept of misfortune, like the concept of happiness, is partially normative; both concepts, that is, stand in some complex relation to a conception of goodness. This is shown by the fact that it is *sometimes* correct to say that a person who claims to be happy is, in fact, not happy and even to see him as the subject of a misfortune if, for example, he falls wildly short of the way we think it is *good* for a person to be. Suppose, for example, he has come to take pleasure in evil, or in an idle, pointless pursuit such as spending every spare moment enjoying pleasurable sensations by operating electrodes. He may be in some sense contented, but he is surely not happy (though he may not be *un*happy either), and is justly described as unfortunate.

The normative concept of misfortune is strongly Aristotelian in its rejection of the idea that the subject's testimony upon his or her own experience is a sufficient criterion of misfortune. It may be argued that death is a misfortune in precisely this sense; that since death is so clearly not in one's best interests, it is a condition for which we reasonably pity others, irrespective of whether or not they feared it. If this is so, the death of an animal must be a great misfortune also; for a dead animal certainly falls short of the way we think it is "good" for animals to be.

I find this unconvincing, however, for it seems to me that death is not a misfortune merely because it is a bad condition to be in, relative to being alive, healthy, and so on; rather it is a misfortune because life is something most of us value, and want to experience for as long as possible. We usually pity a person who has just died for one of two reasons: because that person valued life and wanted to live; or because he or she did *not* value life, and failed to see death as a misfortune. I shall say more about the first reason in a moment. The second reason sheds an interesting complexion on the normative concept of a misfortune. For it suggests that what is unfortunate about the evil or idle person discussed above is that, like the person who did not value life, he does not have the right kinds of *desires or values,* and that we think it in some sense *possible* that he might have had these. The misfortune is not, then, simply his falling short of how we think it good to be; it is also, and I think fundamentally, his failing to desire to be this way. An animal cannot be the subject of a misfortune in this way. He can be better or worse in relation to some conception of what it is to be a good animal; but he cannot be an object of pity because he does not *want* to match up to this conception. It does not make sense to say of an animal, as we say of a person, "It's unfortunate for him that he didn't mind dying." For what this suggests in the case of a person is a condition of depressiveness, or indifference towards life, and a failure to appreciate the richness and interest of life for a creature as complex and sensitive as a person. It follows from the Wittgensteinian argument above that these emotions, and this failure, are not possible for an animal.

The concept of something's being a misfortune *for X* is not adequately captured by identifying a discrepancy between X's "history and possibilities" and X's actual condition, the alleged misfortune. X's misfortune must either be something which X did not want; or it must be something that X *should not* have wanted, because it so obviously conflicted with his interests. Without these qualifications, many conditions could be wrongly considered "X's misfortune," for example, X's failing to be a concert pianist, even though she succeeded in being the teacher she wanted to be. Also, there would be no reason to restrict subjects of misfortune in this sense to persons: an accident could be a misfortune *for my car,* or for the tree which was hit by it. We would of course beg the question unforgivably if we excluded the latter possibility merely by confining the possible subjects of misfortune to persons.

To be a possible subject of misfortunes which are not merely unpleasant experiences, one must be able to desire and value certain things. The kind of misfortune which is in question here is death, and to discover whether this is a misfortune for an animal, we must ask whether, or in what sense, animals don't want to die. Of course, in some sense this is true of virtually all animals, which manifest acute fear when their lives are threatened. Yet blindly clinging on to life is not the same as wanting to live because one *values* life. This is the kind of desire for life of which persons are capable. It is this which gives sense to the claim that death is a misfortune, even a tragedy, for a person. Bernard Williams (in a reply to Nagel) argues a view like this.

Williams introduces the useful concept of a categorical desire. This is a desire which does not merely presuppose being alive (like the desire to eat when one is hungry), but rather answers the question whether one wants to remain alive. It may answer this question affirmatively or not. Williams discusses what he calls a rational forward-looking desire for suicide: this desire is categorical because it resolves (negatively), rather than assumes, the question of one's continued existence. Alternatively one may resolve this question affirmatively with a desire, for example, to raise children or write a book. Such desires give one reason to go on living, they give life so-called point or meaning. Most persons have some such desires throughout substantial periods of their lives.

A person who possesses categorical desires of the second sort is, Williams suggests, vulnerable to the misfortune of death in a way which neither Lucretius nor Nagel grasps. "To want something," says Williams, "is to that extent to have a reason for resisting what excludes having that thing; and death certainly does that, for a very large range of things that one wants." A subject of categorical desires, therefore, "has reason to regard possible death as a misfortune to be avoided, and we, looking at things from his point of view, would have reason to regard his actual death as a misfortune." The fear of death need not grow out of a confused conception of death as a state which is somehow suffered, as Lucretius claims; it may be the entirely rational corollary of the desire to do certain things with one's life. Furthermore we often pity a person who has died on exactly the ground that death prevents the satisfaction of certain desires, and not merely—as Nagel suggests—that death closes certain possibilities that the subject may or may not have wanted to realize.

It will be obvious from the earlier discussion that I reject the suggestion that a categorical desire, or anything of this nature, is attributable to animals. For consider what would have to be the case if this were so. First, animals would have to possess essentially the same conceptions of life and death as persons do. The subject of a categorical desire must either understand death as a condition which closes a possible future forever, and leaves behind one a world in which one has no part as an agent or conscious being of any sort; or he must grasp, and then reject, this conception of death, in favor of a belief in immortality. Either way, the radical and exclusive nature of the transition from life to death must be understood—it must at least be appreciated why people think in these terms—so that the full significance of the idea that "X is a reason for living" may be grasped.

One can only understand life and death in these ways if one possesses the related concepts of long-term future possibilities, of life itself as an object of value, of consciousness, agency and their annihilation, and of tragedy and similar misfortunes. It is only by an imaginative leap that possession of these concepts seems attributable to animals as well as to persons; this leap is all the more tempting, and therefore all the more dangerous, because it is not *obviously* absurd. It is certainly the case, for example, that some animals experience emotions of a relatively sophisticated nature, and that these emotions involve a kind of recognition of such things as human misfortune, impending danger to another, potential loss, and so on. I see no reason to withhold the ascription of sympathy, anxiety, even grief, to some animals; I only want to deny (what may be suggested by an anti-speciesist) that these emotions, and the range of awareness which they presuppose, give us a way into legitimately ascribing to animals an understanding of the finality, and potentially tragic significance, of death. Such understanding is necessary for a subject of categorical desires.

IV. MISFORTUNES AND RIGHTS

If my argument is correct, animals lack the very capacity which is necessary for the right to life: the capacity to have categorical desires. This capacity is necessary for a creature to be a possible subject of the misfortune of death, and *this* possibility is presupposed by the right to life; otherwise the right to life would be a right to be protected from something which could not conceivably be a misfortune, which does not make sense. I want to suggest, furthermore, that the capacity to be a subject of the misfortune of death is *sufficient* for possession of the right to life. I shall try to clarify this last point with reference to an article by Michael Tooley.

Tooley points out that the concepts of a person and human being are usefully prized apart by employing the former as a purely moral concept, entailing the right to life, and the latter to denote membership of the species homo sapiens. The question may then be raised whether all human beings should be regarded as persons (how about fetuses and even newborn infants?), and whether some *non*humans shouldn't be regarded as persons. The distinction is a valuable one, but its usefulness depends upon the discovery of criteria for personhood in this purely moral sense. Tooley suggests that possession of the concept of self as a continuing subject of experiences, and knowledge that one is such a self, are necessary and sufficient for personhood. His claim seems to be that the right to life is entailed by the *desire* for life as a continuing "self," which is present, or explicably absent (for example, through insanity or indoctrination) in most persons. He argues (rather as I have done) that such a desire presupposes a degree of conceptual sophistication which not all humans (for example, fetuses and newborn infants) possess.

Despite resemblances to my own position, there are important differences. For Tooley, a right to *X* is essentially an obligation on the part of others to respect the subject's *desire* for *X*; this is so, it seems, irrespective of whether or not the desire is reasonable or rational, good or evil. However it is most implausible to suggest that the right to life depends on the desire to live; one reason is that one does not forgo this right by *relinquishing* the desire to live. More generally, rights are independent of desires, for people may have desires without corresponding rights (for example, the desire to steal), and rights without corresponding desires (for example, the right to become an American citizen).

The connection between rights and misfortunes is a much more fruitful one. Not all possible misfortunes are matched by rights, though I believe the converse is true. Yet it seems reasonable to suggest that the reason why most human beings (biological concept) have the right to life is related to the fact that death is regarded as possibly a grave misfortune for a human being. The fact that most people desperately do not *want* to die is not what makes death a misfortune, or gives us the right to life; it is rather that this desire is an aspect of a rich understanding of what is not, so to speak, in our "interests" as human beings. Human beings have, we feel, the capacity clearly to recognize what is so appalling about death—its finality and inexorable quality for a self-conscious being—and this recognition is part of what makes death appalling. This, combined with the fact that death is something from which we can to some extent be protected, is part of the reason why we ascribe to human beings the right to life.

I suggest, therefore, that the capacity to *see* death as a misfortune is sufficient for the truth of the claim that death *is* a misfortune for the person in question; also that this capacity is sufficient for the right to life. The concept of capacity in this context has not been examined; I have not, for example, tried to deal with the various ways in which a person may be said to possess an unrealized capacity to be a subject of the misfortune of death. Many awkward cases may be brought up in this connection: what of the incurably comatose, or—Tooley's interest—fetuses and newborn infants? To discuss such cases, and attempt to specify with precision what is meant by "capacity," would be beyond the scope of this paper. I shall close this section with some remarks on the complexity of this concept, and its resistance at certain points to a purely empirical analysis. It is of course an empirical fact that human beings and animals have the capacity to suffer physical pain; yet to claim that an incapacitated (comatose, insane, or whatever) human being nonetheless has the capacity to see death as a misfortune may be plausible, despite the impossibility of verifying this. If this is correct, we are forced to take seriously—much more so than Tooley for example—the biological relationship between human beings and persons (in the purely moral sense), and to observe the fact that, however *uneasy* one may feel about ascribing certain conceptual capacities to, for example, infants, this is not to be confused with the *absurdity* attendant on such attributions to animals. A case can be made (albeit, perhaps, a poor one) for describing the former but not the latter as possible subjects of the misfortune of death. To this extent then, all human beings are properly viewed as *candidates* for the right to life, even though some may be unable, so to speak, to sustain this right, by virtue of their inability to realize in any significant way the capacity we have discussed.

I have suggested, by contrast, that no nonhuman is even a candidate for the right to life. This should be qualified at this point with a distinction between those nonhumans (for example, mice) of which it might be said that this is a logical impossibility, given the primitiveness of their behavior; and those nonhumans of which this cannot quite be said. Chimpanzees and dolphins, for example, are often cited as potential or actual language-users, and it is not *absurd* to suggest that these might turn out to qualify as persons in the purely moral sense. I have serious doubts about this possibility, as I think anyone must who understands the conceptual complexity surrounding our awareness of death, but it is not to be denied that where a small number of unusually sophisticated animals are concerned, the final answer may lie with a critical empirical investigation.

V. IMPLICATIONS FOR VEGETARIANISM

Finally, we must consider the implications of my argument for the practice of meat-eating. This has been a background concern until now: I have been mainly concerned with correcting a certain picture of animals, and the claims they legitimately make upon us. I concluded that animals are deserving of some moral concern, but not as much as persons; that their sufferings, not their (quick and painless) deaths, are morally significant. It remains to be seen just how this affects the vegetarianism issue; I shall close with some suggestions on this point.

My argument, if successful, has pulled the carpet from under the vegetarian ideology which seeks to protect animals from human jaws on the grounds of equal rights. This may reasonably be seen as a disappointing victory for someone who is trying to decide whether or not to eat meat; all it does is remove one argument for *not* eating meat. What is missing, it seems, is some criterion for deciding what kinds of human interests justify causing animals to suffer, or even to die a quick and painless death. With respect to the former, I have already said that certain human interests may outweigh the wrongness of causing animals to suffer; it must now be added that, despite our conclusion that animals are not in any significant sense victims of the misfortune of death, the act of *causing* the quick and painless death of an animal is not necessarily morally neutral. I shall try to clarify these points now in connection with Nozick's example, to which I promised to return.

This example is intended to show that human pleasure inadequately justifies cruelty to animals. The question then arises whether meat-eating is, as the example assumes, reasonably seen as a kind of personal whim, a trivial pleasure with as little justificatory force as the eccentric satisfaction of swinging a baseball bat. If indeed this is the case, it is hard to see how meat-eating justifies either the painful or painless killing of animals. The bat-swinger whose special pleasure had as a (regretted) corollary the instantaneous killing of one, or let us say thirty, animals would, I feel, need to call upon something more than his eccentric pleasure to justify the act. Why this is so is not easy to say. It could of course be the case that the animals in question are valued by someone, or by other animals, and that this would bring us back to a verdict of gratuitous cruelty. Setting this possibility aside, we have to consider the intuition that whimsical bat-swinging, causing instantaneous animal deaths, is, if not a major misdemeanor, pointlessly destructive, perhaps in a way that is akin to the destroying of trees or certain artifacts. It is possible in this way to drive a slim wedge between the moral significance of (or appropriateness of moral concern towards) animal deaths on the one hand, and on the other the acts which bring these about.

The decision to eat or not to eat meat is, I suggest, profitably undertaken with this kind of example in mind. If meat-eating has more justificatory force than whimsical bat-swinging, we need to know what this is; it seems likely that, even if it were proved that meat is nutritively substitutable, a case could be made for according meat-eating more weight as a reason for action than whimsical bat-swinging. After all, insofar as meat-eating is found pleasurable, this pleasure is generally rooted in certain attitudes and traditions of long standing, which many are understandably reluctant to give up. It would of course be conservative in the extreme to give *much* weight to these considerations; the question is whether they carry sufficient weight to justify what I have presented as the morally tolerable, though not insignificant, activity of killing animals quickly and painlessly. My own view is that some such considerations, combined with the contingent fact that the nutritional value of meat is by no means proven to be negligible, successfully justify this activity, though the more usual phenomenon of causing animals to suffer as they are prepared for death is another matter. As long as such suffering persists, and to the extent that one is confident that meat is nutritionally dispensable, vegetarianism may well be the correct course. It is important only to see that this issue cannot be settled in advance, but must be the consequence of many empirical and moral considerations.

QUESTIONS FOR DISCUSSION

1. Singer argues that it is unjust to raise animals for food. It seems doubtful that pigs, chickens, and beef cows would exist at all if they were not raised for food. If their very existence depends on our raising them for food, does that justify, or only somewhat extenuate, what we do to them?

2. Comment on Singer's claim that using range land to grow grains instead of raising livestock would be more efficient in providing protein required for a healthy diet, and would therefore reduce famine. Should our policy toward animals be determined by what is better for us or on what is better for them?

3. If strict laws were passed prohibiting cruel treatment of animals, and they were effectively enforced, would that satisfy Singer's conscience? Would it satisfy yours?

4. What is meant by "speciesism"? What is Cigman's main reply to Singer's analogy between speciesism and racism? Do you agree?

5. Compare Cigman's rejection of animal rights with Mary Anne Warren's rejection of fetal rights. Is one sounder than the other, or are they equally sound or unsound?

6. Do we have a moral obligation not to be cruel to animals? If so, does it follow that animals have a right to compassionate treatment by humans? Does every moral obligation of A to B entail that B has a right to be treated accordingly? For example, it is often claimed that we all have a moral obligation to refrain from littering public spaces. Does that give anyone a right to stop us? For another example: If you have promised your dead grandmother that you will take good care of her cat, then you have a moral obligation to do so. But what would be the correlative right?

SUGGESTED READINGS

BERNSTEIN, M., "Speciesism and Loyalty," *Behavior and Philosophy*, 19, 1 (1991), 43–59.

FINK, C., "The Moderate View on Animal Ethics," *Between the Species*, 7, 4 (1991), 194–200.

FULDA, J., "Reply to an Objection to Animal Rights," *Journal of Value Inquiry*, 26, 1 (1992), 87–88.

NELSON, J., "Autonomy and the Moral Status of Animals," *Between the Species*, 8, 1 (1992), 34–36.

ROLLIN, B., *Animal Rights and Human Morality*, Buffalo: Prometheus, 1992.

SINGER, P., *Animal Liberation*, New York: Avon, 1977.

PART FOUR

*T*HE GOOD LIFE

Until now we have been concerned with issues of right and wrong, and with the standards and rules that should govern our actions toward one another. But ethics includes more than these matters, it also guides us in our self-regarding conduct, by advising us about how to live a full and happy life. This aspect of ethics is often called "value theory," in contrast to "moral theory," although there are philosophers, notably utilitarians, virtue theorists, and pragmatists, who deny any sharp distinction between the two fields.

Any account of what is a good life is also an account of how we *ought* to live. This is a rather hypothetical sense of "ought," meaning that we ought to live that way *if* we want to live a full and happy life. And of course we all want to do that. So any account of what is a good life is a guide to living as well as a definition of happiness and self-fulfillment, which everyone seems to want to some extent. Most people, as Aristotle observed, want this more than anything else.

This last part of the book will not follow the debate format of the first three parts. Chapter 12 offers six discussions of goals of life that most people consider essential ingredients of happiness. Due to the popular belief, echoed by Janice Moulton, that there is a deep division between the two sexes on the subject of sexual fulfillment, a two-sided discussion of this topic is included.

The goals of life discussed in Chapter 12 can hardly be argued for and against. Either we find them desirable or we do not. We are free to choose among them, as we are free to select a house or an apartment in accordance with our needs and preferences. Where we may rationally disagree, and perhaps correct each other's errors of judgment, is in conjecturing how any one of these goals is best achieved, and also in determining its main components and in distinguishing it from a glossy counterfeit. The writers in Chapter 12 distinguish durable and satisfying forms of virtue, pleasure, sexual fulfillment, enlightenment, and self-affirmation.

VIRTUOUS ACTIVITY

Aristotle (384–322 B.C.) formulated a vision of the good life characteristic of the golden age of ancient Greece. Happiness, he tells us, is an ambiguous term having many meanings. People, rational animals, as he calls them, have many different skills and capacities. And it makes them happy to exercise them well;

417

anything that promotes our natural development, our biological and psychic well being, is to that degree a good and contributes to happiness.

Some people, Aristotle notes, identify happiness with pleasure and wealth, others with social honors, still others with "contemplation" (that is, with scientific and philosophical knowledge). While, like Plato, Aristotle places high value on the last of these, he suggests that complete happiness requires the exercise of all our natural capacities, resulting in a varied life that realizes all of these values.

In considering what our "natural capacities" are, Aristotle notes that the human "soul"—by which he means, precisely, our natural capacities—consists of a rational and an irrational part. The irrational part, which man shares with all animals, consists of the faculties of nutrition and nonrational desire (appetite). The intellect and the type of desire that is governed by reason make up the rational and distinctively human part of the soul. Virtue is then defined as the skillful exercise of the rational faculties, and complete happiness as the exercise of all these faculties in virtuous activity. In brief, the good life is one in which all our natural abilities and tendencies are developed and fulfilled. It is not one in which we learn to extinguish all desires or in which we cultivate moderate pleasures and stay out of trouble. It is one in which we acquire the skills to satisfy all our rational, and therefore healthy, desires to a degree that is consistent with our abilities and opportunities, and in which we cease to desire what reason informs us is not worth the cost.

Although Aristotle's dynamic and optimistic vision is intrinsically appealing and avoids excessive preoccupation with any single goal of life, we may question whether his conception of human nature can do all the ethical work he demands of it. Just how "rational," for example, is the pursuit of knowledge of ancient history or the cultivation of the arts or collecting stamps? Is each human activity and its goal equally natural to the individual, or do we all pursue the same natural goals? John Stuart Mill wrote that "all praise of civilization is dispraise of nature." If so, then why should fulfillment of our natural tendencies be essential to happiness? Perhaps some natural tendencies, such as aggression and selfishness, should be suppressed? Aristotle could reply that socially undesirable tendencies are not really natural to us, but that would render "natural" as a criterion of good rather vacuous, since good would also be the criterion of what is natural. Aristotle may have underestimated the importance of individual differences and the enormous variety of personal goals of life, to which Nietzsche's vision of man as the creator of his own values calls attention.

ACTIVE AND PASSIVE PLEASURE

For the utilitarian, positive pleasure and freedom from pain (for oneself, for egoistic utilitarians like Locke and Hume; for as many people as possible, for social utilitarians like J. S. Mill and J. C. Smart) are the supreme goal of human life. And that is largely true for a great many, perhaps most, people a great deal (perhaps most) of the time, whether or not they profess the utilitarian system of ethics. Jeremy Bentham maintained rather persuasively that we are all utilitarians whether we know it or not. Yet there are such profound differences in the ways of life followed by people, not only in different societies, but even in the same family, that the idea of the pursuit of pleasure must be recognized as highly ambiguous. In particular, there is such a vast difference between, for example, the pleasures of the adventurer on the one hand, and the blissful state of the rhapsodic mystic on the other, that at least two distinct meanings of the term "pleasure" and its cognates— "happiness," "joy," and "fulfillment"—should be kept in mind. John Stuart Mill was keenly aware of this in his famous essay on utilitarianism, and took considerable pains to make the distinction as clear as possible. The pleasure of excitement, he reminds us, is not to be confused with the pleasure of tranquility. The former involves more strenuous activity and consequently is more mixed with frustration, fear, and suffering and is by its very nature transient, while the latter is more passive and, if lacking in intensity, may more than compensate for that by its freedom from pain and its capacity to be sustained indefinitely.

Mill also proposes that pleasure be evaluated according to what he calls its "quality" as well as its "quantity," that is, its intensity and duration. Some pleasurable experiences, he maintains, are intrinsically superior to others and, other things being equal, ought to be preferred. The intellectual pleasures of acquiring knowledge, learning new skills, contemplating or creating works of art, the moral pleasures of helping others, and the spiritual joy of feeling at one with nature and/or divinity, all rank higher in quality than the pleasures of the senses. Mill's reason for preferring the higher pleasures is simply that he believes everyone who has experienced both does so; thus no further argument is required.

Just what the relationship is between Mill's two distinctions—between excitement and tranquility, and between lower and higher quality—he does not explain. Surely they do not exactly correspond. The pleasures of mountain climbing and free-fall parachuting, and of achieving great power, wealth, or sexual prowess are intensely exciting. Are they of low quality, compared to the more tranquil satisfactions of aesthetic or religious contemplation? Perhaps that depends on other factors, such as how much knowledge and skill were invested in their pursuit, but if so, it would seem not to be the pleasure that ranks as low or high, but rather (going back to Aristotle's ideal of virtuous activity) the quality of the activity leading to the pleasure in question.

SEXUAL FULFILLMENT (AND PERVERSION)

Judging from the amount of attention paid to matters of sexual satisfaction in the mass media, in popular songs, and even in our dreams, sexual fulfillment would seem to rank high among goals of life except for individuals, like priests and nuns, who have deliberately renounced it. But what constitutes such fulfillment is not as generally agreed upon as its mere desirability. In particular, there seems to be a deep division between those who, in Mill's terms, prefer the pleasure of excitement and those who prefer the pleasure of tranquillity. According to Janice Moulton, this difference of attitude toward sex (and possibly toward other satisfactions) reflects a natural difference between masculine and feminine temperaments. Note that this difference of temperament need not exactly correspond to the related difference of gender.

In his pioneer effort to distinguish clearly between healthy and perverse sexuality, Thomas Nagel analyzes the process of sexual flirtation and mutual conquest as involving many levels of perceptual and emotional interaction between the participants, interactions that the French existentialist, Jean-Paul Sartre, invested with metaphysical significance by calling them modes of "transcendence." According to Nagel, the more numerous and complex the levels of reciprocal perception and arousal, that is, the more A's desire for B is whetted by A's perception of B's response to A's earlier response to B's response, the more distinctively human and fulfilling is the subsequent sexual experience, and, conversely, the fewer such levels of transcendence, the less human and more perverse the experience.

Janice Moulton argues that Nagel's analysis applies only to one aspect of sexual experience, the initial period of flirtation and conquest, and fails to apply, at least to any significant degree of importance, to the sexual experiences of long-term partners such as married couples. Sex between such partners, she maintains, is just as richly fulfilling an experience as that between lovers who have just discovered each other. What may have been lost in excitement and novelty has, she maintains, been more than made up for by deep affection and understanding of each other's needs. Moulton suggests that the emphasis on the excitement of conquest is characteristic of men, while preference for the more tranquil pleasures of enduring love is more typical of women. She does not indicate whether she considers these differences to be biologically rooted or culturally engendered.

ENLIGHTENMENT

Many traditions have placed great value on a state or process called "enlightenment," but Far Eastern religions, preeminently Buddhism, Hinduism, and Taoism, have made enlightenment the supreme goal of human life, far overshadowing any other, and have invested it with metaphysical significance as a state of eternal happiness transcending the *karma* cycle of birth, death, and suffering. While the theme of renunciation of worldly goods runs through all the great religions of the world, it is especially prominent in the teaching of Gautama Siddhartha Buddha (563–483 B.C.) and his disciples. The Buddha's ideal of enlightenment achieved through meditation, self-denial, and ritualistic practices is a state of freedom from desire and therefore from suffering. The cause of suffering is desire and the cause of desire is the illusion of self. When we come to understand fully that the self as an unchanging substance, distinct from other things, does not exist, we cease to care about pleasures, honors, power, and wealth, the pursuit of which produces craving, addiction, frustration, and suffering. When complete self-renunciation has been achieved, the resulting state of *nirvana* is one of perfect happiness. The good life therefore requires training and meditation that leads to nirvana.

It might be objected that the extinction of desire destroys the possibility of pleasure as well as pain and that that is too high a price to pay, but the Buddhist maintains that the very idea of pleasure as a value is part of the illusion of the self and that we are well rid of it. When we do not yet have what we desire, we suffer from frustration; when we have it, we suffer from fear of losing it.

Paradoxically, the renunciation of desire is not thought to produce a neutral state of disinterest, one that is neither happy nor sad, neither pleasant nor painful. On the contrary, Heinrich Zimmer points out in his survey of Buddhist thought that the state of *satori* (Sanskrit for "enlightenment") and the experience of nirvana (self-extinction) constitute the only true happiness. Not that nirvana is observably different from what we ordinarily experience. It is this same world perceived in an enlightened manner. As Zimmer puts it, the Buddhist journey to nirvana is like a ferry ride across a river. But when we reach the farther shore, we find that it is the very place from which we started out. Buddhists often employ such deliberate paradoxes in order to forestall the mistake of thinking that other desires should merely be replaced by the desire to reach nirvana, which is not really a goal, but a release from striving toward goals. The "journey" toward nirvana is an inward journey and thus not literally a journey at all, but a process of increasing enlightenment.

SELF-ASSERTION

Friedrich Nietzsche (1844–1900) was an eloquent spokesman for the nineteenth-century romantic revolt against the sovereignty of reason. He fused elements of idealism, Darwinian evolutionary naturalism, and egoistic psychology into an ideal of life that stressed the "will to power" of the strong and creative individual. Although Hume and the moral sense theorists had already stressed the importance of feelings in motivating conduct, Nietzsche has been one of the few philosophers to denounce conventional morality as inimical to the values of self-assertion and emotional health. In an early work, *The Birth of Tragedy,* he argues that the creative genius of Hellenic art was due to a balance between the force of passion, the "Dionysian" element in man, and formal restraint, the "Apollonian" element. The decline of Hellenic culture began with Socrates (and included Aristotle), Nietzsche asserts, when intellectual and spiritual values became dominant. This overemphasis on rational restraint of passion produced what Nietzsche calls "Alexandrian culture," which has endured ever since. Alexandrian culture is optimistic, theoretical, and rational; it stresses the values of knowledge, self-control, and respect for rules.

In later works, *Beyond Good and Evil* and *The Genealogy of Morals*, Nietzsche attacks Judaeo-Christian religion as the source of a "slave morality" that replaced the superior "master morality" of pre-Socratic Greece, the Roman Republic, and the barbarian tribes of Europe. Master morality, he claims, is the way of life of the naturally superior person, whose instincts and passions create ever new standards of taste and conduct. He concluded that the qualities of such pagan societies are the natural and proper standard of the good life. But the priestly classes of the Western world devised first Judaism and then Christianity to invert the natural moral order and to raise the vices of the weak, such as humility, fear, poverty, and rationality, into pseudo-virtues.

Disregarding Nietzsche's dubious theory of the origin of conventional morality, his criticisms of our excessive emphasis on self-denial and repression of natural instincts are illuminating, if often overblown. The gist of Nietzsche's censure of ascetic and intellectualistic ideals is that they call for unhealthy repression of our desires and emotions, a repression which stifles creativity. Freud and later psychoanalytic theorists have confirmed Nietzsche's insight that long repressed selfish tendencies find abnormal expression in smothering affection, false pity, vindictive hatred of pleasure, and neurotic guilt and seem to support his view that self-assertion is healthier than social conformity. But they tend not to agree with Nietzsche's parallel attack on the values of rational restraint and moderation, which sharply separates his vision of the good life from the "Alexandrian" vision of Aristotle.

12

PATHS TO HAPPINESS

VIRTUOUS ACTIVITY

Aristotle

CHAPTER ONE

It is thought that every activity, artistic or scientific, in fact every deliberate action or pursuit, has for its object the attainment of some good. We may therefore assent to the view which has been expressed that the "good" is "that at which all things aim." Since modes of action involving the practiced hand and the instructed brain are numerous, the number of their ends is proportionately large. For instance, the end of medical science is health; of military science, victory; of economic science, wealth. All skills of that kind which come under a single "faculty"—a skill in masking bridles or any other part of a horse's gear comes under that faculty or art of horsemanship, while horsemanship itself and every branch of military practice comes under the art of war, and in the like manner other arts and techniques are subordinate to yet others—in all these the ends of the master arts are to be preferred to those of the subordinate skills, for it is the former that provide the motive for pursuing the latter.

CHAPTER TWO

Now if there is an end which as moral agents we seek for its own sake, and which is the cause of our seeking all the other ends—if we are not to go on choosing one act for the sake of another, thus landing ourselves in an infinite progression with the result that desire will be frustrated and ineffectual—it is clear that this must be the good, that is the absolutely good. May we not then argue from this that a knowledge of the good is a great advantage to us in the conduct of our lives? Are we not more likely to hit the mark if we have a target? If this be true, we must do our best to get at least a rough idea of what the good really is, and which of the sciences, pure or applied, is concerned with the business of achieving it.

Now most people would regard the good as the end pursued by that study which has most authority and control over the rest. Need I say that this is the science of politics? It is a political science that prescribes what subjects are to be taught in states, which of these the different sections of the population are to learn, and up to what point. We see also that the faculties which obtain most regard come under this science: for example, the art of war, the management of property, the ability to state a case. Since, therefore, politics makes use of the other practical sciences, and lays it down besides what we must do and what we must not do, its end must include theirs. And that end, in politics as well as in ethics, can only be the good of man. For even if the good of the community coincides with that of the individual, the good of the community is clearly a greater and more perfect good both to get and to keep. This is not to deny that the good of the individual is worthwhile. But what is good for a nation or a city has a higher, a diviner, quality.

Such being the matters we seek to investigate, the investigation may fairly be represented as the study of politics.

CHAPTER THREE

In studying this subject we must be content if we attain a high degree of certainty as the matter of it admits. The same accuracy or finish is not to be looked for in all discussions any more than in all the productions of the studio and the workshop. The question of the morally fine and the just—for this is what political science attempts to answer—admits of so much divergence and variation of opinion that it is widely believed that morality is a convention and not part of the nature of things. We find a similar fluctuation of opinion about the character of the good. The reason for this is that quite often good things have hurtful consequences. There are instances of men who have been ruined by their money or killed by their courage. Such being the nature of our subject and such our way of arguing in our discussions of it, we must be satisfied with a rough outline of the truth, and for the same reason we must be content with broad conclusions. Indeed we must preserve this attitude when it comes to a more detailed statement of the views that are held. It is a mark of the educated man and a proof of his culture that in every subject he looks for only so much precision as its nature permits. For example, it is absurd to demand logical demonstrations from a professional speaker, we might as well accept mere probabilities from a mathematician.

Every man is a good judge of what he understands: in special subjects the specialist; over the whole field of knowledge the man of general culture. This is the reason why political science is not a proper study for the young.

The young man is not versed in the practical business of life from which politics draws its premises and its data. He is, besides, swayed by his feelings, with the result that he will make no headway and derive no benefit from a study the end of which is not *knowing* but *doing*. It makes no difference whether the immaturity is in age or in character. The defect is not due to lack of years but to living the kind of life which is a succession of unrelated emotional experiences. To one who is like that, knowledge is as unprofitable as it is to the morally unstable. On the other hand, for those whose desires and actions have a rational basis a knowledge of these principles of morals must be of great advantage. . . .

CHAPTER FOUR

To resume. Since every activity involving some acquired skill or some moral decision aims at some good, what do we take to be the end of politics— what is the supreme good attainable in our actions? Well, so far as the name goes there is pretty general agreement. "It is happiness," say both intellectuals and the unsophisticated, meaning by "happiness" living well and faring well. But when it comes to saying in what happiness consists, opinions differ, and the account given by the generality of mankind is not at all like that given by the philosophers. The masses take it to be something plain and tangible, like pleasure or money or social standing. Some maintain that it is one of these, some that it is another, and the same man will change his opinion about it more than once. When he has caught an illness he will say that it is health, and when he is hard up he will say that it is money. Conscious that they are out of their depths in such discussions, most people are impressed by anyone who pontificates and says something that is over their heads. Now it would no doubt be a waste of time to examine all these opinions; enough if we consider those which are most in evidence or have something to be said for them. Among these we shall have to discuss the view held by some that, over and above particular goods like those I have just mentioned, there is another which is good in itself and the cause of whatever goodness there is in all these others.

We must be careful not to overlook the difference that it makes whether we argue *from* or *to* first principles. Plato used very properly to advert to this distinction. Employing a metaphor from the racecourse, where the competitors run from the starting-point and back to it again, he would ask whether the appropriate procedure in a particular enquiry was *from* or *to* first principles. Of course we must start from what is known. But that is an ambiguous expression, for things are known in two ways. Some are known "to us" and some are known absolutely. For members of the Lyceum there can be little doubt that we must start from what is known to us. So the future student of ethics and politics, if he is to study them to advantage, must have been well brought up. For we begin with the *fact,* and if there is sufficient reason for accepting it as such, there will be no need to ascertain also the *why* of the fact. Now a lad with such an upbringing will have no difficulty in grasping the first principles of morals, if he is not in possession of them already. If he has neither of these qualifications, he had better take to heart what Hesiod says:

> That man is best who sees the truth himself;
> Good too is he who hearkens to wise counsel.
> But who is neither wise himself nor willing
> To ponder wisdom, is not worth a straw.

CHAPTER FIVE

Let us return from this digression. There is a general assumption that the manner of a man's life is a clue to what he on reflection regards as the good—in other words, happiness. Persons of low tastes (always in the majority) hold that it is pleasure. Accordingly they ask for nothing better than the sort of life which consists in having a good time. (I have in mind the three well-known types of life—that just mentioned, that of the man of affairs, that of the philosophic student.) The utter vulgarity of the herd of men comes out in their preference for the sort of existence a cow leads. Their view would hardly get a respectful hearing, were it not that those who occupy great positions sympathize with a monster of sensuality like Sardanapalus. The gentleman, however, and the man of affairs identify the good with honor, which may fairly be described as the end which men pursue in political or public life. Yet honor is surely too superficial a thing to be the good we are seeking. Honor depends more on those who confer than on him who receives it, and we cannot but feel that the good is something personal and almost inseparable from its possessor. Again, why do men seek honor? Surely in order to confirm the favorable opinion they have formed of themselves. It is at all events by intelligent men who know them personally that they seek to be honored. And for what? For their moral qualities. The inference is clear; public men prefer virtue to honor. It might therefore seem reasonable to suppose that virtue rather than honor is the end pursued in the life of the public servant. But clearly even virtue cannot be quite the end. It is possible, most people think, to possess virtue while you are asleep, to possess it without acting under its influence during any portion of one's life. Besides, the virtuous man may meet with the most atrocious luck of ill-treatment; and nobody who was not arguing for argument's sake, would maintain that a man with an existence of that sort was "happy." The third type of life is the "contemplative," and this we shall discuss later.

As for the life of the business man, it does not give him much freedom of action. Besides, wealth obviously is not the good we seek, for the sole purpose it serves is to provide the means of getting something else. So far as that goes, the ends we have already mentioned would have a better title to be considered the good, for they are desired on their own account. But in fact even their claim must be disallowed. We may say that they have furnished the ground for many arguments, and leave the matter at that. . . .

CHAPTER SEVEN

From this digression we may return to the good which is the object of our search. What is it? The question must be asked because good seems to vary with the art of pursuit in which it appears. It is one thing in medicine and another in strategy, and so in the other branches of human skill. We must inquire, then, what is the good which is the end common to all of them. Shall we say it is that for the sake of which everything else is done? In medicine this is health, in military science victory, in architecture a building, and so on—different ends in different arts; every consciously directed activity has an end for the sake of which everything that it does is done. This end may be described as its good. Consequently, if there be some one thing which is the end of all things consciously done, this will be the doable good; or, if there be more than one end, then it will be all of these. Thus the ground on which our argument proceeds is shifted, but the conclusion arrived at is the same.

I must try, however, to make my meaning clearer.

In our actions we aim at more ends than one—that seems to be certain—but, since we choose some (wealth, for example, or flutes and tools or instruments generally) as means to something else, it is clear that not all of them are ends in the full sense of the word, whereas the good, that is the supreme good, is surely such an end. Assuming then that there is some one thing which alone is an end beyond which there are no further ends, we may call *that* the good of which we are in search. If there be more than one such final end, the good will be that end which has the highest degree of finality. An object pursued for its own sake possesses a higher degree of finality than one pursued with an eye to something else. A corollary to that is that a thing which is never chosen as a means to some remoter object, has a higher degree of finality than things which are chosen both as ends in themselves and as means to such ends. We may conclude, then, that something which is always chosen for its own sake and never for the sake of something else is without qualification a final end.

Now happiness more than anything else appears to be just such an end, for we always choose it for its own sake, and never for the sake of some other thing. It is different with honor, pleasure, intelligence, and good qualities generally. We choose them indeed for their own sake in the sense that we should be glad to have them irrespective of any advantage which might accrue from them. But we also choose them for the sake of our happiness in the belief that they will be instrumental in promoting that. On the other hand nobody chooses happiness as a means of achieving them or anything else whatsoever than just happiness.

The same conclusion would seem to follow from another consideration. It is a generally accepted view that the final good is self-sufficient. By "self-sufficient" is meant not what is sufficient for oneself living the life of a solitary but includes parents, wife and children, friends and fellow-citizens in general. For man is a social animal. A self-sufficient thing, then, we take to be one which on its own footing tends to make life desirable and lacking in nothing. And we regard happiness as such a thing. Add to this that we regard it as the most desirable of all things without having it counted in with some other desirable thing. For, if such an addition were possible, clearly we should regard it as more desirable when even the smallest advantage was added to it. For the result would be an increase in the number of advantages, and the larger sum of advantages is preferable to the smaller.

Happiness then, the end to which all our conscious acts are directed, is found to be something final and self-sufficient.

But no doubt people will say, "To call happiness the highest good is a truism. We want a more distinct account of what it is." We might arrive at this if we could grasp what is meant by the "function" of a human being. If we take a flautist or a sculptor or any craftsman—in fact any class of men at all who have some special job or profession—we find that his special talent and excellence comes out in that job, and this is his function. The same thing will be true of man simply as man—that is of course if "man" does have a function. But is it likely that joiners and showmakers have certain functions or specialized activities, while man as such has none but has been left by Nature a functionless being? Seeing that eye and hand and foot and everyone of our members has some obvious function, must we not believe that in like manner a human being has a function over and above these particular functions? Then what exactly is it? The mere act of living is not peculiar to man—we find it even in the vegetable kingdom—and what we are looking for is something peculiar to him. We must therefore exclude from our definition the life that manifests itself in mere nurture and growth. A step higher should come the life that is confined to experiencing sensations. But that we see is shared by horses, cows, and the brute creation as a whole. We are left, then, with a life concerning which we can make two statements. First, it belongs to the rational part of man. Secondly, it finds expression in actions. The rational part may be either active or passive: passive in so far as it follows the dictates of reason, active in so far as it possesses and exercises the power of reasoning. A similar distinction can be drawn within the rational life; that is to say, the reasonable element in it may be active or passive. Let us take it that what we are concerned with here is the reasoning power in action, for it will be generally allowed that when we speak of "reasoning" we really mean *exercising* our reasoning faculties. (This seems the more correct use of the word.) Now let us assume for the moment the truth of the following propositions. (A) The function of a man is the exercise of his non-corporeal faculties or "soul" in accordance with, or at least not divorced from, a rational principle. (B) The function of an individual and of a *good* individual in the same class—a harp player, for example, and a good harp player, and so through the classes—is generically the same, except that we must add superiority in accomplishment to the function, the function of the harp player being merely to play on the harp, while the function of the good harp player is to play on it well. (C) The function of man is a certain form of life, namely an activity of the soul exercised in combination with a rational principle or reasonable ground of action. (D) The function of a good man is to exert such activity well. (E) A function is performed well when performed in accordance with the excellence proper to it.—If these assumptions are granted, we conclude that the good for man is "an activity of soul in accordance with goodness" or (on the supposition that there may be more than one form of goodness) "in accordance with the best and most complete form of goodness."

There is another condition of happiness; it cannot be achieved in less than a complete lifetime. One swallow does not make a summer, neither does one fine day. And one day, or indeed any brief period of felicity, does not make a man entirely and perfectly happy . . .

CHAPTER TWELVE

Now let us see if we can discover whether happiness is something to be *praised* or something to be *valued.* (One thing is clear, it is not a mere potentiality of good.) By a thing to be praised we evidently mean always something that is commended for a certain relation which it bears to something else. Thus we praise the just and the brave and the good and goodness generally on the strength of what they do or produce. In like manner we praise the strong and the swift and so on, on the ground of their possessing certain native gifts and standing in a certain relation to something good and excellent. Another way of apprehending the truth of this is to think of praise addressed to the gods. Praise is relative, and if the gods are praised, it can only be in comparison with us mortals. This shows that to praise them is a manifest absurdity. Since praise is of things capable of being related to other things, it is clear that the supremely good things call not for praise but for something greater and better, as plainly appears in the case of the gods, whom we are content to call "happy" or "blessed," an epithet we apply also to such men as most closely resemble the gods. We see that it is so also with *things* that are good. No one praises happiness as he praises justice—no, we think it something more divine and higher in the scale of values. Hence Eudoxus is held to have made a good point in his plea for awarding the first prize to pleasure when he adduced the following argument. The fact that pleasure (which is one of the things recognized as good) is not praised is evidence that it is superior to the goods that are praised. And this character, he thought, belongs also to God and to the supreme good, which is the standard to which all other goods are referred.

While praise is given to goodness—for goodness is the inspiration to noble actions—panegyrics or encomiums are bestowed on the high deed done, whether bodily feat or intellectual achievement. We must, however, leave the detailed examination of this subject to those who have made a special study of the encomium, for no doubt it is more in their line than in ours. But so far as we are concerned the arguments that have been adduced must have convinced us that happiness is one of those things that are perfect and beyond praise. We might infer as much from the consideration that it is a first principle, as is proved by the fact that everything we do is done with a view to it, and we regard it as fundamental that the first principle and cause of the things called good should be something above price and divine.

CHAPTER THIRTEEN

Happiness, then, being an activity of the soul in conformity with perfect goodness, it follows that we must examine the nature of goodness. When we have done this we should be in a better position to investigate the nature of happiness. There is this, too. The genuine statesman is thought of as a man who has taken peculiar pains to master this problem, desiring as he does to make his fellow-citizens good men obedient to the laws. Now, if the study of moral goodness is a part of political science, our inquiry into its nature will clearly follow the lines laid down in our preliminary observations.

Well, the goodness we have to consider is human goodness. This—I mean human goodness or (if you prefer to put it that way) human happiness—was what we set out to find. By human goodness is meant not fineness of physique but a right condition of the soul, and by happiness a condition of the soul. That being so, it is evident that the statesman ought to have some inkling of psychology, just as the doctor who is to specialize in diseases of the eye must have a general knowledge of physiology. Indeed, such a general background is even more necessary for the statesman in view of the fact that his science is of a higher order than the doctor's. Now the best kind of doctor takes a good deal of trouble to acquire a knowledge of the human body as a whole. Therefore the statesman should also be a psychologist and study the soul with an eye to his profession. Yet he will do so only as far as his own problems make it necessary; to go into greater detail on the subject would hardly be worth the labor spent on it.

Psychology has been studied elsewhere and some of the doctrines stated there may be accepted as adequate for our present purpose and by us here. The soul is represented as consisting of two parts, a rational and an irrational. As regards the irrational part there is one subdivision of it which appears to be common to all living things, and this we may designate as having a "vegetative" nature, by which I mean that it is the cause of nutrition and growth, since one must assume the existence of some such vital force in all things that assimilate food. Now the excellence peculiar to this power is evidently common to the whole of animated nature and not confined to man. This view is supported by the admitted fact that the vegetative part of us is particularly active in sleep, when the good and the bad are hardest to distinguish. Such a phenomenon would be only natural, for sleep is a cessation of that function on the operation of which depends the goodness or badness of the soul. But enough of this, let us say no more about the nutritive part of the soul, since it forms no portion of goodness in the specifically *human* character.

But there would seem to be another constituent of the soul which, while irrational, contains an element of rationality. It may be observed in the types of men we call "continent" and "incontinent." They have a principle—

a rational element in their souls—which we commend, because it encourages them to perform the best actions in the right way. But such natures appear at the same time to contain an irrational element in active opposition to the rational. In paralytic cases it often happens that when the patient wills to move his limbs to the right they swing instead to the left. Exactly the same thing may happen to the soul; the impulses of the incontinent man carrying him in the opposite direction from that towards which he was aiming. The only difference is that, where the body is concerned we see the uncontrolled limb, while the erratic impulse we do not see. Yet this should not prevent us from believing that besides the rational an irrational principle exists running opposite and counter to the other. Yet, as I said, it is not altogether irrational; at all events it submits to direction in the continent man, and may be assumed to be still more amenable to reason in the "temperate" and in the brave man, in whose moral make-up there is nothing which is at variance with reason.

We have, then, this clear result. The irrational part of the soul, like the soul itself, consists of two parts. The first of these is the vegetative, which has nothing rational about it at all. The second is that from which spring the appetites and desire in general; and this does in a way participate in reason, seeing that it is submissive and obedient to it. . . . That the irrational element in us need not be heedless of the rational is proved by the fact that we find admonition, indeed every form of censure and exhortation, not ineffective. It may be, however, that we ought to speak of the appetitive part of the soul as rational, too. In that event it will rather be the rational part that is divided in two, one division rational in the proper sense of the word and in its nature, the other in the derivative sense in which we speak of a child as "listening to reason" in the person of its father.

These distinctions within the soul supply us with a classification of the virtues. Some are called "intellectual," as wisdom, intelligence, prudence. Others are "moral," as liberality and temperance. When we are speaking of a man's character we do not describe him as wise or intelligent but as gentle or temperate. Yet we praise a wise man, too, on the ground of his "disposition" or settled habit of acting wisely. The dispositions so praised are what we mean by "virtues."

ACTIVE AND PASSIVE PLEASURE

John Stuart Mill

WHAT UTILITARIANISM IS

The creed which accepts as the foundation of morals, Utility, or the Greatest Happiness Principle, holds that actions are right in proportion as they tend to promote happiness, wrong as they tend to produce the reverse of happiness. By happiness is intended pleasure, and the absence of pain; by unhappiness, pain, and the privation of pleasure. To give a clear view of the moral standard set up by the theory, much more requires to be said; in particular, what things it includes in the ideas of pain and pleasure; and to what extent this is felt an open question. But these supplementary explanations do not affect the theory of life on which this theory of morality is grounded— namely, that pleasure, and freedom from pain, are the only things desirable as ends; and that all desirable things (which are as numerous in the utilitarian as in any other scheme) are desirable either for the pleasure inherent in themselves, or as means to the promotion of pleasure and the prevention of pain.

Now, such a theory of life excites in many minds, and among them in some of the most estimable in feeling and purpose, inveterate dislike. To suppose that life has (as they express it) no higher end than pleasure—no better and nobler object of desire and pursuit—they designate as utterly mean and grovelling; as a doctrine worthy only of swine, to whom the followers of Epicurus were, at a very early period, contemptuously likened; and modern holders of the doctrine are occasionally made the subject of equally polite comparisons by its German, French, and English assailants.

When thus attacked, the Epicureans have always answered, that it is not they, but their accusers, who represent human nature in a degrading light, since the accusation supposes human beings to be capable of no pleasures except those of which swine are capable. If this supposition were true, the charge could not be gainsaid, but would then be no longer an imputation: for if the sources of pleasure were precisely the same to human beings and to swine, the rule of life which is good enough for the one would be good enough for the other. The comparison of the Epicurean life to that of beasts is felt as degrading, precisely because a beast's pleasures do not satisfy a human being's conceptions of happiness. Human beings have faculties more elevated than the animal appetites, and when once made conscious of them,

FROM *Utilitarianism,* chapters I and II, London, 1863.

do not regard anything as happiness which does not include their gratification. I do not, indeed, consider the Epicureans to have been by any means faultless in drawing out their scheme of consequences from the utilitarian principle. To do this in any sufficient manner, many Stoic, as well as Christian elements require to be included. But there is no known Epicurean theory of life which does not assign to the pleasures of the intellect, of the feelings and imagination, and of the moral sentiments, a much higher value as pleasures than to those of mere sensation. It must be admitted, however, that utilitarian writers in general have placed the superiority of mental over bodily pleasures chiefly in the greater permanency, safety, uncostliness, &c., of the former—that is, in their circumstantial advantages rather than in their intrinsic nature. And on all these points utilitarians have fully proved their case; but they might have taken the other, and, as it may be called, higher ground, with entire consistency. It is quite compatible with the principle of utility to recognize the fact, that some *kinds* of pleasure are more desirable and more valuable than others. It would be absurd that while, in estimating all other things, quality is considered as well as quantity, the estimation of pleasures should be supposed to depend on quantity alone.

If I am asked, what I mean by difference of quality in pleasures, or what makes one pleasure more valuable than another, merely as a pleasure, except its being greater in amount, there is but one possible answer. Of two pleasures, if there be one to which all or almost all who have experience of both give a decided preference, irrespective of any feeling of moral obligation to prefer it, that is the more desirable pleasure. If one of the two is, by those who are competently acquainted with both, placed so far above the other that they prefer it, even though knowing it to be attended with a greater amount of discontent, and would not resign it for any quantity of the other pleasure which their nature is capable of, we are justified in ascribing to the preferred enjoyment a superiority in quality, so far outweighing quantity as to render it, in comparison, of small account.

Now it is an unquestionable fact that those who are equally acquainted with, and equally capable of appreciating and enjoying, both, do give a most marked preference to the manner of existence which employs their higher faculties. Few human creatures would consent to be changed into any of the lower animals, for a promise of the fullest allowance of a beast's pleasures; no intelligent human being would consent to be a fool, no instructed person would be an ignoramus, no person of feeling and conscience would be selfish and base, even though they should be persuaded that the fool, the dunce, or the rascal is better satisfied with his lot than they are with theirs. They would not resign what they possess more than he, for the most complete satisfaction of all the desires which they have in common with him. If they ever fancy they would, it is only in cases of unhappiness so extreme, that to escape from it they would exchange their lot for almost any other, however undesirable in their own eyes. A being of higher faculties requires more to make him happy, is capable probably of more acute suffering, and is certainly accessible to it at more points, than one of an inferior type; but in spite of these liabilities, he can never really wish to sink into what he feels to be a lower grade of existence. We may give what explanation we please of this unwillingness; we may attribute it to pride, a name which is given indiscriminately to some of the most and to some of the least estimable feelings of which mankind are capable; we may refer it to the love of liberty and personal independence, an appeal to which was with the Stoics one of the most effective means for the inculcation of it; to the love of power, or to the love of excitement, both of which do really enter into and contribute to it: but its most appropriate appellation is a sense of dignity, which all human beings possess in one form or another, and in some, though by no means in exact, proportion to their higher faculties, and which is so essential a part of the happiness of those in whom it is strong, that nothing which conflicts with it could be, otherwise than momentarily, an object of desire to them. Whoever supposes that this preference takes place at a sacrifice of happiness—that the superior being, in anything like equal circumstances, is not happier than the inferior—confounds the two very different ideas, of happiness, and content. It is indisputable that the being whose capacities of enjoyment are low, has the greatest chance of having them fully satisfied; and a highly-endowed being will always feel that any happiness which he can look for, as the world is constituted, is imperfect. But he can learn to bear its imperfections, if they are at all bearable; and they will not make him envy the being who is indeed unconscious of the imperfections, but only because he feels not at all the good which those imperfections qualify. It is better to be a human being dissatisfied than a pig satisfied; better to be Socrates dissatisfied than a fool satisfied. And if the fool, or the pig, is of a different opinion, it is because they only know their own side of the question. The other party to the comparison knows both sides.

It may be objected, that many who are capable of the higher pleasures, occasionally, under the influence of temptation, postpone them to the lower. But this quite compatible with a full appreciation of the intrinsic superiority of the higher. Men often, from infirmity of character, make their election for the nearer good, though they know it to be the less valuable; and this no less when the choice is between two bodily pleasures, than when it is between bodily and mental. They pursue sensual indulgences to the injury of health, though perfectly aware that health is the greater good. It may be further objected, that many who begin with youthful enthusiasm for everything noble, as they advance in years sink into indolence and selfishness. But I do not believe that those who undergo this very common change, voluntarily choose the lower description of pleasures in preference to the higher. I believe that before they devote themselves exclusively to the one, they have already become incapable of the other. Capacity for the nobler feelings is in most natures a very tender plant, easily killed, not only by hostile influences, but by mere want of sustenance; and in the majority of young persons it speedily dies away if the occupations to which their position in life has devoted them, and the society into which it has thrown them, are not favourable to keeping that higher capacity in exercise. Men lose their high aspirations as they lose their intellectual tastes, because they have not time or opportunity for indulging them; and they addict themselves to inferior pleasures, not because they deliberately prefer them, but because they are either the only ones to which they have access, or the only ones which they are any longer capable of enjoying. It may be questioned whether any one who has remained equally susceptible to both classes of pleasures, ever knowingly and calmly preferred the lower; though many, in all ages, have broken down in an ineffectual attempt to combine both.

From this verdict of the only competent judges, I apprehend there can be no appeal. On a question which is the best worth having of two pleasures, or which of two modes of existence is the most grateful to the feelings, apart from its moral attributes and from its consequences, the judgment of those who are qualified by knowledge of both, or, if they differ, that of the majority among them, must be admitted as final. And there needs to be less hesitation to accept this judgment respecting the quality of pleasures, since there is no other tribunal to be referred to even on the question of quantity. What means are there of determining which is the acutest of two pains, or the intensest of two pleasurable sensations, except the general suffrage of those who are familiar with both? Neither pains nor pleasures are homogeneous, and pain is always heterogenous with pleasure. What is there to decide whether a particular pleasure is worth purchasing at the cost of a particular pain, except the feelings and judgment of the experienced? When, therefore, those feelings and judgment declare the pleasures derived from the higher faculties to be preferable *in kind,* apart from the question of intensity, to those of which the animal nature, disjoined from the higher faculties, is susceptible, they are entitled on this subject to the same regard.

I have dwelt on this point, as being a necessary part of a perfectly just conception of Utility or Happiness, considered as the directive rule of human conduct. But it is by no means an indispensable condition to the acceptance of the utilitarian standard; for that standard is not the agent's own greatest happiness, but the greatest amount of happiness altogether; and if it may possibly be doubted whether a noble character is always the happier for its nobleness, there can be no doubt that it makes other people happier, and that the world in general is immensely a gainer by it. Utilitarianism, therefore, could only attain its end by the general cultivation of nobleness of character, even if each individual were only benefited by the nobleness of others, and his own, so far as happiness is concerned, were a sheer deduction from the benefit. But the bare enunciation of such an absurdity as this last, renders refutation superfluous.

According to the Greatest Happiness Principle, as above explained, the ultimate end, with reference to and for the sake of which all other things are desirable (whether we are considering our own good or that of other people), is an existence exempt as far as possible from pain, and as rich as possible in enjoyments, both in point of quantity and quality; the test of quality, and the rule for measuring it against quantity, being the preference felt by those who, in their opportunities of experience, to which must be added their habits of self-constituents of a satisfied life appear to be two, either of which by itself is often found sufficient for the purpose: tranquility, and excitement. With much tranquility, many find that they can be content with very little pleasure: with much excitement, many can reconcile them-selves to a considerable quantity of pain. There is assuredly no inherent impossibility in enabling even the mass of mankind to unite both; since the two are so far from being incompatible that they are in natural alliance, the prolongation of either being a preparation for, and exciting a wish for, the other. It is only those in whom indolence amounts to a vice, that do not desire excitement after an interval of repose; it is only those in whom the need of excitement is a disease, that feel the tranquility which follows excitement dull and insipid, instead of pleasurable in direct proportion to the excitement which preceded it. When people who are tolerably fortu-nate in their outward lot do not find in life sufficient enjoyment to make it valuable to them, the cause generally is, caring for nobody but themselves. To those who have neither public nor private affections, the excitements of life are much curtailed, and in any case dwindle in value as the time ap-proaches when all selfish interests must be terminated by death: while those who leave after them objects of personal affection, and especially those who have also cultivated a fellow-feeling with the collective interests of mankind, retain as lively an interest in life on the eve of death as in the vigour of youth and health. Next to selfishness, the principal cause which makes life unsatis-factory, is want of mental cultivation. A cultivated mind—I do not mean that of a philosopher, but any mind to which the foundations of knowledge have been opened, and which has been taught, in any tolerable degree, to exer-cise its faculties—finds sources of inexhaustible interest in all that sur-rounds it; in the objects of nature, the achievements of art, the imaginations of poetry, the incidents of history, the ways of mankind past and present, and their prospects in the future. It is possible, indeed, to become indifferent to all this, and that too without having exhausted a thousandth part of it; but only when one has had from the beginning no moral or human interest in these things and has sought in them only the gratification of curiosity.

Now there is absolutely no reason in the nature of things why an amount of mental culture sufficient to give an intelligent interest in these objects of contemplation, should not be the inheritance of everyone born in a civilised country. As little is there an inherent necessity that any human being should be a selfish egotist, devoid of every feeling or care but those which centre in his own miserable individuality. Something far superior to this is sufficiently common even now, to give ample earnest of what the human species may be made. Genuine private affections, and a sincere interest in the public good, are possible, though in unequal degrees, to every rightly brought up human being. In a world in which there is so much to interest, so much to enjoy, and so much also to correct and improve, every-one who has this moderate amount of moral and intellectual requisites is capable of an existence which may be called enviable, and unless such a person, through bad laws, or subjection to the will of others, is denied the liberty to use the sources of happiness within his reach, he will not fail to find this enviable existence, if he escapes the positive evils of life, the great sources of physical and mental suffering—such as indigence, disease, and the unkindness, worthlessness, or premature loss of objects of affection. The main stress of the problem lies, therefore, in the contest with these calamities, from which it is a rare good fortune entirely to escape; which, as things now are cannot be obviated, and often cannot be in any material degree mitigated. Yet no one whose opinion deserves a moment's consideration can doubt that most of the great positive evils of the world are in themselves removable, and will, if human affairs continue to improve, be in the end reduced within narrow limits. Poverty, in any sense implying suffering, may be completely extinguished by the wisdom of society, combined with the good sense and providence of individuals. Even that most intractable of enemies, disease, may be indefinitely reduced in dimensions by good physical and moral education, and proper control of noxious influences; while the progress of science holds out a promise for the future of still more direct conquests over this detestable foe. And every advance in that direction relieves us from some, not only of the chances which cut short our own lives, but, what concerns us still more, which deprive us of those in whom our happiness is wrapt up. As for vicissitudes of fortune, and other disappointments connected with worldly circumstances, these are principally the effect either of gross imprudence, of ill-regulated desires, or of bad or imperfect social institutions. All the grand sources, in short, of human suffering are in a great degree, many of them almost entirely, conquerable by human care and effort; and though their removal is grievously slow—though a long succession of generations will perish in the breach before the conquest is completed, and this world becomes all that, if will and knowledge were not wanting, it might easily be made—yet every mind sufficiently intelligent and generous to bear a part, however small and inconspicuous, in the endeavor, will draw a noble enjoyment from the contest itself, which he would not for any bribe in the form of selfish indulgence consent to be without.

Sexual Perversion

Thomas Nagel

There is something to be learned about sex from the fact that we possess a concept of sexual perversion. I wish to examine the concept, defending it against the charge of unintelligibility and trying to say exactly what about human sexuality qualifies it to admit of perversions. Let me make some preliminary comments about the problem before embarking on its solution.

Some people do not believe that the notion of sexual perversion makes sense, and even those who do disagree over its application. Nevertheless I think it will be widely conceded that, if the concept is viable at all, it must meet certain general conditions. First, if there are any sexual perversions, they will have to be sexual desires or practices that can be plausibly described as in some sense unnatural, though the explanation of this natural/unnatural distinction is of course the main problem. Second, certain practices will be perversions if anything is, such as shoe fetishism, bestiality, and sadism; other practices, such as unadorned sexual intercourse, will not be; about still others there is controversy. Third, if there are perversions, they will be unnatural sexual *inclinations* rather than merely unnatural practices adopted not from inclination but for other reasons. I realize that this is at variance with the view, maintained by some Roman Catholics, that contraception is a sexual perversion. But although contraception may qualify as a deliberate perversion of the sexual and reproductive functions, it cannot be significantly described as a *sexual* perversion. A sexual perversion must reveal itself in conduct that expresses an unnatural *sexual* preference. And although there might be a form of fetishism focused on the employment of contraceptive devices, that is not the usual explanation for their use.

I wish to declare at the outset my belief that the connection between sex and reproduction has no bearing on sexual perversion. The latter is a concept of psychological, not physiological interest, and it is a concept that we do not apply to the lower animals, let alone to plants, all of which have reproductive functions that can go astray in various ways. (Think of seedless oranges.) Insofar as we are prepared to regard higher animals as perverted, it is because of their psychological, not their anatomical similarity to humans. Furthermore, we do not regard as a perversion every deviation from the reproductive function of sex in humans: sterility, miscarriage, contraception, abortion.

Thomas Nagel, "Sexual Perversion," from *The Journal of Philosophy* LXVI, 1 (January 16, 1969): 5–17. Reprinted by permission of the author and publisher.

Another matter that I believe has no bearing on the concept of sexual perversion is social disapprobation or custom. Anyone inclined to think that in each society the perversions are those sexual practices of which the community disapproves, should consider all the societies that have frowned upon adultery and fornication. These have not been regarded as unnatural practices, but have been thought objectionable in other ways. What is regarded as unnatural admittedly varies from culture to culture, but the classification is not a pure expression of disapproval or distaste. In fact it is often regarded as a *ground* for disapproval, and that suggests that the classification has an independent content.

I am going to attempt a psychological account of sexual perversion, which will depend on a specific psychological theory of sexual desire and human sexual interactions. To approach this solution I wish first to consider a contrary position, one which provides a basis for skepticism about the existence of any sexual perversions at all, and perhaps about the very significance of the term. The skeptical argument runs as follows:

"Sexual desire is simply one of the appetites, like hunger and thirst. As such it may have various objects, some more common than others perhaps, but none in any sense 'natural'. An appetite is identified as sexual by means of the organs and erogenous zones in which its satisfaction can be to some extent localized, and the special sensory pleasures which form the core of that satisfaction. This enables us to recognize widely divergent goals, activities, and desires as sexual, since it is conceivable in principle that anything should produce sexual pleasure and that a nondeliberate, sexually charged desire for it should arise (as a result of conditioning, if nothing else). We may fail to empathize with some of these desires, and some of them, like sadism, may be objectionable on extraneous grounds, but once we have observed that they meet the criteria for being sexual, there is nothing more to be said on *that* score. Either they are sexual or they are not: sexuality does not admit of imperfection, or perversion, or any other such qualification—it is not that sort of affection."

This is probably the received position. It suggests that the cost of defending a psychological account may be to deny that sexual desire is an appetite. But insofar as that line of defense it plausible, it should make us suspicious of the simple picture of appetites on which the skepticism depends. Perhaps the standard appetites, like hunger, cannot be classed as pure appetites in that sense either, at least in their human versions.

Let us approach the matter by asking whether we can imagine anything that would qualify as a gastronomical perversion. Hunger and eating are importantly like sex in that they serve a biological function and also play a significant role in our inner lives. It is noteworthy that there is little temptation to describe as perverted an appetite for substances that are not nourishing. We should probably not consider someone's appetites as *perverted* if he liked to eat paper, sand, wood, or cotton. Those are merely rather odd and very unhealthy tastes: they lack the psychological complexity that we expect of perversions. (Coprophilia, being already a sexual perversion, may be disregarded.) If on the other hand someone liked to eat cookbooks, or magazines with pictures of food in them, and preferred these to ordinary food—or if when hungry he sought satisfaction by fondling a napkin or ashtray from his favorite restaurant—then the concept of perversion might seem appropriate (in fact it would be natural to describe this as a case of gastronomical fetishism). It would be natural to describe as gastronomically perverted someone who could eat only by having food forced down his throat through a funnel, or only if the meal were a living animal. What helps in such cases is the peculiarity of the desire itself, rather than the inappropriateness of its object to the biological function that the desire serves. Even an appetite, it would seem, can have perversions if in addition to its biological function it has a significant psychological structure.

In the case of hunger, psychological complexity is provided by the activities that give it expression. Hunger is not merely a disturbing sensation that can be quelled by eating; it is an attitude toward edible portions of the external world, a desire to relate to them in rather special ways. The method of ingestion: chewing, savoring, swallowing, appreciating the texture and smell, all are important components of the relation, as is the passivity and controllability of the food (the only animals we eat live are helpless mollusks). Our relation to food depends also on our size: we do not live upon it or burrow into it like aphids or worms. Some of these features are more central than others, but any adequate phenomenology of eating would have to treat it as a relation to the external world and a way of appropriating bits of that world, with characteristic affection. Displacements or serious restrictions of the desire to eat could then be described as perversions, if they undermined that direct relation between man and food which is the natural expression of hunger. This explains why it is easy to imagine gastronomical fetishism, voyeurism, exhibitionism, or even gastronomical sadism and masochism. Indeed some of these perversions are fairly common.

If we can imagine perversions of an appetite like hunger, it should be possible to make sense of the concept of sexual perversion. I do not wish to imply that sexual desire is an appetite—only that being an appetite is no bar to admitting of perversions. Like hunger, sexual desire has as its characteristic object a certain relation with something in the external world; only in this case it is usually a person rather than an omelet, and the relation is considerably more complicated. This added complication allows scope for correspondingly complicated perversions.

The fact that sexual desire is a feeling about other persons may tempt us to take a pious view of its psychological content. There are those who believe that sexual desire is properly the expression of some other attitude, like love, and that when it occurs by itself it is incomplete and unhealthy—or at any rate subhuman. (The extreme Platonic version of such a view is that sexual practices are all vain attempts to express something they cannot in principle achieve: this makes them all perversions, in a sense.) I do not believe that any such view is correct. Sexual desire is complicated enough without having to be linked to anything else as a condition for phenomenological analysis. It cannot be denied that sex may serve various functions— economic, social, altruistic—but it also has its own content as a relation between persons, and it is only by analyzing that relation that we can understand the conditions of sexual perversion.

I believe it is very important that the object of sexual attraction is a particular individual, who transcends the properties that make him attractive. When different persons are attracted to a single person for different reasons: eyes, hair, figure, laugh, intelligence—we feel that the object of their desire is nevertheless the same, namely that person. There is even an inclination to feel that this is so if the lovers have different sexual aims, if they include both men and women, for example. Different specific attractive characteristics seem to provide enabling conditions for the operation of a single basic feeling, and the different aims all provide expressions of it. We approach the sexual attitude toward the person through the features that we find attractive, but these features are not the objects of that attitude.

This is very different from the case of an omelet. Various people may desire it for different reasons, one for its fluffiness, another for its mushrooms, another for its unique combination of aroma and visual aspect; yet we do not enshrine the transcendental omelet as the true common object of their affections. Instead we might say that several desires have accidentally converged on the same object: any omelet with the crucial characteristics would do as well. It is not similarly true that any person with the same flesh distribution and way of smoking can be substituted as object for a particular sexual desire that has been elicited by those characteristics. It may be that they will arouse attraction whenever they recur, but it will be a new sexual attraction with a new particular object, not merely a transfer of the old desire to someone else. (I believe this is true even in cases where the new object is unconsciously identified with a former one.)

The importance of this point will emerge when we see how complex a psychological interchange constitutes the natural development of sexual attraction. This would be incomprehensible if its object were not a particular person, but rather a person of a certain *kind*. Attraction is only the beginning, and fulfillment does not consist merely of behavior and contact expressing this attraction, but involves much more.

The best discussion of these matters that I have seen appears in part III of Sartre's *Being and Nothingness*. Since it has influenced my own views, I shall say a few things about it now. Sartre's treatment of sexual desire and of love, hate, sadism, masochism, and further attitudes toward others, depends on a general theory of consciousness and the body which we can neither expound nor assume here. He does not discuss perversion, and this is partly because he regards sexual desire as one form of the perpetual attempt of an embodied consciousness to come to terms with the existence of others, an attempt that is as doomed to fail in this form as it is in any of the others, which include sadism and masochism (if not certain of the more impersonal deviations) as well as several nonsexual attitudes. According to Sartre, all attempts to incorporate the other into my world as another subject, i.e., to apprehend him at once as an object for me and as a subject for whom I am an object, are unstable and doomed to collapse into one or other of the two aspects. Either I reduce him entirely to an object, in which case his subjectivity escapes the possession or appropriation I can extend to that object; or I become merely an object for him, in which case I am no longer in a position to appropriate his subjectivity. Moreover, neither of these aspects is stable; each is continually in danger of giving way to the other. This has the consequence that there can be no such thing as a *successful* sexual relation, since the deep aim of sexual desire cannot in principle be accomplished. It seems likely, therefore, that the view will not permit a basic distinction between successful or complete and unsuccessful or incomplete sex, and therefore cannot admit the concept of perversion.

I do not adopt this aspect of the theory, nor many of its metaphysical underpinnings. What interests me is Sartre's picture of the attempt. He says that the type of possession that is the object of sexual desire is carried out by "a double reciprocal incarnation" and that this is accomplished, typically in the form of a caress, in the following way: "I make myself flesh in order to impel the Other to realize *for-herself* and *for me* her own flesh, and my caresses cause my flesh to be born for me in so far as it is for the Other *flesh causing her to be born as flesh*" (391; italics Sartre's). The incarnation in question is described variously as a clogging or troubling of consciousness, which is inundated by the flesh in which it is embodied.

The view I am going to suggest, I hope in less obscure language, is related to this one, but it differs from Sartre's in allowing sexuality to achieve its goal on occasion and thus in providing the concept of perversion with a foothold.

Sexual desire involves a kind of perception, but not merely a single perception of its object, for in the paradigm case of mutual desire there is a complex system of superimposed mutual perceptions—not only perceptions of the sexual object, but perceptions of oneself. Moreover, sexual awareness of another involves considerable self-awareness to begin with—more than is involved in ordinary sensory perception. The experience is felt as an assault on oneself by the view (or touch, or whatever) of the sexual object.

Let us consider a case in which the elements can be separated. For clarity we will restrict ourselves initially to the somewhat artifical case of desire at a distance. Suppose a man and a woman, whom we may call Romeo and Juliet, are at opposite ends of a cocktail lounge, with many mirrors on the walls which permit unobserved observation, and even mutual unobserved observation. Each of them is sipping a martini and studying other people in the mirrors. At some point Romeo notices Juliet. He is moved, somehow, by the softness of her hair and the diffidence with which she sips her martini, and this arouses him sexually. Let us say that *X senses Y* whenever *X* regards *Y* with sexual desire. (*Y* need not be a person, and *X*'s apprehension of *Y* can be visual, tactile, olfactory, etc., or purely imaginary; in the present example we shall concentrate on vision.) So Romeo senses Juliet, rather than merely noticing her. At this stage he is aroused by an unaroused object, so he is more in the sexual grip of his body than she of hers.

Let us suppose, however, that Juliet now senses Romeo in another mirror on the opposite wall, though neither of them yet knows that he is seen by the other (the mirror angles provide three-quarter views). Romeo then begins to notice in Juliet the subtle signs of sexual arousal: heavy-lidded stare, dilating pupils, faint flush, et cetera. This of course renders her much more bodily, and he not only notices but senses this as well. His arousal is nevertheless still solitary. But now, cleverly calculating the line of her stare without actually looking her in the eyes, he realizes that it is directed at him through the mirror on the opposite wall. That is, he notices, and moreover senses, Juliet sensing him. This is definitely a new development, for it gives him a sense of embodiment not only through his own reactions but through the eyes and reactions of another. Moreover, it is separable from the initial sensing of Juliet; for sexual arousal might begin with a person's sensing that he is sensed and being assailed by the perception of the other person's desire rather than merely by the perception of the person.

But there is a further step. Let us suppose that Juliet, who is a little slower than Romeo, now senses that he senses her. This puts Romeo in a position to notice, and be aroused by, her arousal at being sensed by him. He senses that she senses that he senses her. This is still another level of arousal, for he becomes conscious of his sexuality through his awareness of its effect on her and of her awareness that this effect is due to him. Once she takes the same step and senses that he senses her sensing him, it becomes difficult to state, let alone imagine, further iterations, though they may be logically distinct. If both are alone, they will presumably turn to look at each other directly, and the proceedings will continue on another plane. Physical contact and intercourse are perfectly natural extensions of this complicated visual exchange, and mutual touch can involve all the complexities of awareness present in the visual case, but with a far greater range of subtlety and acuteness.

Ordinarily, of course, things happen in a less orderly fashion—sometimes in a great rush—but I believe that some version of this overlapping system of distinct sexual perceptions and interactions is the basic framework of any full-fledged sexual relation and that relations involving only part of the complex are significantly incomplete. The account is only schematic, as it must be to achieve generality. Every real sexual act will be psychologically far more specific and detailed, in ways that depend not only on the physical techniques employed and on anatomical details, but also on countless features of the participants' conceptions of themselves and of each other, which become embodied in the act. (It is a familiar enough fact, for example, that people often take their social roles and the social roles of their partners to bed with them.)

The general schema is important, however, and the proliferation of levels of mutual awareness it involves is an example of a type of complexity that typifies human interactions. Consider aggression, for example. If I am angry with someone, I want to make him feel it, either to produce self-reproach by getting him to see himself through the eyes of my anger, and to dislike what he sees—or else to produce reciprocal anger or fear, by getting him to perceive my anger as a threat or attack. What I want will depend on the details of my anger, but in either case it will involve a desire that the object of that anger be aroused. This accomplishment constitutes the fulfillment of my emotion, through domination of the object's feelings.

Another example of such reflexive mutual recognition is to be found in the phenomenon of meaning, which appears to involve an intention to produce a belief or other effect in another by bringing about his recognition of one's intention to produce that effect. (That result is due to H. P. Grice, whose position I shall not attempt to reproduce in detail.) Sex has a related structure: it involves a desire that one's partner be aroused by the recognition of one's desire that he or she be aroused.

It is not easy to define the basic types of awareness and arousal of which these complexes are composed, and that remains a lacuna in this discussion. I believe that the object of awareness is the same in one's own case as it is in one's sexual awareness of another, although the two awarenesses will not be the same, the difference being as great as that between feeling angry and experiencing the anger of another. All stages of sexual perception are varieties of identification of a person with his body. What is perceived is one's own or another's *subjection* to or *immersion* in his body, a phenomenon which has been recognized with loathing by St. Paul and St. Augustine, both of whom regarded "the law of sin which is in my members" as a grave threat to the dominion of the holy will. In sexual desire and its expression the blending of involuntary response with deliberate control is extremely important. For Augustine, the revolution launched against him by his body is symbolized by erection and the other involuntary physical components of arousal. Sartre too stresses the fact that the penis is not a prehensile organ. But mere involuntariness characterizes other bodily processes as well. In sexual desire the involuntary responses are combined with submission to spontaneous impulses: not only one's pulse and secretions but one's actions are taken over by the body; ideally, deliberate control is needed only to guide the expression of those impulses. This is to some extent also true of an appetite like hunger, but the takeover there is more localized, less pervasive, less extreme. One's whole body does not become saturated with hunger as it can with desire. But the most characteristic feature of a specifically sexual immersion in the body is its ability to fit into the complex of mutual perceptions that we have described. Hunger leads to spontaneous interactions with food; sexual desire leads to spontaneous interactions with other persons, whose bodies are asserting their sovereignty in the same way, producing involuntary reactions and spontaneous impulses in *them*. These reactions are perceived, and the perception of them is perceived, and that perception is in turn perceived; at each step the domination of the person by his body is reinforced, and the sexual partner becomes more possessible by physical contact, penetration, and envelopment.

Desire is therefore not merely the perception of a preexisting embodiment of the other, but ideally a contribution to his further embodiment which in turn enhances the original subject's sense of himself. This explains why it is important that the partner be aroused, and not merely aroused, but aroused by the awareness of one's desire. It also explains the sense in which desire has unity and possession as its object: physical possession must eventuate in creation of the sexual object in the image of one's desire, and not merely in the object's recognition of that desire, or in his or her own private arousal. (This may reveal a male bias: I shall say something about that later.)

To return, finally, to the topic of perversion: I believe that various familiar deviations constitute truncated or incomplete versions of the complete configuration, and may therefore be regarded as perversions of the central impulse.

In particular, narcissistic practices and intercourse with animals, infants, and inanimate objects seem to be stuck at some primitive version of the first stage. If the object is not alive, the experience is reduced entirely to an awareness of one's own sexual embodiment. Small children and animals permit awareness of the embodiment of the other, but present obstacles to reciprocity, to the recognition by the sexual object of the subject's desire as the source of his (the object's) sexual self-awareness.

Sadism concentrates on the evocation of passive self-awareness in others, but the sadist's engagement is itself active and requires a retention of deliberate control which impedes awareness of himself as a bodily subject of passion in the required sense. The victim must recognize him as the source of his own sexual passivity, but only as the active source. De Sade claimed that the object of sexual desire was to evoke involuntary responses from one's partner, especially audible ones. The infliction of pain is no doubt the most efficient way to accomplish this, but it requires a certain abrogation of one's own exposed spontaneity. All this, incidentally, helps to explain why it is tempting to regard as sadistic an excessive preoccupation with sexual technique, which does not permit one to abandon the role of agent at any stage of the sexual act. Ideally one should be able to surmount one's technique at some point.

A masochist on the other hand imposes the same disability on his partner as the sadist imposes on himself. The masochist cannot find a satisfactory embodiment as the object of another's sexual desire, but only as the object of his control. He is passive not in relation to his partner's passion but in relation to his nonpassive agency. In addition, the subjection to one's body characteristic of pain and physical restraint is of a very different kind from that of sexual excitement: pain causes people to contract rather than dissolve.

Both of these disorders have to do with the second stage, which involves the awareness of oneself as an object of desire. In straightforward sadism and masochism other attentions are substituted for desire as a source of the object's self-awareness. But it is also possible for nothing of that sort to be substituted, as in the case of a masochist who is satisfied with self-inflicted pain or of a sadist who does not insist on playing a role in the suffering that arouses him. Greater difficulties of classification are presented by three other categories of sexual activity: elaborations of the sexual act, intercourse of more than two persons, and homosexuality.

If we apply our model to the various forms that may be taken by two-party heterosexual intercourse, none of them seem clearly to qualify as perversions. Hardly anyone can be found these days to inveigh against oral-genital contact, and the merits of buggery are urged by such respectable figures as D. H. Lawrence and Norman Mailer. There may be something vaguely sadistic about the latter technique (in Mailer's writings it seems to be a method of introducing an element of rape), but it is not obvious that this has to be so. In general, it would appear that any bodily contact between a man and a woman that gives them sexual pleasure, is a possible vehicle for the system of multi-level interpersonal awareness that I have claimed is the basic psychological content of sexual interaction. Thus a liberal platitude about sex is upheld.

About multiple combinations, the least that can be said is that they are bound to be complicated. If one considers how difficult it is to carry on two conversations simultaneously, one may appreciate the problems of multiple simultaneous interpersonal perception that can arise in even a small-scale orgy. It may be inevitable that some of the component relations should degenerate into mutual epidermal stimulation by participants otherwise isolated from each other. There may also be a tendency toward voyeurism and exhibitionism, both of which are incomplete relations. The exhibitionist wishes to display his desire without needing to be desired in return; he may even fear the sexual attentions of others. A voyeur, on the other hand, need not require any recognition by his object at all: certainly not a recognition of the voyeur's arousal.

It is not clear whether homosexuality is a perversion if that is measured by the standard of the described configuration, but it seems unlikely. For such a classification would have to depend on the possibility of extracting from the system a distinction between male and femal sexuality; and much that has been said so far applies equally to men and women. Moreover, it would have to be maintained that there was a natural tie between the type of sexuality and the sex of the body, and also that two sexualities of the same type could not interact properly.

Certainly there is much support for an aggressive-passive distinction between male and female sexuality. In our culture the male's arousal tends to initiate the perceptual exchange, he usually makes the sexual approach, largely controls the course of the act, and of course penetrates whereas the woman receives. When two men or two women engage in intercourse they cannot both adhere to these sexual roles. The question is how essential the roles are to an adequate sexual relation. One relevant observation is that a good deal of deviation from these roles occurs in heterosexual intercourse. Women can be sexually aggressive and men passive, and temporary reversals of role are not uncommon in heterosexual exchanges of reasonable length. If such conditions are set aside, it may be urged that there is something irreducibly perverted in attraction to a body anatomically like one's own. But alarming as some people in our culture may find such attraction, it remains psychologically unilluminating to class it as perverted. Certainly if homosexuality is a perversion, it is so in a very different sense from that in which shoe-fetishism is a perversion, for some version of the full range of interpersonal perceptions seems perfectly possible between two persons of the same sex.

In any case, even if the proposed model is correct, it remains implausible to describe as perverted every deviation from it. For example, if the partners in heterosexual intercourse indulge in private heterosexual fantasies, that obscures the recognition of the real partner and so, on the theory, constitutes a defective sexual relation. It is not, however, generally regarded as a perversion. Such examples suggest that a simple dichotomy between perverted and unperverted sex is too crude to organize the phenomena adequately.

I should like to close with some remarks about the relation of perversion to good, bad, and morality. The concept of perversion can hardly fail to be evaluative in some sense, for it appears to involve the notion of an ideal or at least adequate sexuality which the perversions in some way fail to achieve. So, if the concept is viable, the judgment that a person or practice or desire is perverted will constitute a sexual evaluation, implying that better sex, or a better specimen of sex, is possible. This in itself is a very weak claim, since the evaluation might be in a dimension that is of little interest to us. (Though, if my account is correct, that will not be true.)

Whether it is a moral evaluation, however, is another question entirely—one whose answer would require more understanding of both morality and perversion than can be deployed here. Moral evaluation of acts and of persons is a rather special and very complicated matter, and by no means all our evaluations of persons and their activities are moral evaluations. We make judgments about people's beauty or health or intelligence which are evaluative without being moral. Assessments of their sexuality may be similar in that respect.

Furthermore, moral issues aside, it is not clear that unperverted sex is necessarily *preferable* to the perversions. It may be that sex which receives the highest marks for perfection *as sex* is less enjoyable than certain perversions; and if enjoyment is considered very important, that might outweigh considerations of sexual perfection in determining rational preference.

That raises the question of the relation between the evaluative content of judgments of perversion and the rather common *general* distinction between good and bad sex. The latter discussion is usually confined to sexual acts, and it would seem, within limits, to cut across the other: even some who believed, for example, that homosexuality was a perversion could admit a distinction between better and worse homosexual sex, and might even allow that good homosexual sex could be better sex than not very good unperverted sex. If this is correct, it supports the position that, if judgments of perversion are viable at all, they represent only one aspect of the possible evaluation of sex, even *qua sex*. Moreover, it is not the only important aspect: certainly sexual deficiencies that evidently do not constitute perversions can be the object of great concern.

Finally, even if perverted sex is to that extent not so good as it might be, bad sex is generally better than none at all. This should not be controversial: it seems to hold for other important matters, like food, music, literature, and society. In the end, one must choose from among the available alternatives, whether their availability depends on the environment or on one's own constitution. And the alternatives have to be fairly grim before it becomes rational to opt for nothing.

Sexual fulfillment

Janice Moulton

We can often distinguish behavior that is sexual from behavior that is not. Sexual intercourse may be one clear example of the former, but other sexual behaviors are not so clearly defined. Some kissing is sexual; some is not. Sometimes looking is sexual; sometimes *not* looking is sexual. Is it possible, then, to *characterize* sexual behavior?

Thomas Nagel in "Sexual Perversion" and Robert Solomon in "Sexual Paradigms" each offers an answer to this question. Nagel analyzes sexual desire as a "complex system of superimposed mutual perceptions." He claims that sexual relations that do not fit his account are incomplete and, consequently, perversions.

Solomon claims that sexual behavior should be analyzed in terms of goals rather than feelings. He maintains that "the end of desire is interpersonal communication" and not enjoyment. According to Solomon, the sexual relations between regular partners will be inferior to novel encounters because there is less remaining to communicate sexually.

I believe that sexual behavior will not fit any single characterization; that there are at least two sorts of sexual behavior to characterize. Both Nagel and Solomon have interesting things to say about one sort of sexual behavior. However, both have assumed that a model of flirtation and seduction constitutes an adequate model of sexual behavior in general. Although a characterization of flirtation and seduction can continue to apply to a relationship that is secret, forbidden, or in which there is some reason to remain unsure of one's sexual acceptability, I shall argue that most sexual behavior does not involve flirtation and seduction, and that what characterizes flirtation and seduction is not what characterizes the sexual behavior of regular partners. Nagel takes the developments of what I shall call "sexual anticipation" to be characteristic of all sexual behavior and gives no account of sexual satisfaction. Solomon believes that flirtation and seduction are different from regular sexual relationships. However, he too considers only characteristics of sexual anticipation in his analysis and concludes that regular sexual relationships are inferior to novel ones because they lack some of those characteristics.

Flirtation, seduction, and traditional courtship involve sexual feelings that are quite independent of physical contact. These feelings are increased

Janice Moulton, "Sexual Behavior: Another Position," from *The Journal of Philosophy* LXXIII, 16 (September 16, 1976): 537–46.

by anticipation of success, winning, or conquest. Because what is antici-
pated is the opportunity for sexual intimacy and satisfaction, the feelings of
sexual satisfaction are usually not distinguished from those of sexual anticipation. Sexual satisfaction involves sexual feelings which are increased by
the other person's knowledge of one's preferences and sensitivities, the
familiarity of their touch or smell or way of moving, and not by the novelty
of their sexual interest.

It is easy to think that the more excitement and enthusiasm involved in
the anticipation of an event, the more enjoyable and exciting the event itself
is likely to be. However, anticipation and satisfaction are often divorced.
Many experiences with no associated build-up of anticipation are very satisfying, and others, awaited and begun with great eagerness, produce no
feelings of satisfaction at all. In sexual activity this dissociation is likely to be
frequent. A strong feeling of sexual anticipation is produced by the uncertainty, challenge, or secrecy of novel sexual experiences, but the tension and
excitement that increase anticipation often interfere with sexual satisfaction. The comfort and trust and experience with familiar partners may
increase sexual satisfaction, but decrease the uncertainty and challenge that
heighten sexual anticipation. Given the distinction between anticipation
and satisfaction, there is no reason to believe that an increase of trust and
love ought to increase feelings of sexual anticipation nor that sexual anticipation should be a prerequisite for any long-term sexual relationship.

For some people the processes that create sexual anticipation, the exchange of indirect signals, the awareness of the other person's sexual interest, and the accompanying sexual anticipation may be all that is valued in
sexual behavior. Satisfaction is equated with release, the end of a good time,
and is not considered a process in its own right. But although flirtation and
seduction are the main objects of sexual fantasy and fiction, most people,
even those whose sexual relations are frequently casual, seek to continue
some sexual relationships after the flirtation and seduction are over, when
the uncertainty and challenge are gone. And the motives, goals, and feelings
of sexual satisfaction that characterize these continued sexual relations are
not the same as the motives, goals, and feelings of sexual anticipation that
characterize the novel sexual relations Nagel and Solomon have tried to
analyze. Let us consider their accounts.

Nagel's account is illustrated by a tale of a Romeo and a Juliet who are
sexually aroused by each other, notice each other's arousal and become
further aroused by that:

> He senses that she senses that he senses her. This is still another level of
> arousal, for he becomes conscious of his sexuality through his awareness of
> its effects on her and of her awareness that this effect is due to him. Once
> she takes the same step and senses that he senses her sensing him, it
> becomes difficult to state, let alone imagine, further iterations, though they
> may be logically distinct. If both are alone, they will presumably turn to
> look at each other directly, and the proceedings will continue on another
> plane. Physical contact and intercourse are perfectly natural extensions of

this complicated visual exchange, and mutual touch can involve all the complexities of awareness present in the visual case, but with a far greater range of subtlety and acuteness.

Ordinarily, of course, things happen in a less orderly fashion—sometimes in a great rush—but I believe that some version of this overlapping system of distinct sexual perceptions and interactions is the basic framework of any full-fledged sexual relation and that relations involving only part of the complex are significantly incomplete.

Nagel then characterizes sexual perversion as a "truncated or incomplete version" of sexual *arousal,* rather than as some deviation from a standard of subsequent physical interaction.

Nagel's account applies only to the development of sexual anticipation. He says that "the proliferation of levels of mutual awareness . . . is a type of complexity that typifies human interactions," so he might argue that his account will cover Romeo and Juliet's later relationship as well. Granted that levels of mutual awareness exist in any close human relationship. But it does not follow that the development of levels of awareness *characterizes* all human relationships, particularly sexual relationships between familiar partners. In particular, the sort of awareness Nagel emphasizes—"a desire that one's partner be aroused by the recognition of one's desire that he or she be aroused"—does not seem essential to regular sexual relationships. If we accept Nagel's account for sexual behavior in general, then we must classify as a perversion the behavior of an intimate and satisfying sexual relation begun without any preliminary exchange of multilevel arousals.

Sexual desire can be generated by many different things—a smell, a phrase in a book, a familiar voice. The sexual interest of another person is only on occasion novel enough to be the main cause or focus of sexual arousal. A characterization of sexual behavior on other occasions should describe the development and sharing of sexual pleasure—the creation of sexual satisfaction. Nagel's contribution lies in directing our attention to the analysis of sexual behavior in terms of its perceptions and feelings. However, he characterizes only a limited sort of sexual behavior, flirtation and seduction.

Solomon characterizes sexual behavior by analogy with linguistic behavior, emphasizing that the goals are the same. He says:

> Sexual activity consists in speaking what we might call "body language." It has its own grammar, delineated by the body, and its own phonetics of touch and movement. Its unit of meaningfulness, the bodily equivalent of a sentence, is the *gesture* . . . body language is essentially expressive, and its content is limited to interpersonal attitudes and feelings.

The analogy with language can be valuable for understanding sexual behavior. However, Solomon construes the goals of both activities too narrowly and hence draws the wrong conclusions.

He argues that the aim of sexual behavior is to communicate one's attitudes and feelings, to express oneself, and further, that such self-expression is made less effective by aiming at enjoyment:

That is why the liberal mythology has been so disastrous, for it has rendered unconscious the expressive functions of sex in its stress on enjoyment.... It is thus understandable why sex is so utterly important in our lives, and why it is typically so unsatisfactory.

Does stress on enjoyment hinder self-expression? Trying to do one thing, X, may interfere with trying to do another, Y, for some Xs and Ys. For example, trying to eat peanut butter or swim under water may interfere with vocal self-expression. But enjoyment is a different sort of goal. One isn't trying to do both Y and something else when aiming at Y and enjoyment, but to do one sort of thing, Y, a certain way. Far from interfering, one is more likely to be successful at a venture if one can manage to enjoy oneself during the process.

Solomon claims to refute that enjoyment is the essential aim of sexual activity, but he erroneously identifies enjoyment with orgasm:

No one would deny that sex is enjoyable, but it does not follow that sexuality is the activity of "pure enjoyment" and that "gratification," or "pure physical pleasure," that is, orgasm, is its end.

and consequently he shows merely that orgasm is not the only aim of sexual activity. His main argument is:

If sex is pure physical enjoyment, why is sexual activity between persons far more satisfying than masturbation, where, if we accept recent physiological studies, orgasm is at its highest intensity and the post-coital period is cleansed of its interpersonal hassles and arguments?

One obvious answer is that, even for people who have hassles and arguments, interpersonal sexual activity is more enjoyable, even in the "pure physical" sense. Solomon's argument does not show that enjoyment is not the appropriate aim of sexual activity, only that maximum-intensity orgasm is not. As those recent physiological studies pointed out, participants report interpersonal sexual activity as more enjoyable and satisfying even though their orgasms are less intense. Only someone who mistakenly equated enjoyment with orgasm would find this paradoxical.

One need not claim that orgasm is always desired or desirable in sexual activity. That might be like supposing that in all conversations the participants do, or should, express their deepest thoughts. In sexual, as in linguistic, behavior, there is a great variety and subtlety of purpose. But this is not to say that the desire for orgasm should be ignored. The disappointment and physical discomfort of expected but unachieved orgasm is only faintly parallel to the frustration of not being able to "get a word in edgewise" after being moved to express an important thought. It is usually rude or boorish to use language with indifference to the interests and cares of one's listeners. Sexual behavior with such indifference can be no better.

Solomon does not need these arguments to claim that enjoyment is not the only or the essential goal of sexual behavior. His comparison of sexual behavior with linguistic (or other social) behavior could have been used to do the job. The same social and moral distinctions and evaluations can be applied to both behaviors: hurting and humiliating people is bad; making people happy is good; loyalty, kindness, intelligence, and wit are valued; stupidity, clumsiness, and insincerity are not. The purpose of contact, sexual or otherwise, with other people is not just to produce or receive enjoyment—there are times of sadness, solace, and anguish that are important and meaningful to share, but not enjoyable.

Is self-expression, then, the essential goal of sexual behavior? Solomon lists a number of feelings and attitudes that can be expressed sexually:

- love, tenderness and trust, "being-with," mutual recognition
- hatred, indifference, jealousy, conflict
- shyness, fear, lack of confidence, embarrassment, shame
- domination, submissiveness, dependence, possessiveness, passivity

He claims "some attitudes, e.g., tenderness and trust, domination and passivity are best expressed sexually," and says in his account:

> . . . makes it evident why Nagel chose as his example a couple of strangers; one has far more to say, for one can freely express one's fantasies as well as the truth to a stranger. A husband and wife of seven years have probably been repeating the same messages for years, and their sexual activity now is probably no more than an abbreviated ritual incantation of the lengthy conversations they had years before.

A glance at the list of feelings and attitudes above will show that its items are not independent. Shame, for example, may include components of embarrassment, lack of confidence, fear, and probably mutual recognition and submissiveness. To the extent that they can be conveyed by sexual body language, a mere grunt or whimper would be able to express the whole range of the attitudes and feelings as well, if not better, than sexual gestures. Moreover, it is not clear that some attitudes are best expressed sexually. Tenderness and trust are often expressed between people who are not sexual partners. The tenderness and trust that may exist between an adult and a child is not best expressed sexually. Even if we take Solomon's claim to apply only to sexual partners, a joint checking account may be a better expression of trust than sexual activity. And domination, which in sado-masochistic sexual activity is expressed most elaborately with the cooperation of the partner, is an attitude much better expressed by nonsexual activities such as beating an opponent, firing an employee, or mugging a passerby, where the domination is real, and does not require the cooperation of the other person. Even if some attitudes and feelings (for example, prurience, wantonness, lust) are best expressed sexually, it would be questionable whether the primary aim of sexual activity should be to express them.

The usual conversation of strangers is "small talk": cautious, shallow, and predictable because there has not been time for the participants to assess the extent and nature of common interests they share. So too with sexual behavior; first sexual encounters may be charged with novelty and anticipation, but are usually characterized by stereotypic physical interactions. If the physical interaction is seen as "body language," the analogy with linguistic behavior suggests that first encounters are likely to consist of sexual small talk.

Solomon's comparison of sexual behavior with linguistic behavior is handicapped by the limited view he has about their purposes. Language has more purposes than transmitting information. If all there were to sexual behavior was the development of the sexual anticipation prominent in flirtation and seduction, then Solomon's conclusions might be correct. The fact that people will continue sexual relations with the same partners even after the appropriate attitudes and feelings from Solomon's list have been expressed indicates that sexual behavior, like linguistic behavior, has other functions that are important. Solomon's analogy with linguistic behavior is valuable not because communication is the main goal of sexual behavior but because he directs attention to the social nature of sexual behavior. Solomon's analogy can be made to take on new importance by considering that sexual behavior not only transmits information about feelings and attitudes— something any activity can do—but also, like language, it has a *phatic* function to evoke feelings and attitudes.

Language is often used to produce a shared experience, a feeling of togetherness or unity. Duets, greetings, and many religious services use language with little information content to establish or reaffirm a relation among the participants. Long-term sexual relationships, like regular musical ensembles, may be valued more for the feelings produced than the feelings communicated. With both sexual and linguistic behavior, an interaction with a stranger might be an enjoyable novelty, but the pleasures of linguistic and sexual activity with good friends are probably much more frequent and more reliable.

Solomon's conclusion that sexually one should have more to "say" to a stranger and will find oneself "repeating the same messages for years" to old acquaintances, violates the analogy. With natural language, one usually has more to say to old friends than to strangers.

Both Nagel and Solomon give incomplete accounts because they assume that a characterization of flirtation and seduction should apply to sexual behavior in general. I have argued that this is not so. Whether we analyze sexual behavior in terms of characteristic perceptions and feelings, as Nagel does, or by a comparison with other complex social behavior, as Solomon does, the characteristics of novel sexual encounters differ from sexual relationships between familiar and recognized partners.

What about the philosophical enterprise of characterizing sexual behavior? A characterization of something will tell what is unique about it and how to identify a standard or paradigm case of it. Criteria for a standard or paradigm case of sexual behavior unavoidably have normative implications. It is my position that normative judgments about sexual behavior should not be unrelated to the social and moral standards that apply to other social behavior. Many people, in reaction to old standards, avoid disapproving of sexual behavior that involves deceit or humiliation to another, but will condemn or ridicule sexual behavior that hurts no one yet fails to conform to a sexual standard. Both Nagel and Solomon classify sexual behavior that does not fit their characterizations as perversion, extending this strong negative judgment to behavior that is neither morally nor socially condemned (i.e., sex without multilevel awareness of arousal; sex without communication of attitudes and feelings). Yet perversion can be more accurately accounted for as whatever makes people frightened or uncomfortable by its bizarreness.

Sexual behavior differs from other behavior by virtue of its unique feelings and emotions and its unique ability to create shared intimacy. These unique features of sexual behavior may influence particular normative judgments, but they do not justify applying *different* normative principles to sexual behavior.

ENLIGHTENMENT

Heinrich Zimmer

Buddhism was the only religious and philosophical message of India to spread far beyond the borders of its homeland. Conquering Asia to the north and east, it became in those vast areas the creed of the masses and shaped the civilization for centuries. This tends to conceal the fact that in essence Buddhism is meant only for the happy few. The philosophical doctrine at the root of the numerous fascinating popular features is not the kind of teaching that one would have expected to see made readily accessible to all. In fact, of the numerous answers that have been offered, during the millenniums, in all quarters of the world, as solutions to life's enigmas, this one must be ranked as the most uncompromising, obscure, and paradoxical.

The Buddhist monks of Ceylon tell us how—according to their tradition—the Order of the Buddha, the "Awakened One," was founded. The great princely yogi, Gautama Sakyamuni, departed in secret from the palace and kingdom of his father and devoted himself to austerities for many years, until he arrived at the threshold of absolute Enlightenment. Sitting then beneath the Bo Tree, he was approached and tempted by the god Kama-Mara ("Desire and Death"), the master magician of the world illusion. Having overcome the tempter by remaining immovable in introversion, the prince experienced the Great Awakening, since which time he has been known as the "Awakened One," the Buddha. Absorbed in the vast experience, he remained beneath the Bo Tree, unmoved, untouched, for seven days and seven nights, "experiencing the bliss of the Awakening," then arose, as though to depart from that place, but could not depart. He placed himself beneath a second tree, and there again, for seven days and nights, remained merged in the stream of the bliss of the awakening. A third time, under a third tree, a spell of seven days and nights again absorbed him. He moved from tree to tree in this way for seven weeks, and during the fifth was protected by the hood of the serpent-king, Mucalinda. Following the blessed period of forty-nine days, his glorious glance opened again to the world. Then he understood that what he had experienced was beyond speech; all endeavor to talk about it would be vain. He determined, consequently, not to attempt to make it known.

But Brahma, the Universal Lord of the fleeting processes of life, in his eternal abode at the summit of the egg-shaped cosmos, looking down on the

Awakened One, realized that the decision had been made to withhold the teaching. Brahma, himself a creature, indeed the highest of all creatures, was perturbed to know that the sublime knowledge (knowledge unknown to Brahma) was not to be revealed. He descended from the zenith and with prayer implored the Buddha to become the teacher of mankind, the teacher of the gods, the teacher of the created world. All were enwrapped in the womb of sleep, dreaming a dream known as the waking life of created beings. Brahma implored that the truly Awake should open his path to all. For there might be some, the god urged, some happy few among these deluded beings, whose eyes would not be blinded by the dust of passion, and these would understand. As lotus flowers arising from the dark waters of a lake are to be found in various stages of maturity—some with buds still deep under water, some nearing the surface, some already open, prepared to drink the rays of the sun—just so, there might be among mankind and the gods a few prepared to hear.

The Buddha was moved, thus, to teach the path. Disciples came, an Order assumed shape, and the Buddhist tradition was brought into existence. Nevertheless, from the beginning, by the nature of the problem, the doctrine had been meant only for those prepared to hear. It was never intended to interfere with either the life and habits of the multitude or the course of civilization. In time it might even vanish from the world, becoming incomprehensible and meaningless—for the lack of anyone capable of treading the path to understanding; and this, too, would be right. In contrast, in other words, to the other great teachers of mankind (Zarathustra preaching the religious law of Persia; Confucius commenting on the restored system of early Chinese thought; Jesus announcing Salvation to the world), Gautama, the prince of the royal Sakya clan, is known properly as Sakyamuni: the "silent sage (*muni*) of the Sakyas"; for in spite of all that has been said and taught about him, the Buddha remains the symbol of something beyond what can be said and taught.

In the Buddhist texts there is no word that can be traced with unquestionable authority to Gautama Sakyamuni. We glimpse only the enlightening shadow of his personality; yet this suffices to merge us in a spiritual atmosphere that is unique. For though India in his time, half a millennium before Christ, was a veritable treasure-house of magical-religious lore—to our eyes a jungle of mythological systems—the teaching of the Enlightened One offered no mythological vision, either of the present world or of a world beyond, and no tangible creed. It was presented as a therapy, a treatment or cure for those strong enough to follow it—a method and a process of healing. Apparently Gautama, at least in his terminology, broke from all the popular modes and accepted methods of Indian religious and philosophical instruction. He offered his advice in the practical manner of a spiritual physician, as though, through him, the art of Indian medicine were entering the sphere of spiritual problems—that grand old arena where, for centuries magicians of every kind had been tapping powers by which they and their disciples lifted themselves to the heights of divinity.

Following the procedure of the physician of his day inspecting a patient, the Buddha makes four statements concerning the case of man. These are the so-called "Four Noble Truths" which constitute the heart and kernel of his doctrine. The first, *All life is sorrowful,* announces that we members of the human race are spiritually unhealthy, the symptom being that we carry on our shoulders a burden of sorrow; the disease is endemic. No discussion of any question of guilt goes with this matter-of-fact diagnosis; for the Buddha indulged in no metaphysical or mythological dissertations. He inquired into the cause on the practical, psychological level, however; hence we have, as the second of the "Four Noble Truths," *The cause of suffering is ignorant craving.*

As in the teaching of the Sankhya, an involuntary state of mind common to all creatures is indicated as the root of the world-disease. The craving of nescience, not-knowing-better (*avidya*), is the problem—nothing less and nothing more. Such ignorance is a natural function of the life-process, yet not necessarily ineradicable; no more ineradicable than the innocence of a child. It is simply that we do not know that we are moving in a world of mere conventions and that our feelings, thoughts, and acts are determined by these. We imagine that our ideas about things represent their ultimate reality, and so we are bound in by them as by the meshes of a net. They are rooted in our consciousness and attitudes; mere creations of the mind; conventional, involuntary patterns of seeing things, judging, and behaving; yet our ignorance accepts them in every detail, without question, regarding them and their contents as the facts of existence. This—this mistake about the true essence of reality—is the cause of all the sufferings that constitute our lives.

The Buddhist analysis goes on to state that our other symptoms (the familiar incidents and situations of our universal condition of non—well being) are derivatives, one and all, of the primary fault. The tragedies and comedies in which we get ourselves involved, which we bring forth from ourselves and in which we act, develop spontaneously from the impetus of our innermost condition of non-knowing. This sends us forth in the world with restricted senses and conceptions. Unconscious wishes and expectations, emanating from us in the shape of subjectively determined decisions and acts, transcend the limits of the present; they precipitate for us the future, being themselves determined from the past. Inherited from former births, they cause future births, the endless stream of life in which we are carried along being greater by far than the bounds of individual birth and death. In other words, the ills of the individual cannot be understood in terms of the individual's mistakes; they are rooted in our human way of life, and the whole content of this way of life is a pathological blend of unfulfilled cravings, wrong longings, fears, regrets, and pains. Such a state of suffering is something from which it would be only sensible to be healed.

This radical statement about the problems that most of us take for granted as the natural concomitants of existence, and decide simply to endure, is balanced in the doctrine of the Buddha by the third and fourth of the "Four Noble Truths." Having diagnosed the illness and determined its cause, the physician next inquires whether the disease can be cured. The Buddhist prognostication is that a cure is indeed possible; hence we hear: *The suppression of suffering can be achieved;* and the last of Four Truths prescribes the way: *The way is the Noble Eightfold Path*—Right View, Right Aspiration, Right Speech, Right Conduct, Right Means of Livelihood, Right Endeavor, Right Mindfulness, and Right Contemplation.

The Buddha's thoroughgoing treatment is guaranteed to eradicate the cause of the sickly spell and dream of ignorance, and thus to make possible the attainment of a state of serene, awakened perfection. No philosophical explanation of man or the universe is required, only this spiritual physician's program of psychodietetics. And yet the doctrine can hardly appeal to the multitude; for these are not convinced that their lives are as unwholesome as they obviously are. Only those few who not only would like to try, but actually feel acutely a pressing need to undertake some kind of thorough-going treatment, would have the will and stamina to carry to the end such an arduous, self-ordained discipline as that of the Buddhist cure.

The way of Gautama Sakyamuni is called the "middle path"; for it avoids extremes. One pair of extremes is that of the outright pursuit of worldly desires, on the one hand, and the severe, ascetic, bodily discipline of such contemporaries of the Buddha as the Jainas, on the other, whose austerity was designed to culminate in annihilation of the physical frame. Another pair of extremes is that of skepticism, denying the possibility of transcenden-tal knowledge, and the argumentative assertion of undemonstrable meta-physical doctrines. Buddhism eschews the blind alleys to either side and conduces to an attitude that will of itself lead one to the transcendental experience. It rejects explicitly *all* of the contending formulae of the intel-lect, as inadequate either to lead to or to express the paradoxical truth, which reposes far, far beyond the realm of cerebral conceptions.

A conversation of the Buddha, recorded among the so-called "Long Dialogues," enumerates an extended list of the practical and theoretical disciplines by which people master various skills, crafts, and professions, or seek some understanding of their own nature and the meaning of the uni-verse. All are described and then dismissed without criticism, but with the formula: "Such Knowledge and opinions, if thoroughly mastered, will lead inevitably to certain ends and produce certain results in one's life. The Enlightened One is aware of all these possible consequences, and also of what lies behind them. But he does not attach much importance to this knowledge. For within himself he fosters another knowledge—the knowl-edge of cessation, of the discontinuance of worldly existence, of utter re-pose by emancipation. He has perfect insight into the manner of the spring-ing into existence of our sensations and feelings, and into the manner of their vanishing again with all their sweetness and bitterness, and into the way of escape from them altogether, and into the manner in which, by non-attachment to them through right knowledge of their character, he has himself won release from their spell."

Buddhism attaches no serious importance to such knowledge as entangles men more tightly in the net of life, knowledge that adds a comfortable material or interesting spiritual background to existence and thereby only contributes additional substance to the maintenance of the personality. Buddhism teaches that the value attributed to a thing is determined by the particular pattern of life from which it is regarded and the personality concerned. The weight of a fact or idea varies with the unenlightenment of the observer—his spontaneous commitment to certain spheres of phenomena and ranges of human value. The atmosphere, nay the world, surrounding and overpowering him, is continually being produced from his own unconscious nature, and affects him in terms of his commitment to his own imperfections. Its traits are the phenomenal projections of his inner state of ignorance sent out into the realm of sense-perception and there, as it were, discovered by an act of empirical experience. Hence Buddhism denies, finally, the force and validity of everything that can be known.

A Tibetan author—a Buddhist Dalai-Lama—puts it this way: The one substance, which fundamentally is devoid of qualities, appears to be of various, completely differing flavors, according to the kind of being who tastes it. The same beverage which for the gods in their celestial realm will be the delightful drink of immortality, for men on earth will be mere water, and for the tormented inmates of hell a vile, disgusting liquid which they will be loath to swallow even though tortured with intolerable pangs of thirst. The three qualities of, or ways of experiencing, the one substance are here nothing more than the normal effects of three orders of karma. The senses themselves are conditioned by the subjective forces that brought them into being and hold them under strict control. The world without is no mere illusion—it is not to be regarded as nonexistent; yet it derives its enchanting or appalling features from the involuntary inner attitude of the one who sees it. The alluring hues and frightening shadows that form its very tissue are projected reflexes of the tendencies of the psyche.

One lives, in other words, enveloped by the impulses of the various layers of one's own nature, woven in the spell of their specific atmosphere, to which one submits as to an outside world. The goal of the techniques of the Buddhist therapy is to bring this process of self-envelopment to a stop. The living process is likened to a fire burning. Through the involuntary activity of one's nature as it functions in contact with the outer world, life as we know it goes on incessantly. The treatment is the extinction (*nirvana*) of the fire, and Buddha, the Awake, is the one no longer kindled or enflamed. The Buddha is far from having dissolved into nonbeing; it is not He who is extinct but the life illusion—the passions, desires, and normal dynamisms of the physique and psyche. No longer blinded, he no longer feels himself to be conditioned by the false ideas and attendant desires that normally go on shaping individuals and their spheres, life after life. The Buddha realizes himself to be void of the characteristics that constitute an individual subject to a destiny. Thus released from karma, the universal law, he reposes beyond fate, no longer subject to the consequences of personal limitations. What other people behold when they look upon his physical presence is a sort of mirage; for he is intrinsically devoid of the attributes that they venerate and are themselves striving to attain.

Buddhist art has attempted to render this paradoxical experience of the Enlightened One in certain curious works of sculpture, which represent the scene of the temptation of the Buddha. The fierce hosts of Kama-Mara, the tempter, assail the meditation of the one about to be enlightened as he sits beneath the holy tree. They brandish weapons, fling uprooted trees and prodigious rocks against him, and attempt by every means to break the calm of his meditation. By threats they strive to arouse in him some fear of death, the trace of an impulse of self-preservation, a wish to cling to the perishable frame of the body, which they are menacing with destruction. Simultaneously, the charm of life—all its loveliness—in the guise of divine women, is displayed before him; so that the allure of the senses should move him—not literally bring him from his place, but only provoke the least stir of a will to enjoy, which would amount to a step back into the thralldom of life. But both temptations fail. The powers work in vain to discover in his nature some flaw, some last reminder of fear and desire. The menacing and the enticing gestures equally fail to touch him; for he was vanished from the sphere of the currents and cross-currents of delight and despair, which constitute the warp and woof of life. In the works of sculpture in question, this unassailable state of the "one who cannot be reached any more" is expressed by omitting the Buddha-image from the composition. Amid the turmoil of the hosts and the captivating attitudes of the daughters of the tempter, the holy seat beneath the Bo Tree is empty; the Buddha is not to be seen.

The De-spirited One is never depicted through visible or tangible features in the early Buddhist monuments; for anything tangible or visible would amount to a description of him—either as a man or as a god. He would be endowed then with such features as befit beings shaped by the influences of former lives, beings brought by the law of karma into human or celestial forms. Any shape would by its nature communicate a wrong notion of his essence, which is on a nondepictable plane. A shape would show him to be tied by the subtle bonds of karma to the sphere of some set of limiting and transitory qualifications, whereas the whole sense of his being is that he is released from such symptoms of ignorance and desire. In viewing these early works of Buddhist sculpture one is to think of the Buddha as truly there, on the throne of Enlightenment, but as though he were a bubble of emptiness. Footprints on the ground and a slight hollowing of the cushion betray his presence, but no visible trait could possibly render the essence of his nature. Visible traits (beauty and grandeur, for example, or the dazzling charm of a divinity) are the signs of ordinary beings, and reveal their karma. But the Buddha is without karma and therefore must be rendered without determinable form. That is the most consistent, nay the only perfectly adequate way to designate his absolute emancipation from the law that enjoins all to go on assuming the varying transitory garbs of renewed existences.

The Buddha's doctrine is called *yana.* The word means "a vehicle," or, more to the point, "a ferryboat." The "ferryboat" is the principal image employed in Buddhism to render the sense and function of the doctrine. The idea persists through all the differing and variously conflicting teachings of the numerous Buddhist sects that have evolved in many lands, during the long course of the magnificent history of the widely disseminated doctrine. Each sect describes the vehicle in its own way, but no matter how described it remains always the ferry.

To appreciate the full force of this image, and to understand the reason for its persistence, one must begin by realizing that in everyday Hindu life the ferryboat plays an extremely prominent role. It is an indispensable means of transportation in a continent traversed by many mighty rivers and where bridges are practically nonexistent. To reach the goal of almost any journey one will require a ferry, time and time again, the only possible crossing of the broad and rapid streams being by boat or by a ford. The Jainas called their way of salvation the ford (*tirtha*), and the supreme Jaina teachers were *Tirthankaras,* "those making, or providing, a ford." In the same sense, Buddhism, by its doctrine, provides a ferryboat across the rushing river of samsara to the distant bank of liberation. Through enlightenment (*bodhi*) the individual is transported.

The gist of Buddhism can be grasped more readily and adequately by fathoming the main metaphors through which it appeals to our intuition than by a systematic study of the complicated superstructure, and the fine details of the developed teaching. For example, one need only think for a moment about the actual, everyday experience of the process of crossing a river in a ferryboat, to come to the simple idea that inspires and underlies all of the various rationalized systematizations of the doctrine. To enter the Buddhist vehicle—the boat of the discipline—means to begin to cross the river of life, from the shore of the commonsense experience of non-enlightenment, the shore of spiritual ignorance (*avidya*), desire (*kama*), and death (*mara*), to the yonder bank of transcendental wisdom (*vidya*), which is liberation (*moksa*) from this general bondage. Let us consider, briefly, the actual stages involved in any crossing of a river by ferry, and see if we can experience the passage as a kind of initiation-by-analogy into the purport of the stages of the Buddhist pilgrim's progress to his goal.

Standing on the nearer bank, this side of the stream, waiting for the boat to put in, one is a part of its life, sharing in its dangers and opportunities and in whatever may come to pass on it. One feels the warmth or coolness of its breezes, hears the rustle of its trees, experiences the character of its people, and knows that its earth is underfoot. Meanwhile the other bank, the far bank, is beyond reach—a mere optical image across the broad, flowing waters that divide us from its unknown world of forms. We have really no idea what it will be like to stand in that distant land. How this same scenery of the river and its two shorelines will appear from the other side we cannot imagine. How much of these houses will be visible among the trees? What prospects up and down the river will unfold? Everything over here, so tangible and real to us at present—these real, solid objects, these tangible forms—will be no more than remote, visual patches, inconsequential optical effects, without power to touch us, either to help or to harm. This solid earth itself will be a visual, horizontal line beheld from afar, one detail of an extensive scenic view, beyond our experience, and of no more force for us than a mirage.

The ferryboat arrives; and as it comes to the landing we regard it with a feeling of interest. It brings with it something of the air of that yonder land which will soon be our destination. Yet when we are entering it we still feel like members of the world from which we are departing, and there is still that feeling of unreality about our destination. When we lift our eyes from the boat and boatman, the far bank is still only a remote image, no more substantial than it was before.

Softly the ferryboat pushes off and begins to glide across the moving waters. Presently one realizes that an invisible line has been recently, imperceptibly passed, beyond which the bank left behind is assuming gradually the unsubstantiality of a mere visual impression, a kind of mirage, while the farther bank, drawing slowly nearer, is beginning to turn into something real. The former dim remoteness is becoming the new reality and soon is solid ground, creaking under keel—real earth—the sand and stone on which we tread in disembarking; whereas the world left behind, recently so tangible, has been transmuted into an optical reflex devoid of substance, out of reach and meaningless, and has forfeited the spell that it laid upon us formerly—with all its features, all its people and events—when we walked upon it and ourselves were a portion of its life. Moreover, the new reality, which now possesses us, provides an utterly new view of the river, the valley, and the two shores, a view very different from the other, and completely unanticipated.

Now while we were in the process of crossing the river in the boat, with the shore left behind becoming gradually vaguer and more meaningless—the streets and homes, the dangers and pleasures, drawing steadily away—there was a period when the shoreline ahead was still rather far off too; and during that time the only tangible reality around us was the boat, contending stoutly with the current and precariously floating on the rapid waters. The only details of life that then seemed quite substantial and that greatly concerned us were the various elements of the ferryboat itself: the contours of the hull and gunwales, the rudder and the sail, the various ropes, and perhaps a smell of tar. The rest of existence, whether out ahead or left behind, signified no more than a hopeful prospect and a fading recollection—two poles of unrealistic sentimental association affiliated with certain clusters of optical effects far out-of-hand.

In the Buddhist texts this situation of the people in a ferryboat is compared to that of the good folk who have taken passage in the vehicle of the doctrine. The boat is the teaching of the Buddha, and the implements of the ferry are the various details of Buddhist discipline: meditation, yoga-exercises, the rules of ascetic life, and the practice of self-abnegation. These are the only things that disciples in the vehicle can regard with deep conviction; such people are engrossed in a fervent belief in the Buddha as the ferryman and the Order as their bounding gunwale (framing, protecting, and defining their perfect ascetic life) and in the guiding power of the doctrine. The shoreline of the world has been left behind but the distant one of release not yet attained. The people in the boat, meanwhile, are involved in a peculiar sort of middle prospect which is all their own.

Among the conversations of the Buddha known as the "Medium-length Dialogues," there appears a discourse on the value of the vehicle of the doctrine. First the Buddha describes a man who, like himself or any of his followers, becomes filled with a loathing of the perils and delights of secular existence. That man decides to quit the world and cross the stream of life to the far land of spiritual safety. Collecting wood and reeds, he builds a raft, and by this means succeeds in attaining the other shore. The buddha confronts his monks, then, with the question.

"What would be your opinion of this man," asks the Buddha, "would he be a clever man, if, out of gratitude for the raft that has carried him across the stream to safety, he, having reached the other shore, should cling to it, take it on his back, and walk about with the weight of it?"

The monks reply. "No, certainly the man who would do that would not be a clever man."

The Buddha goes on. "Would not the clever man be the one who left the raft (of no use to him any longer) to the current of the stream, and walked ahead without turning back to look at it? Is it not simply a tool to be cast away and forsaken once it has served the purpose for which it was made?"

The disciples agree that this is the proper attitude to take toward the vehicle, once it has served its purpose.

The Buddha then concludes. "In the same way the vehicle of the doctrine is to be cast away and forsaken, once the other shore of Enlightenment (*nirvana*) has been attained."

The rules of the doctrine are intended for beginners and advanced pupils, but become meaningless for the perfect. They can be of no service to the truly enlightened, unless to serve him, in his role of teacher, as a convenient medium by which to communicate some suggestion of the truth to which he has attained. It was by means of the doctrine that the Buddha sought to express what he had realized beneath the tree as inexpressible. He could communicate with the world through his doctrine and thus help his unprepared disciples when they were at the start, or somewhere in the middle, of the way. Talking down to the level of relative or total ignorance, the doctrine can move the still imperfect yet ardent mind; but it can say nothing any more, nothing ultimately real, to the mind that has cast away darkness. Like the raft, it must be left behind, therefore, once the goal has been attained; for it can thenceforth be no more than an inappropriate burden.

Moreover, not the raft only, but the stream too, becomes void of reality for the one who has attained the other shore. When such a one turns around to look again at the land left behind, what does he see? What *can* one see who has crossed the horizon beyond which there is no duality? He looks—and there *is* no "other shore"; there is no torrential separating river; there is no raft; there is no ferryman; there can have been no crossing of the nonexistent stream. The whole scene of the two banks and the river between is simply gone. There can be no such thing for the enlightened eye and mind, because to see or think of anything as something "other" (a distant reality, different from one's own being) would mean that full Enlightenment had not yet been attained. There can be an "other shore" only for people still in the spheres of dualistic perception; those this side of the stream or still inside the boat and heading for the "other shore"; those who have not yet disembarked and thrown away the raft. Illumination means that the delusory distinction between the two shores of a worldly and a transcendental existence no longer holds. There *is* no stream of rebirths flowing between two separated shores: no samsara and no nirvana.

Thus the long pilgrimage to perfection through innumerable existences, motivated by the virtues of self-surrender and accomplished at the cost of tremendous sacrifices of ego, disappears like a landscape of dreams when one awakes. The long-continued story of the heroic career, the many lives of increasing self-purification, the picture-book legend of detachment won through the long passion, the saintly epic of the way to become a savior—enlightened and enlightening—vanishes like a rainbow. All becomes void; whereas once, when the dream was coming to pass step by step, with ever-recurrent crises and decisions, the unending series of dramatic sacrifices held the soul completely under its spell. The secret meaning of Enlightenment is that this titan-effort of pure soul-force, this ardent struggle to reach the goal by acts, ever-renewed, of beautiful self-surrender, this supreme, long strife through ages of incarnations to attain release from the universal law of moral causation (*karma*)—is without reality. At the threshold of its own realization it dissolves, together with its background of self-entangled life, like a nightmare at the dawn of day.

For the Buddha, therefore, even the notion of nirvana is without meaning. It is bound to the pairs-of-opposites and can be employed only in opposition to samsara—the vortex where the life-force is spellbound in ignorance by its own polarized passions of fear and desire.

The Buddhist way of ascetic training is designed to conduce to the understanding that there is no substantial ego—nor any object anywhere—that lasts, but only spiritual processes, welling and subsiding: sensations, feelings, visions. These can be suppressed or set in motion and watched at will. The idea of the extinction of the fire of lust, ill will, and ignorance becomes devoid of meaning when this psychological power and point of view has been attained; for the process of life is no longer experienced as a burning fire. To speak seriously, therefore, of nirvana as a goal to be attained is simply to betray the attitude of one still remembering or experiencing the process as the burning of the fire. The Buddha himself adopts such an attitude only for the teaching of those still suffering, who feel that they would like to make the flames extinct. His famous Fire Sermon is an accommodation, not by any means the final word of the sage whose final word is silence. From the perspective of the Awake, the Illumined One, such opposed verbalizations as nirvana and samsara, enlightenment and ignorance, freedom and bondage, are without reference, void of content. That is why the Buddha refused to discuss nirvana. The pointlessness of the connotations that would inevitably seem to be intended by his words would confuse those trying to follow his mysterious way. They being still in the ferryboat framed of these conceptions and requiring them as devices of transport to the shore of understanding, their teacher would not deny before them the practical function of such convenient terms; and yet would not give the terms weight, either, by discussion. Words like "enlightenment," "ignorance," "freedom," and "entanglement" are preliminary helps, referring to no ultimate reality, mere hints or signposts for the traveler, which serve to point him to the goal of an attitude beyond their own suggestions of a contrariety. The raft being finally left behind, and the vision lost of the two banks and the separating river, then there is in truth neither the realm of life and death nor that of release. Moreover, there is no Buddhism—no boat, since there are neither shores nor waters between. There is no boat, and there is no boatman—no Buddha.

The great paradox of Buddhism, therefore, is that no Buddha has ever come into existence to enlighten the world with Buddhist teachings. The life and mission of Gautama Sakyamuni is only a general misunderstanding by the unenlightened world, helpful and necessary to guide the mind toward illumination, but to be discarded when—and if—enlightenment is to be attained. Any monk failing to get rid of such ideas clings (by clinging to them) to the general mundane delusion which he imagines himself to be striving to leave behind. For, briefly, so long as nirvana is looked upon as something different from samsara, the most elementary error about existence still has to be overcome. These two ideas mirror contrary attitudes of the semiconscious individual toward himself and the outer sphere in which he lives; but beyond this subjective range they have no substantiation.

Buddhism—this popular creed which has won the reverence of all Eastern Asia—contains this boldest paradox at its very root; the most startling reading of reality ever whispered into human ear. All good Buddhists tend to avoid, therefore, statements about existence and nonexistence. Their "Middle Path" goes between by simply pointing out that the validity of a conception is always relative to one's position along the road of progress from Ignorance to Buddhahood. Attitudes of assertion and negation belong to worldly beings on the hither bank of ignorance, and to pious people making headway in the crowded ferryboat of the doctrine. Such a conception as Voidness (*sunyata*) can have meaning only for an ego clinging to the reality of things; one who has lost the feeling that things are real can make no sense of such a word. And yet words of this kind remain in all the texts and teachings. Indeed, the great *practical* miracle of Buddhism is that terms of this kind, used successfully as steppingstones, do not become rocks on which to found and build a creed.

The greater portion of the Buddhist literature that has become available and familiar to us in translation is adjusted in this way, pedagogically, to the general human attitude of partial ignorance. It is intended for the teaching and guidance of disciples. It outlines and points the way along the path of the Buddhas (*buddha-marga*), depicting the career of the hero "going to enlightenment" (*bodhicarya*). Its position, therefore, is comparable to that of the ferryman inviting people on our hither bank to enter his boat and cross the waters, or guiding his crew in their handling of the craft during the passage. The yonder bank is represented only in a preliminary, very sketchy way; only hinted at and attractively suggested, for the captivation and continued inspiration of those still spellbound by the notions of this dualistic shore—men and women trying to make up their minds to leave, or else in the toilsome stages of crossing to an absolute contrary point of view, which they will perceive presently to be utterly inconsistent with their expectation.

This pedagogical interest of Buddhism entails, unavoidably, a screening of the ultimate essence of the doctrine. The introductory statements, graded as they are, lead right up to the goal—but then have to be put behind, or the goal itself will never be attained. Anyone wishing to gain some inkling of the transformation of perspective intended will have to turn from the great volumes of initiatory conversations, questions, analyses, and codifications to a somewhat less conspicuous, curious, special branch of Buddhist writings, in which an attempt is made actually to state something of the supreme experience.

One may well marvel at the bold experiment—an effort to represent the ultimate essence of an incommunicable intuition through words and conceptions familiar to the usual philosophical and pious understanding. But, wonderful to relate, a vivid sense of the ineffable reality known in "extinction" (*nirvana*) is actually conveyed in this unexampled body of strange, esoteric texts. They are named *Prajna-paramita:* "The Accomplishment of Transcendental Wisdom," or "The Wisdom (*prajna*) Gone to the Other Shore (*param-ita*)." And they are a series of the most curious dialogues, conducted in a sort of conversation-circle of Buddhas and Bodhisattvas—mostly legendary beings, superhuman saviors, without a single merely human, still half-bewildered aspirant-to-enlightenment among them.

The Illumined Ones behave in a way that should be rather shocking and confusing to any sound thinker, who, from habit and firm determination, is resolved to keep his feet on the ground. In a sort of mocking conversation, these Buddhas and Bodhisattvas entertain themselves with enigmatical statements of the unstatable truth. They delight in declaring, time and again, that there is no such thing as Buddhism, no such thing as Enlightenment, nothing remotely resembling the extinction of nirvana, setting traps for each other and trying to trick each other into assertions that might imply—even remotely—the reality of such conceptions. Then, most artfully, they always elude the cleverly placed hazards and hidden pitfalls—and all engage in a glorious, transolympian laugh; for the merest hint of a notion of nirvana would have betrayed a trace of the vestige of the opposite attitude, samsara, and the clinging to individual existence.

For example, in one of the texts the Buddha makes the following declaration to his pupil Subhuti. "Whosoever stands in the ferryboat of the saviors-who-lead-to-the-far-bank shall bear in mind the rescue of all living beings, conducting them to release-and-extinction in the pure and perfect nirvana. And when, by virtue of this attitude, he has rescued all living beings, no being whatsoever has been made to reach nirvana."

Following this paradoxical remark, the Buddha supplies his explanation. "Why, O Subhuti, is this so? Because, if this savior had the notion of the actual existence of any being, he could not be called a perfect Enlightened One. If there could occur to him the conception of a living being donning the garb of various bodies and migrating through numerous existences, or the idea of an individual personality, then he could not be called a Bodhisattva, 'a being whose essence is Enlightenment.' And why is this so? Because there is no such thing as anything or anybody standing in the vehicle of the Enlightened Ones."

Another text states that on a certain day, when myriads of gods had flocked together to celebrate with a great feast the solemn occasion of the Buddha's preaching of a sermon, they were all saying joyfully: "Forsooth, this is the second time that the wheel of the true law has been set in motion on Indian soil, let us go and watch!" But the Buddha, turning stealthily to Subhuti, whispered something that he would not tell the gods; for it was beyond their power of understanding. "This is not the second time that the wheel of the true law has been set in motion; there is not setting in motion of anything, nor any stopping of the motion of anything. Knowing just that, is the perfection of wisdom (*prajna-paramita*), which is characteristic of the beings whose essence is enlightenment."

These bewildering texts, with their explicit teaching of the Wisdom of the Far Bank (*prajna-paramita*), belong to a later period of the Buddhist tradition, the stage of the so-called "Great Ferryboat," or Mahayana, which teaches that the secret meaning and goal of the doctrine is the universal Buddhahood of *all* beings. This is in contrast to the earlier doctrine of the so-called "Little Ferryboat," the Hinayana, where, though an effective way to *individual release* is disclosed, the accomplishment of *Buddhahood* is regarded as a goal attained only by very few throughout the cycling ages. The *Prajna-paramita* texts of the Mahayana were intended to counteract what their authors regarded as a basic misunderstanding, in the Hinayana, of the very essence of the wisdom of the Buddha, a misunderstanding caused by thinking that the preliminary teaching was an expression of the Buddha's transcendental realization. The emphasis on the means, the path, the rules of the order, and the ethical disciplines of the ferry-ride was stifling the essence of the tradition within the very fold of Buddhism itself. The Mahayana way, on the other hand, was to reassert this essence by means of a bold and stunning paradox.

"The Enlightened One," we read, "sets forth in the Great Ferryboat; but there is nothing from which he sets forth. He starts from the universe; but in truth he starts from nowhere. His boat is manned with all the perfections; and is manned by no one. It will find its support on nothing whatsoever and will find its support on the state of all-knowing, which will serve it as a non-support. Moreover, no one has ever set forth in the Great Ferryboat; no one will ever set forth in it, and no one is setting forth in it now. And why is this? Because neither the one setting forth nor the goal for which he sets forth is to be found: therefore, who should be setting forth, and whither?"

The conceptions that go to make up the communicated doctrine are, from the point of view of the Enlightened One, without corresponding ultimate realities. They are part of a raft, which is good and helpful for the crossing of a stream of ignorance and indispensable for disciples on the way, but they are devoid of meaning for the finished master whose crossing is accomplished. They mirror shapes of the transitory processes of life, and so have no lasting substance. They lead to enlightenment, and yet are fallacious, broken reflections of its truth. Indeed, they are different from what is known to the enlightened; just as the boat, or raft, is different from the farther shore. Such helpful concepts emerge, together with all the rest of these visible and thinkable things round about us, from an infinitely pure reality, which is beyond conceptions, void of limiting qualities, undifferentiated, and untouched by the dialectic of the pairs-of-opposites, of which it is the ground—just as the heavens and the atmosphere, which are visible, stand as apparitions on the fundamentally pure void of ether.

"Just as, in the vast ethereal sphere, stars and darkness, light and mirage, dew, foam, lightning, and clouds emerge, become visible, and vanish again, like the features of a dream—so everything endowed with an individual shape is to be regarded." Thus we read in one of the most celebrated of these Mahayana texts of meditation. From the intangible matter that pervades the universe, tangible shapes emerge as its ephemeral transformations. But their breaking into existence and their vanishing away does not affect the limpid, profound serenity of the basic element, the space of which they fill for their short spell of being. Comparably, the Enlightened Ones, with unruffled self-composure, watch their own sensations, feelings, and other experiences of the outer world and their inner life, remaining untouched by them, beyond the changes continually coming to pass in them, like the reposeful ether beyond the changes of the forms within its infinite space.

So far as the Awakened One is concerned, the notion of Awakening is at bottom as devoid of meaning as the notion that there is a dreamlike state that precedes it (the state of ordinary life—our own attitude and atmosphere). It is unreal. It does not exist. It is the sail of the nonexistent raft. The Buddhist yogi is taught, by means of the disciplines, to realize, within, such a peace as one perceives looking outward into the vast ethereal realm with its sublime display of transient forms. He is taught to experience, gazing inward, through successive stages of self-control and meditation, an ethereal essence of his own—sheer voidness, unsullied by any process of the mind and not changed by any effect of the senses in their contact with the outer world. By imbuing himself completely with an utter aloofness comparable to that of the celestial atmosphere in relation to the various luminous and darkening phenomena that pass through it, he realizes the real meaning of the Buddhist transcendental wisdom, the nature of the view from the yonder shore. He comes to know that fundamentally nothing whatsoever is happening to the true essence of his nature, nothing to give cause for either distress or joy.

The disciple Subhuti said: "Profound, O Venerable One, is the perfect Transcendental Wisdom."

Quoth the Venerable One: "Abysmally profound, like the space of the universe, O Subhuti, is the perfect Transcendental Wisdom."

The disciple Subhuti said again: "Difficult to be attained through Awakening is the perfect Transcendental Wisdom, O Venerable One."

Quoth the Venerable One: "That is the reason, O Subhuti, why no one ever attains it through Awakening."

And the two—we may imagine—roared with laughter. Here is metaphysics as the intellect's greatest game.

SELF-ASSERTION

Friedrich Nietzsche

FROM *"THE BIRTH OF TRAGEDY"*

It is an eternal phenomenon: the insatiate will can always, by means of an illusion spread over things, detain its creatures in life and compel them to live on. One is chained by the Socratic love of knowledge and the delusion of being able thereby to heal the eternal wound of existence; another is ensnared by art's seductive veil of beauty fluttering before his eyes; still another by the metaphysical comfort that beneath the flux of phenomena eternal life flows on indestructibly: to say nothing of the more ordinary and almost more powerful illusions which the will has always at hand. These three planes of illusion are on the whole designed only for the more nobly formed natures, who in general feel profoundly the weight and burden of existence, and must be deluded by exquisite stimulants into forgetfulness of their sorrow. All that we call culture is made up of these stimulants; and, according to the proportion of the ingredients, we have either a dominantly *Socratic* or *artistic* or *tragic* culture: or, if historical exemplifications are wanted, there is either an Alexandrian or a Hellenic or a Buddhistic culture.

Our whole modern world is entangled in the net of Alexandrian culture. It proposes as its ideal the theoretical man equipped with the greatest forces of knowledge, and laboring in the service of science, whose archetype and progenitor is Socrates. All our educational methods have originally this ideal in view: every other form of existence must struggle on wearisome beside it, as something tolerated, but not intended. In an almost alarming manner, the cultured man was for a long time found only in the form of the scholar: even our poetical arts have been forced to evolve from learned imitations, and in the main effect, that of rhyme, we still recognize the origin of our poetic form from artistic experiments with a nonindigenous, thoroughly learned language. How unintelligible must *Faust,* the modern cultured man, who is in himself intelligible, have appeared to a true Greek—Faust, storming unsatisfied through all the faculties, devoted to magic and the devil from a desire for knowledge; Faust, whom we have but to place beside Socrates for the purpose of comparison, in order to see that modern man is beginning to divine the limits of this Socratic love of perception and yearns for a coast in the wide waste of the ocean of knowledge. When Goethe on one occasion said to Eckermann with reference to Napoleon: "Yes, my good friend, there is also a productiveness of deeds," he reminded us in a charmingly naive manner that the non-theorist is something incredible and astounding to modern man; so that we again have need of the wisdom of Goethe to discover that such a surprising form of existence is not only comprehensible, but even pardonable.

Now, we must not hide from ourselves what is concealed at the heart of this Socratic culture: Optimism, with its delusion of limitless power! Well, we must not be alarmed if the fruits of this optimism ripen—if society, leavened to the very lowest strata by this kind of culture, gradually begins to tremble with wanton agitations and desires, if the belief in the earthly happiness of all, if the belief in the threatening demand for such an Alexandrian earthly happiness, into the conjuring up of a Euripidian *deus ex machina*. Let us mark this well: the Alexandrian culture, to be able to exist permanently, requires a slave class, but, with its optimistic view of life, it denies the necessity of such a class, and consequently, when the effect of its beautiful seductive and tranquilizing utterance about the "dignity of man" and the "dignity of labor" is over, it gradually drifts toward a dreadful destruction. There is nothing more terrible than a barbaric slave class, who have learned to regard their existence as an injustice, and now prepare to avenge, not only themselves, but all future generations. In the face of such threatening storms, who dares to appeal with any confidence to our pale and exhausted religions, whose very foundations have degenerated into "learned" religions?—so that myth, the necessary prerequisite of every religion, is already paralyzed everywhere, and even in this domain the optimistic spirit—which we have just designated as the destroying germ of society—has attained the mastery.

While the evil slumbering in the heart of theoretical culture gradually begins to disquiet modern man, while he anxiously ransacks the stores of his experience for means to avert the danger, though he has no great faith in these means; while he, therefore, begins to divine the consequences of his position: great, universally gifted natures have contrived, with an incredible amount of thought, to make use of the paraphernalia of science itself, in order to point out the limits and the relativity of knowledge generally, and thus definitely to deny the claim of science to universal validity and universal aims: with which demonstration the illusory notion was for the first time recognized as such, which pretends, with the aid of causality, to be able to fathom the innermost essence of things. The extraordinary courage and wisdom of *Kant* and *Schopenhauer* have succeeded in gaining the most difficult victory, the victory over the optimism hidden in the essence of logic, which optimism in turn is the basis of our culture. While this optimism, resting on apparently unobjectionable *aerternae veritates,* had believed in the intelligibility and solvability of all the riddles of the universe, and had treated space, time, and causality as totally unconditioned laws of the most universal validity, Kant, on the other hand, showed that in reality these served only to elevate the mere phenomenon, the work of Maya, to the position of the sole and highest reality, putting it in place of the innermost and true essence of things, and thus making impossible any knowledge of this essence or, in Schopenhauer's words, lulling the dreamer still more soundly asleep. With this knowledge a culture is inaugurated which I venture to call a tragic culture; the most important characteristic of which is that wisdom takes place of science as the highest end, wisdom, which uninfluenced by the seductive distractions of the sciences, turns with unmoved eye to a comprehensive view of the world, and seeks to conceive therein, with sympathetic feelings of love, the eternal suffering as its own. Let us imagine a rising generation with this bold vision, this heroic desire for the magnificent, let us imagine the valiant step of these dragonslayers, the proud daring with which they turn their backs on all the effeminate doctrines of optimism that they may "live resolutely," wholly, and fully: Would it not be necessary for the tragic man of this culture, with his self-discipline of seriousness and terror, to desire a new art, the art of metaphysical comfort—namely, tragedy—to claim it as Helen, and exclaim with Faust:

Und sollt ich nicht, sehnsuechtigster Gewald,
Ins Leben ziehn die einzigste Gestalt?
[And must I not satisfy my longing,
By bringing this incomparable beauty to life?]

But now that the Socratic culture can only hold the scepter of its infallibility with trembling hands; now that it has been shaken from two directions—once by the fear of its own conclusions which it at length begins to surmise, and again, because it no longer has its former naive confidence in the eternal validity of its foundations—it is a sad spectacle to see how the dance of its thought rushes longingly on ever-new forms, to embrace them, and then, shuddering, lets them go suddenly as Mephistopheles does the seductive Lamaiae. It is certainly the sign of the "breach" which all are wont to speak of as the fundamental tragedy of modern culture that the theoretical man, alarmed and dissatisfied at his own conclusions, no longer dares entrust himself to the terrible ice-stream of existence: he runs timidly up and down the bank. So thoroughly has he been spoiled by his optimistic views, that he no longer wants to have anything whole, with all of nature's cruelty attaching to it. Besides, he feels that a culture based on the principles of science must be destroyed when it begins to grow *illogical,* that is, to retreat before its own conclusions. Our art reveals this universal trouble: in vain does one depend imitatively on all great productive periods and natures; in vain does one accumulate the entire "World-Literature" around modern man for his comfort; in vain does one place one's self in the midst of the art-styles and artists of all ages, so that one may give names to them as Adam did to the beasts: one still continues eternally hungry, the "critic" without joy and energy, the Alexandrian man, who is at bottom a librarian and corrector of proofs, and who, pitiable wretch, goes blind from the dusty books and printers' errors.

FROM *"BEYOND GOOD AND EVIL"*

In a tour through the many finer and coarser moralities which have hitherto prevailed or still prevail on the earth, I found certain traits recurring regularly together, and connected with one another, until finally two primary types revealed themselves to me, and a radical distinction was brought to light. There is *master-morality* and *slave-morality.* I would at once add, however, that in all higher and mixed civilizations, there are also attempts at the reconciliation of the two moralities; but one finds still oftener the confusion and mutual misunderstanding of them, indeed, sometimes their close juxtaposition—even in the same man, within one soul. The distinctions of moral values have either originated in a ruling caste, pleasantly conscious of being different from the ruled—or among the ruled class, the slaves and dependents of all sorts. In the first case, when it is the rulers who determine the conception "good," it is the exalted, proud disposition which is regarded as the distinguishing feature, and that which determines the order of rank. The noble type of man separates from himself the beings in whom the opposite of this exalted, proud disposition displays itself: he depises them. Let it at once be noted that in this first kind of morality the antithesis "good" and "bad" means practically the same as "noble" and "despicable"; the antithesis "good" and *"evil"* is of a different origin. The cowardly, the timid, the insignificant, and those thinking merely of narrow utility are despised; moreover, also, the distrustful, with their constrained glances, the self-abasing, the doglike kind of men who let themselves be abused, the mendicant flatterers, and above all the liars:—it is a fundamental belief of all aristocrats that the common people are untruthful. "We truthful ones"—the nobility in ancient Greece called themselves. It is obvious that everywhere the designations of moral value were at first applied to *men,* and were only derivatively and at a later period applied to *actions;* it is a gross mistake, therefore, when historians of morals start questions like, "Why have sympathetic actions been praised?" The noble type of man regards *himself* as a determiner of values: he does not require to be approved of; he passes the judgment: "What is injurious in itself"; he knows that it is he himself only who confers honor on things; he is a *creator of values.* He honors whatever he recognizes in himself: such morality is self-glorification. In the foreground there is the feeling of plenitude, of power which seeks to overflow, the happiness of high tension, the consciousness of a wealth which would fain give and bestow: the noble man also helps the unfortunate, but not—or scarcely—out of pity, but rather from an impulse generated by the super-abundance of power. The noble man honors in himself the powerful one, him also who has power over himself, who knows how to speak and how to keep silence, who takes pleasure in subjecting himself to severity and hardness and has reverence for all that is severe and hard. "Wotan placed a hard heart in my breast," says an old Scandinavian Saga: it is thus rightly expressed from the soul of a proud Viking. Such a type of man is even proud of *not* being made for sympathy; the hero of the Saga therefore adds warningly: "He who has not a hard heart when young, will never have one." The noble and brave who think thus are the furthest removed from the morality which sees precisely in sympathy, or in acting for the good of others, or in *désinteressement,* the characteristic of the moral; faith in oneself, pride in oneself, a radical enmity and irony towards "selflessness," belong as definitely to noble morality, as do a careless scorn and precaution in presence of sympathy and the "warm heart"—it is the powerful who *know* how to honor, it is their art, their domain for invention. The profound reverence for age and for tradition—all law rests on this double reverence, the belief and prejudice in favor of ancestors and unfavorable to newcomers, is typical in the morality of the powerful; and if, reversely, men of "modern ideas" believe almost instinctively in "progress" and the "future," and are more and more lacking in respect for old age, the ignoble origin of these "ideas" has complacently betrayed itself thereby. A morality of the ruling class, however, is more especially foreign and irritating to present-day taste in the sternness of its principle that one has duties only to one's equals; that one may act towards beings of a lower rank, towards all that is foreign, just as seems good to one, or "as the heart desires," and in any case "beyond good and evil": it is here that sympathy and similar sentiments can have a place. The ability and obligation to exercise prolonged gratitude and prolonged revenge—both only within the circle of equals, artfulness in retaliation, *raffinement* of the idea in friendship, a certain necessity to have enemies (as outlets for the emotions of envy, quarrelsomeness, arrogance—in fact in order to be a good *friend*): all these are typical characteristics of the noble morality, which, as has been pointed out, is not the morality of "modern ideas," and is therefore at present difficult to realize, and also to unearth and disclose. It is otherwise with the second type of morality, *slave-morality.* Supposing that the abused, the oppressed, the suffering, the unemancipated, the weary, and those uncertain of themselves, should moralize, what will be the common element in their moral estimates? Probably a pessimistic suspicion with regard to the entire situation of man will find expression, perhaps a condemnation of man, together with this situation. The slave has an unfavorable eye for the virtues of the powerful; he has a skepticism and distrust, a *refinement* of distrust of everything "good" that is there honored—he would fain persuade himself that the very happiness there is not genuine. On the other hand, *those* qualities which serve to alleviate the existence of sufferers are brought into prominence and flooded with light; it is here that sympathy, the kind, helping hand, the warm heart, patience, diligence, humility, and friendliness attain to honor; for here these are the most useful qualities, and almost the only means of supporting the burden of existence. Slave-morality is essentially the morality of utility. Here is the seat of the origin of the famous antithesis "good" and "evil": power and dangerousness are assumed to reside in the evil, a certain dreadfulness, subtlety, and strength, which do not admit of being despised. According to slave-morality, therefore, the "evil" man arouses fear; according to master-morality it is precisely the "good" man who arouses fear and seeks to arouse it, while the bad man is regarded as the despicable being. The contrast attains its maximum when, in accordance with the logical consequences of slave-morality, a shade of depreciation—it may be slight and well-intentioned—at last attaches itself to the "good" man of his morality; because, according to the servile mode of thought, the good man must in any case be the *safe* man: he is good-natured, easily deceived, perhaps a little stupid, *un bonhomme.* Everywhere that slave-morality gains the ascendency, language shows a tendency to approximate the significations of the words "good" and "stupid." A last fundamental difference: the desire for *freedom,* the instinct for happiness, and the refinements of the feeling of liberty belong as necessarily to slave-morals and morality, as artifice and enthusiasm in reverence and devotion are the regular symptoms of an aristocratic mode of thinking and estimating. Hence we can understand without further detail why love *as a passion*—it is our European speciality—must absolutely be of noble origin; as is well known, its invention is due to the Provençal poet-cavaliers, those brilliant ingenious men of the *"gaisaber,"* to whom Europe owes so much, and almost owes itself.

FROM *"THE GENEALOGY OF MORALS"*

The revolt of the slaves in morals begins in the very principle of *resentment* becoming creative and giving birth to values—a resentment experienced by creatures who, deprived as they are of the proper outlet of action, are forced to find their compensation in an imaginary revenge. While every aristocratic morality springs from a triumphant affirmation of its own demands, the slave morality says "no" from the very outset to what is "outside itself," and "not itself": and this "no" is its creative deed. This volte-face of the valuing standpoint—this *inevitable* gravitation to the objective instead of back to the subjective—is typical of "resentment": the slave-morality requires as the condition of its existence an external and objective world; to employ physiology terminology, it requires objective stimuli to be capable of action at all—its action is fundamentally a reaction. The contrary is the case when we come to the aristocrat's system of values: it acts and grows spontaneously, it merely seeks its antithesis in order to pronounce a more grateful and exultant "yes" to its own self; its negative conception, "low," "vulgar," "bad," is merely a pale lateborn foil in comparison with its positive and fundamental conception (saturated as it is with life and passion), of "we aristocrats, we good ones, we beautiful ones, we happy ones."

When the aristocratic morality goes astray and commits sacrilege on reality, this is limited to that particular sphere, with which it is *not* sufficiently acquainted—a sphere, in fact, from the real knowledge of which it disdainfully defends itself. It misjudges, in some cases, the sphere which it despises, the sphere of the common vulgar man and the low people: on the other hand, due weight should be given to the consideration that in any case the mood of contempt, of disdain, of superciliousness, even on the supposition that it *falsely* portrays the object of its contempt, will always be far removed from that degree of falsity which will always characterize the attacks—in effigy, of course—of the vindictive hatred and revengefulness of the weak in onslaughts on their enemies. In point of fact, there is in contempt too strong an admixture of nonchalance, of casualness, of boredom, of impatience, even of personal exultation, for it to be capable of distorting its victim into a real caricature or a real monstrosity. Attention again should be paid to the almost benevolent *nuances* which, for instance, the Greek nobility imparts into all the words by which it distinguishes the common people from itself; note how continuously a kind of pity, care, and consideration imparts its honeyed *flavor,* until at last almost all the words which are applied to the vulgar man survive finally, as expressions for "unhappy," "worthy of pity"—and how, conversely, "bad," "low," "unhappy" have never ceased to ring in the Greek ear with a tone in which "unhappy" is the predominant note: this is a heritage of the old noble aristocratic morality, which remains true to itself even in contempt. The "well-born" simply *felt* themselves the "happy"; they did not have to manufacture their happiness artificially through looking at their enemies, or in cases to talk and lie themselves into happiness (as is the custom with all resentful men); and similarly, complete men as they were, exuberant with strength, and consequently *necessarily* energetic, they were too wise to dissociate happiness from action—activity becomes in their minds necessarily counted as happiness—all in sharp contrast to the "happiness" of the weak and the oppressed, with their festering venom and malignity, among whom happiness appears essentially as a narcotic, a deadening, a quietude, a peace, a "Sabbath," an enervation of the mind and relaxation of the limbs, in short, a purely *passive* phenomenon. While the aristocratic man lived in confidence and openness with himself, the resentful man, on the other hand, is neither sincere nor naive, nor honest and candid with himself. His soul *squints;* his mind loves hidden crannies, tortuous paths and backdoors, everything secret appeals to him as *his* word, *his* safety, *his* balm; he is past master in silence, in not forgetting, in waiting, in provisional self-depreciation and self-abasement. A race of such *resentful* men will of necessity eventually prove more *prudent* than any aristocratic race, it will honor prudence on quite a distinct scale, as, in fact, a paramount condition of existence, while prudence among aristocratic men is apt to be tinged with a delicate flavor of luxury and refinement; so among them it plays nothing like so integral a part as that complete certainty of function of the governing *unconscious* instincts, or as indeed a certain lack of prudence, such as a vehement and valiant charge, whether against danger or the enemy, or as those ecstatic bursts of rage, love, reverence, gratitude, by which at all times noble souls have recognized each other. When the resentment of the aristocratic man manifests itself, it fulfills and exhausts itself in an immediate reaction, and consequently instills no *venom:* on the other hand, it never manifests itself at all in countless instances, when in the case of the feeble and weak it would be inevitable. An inability to take seriously for any length of time their enemies, their disasters, their *misdeeds*—that is the sign of the full strong natures who possess a superfluity of molding plastic force, that heals completely and produces forgetfulness: a good example of this in the modern world is Mirabeau, who had no memory for any insults and meannesses which were practised on him, and who was only incapable of forgiving because he forgot. Such a man indeed shakes off with a shrug many a worm which would have buried itself in another; it is only in characters like these that we see the possibility (supposing, of course, that there is such a possibility in the world) of the real "*love* of one's enemies." What respect for his enemies is found, forsooth, in an aristocratic man—and such a reverence is already a bridge to love! He insists on having his enemy to himself as his distinction. He tolerates no other enemy but a man in whose character there is nothing to despise and much to honor! On the other hand, imagine the "enemy" as the resentful man conceives him—and it is here exactly that we see his work, his creativeness; he has conceived "the evil enemy," the "evil one," and indeed that is the root idea from which he now evolves as a contrasting and corresponding figure, a "good one," himself—his very self!

The method of this man is quite contrary to that of the aristocratic man, who conceives the root idea "good" spontaneously and straight away, that is to say, out of himself, and from that material then creates for himself a concept of "bad"! This "bad" of aristocratic origin and that "evil" out of the cauldron of unsatisfied hatred—the former an imitation, an "extra," an additional nuance; the latter, on the other hand, the original, the beginning, the essential act in the conception of a slave-morality—these two words "bad" and "evil," how great a difference do they mark, in spite of the fact that they have an identical contrary in the idea "good." But the idea "good" is *not* the same: much rather let the question be asked, "Who is really evil according to the meaning of the morality of resentment?" In all sternness let it be answered thus: *just* the good man of the other morality, just the aristocrat, the powerful one, the one who rules, but who is distorted by the venomous eye of resentfulness, into a new color, a new signification, a new appearance. This particular point we would be the last to deny: the man who learned to know those "good" ones only as enemies, learned at the same time not to know them only as *"evil enemies,"* and the same men who *inter pares* were kept so rigorously in bounds through convention, respect, custom, and gratitude, though much more through mutual vigilance and jealousy *inter pares,* these men who in their relations with each other find so many new ways of manifesting consideration, self-control, delicacy, loyalty, pride and friendship, these men are in reference to what is outside their circle (where the foreign element, a *foreign* country, begins) not much better than beasts of prey, which have been let loose. They enjoy their freedom from all social control, they feel that in the wilderness they can give vent with impunity to that tension which is produced by enclosure and imprisonment in the peace of society, they *revert* to the innocence of the beast-of-prey conscience, like jubilant monsters, who perhaps come from a ghostly bout of murder, arson, rape, and torture, with bravado and a moral equanimity, as though merely some wild student's prank had been played, perfectly convinced that the poets have now an ample theme to sing and celebrate. It is impossible not to recognize at the core of all these aristocratic races a beast of prey; the magnificent *blond brute,* avidly rampant for spoil and victory; this hidden core needed an outlet from time to time, the beast must get loose again, must return into the wilderness—the Roman, Arabic, German, and Japanese nobility, the Homeric heroes, the Scandinavian Vikings, are all alike in this need. It is the aristocratic races who have left the idea "Barbarian" on all the tracks in which they have marched; nay, a consciousness of this very barbarianism, and even a pride in it, manifests itself even in their highest civilization (for example, when Pericles says to his Athenians in that celebrated funeral oration, "Our audacity has forced a way over every land and sea, rearing everywhere imperishable memorials of itself for *good* and for *evil*").

... Granted the truth of the theory now believed to be true, that the very *essence of all civilizations is* to *train* out of man the beast of prey, a tame and civilized animal, it follows indubitably that we must regard as the real tools of civilization all those instincts of reaction and resentment, by the help of which the aristocratic races, together with their ideas, were finally degraded and overpowered; though that has not yet come to be synonymous with saying that the bearers of those tools also *represented* the civilization. It is rather the contrary that is not only probable—nay, it is *palpable* today; these bearers of vindictive instincts that have to be bottled up, these descendants of all European and non-European slavery, especially of the pre-Aryan population—these people, I say, represent the *decline* of humanity! These "tools of civilization" are a disgrace to humanity, and constitute in reality more of an argument against civilization, more of a reason why civilization should be suspected. One may be perfectly justified in being always afraid of the blond beast that lies at the core of all aristocratic races, and in being on one's guard: but who would not a hundred times prefer to be afraid, when one at the same times admires, than to be immune from fear, at the cost of being perpetually obsessed with the loathsome spectacle of the distorted, the dwarfed, the stunted, the envenomed? And is that not our fate? What produces today our repulsion towards "man"? for we *suffer* from "man," there is no doubt about it. It is not fear; it is rather that we have nothing more to fear from men; it is that the worm "man" is in the foreground and pullulates; it is that the "tame-man," the wretched mediocre and unedifying creature, has learned to consider himself a goal and a pinnacle, an inner meaning, an historic principle, a "higher man"; yes, it is that he has a certain right so to consider himself, in so far as he feels that in contrast to that excess of deformity, disease, exhaustion, and effeteness whose order is beginning to pollute present-day Europe, he at any rate has achieved a relative success, he at any rate still says "yes" to life. . . .

But let us come back to it; the problem of *another* origin of the good—of the good, as the resentful man has thought it out—demands its solution. It is not surprising that the lambs should bear a grudge against the great birds of prey for taking the little lambs. And when the lambs say among themselves, "Those birds of prey are evil, and he who is far removed from being a bird of prey, who is rather its opposite, a lamb—is he not good?" then there is nothing to cavil at in the setting up of this ideal, though it may also be that the birds of prey will regard it a little sneeringly, and perchance say to themselves, "We bear no grudge against them, these good lambs, we even like them: nothing is tastier than a tender lamb." To require of strength that it should *not* express itself as strength, that it should not be a wish to overpower, a wish to overthrow, a wish to become master, a thirst for enemies and antagonisms and triumphs, is just as absurd as to require of weakness that it should express itself as strength. A quantum of force is just such a quantum of movement, will, action; rather it is nothing else than just those very phenomena of moving, willing, acting, and can only appear otherwise in the misleading errors of language (and the fundamental fallacies of reason which have become petrified therein), which understands, and understands wrongly, all working as conditioned by a worker, by a "subject." And just exactly as the people separate the lightning from its flash, and interpret the latter as a thing done, as the working of a subject which is called lightning, so also does the popular morality separate strength from the expression of strength, as though behind the strong man there existed some indifferent neutral *substratum,* which enjoyed a *caprice and option* as to whether or not it should express strength. But there is no such *substratum,* there is no "being" behind doing, working, becoming; "the doer" is a mere appanage to the action. The action is everything. In point of fact, the people duplicate the doing, when they make the lightning lighten, that is a "doing-doing"; they make the same phenomenon first a cause, and then, secondly, the effect of that cause. The scientists fail to improve matters when they say, "Forces move, forces cause," and so on. Our whole science is still, in spite of all its coldness, of all its freedom from passion, a dupe of the tricks of language, and has never succeeded in getting rid of that superstitious changeling "the subject" (the atom, to give another instance, is such a changeling just as the Kantian "Thing-in-itself"). What wonder if the suppressed and stealthily simmering passions of revenge and hatred exploit for their own advantage their belief, and indeed hold no belief with a more steadfast enthusiasm than this—"that the strong has the *option* of being weak, and the bird of prey of being a lamb." Thereby do they win for themselves the right of attributing to the birds of prey the *responsibility* for being birds of prey: when the oppressed, downtrodden, and overpowered say to themselves with the vindictive guile of weakness, "Let us be otherwise than the evil, namely, good! and good is everyone who does not oppress, who hurts no one, who does not attack, who does not pay back, who hands over revenge to God, who holds himself, as we do, in hiding; who goes out of the way of evil, and demands, in short, little from life; like ourselves the patient, the meek, the just"—yet all this, in its cold and unprejudiced interpretation, means nothing more than "once for all, the weak are weak; it is good to do *nothing for which we are not strong enough*"; but this dismal state of affairs, this prudence of the lowest order, which even insects possess (which in a great danger are fain to sham death so as to avoid doing "too much") has, thanks to the counterfeiting and self-deception of weakness, come to masquerade in the pomp of an ascetic, mute, and expectant virtue, just as though the *very* weakness of the weak—that is, forsooth, its *being,* its working, its whole unique inevitable inseparable reality—were a strong result, something wished, chosen, a deed, an act of *merit.* This kind of man finds the belief in a neutral, free-choosing "subject" *necessary* from an instinct of self-preservation, of self-assertion, in which every lie is fain to sanctify itself. The subject (or to use popular language, the *soul*) has perhaps proved itself the best dogma in the world simply because it rendered possible to the horde of mortal, weak, and oppressed individuals of every kind, that most sublime specimen of self-deception, the interpretation of weakness as freedom, of being this, or being that, *as merit.*

QUESTIONS FOR DISCUSSION

1. Comment on Aristotle's opening remark, that "the good is that at which all things aim." Does he mean that whatever anything aims at is by that very fact good, including theft and murder? Or that all things aim at what they believe to be good? Or that the aim of any *natural* activity is toward what is really good?

2. What is Aristotle's definition of happiness? How close is it to what you understand by the word, "happiness"?

3. When, for Aristotle, are our desires "rational" in a derivative sense of "rational"? Do you agree that some desires are more rational than others? Which, for instance?

4. Explain Mill's distinction between the quality and the quantity of pleasure. How does he determine whether one pleasure is of higher quality than another?

5. Explain Mill's distinction between the pleasures of excitement and the pleasures of tranquility. Does he rate one more highly than the other?

6. What is Nagel's definition of sexual perversion? Why are levels of reciprocal arousal so important?

7. Is homosexual experience perverse, according to Nagel? Is masturbation? Why or why not?

8. Which two types of sexual experience do Nagel and Solomon overemphasize, according to Moulton? Why does she believe that they make this mistake?

9. Comment on Moulton's definition of perversion as "whatever makes people frightened or uncomfortable by its bizarreness." Is it a perversion to wear a Mohawk hairdo?

10. What is *nirvana* and why is it supremely good? How is it achieved?

11. Buddhism holds that evil cannot be overcome by changing the world, but only by changing ourselves. Is this a recipe for ostrichlike turning away from problems rather than solving them? Is this view more appropriate to some evils, such as incurable illness, than to others?

12. What is the point of the Buddhist metaphor of the ferry? If the two shores are really one, then what is the purpose of the journey?

13. What do you think Nietzsche means by "morality"? Is he defending immorality, or arguing for a higher kind of morality than most people follow?

14. Discuss Nietzsche's distinction between "master" and "slave" morality. How was it possible for the latter to defeat the former? When did this happen?

SUGGESTED READINGS

Virtuous Activity

ANTON, J. and MODRAK, D., *Aristotle on Reason, Practical Reason, and Living Well,* Albany: SUNY Press, 1991.

KENNY, A., *Aristotle and the Perfect Life,* Oxford: Clarendon Press, 1992.

LAWRENCE, G., "Aristotle and the Ideal Life," *Philosophical Review,* 102, 1 (1993), 1–34.

PAUL, E. and F. MILLER, *The Good Life and the Human Good,* New York: Cambridge University Press, 1991.

SCHULTE, J., ed., *The Happy Man in Criss-Crossing a Philosophical Landscape,* Amsterdam: Rodopi, 1992.

Active and Passive Pleasure

PENELHUM, T., "The Logic of Pleasure," *Philosophy and Phenomenological Research* (1957).

RIST, J., *Epicurus: An Introduction,* London: Cambridge University Press, 1972.

RYLE, G., *The Concept of Mind,* New York: Barnes & Noble, 1949.

SUMNER, L. W., "Welfare, Happiness and Pleasure," *Utilitas,* 4, 2 (1992), 199–223.

Sexual Fulfillment (and Perversion)

ATKINSON, R. F., *Sexual Morality,* New York: Harcourt, Brace, 1965.

DE BEAUVOIR, S., *The Second Sex,* trans. H. Parshley, New York: Bantam, 1961.

ELLIS, H., *Studies in the Psychology of Sex,* New York: Random House, 1942.

FREUD, S., *Three Contributions to the Theory of Sex,* trans. A. Brill, New York: Dutton, 1962.

FROMM, E., *The Art of Loving,* New York: Harper & Row, 1956.

GAGNON., J., and SIMON, W., eds., *Sexual Deviance,* New York: Harper & Row, 1967.

HOFFMAN, H., *Sex Incorporated: A Positive View of the Sexual Revolution,* Boston: Beacon, 1967.

MONTAGU, A., *Sex, Man and Society,* New York: Putnam, 1969.

RUDDICK, S., "On Sexual Morality," in J. Rachels, ed., *Moral Problems,* 2nd ed., New York: Harper & Row, 1975.

RUSSELL, B., *Marriage and Morals,* New York: Bantam, 1968.

SOBLE, A., *The Philosophy of Sex,* Totowa, N.J.: Rowman & Littlefield, 1991.

VATSAYANA, *The Kama Sutra,* trans. R. Burton, New York: Dutton, 1962.

WILSON, J., *Logic and Sexual Morality,* Baltimore: Penguin, 1965.

Enlightenment

CONZE, E., *Buddhism: Its Essence and Development,* New York: Harper & Row, 1951.

HUMPHREYS, C., *An Invitation to the Buddhist Way of Life for Western Readers,* New York: Schocken, 1969.

MITCHELL, D., *Spirituality and Emptiness,* Mahwah, N.J.: Panhit Press, 1991.

Self Assertion

CARUS, P., *Nietzsche,* New York: Haskell House, 1972.

DANTO, A., *Nietzsche as a Philosopher,* New York: Macmillan, 1965.

KAUFMAN, W., *Nietzsche: Philosopher, Psychologist, Antichrist,* New York: Random House, 1968.

LEA, F. A., *The Tragic Philosopher,* New York: Methuen, 1957.

NIELSEN, K., "Nietzsche as a Moral Philosopher," *Man and World,* 6 (1973).

Name Index

SUBJECT INDEX